The Blackwell Dictionary of
Historians

The Blackwell Dictionary of
Historians

Edited by
John Cannon

R.H.C. Davis
William Doyle
Jack P. Greene

Blackwell Reference

First published 1988
First published in USA 1988

Basil Blackwell Ltd
108 Cowley Road, Oxford, OX4 1JF, UK

Basil Blackwell Inc.
432 Park Avenue South, Suite 1503
New York, NY 10016, USA

British Library Cataloguing in Publication Data

The Blackwell dictionary of historians.
1. Historiography. Biographies. Collections.
I. Cannon, John, *1926–*
907'.2022

ISBN 0–631–14708–X

Library of Congress Cataloging in Publication Data

The Blackwell dictionary of historians.

Includes index.
1. Historians—Biography—Dictionaries. I. Cannon,
John Ashton.
D14.B58 1988   907'.202'2 [B]   88–19361

ISBN 0–631–14708–X

Typeset in 9½ on 11pt Ehrhardt
by Setrite Typesetters Ltd, Hong Kong
Printed in Great Britain by Butler and Tanner Ltd, Frome, Somerset

Contents

Preface

The *Blackwell Dictionary of Historians* has been designed for all who read history, whether for academic purposes or pure pleasure. It contains over 450 biographical entries which indicate the scholarly reputation of historians, the circumstances in which they worked and the extent to which their work has subsequently been confirmed or refuted. The biographies include all the historians who are most widely read together with many others who, though rarely perused are often cited. Footnotes referring to Droysen, Fustel de Coulanges, Hauck, Klyuchevsky or Srbik, whose works are no longer found on the open shelves of the average library, can be meaningless unless the reader has some idea of who they were and what they did.

There are more than fifty entries referring to living historians. We started by deciding that fifty should be the absolute maximum, and spent much time discussing inclusions and exclusions. In the event, however, we received a good deal of advice from contributors, some of it couched in lively or reproachful terms, so that (in accordance with the spirit of this inflationary age) we allowed the number to increase slightly above our original target. Since selection is not an exact science, we cannot hope to have pleased everybody or to have been absolutely correct in our judgements, but we have done our best.

We have presumed that a dictionary printed in English would be read mainly in Britain and America, and have accepted this as a guiding principle. But other areas and traditions have not been ignored. Sixty of the individual entries refer to French historians, forty to German and twenty to Italian. In addition there are historiographical surveys – African, Chinese, Hispanic, Russian and so on, for those countries or regions with which our readers may be less familiar. We have also included thirty classical historians, such as Herodotus, Livy, Tacitus or Xenophon, together with a survey of classical historiography.

Finally there are entries to explain some of the more baffling terms used, or misused, by working historians – cliometrics, historicism, historical materialism or the Marxist interpretation of history. Curiously enough the definition of such terms is also still liable to be controversial.

PREFACE

Each entry is intended to be complete in itself, but where it might be helpful to consult other entries, cross-references are printed in the text in capital letters. The reader can trace all references to a specific individual or topic through the general index which appears at the end of the volume.

We thank our contributors for the boldness and learning with which they have carried out their tasks, and are grateful to them for their forbearance and understanding.

JAC
RHCD
WD
JPG
June, 1988

Contributors

David Abulafia **DSHA**
Gonville and Caius College, Cambridge

B. W. E. Alford **BWEA**
University of Bristol

A. V. Antonovics **AVA**
University of Bristol

Joyce O. Appleby **JOA**
University of California, Los Angeles

Yehoshua Arieli **YA**
The Hebrew University of Jerusalem

R. F. Atkinson **RFA**
University of Exeter

Theo Barker **TCB**
*The London School of Economics
and Political Science*

T. H. Barrett **THB**
*School of Oriental and African Studies,
University of London*

Derek Beales **DEDB**
Sidney Sussex College, Cambridge

John V. Beckett **JVB**
University of Nottingham

Richard Bellamy **RPB**
Jesus College, Cambridge

Michael Bentley **MB**
University of Sheffield

John G. Bernasconi **JGB**
University of Hull

Michael D. Biddiss **MDB**
University of Reading

A. R. Birley **ARB**
University of Manchester

Geoffrey Blainey **GB**
University of Melbourne

Tim Blanning **TCWB**
Sidney Sussex College, Cambridge

Richard Bonney **RB**
University of Leicester

Christopher Brooke **CNLB**
Gonville and Caius College, Cambridge

A. A. M. Bryer **AAMB**
University of Birmingham

D. A. Bullough **DB**
University of St Andrews

Robert Burchell **RAB**
University of Manchester

Peter Burke **UPB**
Emmanuel College, Cambridge

Amy Turner Bushnell **ATB**
University of South Alabama

R. van Caenegem **RCv C**
State University of Ghent

CONTRIBUTORS

John C. Cairns **JCC**
University of Toronto

Averil Cameron **AMC**
Kings College London

A. E. Campbell **AEC**
*Keble College, Oxford, and
University of Birmingham*

James Campbell **JC**
Worcester College, Oxford

Peter Robert Campbell **PRC**
University of Sussex

John Cannon **JAC**
University of Newcastle upon Tyne

Henry Chadwick **HC**
Peterhouse, Cambridge

Muriel E. Chamberlain **MEC**
University College of Swansea

John Channon **JCh**
*School of Slavonic and East European Studies,
University of London*

Marjorie Chibnall **MMC**
Clare Hall, Cambridge

Michael Clanchy **MTC**
Westfield College, University of London

Peter Clark **PAC**
University of Leicester

C. G. A. Clay **CC**
University of Bristol

Guadalupe Jiménez Codinach **GJC**
Mexico City

David William Cohen **DWC**
The Johns Hopkins University

T. J. Cornell **TJC**
University College London

David Corner **DJC**
University of St Andrews

H. E. J. Cowdrey **HEJC**
St Edmund Hall, Oxford

Geoffrey Crossick **GC**
University of Essex

Gordon Daniels **GD**
University of Sheffield

N. S. Davidson **NSD**
University of Leicester

K. G. Davies **KGD**
Trinity College, Dublin

R. R. Davies **RRD**
The University College of Wales, Aberystwyth

R. W. Davies **RWD**
University of Birmingham

R. H. C. Davis **RHCD**
*Merton College, Oxford, and
University of Birmingham*

John Derry **JWD**
University of Newcastle upon Tyne

H. T. Dickinson **HTD**
University of Edinburgh

William Doyle **WD**
University of Bristol

Seymour Drescher **SD**
University of Pittsburgh

Paul Dukes **PD**
University of Aberdeen

Jean Dunbabin **JHD**
St Anne's College, Oxford

William Dusinberre **WWD**
University of Warwick

Christopher Dyer **CCD**
University of Birmingham

Peter W. Edbury **PWE**
University College, Cardiff

A. S. Eisenstadt **ASE**
Brooklyn College of the City of New York

Christopher Elrington **CRE**
University of London

Geoffrey Elton **GRE**
Clare College, Cambridge

Stanley L. Engerman **SLE**
University of Rochester, New York

R. J. W. Evans **RJWE**
Brasenose College, Oxford

H. S. Ferns **HSF**
University of Birmingham

Roderick C. Floud **RCF**
Birkbeck College, London

James Friguglietti **JF**
Eastern Montana College

Peter Garnsey **PDAG**
Jesus College, Cambridge

Martin Gilbert **MG**
London

John Grenville **JASG**
University of Birmingham

Philip Grierson **PG**
Gonville and Caius College, Cambridge

Ira D. Gruber **IDG**
Rice University, Houston

B. A. Haddock **BAH**
University College of Swansea

K. H. D. Haley **KHDH**
University of Sheffield

Bernard Hamilton **BH**
University of Nottingham

Norman Hampson **NH**
University of York

D. W. Harkness **DWH**
The Queen's University of Belfast

Gerald L. Harriss **GLH**
Magdalen College, Oxford

Gary R. Hawke **GRHk**
Victoria University of Wellington, New Zealand

Gerald R. Hawting **GRHt**
School of Oriental and African Studies, University of London

Denys Hay **DH**
University of Edinburgh

David Hayton **DWHn**
History of Parliament, *Institute of Historical Research, University of London*

E. D. Hunt **EDH**
University of Durham

Ronald Hutton **RH**
University of Bristol

J. K. Hyde **JKH**
Late of *University of Manchester*

Kenneth Ingham **KI**
University of Bristol

Robert Irwin **RGI**
London

E. W. Ives **EWI**
University of Birmingham

Edward F. James **EFJ**
University of York

J. Jervis **JJ**
University of Kent at Canterbury

David A. Johnson **DAJ**
Portland State University

Douglas Johnson **DJ**
University College London

Richard R. Johnson **RJ**
University of Washington

Michael Jones **MCEJ**
University of Nottingham

H. A. F. Kamen **HK**
University of Warwick

Mark Kaplanoff **MDK**
Pembroke College, Cambridge

CONTRIBUTORS

Maurice Keen **MHK**
Balliol College, Oxford

Ian Keil **IJEK**
Loughborough University

Linda K. Kerber **LKK**
University of Iowa

Edmund L. King **ELK**
Princeton University

Edmund King **EK**
University of Sheffield

Milton M. Klein **MMK**
University of Tennessee

Franklin W. Knight **FWK**
The Johns Hopkins University

William M. Lamont **WML**
University of Sussex

Gordon Leff **GL**
University of York

K. J. Leyser **KJL**
All Souls College, Oxford

Peggy K. Liss **PKL**
Washington, DC

Peter Llewellyn **PABL1**
University College of North Wales, Bangor

Howell A. Lloyd **HAL1**
University of Hull

D. M. Loades **DML**
University College of North Wales, Bangor

Derek W. Lomax **DWL**
University of Birmingham

Donald Low **DAL**
University of Stirling

Alan Macfarlane **ADJM**
King's College, Cambridge

Michael Maclagan **MM**
Richmond Herald, College of Arms, London

Duncan MacLeod **DMacl**
St Catherine's College, Oxford

G. H. Martin **GHM**
Public Records Office, London

J. F. A. Mason **JFAM**
Christ Church, Oxford

John Matthews **JFM**
The Queen's College, Oxford

Norman McCord **NMcC**
University of Newcastle upon Tyne

Thomas K. McCraw **TKMc**
Harvard University

Patrick McGrath **PVM**
University of Bristol

Rosamond McKitterick **RMcK**
Newnham College, Cambridge

David McLellan **DTM**
University of Kent at Canterbury

Joseph C. Miller **JCM**
University of Virginia, Charlottesville

Joel Mokyr **JM**
Northwestern University

R. I. Moore **RIM**
University of Sheffield

D. O. Morgan **DOM**
School of Oriental and African Studies, University of London

Colin Morris **CM**
University of Southampton

J. N. L. Myres **JNLM**
Oxford

Aubrey Newman **AN**
University of Leicester

Edward Norman **ERN**
University of Cambridge

Stewart P. Oakley **SPO**
University of East Anglia

Peter S. Onuf **PSO**
Southern Methodist University, Dallas

Mark Overton **MO**
University of Newcastle upon Tyne

Peter J. Parish **PJP**
University of London

David Parker **DP**
University of Leeds

Paul F. Paskoff **PFP**
Louisiana State University, Baton Rouge

J. J. Paterson **JJP**
University of Newcastle upon Tyne

James T. Patterson **JTP**
Brown University

Christopher Pelling **CBRP**
University College, Oxford

John Percival **JP**
University College, Cardiff

C. V. Phythian-Adams **CVP-A**
University of Leicester

Stuart Piggot **SP**
Wantage, Oxfordshire

Andrei Pippidi **AP**
University of Bucharest

Roy Porter **RP**
The Wellcome Institute for the History of Medicine, London

Leslie Price **JLP**
University of Hull

Roger D. Price **RDP**
University of East Anglia

Brian S. Pullan **BSP**
University of Manchester

Tessa Rajak **TRk**
University of Reading

Agatha Ramm **AR**
Somerville College, Oxford

Orest Ranum **OR**
The Johns Hopkins University

T. Raychaudhuri **TRi**
St Antony's College, Oxford

Jane Rendall **JR**
University of York

Timothy Reuter **TAR**
Monumenta Germaniae Historica, Munich

Martin Ridge **MR**
The Huntington Library, San Marino, California

K. G. Robbins **KGR**
University of Glasgow

D. W. Rollason **DWR**
University of Durham

I. A. Roots **IAR**
University of Exeter

William T. Rowe **WTR**
The Johns Hopkins University

A. J. R. Russell-Wood **AJRR-W**
The Johns Hopkins University

David Saunders **DBS**
University of Newcastle upon Tyne

John Saville **JS**
University of Hull

Clemence Schultze **CES**
The Queen's University of Belfast

H. M. Scott **MS**
University of St Andrews

W. J. Sheils **WJS**
University of York

George Shepperson **GS**
University of Edinburgh

Lawrence Shore **LS**
Queen's University, Kingston, Canada

Paul Slack **PAS**
Exeter College, Oxford

CONTRIBUTORS

Peter Slee **PRHS**
University of Durham

J. D. Smart **JDS**
University of Leeds

Dennis Smith **DS**
Aston University

W. A. Speck **WAS**
University of Leeds

A. T. Q. Stewart **ATQS**
The Queen's University of Belfast

Traian Stoianovich **TS**
Rutgers University

H. F. A. Strachan **HFAS**
Corpus Christi College, Cambridge

Birgit Strand-Sawyer **BSS**
University of Gothenburg, Sweden

John Styles **JAS**
University of Bristol

Robert P. Swierenga **RPS**
Kent State University

Joan Taylor **JMT**
University of Newcastle upon Tyne

Rodney M. Thomson **RMT**
The University of Tasmania

Hugh Tulloch **HT**
University of Bristol

Christopher Tuplin **CJT**
University of Liverpool

Timothy Unwin **PTHU**
Royal Holloway and Bedford New College, London

Malcolm Vale **MV**
St John's College, Oxford

Sally N. Vaughn **SNV**
University of Houston

F. W. Walbank **FWW**
Peterhouse, Cambridge

Andrew Wallace-Hadrill **AW-H**
University of Reading

James P. Walsh **JPW**
Central Connecticut State University

W. R. Ward **WRW**
University of Durham

Wilcomb E. Washburn **WEW**
Smithsonian Institution, Washington, DC

Stephen Saunders Webb **SSW**
Syracuse University

John R. Whittam **JRW**
University of Bristol

Glanmor Williams **GW**
Swansea, Wales

Chris Wilson **CW**
The London School of Economics and Political Science

Daniel J. Wilson **DJW**
Muhlenburg College, Allentown, Pennsylvania

T. P. Wiseman **TPW**
University of Exeter

A. J. Woodman **AJW**
University of Durham

Jenny Wormald **JW**
St Hilda's College, Oxford

Patrick Wormald **PW**
University of Glasgow

Chris Wrigley **CJW**
University of Nottingham

A. Zakai **AZ**
The Hebrew University of Jerusalem

W. H. Zawadzki **WHZ**
Abingdon School, Oxfordshire

A

Acton, Lord John Emerich Edward Dalberg (b.1834, d.1902) Few professional historians can have had so intermittent a career as Acton: for a dozen or so years, up to 1870 when he was thirty-six, he was a prolific writer of rather polemical essays in Catholic journals; he then did very little until the last seven years of his life, when, as regius professor of history at Cambridge (an appointment he owed to Lord Rosebery), he plunged into the task of preparing the Cambridge Modern History. He was better known to his contemporaries as a Catholic controversialist, notorious for his assaults upon the ultramontane claims of the papacy, than as an historical writer. Born in Naples, the son of a diplomat, Acton's intellectual formation was dominated by a six-year period of study under Döllinger at Münich. In 1859 he was elected to parliament as a Liberal. It was to Gladstone, with whom he maintained an enduring *rapport*, that he owed his peerage in 1869.

Acton's consistent theme was the moral superiority of liberal institutions, and his essays and lectures ransacked the history of the Catholic church to show, as he contended, the baneful effects of autocracy. He never published a single book, and it was his executors who later prepared collections of essays. The essentially eclectic nature of his scholarship may be judged from the enormous stacks of card-indexes of memorable quotations, culled from his vast reading, now in the Cambridge University Library. A definitive 'History of Liberty', which he projected in his later years, was never written.   ERN

Main publications

Lectures on Modern History (London: Macmillan,

1906); *Essays on Church and State by Lord Acton*, ed. D. Woodruff (London: Hollis & Carter, 1952).

Reading

Gasquet, A. F.: *Lord Acton and his Circle* (London: George Allen, 1906).
Noack, U.: *Geschichtswissenschaft und Wahrheit: nach den Schriften von J. Dalberg Acton* (Frankfurt: 1935).
Himmelfarb, G: *Lord Acton: a Study in Conscience and Politics* (London: Routledge & Kegan Paul, 1952).

Adam of Bremen (d.1081/1085) Adam was *scholasticus* at the cathedral school of Bremen. His only surviving work, the *Gesta Hammaburgensis ecclesiae pontificum*, was compiled from a very wide range of sources, many now lost, and completed by 1075, though Adam continued revising it until 1081. The *Gesta* is a history of the church of Bremen; the third book is an extended character portrait of Archbishop Adalbert, in effect one of the earliest biographies in European historical writing.   TAR

Main writings

Gesta Hammaburgensis ecclesiae pontificum (Deeds of the archbishops of Bremen), ed. B. Schmeidler (Hanover: Monumenta Germaniae Historica, scriptores rerum Germanicarum, 1917).

Reading

Schmale, F.-J.: Adam von Bremen. In *Verfasserlexikon des deutschen Mittelalters* (Dictionary of medieval German authors), ed. W. Stammler and K. Langosch, 2nd edn (Berlin: De Gruyter, 1978), 50—4.

Adams, Henry (b.1838, d.1918) Although Adams is most famous for his third-person autobiography *The Education of Henry Adams*

1

(1918) and is also well known for *Mont-Saint-Michel and Chartres* (1913), his nine-volume *History of the United States during the Jefferson and Madison Administrations* (published 1889–90) is the principal basis for his reputation as a historian. In this work he sought to marry the new German scientific history to an older British literary tradition. The *History* has been admired by some historians though it has not won popular acclaim, and Adams has become known as a thwarted politician and prophet of twentieth-century disillusion; his historical masterpiece is neglected by all except specialists and those who cherish his mastery of the English language.

He profited, but also suffered, from being a member of America's best-known family. Presidents, diplomats, public figures – John Adams, John Quincy Adams, Charles Francis Adams, Charles Francis Adams, Jr – all contributed indirectly or directly to shaping his mind. After graduating from Harvard College in 1858 Henry Adams studied for two years in Germany and worked for seven years as his father's secretary in the American legation in London; this long sojourn gave him a deeper acquaintance with European literary and historical culture than most of his countrymen. After two years as a political journalist and six years as Harvard teacher, Adams worked almost without interruption from 1877 to 1890 upon the *History*.

A diplomatic, military, and political narrative in the traditional mould, the *History* is distinguished for the depth and relative soundness of its research, the balance of its author's judgement, and the felicity of its style. Adams's work in American, British, Spanish, French, and Canadian archives has probably stood the test of time better than that of any other nineteenth-century American historian, and the course he steered between Federalist and Democratic partisanships, between British and American chauvinisms, sets a model for objective yet engaged scholarship. He later pretended to have been a dilettante, but actually had worked with painstaking care upon verbal expression, normally reconsidering every chapter 'pen in hand, full thirty' times. What might otherwise be the tedious political annals of a then third-rate power are elevated by Adams's intelligence, the depth of his humour, and his literary skill into an enduring work of art.

Adams was married to Marian Hooper Adams, a woman of outrageous wit and intellectual vivacity, who suffered from recurrent depressive illness and killed herself in 1885. This marriage had been exceptionally happy and his wife's death left him a changed man. During the last part of his life he wrote the two books which ironically won him the fame he had hoped for with the *History*. *Mont-Saint-Michel and Chartres* – in part a convoluted autobiographical confession and in part a superior guidebook – is also a wide-ranging, suggestive, but rather amateurish essay on medieval French cultural history. *The Education of Henry Adams*, a rich and shrewd autobiography, also contains portentous, half-playful speculations about the confusing complexity of modern life. But historians are likely to value Adams primarily for the acuity and art with which he narrated early nineteenth-century American history.   WWD

Main publications

History of the United States during the Jefferson and Madison Administrations, Series in 9 vols (New York: Charles Scribner's Sons, 1889–90); *Mont-Saint-Michel and Chartres* (Boston: Houghton Mifflin, 1913); *The Education of Henry Adams* (Boston: Houghton Mifflin, 1918).

Reading

Dusinberre, W. W.: *Henry Adams: the Myth of Failure* (Charlottesville: University Press of Virginia 1980).

Jordy, W. H.: *Henry Adams: Scientific Historian* (New Haven, Conn.: Yale University Press 1952).

Adams, Herbert Baxter (b.1850, d.1901) Born in Shutesbury, Massachusetts, Adams received his undergraduate degree from Amherst, his doctorate at the University of Heidelberg in 1876, and accepted an appointment in history at the newly established Johns Hopkins University. Adams introduced the German scientific or critical approach and was one of the first to apply it to American historical sources. An advocate of the 'germ theory' of historical origins, he argued that new world institutions had their roots in Teutonic political, economic and social structures. His seminar soon became noted as a training ground for historians. To foster the new scholarship, Adams established in 1882 the Johns Hopkins studies in historical and political science. Two years later he helped to create the American Historical Association. Adams's importance lies more in the encouragement he gave to scientific history, and to the professionalization of the discipline, than in his own scholarship.   DJW

Main publications

The German Origin of New England Towns (Baltimore: The Johns Hopkins University Press, 1882); *The Life and Writings of Jared Sparks* (Boston: Houghton Mifflin, 1893).

advertising history Becoming identified as a distinct component of business history during the 1970s, advertising history aims to show, where evidence exists, the interconnections between agencies, various communications media, marketing and consumers' perspectives. Currently much effort is devoted to establishing archives to provide sources both for historians and advertising practitioners. In London, the History of Advertising Trust (HAT) was founded in 1977 by members of advertising agencies and users of advertising; the same year it established the learned *Journal of Advertising History*. The purpose of HAT is to encourage the study of the contributions of advertising to many aspects of social and economic life; it has its own archive depository and records the locations of other collections. In North America too, the systematic study of the history of advertising emerged during the 1970s when business history took greater account of marketing, communications, and firms selling products and services. The first archive of advertising at the University of British Columbia had close connections with business studies.

Linked with advertising history is the study of the use of advertising in political life: both for party political campaigns and as propaganda. Analyses of political advertising have employed the techniques of political scientists and psychologists. For example, S. Constantine examined how the British government sought to influence opinion on trade between 1926 and 1933 with its Empire Marketing Board in a collection of essays, *Imperialism and Popular Culture*, edited by J. M. Mackenzie (1986). Effective use of television for political persuasion involved American advertising specialists, as S. Mickelson showed in *The Electric Mirror: Politics in the Age of Television* (1972).

The concepts and methods of business and economic historians have served the needs of advertising historians. Much incidental commentary on the consequences of advertising appears in studies of companies dependent on sustained advertising to market their products. For example B. W. E. Alford showed in *W. D. & H. O. Wills and the Development of the UK Tobacco Industry* (1973) how the firm pioneered the successful use of brand names in selling. The growth of pharmaceutical retailing in England made extensive use of advertising as S. D. Chapman demonstrated in *Jesse Boot of Boots the Chemists: a Study in Business History* (1974).

Advertising history has intimate involvement with the history of the press, cinema, radio and television. For example, see the essays in B. Henry (editor), *British Television Advertising: the First 30 Years* (1986), which provides insights into the ways in which funding from advertisements shaped the development of British television.   IJEK

Reading

Henry, B. ed.: *British Television Advertising: the First 30 Years* (London: Century Benham, 1986).
Journal of Advertising History, 1977– .
Nevett, T.: *Advertising in Britain: a History* (London: Heinemann, 1982).

African historiography The history of black Africans, as opposed to the history of Africa's visitors and invaders, was scarcely written at all before the second world war. As late as 1963 the regius professor of modern history at Oxford University claimed, albeit by that time a little anachronistically, that there *was* no African history.

The initiative for the new, post-war study of the history of Africa came from scholars in the metropolitan countries, Britain, France and Belgium, but their work flourished because of the creation of university institutions for Africans in colonial Africa itself and because of the growing campaign for independence among Africa's emergent political leaders. University students in Africa wanted to know about the origin of their own societies and not just of those of their teachers, while political leaders were anxious to demonstrate that they had their own cultures and were not simply the creation of a colonial system.

The primary aim of historians of Africa during this early period of research was to extend their knowledge of Africa's peoples into the era before colonization. Their sources ranged from the writings of anthropologists and ethnographers to missionary records, the journals of explorers and even slave traders, the reports of early administrators and to ORAL HISTORY. A number of significant monographs were produced, some of them by Africans with special knowledge of the language and culture of the areas about which they were writing, but progress in different parts of the country was uneven and comparisons between different areas were difficult to draw. Some broader themes of a pre- or-proto-historical character were opened up by archaeologists, often working in close association with historians. Notable among these was the research undertaken into the spread of the iron age in Africa and the development of pastoralism and agriculture. These topics, however, were of limited interest to the majority of Africans.

It was the politicians who provided the impetus for the next development in African historiography. African political leaders in the Gold Coast had been happy to revive the ancient name of Ghana and apply it to the independent nation over which they came to rule, although the name itself had little geographical or historical connection with their country. But something more was needed to arouse popular interest in the independence movement. Something had to be said about African, rather than colonial, endeavour and achievement. Historians provided the necessary information. In the late 1950s and early 1960s two words — resistance and exploitation — became the constant refrain in books and articles which no longer concentrated on the pre-colonial period but focused specifically upon the relations between Africans and their alien overlords. Africans, it was demonstrated, had not always accepted the superiority of foreign invaders. They had resisted in defence of their own societies and way of life and, by implication, they could and should continue to resist the imposition of alien cultures. Economic historians made their contribution by drawing attention to the way in which colonial powers had developed the resources of their dependencies in their own interests and often to the detriment of the peoples they administered.

This dual theme of resistance and exploitation was powerfully developed by white radical historians who saw the African independence movement as part of the process of overthrowing capitalism. Their assumption was that, on achieving independence, African countries would reject the capitalist system introduced in the colonial period. In Tanzania, for example, Julius Nyerere sought to reduce his country's dependence upon external aid by trying to revive traditional African communalism as a means of ensuring maximum economic effort with a minimum of economic inequality.

The generation of Africans trained as historians during the 1950s and early 1960s was scarcely involved in this new movement. The preoccupation of these scholars continued to be the production of histories of their own peoples up to the early years of the colonial period, or other pre-colonial themes such as the impact of the Atlantic slave trade on West Africa, a topic to which American historians had brought new statistical insights. It was a later generation of African historians who joined in the most recent development in African historiography, the promulgation of the theory of underdevelopment.

Once again politicians provided, if not the stimulus, at least the justification for this new interpretation of African history and again radical historians took the lead in promoting the theory. It was clear that an explanation was needed as to why, after two decades of self-government, African countries were still unable to provide the prosperity which the people had confidently expected would result from independence. The argument now put forward was that, in the effort to exploit the resources of their dependencies, the colonial powers had destroyed or distorted the countries' natural economic character, leaving them exposed and defenceless in face of the neocolonialist ambitions of the wealthier nations.

Although this type of historical writing is too clearly the handmaid of political theory, it has contributed significantly to the study of African history. It has, conspicuously, turned a critical eye upon colonial policies and practices. More important, it has drawn attention to the importance of understanding the economic history of a continent in which population growth has rapidly outstripped productivity. That is not to say that the picture thus presented is not distorted. There is still a need to insist that history is an academic discipline in its own right and is not susceptible to the theorizing common to certain other disciplines. It is not, for example, easy to generalize about the African continent. Multi-volume 'histories' of Africa tend still to be collections of essays on individual countries or regions. Historical parallels, comparisons and contrasts may often be more usefully drawn from outside the African continent than from within.   KI

Reading

Fyfe, C. ed.: *African Studies since 1945*. (London: Longman, 1976).

Jewsiewicki, B. and Newbury, D. eds: *African Historiographies* (London: Sage, 1986).

Oliver, R.: *African History for the Outside World* (London: University of London, School of Oriental and African Studies, 1964).

Temu, A. and Swai, B.: *Historians and Africanist History*. (London: Zed, 1981).

Vansina, J., Mauny, R. and Thomas, L.V.: *The Historian in Tropical Africa* (London: Oxford University Press, 1964).

agrarian history The boundaries of agrarian history are not clearly defined, and tracing the development of the subject depends in part on how it is conceived. Studies of agriculture and rural economies have always found a place in ECONOMIC HISTORY and HISTORICAL GEOGRAPHY but general historical writing about agrarian matters can be traced back to the pastoral tradition of the ancient Greeks.

Nevertheless it is possible to distinguish two main themes in agrarian historiography: the study of the practicalities of farming (with links to both archaeology and the history of science and technology); and the institutional structures under which farming is carried out (with links to economic, social, political, and legal history). Towards the end of the eighteenth century both themes are found in the earliest books on agrarian history published in Europe and in entries on agrarian history in general encyclopaedias in England. Separate agrarian histories appear in England after the mid-nineteenth century but agriculture had already found a place in general histories, most notably perhaps in MACAULAY's description of England in 1685 in the third chapter of his *History*.

The theme of institutional change is evident in the work of Karl MARX who saw the parliamentary enclosure movement of the eighteenth and nineteenth centuries as the mechanism responsible for creating the English proletariat. In a different vein, but still with an emphasis on institutions, a group of late nineteenth-century historians (including SEEBOHM, VINOGRADOFF, and MAITLAND) considered the problem of the origin and development of the manor in England. Two of the most influential works of the next generation of English agrarian historians tackled the origins and consequences of capitalist agriculture: R. H. TAWNEY, *The Agrarian Problem in the Sixteenth Century* (1912), and J. L. LE B. and B. HAMMOND, *The Village Labourer* (1911). They are classic works still serving as a stimulus for new research.

Agricultural technology was described in the earliest agrarian histories, but the chapter on agriculture in A. Toynbee's posthumous *Lectures on the Industrial Revolution* (1884) is noteworthy for its description of eighteenth-century changes in crop rotations and livestock breeding that later became known as the 'agricultural revolution'. Farming practice was also considered in the most influential (but not the first) text on English agrarian history: R. L. Prothero (later Lord Ernle), *English Farming Past and Present*, published in 1912.

Institutional and technological change have been merged in studies with a more explicitly economic framework. The forerunner of these studies is J. E. T. ROGERS's compilation *A History of Agriculture and Prices in England*, but subsequent writing in this vein (which is much more analytical than Rogers) has tended to be European rather than British. The study by W. Abel, *Agricultural Fluctuations in Europe from the Thirteenth to the Twentieth Centuries* (first published in German in 1935) was path-breaking in its departure from the German historical tradition and in its employment of quantitative data and explicit economic concepts. The tradition continued with B. H. SLICHER VAN BATH, *The Agrarian History of Western Europe AD 500–1850* (first published in Dutch in 1959). There is a long tradition of writing on rural matters in France which has been dominated for many years by the distinctive ANNALES SCHOOL and particularly by the work of M. BLOCH, F. BRAUDEL, and E. B. LE ROY LADURIE.

In the United States agrarian history grew with economic history: the Carnegie institution in Washington published P. W. Bidwell and J. I. Falconer, *History of Agriculture in the Northern United States 1620–1860* in 1925 and L. C. Gray, *History of Agriculture in the Southern United States to 1860* in 1933, but agrarian history has been subsumed within other themes of American historiography such as the frontier, environmentalism, and slavery. Nevertheless it was in the United States that the first specialist journal, *Agricultural History*, was established by the Agricultural History Society in 1927. Other journals followed after the second world war with the *Agricultural History Review* published by the British Agricultural History Society from 1953, and *AAG Bijdragen* published from the department of rural history at the Agricultural University of Wageningen in the Netherlands from 1958. Small institutes of agrarian history have also been established at Reading in England and at the University of California, Davis in the USA, but many countries now boast agricultural museums which are to varying degrees concerned with research in agrarian history.

For the last 30 years or so agrarian history in England has been dominated by the 'Leicester School' of historians and their followers, under the leadership of such scholars as H. P. R. Finberg, W. G. HOSKINS, and Joan THIRSK. They steered the subject away from national studies dealing mainly with legal and institutional matters towards local studies emphasizing farming practice. This approach to agrarian history characterizes volumes IV and V of the *Agrarian History of England and Wales* under Thirsk's general editorship. Work on the medieval period has been more broadly based, stressing both the institutional and practical sides of farming. This work is also characterized by a concern with more general models of agrarian change so that, for example, M. M. POSTAN invokes Malthusian ideas to link agrarian and demographic change, while part of R. R. HILTON's work explores Marxian concepts of feudalism.

There have been recent calls in the United States for a 'new rural history', as agrarian historians are being urged to adopt concepts and techniques from other branches of history. Indeed agrarian history has not been particularly innovative in recent years, watching from the sidelines as initiatives have been taken elsewhere, in such fields as social history and CLIOMETRICS; but there are signs that some of these new developments are spilling into agrarian history.   MO

Reading

Abel, W.: *Agrarkrisen und Agrarkonjunktur* (Hamburg: Paul Parey, 1935).

Bidwell, P. W. and Falconer, J. I.: *History of Agriculture in the Northern United States 1620–1860* (Washington: Carnegie Institution, 1925).

Fussell, G. E.: *Agricultural History in Great Britain and Western Europe before 1914: a Discursive Bibliography* (London: Pindar Press, 1983).

Gray, L. C.: *History of Agriculture in the Southern United States to 1860* (Washington DC: Carnegie Institution, 1933).

Hammond, J. L. Le B. and Hammond, B.: *The Village Labourer 1760–1832* (London: Longmans Green, 1913).

Hilton, R. H.: The content and sources of English agrarian history before 1500. *Agricultural History Review* 3 (1955) 3–19.

Prothero, R. L.: *English Farming Past and Present* (London: Longmans Green, 1912).

Rogers, J. E. T.: *A History of Agriculture and Prices in England* (Oxford: Oxford University Press, 1866–1902).

Slicher van Bath, B. H.: *De agrarische geschiedenis*

van West-Europa (500–1850) (Uitgeuerij Het Spectrum NV, 1959).

Swierenga, R. P.: Theoretical perspectives on the new rural history: from environmentalism to modernisation. *Agricultural History* 56 (1982) 495–502.

Tawney, R. H.: *The Agrarian Problem in the Sixteenth Century* (London: Longmans Green, 1912).

Thirsk, J.: The content and sources of English agrarian history after 1500. *Agricultural History Review* 3 (1955) 66–79.

Thirsk, J. ed.: *The Agrarian History of England and Wales* (Cambridge: Cambridge University Press, 1967–).

Toynbee, A.: *Lectures on the Industrial Revolution in England* (London: Rivingtons, 1884).

Alison, Archibald (b.1792, d.1867) A lawyer by profession, Alison was an active controversialist, writing on contemporary questions from a strongly Tory standpoint. Despite his opposition to Catholic emancipation and the 1832 Reform Act he was quick to urge the Tory party to come to terms with the post-reform situation.

Alison wrote a study of Marlborough and the official life of Castlereagh, but his chief historical work was *A History of Europe from the Commencement of the French Revolution to the Restoration of the Bourbons*. First published between 1833 and 1843, and frequently revised and reprinted, this was on a vast scale: the 1847 edition ran to twenty volumes. The book was popular in Britain and in America and was translated into several languages. Alison believed that one reason for his success was the fact that his was the first serious study in English of the French Revolution. He was enthusiastic in hunting out sources but was insufficiently critical in his treatment of them. His main purpose in writing the *History* was to uncover the workings of Providence in human affairs and to defend regulated freedom, by which he meant the English constitution. His Tory convictions are most obvious when he is drawing parallels between events in France and contemporary issues, but in other respects he was fair-minded and perceptive. On the resistance of the French nobility to reform, the significance of the emigrations, the humanitarian reforms of the Constituent Assembly, the reception of the Revolution in the provinces, the role of shopkeepers and artisans in popular politics, or the integrity of Robespierre compared with those who overthrew him, Alison showed considerable judgement. Nor did he limit himself to events in western Europe, devoting much space to Russia, Poland, the Americas and the near east. His work contained a wealth of information communicated in a vigorous though wordy style, and may still be read with profit.   JWD

Main publications

(All published by Blackwood: Edinburgh and London)
A History of Europe from the Commencement of the French Revolution to the Restoration of the Bourbons (1833–43); *The Military Life of John, Duke of Marlborough* (1847); *The Lives of Lord Castlereagh and Sir Charles Stewart* (1861).

Ammianus Marcellinus (b.*c*.330, d.*c*.395) A native of Antioch in Syria, Ammianus Marcellinus entered military service aged about 20 as a member of the elite corps of protectores domestici. Receiving his commission from the emperor Constantius II, he was assigned to the personal service of the general Ursicinus, whom he attended in north Italy, Gaul and Germany, Illyricum and Mesopotamia. The climax of Ammianus' service was the Persian siege and capture of Amida (modern Diarbekir) in 359, from which he escaped at the moment of its fall, and subsequently the disastrous Persian invasion of the emperor Julian (363), after which he seems to have left active service. He can be glimpsed at Antioch and in visits to Egypt and the Black Sea, southern Greece and possibly Thrace, before coming to Rome in the mid-380s. It was here, in or very shortly after 390, in Latin rather than his native Greek, that he completed his history.

Ammianus' work is composed in 31 books, of which the first 13 books, covering the period from AD 96 to 353, were apparently already lost by the early sixth century. To judge by references made to them, the earlier of the lost books were neither very full nor very original in character, but became more so as they approached the historian's own day. The surviving 18 books describe in detail the political and military events of Ammianus' lifetime down to the death of Julian and the brief reign of his successor Jovian (books

14–25) and, in somewhat less detail (books 26–31), the joint reigns of Valentinian and Valens until the battle of Hadrianople (9 August, 378) and its immediate aftermath. Ammianus himself features prominently in the earlier of these books, which sometimes resemble personal memoir rather than formal history. The contemporary narrative was based on personal knowledge and accounts of eye-witnesses, some of whom — such as the senator Praetextatus and the imperial eunuch Eutherius with the 'immense memory', whom Ammianus knew in old age at Rome — can be persuasively identified. The centre-piece of the history was the regime, first in Gaul as Caesar and subsequently in the east as sole Augustus, of the emperor Julian (the Apostate). Ammianus admired emperor Julian for his military and administrative capacities, but was very critical of many aspects of his religious policies, especially his superstitious devotion to endless sacrifice. Himself a pagan of a more traditional cast, Ammianus did not adopt the openly polemical stance against Christianity of his younger contemporary, the Greek historian Eunapius, whose work survives in the later history of ZOSIMUS. Ammianus is however scathing of the ostentation of the bishops of Rome and ironically critical of Christianity for its failure to live up to its own 'pure and simple' professions.

Ammianus' work, written in an elaborate, idiosyncratic and often intense style, has moments of profound expressiveness, a highly developed pictorial sense and a remarkable ability to portray character in action, particularly under the stress of physical danger — of which Ammianus had much personal experience in his career — and subject to the moral demands of political office. It is dense with situations and personalities observed vividly and at close quarters, with fine military narrative (its main subject) and passages of brilliant moralizing satire, as when denouncing the conduct of the senatorial class and populace of Rome. The range of subject matter is wide, touching the non-Roman as well as the Roman worlds, and the work contains many geographical, ethnographic, antiquarian and scientific digressions, in the last of which Ammianus' Greek background is acknowledged, with quotations of technical Greek words. The book is nevertheless a masterpiece of Latin historiography, more than worthy of the tradition of TACITUS, as whose formal successor Ammianus should be seen. The further extent of Tacitus' influence upon Ammianus is doubtful: the influences of Sallustius Crispus (see SALLUST) and, above all, CICERO, are much more evident. Other authors, such as HERODOTUS, THUCYDIDES and POLYBIUS, are mentioned at appropriate points without exercising a more general influence upon Ammianus' manner, and Homer and Virgil are deployed to add epic scale and colour to the narrative. The most obvious feature of Ammianus' style is however its independence and originality.   JFM

Main writings

Ammianus Marcellinus: Works, 3 vols, trans. J. C. Rolfe (Cambridge, Mass.: Loeb Classical Library/ Heinemann, 1935–40); *Ammianus Marcellinus: Later Roman Empire*, trans. and ed. W. Hamilton, intro. A. Wallace-Hadrill (Harmondsworth: Penguin, 1986).

Reading

Blockley, R. C.: *Ammianus Marcellinus: a Study of his Historiography and Political Thought* (Brussels: Coll. Latomus 141, 1975).

Crump, G. A.: *Ammianus Marcellinus as a Military Historian* (Wiesbaden: Historia, Einzelschriften 27, 1975).

Matthews, J. F.: Ammianus Marcellinus. In *Ancient Writers: Greece and Rome*, Vol. 2, ed. T. J. Luce (New York: Scribner, 1982) pp. 1117–38.

The Roman Empire of Ammianus (London: Duckworth, 1988).

Sabbah, G.: *La Méthode d'Ammien Marcellin: recherches sur la construction du discours historique dans les Res Gestae* (Paris: Les Belles Lettres, 1975).

Thompson, E. A.: *The Historical Work of Ammianus Marcellinus* (Cambridge: Cambridge University Press, 1947).

Anderson, Perry (b.1938) Anderson became editor of the *New Left Review* in 1962, a position which he held for 20 years. He is currently teaching at the New School for Social Research in New York. His writing, which straddles the realms of history, philosophy and political theory, reflects his own commitment to the New Left at a time when British Marxists were involved in a major reassessment of their political strategies and theoretical inheritance. To this process Anderson brought not only an extensive knowledge of the diverse and shifting currents within modern Marxism but equally remarkable powers of synthesis.

These powers were fully demonstrated with the publication in 1974 of two volumes devoted to the history of both western and eastern Europe from classical antiquity to the nineteenth century. The first, *Passages from Antiquity to Feudalism*, offers not only a highly individual perspective on the genesis and character of feudal social formations but a commentary on the diverging evolutions of western Europe, Scandinavia and eastern Europe. The contrast between eastern and western Europe assumes even greater prominence in the second volume, *Lineages of the Absolutist State*, as Anderson seeks both to establish a regional typology of monarchical absolutism and to explore its role during the long transition to capitalism. For this purpose he combines empirical observation and a theoretical approach to the question of the relative autonomy of the superstructure which owes much to Althusser. Two years later Anderson produced *Considerations on Western Marxism*, an 'elegant and acute' essay in modern intellectual history. In 1980 *Arguments within English Marxism* was published. Focusing on E. P. THOMPSON's polemic with Althusser, this brilliantly succinct study includes a discussion of history as a discipline; the role of human agency in history; the nature of class, the function of the law; and the intellectual roots of Stalinism. It is probably the most penetrating and effective critique of Thompson's historical writings to be found anywhere.   DP

Main publications

(All published by New Left Books, London.)
Passages from Antiquity to Feudalism (1974); *Lineages of the Absolutist State* (1974); *Considerations on Western Marxism* (1976); *Arguments within English Marxism* (1980).

Reading

Thompson, E. P.: *The Poverty of Theory and other Essays* (London: Merlin, 1978).

Andrews, Charles McLean (b.1863, d.1943)
Andrews's career coincided with the rise and spread of professional history in the United States during the late nineteenth and early twentieth centuries. Reacting against what they deemed questionable in the 'amateur' historiography of the preceding decades, the leaders of professional history put forward three aims: to strive for objectivity and past-mindedness and to contribute to both by canvassing thoroughly the primary materials; to focus on the study of institutions rather than individuals; and to communicate with fellow historians through monographic works, thereby making historiography a co-operative venture. Andrews achieved each of these aims; together they made up his contribution to American historical writing.

Entering the new discipline of professional history early, Andrews assiduously pursued its varied activities all his life. He took his PhD at Johns Hopkins, the first American institution to concentrate on postgraduate studies, and subsequently held teaching positions at Bryn Mawr (1889–1907), at Johns Hopkins (1907–10), and at Yale (1910–33), where he was Farnam professor of American history. Tall, magisterial, handsome, intently serious yet open and affable, he was a master teacher and a master seminarian. At Yale he founded his famous school of American colonial history, the products of which appeared in the notable monographic series that he edited from 1913 to 1933. He served on several important national historical committees and as president of the American Historical Association in 1924 and 1925.

Andrews was the foremost spokesman of the imperial school of early American history, the other prominent figures being Herbert Levi OSGOOD and George Louis Beer. Attempting to undo what they held to be the errors of the 'patriotic' historians of earlier generations, Andrews and his colleagues insisted that the American colonial and revolutionary past could be grasped only by placing the colonies within the context of the larger British empire to which they belonged, and by understanding the imperial agencies and policies that governed colonial life. How the empire worked, they said, could best be discovered in the records on deposit in the British archives, and that is where Andrews laboured arduously for more than a decade on the production of the two works he regarded as his lasting contribution to the new American colonial history: the one-volume *Guide to the Manuscript Materials for the History of the United States to 1783* (1908) and the two-volume *Guide to the Materials for American History to 1783* (1912−14).

He presented the imperial viewpoint in three key works: *The Colonial Period* (1912); *The Colonial Background of the American Revolution* (1924); and the authoritative tetralogy *The Colonial Period of American History* (1934−8), for which he won a Pulitzer prize in 1935 and a National Institute of Arts and Letters gold medal in 1937. Creating colonies in North America, he argued, figured prominently in England's seventeenth-century commercial expansion. America was England's frontier. American institutions were English transplantations. From the 1650s onwards, England tried to rough-shape a policy of colonial management, one that would more effectively relate the colonies to the needs of the mother country, and particularly to her ongoing conflicts with the Dutch republic and with France. The end of interdependence between colonial North America and Britain came with the American Revolution, which was best perceived as an event in British colonial history. Its causes lay deep in the relation between the mother country and the colonies, and principally in the fact that, for a century, the former had been moving towards greater imperial control and the latter towards more insistent self-government. Still, the revolution came in the end because extremists, grim and unyielding, had taken command on both sides of the Atlantic and because Britain's leaders decided on a policy of coercion rather than accommodation.

Andrews defined his goal early on as putting the 'colonial' back into 'American colonial history'. He did so by digging deep into the English government's records of the seventeenth and eighteenth centuries. Here lay the success and limitations of his achievement. His four-volume masterpiece appeared in the last decade of his life, at a time when historical studies had moved on to other perspectives and interests. His view of colonial America was then criticized for having centred too much on the 'colonial' and too little on the 'American', and for having glossed over many of its important social and economic aspects and movements. But for all the criticism and the subsequent changing fashions of historiography, Andrews's achievement remains impressive. Working relentlessly over half a century, he amassed the myriad facts of the early American past. From these he drew a monumental, enduring portrait of the constitutional and political institutions that he considered the essential framework of American colonial life.   ASE

Main publications

The Old English Manor (Baltimore: Johns Hopkins University Studies in Historical and Political Science, extra vol. XII, 1892); *Colonial Self-Government, 1652−89* (New York: Harper, 1904); (with Frances G. Davenport) *Guide to the Manuscript Materials for the History of the United States, to 1783, in the British Museum, in Minor London Archives, and in the Libraries of Oxford and Cambridge* (Washington: Carnegie Institution of Washington, 1908); *The Colonial Period* (New York: Holt, 1912); *Guide to the Materials for American History to 1783, in the Public Record Office of Great Britain*, 2 vols (Washington: Carnegie Institution of Washington, 1912−14); *The Colonial Background of the American Revolution: Four Essays in American Colonial History* (New Haven, Conn: Yale University Press, 1924, rev. edn 1931); *The Colonial Period of American History*, 4 vols (New Haven, Conn.: Yale University Press, 1934−38).

Reading

Eisenstadt, A. S.: Charles McLean Andrews. In *Some Modern Historians of Britain*, ed. H. Ausubel, J. B. Brebner, and E. M. Hunt (New York: Dryden Press, 1951).

——:*Charles McLean Andrews: a Study in American Historical Writing* (New York: Columbia University Press, 1956).

Gipson, L. H.: Charles McLean Andrews and the re-orientation of the study of American colonial history. *Pensylvania Magazine of History and Biography* 59 (1935) 209−22.

Labaree, L. W.: Charles McLean Andrews: Historian. *William and Mary Quarterly* 3.1 (1944) 3−14.

Annales school   If a school is a group committed to the production of a homogeneous body of thought, there is no Annales school. If, on the other hand, a school is understood as a milieu of intellectual exchange with a preference for certain kinds of questions, as a way of thinking rather than as consensus, there has been an Annales school since 1929.

Challenging the authority of 'idols', especially the idol of narrative chronological history, the Annales school had little impact outside France during the first two decades of its existence. In the subsequent two decades, Annales approaches received a sympathetic hearing in countries with an appreciation of French culture, such as Spain, Portugal, Latin America, Quebec, Belgium, Poland, Hungary, Romania, Greece, and Turkey. They also found disciples in Italy, where Italy's Crocean idealist and Gramscian Marxist traditions were an obstacle, however, to their deep penetration. In empiricist Britain and Anglo-America the reception was cooler. One vehicle of circulation of Annales ideas in Britain was the scholarly journal *Past and Present*. Scholars in the United States esteemed the work of Marc BLOCH, an advocate of comparative history and one of the two founders of the *Annales* review from which the school takes its name. Apart from sixteenth-century specialists and scholars with geographic perspectives, few Americans knew the work of Bloch's senior collaborator, Lucien FEBVRE. Though they admired Fernand BRAUDEL, chief propagator of Annales methods, for the brilliance of his *Méditerranée* (1949), they spurned his methods as a model. Braudel's popularity in America dates back only to the translation into English between 1970 and 1973 of his article on 'la longue durée' and of the revised and enlarged two-volume edition of *Méditerranée*. Familiarity with his work came to Americans only after the French student rebellion against consensus and authority in May 1968, in the wake of which followed a challenge to Annales approaches.

The following events chart the institutionalization of an Annales school: the foundation in 1929 by Lucien Febvre and Marc Bloch of the *Annales d'histoire économique et sociale* at the new French University of Strasbourg; the renaming in 1946 of the then (1930s) Paris-centred journal, already renamed several times since 1939, as *Annales: économies, sociétés, civilisations*, in reflection of the expanded scope of its interests; the organization in 1947–8, by Lucien Febvre, at the École Pratique des Hautes Études, of the Sixième section for economic and social history; Braudel's succession in 1949 to Febvre's chair of modern civilization at the Collège de France; Braudel's appointment in 1956 (until 1970) as president of the Sixième section; the creation in 1962–3 of the Maison des Sciences de l'Homme, of which Braudel became Administrateur, a post he held until he died in 1985; Braudel's relinquishment of editorial control to the collective management of a 'new *Annales*' in 1969 as a result of the crucial events of May 1968; the physical integration in 1970 of the hitherto dispersed Maison des Sciences de l'Homme; and, in 1975, the transmutation of the Sixième section into a school with university status, the École des Hautes Études en Sciences Sociales.

Since 1968 the Annales school has undergone an identity crisis. On the one hand the perspectives of 1929–68 persist; on the other the orientations of the 'new *Annales*' scholars. Partly under the attraction of Anglo-American models the latter prefer to study small, often marginal groups, without attempting to ascertain the relationship between such groups and a whole culture. Some of the 'new *Annales*' scholars, among them François FURET, believe that the study of large units of integration should be postponed until more data are available. Others contend that what, in Gaullist terminology, Lucien Febvre called 'une histoire à part entière', and what Braudel called total history or 'histoire globale', is a chimerical goal. Yet others, under the inspiration of France's libertarian 'new philosophers', denounce total history as a totalitarian endeavour, glorying instead in the *émiettement* of history as a discipline – its fragmentation under the impact of professionalization. However the dialectic ultimately evolves, its existence obliges us to distinguish between an Annales school, in evidence since 1929, and an Annales paradigm, conceived by that school between 1929 and 1968 and subsequently refined but subject since 1968 to critique by members of that same school.

The Annales paradigm has been progressively restated and made ever more comprehensive. Braudel's three main temporalities –

a time of long duration, a time of intermediate duration marked by fluctuations, and a time of short duration — have been maintained. The changes and patterns included in each kind of time were redefined, however, many of them by Braudel himself. Long duration ceased to be identified almost exclusively with geography, and several *Annalistes*, including Braudel, shifted the emphasis from geography to location theory. Other Annales scholars distinguished between various categories of events, some of them creative of situations of long or intermediate duration. In the process, the goal of political history was altered. Berated hitherto (although firmly in place in Braudel's *Méditerranée*) as a chronological narrative of brief events, political history was reconceived as a study of power relationships. As higher education became accessible in France to a larger number of persons, interest in an 'almost immobile' history declined. In 1963 Jean Lacouture called for the inclusion of a neglected *histoire immédiate* of contemporary events, paradoxically often mediated by the new media, agents for the transformation of current events into standardized objects of mass consumption. Febvre's goal of grasping the *outillage mental* of human groups, redefined as a study of *mentalités*, became too vague a concept for some *Annalistes*. They strove to achieve a historical anthropology simultaneously social, cultural, and physical; a historical anthropology of material culture and value orientations alike.

The separation between the Annales school and Annales paradigm became almost inevitable as the paradigm became more comprehensive and the school more inclusive. As specialization became more necessary, many members of the Annales school lowered their sights so as not to exceed history-as-problem.

The great weakness of the paradigm, affirm Marxists, is its lack of a satisfactory theory of change. Its practitioners, they claim, rarely show how structures, conjunctures (such as business cycles) and events interact, and they overemphasize Malthusian explanations. The Annales paradigm continues nevertheless to tantalize scholars.   TS

Reading

Burguière, André; Histoire d'une histoire: la naissance des 'Annales'. *Annales: économies, sociétés, civilisations* 34 (1979) 1347–59.

——: The fate of the history of 'mentalités' in the 'Annales'. *Comparative Studies in Society and History* 24 (1982) 424–37.

——: Annales (école des). In *Dictionnaire des sciences historiques*, ed. A. Burguière (Paris: Presses Universitaires de France, 1986) 46–52.

Cedronio, Marina et al.: *Storiografia francese di ieri e di oggi* (Napoli: Guida, 1977).

Coutau-Bégarie, Hervé: *Le phénomène 'nouvelle histoire': stratégie et idéologie des nouveaux historiens* (Paris: Economica, 1983).

Furet, François: Beyond the 'Annales'. *Journal of Modern History* 55 (1983) 389–410.

Hexter, Jack: Fernand Braudel and the 'monde braudellien'. *Journal of Modern History* 44 (1972) 480–539.

Hunt, Lynn: French history in the last twenty years: the rise and fall of the 'Annales' paradigm. *Journal of Contemporary History* 21 (1986) 209–24.

Le Roy Ladurie, Emmanuel: L'histoire immobile. *Annales: économies, sociétés, civilisations* 29 (1974) 673–92.

Revel, Jacques: Histoire et sciences sociales: les paradigmes des 'Annales'. *Annales: économies, sociétés, civilisations* 34 (1979) 1360–76.

Review: a Journal of the Fernand Braudel Center for the Study of Economies, Historical Systems, and Civilizations 1.3/4 (1978): The impact of the 'Annales' school on the social sciences.

Stoianovich, Traian: *French Historical Method: the 'Annales' Paradigm* (Ithaca and London: Cornell University Press, 1976).

anthropology and history The roots of much of modern anthropology and history lie in the writers of the Scottish Enlightenment. Kames, Millar, SMITH, ROBERTSON, HUME and others speculated in a comparative and historical manner about the development of societies in Europe and elsewhere. Throughout the nineteenth century there was much cross-stimulation between disciplines which were seen as having the same aims and methods, as in the work of Sir Henry Maine. It was only with the rejection of evolutionary and diffusionist frameworks in anthropology and a growing preoccupation with intensive fieldwork that the discipline of anthropology withdrew from the association. 'Conjectural' history was rejected and the past largely ignored in the functionalist era pioneered by Malinowski and Radcliffe-Brown. This lasted from about 1910 to 1960. During the same period many historians showed a growing absorption with documentary analysis and a concentration on the upper, literate classes and on political and constitutional history. This further widened the gap between the disciplines. It was believed that anthropology was a science looking for general laws, history an art concerned with the particular. The accepted form of explanation in anthropology was in terms of context or function, in history it was in terms of antecedent events.

From about 1960 onwards, first heralded in important articles by the anthropologist E. E. Evans-Pritchard and the historian Keith THOMAS, the unity and overlapping nature of the disciplines has been stressed. A tradition which had never died out in France, with the work of BLOCH, FEBVRE and the 'ANNALES' SCHOOL, was reasserted. It became apparent that the aims of the two disciplines, namely the understanding of man in society, overlapped and that the methods were complementary rather than opposed. Historians were increasingly ready to learn from the insights provided by a classic period of anthropological study.

Social anthropology is based on the intensive study of small communities. This has reinforced the pioneering work of local history and made the period between 1960 and 1980 a golden age of historical community studies in England, France, America and elsewhere. Combined with the post-war archival revolution which gave historians a far wider range of sources, it was now possible to attempt 'total' reconstructions of past communities over long periods. This immersion in the multiple social relationships which link individuals drew consciously on the work of anthropologists.

Anthropology helped to provide insights into features of the past which were so strange that modern historians had found them difficult to comprehend or examine. Complex rituals, blood-feuds, trance and ecstasy, millennarianism, oath-taking, the divine right of kings, and particularly magical and witchcraft beliefs became legitimate and fruitful topics for study. In the last of these, for instance, models from African witchcraft provided a stimulus for many important works on English, French, Spanish, North American and German witchcraft. Again, a newly stimulated interest was combined with the opening up of the immensely rich archives of the judicial authorities, and in particular the records of the Catholic Inquisition.

Anthropological works also had the effect of distancing the familiar, making historians aware that much of what they had regarded as normal in the past really required investigation because it was, cross-comparatively, unusual. A particularly striking example of this was in the field of family relationships. Much of anthropology is concerned with kinship and marriage. These works helped to stimulate many of the studies of such topics as sexuality, marriage, childhood, parental ties, domestic groups, women, love and incest. The anthropological inspiration joined up with interests from historical demography and from women's studies, and thereby opened the whole field of interpersonal relationships and sentiment.

Historical research into many other topics was stimulated by anthropological inquiries; among these were conflict, ceremony, work discipline, time, space, myths, folklore, style and fashion, oral and literate culture, birth, death, dreams, suicide and animals. The formal historical documents usually conceal such topics, so that it was largely under the pressure of anthropology that a vigorous development of the study of past mentality and emotional structures took place, exemplified in the work of historians such as Eric HOBSBAWM, E. LE ROY LADURIE, E. P. THOMPSON and Keith THOMAS.

Anthropology is an explicitly comparative discipline and this has forced historians to look at their particular studies in a wider context, noting the differences between features of European and American society on the one hand and Asia and Africa on the other. It has helped to prevent the easy assumption that like causes will lead to like effects. It has become possible to avoid some of the dangers of ethno- and tempero-centric views that make an analyst judge the past by the present standards of his or her own society. Social anthropology has made certain features of the past apparent for the first time and provided a logic in what was otherwise incomprehensible.

As in any other marriage, there are dangers to be avoided: some of the analogies drawn between the western past and third world societies are too glib; there is a danger of over-stressing the functionality of beliefs; there is a temptation to search for features (e.g. taboos, caste, peasants) which have been found elsewhere and which are therefore presumed to have existed in the past. There is a tendency for all societies to be lumped together, and hence to assume that, as Maine believed, we can infer that the current state of affairs in India or China will tell us something about early European history. There is also the danger that when something is found to be cross-comparatively very unusual, for example the 'romantic love complex' or 'capitalism', we are led to believe that it must be a recent product of those revolutionary events, the industrial and urban developments of the eighteenth and nineteenth centuries, which separate off the west.

Yet on the whole the renewed association of the two disciplines has been mutually enriching. Both seek to interpret the basic patterns in societies, to contrast and compare in order to separate the universal from the particular, to explain both the single event and the broad institution. Both are interested in continuity and in change, in how things came to be as they are and why they persist. Anthropology stresses the interdependence of spheres, the overlap of economics, politics, religion and kinship, which have superficially been separated in the modern industrial world. It proposes paradoxical and ingenious causes for unquestioned institutions. It stresses the importance of context and the difficulty of ascribing meaning. It is particularly concerned with the symbolic, ritual and conceptual, while being equally interested in the material world and ecology.

In the hands of a particularly brilliant group of individuals, anthropology has analysed the workings of three of the four major forms of human civilization, namely hunters and gatherers, tribal societies and peasant societies. For the understanding of a past which may have features of these types of social organization, anthropology has proved an irreplaceable guide. As a mirror in which we can now look more dispassionately at the history of advanced industrial societies it has equal promise. Finally, in its analysis of myth, legend and history, and their overlap, it suggests that history and historians need to be constantly aware of the ways in which their own insights are legitimations which are subtly affected by the political, economic and social worlds which they inhabit. The anthropology of historical research has still to be written, but it would be a fruitful area of study. There can be little doubt that of all the disciplines which lie adjacent to history, anthropology has had the most marked influence in the period between 1960 and 1985.   ADJM

Reading

Gaunt, David: Memoir on history and anthropology (Stockholm, Sweden: Council for Research in Humanities in Social Sciences, Swedish Research Councils, 1982).

Lewis, I. M.: *History and Social Anthropology* (London: Tavistock, 1968).

Rabb, T. K. and Rotberg, R. eds: *The New History: the 1980s and Beyond* (Princeton, NJ: Princeton University Press, 1982) [essays by J. W. Adams, B. Cohn and N. Z. Davis].

Thomas, Keith: History and anthropology. *Past and Present* 24 (1963) 3–24.

antiquarianism The use of artefacts (including works of art, architecture and coins) as evidence for the human past first emerged in early modern Europe as antiquarianism, ancestral to archaeology and distinguished from history, using documentary sources. It began with the study of classical antiquities by Italian humanists such as Flavio Biondo (1392–1463) or Cyriac of Ancona (1391–1455) and was soon taken up in France, where the classical scholar Guillaume Budé made an outstanding contribution to Roman numismatics in his *De asse et partibus eius* (1515). The antiquarian tradition developed, with scholars such as Jacques Spon (*Miscellanea eruditae antiquitatis,*

1679) and the great compilations of the MAURIST Bernard de Montfaucon (*L'Antiquité expliquée* in 15 vols, 1718) and of the Comte de Caylus (*Recueil d'antiquités* in 7 vols, 1752−67). An outstanding early Scandinavian antiquary was the Dane, Ole Worm (1588−1654).

In Britain antiquarianism was closely associated with the topographers such as John Leland (1506−52) and found a triumphant early exponent in William CAMDEN (1551−1623). In the later seventeenth century the study of prehistoric monuments in the field began: Inigo Jones's interest as an architect in Stonehenge (his notes were published posthumously in 1655), the fundamental work of John Aubrey (1626−97), the early work of William STUKELEY (1687−1765), and the surveys associated with the Royal Society's classificatory approach to natural phenomena such as those of Aubrey himself, Robert Plot (1640−96) or Edward Lhwyd (1660−1709). The scientific principles of taxonomy here were promisingly applied to antiquities and in the 1670s Aubrey produced the first (unpublished) classificatory sequence of medieval building styles.

Changing tastes, which in eighteenth-century France led the *philosophes* to ridicule the *érudits* and in England the Virtuosi to be laughed at by the Wits, mark a decline in antiquarian standards, though in Britain a sound tradition of Romano-British field studies continued in the work of John Horsley (1685−1732) and General William Roy (1726−90). Caught up in the Romantic Movement and prompted by fantasies of Stukeley's later writings, Druids and Ancient Britons appear as noble savages in an antiquarianism of a far lower standard than that of Camden or Aubrey. The same mood, however, with its new interest in earlier English poetry, led Thomas Warton (1728−90) to publish in his 1762 edition of the *Faerie Queene*, the first sequence of medieval architecture in print. The resulting romantic antiquarianism profoundly influenced art and literature and, combined with contemporary religious movements, brought about the Gothic Revival in architecture and ornament. From the later eighteenth century antiquarianism fuelled the invention of national traditions and racial myths, harmlessly in Wales, less creditably in Ireland and disastrously in Germany. Empirical antiquarianism expressed in field work and excavation led to the recognition of pagan Saxon antiquities by James Douglas (1753−1819) and of pre-Roman Britain by Sir Richard Colt Hoare (1758−1838) and William Cunnington (1754−1810). In parallel with geology and history, antiquarianism as archaeology became a professional discipline late in the nineteenth century.   SP

Reading

Daniel Glyn: *Origins and Growth of Archaeology*. Harmondsworth: Penguin, 1967.

Piggott, S.: *Ruins in a Landscape*. Edinburgh: Edinburgh University Press, 1976.

Appian (b.*c.*90, d.*c.*165)   Born in Alexandria in Egypt, where in his youth he claimed to have achieved some prominence, Appian subsequently came to Rome, received citizenship, and practised as a legal advocate. Late in life he obtained the post of procurator Augusti through the good offices of Fronto, a leading orator. Appian's *Roman History*, written in Greek, was unusual in its structure. In rough chronological order he dealt in separate books with the wars which Rome had with each of the major nations with whom it came into contact, and with the civil wars of the late Republic. Covering the period down to his own day, the work consisted of 24 books, of which 11 survive. No great stylist, Appian nevertheless is an important source of historical information.   JJP

Main writings

Roman History, 4 vols, trans. Horace White (Cambridge, Mass.: Loeb, 1912).

Reading

Gabba, E.: *Appiano e la storia delle Guerre Civili* (Florence: La Nuova Italia, 1956).

Arbois de Jubainville, Marie-Henry d' (b.1827, d.1910)   From old noble stock originating in Lorraine and destined for the law, Henry went to school in Nancy and then enrolled in the recently founded École des Chartes in Paris (1846). While still pursuing legal studies he also thought of entering the church, but abandoned both callings to become archivist of the *département* of Aube. At Troyes from 1852 to 80 his output was enormous, notably inventories of documents in his care and works principally but not exclusively on the medieval history of Champagne. Simultaneously he began to develop a consuming passion. Hardly pausing in his archival work, he plunged into Celtic philology under the influence of German scholars and Joseph Loth. The appearance of *Les premiers habitants de l'Europe* (1877) brought his name to a wider public. In 1880 he resigned his post at Troyes and took up the newly founded chair of Celtic language and literature in the Collège de France. From 1885 he directed the *Revue celtique*. His teaching and writing covered every aspect of Celtic studies. A man of prodigious learning and intellectual curiosity, who defended his views with passion, he remained to the last open to new ideas and approaches and was his own severest critic.   MCEJ

Main publications

With M. L. Pigeotte: *Histoire des ducs et comtes de Champagne depuis le VIe siècle jusqu'à la fin du XIe*, 7 vols (Paris, 1859–67); *Les premiers habitants de l'Europe d'après les auteurs de l'antiquité et les recherches les plus récentes de la linguistique* (Paris, 1877); *Cours de littérature celtique*, 12 vols (Paris, 1883–1902).

Reading

Chénon, E.: *Notice nécrologique sur Henri d'Arbois de Jubainville* (Paris, 1912).

archaeology and history In the course of the twentieth century archaeology and history, though never completely separated in practice, have developed distinct patterns of organization. In universities it is common for them to be studied in separate departments, sometimes even within different faculties. Distinct national institutions evolved, such as (in Britain) the Historical Association and the Council for British Archaeology.

This separate institutional framework reflected the different routes by which history and archaeology developed into well-established academic subjects. Archaeology is the younger discipline, despite its antiquarian antecedents. Until well into the nineteenth century, the full development of the archae-

ological approach to the past was prevented by the general acceptance of a Creation believed to be only a few thousand years old. The occasional discovery of huge bones could be accommodated within the scriptural evidence for the early existence of giants. The acceptance of the theory of evolution made possible for the first time the application of archaeological techniques over a very wide time span. Indeed, the wider chronology which the development of prehistoric studies has brought is one of archaeology's most distinctive contributions to scholarship.

This was not the only way in which the early development of archaeology was affected by prevailing modes of thought. The influence of religion led to an early concentration of interest upon the near east; the prominent place which the classical Mediterranean civilizations held in the culture of the dominant groups in society also played an important part in determining the areas to which the developing archaeological techniques were directed. Ancient history followed a similar pattern of interest, which often led to an organizational break between medieval and modern history and an ancient history closely tied to the world of religious or classical studies. Other branches of archaeology developed by a route very different from mainstream history; in North America, for instance, archaeological studies of early Indian societies were orginally very much a by-product of anthropology.

The institutional separation of history and archaeology was reinforced by the increasing use in archaeology of sophisticated scientific techniques which have no relevance to the ordinary practices of history. Examples of this development include aerial photography, and dating by the study of tree rings and by radiocarbon or thermoluminescence methods. Meanwhile, mainstream history concentrated on refining techniques which relied upon a wide range of written or printed material. Since the actual techniques employed in the two approaches to reconstructing the past varied a great deal, the persistence of a parallel but separate development is understandable.

For a number of good reasons this separation has become less viable in recent years. Moreover, it was never complete, for archaeologists in a number of major fields of interest continued to rely in part upon documentary evidence, blending this with the results of more strictly archaeological techniques. For example, in the archaeology of London a substantial and distinctive destruction level is well established as an invaluable stratigraphical datum: it is history which provides the evidence to associate that destruction with a closely dated event, Boudicca's rising of AD 60–1.

In recent years it has become more difficult to maintain that archaeology should concentrate on sections of the past with which mainstream history does not concern itself. Archaeology is now applied throughout the world, taking in a very wide range of different cultural sequences, with accompanying historical traditions. Glyn Daniel has claimed that 'archaeology begins yesterday'. Fifty years ago the concept of 'industrial archaeology' scarcely existed, and the spread of archaeology even into the medieval period had not gone very far. Now it is well established that a cotton mill, chapel or railway station can be a valid subject for archaeological investigation. Long experience of studying topics in which documentary and non-documentary evidence can together be fruitfully employed has increased the level of liaison between archaeologists and historians, without as yet doing much to erode the distinct institutional structures which past developments determined.

History and archaeology in terms of subject matter are complementary approaches to the study of the past. Most historians depend essentially on written or printed source material and in some cases, such as the history of law, it is unlikely that other forms of evidence can ever make anything like an equivalent contribution. Archaeology, on the other hand, is primarily concerned with such matters as topography and the study of structures and artefacts. In some major fields, such as the study of very early societies, documents can offer no significant help. Faced with such important problems in the history of mankind as the early development of settled agriculture or the creation of the first towns, the orthodox historian is helpless, and only through archaeology can anything very useful be discovered.

More recently, the common ground between history and archaeology has come to be more fully and overtly appreciated. There are now many areas, by no means confined to such well-established instances as the classical Mediterranean civilizations, where documentary and non-documentary materials have been successfully combined. Work in England on deserted medieval villages, where documentary study has reinforced archaeological investigations, has produced a fuller understanding of these communities. In such contexts documents can often provide precise dating evidence, while excavation may contribute details of past life styles too mundane to engage the interest of contemporary scribes. Equally striking has been the introduction of what has sometimes been called 'total archaeology', which might with equal propriety be termed 'total history', in which all of the evidence relating to a given piece of territory is brought into account, including all periods of human activity. Such investigations may include aerial photography, field-work and excavation, but also manorial records, ratebooks and the enumerators' books of the modern census. This development has obvious parallels with modern developments in historical techniques (see BRAUDEL).

However, the most important link between history and archaeology is of a different but related kind. The end product of any archaeological investigation must be some kind of historical account; this applies even where the study is comprehended under that rather misleading term 'prehistory' ('pre-literate' would be more helpful). There is no archaeology of bronze or iron, pottery or marble, but ultimately only an archaeology of people. The conclusions of a competent piece of archaeological work must, directly or indirectly, embody some kind of historical account of the contribution of the investigation to our understanding of a past society. This is a crucial common ground between history and archaeology. A great archaeologist makes men and women from the past come alive to us, as does a great historian, and their fundamental aims are identical. In this context the existence of distinct institutional patterns of specialist techniques is relatively unimportant. While not all archaeologists would accept such a prescription, archaeology may now be properly defined as that branch of history which is primarily concerned with the study and interpretation of the physical remains of the past.

NMcC

Reading

Daniel, G.: *A Hundred and Fifty Years of Archaeology* 2nd edn (London: Duckworth, 1975).

Dymond, D. P.: *Archaeology and History* (London: Thames & Hudson, 1974).

Finley, M. I.: *The Uses and Abuses of History* (London: Chatto & Windus, 1975), ch.5.

Piggott, S.: *Approach to Archaeology* (London: Adam & Charles Black, 1959).

Ariès, Philippe (b.1914, d.1984) A part-time historian, Philippe Ariès managed during most of his life a family import business of tropical fruits. He became a director of studies at the École des Hautes Études en Sciences Sociales (founded in 1975) only when he was more than 60 years old. While born into a family of the moderate monarchist right, he admired scholars of republican persuasion, namely, Lucien FEBVRE, Marc BLOCH, and Émile Durkheim.

With ANNALES SCHOOL historians and kindred spirits, he helped to fashion a history of *mentalités*, that is, a history of values and representations. Unsympathetic to the general propensity in France after the second world war for socio-economic history, he made use of DEMOGRAPHIC HISTORY as a means to understanding the persistences and shifts in French and western attitudes toward life and death. As demographic history became a separate subdiscipline after the mid-1950s, he maintained his focus on *mentalités*. After the student unrest of 1968, the study of *mentalités* itself became an autonomous field of research. But distrustful of the European experience and of notions of progress and economic growth, many young scholars shied away from *mentalités* to elaborate a subdiscipline of historical anthropology. Ariès, however, continued to stress the primacy of *mentalités* as the determining field of force in which economic, social and cultural change occurs.

Facts of population, he affirmed, correspond to facts of civilization. They thus allow us to distinguish between a pre-eighteenth-century European 'civilization of the instinct' and a post-eighteenth-century 'civilization of the object' and consciousness.

The transition from the first civilization to the second occurred in several steps. Around the year 1000, European civilization was characterized by family fluidity; the protection of the inheritance rights of women; the simultaneous practice and denunciation of greed; and the valuation of tame death (*la mort familière et apprivoisée*), which was defined not by lack of violence but by a charitable view of salvation. By 1300, in what was still essentially a civilization of the instinct, there had appeared a different configuration of attitudes: a continuing participation by children in the play and work of adults, but the placing of restrictions upon the inheritance rights of women; the introduction of Roman conceptions of justice; and a view of death as death of the self (*la mort de soi*), requiring individual punishment and reward in the after-life. Then, from about 1500, there was a growing appreciation of the household and conjugal family and a growing perception of childhood as a special age category which, during the seventeenth and eighteenth centuries, culminated in a dialectic between advocates of childhood innocence and partisans of discipline. Soon there was an identification of adolescence. At the same time, there was a shift in some parts of France from a system limiting inheritance to one or two heirs to one of greater equity in the division of property. The more customary perception of death was now as death of the other (*la mort de toi*), perceived as the loss of a friend or dear one who should be both grieved and remembered.

The transition to a civilization of the object and consciousness was thus made before 1789. But a 'Malthusian mentality' or desire to limit births was manifest in France from the middle of the eighteenth century. Soon there was a desire to subject the body in general to rational corrective intervention. As the body became an object of increasing concern and as it became possible to separate sex from reproduction, awaken desire, and turn sex into a source of repeatable pleasure, vaguely intimates Ariès, the foundations were laid for the quest of the twentieth century: to find a successor to the civilization of the object.   TS

Main publications

Histoire des populations françaises et de leurs attitudes devant la vie depuis le XVIIIe siècle (Paris: Editions Self, 1948); *Le Temps de l'histoire* (Monaco: Editions du Rocher, 1954); *L'Enfant et la vie familiale sous l'ancien régime* (Paris: Plon, 1960), trans. Robert Baldick as *Centuries of Childhood: a Social History of Family Life* (London: Jonathan Cape; New York: Alfred A. Knopf, 1962); *L'Homme devant la mort* (Paris: Éditions du Seuil, 1977), trans. Helen Weaver as *The Hour of our Death* (New York: Alfred A. Knopf, 1981); L'Histoire des mentalités. In *La Nouvelle Histoire*, ed. Jacques Le Goff, Roger Chartier and Jacques Revel (Paris: La Bibliothèque du CEPL, Les encyclopédies du savoir moderne 1978) pp. 402–23; *Un Historien du dimanche* (Paris: Éditions du Seuil, 1980).

Reading

Burguière, André: Ariès (Philippe), 1914–1984. In *Dictionnaire des sciences historiques*, ed. A. Burguière (Paris: Presses Universitaires de France, 1986) pp. 67–70.

Arneth, Alfred Ritter von (b.1819, d.1897)

Arneth spent his life in Austrian government service, first at the foreign office and then at the state archives (vice-director 1860, director 1868), combining liberal politics with loyalty to the Habsburg dynasty. His major achievement as an historian was his ten-volume life of Maria Theresa, still the standard work. He was also the tireless (and, on occasions, selective) editor of numerous volumes of correspondence, most notably of Maria Theresa, Joseph II, Catherine II, Leopold II, Marie Antoinette and Kaunitz.   TCWB

Main publications

Prinz Eugen von Savoyen, 3 vols (Vienna, 1858); *Geschichte Maria Theresias*, 10 vols (Vienna, 1863–79).

Arrian (b.c.85, d. after 145)

An inscription from Athens, 'L[ucius] Flavius Arrianus, consular, philosopher', neatly sums up the two strands of Arrian's career: on the one hand was the Greek aristocrat in the service of Rome; on the other, the scholar whose writings, by his own assessment, 'could bear comparison with the virtuosi of the Greek language'. Arrian was born into the wealthy municipal aristocracy of Nicomedia in Bithynia in north-west Asia Minor. There he moved among men who were rich, self-confident, and devoted to an exuberant revival of Greek culture. His family had Roman citizenship; however, despite being part of the elite of Rome's empire, contemporary Greek aristocrats by no means considered a public career at Rome as a necessary or even particularly desirable objective. Arrian, indeed, was the first of only a handful of men from his region to hold high office in Rome.

He is probably to be found in the entourage of C. Avidius Nigrinus, governor of Achaea, about AD 110 and it is a reasonable supposition that this Roman noble, from a family with close contacts with the Greek world, sponsored Arrian's career. It is not possible to recover with certainty the stages of that career. A curious metrical inscription in Greek from Cordoba in Spain is almost certain testimony to Arrian's governorship there about 125. He went on to hold the consulship in 129 or 130. Then came an unusually long stint of six or seven years as governor of Cappadocia in eastern Asia Minor. Shortly after his arrival he carried out an inspection of the Black Sea coast of his province and later used his official report in Latin as the basis for his *Periplus* (Voyage round the Black Sea), composed in Greek. In 135 he repulsed an invasion of Alans. He commemorated his achievement in a lost history and in a pamphlet *On the Battle Formation against the Alans*; he also wrote an *Essay on Tactics*. After the Cappadocian command Arrian settled in Athens, where he was granted citizenship and even held the senior magistracy there. So rarely do personal details survive about the writers of classical antiquity that it is impossible to pass over the vignette of 'Arrian the consul' – reasonably to be identified with the historian – which the medical writer, Galen, preserves, of his habit of cupping his hand behind his ear to counteract his deafness.

Arrian was a prolific writer and with amiable affectation styled himself 'the new XENOPHON'. The influence of his predecessor is obvious in works like his *On Hunting*. In his youth Arrian had studied with the noted Stoic philosopher, Epictetus, and produced both an *Encheiridion*

(Manual) of his master's ideas and eight books of *Discourses* (of which four survive) after the manner of Xenophon's *Memorabilia* of Socrates. There is little elsewhere in his works to suggest that Arrian's attachment to Stoicism was particularly profound. His *Indike* (On India) was a study which came into his mind when he was writing about Alexander's campaigns there. The Indians had inspired a long list of more or less fanciful works about the wonders of their land, which went back to HERODOTUS, another important influence on Arrian. Of his major historical works several survived well into the Byzantine period, but are now known only from quotations. There was a history of his home region, Bithynia, a long study of Rome's wars with Parthia, and a study in depth of the struggles of the successors to Alexander. However, Arrian's fame rests upon his *Anabasis of Alexander*, which in seven books provides the fullest surviving account of the campaigns of Alexander the Great. Although there had been many narratives of Alexander and his achievements by his contemporaries, none has come down to us. This fact gives Arrian's work its importance. Arrian had read widely in the sources; but he chose to base his work on the accounts of Aristobulus, a companion of Alexander, and Ptolemy who became ruler of Egypt after Alexander's death. His reason for picking Ptolemy was that since he was a king he was less likely to tell lies, which is a nice illustration of the strand of naivety which runs through his history. Arrian's clear narrative eschews many of the stories of wonders associated with Alexander. Some of Alexander's actions — the occasional brutality, violent anger, and drunkenness — had become the standard exemplum for moral philosophers. While Arrian does not avoid these incidents and, on occasion, expresses his disgust, his history is ultimately a long encomium of its hero, which culminates in book 7.30 with a sharp condemnation of anyone who might try to criticize Alexander, whose faults were minor but whose repentance for misdeeds was a sign of true nobility.   JJP

Main Writings

Anabasis of Alexander, principal edn of the text by A. G. Roos (2nd edn rev. by G. Wirth, Teubner, 1967–8); *Arrian: History of Alexander and Indica*, text and trans. P.A. Brunt (Cambridge, Mass.: Loeb, 1976, 1983).

Reading

Stadter, P.: *Arrian of Nicomedia* (Chapel Hill: University of North Carolina Press, 1980).

Bosworth A. B.: *A Historical commentary on Arrian's History of Alexander*, vol. 1 (Oxford: Oxford University Press, 1980).

art history The branch of history concerned with the visual arts. It can claim descent from the anecdotal biographies of painters and sculptors in the elder Pliny's (AD *c*.23–79) *Historia Naturalis* (*Natural History*). More realistically, it developed from the writers on art in the Italian Renaissance. Lorenzo Ghiberti (1378–1455) in his *Commentarii* prefaced the account of his own work as a sculptor with an outline of antique art which drew on Pliny and an account of the work of his Florentine predecessors. He and others elaborated the idea, implicit in Pliny, of individual artists seen not simply in isolation but as contributing to a general progress in art. Giorgio VASARI (1511–1574) perhaps best deserves the title of father of art history. In his *Vite* he described the development of Florentine art to its culmination in Michelangelo. Others followed Vasari in providing accounts of their schools of art. Carel van Mander (1548–1606) in his *Het schilderboeck* (The Painter's Book) of 1604 provided a systematic account of Netherlandish and German artists. Later writers of the seventeenth century included: Carlo Ridolfi (1594–1658) who provided an account of Venetian art; André Félibien des Avaux (1619–1695) on French painting; Giovanni Bellori (1615–1696) on baroque art; and Joachim von Sandrart (1606–1688) who added much material on German artists.

It was Johann Joachim WINCKELMANN (1717–1768), a librarian working in Rome, who in many respects was the founder of modern art history, and for over a century the chief language of art historical writing was German. In his *Geschichte der Kunst des Altertums* (*History of Ancient Art*) of 1764 Winckelmann categorized and interpreted the styles of classical art. He was concerned less with the biographies of individual artists than with the stylistic development of the Greek ideal of beauty. He further characterized their art as expressing the whole spirit of the Greeks. In the 1820s this concept was taken further by G. W. F. HEGEL (1770–1831) who in his *Aesthetik* (1820–9) (*Aesthetics: Lectures on Fine Art*) saw the entire history of art as a coherent whole, in terms of his vision of the development of the human spirit. The idea that works of art could be the highest embodiment of a historical period gave added importance to the study of art and greatly influenced later art historians. Jacob BURCKHARDT's (1818–1897) conception of the Renaissance owed much to his deep study of Italian Renaissance art though he never produced a history of Renaissance art to complement his *Die Kultur der Renaissance in Italien* (1860) (*The Civilization of the Renaissance in Italy*).

Karl Fredrich von Rumohr (1785–1843) can be regarded as having initiated systematic archival research in art history with his *Italienische Forschungen* of 1827–32. For Rumohr, along with the discovery and interpretation of documents there went a concern for the correct authorship of works of art. However, the important task of the attribution and dating of works could often only be done on the basis of stylistic evidence. Sir Joseph Crowe (1825–1896) and the Italian G. Cavalcaselle (1820–1897) combined archival research with connoisseurship in their joint publications establishing the body of work of Italian painters. Others came to rely more exclusively on the internal evidence of the works. Giovanni Morelli (1816–1891) applied his early training in anatomy to connoisseurship, identifying artists by their treatment of physiological details like earlobes and fingernails. He was also one of the earliest art historians to make use of what has become the essential tool of art historical research and teaching – photography. Bernard Berenson (1865–1959) became perhaps the most celebrated and controversial of the great art historian connoisseurs, relying on intuition and a superb visual memory where now scientific examination plays a much greater role. Other art historians were more concerned with analysing the stylistic development of art from one period to another. Alois Riegl (1858–1905) closely analysed changes in artistic forms and intentions which he saw as a purely internal process, isolated from the context and functions of the works which were seen as representing stages in the continuous evolution of art. He and Heinrich WÖLFFLIN (1864–1945), in concentrating on the analysis of artistic forms, developed a new and valuable terminology for defining changes in style more precisely.

There was an inevitable reaction against both connoisseurship and formal analysis with their concentration on style at the expense of content. Émile Mâle (1862–1954) in his pioneering studies explored the subject matter of French medieval art and its sources. The study of the subject matter and symbolism of works of art, iconography, became particularly important in the United States through the influence of Charles Rufus Morley (1877–1955) at Princeton. In Germany, Aby Warburg's (1866–1929) iconographic interests were broader in scope and were concerned with relating the works to their historical context. Among Warburg's many distinguished followers was Erwin Panofsky (1892–1968). Panofsky developed a distinction between 'iconography', the study of what a work of art symbolizes, and 'iconology', the study of what the subject matter expresses within the cultural tradition of the symbols. His *Studies in Iconology* (1939) influenced a generation of American scholars. Max Dvořák (1874–1921) in Vienna developed history of art as the history of ideas and two of his students, Fredrich Antal (1887–1954) and Arnold Hauser (1892–1978), produced Marxist-based social histories of art.

A professorship in art history had been established at Göttingen as early as 1813 and the academic discipline of *Kunstgeschichte* became firmly established in German, Austrian and Swiss universities. Its spread in the United States dates from the early twentieth century and there was a chair at Edinburgh in 1879; but it was not until 1932 that England saw a department of art history with the establishment of the Courtauld Institute of Art in London. In 1934 Warburg's library and institute for the study of the classical tradition was transferred to London. The different outlooks of the two institutes are reflected in the organization of their photographic collections: the Courtauld's by artist and the Warburg's by subject. Both institutes achieved a high international reputation particularly under the directorships of Anthony Blunt (1907–1983) at the Courtauld (1947–74) and Sir Ernst Gombrich (b.1909) at the Warburg (1959–76). Gombrich, like the architectural historian Sir Nikolaus Pevsner, was one of many central European scholars who by their presence abroad greatly enriched the spread of the discipline. The rise of Nazism caused an exodus of art historians. Max J. Friedländer (1867–1957) from 1937 worked in Holland on early northern European painting. Of the many important scholars who settled in the United States Erwin Panofsky was the most influential. Edgar Wind (1900–1971) was also concerned with Renaissance humanism and iconography and was an influential teacher both in America and at Oxford. At the Courtauld, Johannes Wilde (1891–1970) influenced a generation of British art historians with his emphasis on the importance of the work of art itself and the need to reconstruct its original appearance and physical context.

In British universities art history remained a relatively small subject, though larger departments have developed in art colleges and polytechnics. Much research of a high order has been carried out by art historians working in museums and art galleries. Sir Martin Davies's (1908–1975) catalogues of the National Gallery established new standards and one can point to the writings of Sir John Pope-Hennessy (b.1913) while at the Victoria and Albert Museum.

Most recently, art history in the English-speaking world has shown an increasing tendency towards specialization both in terms of chronological periods covered and in subject matter. Architectural history and design history have both become virtually separate disciplines. There has been at the same time a growing diversity of approaches with increasing interest in the social history of art and the study of taste and patronage, as well as a desire to apply lessons from semiotics, feminism and psychoanalysis. But what continues to distinguish art history from other forms of history is that the art historian's usual starting point and primary source material is a physical object or building that is also a work of art.   JGB

Reading

Berenson, B.: Rudiments of connoisseurship. In *The Study and Criticism of Italian Art*, 2nd series (London: G. Bell, 1902).

Clark, K.: *The Study of Art History*, repr. from *Universities Quarterly* 10.3 (London: Turnstile Press, 1956).

Gombrich, E. H.: *Aby Warburg: an Intellectual Biography* (London: Warburg Institute, 1970).

——: *Tributes: Interpreters of our Cultural Tradition* (Oxford: Phaidon, 1984).

Hauser, A: *The Philosophy of Art History* (New York: Knopf, 1959).

Holly, M.: *Panofsky and the Foundations of Art History* (Ithaca and London: Cornell University Press, 1984).

Kleinbauer, W. E. and Slavens, T. P.: *Research Guide to the History of Western Art* (Chicago: American Library Association, 1982).

Panofsky, E.: *Meaning in the Visual Arts: Papers in and on Art History* (New York: Doubleday, 1955).

Podro, M.: *The Critical Historians of Art* (London: Yale University Press, 1982).

Roskill, M.: *What is Art History?* (London: Thames & Hudson, 1976).

Ashley, William James (b.1860, d.1927) An Oxford history scholar and fellow, Ashley became interested in the application of historical method (as distinct from mere theory) to economic matters. He was much influenced by Gustav Schmoller and Arnold TOYNBEE whose influential *Lectures on the Industrial Revolution*, posthumously issued in 1884, were derived largely from Ashley's notes. After publishing a volume on the early history of the English woollen industry (in the United States, 1887) and the first part of a textbook (1888), he was appointed to a chair of political economy in Toronto (1888). He then became holder of the first chair of economic history in the English-speaking world, at Harvard (1892–1901).

Impressed by the value of tariffs to the USA, he was an obvious recruit to establish, and rule over (until his retirement in 1925), the new faculty of commerce — in fact, England's first university business school — at Birmingham, then much under the influence of Joseph Chamberlain, would-be tariff reformer. Despite university administration and government committees (he was knighted in 1917), and although he then described himself as an economist, his original interest in history persisted and he wrote two further books of significance to economic historians. An acknowledged pioneer in the subject, he became involved in the International Congress's one and only meeting in England (1912). This austere workaholic did not, however, endear himself to many younger members of the profession. Nonconformist by upbringing, he turned Anglican and retired to Canterbury where he died.   TCB

Main publications

(Published by Longmans Green, London, unless otherwise stated.) *The Early History of the English Woollen Industry* (Baltimore: American Economic Association, vol. 2.4, 1887); *An Introduction to English Economic History and Theory*, part 1, *The Middle Ages* (1888); part 2, *The End of the Middle Ages* (1893); *Surveys, Historic and Economic* (1900); Survey of the past history and present position of political economy (1907), in *Essays in economic method*, ed. R. L. Smyth (London: Duckworth 1962); *The Economic Organisation of England: an Outline History (1914); Bread of our Forefathers* (Ford lectures 1923, but not delivered because of pressure of government work; published posthumously) (Oxford: Clarendon Press, 1928).

Reading

The Times, 25 July 1927.

Ashton, Thomas Southcliffe (b.1889, d. 1968) A down-to-earth Lancastrian and proud of it, the son of the Trustee Savings Bank manager at Ashton-under-Lyne, Ashton won a scholarship to Manchester University where he read history and political economy and, after a spell as schoolteacher, extramural lecturer and university lecturer elsewhere, returned to Manchester as senior lecturer in 1921 (reader in currency and public finance in 1927). He had become much influenced by the magnetic personality of George UNWIN, Manchester's professor of economic history, and later recalled that 'one by one the young theorists ceased to twitter in their nests of indifference curves and fluttered down to earth'. His research and writing concentrated upon economic, and particularly industrial, history, though he also wrote the centenary

history of the Manchester Statistical Society. In 1944, on R. H. Tawney's initiative, he was appointed to the prestigious chair of economic history in London, tenable at the London School of Economics, for the remaining ten years of his teaching life. Here, despite his natural reticence, he became the dominating figure in the subject during its period of rapid post-war growth. His short, brilliantly written textbook, *The Industrial Revolution* (1948), brought him fame not only throughout the English-speaking world but also among readers of the six other languages into which it was translated. He was an active participant in the debate about the standard of living in the Industrial Revolution, decidedly on the side of the optimists. He was elected a fellow of the British Academy in 1951 and appointed Ford's lecturer in history at Oxford for 1953. He had a great influence upon the growing ranks of younger teachers in the subject who frequently made pilgrimages to visit him in his retirement at Blockley, Gloucestershire. In 1960 he succeeded Tawney as president of the Economic History Society in which he had long played a leading part.   TCB

Main publications

Iron and Steel in the Industrial Revolution (Manchester: Manchester University Press, 1924; with Joseph Sykes, *The Coal Industry in the Eighteenth Century* (Manchester: Manchester University Press, 1929); *Economic and Social Investigations in Manchester* (London: P. S. King, 1934); *The Industrial Revolution* (Oxford: Home University Library, 1948); The treatment of capitalism by historians, and The standard of life of the workers in England, 1790–1830, in *Capitalism and the Historians*, ed. F. A. Hayek (London: Routledge & Kegan Paul, 1954); *An Economic History of England in the Eighteenth Century* (London: Methuen, 1955); *Economic Fluctuations in England, 1700–1800* (Oxford: Clarendon Press, 1959).

Reading

Sayers R. S.: Thomas Southcliffe Ashton, 1889–1968. *Proceedings of the British Academy* 56 (1972) 263–81.

Ashworth, William (b.1920) Born in Yorkshire and educated at Todmorden Grammar School and the London School of Economics, Ashworth joined the staff of the LSE in 1948, was elected reader in economic history in the

University of London in 1955 and was professor of economic and social history in the University of Bristol from 1958 until his retirement in 1982.

Ashworth's major work focused on the development of the British economy since the late Victorian period. His *Economic History of England 1870–1939* (1960) set new standards in the application of economic concepts to historical analysis; it was a major influence on generations of students and it is still the leading text on the period. He has made significant contributions to urban history, especially in relation to the role of planning and the impact of industrialization on urban change, and has published on international and comparative history, including one of the most successful textbooks on this subject. His most recent work is a comprehensive study of the political and economic history of the nationalized coal industry in Britain.   BWEA

Main publications

A Short History of the International Economy (1952), 4th edn (London: Longman, 1987); *The Genesis of Modern Town Planning* (London: Heinemann, 1954); *An Economic History of England, 1870–1939* (London: Methuen, 1960); contributor to *London Aspects of Change*, ed. Centre for Urban Studies (London: MacGibbon & Kee, 1964); contributor to *Victorian County History of Essex* (Oxford: Oxford University Press, 1966); Typologies and evidence; has nineteenth century Europe a guide of economic growth?. *The Economic History Review*, 30 (1977) 140–58; *The History of the British Coal Industry*. Vol. 8, *1946–1982: The Nationalized Industry* (Oxford: Clarendon Press, 1986).)

Asser (b. before 855, d.908/909)   The biographer of King Alfred, Asser was a cleric from St David's in Wales. From *c.*885 he was one of the scholars who assisted Alfred in his search for learning. Sometime between 892 and 900 he became bishop of Sherborne. His life of Alfred, completed in 893, tells much which would otherwise be unknown, especially about the king's early life and non-military activities. Partly modelled on EINHARD's life of Charlemagne, it more closely resembles that of Louis the Pious by Thegan. Its authenticity, formerly questioned, is fully proved.   JC

Main writings

Asser's Life of Alfred, W. H. Stevenson (1906; new impression, with an article by D. Whitelock on recent work, Oxford: Oxford University Press, 1951).

Reading

Keynes, S. and Lapidge M.: eds *Alfred the Great*. (Harmondsworth Penguin, 1983); incl. intro., trans. and notes.

Aulard, François Victor Alphonse (b.1849, d.1928)   From an academic family, Aulard was educated under the Second Empire in the French provinces and at the École Normale Supérieure. He saw service during the Franco-Prussian war and emerged from it as a radical socialist republican. His early work was on Italian literature, but by the 1880s his interests had focused on the French Revolution. In 1886 he moved from his position as a schoolteacher to the first chair in the history of the French Revolution at the Sorbonne, which he occupied until 1922. From 1887 until he died, he edited a learned journal, *La Révolution française*, and contributed regularly to the left-wing periodical press.

Aulard published prolifically on all aspects of the Revolution. Among his more notable contributions were his devastating critique of TAINE (1907), his unjustly neglected study of the Revolution and feudalism (1919) and his 26-volume edition of the Acts of the Committee of Public Safety (1889–1923). His hero was Danton, whom he was determined to exonerate from the charges of moral and financial corruption on which he had been condemned in 1794. In 1907 this admiration caused a spectacular rift with his most brilliant pupil, MATHIEZ, who set up a rival journal, *Annales révolutionnaires*, dedicated to the memory of Robespierre. Mathiez attacked his former master unremittingly for the rest of his life. Aulard never replied, and as a result died in scholarly eclipse. Even his journal did not survive him long, while that of Mathiez became (in 1924) the *Annales historiques de la révolution française*, which is still prestigious. Nor will Danton's reputation ever recover from the onslaughts of Mathiez. Yet Aulard's knowledge was encyclopaedic, his insights often shrewd, and nobody did more to establish scholarly standards in the study of the French Revolution. As the legacy of Mathiez crumbles, Aulard's reputation seems ripe for reappraisal. WD

Main publications

The French Revolution: a Political History (1901, English trans. London: Benn, 1910); *Taine, historien de la révolution française* (Paris: Félix Alcan, 1907); *La Révolution française et le régime féodal* (Paris: Félix Alcan, 1919); *Christianity and the French Revolution* (London: Benn, 1925, English trans. 1927).

Reading

Belloni, G.: *Aulard, historien de la révolution française* (Paris: Presses Universitaires de France, 1949).

Aurelius Victor (*fl.* fourth century AD) An African of self-professed humble origins, Sextus Aurelius Victor rose high in the service of the Roman empire, becoming prefect of Rome in 389. His so-called *Liber de Caesaribus* (Book of the Caesars) is a summary account of four centuries of Roman history from the reign of Augustus to 360 AD. It is a series of very brief, and frequently erroneous, imperial biographies, with a penchant for moralizing digressions. EDH

Main writings

Livre des Césars, ed. and trans. P. Dufraigne (Paris: Les Belles Lettres, 1975) English trans. E. C. Echols, *Brief Imperial Lives* Exeter: 1962).

Reading

Bird, H. W.: *Sextus Aurelius Victor: a historiographical study* (Liverpool: Francis Cairns, 1984).

Australian historiography The first British settlement at Sydney in 1788 consisted largely of convicts; and as a gaol by its very nature is a record-keeping institution, early Australia gave historians an abundance of records. The wealth of official archives continued, because by 1860 six Australian colonies were busily serving a population which had just passed one million.

The first creditable history based on research was John West's two-volume *History of Tasmania*, published in 1852. A Congregational minister and journalist, West wrote lucidly, was alert to economic as well as political events, and was impressively fair except when discussing the recent transportation of convicts, of which he was an ardent opponent. His book, admired by many historians, has been republished twice in the last twenty years. From George Rusden, a retired civil servant, came in 1883 the first comprehensive history of the Australian colonies. In the second edition (1897) Rusden revealingly observed: 'If he tells the truth an author cannot avoid making enemies; and if he palter with it he can deserve no friends.' In his 1,800 pages he primarily displayed what R. G. Collingwood in *The Idea of History* called 'scissors and paste'. Most Australian histories written in the nineteenth century depicted, in their more flowery paragraphs, a Providence which was eager to punish and reward.

The nationalism spurred by the first world war and the Gallipoli campaign of 1915 was expressed in a bold official war history of which Charles Bean eventually wrote six volumes. Unusual among Great War histories, it was free from official censorship and also gave unusual emphasis to the private soldier and no undue credence to the generals and their despatches.

Professional historians in Australia could be counted on the fingers of two hands until the 1920s. Their teaching load was heavy and they wrote few books. John Simeon Elkington, professor of history and political economy at the University of Melbourne from 1879 to 1912, often confided that he was about to write a book: he died with it unfinished. His successor, Ernest Scott, had written on the French sea explorers of Australia while working as a *Hansard* reporter, and soon after taking the chair he produced his *Short History of Australia* which for three decades was a quietly-stimulating influence on Australian schools. The history chair at the other large Australian university, Sydney, was held from 1899 by George Arnold Wood, who also wrote on navigators at a time when the early exploration of the continent was seen as the most heroic of history topics. One of Wood's students, R. Max Crawford, succeeded Scott at Melbourne (1937–70) and made it the country's main recruiting ground for academic historians. Crawford, like Wood, was a Balliol man; of overseas universities, Oxford had the strongest influence on the profession of history in Australia.

A milestone in the writing of Australian history came in the year 1930. E. O. G. Shann at the University of Western Australia produced his *Economic History of Australia*, elegant and thoughtful but deemed Toryish and too much a freetrader's firearm to be tolerated in a citadel of protectionism, while in the same year Keith Hancock's stylish *Australia* was promptly acclaimed as relevant to present as well as past. Hancock was also the first major historian to worry about those conservation issues that became the vogue among younger historians in the 1970s when the counterculture held sway. 'The very soil has suffered from the ruthlessness of the invaders', wrote Hancock in 1930. In *Discovering Monaro* he returned to this theme more than four decades later.

Australian historians have tended to see economic events as watersheds: the wool expansion beginning about 1815, the first gold rush in 1851, the bank crashes and slump in the 1890s, the depression of the 1930s, and the post-war immigration from diverse lands. Timothy A. Coghlan was the first specialist in economic history, and his work of 2,400 pages described nearly every strike, rise in the price of bread and new railway. His preface proudly announced: 'For the statistics I am my own authority.' In the 1930s important economic histories appeared by Brian Fitzpatrick, who took the opposite side from Shann, and from the 1950s the Butlin brothers made the running, S. J. writing banking history while N. G. pioneered his 'scoreboard school' which rewrote the economic history of 1860–1900.

In the quarter century 1950–75 the number of full-time historians multiplied many times; prehistory under D. J. Mulvaney became influential; neglected fields ranging from the history of sport and women to business and shipping were explored; and by the 1970s too many historians were concentrating on little, walled, proprietary fields. One day the walls will fall and the new densely-stacked knowledge will tumble out. Of the synthesizing historians, Manning Clark was a celebrated national figure, and in 1987 his sixth large volume took Australia's story to 1935. Waves of nationalism and anti-nationalism were giving historical arguments a high place in national controversy; and History was seen as both an ammunition dump and as arbiter. GB

Reading

Bean, C. E. W. ed: *The Official History of Australia in the War of 1914–18*, 12 vols (Sydney, Angus & Robertson 1921–42).

Clark, C. M. H.: *A History of Australia*, 6 vols (Melbourne: Melbourne University Press, 1961–87).

Coghlan, T. A. *Labour and industry in Australia*, 4 vols. (London, Oxford University Press, 1918).

Crawford, R. M. *'A bit of a rebel': the life and work of George Arnold Wood* (Sydney, Sydney University Press, 1975).

Crawford, R. M., Clark, M. and Blainey, G. *Making History* (Melbourne: McPhee Gribble, and Penguin, 1985).

Hancock, W. K. *Australia* (London: Benn 1930).

Inglis, K. S. *C. E. W. Bean, Australian Historian* (Brisbane: University of Queensland Press, 1970).

Pascoe, R.: *The Manufacture of Australian History* (Melbourne: Oxford University Press, 1979).

Rusden, G. W.: *A History of Australia* 2nd edn, 3 vols (Melbourne: Melville, Mullen & Slade, 1897).

Shann, E. *An Economic History of Australia* (Cambridge, Cambridge University Press, 1930).

West, J. *The History of Tasmania*, 2 vols (Launceston: Henry Dowling, 1852).

Austrian historiography Also known as Habsburg historiography because it grew out of the court historiography of the Habsburg dynasty, the 'House of Austria', as Holy Roman Emperors and kings of Bohemia and Hungary. Until the mid-nineteenth century it remained correspondingly deferential and second-rate, although it had already begun to yield major achievements in a few areas of special concern (for example Hammer-Purgstall's volumes on the Ottoman Empire). Austrian historiography took off after the 1848 revolution, with the foundation of the Institute for Austrian Historical Research (Institut für Österreichische Geschichtsforschung) and of historical societies and journals throughout the empire, alongside a fuller exploitation of the resources of the imperial archives (Haus-Hof- und Staatsarchiv). Austria now began to make a large contribution to the advances in German *Quellenforschung*, especially for the middle ages. Work on later periods by German Austrians tended to remain conservative, though it could be distinguished, as with the splendid lives of Maria Theresa and Prince Eugene by the court archivist ARNETH, the astounding one-man biographical achievement of Constantin von Wurzbach, the accounts of high politics by FRIEDJUNG, and the Catholic historiography of PASTOR. Liberal critique was rare: its first and most brilliant exponent, Anton Springer, settled in Germany to write his history of Austria since the Peace of Vienna (*Geschichte Oesterreichs seit dem Wiener Frieden 1809*, 1863–5).

Meanwhile the very notion of a unified 'Habsburg' historiography, embracing the whole Monarchy, soon proved fragile. German writings were increasingly tinged by nationalism. In Hungary there was an early phase of Latin, then of German-language historians – I. Katona, *Historia critica regum Hungariae* (42 volumes, 1779–1817): J. C. Engel, *Geschichte des ungrischen Reichs* (1796); I. A. Fessler, *Die Geschichte der Ungern und ihrer Landsassen* (1815–25). Following these a national school, around Horváth and Szalay, turned to the Magyar vernacular and largely patriotic concerns, though professional scholars of the next generation (see MARCZALI) still owed much to the Viennese connection, which was later explicitly stressed by SZEKFÜ. The Slavs of the Monarchy developed their own historical preoccupations (see SLAVONIC HISTORIOGRAPHY), and PALACKÝ in Bohemia evolved a scheme of interpretation with a radically anti-German edge. Here too, however, the bond of the Monarchy and its traditions retained influence: witness GINDELY's pioneering research on the travails of the seventeenth-century Empire, or the work of the Cracow school among the Poles.

The break-up of Austria–Hungary in 1918, though it stimulated much good research on a regional or national base, crippled historical study of the old Monarchy, even in rump Austria, where the cogent radical-liberal reflections of REDLICH gave way to the pan-German vision of SRBIK, which itself soon

suffered shipwreck, leaving as central figures of the next generation a medievalist, BRUNNER, and a Benedictine monk, Hugo Hantsch. But the combination, inherited from the nineteenth century, of rigorous training, well-established professional institutions and outlets, and the controversiality and topicality of many aspects of the past, has sustained historiography as a major intellectual endeavour in all the successor states.

The difficulty of embracing the problems of the Austrian or Habsburg past from within, in an age of rival nationalisms which drew heavily on history for their political claims and integrative myths, left much of the best synthetic work to be accomplished by outsiders. French historians were prominent, with DENIS's special feel for Bohemian developments and EISENMANN's larger view of the nineteenth-century constitutional evolution. Subsequently British and American writers took the lead, at first much swayed by international politics in the vigorous *haute vulgarisation* of SETON-WATSON, then in the more objective work of three scholars born around 1900. All concentrated on the nineteenth century: A. J. P. TAYLOR presenting a sparkling, merciless, somewhat *outré* reworking of the Springer and Eisenmann theses; MACARTNEY combining many virtues of Austrian and Hungarian historiography in the most successful comprehensive treatment; R. A. Kann, born in Vienna but settled in the USA, adapting and developing the insights of Redlich for an American audience. Much of the best writing on the history of old Austria continues to come from the USA, where problems of ethnic interplay and modernization under imperial aegis elicit particular interest.   RJWE

Reading

Fichtner, P. S.: Americans and the disintegration of the Habsburg Monarchy. In *The Habsburg Empire in World War I*, ed. R. A. Kann et al. (New York: Columbia University Press, 1977) pp. 221–34. Lhotsky, A.: *Geschichte des Instituts für Österreichische Geschichtsforschung – Mitteilungen des Instituts für Österreichische Geschichtsforschung*, Ergänzungsband 17 (1954). Idem: *Österreichische Historiographie* (Vienna: Österreich-Archiv, 1962).

B

Bacon, Francis, Lord Verulam (b.1561, d.1626)   Bacon's career falls mainly in the public domain. As a lawyer he became solicitor general and attorney general (1613); from 1601 he was a prominent MP and in 1618 he became Lord Chancellor. However, in 1621 he was accused of bribery, imprisoned and heavily fined. This put an end to his political career and for the remainder of his life he devoted himself to writing and research. His reputation as a writer and thinker lay almost entirely in philosophy and what was to be called 'natural philosophy'. His histories, actual or projected, were mainly analyses of natural phenonema. His eminence as a philosopher, his establishment of induction as a means of reasoning, have little to do with historiography. Yet, limited as was his role as a practising historian, this was nevertheless of some importance. In two respects he resembled, perhaps emulated the 'new' Florentine historians, MACHIAVELLI and GUICCIARDINI. He resembled them in that he was, as they were, a man of affairs and he only took to writing history when deprived of political influence. In the second place his interest in political history was in the *politics* and not merely, as with chroniclers, in narrating *res gesta*. He shared with his Italian predecessors a desire to make the past yield lessons for the future. In the middle ages the writer of reflective history tried to show what made men, and especially kings and 'governors', able to be virtuous; the novelty of the politicians-turned-historians was their attempts to make the great learn from experience. This has been called 'politic' historiography − a good term to express its pragmatic nature. In this genre Bacon only wrote one book, though that was influential: *The History of Henry VII* (1622). In this can be seen the characteristics of the new mode, admiring Tacitus and brevity rather than Livy and rotund prose; but it was a relatively slender work, heavily dependent on Polydore Vergil and Hall's *Chronicles*. Bacon's genius did not spill over into his *History*.   DH

Main writings

The History of Henry VII (1622); *Philosophical Works* (1857−74), ed. John M. Robertson (London: Routledge, 1965).

Reading

Busch, W.: *England under the Tudors*, I, *Henry VII* [pub. in full], trans. A. H. Johnson and Alice M. Todd (London: A. B. Innes, 1895).

Levy F. J.: *Tudor Historical Thought* (San Marino: The Huntingdon Library, 1967), ch. 7.

Bailyn, Bernard (b.1922)   After studying with Oscar Handlin and completing his PhD at Harvard in 1953, Bailyn joined the Harvard history department. Through his own writings and those of his many students, Bailyn has played a decisive role in shaping the study of American colonial history. Winner of numerous prizes and honours, he was elected president of the American Historical Association in 1981.

Bailyn's work is characterized by its unusual range and openness to a wide variety of influences and methodologies. His first book, a study of early New England merchants (1955), moved beyond the conventional limits of economic history to a consideration of transatlantic social and cultural exchanges. Another early work, a seminal essay relating unfavourable demographic conditions to political instability in seventeenth-century Virginia, demonstrated the importance of avoiding a narrow focus on politics. A short monograph on the early history of education also had a profound impact. Bailyn's common-sense assertion that the 'family', rather than schools or 'other public instruments of communication', was most crucial to 'the transfer of culture' led historians of education to redefine their subject; meanwhile, social historians have accorded Bailyn's 'family' a central role in their reconstruction of colonial community life. In these early works Bailyn emphasized the importance of relationships between mature colonial societies (or 'provinces') and the British metropolis. While a number of historians had previously charted the transformation of the first settlements into stable political societies, Bailyn's influential studies showed the value of social scientific analysis in explaining these changes.

The second great phase of Bailyn's career began with his collection of pamphlets from the pre-revolutionary era. His lengthy introduction (1965) was subsequently expanded and republished as *The Ideological Origins of the American Revolution* (1967), his best-known and most influential book. At first, Bailyn's new interest in the development and diffusion of revolutionary ideas looked like a radical departure from his earlier work. Indeed, his brilliant evocation of what colonists saw as a struggle between liberty and power and his emphasis on the importance of the tradition of English 'republican' dissent (as reconstructed by Caroline Robbins) gave the languishing field of intellectual history a significant boost. But Bailyn's concern with social context was never far below the surface. *The Ideological Origins* emphasized the importance of the colonists' predisposition to receive, reformulate, and act on, resistance principles. A companion volume, *The Origins of American Politics*, showed how the structure of imperial authority (notably in the disjunction between royal governors' theoretical and actual power) encouraged the spread of dissenting ideas well before the onset of the imperial crisis.

During the 1970s Bailyn came under fire from New Left historians for promoting what they took to be a 'consensus' view of ideology and playing down the revolutionary struggle among Americans as well as the distinctive world views of non-elite colonists. His sympathetic biography of Governor Thomas Hutchinson reinforced this hostile reading. But the rehabilitation of one loyalist's 'ordeal' was consistent with Bailyn's larger goal of grounding revolutionary and counter-revolutionary ideas in political and personal contexts. And notwithstanding Bailyn's alleged elite bias, the ideological interpretation has proved remarkably adaptable to efforts to reconstruct the ideas and assumptions of the 'inarticulate'. In retrospect, the revisionists' work looks more like an extension of the 'republican synthesis' than a challenge to it.

Recently, Bailyn has issued preliminary chapters introducing a third great phase of his work: *The Peopling of British North America* (1986) sketches his magisterial approach to the continuing settlement and development of colonial America. Once again, his concern with questions of the broadest scope and his impatience with specialization are apparent. In the multivolume *Peopling* series Bailyn clearly intends to heed his own call in his presidential address to the American Historical Association for analytically rigorous but 'comprehensive history' that will 'explain some significant part of the story of how the present world came to be the way it was'.   PSO

Main publications

(Published by Harvard University Press, Cambridge, Mass., unless otherwise stated.)
The New England Merchants in the Seventeenth Century (1955), Politics and social structure in Virginia, in *Seventeenth-Century America*, ed. James Morton Smith (Chapel Hill: University of North Carolina Press, 1959); *Education in the Forming of American Society* (Chapel Hill: University of North Carolina Press, 1960); *The Pamphlets of the American Revolution* (1965); *The Ideological Origins of the American Revolution* (1967); *The Origins of American Politics* (New York: Knopf, 1968); The central themes of the American Revolution: an interpretation, in *Essays on the American Revolution*, ed. Stephen G. Kurtz and James H. Hutson (Chapel Hill: University of North Carolina Press, 1974); *The Ordeal of Thomas Hutchinson* (1974); The challenge of modern historiography. *American Historical Review* 87 (1982) 1–24; *The Peopling of British North America* (New York: Knopf, 1986).

29

BAIN, ROBERT NISBET

Reading

Shalhope, Robert E.: Toward a Republican synthesis: the emergence of an understanding of Republicanism in American historiography. *William and Mary Quarterly* 3.29 (1972) 49−80.

——: Republicanism and early American historiography. *William and Mary Quarterly* 39 (1982) 33456.

Bain, Robert Nisbet (b.1854, d.1909) Bain was born in London and spent the whole of his life there. After working for some time in a solicitor's office, he entered the British Museum (Department of Printed Books) in 1884 and eventually rose to the rank of first class assistant. A prodigious worker, he mastered some twenty languages but spent only four brief periods outside England. The first of these was in the summer of 1884, when he visited Denmark and Sweden, as a result of which he developed a particular interest in the history of northern and eastern Europe in the seventeenth and eighteenth centuries. His first and in many ways his most important publication was a two-volume study of Gustav III of Sweden, still the only work in English. Apart from a life of Charles XII and a political history of Scandinavia, Bain's other historical works were devoted to Russia and Poland (neither of which he ever visited), beginning with *The Pupils of Peter the Great* (1897) and ending in the year of his death with a study of Stanislav Poniatowski, last king of Poland. He was also interested in the literature of the same area and produced a number of translations from Danish, Hungarian, Finnish and Russian. Although a gymnast and boxer in his early life and a keen cyclist, overwork brought about his premature death.   SPO

Main publications

Gustav III and his Contemporaries (London: Kegan Paul, 1894); *Daughter of Peter the Great* (London: Constable, 1899); *Peter III* (Constable, 1902); *The First Romanovs* (Constable, 1905).

Baluze, Dom Étienne See MAURISTS.

Bancroft, George (b.1800, d.1891) After graduating from Harvard at the age of 16 Bancroft proceeded to Göttingen, gaining his doctorate in 1820, and becoming a lifelong admirer of Germany. By 1831 he had embarked upon a dual career in Democratic politics and historical scholarship. His commitment to the egalitarian faith of the Democratic party not only dictated his political allegiance (and secured him several political appointments), but also provided the principal thrust of his scholarly writings.

In 1834 Bancroft published the first volume of a projected history of the United States from its beginnings to his own day. He stated his main theme unambiguously in the preface: 'The spirit of the colonies demanded freedom from the beginning.' And he insisted that the America of his own day was foremost in the defence of equal rights. By 1874 the *History* had reached ten volumes culminating in the American Revolution. Bancroft subsequently pruned it to six volumes and added two on the formation of the US Constitution.

A sensational success, the *History* appealed particularly to those who shared Bancroft's political beliefs not least because it linked the past indelibly to the present. Bancroft saw the history of his country as one of unending progress, the essence of which was a drive towards ever greater liberty. That drive gave impetus to the 'manifest destiny' of the United States to spread its institutions and values world-wide.

Bancroft has been labelled the 'father of American history' although his works are now scoured more for the light they cast upon the times in which he wrote than for the times which were his subject matter.   DMacI

Main publications

History of the United States from the Discovery of the American Continent, 10 vols (Boston, 1834−74); *History of the Formation of the Constitution of the United States of America*, 2 vols (Boston, 1882).

Reading

Nye, Russell B.: *George Bancroft: Brahmin Rebel* (New York: Knopf, 1944).

Barnave, Antoine Pierre Joseph Marie (b.1761, d.1793) A Protestant lawyer from Grenoble, Barnave was elected to the Estates General in 1789 and took a leading role in the early years of the French Revolution. Beginning as a radical, by 1791 he had turned conservative and eventually became the royal family's secret adviser. Arrested after the fall of the monarchy, he spent 15 months in prison before execution. During this time he wrote an *Introduction to the French Revolution* in which he argued that the Revolution had been prepared by a new distribution of wealth and property within French society. It was not published until 1843, and remained little known until JAURÈS used it to support his own Marxist interpretation of the Revolution. It has often been invoked by Marxists since.   WD

Main publications

Barnave, A. P. J. M.: Introduction à la Révolution française (1843), ed. F. Rude (Paris: A. Colin, 1960), trans. E. Chill (New York, 1971).

Barraclough, Geoffrey (b.1908, d.1984) Born a Yorkshireman, educated at Bootham School, York (a Quaker foundation), and Oriel College, Oxford, Barraclough owed his training in research to professor von Heckel of Munich and to the British School at Rome. His first book *Public Notaries and the Papal Curia* (1934) was a calendar of documents with 132 pages of learned introduction. *Papal Provisions: Aspects of Church History . . . in the Later Middle Ages* (1935) is still authoritative. From 1934 to 1936 he was fellow and tutor at Merton College, Oxford. He then moved to Cambridge where he was fellow and tutor at St John's College and university lecturer. Barraclough was disturbed by the ignorance among undergraduates and colleagues alike of the work of continental scholars and *Medieval Germany, 911–1250* (1938) contained nine important essays by German historians translated into English, with a long introduction.

At the outbreak of war in 1939 he joined the political intelligence department of the Foreign Office but from 1942 to 1945 served in the RAF. He resumed historical study as professor of medieval history at Liverpool and, turning to English history, published *The Earldom and County Palatine of Chester* (1953) and edited a collection of related charters. He wrote a fluent, succinct and elegant prose and now began to use his medieval knowledge to explain

to the student and general reader the broad reasons determining the shape of twentieth-century Europe. He pleaded for 'a deeper understanding of the continuity of history and its underlying currents'. His greatest achievement was to further in a scholarly way precisely this understanding. In 1946 he published, almost simultaneously, *The Origins of Modern Germany* and *Factors in German History*. For the period 1519–1946 both had virtually the same text, though in *The Origins* this text accounted for only the last quarter of the book, while in *Factors* it constituted three-quarters. In *History in a Changing World* (1957) he explained that since the siege of Stalingrad, all history had to be global and relevant to the present, as was shown also in his *Introduction to Contemporary History* (1964).

In 1956 he succeeded Arnold Toynbee as Stevenson research professor at the Royal Institute of International Affairs. He was therefore responsible for the preparation and publication of its *Annual Survey of International Affairs*. In 1962 he resigned from Chatham House and among later appointments held chairs at the university of California and Brandeis university. He was president of the Historical Association and his presidential address in 1966 *History and the Common Man* was characteristic. From 1970 to 1974 Barraclough was Chichele professor at Oxford. In 1978 he edited *The Times Atlas of World History*. His last work, *The Charter of the Norman Earls of Chester* was published posthumously by the Record Society of Lancashire and Cheshire in 1988.   AR

Main publications

(Published by Blackwell, Oxford, unless otherwise stated.)
Papal Provisions: Aspects of Church History, Constitutional, Legal and Administrative in the Later Middle Ages (1935); *Medieval Germany, 911–1250 Essays by German Historians*, 2 vols (1938); *Origins of Modern Germany* (1946); *Factors of German History* (1946); *History in a Changing World* (1957); *European Unity in Thought and Action* (1963); *Introduction to Contemporary History* (London: C. A. Watt, 1964); *The Medieval Papacy* (London and New York: Library of European Civilization, 1968); *The Crucible of Europe. The Ninth and Tenth Centuries of European History* (London: Thames & Hudson, 1976); editor, *The Times Atlas of World History* (London: 1978).

Barruel, Augustin de (b.1741, d.1820) From a family of old Languedoc nobility, Barruel was educated by the Jesuits, joined the order, and taught in its schools. After the Jesuits' expulsion from France he travelled extensively, returning in 1773 as a secular priest. He served in various aristocratic households, then took up journalism and wrote for conservative periodicals hostile to the Enlightenment. *Les Helviennes*, published in two parts (1781 and 1788) was a substantial attack on the *philosophes* as enemies of religion. Barruel continued to press this theme as editor of the *Journal Ecclesiastique* between 1788 and 1792, blaming philosophic ideas for the French Revolution's attack on the church.

By 1797, in exile in England, he had become convinced that before 1789 a philosophic conspiracy had worked to overthrow the *ancien régime* through the network of Masonic lodges, and that the Jacobin clubs were merely the culminating manifestations of a far-flung and deeply laid plot. He expounded this argument at length in the six volumes of *Mémoires pour servir à l'histoire du Jacobinisme* (1797–8), which was an immediate success and eventually translated into six languages. Gratifying the desire for simple, all-embracing explanations of the revolutionary upheaval, it drew on and wove together a wide range of plot theories to demonstrate that the *ancien régime* had not been unsound, but subverted. It attributed to Freemasonry a republican, anti-Christian purpose that it had certainly lacked before 1789; yet despite the patent absurdity of many of his assertions and complete lack of scholarly standards, Barruel's general thesis was enormously influential, casting permanent suspicion upon Freemasonry and its purposes and encouraging conspiratorial explanations of revolution.   WD

Main publications

Mémoires pour servir à l'histoire du Jacobinisme, 6 vols (London: 1797–8).

Reading

Roberts, J. M.: *The Mythology of the Secret Societies* (London: Secker & Warburg, 1980) ch. 6.

Barthold, Wilhelm (b.1869, d.1930) Vasilii Vladimirovich Bartol'd was born in Russia though of German descent; he was the greatest historian of central Asia, and indeed the virtual founder of the modern study of central Asian history. He spent his career as a professor at the University of St Petersburg, where in 1900 he presented the thesis which subsequently became his most important book, *Turkestan down to the Mongol Invasion*. He was an extremely prolific scholar: the collected edition of his works runs to some 7,000 pages, much of it still available only in the Russian language.

The Russian conquest of central Asia in the late nineteenth century was perceived by Barthold as affording the historian a unique opportunity to place the history of the region on a sound scholarly basis – a task which had hardly been attempted previously. He brought to his studies a mastery of the most necessary languages, Arabic, Turkish and Persian, and a highly developed critical sense. For many years he travelled almost annually to central Asia. He was the first scholar to make effective use of many of the sources which are now regarded as basic to the study of the region.

Barthold fell under something of an official cloud after the Russian Revolution. He was not a Marxist – though he inclined towards an economic interpretation of history – and he refused to make concessions to the current dogma. It is said that at one of his lectures he was asked: 'How did Marx consider this problem?' He replied: 'Marx? I do not know this orientalist.' Partly for this reason, and perhaps partly because he does not seem to have had an especially endearing personality, he left no school of disciples. Nevertheless, his influence on subsequent scholarship has been considerable, no less in the west than in the Soviet Union. There, his work swung back into favour within a few years of his death, when his emphasis on the positive results of tsarist imperialism in central Asia came to coincide with Stalinist orthodoxy. Soviet historians of the Orient continue to view him with respect, despite his anti-Marxism. Many of Barthold's works remain standard, above all *Turkestan down to the Mongol Invasion* (though not everything he wrote is of that book's quality). This durability is a tribute to the excellence of his scholarship as well, it should be said, as a comment on the slow pace at which the historical study of the Middle East and Central Asia has advanced since his time. DOM

Main publications

Collected Works (in Russian), 9 vols in 10 (Moscow 1963–77); *Turkestan down to the Mongol Invasion*, 3rd expanded edn (London: Luzac, 1968); *Four studies on the History of Central Asia*, 3 vols, trans. V. and T. Minorsky (Leiden: E. J. Brill, 1956–62); *An historical geography of Iran*, trans. S. Soucek, ed. C. E. Bosworth (Princeton: Princeton University Press, 1984); *Zwölf Vorlesungen über die Geschichte der Türken Mittelasiens* (Darmstadt: Wissenschaftliche Buchgesellschaft, 1962), French trans. M. Donskis, *Histoire des Turcs d'Asie centrale* (Paris: Adrien-Maisonneuve, 1945); *La découverte de l'Asie, histoire de l'orientalisme en Europe et en Russie* (Paris: Payot, 1947).

Reading

Bosworth, C. E.: Introduction. In W. Barthold, *An historical geography of Iran* (see above).
Bregel, Y.: Barthold and modern oriental studies. *International Journal of Middle East Studies* 12 (1980) 385–403.

Basin, Thomas (b.1412, d.1491) Born a Norman, fiercely attached to his native province, widely travelled and highly educated, Basin was bishop of Lisieux (1447–74) and then titular archbishop of Caesarea. A lifelong reformer, capable administrator and active polemicist, he is best known for two contrasting Latin histories in humanist style of Charles VII and Louis XI of France, written in exile in the Low Countries (1471–5, revised after 1483). The former gives a generally sympathetic portrait, but the latter is a vitriolic indictment of the rule of a man to whom Basin attributed all his personal misfortunes, recounted at length elsewhere in an *Apologia*. He is buried at Utrecht. MCEJ

Main writings

(Dates are of editions published by Les Belles Lettres, Paris.)
Histoire de Charles VII, ed. and trans. C. Samaran and H. de Surirey de St Rémy, 2 vols (1933–44); *Histoire de Louis XI*, ed. and trans. C. Samaran and M. C. Garand, 3 vols 1963–72); *Apologie ou plaidoyer pour moi-même*, ed. and trans. C. Samaran and G. de Groër (1974).

Reading

Maurice, A.: *Un grand patriote: Thomas Basin, évêque de Lisieux* (Rouen; 1963).

Bayle, Pierre (b.1647, d.1706) Though not strictly a historian, Bayle had considerable influence upon writers such as VOLTAIRE, HUME and GIBBON. Born in southern France, the son of a Huguenot pastor, Bayle taught at the Protestant academy at Sedan until 1681, before moving to Rotterdam, where he spent the rest of his life. In 1682 he published a letter on the comet of 1680, insisting that it was a natural phenomenon, devoid of portent. In 1686 he wrote a commentary on the text 'Compel them to come in', a plea for religious toleration. But his most influential work was the *Dictionnaire historique et critique* (1695–7). It had an immediate success and held the field throughout the eighteenth century. Bayle's approach was sceptical and iconoclastic, and he treated the Bible as a historical document rather than a divine text. In his article on Remond, Bayle wrote that the historian must rid himself of religious zeal and dedicate himself to the pursuit of truth: 'an historian can never stand too much upon his guard'. Gibbon paid tribute to Bayle's 'wonderful power of . . . assembling doubts and objections'. JAC

Main publications

Pensées diverses à l'occasion de la comète . . . de 1680, (1682); *Commentaire philosophique sur ces paroles de Jésus-Christ, contrain-les d'entrer* (1686); *Dictionnaire historique et critique* (Rotterdam, 1695–7); *Oeuvres diverses* (1727–31).

Reading

Labrousse E.: *Pierre Bayle* (The Hague: Mouton, 1963).
Mason H. T.: *Pierre Bayle and Voltaire* (London: Oxford University Press, 1963).

Baynes, Norman Hepburn (b.1877, d.1961) Baptist by family and Londoner by adoption, Baynes went up to New College, Oxford to read Greats in 1896 and then presented historical prize essays on Constantine and Heraclius, subjects which were to exercise him throughout his life. He digressed until 1916 by studying and teaching law, and there were lures of a New College fellowship and of a Liberal constituency. But he decided for ancient history and University College London, where he had been teaching Evening School since 1913 and which gave him a

33

personal chair of Byzantine history from 1931 to 1942.

Baynes published sparingly, but his work is refined gold, which endures in a shifting field. He regarded J. B. BURY (to whom he paid judicious tribute) as a mentor. Baynes's outlying works include *Israel among the Nations* (1927) and his careful hand is evident in volume XII of the *Cambridge Ancient History* and, from 1924, in time-consuming notices in the *Byzantinische Zeitschrift*. Baynes was really an ancient historian who strayed into Byzantium by way of the conversion of the Roman Empire: his Raleigh Lecture on Constantine (1929) was an entry which he opened for others. How subtly he understood the transition to Christianity is shown in his essays of 1947 on Hellenistic civilization and on what he called the 'thought world' of East Rome. These came after his retirement, for which he had always planned a social history of Byzantium and held in reserve a study of St Augustine. Baynes's own 'thought-world' was, as he put it, that of a Victorian individualist. He looked the part. A Gladstonian orator, he suited the stage of University College (on which he could be very funny), and gave it his bachelor devotion. On his retirement in 1942 its students responded by inviting Baynes to give the Foundation Address to the College, then evacuated to Bangor. Fresh from his wartime Intelligence chore (a meticulous edition of Hitler's speeches), this recessional lecture on 'The Custody of a Tradition' is a peculiarly vivid testament to liberal academic values.

The mark of such legendary teachers is apt to evaporate, but in this case it survives. Typically, Baynes was an enthusiast for discussion groups, which gathered friends of all sorts. His Nearer East Group still meets at 'Baynes Weekends' to preserve the scholarly conviviality which was his mark.   AAMB

Main publications

Byzantine Studies and other essays (London: Athlone Press, 1955) includes the 1942 address and 1947 essays; *An Address presented to Norman Hepburn Baynes* (Oxford: privately printed at Oxford University Press, 1942) with bibliography to 1942; with H. St L. B. Moss, *Byzantium: an introduction to East Roman civilisation*, (Oxford: Clarendon Press, 1948).

Reading

Hussey, J. M.: *Proceedings of the British Academy* 49 (1963) [an appreciation].
——: *Bulletin of Dr Williams's Library* 72 (1967) [an appreciation].
Journal of Roman Studies 37 (1947) [a festschrift].

Beard, Charles Austin (b.1874, d.1948) During a career that spanned the first half of the twentieth century, Beard was noted for writings in four areas: the economic interpretation of American history, urban planning and reform, the philosophy of history, and foreign affairs. An acclaimed speaker and prolific writer, he published scores of scholarly books and essays, reports on urban government and, for general audiences, articles on politics and public affairs. Even after his death, Beard's work continued to be a controversial touchstone for American historians.

Raised in rural Indiana, Beard's collegiate education took place at Depauw University. A gifted student and committed young reformer, he moved to Oxford in his twenties. There he studied English constitutional history and devoted himself to industrial reform and workers' education. With Walter Vrooman he founded Ruskin Hall (now College), a working men's college at Oxford, in 1899. During his stay at Ruskin Hall he spoke to labour unions and co-operative societies throughout England. These lectures formed the basis of his first book, *The Industrial Revolution* (1901), a lively study that displayed a Ruskinian preoccupation with the prospects of, as well as obstacles to, creating an industrial society that improved the quality of human life.

In 1902 Beard returned to the United States and, two years later, received a doctorate from Columbia University. For the next 15 years he taught history and politics at Columbia where, with James Harvey Robinson, he was a leading proponent of the 'new history'. Beard resigned from the faculty in 1917 in protest against the university's firing of two teachers who opposed American involvement in the first world war. He then helped found the New School for Social Research and, until the early 1920s, directed the training school of the New York Bureau of Municipal Research. Thereafter he worked as an independent writer and lecturer, living in New Milford, Connecticut, and New York City.

At Columbia, Beard came to prominence through a series of books on the founding period in American politics. His best-known book, *An Economic Interpretation of the Constitution* (1913), reshaped scholarly debate and reinforced calls for constitutional reform. He drew upon James Madison's contention that politics in a republic revolved around conflict between property-based factions. In Beard's view, two competing interests had been embedded in American political culture with the writing of the Constitution: the 'Hamiltonian' and the 'Jeffersonian'. The former consisted primarily of northerners whose wealth was in liquid capital and whose vision of the United States was of an urban, commercial, civilization. The latter was composed of slave-owning southerners who, tied to landed property and a culture of self-sufficient agriculture, wished to create a rural republic.

Beard's greatest work, *The Rise of American Civilization* (1927), co-authored by his wife and frequent collaborator, Mary Ritter Beard, extended these themes to encompass all of United States history. According to the Beards, the conflict of interests that marked the early republic reached a climax with the Civil War. The war suppressed Jeffersonianism, unleashing the industrial revolution and its intellectual counterpart, scientific reasoning. The resulting industrial civilization, while marred by poverty and oppression, promised a new stage in United States history, 'industrial democracy'. As the Beards saw it, unprecedented productivity, the principle of planning inherent in science, and the nation's democratic traditions made possible, indeed likely, a future of equality and material plenty.

Published during the progressive era, Beard's early histories bolstered activists' calls for systematic reform. In the 1910s and 1920s he also tried to demonstrate how the principles of science could in practice be applied to democratic government. As a staff member of the Bureau of Municipal Research, and later as director of its training school, he promoted governmental reform and the modernization of urban services. This gained him an international reputation. He travelled widely, published a respected study of Tokyo and, following that city's 1923 earthquake, was called to Japan to help redesign the city.

Initially confident that Tokyo's reconstruction would demonstrate the value of scientific planning, Beard was deeply disappointed when the new city replicated the faults he had found in the old. As a result of this experience − and the constant opposition of entrenched interests to his work at the Bureau of Municipal Research − Beard concluded that planning had to begin at the national level. *The Rise* implied that this would occur. But shortly afterwards, the great depression of the 1930s dashed Beard's faith in science and technology. As a result, he turned his attention to two complementary questions: the philosophical grounds of knowledge and the sources of the economic collapse.

In constructing his philosophical position, which he considered a necessary first step in attacking the depression, Beard turned to continental idealism, in particular the work of Benedetto CROCE, Karl Heussi, Kurt Mannheim, Hans Vaihinger and Kurt Riezler. Emphasizing the indeterminacy of knowledge and the role of interpretation and speculation in thought, he departed from the implicit positivism of most American historians, initiating a controversy that continued long after his death.

Beard's conviction that the depression was a 'crisis in thought as well as economy' is evident in two books of 1934, *The Idea of National Interest* and *The Open Door at Home*. He argued that the economic breakdown originated in the belief − falsely held as fact by the heirs of both the Hamiltonian and Jeffersonian traditions − that domestic prosperity depended upon international trade. For Beard, internationalism required the national government to protect private interests abroad; as such it led inevitably to conflict with other foreign powers. Recovery, he held to the contrary, demanded a new conception of the nation's interest, one that forswore global entanglements and emphasized national planning to rectify the nation's unbalanced distribution of wealth.

In the first years of the New Deal, Beard viewed the Roosevelt administration hopefully, believing that the president was moving towards the kind of national planning he favoured. By the middle of the decade, however, he concluded that Roosevelt had abandoned domestic reform in favour of fanciful plans to reconstruct the international order; schemes, he believed, that pointed to war. Following the second world war he evaluated Rooseveltian diplomacy critically, denouncing the president's internationalism in his last book, *President Roosevelt and the Coming of the War* (1948).

Beard's critique of Roosevelt was condemned by many, including many old friends within liberal circles. In the decade following his death, former allies as well as younger American historians subjected his life's work to close and mostly negative scrutiny. To these critics, Beard's division of the nation's political culture along Jeffersonian – Hamiltonian lines was simplistic. His relativism they found naive, and his criticism of Roosevelt they denounced as vindictive. However, in the 1960s and after, Beard's reputation was revived by American historians of the 'new left', who shared his concern with – and approach to – the relationship between economic interests, politics and foreign affairs. Seeking a history that would guide political activism, they used as their starting point Beard's writing on the Constitution, American politics, and diplomacy. In many ways, his thought served as a foundation of new left historiography.

Both post-war views of Beard – the negative and the positive – persist. In the 1980s he still exemplifies a mode of historical interpretation and a style of scholarly activism that is for some a dangerous, for others an inspiring, model. DAJ

Main publications

The Industrial Revolution (1901) (Westport, Conn.: Greenwood, 1975); *An Economic Interpretation of the Constitution* (1913) (New York: Free Press, 1986); *The Economic Origins of Jeffersonian Democracy* (1914) (New York: Free Press, 1965); *The Economic Basis of Politics* (1922) (Salem, NH: Ayer, 1970); *The Administration and Politics of Tokyo* (New York: Macmillan, 1923); *The Rise of American Civilization*, 2 vols (1927, rev. and enlarged New York: Macmillan, 1933); *The Idea of National Interest* (1934) (Westport, Conn.: Greenwood, 1977); *The Open Door at Home* (New York: Macmillan, 1934); Written history as an act of faith *American Historical Review* 39, 219–31 (repr. El Paso, Tex.: Texas Western Press, 1960); That noble dream *American Historical*

Review 41, 74–87; *President Roosevelt and the Coming of the War, 1941* (New Haven: Yale University Press, 1948).

Reading

Brown, R.: *Charles Beard and the Constitution*. (Princeton: Princeton University Press 1956).

Hofstadter, R.: *The Progressive Historians* (New York: Knopf, 1968).

Nore, E.: *Charles A. Beard* (Carbondale: Southern Illinois University Press, 1983).

Strout, C.: *The Pragmatic Revolt in American History* (Ithaca: Cornell University Press, 1958).

Becker, Carl Lotus (b.1873, d.1945) Born near Waterloo, Iowa, Becker attended Cornell College in Iowa but soon transferred to the University of Wisconsin. Here he came under the influence of Frederick Jackson TURNER, the historian of the frontier. From his mentor Becker learned less about history than about the teaching and writing of history. Turner understood history not as a matter of fact, but as a never-ending series of questions about the past, a recurring reinterpretation of past events to suit the needs of contemporary generations. From Turner's notion that every age rewrites history to serve its own purposes, Becker acquired his own belief, later made famous in a classic address to the American Historical Association in 1931, that 'everyman' was 'his own historian'. The address represented the apotheosis of the progressive school of historiography and reflected the triumph of historical relativism in a profession that had been guided before then by a 'scientific' approach to the writing of history.

Although Becker considered himself a historiographer rather than a historian, he made significant contributions to both American and European history. His doctoral dissertation, the *History of Political Parties in the Province of New York* (1909), propounded a view of American colonial history that became a standard interpretation for at least half a century. It suggested that because colonial society was sharply divided between upper and lower classes, the American Revolution was as much an internal struggle for democracy as a contest for independence of the colonies from the mother country. Becker's thesis dealt only with New York, but the idea of a 'dual revolution' was quickly taken up by other historians and reiterated by Becker himself so that it acquired intercolonial applicability.

On the European side, Becker's interpretive lectures on *The Heavenly City of the Eighteenth-Century Philosophers* (1932) challenged the traditional view that Enlightenment thinkers were forerunners of modernism in their attacks on revealed religion and argued that the *philosophes* merely replaced one set of dogmatic beliefs with a new orthodoxy, a faith in reason.

Becker is not easily categorized as either an American or a European historian. He wrote textbooks in both fields but claimed to know little about the teaching of history. He wrote two substantial monographs on American history but taught European history at Cornell University, where he served on the faculty from 1917 to his retirement in 1941. He trained a large number of important European historians, but they represented no 'Becker school' of historiography. He enjoyed the appellation 'man of letters' which Charles A. BEARD conferred upon him, perhaps more than the presidency of the American Historical Association which he secured in 1930.

Becker always insisted that he was less a historian than a thinker about history and historians. In his later days, he penned a large number of essays on contemporary affairs, most of which in retrospect appear to be more timely than timeless. Perhaps the one constant that runs through these writings is his belief that despite its limitations, the free mind, engaged in the continuous pursuit of knowledge, is both the hallmark of civilization and the only guarantor of the humane society of the eighteenth century whose principal figures in America and in Europe he studied so avidly.   MMK

Main publications

The History of Political Parties in the Province of New York, 1760–1776 (Madison: University of Wisconsin Press, 1909); *The Beginnings of the American People* (Boston: Houghton Mifflin, 1915); *The Eve of the Revolution* (New Haven, Conn.: Yale University Press, 1920); *The United States: an Experiment in Democracy* (New York and London: Harper, 1920); *The Declaration of Independence* (New York: Harcourt, Brace, 1922); *Modern History* (New York: Silver Burdett, 1931); *The Heavenly City of the Eighteenth-Century Philosophers* (New Haven, Conn.: Yale University Press, 1932); *Everyman his own Historian* (New York: Crofts, 1935); *Progress and Power* (London: Oxford University Press, 1936); *The Story of Civilization* (New York: Silver Burdett, 1938); *Modern Democracy* (London: Oxford University Press, 1941); *New Liberties for Old* (London: Oxford University Press, 1941); *Cornell University: Founders and the Founding* (Ithaca, NY: Cornell University Press, 1943); *How New will the Better World be?* (New York: Knopf, 1944); *Freedom and Responsibility in the American Way of Life* (New York: Knopf, 1945).

Reading

Brown, Robert E.: *Carl Becker on History and the American Revolution.* (East Lansing, Mich,: Spartan Press, 1970).

Rockwood, Raymond O. ed.: *Carl Becker's Heavenly City Revisited* (Ithaca, NY: Cornell University Press, 1958).

Smith, Charlotte: *Carl Becker: on History and the Climate of Opinion* (Ithaca, NY: Cornell University Press, 1956).

Wilkins, Burleigh T.: *Carl Becker: a Biographical Study in American Intellectual History* (Cambridge, Mass.: MIT Press, 1961).

Beckett, James Camlin (b.1912) Beckett is emeritus professor of Irish history at the Queen's University of Belfast, and one of that distinguished pleiad of Irish historians who graduated in the 1930s and who, though coming from different political and religious traditions, pioneered a revolution in Irish historical study. Their natural leader was the late T. W. MOODY, and partly inspired by his example, they sought to give Irish history new aims and a new methodology. Reacting to the polemical and often blatantly biased tone of so much writing on Irish history, they insisted on a uniformly cool and analytical approach, based on meticulous research, and conforming to the most rigorous standards of scholarship. This gospel was expounded in the pages of the journal *Irish Historical Studies*, launched in 1939, which has profoundly influenced the work of Irish historians down to the present.

Beckett was born in Belfast and educated at the Royal Belfast Academical Institution and the Queen's University, where he graduated with first class honours in modern history in 1934. For the next 11 years he taught history and English in the Belfast Royal Academy. This was not his own school (the somewhat similar names are a source of confusion to all except natives of Belfast) but the oldest of the city's grammar schools, founded in 1785 by the Protestant dissenters, i.e. the Presbyterians.

This may help to explain why he chose, as the subject of his MA thesis, the efforts of the dissenters in the eighteenth century to bring about the repeal of legislation imposing disabilities on them similar to those endured by Catholics. His own background, however, was solidly Church of Ireland. His mother's family came from Dublin; his father, a civil servant, was a northerner from County Armagh. The blending of these northern and southern strains first stimulated Beckett's interest in Irish history, and the study of the Protestant Anglo-Irish is the central theme of his work. In 1945 he was appointed lecturer at the Queen's University, Belfast. In 1948 *Protestant Dissent in Ireland, 1687–1780* was published by Faber as the first of their series of studies in Irish History. *A Short History of Ireland* appeared in the Hutchinson University Library series in 1952. This little work, which first demonstrated his mastery of concise historical analysis, has gone through many editions and been translated into German and Japanese.

Beckett's abilities as a historian rapidly found recognition, both in his own university and further afield. He became reader in modern history at Queen's in 1952, and for a year was fellow commoner at Peterhouse, Cambridge (1955–6). In 1958 he was appointed to a personal chair of Irish history, later made an established chair. Election to membership of the Irish Historical Manuscripts Commission and the Royal Commission on Historical Manuscripts soon followed, and he was also elected fellow of the Royal Historical Society and member of the Royal Irish Academy.

These years saw a steady stream of articles and reviews. Most were the product of his deep research into Irish history in the eighteenth century, but in time he became more and more interested in the seventeenth century. Meanwhile, with T. W. Moody, he wrote the magisterial two-volume history of the Queen's University, Belfast; this was a long and arduous task, not made easier by Moody's meticulous rules, which might necessitate writing to New Zealand to determine where a comma should come in a particular sentence. Praise for this fine work must be tinged with some regret that it engaged the energies of two outstanding Irish historians for so long. *The Making of Modern Ireland, 1603–1923*, published in 1966, is Beckett's master-work. In it, his qualities are seen to the fullest advantage: accuracy, a scrupulous objectivity, analytical power and, not least, the gift of conveying his thought in clear incisive writing. The work was received with critical acclaim, and is now a standard textbook.

Much of Beckett's work is to be found in editing – or in contributions to – other books on Irish history, not least in his chapters in volume 4 of *The New History of Ireland*. He is also a notable contributor to studies on Swift, and his broad literary interests range from Jane Austen to Norwegian poetry.   ATQS

Main publications

Protestant Dissent in Ireland, 1687–1780 (London: Faber & Faber, 1948); *A Short History of Ireland* (London: Hutchinson, 1952); with T. W. Moody, *Ulster since 1800: a Political and Economic Survey* (Belfast: BBC, 1954); with T. W. Moody, *Ulster since 1800: a Social Survey* (Belfast: BBC, 1957); with T. W. Moody, *Queen's, Belfast*, 2 vols (London: Faber & Faber, 1959); *The Making of Modern Ireland, 1603–1923* (London: Faber & Faber, 1966); with R. E. Glasscock, *Belfast: the Origin and Growth of an Industrial City* (London: BBC, 1966); *Confrontations* (London, Faber & Faber, 1973); *The Anglo-Irish Tradition* (London, Faber & Faber, 1976).

Bede (b.672/673, d.735) Bede's life, from the age of seven, was spent in the monastic community of Monkwearmouth-Jarrow. His learning derived from the large library provided by Benedict Biscop when he founded these twin monasteries (Monkwearmouth 674, Jarrow 681–2). A prolific scholar, most of Bede's works were biblical commentaries, but he also wrote on grammar, metrics, chronology and the lives of saints. His historical works comprise only the *Ecclesiastical History*, the *Lives* of the abbots of his monastery and two chronicles (lists of dated events). He also wrote two lives of St Cuthbert (one prose, one verse), very much in a hagiographical style.

The *Historia ecclesiastica gentis anglorum* was completed in 731 or 732. In some 85,000 words Bede sought to relate the history of the church in his own land from Roman times onwards. It was a great success, which is why early manuscripts of it are relatively common; two, the Moore and Leningrad manuscripts, come from near the date of composition. It has remained famous and in favour. No book, except the Bible, has had such a long history of continuous regard in England.

Its virtues are indeed great. Bede was active in the search for materials, as he tells us in his preface. He included many documents in his text and wrote with clarity and vividness; the most skilled chronologist of his day, he took great pains over dates (he was responsible for the AD system of dating coming into common use) and handled with skill the problems of describing simultaneous series of events in several kingdoms. His tone is judicious and the modern reader can feel a kind of rapport seldom felt in reading a Dark Age author.

Bede followed no single model. He imitated OROSIUS in providing a geographical introduction, but the strongest single influence on him was that of EUSEBIUS. Bede's *Ecclesiastical History* resembles that of Eusebius in its concern to record the succession of bishops and the fate of heresies, and, not least, in the frequent inclusion of documents. It is sometimes forgotten that the term 'ecclesiastical history', for Bede as for Eusebius, meant what it says. Bede seldom recorded secular events for their own sake but usually did so in ecclesiastical contexts or to show the hand of God at work. It is likely that there were many major events of which Bede knew but of which he tells us nothing at all.

Bede was inevitably to a large extent at the mercy of his sources: a mixed bag. Papal letters (some obtained from Rome) provided the backbone of his account of St Augustine's mission. For the period after 597 he had *Vitae* of Fursey, Cuthbert, Aethelburh, Ceolfrith and, probably, Wilfrid. A number of regnal lists, genealogies and annals were available. His preface shows that much information came to him by correspondence. A lot of what he gleaned derived from oral tradition. He said that he had followed a 'true law of history' in simply committing to writing what he had gathered from common report for the instruction of posterity.

The instruction he had in mind was chiefly that of teaching by examples. Some of these were for the clergy. Bede's *Letter to Egbert*, written not long after the *Ecclesiastical History*, shows that he found much to blame in the contemporary church. For example some of the bishops were neglectful and avaricious. The vigorous emphasis in the *History* on the virtues of such model bishops of the past as Aidan was strongly homilectic. Bede sought similarly to instruct the laity. His book is dedicated to a king and part of its purpose is to indicate the true role of a Christian monarch. There is repeated emphasis on the practical benefits of religion, on how a most Christian king could become a most victorious king (though Bede approved also of kings who withdrew from the world).

On the rare occasions when we have another source, such as Eddius's *Life of Wilfrid* to set beside Bede, it can be seen that, for all his virtues, Bede could be discreet up to and beyond the point of evasiveness. He was inclined to suppress that which could not edify. It is interesting that he had less to say about the immediate past than about what he believed to have happened a hundred years before. His own day did not provide such good example.

A subject of special interest to Bede, prominent in the *Ecclesiastical History*, was the dispute over the date of Easter. This arose because Irish missionaries adhered to systems of calculation other than those which were, by the seventh century, used at Rome and elsewhere. Bede was the great expert on such subjects. His monastery had strong links with Canterbury and with Rome. His theology was such that he gave getting right the date of Easter an almost sacramental significance. So an event such as Oswy's acceptance of the Roman Easter in 664 is given an importance which modern commentators sometimes find hard to understand; so much so that some have been, wrongly, tempted to rationalize Bede by assuming that he was 'really' concerned with something other than Easter.

Bede's work is often more sophisticated than a first impression suggests; for example, in its treatment of miracles. The *Ecclesiastical History* is full of miracles, shining, one may suppose, with Bede's simple faith. In fact the nature of the miracles he included indicates that he had made a careful selection, for they do not include types of miracle common in the works of other Dark Age writers: starkly flabbergasting or cruel miracles or miracles to show that the author's own monastery was under heavenly protection. Very remarkably Bede related only one miracle from Monkwearmouth-Jarrow, and it is not much of a miracle either. But then, Bede was a very remarkable man.   JC

Main writings

Chronica minora et majora, ed. T. Mommsen, (Hanover: *Monumenta Germaniae Historica, Auctores Antiquissimi*, 1898): *Baedae Opera Historica*, ed. C. Plummer, 2 vols (Oxford: Oxford University Press, 1896); *Bede's Ecclesiastical History of the English People*, ed. and trans. B. Colgrave and R. A. B. Mynors (Oxford University Press, 1969); *Two Lives of St Cuthbert*, ed. and trans. B. Colgrave (Cambridge: Cambridge University Press, 1940).

Reading

Bonner, G. ed.: *Famulus Christi: essays in commemoration of the thirteenth centenary of the birth of the Venerable Bede* (London: SPCK, 1976).

Farrell, R. T. ed.: *Bede and Anglo-Saxon England: papers in honour of the 1300th anniversary of the birth of Bede, given at Cornell University in 1973 and 1974* (Oxford: British Archaeological Reports, British Series 46, 1978).

Belgian historiography See LOW COUNTRIES, HISTORIOGRAPHY OF.

Benedict of Peterborough See ROGER OF HOWDEN.

biography Writing an account of someone's life is almost as old as the writing of history. In the west the most notable ancient biographer, PLUTARCH, composed in Greek around AD 110 a collection of short *Parallel Lives of the Noble Grecians and Romans* which inspired many subsequent writers. He considered history and biography the same in form, but different in content, the former supplying a detailed account of events, the latter delineating individuals' characters. SUETONIUS's Latin *Lives of the Caesars*, written around AD 120, though gossipy and undiscriminating, was for many centuries even more influential, exercising for example a strong influence on Einhard's *Life of Charlemagne*.

Until the eighteenth century, since history was seen as essentially the story of the deeds of individuals, it had much in common with biography. But as historiography became more concerned with identifying and describing impersonal forces, trends and tendencies, biography became more independent of it. One of the earliest of modern biographies — often thought the best of all — was James Boswell's *Life of Samuel Johnson* (1791). Its author sought not merely to delineate the character of the subject, to trace in detail the story of his life, to describe his writings and to pass on a record of his conversation, but also to supply 'a view of literature and literary men in Great Britain, for near half a century during which he flourished'. In the nineteenth century, Thomas CARLYLE, contending that great heroes are the dominant forces of history, wrote classic biographies of Oliver Cromwell (1845) and Frederick the Great (1858–65). It became usual for biographers to try to deal with both the life and times of their subject; and, especially in Britain, numerous biographies appeared of public men, often in several volumes, full of undigested documents, prudish and uncritical. Such works were effectively debunked by Lytton Strachey in *Eminent Victorians* (1918).

In the twentieth century 'popular biography' has flourished, but many examples are too imaginative, romantic, amateurishly psychological and lacking in historical awareness to be of much value to the historian. In numerous 'scholarly' biographies, on the other hand, the techniques of the professional historian have been applied to the life of an individual rather than to a period or theme. British historians have been especially prolific and successful in this genre, for example, G. M. TREVELYAN with his trilogy on Garibaldi (1907–11) and J. H. PLUMB in his still unfinished *Sir Robert Walpole* (1956–60).

Collective biography is often attempted. Notable examples are Vasari's *Lives of the Painters* (1550), Johnson's *Lives of the Poets* (1779–81) and Keynes's *Studies in Biography* (1933). The vast series started by NAMIER under the title The History of Parliament consists of short biographies of all MPs.

Autobiographies are of special value to the historian, and of course to the biographer, as revealing what only the writer can know; but they are particularly difficult to use, as they tell only what the writer wants known. Some autobiographies, however, because of their authors' acute perception of their age, are unrivalled historical sources, such as the *Confessions* of St Augustine (*c*.420), Goethe's *Dichtung und Wahrheit* (1811–31) and John Stuart Mill's *Autobiography* (1873).

Some historians, such as E. H. CARR and G. R. ELTON, doubt the historical value of biography, or regard the writing of history and biography as distinct enterprises. Seeing history as a matter of impersonal (especially social and economic) trends, or as essentially the study of institutions, they consider concentration on individual historical figures distorting. The form is inherently biased: we possess significant amounts of information about relatively few personages of the past, and the great majority of these were at the top of the social scale, political actors or writers and artists, and male.

The focus of the biographer is certainly different from that of general historians or historians of politics, the economy, or a locality. Biographies vary in their emphasis: some concentrate on the subject's personality, deeds or writings; others pay more attention to the historical background. But history is not so much the study of disembodied trends and institutions as the study of their relation to people, and all its evidence derives from individuals. Hence authentically documented biographies always have something to tell the historian, and those that are written with due awareness of the subject's historical context form a central branch of historical writing. DEDB

Reading

Beales, Derek: *History and Biography* (Cambridge: Cambridge University Press, 1981).

Garraty, John A.: *The Nature of Biography* (London: Jonathan Cape, 1958).

Gash, Norman: A modest defence of historical biography. In *Pillars of Government* (London: Edward Arnold, 1986) pp. 179–85.

Taylor, A. J. P.: The historian as biographer *Wiener Beiträge zur Geschichte der Neuzeit* 6 (1979) 254–61.

black historiography With the growth of the civil rights movement in the United States and the increasing anger of Afro-Americans against the slavery-derived term 'Negro', the expression black historiography arose in the 1960s to describe writing by persons of African descent about the part played by blacks in the history of North America. The expression is occasionally widened to include work on the African Diaspora and is sometimes applied to the study of writing by sympathetic whites on the black experience in the New World.

Before the emancipation of the slaves in the United States between 1863 and 1865, writing by blacks about their past in either Africa or America was limited to blacks who had either been born free or had acquired freedom through manumission or escape. The first comprehensive attempt at black historiography appears to have been the publication in 1841 by a fugitive slave who became a Congregational minister in Connecticut: James W. C. Pennington, *Text Book of the Origin and History, &c. &c. of the Colored People*. Earlier Afro-American writers, however, had stressed the importance of black history for the liberation of persons of African descent, notably David Walker of Boston in 1829 in his militant *David Walker's Appeal . . . to the Colored Citizens of the World*.

Black historiography as an adjunct to Afro-American nationalism developed before the American Civil War in such works as Martin R. Delany, *The Condition, Elevation, Emigration and Destiny of the Colored People of the United States, Politically Considered* (Philadelphia, 1852). Yet integration into American life through the examination of patriotic episodes in the Afro-American past was also an important motive of black historians at this time: for example, William C. Nell's *The Colored Patriots of the American Revolution* (Boston, 1855).

Early Afro-American historians often suffered from inadequate documentary materials. But the autobiographical narratives by escaped slaves, which were published in the fight for civil rights in the United States before and after the Civil War, helped both contemporary and later writers on black history. One such writer, William Wells Brown, produced four historical works which were notable contributions to the preservation of black history, ranging from *St. Domingo: its Revolution and its Patriots* (1855) to *The Rising Son, or the Antecedents and Advancement of the Colored Race* (1874).

After the Civil War and emancipation, as Afro-American educational institutions, particularly Howard and Fisk Universities, were established and entry into white universities became possible for Afro-Americans, black historiography was able to develop on a more scholarly basis. George Washington Williams's two-volume *History of the Negro Race in America from 1619 to 1880* (New York, 1883) and his *History of the Negro Troops in the War of the Rebellion* (New York, 1887) could be compared favourably with other historical works of the period. And when the first volume of the Harvard Historical Series to be published in 1896, *The Suppression of the African Slave Trade to the United States of America, 1638–1870*, was written by an Afro-American scholar, W. E. B. Du Bois, it could be claimed that black historiography, at last, had made an entry into the American historical profession.

Nevertheless, at the turn of the century, black historiography had still to fight for acceptance as a valid academic subject in America. Afro-American intellectuals, in the attempt to overcome prejudice against them and their writings, founded learned societies, notably the American Negro Academy in 1897, the Negro Society for Historical Research in 1911, and the Association for the Study of Negro Life and History in 1915. Carter G. Woodson, a Harvard PhD in history like Du Bois, the founder of the Association, was editor of the influential *Journal of Negro History* from 1916 to his death in 1950. Woodson wrote and edited more books on black history than any other scholar of his time. Arthur A. Schomburg, the Puerto Rican bibliophile and pioneer of the Negro Society of 1911, assembled a unique collection of primary and secondary sources for black historiography which was bought for the New York Public Library by the Carnegie Corporation in 1926. Today, as the Schomburg Center for Research in Black Culture, it is one of the world's major institutions for the study of the past of peoples of African descent everywhere.

The growth of American sociology, the Depression of the 1930s and the stimulus of Marxism encouraged Afro-American writers to explore new areas of black history: for example, Horace Mann Bond, *Negro Education in Alabama: a Study in Cotton and Steel* (Washington, DC, 1939) and Horace R. Cayton and St Clair Drake, *Black Metropolis: A Study of Negro Life in a Northern City* (Chicago, 1946). The study of black revolt against slavery was pioneered by white writers: Thomas Wentworth Higginson in five articles in the mid-nineteenth century and Herbert Aptheker in his seminal *American Negro Slave Revolts* (New York, 1943).

By the second world war, black historiography had come of age. Another Harvard PhD in history, John Hope Franklin, published his first book in wartime America: *The Free Negro in North Carolina, 1790–1860* (Chapel Hill, 1943). Four years later, the first edition of his influential textbook of Afro-American history, *From Slavery to Freedom*, appeared. This began the reputation that made Franklin the first Afro-American Pitt professor of American history and institutions at Cambridge University and the respected promoter of black historiography around the world.

From the beginnings of black historiography, the question of African survivals in the New World has challenged scholars. Some, such as the Afro-American sociologist, E. Franklin Frazier (1894–1962) were sceptical that African survivals had much significance for America, in spite of the arguments to the contrary by the white anthropologist, Melville J. Herskovits, and the impressive linguistic evidence collected by the black scholar, Lorenzo Dow Turner, in his *Africanisms in the Gullah Dialect* (Chicago, 1949). A new generation of black historians now address themselves to this debate. The Afro-American historian, Sterling Stuckey, in his *Slave Culture: Nationalist Theory and the Foundations of Black America* (New York, 1987) argues decisively for the existence of African survivals as basic elements in black American culture.

It was not, however, until after the second

world war that the study of the African Diaspora burgeoned among black scholars. Although it had begun as early as 1887 — with Afro-Caribbean Edward Blyden's *Christianity, Islam and the Negro Race*, and had produced two heavily learned volumes, *The African Abroad*, in 1913 by Afro-American William Henry Ferris, and one masterpiece by Trinidadian C. L. R. James, *The Black Jacobins* (London, 1935) — the significance of the African Diaspora did not capture the imagination of black scholars until much later. At the end of the twentieth century, however, the work of Joseph E. Harris of Howard University, as demonstrated in *Global Dimensions of the African Diaspora* (Washington, DC, 1982), which he edited, and the publication of St Clair Drake's *Black Folk Here and There* (Los Angeles, 1987), indicate that African Diaspora studies are very much alive among Afro-Americans.

Another aspect of black historiography which has had to wait until after the second world war for adequate exploration is the study of the African presence in Canada. This was not put upon scholarly foundations until the publication of the white American historian Robin Winks's *The Blacks in Canada: a History* (New Haven, 1971). The study of the role of black women in American history is also largely a post-1945 product. But such books as Jacqueline Jones's *Labor of Love, Labor of Sorrow: Black Women, Work and the Family from Slavery to the Present* (New York, 1985) demonstrate that the subject is no longer neglected.

Similarly, the documentary foundations of black historiography have been greatly improved in the post-war period. Black and white scholars have collaborated in multi-volume editions of basic documents. Notable here are the scholarly editions of the papers of Frederick Douglass (ed. John Blassingame), Booker T. Washington (ed. Louis R. Harlan), W. E. Du Bois (ed. Herbert Aptheker) and Marcus Garvey (ed. Robert A. Hill). They indicate that black historiography has now the scholars, the materials and the techniques to face the future with confidence.   GS

Reading

Drimmer, Melvin, ed: *Black History: a Reappraisal* (Garden City, NY: Doubleday, 1968).

Franklin, John Hope: *From Slavery to Freedom: a History of Negro Americans*, 3rd edn (New York: Knopf, 1967).

——: *George Washington Williams: a Biography* (Chicago: University of Chicago Press, 1985).

Lerner, Gerda, ed.: *Black Women in White America: a Documentary History* (New York: Pantheon, 1972).

Shepperson, George: The Afro-American contribution to African studies. *Journal of American Studies* 8 (1974) 281–301.

Thorpe, Earl E.: *Negro Historians in the United States* (Baton Rouge, Louis.: Fraternal Press, 1958).

Blanc, Louis (b.1811, d.1882) Blanc was an active French socialist. His tract on the 'Organisation du travail', published in the *Revue du progrès* in 1839, blamed poverty upon unregulated competition and advocated state-supported producer co-operatives, which would eventually become the 'fundamental units of society'. After the revolution of February 1848 he served as a member of the Provisional Government, was the author of its decree guaranteeing the right to work, and president of the short-lived Luxembourg Commission established to inquire into workers' conditions and social reform.

Although he made a considerable effort to evaluate the sources used in his historical works Blanc, like such contemporaries as de Bonald, Thierry, GUIZOT, Thiers and MICHELET, rejected 'cold impartiality' and approached the study of the past as a propagandist rather than as an objective historian. In his case, inspired by the democratic idealism of the 1830s and 1840s, this was in the cause of Jacobin socialism. It was also an attempt to explain French politics in terms of class conflict. Blanc believed that the course of history was determined by a succession of fundamental ideas, each defining a distinctive period with its characteristic political, social and economic structures. In his major study of the French Revolution he was concerned to explain the rise of the bourgeoisie and tried to prove that this was, as the eventual demise of bourgeois society would be, the product of 'the ineluctable laws of history'.   RDP

Main publications

Organisation du travail (Paris, 1840); *Histoire de dix ans, 1830–1840* (Brussels, 1844); *Histoire de la*

43

BLOCH, MARC

Révolution française, 12 vols (Paris: Langlois & Leclerq, 1847—62).

Reading

Loubère, L. A.: *Louis Blanc: his Life and his Contribution to the Rise of French Jacobin-Socialism* (Buffalo, NY: Northwestern University Press, 1961)

Bloch, Marc (b.1886, d.1944) Of few historians can it be said that the quality of their lives and convictions has had almost as great an influence and appeal as their historical writings. But Marc Bloch is one such. The son of a distinguished ancient historian, Bloch was trained at the École Normale Supérieure at Paris and thereafter at Leipzig and Berlin. His early academic career was interrupted by four years of war service, but by the age of 33 he had been appointed professor at Strasburg and subsequently in 1936 moved to the chair of economic history at the Sorbonne. His career was again interrupted by war in 1939: he enlisted once more, 'the oldest captain in the French army' in his own words; then, after the defeat of 1940, retired to teach in Vichy France; in 1943, fully in line with his own intense patriotism and deep moral convictions, he joined the Resistance. He was captured by the Nazis and shot on 16 June 1944.

Bloch's output as a historian was prolific. His early work concentrated on the evolution of landscape and society and the relationship between the two in northern France in the middle ages. His next major book, *Les Rois thaumaturges* (1924), indicated, however, that Bloch was more than an economic historian and that his interest lay also in the history of collective mentalities and in the interplay between myths and beliefs on the one hand and political and social institutions on the other. The year 1931 saw the appearance of the book which brought him European-wide fame, *Les Caractères originaux de l'histoire rurale française*. In it he explored the intricate counterpoint between man's physical setting and his social institutions from early medieval times to the French Revolution, drawing on a remarkably wide range of documentation and confronting some of the central issues in the history of the making of European rural society. It was to the medieval period itself that Bloch returned for what was to prove his last and probably best-known work, *La Société féodale* (1939—40). Its 'exhilarating competence' and 'its controlled breadth' — two phrases used about it by English reviewers — are as evident today as they were on its first appearance. It has naturally attracted criticism — for its over-schematism and unmanageability, its failure to pay sufficient attention to the political framework of events, and its essentially mistaken chronology of the development of feudal relationships. But as a breath-takingly ambitious attempt to understand a medieval society in the round and to explain the multi-faceted nature of social change and relationships, it still has few equals and no superior.

Bloch's own corpus of published work would of itself give him a commanding position in twentieth-century historiography. But his role in re-orienting the direction of French and thereby European academic history was, arguably, even more important. The organ for his views was the journal he founded with Lucien FEBVRE in 1929, *Annales d'histoire économique et sociale* (see ANNALES SCHOOL). Bloch set out to counter what he saw, sometimes uncharitably and often exaggeratedly, as the document-centred, political and administrative character of current French historiography. History, so he claimed, was the study of the past, not of documents; the historian's prime duty was to ask questions, not to assemble facts; only thus could he achieve 'rational classification and progressive intelligibility'. The historian's questions must be large ones: about the relationship between man and his environment, the reasons for the decline of slavery or the development of serfdom, the impact of technological innovation on patterns of authority, the nature and chronology of seignorial power, or the interplay between intellectual changes and social and political attitudes. In order to pose and to answer such questions, the historian must make use of the insights of allied disciplines, such as anthropology, sociology, collective psychology or etymology, as well as of the historical evidence itself. Such understanding could be further advanced by taking a long-term view of social phenomena (rather than the short-term perspective frequently adopted by historians), by arguing back from the better-known and better-documented to the less well-known (the 'retrogressive method') and by frequent recourse to comparisons across regional, national and international boundaries. When asked in 1933 what his programme was, Bloch answered crisply 'the comparative study of European societies'.

He crystallized his views on history in the unfinished *Apologie pour l'histoire*, published posthumously in 1949. The *Apologie* is as striking a memorial to Bloch the man as to Bloch the historian. That is why it has worn so well. Its appeal is as much poetic as it is academic. It was written in the dark days of war and despair by a scholar who was a man of action as well as of words and who saw past and present as one reality. Bloch wrote as tellingly and movingly on the collapse of France in 1940 in *L'Étrange défaite* as of the impact of invasions on early medieval Europe; likewise, his remarkable essay on the transmission of news and rumour in medieval Europe sprang directly from his experience in the trenches of the first world war. This firm grasp on the present and his recognition of the intangibility of reality – 'the knot of reality' as he himself called it – saved Bloch from the aridities and abstractions of some latter-day *annalistes*. *'L'histoire humaine'* or 'the history of men in societies' were his favourite definitions of his subject. Vacuous or unattainable they may sound as definitions, but in his life, as in his writings, they have a certain undeniable appropriateness.   RRD

Main publications

L'Île de France (1913; English trans., London: Routledge & Kegan Paul, 1971; New York: Cornell University Press, 1971); *Roi et serfs* (1920; Coronet reprint); *Les rois thaumaturges* (1924) trans. as *The Royal Touch* (London: Routledge & Kegan Paul, 1973); *Les Caractères originaux de l'histoire rurale française* (1931) trans. as French Rural History (London: Routledge & Kegan Paul, 1966; Berkeley and Los Angeles: University of California Press, 1966; *La Société féodale* (1939–40; English trans.: Routledge & Kegan Paul, 1966; University of Chicago Press, 1961; *Apologie pour l'histoire* (1949) trans. as *The Historian's Craft* (Manchester: Manchester University Press, 1954; New York: Random House, 1964); *Mélanges historiques* (Paris: SEVPEN, 1963), with full bibliography; several essays in trans. in *Land and Work in Medieval Europe* (London:

Routledge & Kegan Paul, 1967) and *Slavery and Serfdom in the Middle Ages* (London: Routledge & Kegan Paul; Berkeley University of California Press, 1978).

Reading

Davies, R. R.: Marc Bloch. *History* 52 (1967) 265–86.
Loyn, H. R.: Marc Bloch. In *The Historian at Work*, ed. J. Cannon (London: Allen & Unwin, 1980).
Perrin. Ch.-E.: L'oeuvre historique de Marc Bloch. *Revue Historique* 199 (1948) 161–88.

Bobrzyński, Michał (b.1849, d.1935) A leading conservative political and educational figure in Austrian Poland, Bobrzyński was professor of history in Cracow, member of the Australian council of state and, from 1908 to 1913, viceroy of Galicia. He did much to raise the standard of education in the province and tried to reconcile Poles and Ukrainians. His research centred on legal and medieval history. He rejected LELEWEL's Romanticism and proposed a new periodization of Polish history following political-constitutional criteria: primitive (to 1241), medieval (1241–1505) and modern (1505–1795). He co-founded the Cracow school of history which identified the Poles' irresponsible republicanism as the main cause of Poland's downfall. Bobrzyński's 'pessimistic' interpretation was challenged by KORZON.   WHZ

Main publications

Dzieje Polski w zarysie (An Outline of Polish History) (Cracow: 1877).

Reading

Serejski, M. H.: L'école historique de Cracovie et l'historiographie européenne. *Acta Poloniae Historica* 26 (1972) 127–52.

Bodin, Jean (b.1529/30, d.1596) French legal theorist. An Angevin by birth, Bodin studied and taught civil law at Toulouse before practising in the 1560s at the Paris bar. Having served the Duke of Alençon, he became in 1587 attorney-general for Laon where he ran into trouble through collaborating with the Catholic League. His own religious views seem to have veered towards Judaism. Early in his career Bodin became convinced, with other humanist scholars, of the need for a new systematization of law on the basis of an historical methodology. This meant treating the civilian texts as imperfect records compiled by fallible jurists of laws which in any case were the products of a particular society. Other societies had laws of their own; and all societies changed with the passage of time. Critical evaluation of the sources and a comparative approach to jurisprudence were therefore essential to the task of specifying and systematizing the universal principles of law as such. Bodin set out his prescription in his *Classification of Universal Law* (written *c.*1560) and his *Method*. He applied it to the sphere of public law in his *Six Bookes*, a seminal work famous for its recognition of legislative sovereignty as the prime characteristic of state power.   HALI

Main publications

Methodus ad facilem historiarum cognitionem (1566) trans. as *Method for the Easy Comprehension of History* (New York: Columbia University Press, 1945); *Les six livres de la république* (1576) trans. as *The Six Bookes of a Commonweale*, (Cambridge, Mass.: Harvard University Press, 1962).

Reading

Denzer, H. ed.: *Jean Bodin: proceedings of the international conference on Bodin in Munich* (Munich: C. H. Beck 1973) [valuable essays including three on Bodin's historical thought].
Franklin, J. H.: *Jean Bodin and the Sixteenth-Century Revolution in the Methodology of Law and History* (New York: Columbia University Press, 1963).

Bolingbroke, Lord Henry St John (b.1678, d.1751) Excluded from politics by his flirtations with Jacobitism, Bolingbroke turned to the study of history both as a consolation and as a means of attacking his political opponents. His enlightened scepticism led him to doubt the historian's ability to recover the past. He repeatedly expressed his distrust of the history of biblical and ancient times, which he regarded as little more than myths and fables. Nor did he have any patience with antiquarians who simply amassed facts and placed them in chronological order. On the other hand Bolingbroke's humanist side led him to argue that the chief value of studying history was the constant improvement of private and public virtue. History inculcated moral and practical lessons, promoted social virtues and provided

a guide to future action. This utilitarian view of history encouraged Bolingbroke to use the past for partisan purposes. He used historical examples to repudiate Walpole's factious government which depended upon political corruption and threatened England's ancient constitution and the liberties of the subject, and to stress the importance of the balance of power in Europe. In attempting to explain historical change, Bolingbroke vacillated between an emphasis on the actions of great men and a belief in the crucial influence of social structure and economic change.   HTD

Main publications

Remarks on the History of England, first appeared as 24 essays contributed to *The Craftsman* 1730–31 (London: R. Franklin, 1743); *Letters on the Study and Use of History* (London, 1752); *Lord Bolingbroke: Historical Writings*, ed. I. Kramnick (Chicago, Ill.: University of Chicago Press, 1972).

Reading

Dickinson, H. T.: *Bolingbroke* (London: Constable, 1970).
Kramnick, I.: Introduction to *Historical Writings* (see above).

Bollandists La Société des Bollandistes is a group of Jesuit scholars engaged in the critical examination of hagiographical sources. They take their name from Jean Bolland (d.1665) who carried out the idea of Héribert Rosweyde (d.1625) that a scholarly edition of the *Acta Sanctorum* should be produced. Bolland arranged the lives of the saints in accordance with the liturgical calendar and published the two volumes of the January *Acta* in 1643. He had two distinguished collaborators, Godefroid Henskens (d.1681) and Daniel Van Papenbroeck (d.1714), under whose direction the work continued smoothly after his death. When the Society of Jesus was dissolved in 1773 the Bollandists continued to function under the auspices first of the Austrian government and then of the abbeys of Caudenberg and Tongerloo, until the French invasion of Belgium in 1794 brought their work to an end. Volume VI of the October *Acta* had been published in that year.

The Jesuits were reconstituted in 1814 and the Bollandists refounded in 1837 with their headquarters at Brussels. By 1883 they had produced volumes VII–XIII of the October *Acta*. In 1882 they began publication of a quarterly journal, *Analecta Bollandiana*, and soon after this issued a series of *Subsidia* volumes. These works dealt with hagiographical questions unrelated to the current volume of the *Acta* on which the fathers were working. This diversification of the activities of the Society made its publication of the *Acta* slower, as did the great increase in source material which resulted from the opening of archives to the public throughout western Europe. The scope of the *Acta* was also broadened as members of the Society acquired new linguistic skills enabling them to edit, for example, Armenian and Celtic texts. The work remains incomplete: the first four volumes of the November *Acta* have been published and the introductory volume to the December *Acta*, an edition of the Roman Martyrology, appeared in 1940.

The Bollandists' chief concern has always been to establish the truth about the cult of the saints, but in the process they have also solved many general historical problems, as the dissertations with which their volumes are embellished bear witness. Through careful editing they have turned hagiographical texts into valuable historical sources, for even the most fanciful saint's life may tell scholars something about the society in which it originated. No end to the Bollandists' activity is in sight; when they publish the last volume of the December *Acta* the January volumes of 1643 will await revision.   BH

Main publications

Published by the Society of Bollandists: *Acta Sanctorum, quotquot in toto orbe coluntur*, 67 vols (Antwerp and Brussels: 1643–1940); *Bibliotheca hagiographica graeca*, ed. F. Halkin, 3rd edn, 3 vols (1957); F. Halkin, *Auctarium Bibliothecae hagiographicae graecae* (1969); *Bibliotheca hagiographica latina*, 2 vols (1898–1901, repr. 1949); *Supplementum*, 2nd edn (1911); *Bibliotheca hagiographica orientalis*, ed. P. Peeters, 1910, repr. 1954).

Reading

Delehaye, H.: *A Travers trois siècles: l'oeuvre des Bollandistes* (Brussels 1920) English trans. *The Work of the Bollandists through Three Centuries, 1615–1915* (Princeton, NJ: Princeton University Press, 1922).

Knowles, D.: The Bollandists. In *Great Historical Enterprises* (London: Nelson, 1963) pp. 1–32.

Bolton, Herbert Eugene (b.1870, d.1953) Born on a farm in Wisconsin, Bolton went to the University of Pennsylvania for his doctorate in medieval history. Earlier, he had taken a master's degree in American history at the University of Wisconsin under the young Frederick Jackson TURNER, who had just stated his important thesis on the formative frontier.

It was while editing the state historical quarterly at the University of Texas that Bolton found his own frontier, a Spanish-American one. It was a happy discovery. His efforts to locate the accounts of missionaries and conquistadors led to the monumental *Guide to Materials for the History of the United States in the Principal Archives of Mexico* and the first of many volumes of translations.

In 1909 Bolton and his family went to California. After two years at Stanford University he moved to Berkeley as the professor in American history, in his words, 'the academic position in history of most influence west of the Mississippi'. At Berkeley Bolton became curator of the Bancroft Library, Sather Professor, and chairman of his department. He made a rare foray into theory with a lecture on 'The mission as a frontier institution in the Spanish-American colonies'. As a member of the council of the American Historical Association, he helped to launch the *Hispanic American Historical Review*.

Bolton dreamed of dramatizing the Spanish presence in North America as Francis PARKMAN had the French. In *The Spanish Borderlands: a Chronicle of Old Florida and the Southwest* (1921) he applied the term 'Borderlands' to all the areas once Spanish, yet he was more interested in the Southwestern explorers whose routes he followed on horseback than in defining a new field of inquiry. His academic progeny concerned themselves mainly with archival discovery and recounting the particulars of the past.

At the same time Bolton was making history as a teacher. In 1919 he announced a lower division course on the history of the Americas similar to a survey of Europe. He expected no students, but 772 registered. He mimeographed their syllabus one page at a time, drawing maps on manila paper. Bolton's 'History of the Americas', filled with heroic figures and romance, drew more than a thousand students every semester for a quarter of a century. His presidential address to the American Historical Association in 1932, 'The epic of greater America', succinctly states its premises that the Spanish past is an essential part of United States history and that the two American continents can be studied together.

These simple premises were more acceptable to undergraduates than to the guild of historians. Bolton was charged with claiming that the Americas have a common history — something he did not say but which has been refuted by historians both of the US and of Latin America as the 'Bolton Thesis'. Despite the output of the Bolton school, the Borderlands have not been integrated into US colonial history but excluded from it as something base and alien. For this, Bolton himself is largely responsible. Unconsciously influenced by a tradition of sombre Spanish exceptionalism, he neglected the opportunity to apply the Turner thesis to a non-Anglo frontier. The dramatist of the Borderlands did not inquire into the influence of the frontier upon Spaniards, for everywhere he found only what he had expected: Spanish absolutism unaltered.   ATB

Main publications

Guide to Materials for the History of the United States in the Principal Archives of Mexico (Washington, DC: Carnegie Institution, 1913); The mission as a frontier institution in the Spanish American colonies. *American Historical Review* 23 (1917) 42–61; *The Spanish Borderlands: a Chronicle of Old Florida and the Southwest* (New Haven, Conn.: Yale University Press, 1921); *History of the Americas: a Syllabus with Maps* (Boston and New York: Ginn, 1928); The epic of Greater America. *American Historical Review* 38 (1933) 448–74; *Rim of Christendom: a Biography of Eusebio Francisco Kino, Pacific Coast Pioneer* (New York: Macmillan, 1936).

Reading

Bannon, John Francis: *Herbert Eugene Bolton: the Historian and the Man, 1870–1953* (Tucson: University of Arizona Press, 1978).

Hanke, Lewis ed.: *Do the Americas have a Common History? a Critique of the Bolton Theory* (New York: Knopf, 1964).

Scardaville, Michael C.: Approaches to the study of the southeastern Borderlands. In *Alabama and the Borderlands from Prehistory to Statehood*, ed. R. Reid Badger and Lawrence A. Clayton (Tuscaloosa: University of Alabama Press, 1985).

Weber, David J.: Turner, the Boltonians, and the Borderlands. *American Historical Review* 91 (1986) 66–81.

Boorstin, Daniel J. (b.1914) A graduate of Harvard and Oxford, Boorstin was awarded his doctorate by Yale in 1940. After teaching at Harvard and Swarthmore for six years he moved to the University of Chicago where he spent the bulk of his academic career. He has taught as a visitor in many American and overseas universities and in 1975 became librarian of Congress. The successive publication of the three volumes of his major work, *The Americans*, brought him numerous prizes including the Bancroft (1959), the Francis Parkman (1966) and a Pulitzer (1974).

Boorstin has been the primary proponent of the so-called consensus school of American history. He interpreted the American past in terms of consensus and celebrated it for the same reason. Reacting against the ideological struggles of the McCarthy era he produced *The Genius of American Politics*, first as a lecture series and then as a book. Its main theme is that the American experience has been unique and has promoted the development of unique institutions and democratic values peculiar to the United States. Indeed, American institutions are so impregnated with values deriving from the American experience that the nation has neither developed an explicit political theory nor needed one. 'For the belief that an explicit political theory is superfluous precisely because we already possess a satisfactory equivalent', he writes, 'I propose the name of "givenness"' (p. 8). He defined 'givenness' as 'the belief that values in America are in some way or other automatically defined: *given* by certain facts of geography or history peculiar to us' (p. 9).

In *The Americans* Boorstin sets out, through a thematic approach, to illuminate the process by which uniquely American institutions and values developed. In places the analysis is Turnerian, emphasizing the importance of geography and environment. Elsewhere he is more concerned to note the interaction of inherited English institutions and values with the American environment, an interaction which proved to be transforming. At the centre of his schema is the community, the development of which he sketches against an implicit and contrasting backcloth of European development. Treating the American Revolution as a distinctly non-revolutionary event, and largely ignoring the Civil War, Boorstin's account has been strongly criticized for the way it avoids discussion of conflict in the American past. His repudiation of theory has struck many as evidence of a distinctly anti-intellectual bias and that charge gained greater weight as a result of the later publication of political tracts aimed at the dissenting movements of the 1960s. Nevertheless, *The Americans* was a major interpretative achievement and stands as an exemplar of the consensus school.

Boorstin's first publications were in the field of intellectual history. Beginning in English history with a study of Blackstone's *Mysterious Science of the Law* (1941), he turned to America with *The Lost World of Thomas Jefferson* (1948) and has, most recently, taken the whole world as his canvas in *The Discoverers* (1983). In all these works Boorstin keeps before the reader the importance of local circumstance and experience. Respectful of the overall integrity of Blackstone's purpose, Boorstin was, ironically in view of his later publications, inclined to slight the Jeffersonians for their lack of a critical intellectual framework. Equally ironically, the equivalent absence of such a framework characterizes *The Discoverers*.

A long book, and fascinating in its details, *The Discoverers* explores the process of invention and discovery around the world and through the ages, paying particular attention to the precise circumstances of time and place. It may be that there is inherent in such an approach a tendency to produce a chronicle rather than a work of coherent interpretation. Certainly Boorstin's particularism is cumulative in a wholly arithmetical way. Nowhere does he suggest the possibility of a geometrical accumulation leading to a situation in which discovery takes place in a denser medium which might suggest the necessity for a different perspective on the very process and control of exploration. There is thus a high degree of consistency in Boorstin's considerable output. He stresses throughout the controlling influence of time, place and circumstance upon historical process.   DMacl

Main publications

(Published by Random House, New York, unless otherwise stated.)
The Mysterious Science of the Law (Cambridge, Mass.: Harvard University Press, 1941); *The Lost World of Thomas Jefferson* (New York: H. Holt, 1948); *The Genius of American Politics* (Chicago: University of Chicago Press, 1953); *The Americans: the Colonial Experience* (1958); *The Americans: the National Experience* (1965); *The Americans: the Democratic Experience* (1973); *The Discoverers* (1983).

Reading

Pole, J. R.: Daniel J. Boorstin. In *Pastmasters. Some Essays on American Historians*, ed. Marcus Cunliffe and Robin W. Winks (New York: Harper & Row, 1969) pp. 210–38.

Bouquet, Dom   See MAURISTS.

Boxer, Charles R. (b.1904) Boxer was educated at Sandhurst and saw extensive service in East Asia as an army officer (1923–47). His academic career was primarily at London University (Camões Chair of Portuguese, 1947–51 and 1953–67; professor of the history of the Far East, School of Oriental and African Studies, 1951–53). After retirement, he held appointments at Yale (1969–72) and at Indiana (1967–79). Honoured by Portugal (Grand Cross of the Order of the Infante Dom Henrique), Knight of the Order of St Gregory the Great, in 1986 Boxer was only the eighth recipient (in 150 years) of the Gold Medal of Dom Pedro II of the Instituto Histórico e Geográfico Brasileiro.

A superb linguist, a prolific author, Boxer's scholarship focuses on the history of Europe overseas. He demonstrated how the interplay of diplomatic, economic, social, religious, and institutional factors in Europe impinged on policies and events overseas. His histories of the Portuguese and Dutch seaborne empires traced their formation, consolidation and decline, and the rivalries between Portugal, Spain and the United Provinces, both in Europe and in Africa, Asia, and the Americas.

Boxer emphasized the corresponding complexity of interaction between non-European peoples. A central theme is the relations (commercial, religious, political, diplomatic) between European interlopers and indigenous peoples; cultural, social, sexual and linguistic exchanges; and reciprocity of influences. His major interests are missionary (most notably the Jesuits in Japan) and maritime history, cartography, numismatics, naval architecture, and military fortifications. Boxer does not scorn the heroic, but his is not drum and trumpet history. He delves below the surface to examine institutional infrastructures (town councils, philanthropic organizations) and to give prominence to ordinary people. His revisionist views on Portuguese race relations and treatment of slaves stirred controversy. Pervading his writings is a keen and sympathetic interest in the human condition and how people cope with adversity. An avid bibliophile, he is famous for his encyclopaedic knowledge of contemporary sources, his meticulous research, enthusiasm, and willingness to share his knowledge. In addition to narrative histories, Boxer has written biographies, and translated and edited texts with critical commentaries. His sources are more qualitative than quantitative, his approach more narrative than analytical. An inspiring and demanding teacher and much sought-after lecturer, Boxer is a truly active participant through personal contacts and voluminous correspondence in the international community of scholars.   AJRR-W

Main publications

Jan Compagnie in Japan (The Hague: Nijhoff, 1936); *Fidalgos in the Far East* (The Hague: Nijhoff, 1948); *The Christian Century in Japan* (Berkeley: University of California Press; London: Cambridge University Press, 1951); *Salvador de Sá and the Struggle for Brazil and Angola* (London: Athlone, 1952); *South China in the Sixteenth Century* (London: Hakluyt Society, 1953); *The Dutch in Brazil* (Oxford: Clarendon Press, 1957); *The Great Ship from Amacon* (Lisbon: Centro de Estudos Historicos, 1959); *The Tragic History of the Sea* (London: Cambridge University Press, 1959); *The Golden Age of Brazil* (Berkeley and Los Angeles: University of California Press, 1962); *Race Relations in the Portuguese Colonial Empire* (London: Oxford University Press, 1963); *The Dutch Seaborne Empire* (London: Hutchinson, 1965); *Portuguese Society in the Tropics* (Madison and Milwaukee: Wisconsin University Press, 1965); *The Portuguese Seaborne Empire* (London: Hutchinson, 1969); *The Anglo-Dutch Wars of the Seventeenth Century* (London: HMSO, 1974).

Reading

West, S. George: *A List of the Writings of Charles Ralph Boxer Published between 1926 and 1984 Compiled for his Eightieth Birthday* (London: Tamesis Books, 1984).

Braudel, Fernand (b.1902, d.1985) Braudel was born in Lorraine. Before the first world war, he taught in schools in Algeria (1923−32), and at the university of São Paulo (1935−8); these years of residence outside Europe helped to give him a global view of human history. Braudel spent the second world war in a German prison camp, writing his doctoral thesis, despite his lack of access to books (he had a phenomenal memory). After the war he became professor at the Collège de France (1949), editor of the journal *Annales* (1956) and president of the sixième section of the École Pratique des Hautes Études. A man of dignified and commanding presence, Braudel remained, even after his retirement, the most influential man in what is still in France an influential profession.

Braudel's reputation rests essentially on his first book, planned as a study of the foreign policy of Philip II, but, with the encouragement of Lucien FEBVRE, transformed to give pride of place to the sea. It is a vast book on a vast subject, but not big enough for its author who, faithful to his maxim that to understand something it is necessary to see it as part of a larger whole, extended his intellectual frontiers from the Atlantic to the Sahara. *The Mediterranean* (1972−3) is best known, however, for its concern with what Braudel called *la longue durée*, the long term, and divided into the extremely slow-moving time of historical geography (or as he preferred to call it, geohistory), and the somewhat more rapidly moving time of institutions − economic systems, societies and states. As for the short term, the time of events, Braudel thought it superficial. In a famous image, appropriate to the subject, he described events as mere 'crests of foam that the tides of history carry on their strong backs'. He did not exactly despise events; he recognized their human interest. All the same, in contrast to what might be called the 'classical tradition' of historical writing, from Thucydides to Ranke, he thought events worthy of study only in so far as they revealed underlying structures. Braudel has sometimes been accused of being a geographical determinist, uninterested in individuals. A determinist he was not, in the strict sense; he was certainly fascinated by the mysterious Philip II. However, he certainly regarded geographical and other structural factors as being of crucial importance in the long run.

In the years which followed the publication of *The Mediterranean* Braudel was concerned with revising and enlarging it. The second edition (published in 1966) betrays the influence of Ernest LABROUSSE and takes much more account of statistical data on prices and population. Braudel went on revising his work almost all his life, but in the 1960s and 1970s most of his still abundant energies went into a study originally commissioned by Lucien Febvre, concerned with the material culture and economic life of Europe from 1400 to 1800. What had been planned as one volume ended up as three, concerned with three levels of economic history. On the ground floor (Braudel's metaphor, not far removed from Marx's 'base'), is *civilisation matérielle*, defined as 'repeated actions, empirical processes, old methods, and solutions handed down from time immemorial'. On the next floor there is *vie économique*, economic life in the strict sense, involving calculation and the following of rules. At the top (not to say 'superstructure') there is capitalism. At all these levels Europe is placed in typical Braudelian fashion in the context of world developments in the same period.

By the time these three volumes were published, Braudel was seventy-seven. He was by this time hard at work on another book, this time a history of France, which was left half-finished at his death. The first volume deals, as one might have guessed, with geo-history. It discusses the diversity of France, and also the forces making for its cohesion, such as communication systems. The old Braudel describes the new autoroutes with the same

enthusiasm that the young Braudel had given to timing the speed of galleys and of sailing-ships across the Mediterranean in the age of Philip II.

Unlike most of his colleagues, Braudel was at his best when dealing with great sweeps of time and space, though he had a sharp eye for the revealing detail. He read a good deal outside his subject, vast as it was, and he was adept at picking up ideas from others, putting them to new uses and making them his own. His early work, for example, draws on historical geographers such as Maximilien Sorre, historical demographers such as Alfred Sauvy, and historical sociologists such as the Brazilian Gilberto FREYRE, while his late work owes much to the economic historians Witold Kula and Immanuel Wallerstein. Braudel was not always accurate on points of detail and there were surprising gaps in his knowledge. In a book which had occasion to refer again and again to Chinese technology, he failed to mention Joseph Needham. Yet his contribution to the renewal of historical studies in our time was greater than that of either Marc Bloch or Lucien Febvre, and possibly greater than that of the two scholars together.   UPB

Main publications

La Méditerranée et le monde méditerranéen à l'époque de Philippe II (1949) (London: Collins, 1972–3); *Écrits sur l'histoire* (1969) (Chicago: Chicago University Press, 1980); *Civilisation matérielle, économie et capitalisme* (1967–79) (London: Collins, 1981–4); *L'identité de la France* (Paris: Arthaud-Flammarion, 1986).

Reading

Burke, P: Braude. In *The Historian at Work*, ed. J. Cannon (London: Allen & Unwin, 1980).

Hexter, J. H.: Fernand Braudel and the monde braudelien. *Journal of Modern History* 44 (1972) 480–537.

Wallerstein, I. et al: *Review* 2 (1978) [special issue].

Wesseling, H. et al: Fernand Braudel. *Itinerario* 5 (1981) 15–52.

Briggs, Asa (b.1921) Born at Keighley in Yorkshire, Briggs characterized social history as history, not with the politics left out, but with the economics put in. This view, acceptable when Labour governments were funding the development of economic and social studies, underlay an outstanding text-book, *The Age of Improvement*, and many popular and scholarly works, including important contributions to the development of urban history. A lifelong don in Oxford, Leeds and Sussex, Briggs also became a public figure (and a life peer in 1976) and transmuted public service into scholarship in his *History of Broadcasting in the United Kingdom*, a study of a monopoly in a liberal society.   WRW

Main publications

A History of Birmingham 1865–1938 (Oxford: Oxford University Press, 1952); *The Age of Improvement* (London: Longmans Green, 1959); *A History of Broadcasting in the United Kingdom*, 4 vols (Oxford University Press, 1960–77); *Victorian Cities* (London: Longmans Green, 1963; Harmondsworth: Penguin, 1968).

Brinton, Crane (b.1898, d.1968) Educated at Harvard and Oxford (where he spent three years as a Rhodes scholar), Brinton became one of the foremost American exponents of European intellectual history. His rationalism, optimism and tolerance, as well as the influence that his undergradute instructors Harold Laski and Irving Babbitt exerted on him, drew him naturally to the study of the Enlightenment and the French Revolution. As he later declared: 'I have kept to the basic belief of my youth in the rightness...of human reason. You may write me down as born in the eighteenth century and yet not too uncomfortable...in the mid-twentieth.' During a long teaching career at Harvard (1923–68), his wide reading in the original texts enabled him to produce numerous studies of English and French thought. His lucid, familiar, and sometimes flippant style won him a considerable audience outside academic circles and thereby shaped American understanding of Europe's intellectual heritage. Despite the advance of totalitarianism during the 1930s and 1940s, Brinton maintained his faith in the benefits that liberal, democratic society offered humanity. This enlightened spirit permeated all his historical writings, particularly his later works of synthesis.   JF

Main publications

The Jacobins (New York: Macmillan, 1930); *English Political Thought in the Nineteenth Century* (London: Benn, 1933); *A Decade of Revolution, 1789–1799* (New York: Harper, 1934); *The Anatomy of Revolution* (New York: Norton, 1938); *Ideas and Men: the Story of Western Thought* (New York: Prentice-Hall, 1950).

Reading

American Historical Review 74 (1968) 854–5 [an appreciation].
Bien, David D.: Crane Brinton. *French Historical Studies* 6 (1969) 113–19.

Brogan, Denis William (b.1900, d.1974) Although of Irish stock, Brogan was born in Glasgow and received his early education in Scotland. From Glasgow University he went to Balliol College, Oxford, and thence as a research fellow to Harvard. But the major part of his working life was spent as professor of political science at Cambridge, a chair which he occupied from 1939 until his retirement in 1968. The list of his publications shows his life-long concern to bring to English readers an understanding of the history and institutions of the United States and France. His major works appeared at historically opportune moments: *The American Political System* (1933) coincided with an increasing British awareness of the importance of the United States in international affairs; *The Development of Modern France* (1940), published when many were seeking to understand the collapse of the Third Republic, provided a much-needed analysis of its history and politics and has remained an indispensable tool for serious students; *The French Nation: Napoleon to Pétain* (1957) surveys a longer period more briefly, with clarity and wit.

As a broadcaster in the war-time Transatlantic Quiz, and as a frequent contributor to the *Guardian* and many periodicals, he became known to a wide public. As a speaker, he combined historical insight with a sparkle and deftness of touch that appeared less often in his writings.

Brogan became a Fellow of the British Academy in 1955 and was knighted in 1963.   JMT

Main publications

The American Political System (London: Hamish Hamilton, 1933); *The Development of Modern France* (Hamish Hamilton, 1940; rev. edn, 1967); *The Era of Franklin D Roosevelt* (New Haven, Conn.: Yale University Press, 1950; English edn, *Roosevelt and the New Deal*, Hamish Hamilton, 1952); *The French Nation: Napoleon to Pétain* (Hamish Hamilton, 1957)

Reading

Nicholas, H. G.: Memoir. *Proceedings of the British Academy* 53 (1976) 399–412.

Bruni, Leonardo (b.*c.*1374, d.1444)   Bruni's Latin style was greatly admired and gave him a preponderant role in the chancery of Florence of which he became head in 1427. Earlier he had been employed in the papal curia and his successors as Florentine chancellors included several humanist scholars of note. His Greek studies were influential and included many translations into Latin of Plato and Aristotle. His chief reputation was as a servant of the republic, drafting many dispatches which (so it was claimed) were more potent than a regiment of cavalry. In this vein he also wrote a work in praise of Florence (the *Laudatio florentinae urbis*) and a similar propaganda motive lay behind his very substantial historical works. The 'commentary on the Punic war' (1421) was in fact a version of Polybius, i and ii; the 'commentary on the Italian wars against the Goths' (1442) is derived from Procopius. But above all he wrote a 'History of the Florentine people' in twelve books (down to 1404). This was ordered by the government to be translated into Italian by Donato Acciauoli, and thus had even wider influence. It was in effect continued in his 'History of his own time' (1378–1440). This combination of diplomacy and stylish history was emulated throughout Europe in the fifteenth and sixteenth centuries. It is also worth recording his brief Italian life of Dante, a short but telling view of Dante as a representative of what later scholars have called 'civic humanism'.   DH

Main writings

Rerum Italica rum Scriptores, 2nd ser., vol. 19, part 3, ed. Emilio Santini.

Reading

Baron, Hans: *The Crisis of the Early Italian Renaissance*, 2nd edn (Princeton, NJ: Princeton University Press, 1966).
Santini, E.: Introduction to *Rerum Italicarum Scriptores*, 2nd ser., vol. 19 (see above).

Brunner, Heinrich (b.1840, d.1915)   Legal historian born at Wels (Austria), Brunner was professor at Lemberg (1866), Prague (1870), Strasburg (1872) and from 1874 at Berlin. In his studies of the early Germanic laws he showed the influence of the Theodosian Code and the importance of 'vulgar Roman law' (a phrase which he coined himself). His great work was his *History of German Law* (2 vols, 1887–92) but from 1886 he also supervised the 'Leges' section of the *Monumenta Germaniae Historica*. In England he is best-known for his work on the origin of the jury (1872) which was endorsed by STUBBS and MAITLAND and which is still important. For medievalists generally, Brunner's most challenging work was his article (1887) on knight-service and the origins of feudalism, in which he connected Charles Martel's need for mounted knights against the Saracens with his spoliation of church lands in order to provide benefices for his retainers. With various modifications concerning the invention of stirrups or horsebreeding, this theory still has many supporters.   RHCD

Main publications

Die Entstehung der Schwurgerichte (Berlin: 1872); *Deutsche Rechtsgeschichte*, 2 vols (Leipzig: 1887–92; 2nd edn 1906–28); Die Reiterdienst und die Anfänge den Lehnwesen. *Zeitschrift der Savigny Stiftung* 8 (1887) 1–38; Geschichte der englischen Rechtsquellen in Grundriss [originally an article in a legal encyclopaedia], trans. W. Hastie as *The Sources of the Law of England* (Edinburgh: T. and T. Clark, 1888) [incl. a biographical appendix].

Brunner, Otto (b.1898, d.1982)   After serving in the first world war, Brunner studied history and geography at Vienna, and took the course for historians and archivists at the Institut für Österreichische Geschichtsforschung in 1921–2. From 1923 to 1931 he was archivist at the Haus- Hof- und Staatsarchiv in Vienna; in 1931 he succeeded his teacher Redlich as professor for Austrian history in

Vienna; after 1936 he was also responsible for economic and social history; and in 1940 he succeeded Hirsch as director of the Institut für Österreichische Geschichtsforschung. Brunner was deprived of his chair after the end of the second world war, and returned to academic life only in 1954, when he succeeded Hermann Aubin at Hamburg.

Brunner's most important work was *Land und Herrschaft*, which first appeared in 1939 and has gone through no less than eight editions. It is a study of the origins and development of territorial lordship in the late middle ages in what is now Austria. What made it so influential was the attempt to discuss the reality of medieval political and constitutional history in its own terms rather than apply a conceptual framework drawn from the modern state. The work begins, for example, with a long discussion of the role of feud in the late medieval polity, and shows how important it was for contemporary notions of law, right and order. Although the book gave rise to considerable controversy and is not without a certain contemporary flavouring (most of which was removed in subsequent revisions), it has had immense influence on the study of late medieval Germany (perhaps too much: Brunner himself protested against an uncritical application of his conclusions to other areas of the Reich).

His later scholarly work applied sociological techniques to the study of constitutional history and showed an increasing interest in *mentalités*: his *Adeliges Landleben und europäischer Geist* is a study of the Austrian aristocrat Wolf Helmhard von Hohberg (1612–88) set in a broad context, while his collected essays on constitutional and social history set a very broad framework for the study of pre-industrial Europe.   TAR

Major works

Land und Herrschaft (Baden: Röhrer, 1939); *Adeliges Landleben und europäischer Geist* (Salzburg: Müller, 1949); *Neue Wege der Verfassungs- und Sozialgeschichte* (Göttingen: Vandenhoeck & Rupprecht, 1968).

Reading

Zöllner, E.: Otto Brunner *Mitteilungen des Instituts für Österreichische Geschichtsforschung* 90 (1982) 519–22.

Zum Gedenken an Otto Brunner (1898–1982) (Hamburg: Pressestelle der Universität, 1983).

Brut-y Tywsogym See WELSH HISTORIO-GRAPHY.

Bryant, Arthur (b.1899, d.1985) For over half a century Bryant was one of the most widely read of English historians. The fluency of his prose and his ability to convey the excitement of past events did much to explain his popularity, but the apparently effortless style was the result of painstaking and scrupulous revision. Combining social and political history in a single vision of the past, Bryant was always conscious of the historian's duty to communicate to a non-specialist audience. After establishing his reputation with a brilliantly partisan biography of Charles II and a humane and scholarly trilogy on Pepys, he went on to write a general history of England from 1840 and a highly acclaimed series of books on the Revolutionary and Napoleonic wars and their aftermath. In all of these his remarkable gift for narrative was evident, as well as his ability to evoke the social life of an earlier age. Although his edition of the Alanbrooke diaries confirmed that few historians could equal him in writing a sustained and detailed military narrative, for much of the rest of his life he devoted himself to the history of England from the earliest times. Bryant was appreciative in his acknowledgement of the work of other historians, confessing the debt he owed to specialists, particularly in fields other than his own. This generosity of spirit was not always reciprocated by academic historians, some of whom distrusted Bryant's fondness for bright historical colour, while others found his narrative lacking in analysis. Believing history to be a branch of literature he placed himself boldly in the tradition of Macaulay and Trevelyan. Bryant was knighted in 1954.   JWD

Main publications

(All published by Collins, London, unless otherwise stated.)
King Charles II (London: Longmans Green, 1931); *Macaulay* (London: Peter Davies, 1932); *Samuel*

Pepys, the Man in the Making (Cambridge: Cambridge University Press, 1933); *Samuel Pepys, the Years of Peril* (Cambridge University Press 1935); *Samuel Pepys, the Saviour of the Navy* (Cambridge University Press, 1938); *English Saga* (1940); *The Years of Endurance* (1942); *Years of Victory* (1944); *The Age of Elegance* (1950); *The Turn of the Tide* (1957); *Triumph in the West* (1959); *Set in a Silver Sea* (1984); *Freedom's Own Island* (1986).

Bryce, James (b.1838, d.1922) Traveller, jurist, historian and Liberal statesman, Bryce was born in Belfast of Ulster-Scots parents who moved to Glasgow in 1846. Graduating from Glasgow University he entered Trinity College, Oxford, in 1857, was elected a fellow of Oriel in 1862 and crowned a dazzling academic career with his appointment as Regius professor of civil law in 1870.

The Holy Roman Empire (1864) established his reputation: a graphic saga encompassing over 1800 years of European civilization, it exemplified those principles of racial and institutional continuity which Bryce had imbibed from his two Oxford mentors, Goldwin Smith and E. A. FREEMAN. A contribution to *Essays on Reform* followed in 1867, surveying the history of democracy and urging the necessity of a moderate extension of the suffrage. In 1888 he published his masterpiece, *The American Commonwealth*. While ostensibly a microscopic study of the Gilded Age which gave an immense fillip to progressive reform in America and helped to create the intellectual rationale for a special Anglo-American relationship in Britain, Bryce's interpretation of the American past was profoundly conservative. He argued that the republic's history was in essence an organic enlargement upon English traditions of ordered liberty, and his insistence that the revolution of 1776 marked a continuity with the past led Lord Acton to accuse him of being a 'bewildered whig'. Bryce planned a second major work on Justinian. Fragments of this surfaced in his *Studies in History and Jurisprudence* (1901), but the book remained unwritten and the crippling burden of public life (he had entered parliament as a Gladstonian Liberal in 1880) increasingly hindered his scholarship. He was created viscount for political services in 1914. *South Africa* (1897) and *South America* (1912)

were the products of extensive travel and historical investigation, as was his last book, *Modern Democracies* (1921), a comparative study which reflected the growing pessimism of old age and the tragic collapse of his liberal values in the wake of the first world war.   HT

Main publications

(Published by Macmillan, London.)
The Holy Roman Empire (1864); *The American Commonwealth* (1888).

Reading

Fisher, H. A. L.: *James Bryce, Viscount Bryce of Dechmont*, 2 vols (London: Macmillan, 1927).
Ions, Edmund: *James Bryce and American Democracy 1870–1922* (Macmillan, 1968).
Tulloch, Hugh: *James Bryce's 'American Commonwealth'* (London: Royal Historical Society, 1988).

Buarque de Holanda, Sérgio (b.1902, d.1982) Educated in São Paulo and Rio de Janeiro, Buarque de Holanda was active in the modernist movement, co-founder of the review *Estética*, and European correspondent (1929–30) for *O Jornal*. He had a multifaceted career as journalist, civil servant, active socialist, museum director, cultural attaché, and held academic posts in Brazil and the United States. He resigned (1969) from the chair of the history of Brazilian civilization at São Paulo to protest against government intervention.

A versatile man of letters, Buarque de Holanda applied to history tools of analysis and interpretation derived from social sciences. He founded the interdisciplinary Instituto de Estudos Brasileyiros. *Raizes do Brasil*, his best-known work, evidences his familiarity with German historians and sociologists, and is a powerful interpretive essay on the development of Brazilian mores and institutions. His studies of colonial Brazil broke with traditional patriotic glorification of the past, stressing the Indian contribution and demythifying the *bandeirantes*. A central theme was the move from littoral to interior and the break with Portuguese antecedents and seigneurial tradition. He analysed Portuguese Edenic visions of Brazil, and provided a contrast between beliefs and experience and between Spanish and Portuguese views of America. His capacity for rich political history was shown by his contribution *Do Império à República* to the *História Geral da Civilização Brasileira*, of which he was editor, describing events leading to the fall of the Empire. Buarque de Holanda was keenly conscious of the nexus between past and present and historical antecedents of contemporary issues.   AJRR-W

Main publications

(Published by José Olympio, Rio de Janeiro, unless otherwise stated.)
Raizes do Brasil (1936); *Monções* (Rio de Janeiro: Casa do Estudante, 1945); *Caminhos e Fronteiras* (1957); *Visão do Paraiso* (1959); *Do Império à República* (São Paulo: Difusão Europeia do Livro, 1972).

Reading

da Silva Dias, Maria Odila Leite, ed.: *Sérgio Buarque de Holanda, História* (São Paulo: Atica, 1985) pp. 7–64.

Buckle, Henry Thomas (b.1821, d.1862) Buckle was a bachelor gentleman scholar and a striking example of a one-book author, for though his *Miscellaneous and Posthumous Works* were published in 1872, they are no more than research notes. Buckle did not regard himself as a disciple of COMTE but was greatly influenced by POSITIVISM and his ambition was 'to accomplish for the history of man something equivalent, or at all events analogous, to what has been effected by other enquirers for the different branches of natural science'. He intended to rescue history 'from the hands of biographers, genealogists and collectors of anecdotes, chroniclers of courts and princes and nobles, those babblers of vain things' and to place it on a sound methodological footing.

His *History of Civilization in England*, the first volume of which appeared in 1857, is in the tradition of the grand schematizers, from Montesquieu to Toynbee and Braudel. It received great attention, but Buckle died soon after the publication of the second volume in 1861 having developed a fever on a trip to the Middle East. There is, in fact, very little about civilization in England: the first volume is a general introduction, expounding Buckle's views on method, while the second is concerned with Spain and Scotland. This rather excessive clearing of the throat, in best Casaubon style, was perhaps the hallmark of the self-taught and isolated scholar, as was the confidence with which Buckle put forward his own opinions and his lack of interest in objections to them. He saw the critical choice as whether 'the actions of man, and therefore of societies, are governed by fixed laws, or are the result of chance or supernatural interference': this is too stark an antithesis. He leaned heavily upon statistical regularity, particularly in crime, without a corresponding acknowledgement of the important areas where statistics do not illuminate. Though unduly disparaged by Leslie Stephen in the Dictionary of National Biography, it remains true that Buckle's book has been more admired by sociologists than historians.   JAC

Main publications

The History of Civilization in England (1857, 1861); *Miscellaneous and Posthumous Works*, 3 vols ed. H. Taylor (1872).

Reading

Hanham, H. J.: *Buckle on Scotland and the Scottish Intellect* (Chicago, Ill.: University of Chicago Press, 1970).
Robertson, J. M.: *Buckle and his Critics* (London: Sonnenschein, 1895).
St. Aubyn, G.: *A Victorian Eminence* (London: Barrie, 1958).

Buonarroti, Filippo Michele (b.1761, d.1837) During his long and eventful life, Buonarroti produced only one historical work, his *Conspiration pour l'égalité, dite de Babeuf*, originally published in 1828. Part memoir, part narrative, part apology, it was written by a man who has been called the 'first professional revolutionist'. Born of a wealthy noble Tuscan family, Buonarroti welcomed the French Revolution, served with the Jacobins, and suffered imprisonment in the Thermidorean reaction. In 1796 he joined Babeuf in an unsuccessful coup against the Directory and was kept in confinement until Napoleon's fall. In the post-war period he acquired something of a legendary reputation among a new generation of radicals.

In the first volume of *Conspiration pour l'égalité* Buonarroti showed that the democratic and egalitarian hopes of the French people were dashed by the fall of Robespierre and the institution of the reactionary constitution of 1795. After describing the wretched conditions of the time, he explained the genesis of Babeuf's scheme for a regenerated France. He devoted considerable attention to detailing its organization and membership as well as throwing light on its plan to seize power by means of an underground network of dedicated agents. The conspiracy aimed to restore the democratic constitution of 1793 and proceed to expropriate and redistribute property on a communal basis. Volume one concluded with the betrayal of the conspirators and their arrest. The second volume chronicled the imprisonment, transportation to Vendôme, trial and condemnation of Babeuf and his associates. Buonarroti supplemented his narrative with an extensive collection of original documents concerning the aims of the conspirators.

Conspiration pour l'égalité remains an important historical document. As Samuel Bernstein has observed, the book is the 'most reliable single source on the movement he assisted in setting on foot'. More important, the history and the ideals it contained were taken up by French and foreign radicals during the 1830s and 1840s, becoming a veritable 'revolutionist's handbook'. In this way it served as a link between the utopian dreams of such Enlightenment thinkers as Mably and Rousseau and the radical democracy of the nineteenth century. Although the fact has been contested, Georges LEFEBVRE has insisted that the work 'exerted a profound influence over revolutionary opinion symbolized by the name of Blanqui'. An English translation, published by the Irish radical O'Brien in 1836, further extended Buonarroti's influence. Marx is known to have read the history in 1844 and planned to translate it into German. Its ideological consequences extended much further. Arthur Lehning has declared that Buonarroti 'introduced for the first time the ideology of state communism and dictatorship in the history of European socialism'. The historian J. L. Talmon deplored this fact, awarding the work a 'place of honour' in the 'nascent religion of the

totalitarian-democratic Revolution'. That the book was reisssued in 1957 by a French Communist publishing house indicates how strongly Buonarroti's ideas and reputation have continued to inspire twentieth-century ideology.   JF

Main publications

Conspiration pour l'égalité, dite de Babeuf (Brussels: Librairie Romantique, 1828; English trans. and notes, J. B. O'Brien (London: Hetherington, 1836); English trans., new edn (Paris: Éditions Sociales, 1957).

Reading

Bernstein, S.: *Buonarroti* (Paris: Hier et Aujourd'hui, 1949).

——: Buonarroti's classic history of Babouvism *Science and Society* 21 (1957) 346–52.

Eisenstein, E. L.: *The First Professional Revolutionist: Filippo Michele Buonarroti (1761–1837)* (Cambridge, Mass.: Harvard University Press, 1959).

Lehning, A.: Buonarroti's ideas on communism and dictatorship *International Review of Social History* 2 (1957) 266–87.

Burckhardt, Jacob (b.1818, d.1897) The son of a clergyman from a patrician family of Basle, Burckhardt studied theology before losing his faith. Between 1839 and 1842 he attended RANKE's famous seminars at the university of Berlin, but Ranke's kind of history did not appeal to him. It was his visits to Italy in 1838, 1846 and 1853 that fired him with enthusiasm for cultural history and for the classical and Renaissance world. In the mid-1840s he edited a conservative paper, the *Basler Zeitung*, but he came to feel a strong dislike for politics and the 'degrading *métier* of journalism' and turned to an academic career. He lectured at Basle from 1845 until he moved to the Zürich Polytechnic when it opened in 1855. He returned to Basle in 1858 and remained there for the rest of his life, lecturing on history and art history and refusing the invitation to succeed Ranke in Berlin.

Burckhardt's life was outwardly uneventful. The long-haired romantic young man of the 1840s who had wanted to expatriate himself from Switzerland turned imperceptibly into the elderly professor who, despite his dislike for 'the new railway-Basle', was devoted to his native city. He continued to write poems, sketch, and play the piano. A bachelor of simple tastes, he lived in two rooms above a baker's shop in the old town. He was a familiar figure in Basle, walking to his lectures with a large portfolio of illustrations under his arm. After the publication of his study of the Renaissance, which eventually made him famous though it attracted little notice at first, Burckhardt, in his own words, 'lived exclusively for his work as a teacher', lecturing to a handful of students during the week and to the general public on Saturdays. His posthumously-published book on the cultural history of Greece and his reflections on world history are in fact printed versions of his lectures. As a lecturer he was incisive, ironic, and caustic, and his discussion of 'historical greatness' impressed even the twenty-four-year-old Nietzsche.

Burckhardt has many claims to fame. It was *Der Cicerone* (1855), his guide to the art treasures of Italy, which first made his reputation, and gives him a place in the history of art history, a new discipline in his day. His cultural history of Greece is still considered important by classical scholars. Like Tocqueville, he may be regarded as a 'prophet of a mass age', since his reflections on world history, like his letters, are full of acute, pessimistic observations on the present and the future. He disliked democracy, industrialism, militarism, nationalism, and what he called 'the whole power and money racket', but he saw these developments as connected and inevitable.

Burckhardt's reputation rightly rests on the 'essay', as he called it, on the Italian Renaissance which he published at the age of forty-two. He once wrote that a great historical subject 'must needs cohere sympathetically and mysteriously to the author's inmost being', and this was certainly true for him in this case, since he was drawn to Italy and to a period when 'culture' was for once more important than religion or politics. The aim of his book was not, like most nineteenth-century works of history, to tell a story, but to paint the portrait of an age by cutting what the author called 'cross-sections' through the period and emphasizing 'the constant, the recurrent, and the typical'. It dealt with major themes such as Renaissance 'individualism' and 'the discovery

of the world and of man' at the expense of developments within the period. After more than 120 years, it is easy to criticize Burckhardt's essay for its lack of concern with change and with the economic foundations of cultural life and its lack of sympathy with the middle ages, in contrast to which the Renaissance is defined. Yet however they modify his picture, historians continue to find Burckhardt's conception of the Renaissance inescapable – and inspiring.   UPB

Main publications

Die Zeit Constantin des Grossens (1852, English trans. New York: Pantheon, 1949); *Der Cicerone* (Basle: 1855, English trans. London: 1873); *Die Kultur der Renaissance in Italien* (1860, English trans. London: 1878); *Die Baukunst der Renaissance in Italien* (Stuttgart: Ebner und Seubert, 1867; English trans. London: 1985); *Erinnerungen aus Rubens* (1898), (English trans. London: Phaidon, 1950); *Beiträge zur Kunstgeschichte von Italien* (Basle: Lendorff, 1898); *Griechische Kulturgeschichte* (3 vols, Basle: 1898–1902); *Weltgeschichtliche Betrachtungen* (Basle: 1906), English trans. London: Allen & Unwin, 1943); *Historische Fragmente* (1929), English trans. London: Allen & Unwin, 1959).

Reading

Baron, H., Burckhardt's *Civilisation of the Renaissance* a century after its publication. *Renaissance News* (1960) 207–22.

Dru, A.: Introduction. In *The Letters of Jacob Burckhardt* (London: Routledge & Kegan Paul, 1955).

Gay, P.: Burckhardt: the poet of truth. In *Style in History* (London: Jonathan Cape, 1975).

Kaegi, W: *Jacob Burckhardt: eine Biographie*, 7 vols (Basle: Schwabe, 1947–82).

Momigliano, A: Introduction to the *Griechische Kulturgeschichte* by Jacob Burckhardt (1955) (English trans. in his *Essays in Ancient and Modern Historiography*, Oxford: Blackwell, 1977) ch. 17.

White, H.: Burckhardt: the ironic vision. In *Metahistory* (Baltimore and London: Johns Hopkins University Press, 1973).

Burnet, Gilbert (b.1643, d.1715) Burnet came from a well-connected Scottish legal family, was educated at Marischal College, Aberdeen, and appointed professor of divinity at Glasgow in 1669. A big, vigorous, bustling man, with great powers of scholarly application, Burnet moved to London during the 1670s and became involved in political and ecclesiastical controversy. He was an associate of Lord Russell, whom he attended on the scaffold, and after the Rye House plot thought it prudent to travel on the European continent. In 1687 he arrived in Holland and rapidly became a zealous supporter of William of Orange. He accompanied William on the expedition in 1688, wrote the declaration and, after the successful march to London, was at once rewarded with the bishopric of Salisbury. He continued in high favour during William's reign and was governor to Prince William of Gloucester, Princess Anne's only surviving son.

As a historian, Burnet is best known for his *History of my own Time*, which was based upon his journal, and offered a commentary on events from the Restoration to the treaty of Utrecht. It was published posthumously in two parts: the first in 1723; the second in 1734. Though heavily criticized for its whiggish partisanship, it has remained an important source and was much used by Macaulay. But his more important work was a *History of the Reformation in England*, the first volume of which came out in 1679 and was greeted with acclaim. It has been called a milestone in English historiography, mainly because of the trouble Burnet took to consult archival and documentary sources. It held the field for two hundred years and was still being reprinted in 1872.   JAC

Reading

Davis, H. W. C.: Burnet. In *Typical English Churchmen*, ed. W. E. Collins (London: SPCK, 1902).

Clarke, T. E. S. and Foxcroft, H. C.: *A life of Gilbert Burnet* (Cambridge: Cambridge University Press, 1907).

Hamilton, K. G.: Two Restoration prose writers: Burnet and Halifax. In *Restoration Literature: Critical Approaches*, ed. H. Love (London: Methuen, 1972).

Kenyon, J. P.: *The History Men* (London: Weidenfeld & Nicolson, 1983).

Bury, John Bagnell (b.1861, d.1927) Bury was born in Co. Monaghan and educated at Foyle College, Londonderry, and Trinity College, Dublin, from which he graduated in 1882 with a double first in classics and mental and moral philosophy, becoming a fellow in 1885. As a student he specialized in classical philology, but also revealed a passionate interest in poetry, in particular the work of Swinburne and Browning. But it was to the study of history that he became increasingly devoted, and in 1889 appeared the work which established his reputation as a historian: the *History of the Later Roman Empire from Arcadius to Irene*. In 1893 he became professor of modern history at Trinity, and in 1902 was appointed to the regius chair of modern history at Cambridge, a post which he held until his death in 1927.

The range of Bury's scholarship was enormous. His publications cover the whole of Greek and Roman history from the Minoan age of Crete to ninth-century Byzantium. He edited Euripides and Pindar, wrote a *Life of St Patrick*, and published volumes on *The History of Freedom of Thought* and *The Idea of Progress*. He was an editor of the *Cambridge Ancient History* (and planned the *Cambridge Modern History*), and produced what is still the standard scholarly edition of Gibbon's *Decline and Fall*. His last work, a volume of lectures published shortly after his death, was devoted to the history of the papacy in the nineteenth century.

Underlying this range of interest were three main unifying factors: a belief in the unity of history, exemplified by his concept of Rome, and more particularly Byzantium, as the bridge whereby Hellenic culture became part of the culture of Europe; an early training in philology, which led to the rigorous handling of historical sources and to a firm belief in history as a science, with its own techniques and procedures for the pursuit of truth; and an interest in the philosophy of history, deriving ultimately from his undergraduate studies and in particular from an early concern with Hegel, whose influence is evident throughout his work. Bury was interested in the broad sweep of history, and was concerned with institutions more than with individuals. He was hostile to those influences on historians — rhetorical, nationalistic, religious — which he saw as hindrances to their task of establishing the objective truth as far as was possible. Though committed to a view of history as an essential guide to the present, and to the concept of progress as at least a theoretical possibility, he came increasingly to believe in the role of contingency, even accident, in history, and was therefore reluctant to commit himself wholeheartedly to a belief in underlying causes. JP

Main publications

(Published by Macmillan, New York and London, unless otherwise stated.)
History of the Later Roman Empire from Arcadius to Irene (1889) (New York: Dover, 1958); (editor) Gibbon's *Decline and Fall of the Roman Empire* (1896–1900) London: Dent, 1978; *History of Greece to the Death of Alexander the Great* (1900, 4th edn 1975); *Life of St Patrick* (1905); *The Ancient Greek Historians* (1909) (New York: Dover, 1958); *History of the Eastern Roman Empire from the Fall of Irene to the Accession of Basil I* (1912); *History of Freedom of Thought* (1914) (2nd edn, Oxford: Oxford University Press, 1952); *Idea of Progress* (1920); *History of the Later Roman Empire from the Death of Theodosius I to the Death of Justinian* (1923).

Reading

Baynes, N. H.: John Bagnell Bury. *Papers of the British Academy* XIII (1927).
——: *A Bibliography of the Works of J. B. Bury, compiled with a Memoir* (Cambridge: Cambridge University Press, 1929).
Temperley, H.: Introduction to *Selected Essays of J. B. Bury* (Cambridge: Cambridge University Press, 1930, repr. Amsterdam: Hakkert, 1964).

business history Having its origins in ECONOMIC HISTORY, business history attracted attention during the 1920s in both Britain and the USA. The first academic journal devoted to the subject was *Business History Review*. This began at Harvard in 1926 (originally called *Bulletin*) and followed the formation of the Business History Society at Harvard. In Britain, research at several universities in business history encouraged the inauguration of a specialized journal in 1959, *Business History*; but it was not until 1978 that the first British chair in business history was established in association with the Business History Unit at the London School of Economics. Popular interest in business history began during the nineteenth century on each side of the Atlantic with the publication of autobiographies and biographies of successful entrepreneurs, perhaps the most famous being the works of Samuel Smiles. A long-established firm implied success and in its turn this was thought to imply probity and quality. This encouraged a large number of publications which gave accounts of an industry and emphasized the qualities of a particular firm. Such works were written by authors from diverse backgrounds and often presented the life of the firm's founder in hagiographical terms.

As economic history has spread as a substantial discipline in higher education, room has been made for business history. The relationship of business history to management studies has encouraged more sophisticated research not only into the development of entrepreneurship but also into the growth of organizations and the role of the firm within an industry. During the twentieth century mergers and diversification by large companies have attracted studies of concentration of ownership and the relationship of these major companies to the working of the economy. Multinational companies with markets in many countries have become more conspicuous, especially since the middle of the twentieth century, so the scope of business history has had to take account of international relations in the formulation of corporate policies.

The aspects of business history attracting research depended upon the questions that engaged economists and economic historians at any particular time but with important constraints of access to sources. Recognition of this problem led to the formation in 1932 of the Business Archives Council in London. This has stimulated successfully some parts of the business community to take active steps to preserve and make available records, either by establishing their own archive or by sending their muniments to a public archive depository.

Many areas of commerce and manufacture have been examined in terms of questions about growth, responses to innovations in technology or organization, and markets. This has led to most studies concentrating on periods since the late eighteenth century. For the eighteenth century and earlier the history of the firm has often given way to studies of important individuals such as R. H. Tawney's biography of Lionel Cranfield in *Business and Politics under James I* (1958), or J. R. Harris's biography of Thomas Williams, the copper monopolist of the eighteenth century, in *The*

Copper King (1964). In *The History of the Hudson's Bay Company* (1958–9), E. E. Rich related the contribution of trading companies.

Increasingly rapid changes in economic life since 1750 in Britain and the survival of convenient sources have coincided to make certain aspects of business activity important for business history. Among the sectors of the economy attracting particular attention have been transport, textiles, finance, some branches of mining and metalworking and heavy engineering. Differences of approach to these subjects depended partly on the questions posed but also on the sources and research techniques employed. The history of transport has used industrial archaeological techniques is writing the history of canal and railway companies. This has enabled the problems of initiating new forms of transport including the costs both financial and organizational to be examined. A different emphasis, facilitated by more elaborate data survival, permitted the rigorous use of financial analysis and econometric models as in R. J. Irving, *The North Eastern Railway Company, 1870–1914* (1976). Earlier in the field were Americans who utilized business analysis techniques and used computers to handle large amounts of data: for example, in 1968 the development of efficient manning and organization by D. C. North in 'Sources of productivity changes in ocean shipping, 1600–1850', *Journal of Political Economy* (76, 953–970). More traditional methods were used by historians of various Liverpool based shipping companies of which the first was F. E. Hyde, *Blue Funnel: a history of Alfred Holt and Company of Liverpool from 1865 to 1914* (1956).

The evolution of the complex business organization of multinationals was examined in the pioneering work of Charles WILSON, *The History of Unilever* (vols 1 and 2, 1954, and vol. 3, 1968). Comparisons of European and American experience demonstrate how far the problems ramified in the essays in *Managerial Hierarchies* (1982) (ed. A. D. Chandler and H. Daems). The nature of businesses whose histories have been written has been as eclectic as the research methods adopted. To some extent this is because the field has interest for business people: the history of business

provides validation and even inspiration. The newly emerging study of advertising history illustrates this process (see ADVERTISING HISTORIOGRAPHY). The disdain of academia for the biographies of business leaders has given way to serious academic consideration of the qualities of entrepreneurs and senior managers with the publication of the *Dictionary of Business Biography*, which has used the full range of research techniques including oral history. Though there is no comprehensive bibliography of business history, for British studies see F. Goodall, *A Bibliography of British Business Histories* (1987).   IJEK

Reading

Chandler, A. D.: *Strategy and Structure: Chapters in the History of Industrial Enterprises* (Cambridge, Mass.: MIT press, 1962).

Hannah, L.: New issues in business history. *Business History Review* 57 (1983) 165–174.

Teichova, A. and Cottrell, P. eds: *International Business and Central Europe* (Leicester: Leicester University Press, 1983).

Butterfield, Herbert (b.1900, d.1979) Educated at Keighley Grammar School, Yorkshire, Butterfield arrived at Peterhouse, Cambridge, as a scholar in 1919, and spent all his adult life in the university of Cambridge; he was master of Peterhouse from 1955 to 1968. His Yorkshire methodist background was of great importance to him; he served for some years as a lay preacher around Cambridge and was preoccupied with the relationship between his Christian beliefs and his historical practice. A small, alert man, with a gentle manner and shy charm, he was a gifted and vigorous lecturer, particularly on European history, with a penchant for lurid phraseology which occasionally spilled over into his printed work.

Butterfield's historical interests were wide. He began in diplomatic history under the influence of Harold Temperley, developed an interest in historiography, and then turned to eighteenth-century English history. After 1945 he wrote with success on the origins of modern science but turned increasingly to a consideration of the role of the Christia historian. By far his best-known volume was

BYZANTINE HISTORIOGRAPHY

a slim work of 1931 entitled *The Whig Interpretation of History* in which certain unidentified historians (believed to be ACTON or TREVELYAN) were taken to task for a teleological approach to their subject. He was particularly concerned to put down what he regarded as the 'cardinal sin' in writing history – that of studying the past with one eye on the present. Though marred by repetition and a curiously narrow range of example the book enjoyed great success and was much quoted, particularly in entrance examination papers. In a later and even slimmer work, written during the war, Butterfield seemed to many to have made a total recantation.

For many years Butterfield was understood to be working on Charles Fox. No definitive book appeared but in 1949 Butterfield published *George III, Lord North and the People*, an analysis of the Association movement and crisis of 1780. His view that the events were 'quasi-revolutionary' in character did not win widespread support. It was followed in 1957 by Butterfield's strangest volume, *George III and the Historians*. After a historiographical prologue, Butterfield launched a severe attack upon NAMIER and the method of structural analysis, arguing that it could lead to desiccated and distorted history. So fierce an onslaught from so mild a man reverberated around the historical world for some years.

Butterfield's later attempts to reconcile his personal religious views with his professional history have been variously assessed. As a Christian Butterfield was anxious to testify to the intervention of God in everyday life while accepting, as a historian, that it could not be brought into interpretation. It is doubtful whether he succeeded in bringing the two attitudes into harmony.

Butterfield was married and had a family. Elected to the chair of modern history at Cambridge in 1944, he became regius professor in 1963, and was knighted in 1968. A fellow of the British Academy from 1963, he took a keen interest in the Historical Association, and was its president from 1955 to 1958.   JAC

Main publications

The Historical Novel (Cambridge: Cambridge University Press, 1924); *The Peace Tactics of Napoleon* (Cambridge University Press, 1929); *The Whig Interpretation of History* (London: Bell, 1931); *Napoleon* (London: Duckworth, 1939); *The Statecraft of Machiavelli* (Cambridge University Press, 1940); *The Englishman and his History* (Cambridge University Press, 1944); *George III, Lord North and the people* (London: Bell, 1949); *The Origins of Modern Science* (London: Bell, 1949); *Christianity and History* (London: Bell, 1949); *Man on his Past* (Cambridge University Press, 1955); *George III and the Historians* (London: Collins, 1957).

Reading

Cowling, M.: Memoir: Herbert Butterfield. *Proceedings of the British Academy* 65 (1979) 595–609.

Derry, J. W.: Herbert Butterfield. In *The Historian at Work*, ed. J. A. Cannon (London: Allen & Unwin, 1980).

Elliott, J. H. and Koenigsberger, H. G.: *The Diversity of History: Essays in Honour of Sir Herbert Butterfield* (London: Routledge & Kegan Paul, 1970).

Elton, G. R.: Herbert Butterfield and the study of history. *Historical Journal* 27.3 (1980) 729–43.

McIntire, C. T., ed.: Introduction. In *Herbert Butterfield: Writings on Christianity and History* (New York: Oxford University Press, 1979).

Thompson, K. W., ed.: *Herbert Butterfield: the Ethics of History and Politics* (Lanham, MD: University Press of America, 1980).

Byzantine historiography The study of the history of the lands and peoples of the East Roman Empire from its inauguration at Byzantium on 11 May 330 to the fall of Constantinople to the Ottomans on 29 May 1453. Among the attractions of the subject are that it is traditionally woven into a seamless robe of Byzantine Studies, involving many disciplines (which are only recently showing signs of coming apart); that no national historiographical school can claim Byzantium as its exclusive preserve (although all Slav and Balkan countries, Greece especially, have adopted and adapted it to national historiographical needs); and that the era of the writing of Byzantine history is now longer than the span of the Empire itself and shows no sign of abating. Following the Byzantines' own penchant, it may be divided into seven overlapping ages, of which the First Age is that of their own introspection in their past, exemplified by such encyclopaedists as Constantine VII Porphyrogenitus (913–59).

The Humanist Age coincided with the work of Byzantines in the west, such as the Trapezuntine Cardinal Bessarion (1403–72) and the Uniat Leo Allatius (1586–1669), and led to a Third, and continuing, Age of Edition. It was Hieronymus Wolf (1516–80), Melanchthon's pupil and librarian to the Fuggers, who first proposed a *Corpus Byzantinae Historiae*, which was partly achieved from 1645 in the majestic Paris *Corpus*, edited notably by François Combéfis (1605–97) and C. Ducange (1610–88) (see MAURISTS). The 33-volume Paris *Corpus* was re-edited as the Venice *Corpus* and passed into the more extensive Bonn *Corpus* (1828–97), which from 1967 is being overhauled by the international *Corpus Fontium Historiae Byzantinae*. Meanwhile the BOLLANDISTS took an early interest in Byzantine hagiography; from 1643 their awesome undertaking of the *Acta Sanctorum* antedates, and threatens to outlast, all Byzantine *Corpora*.

The Age of Reason was unsympathetic to Byzantium and saw a suspension of the Paris *Corpus*. It was not until the dispersal of Greek manuscripts during the Napoleonic wars brought to light Bessarion's library in Venice that there came the last flicker of the Paris *Corpus* and first of a new generation, in Hase's edition of *Leo the Deacon* in 1819. In this atmosphere it is a widely held opinion that since 1776 Byzantine historiography has been fighting a rearguard action against the supposed views of GIBBON – to the extent that popular revisionism inveighs against the misdeeds of the Fourth Crusade which took Constantinople in 1204. In fact entry to Byzantine history through the Crusades has all the drawbacks of constructing Mongol history from Marco Polo, while Gibbon's great work had curiously little impact upon Byzantine historiography until BURY's editions of it from 1896 to 1914. Far more influential was C. Lebeau's plodding *Bas Empire* (1757–86).

The nineteenth century brought the real start to the continuing Age of Byzantine Archaeology, initially on the back of classical exploration, founded by Cyriac of Ancona (d.1452), who was the first to ignore living Mistra for what was left of the stones of Sparta. Pierre Gylles began a minor industry in the topography of Constantinople itself in 1540–61, which was extended by Sir William Ramsay (1851–1939), perhaps Britain's greatest Byzantinist, to the foundation of Byzantine historical geography. Gabriel Millet and Henri GRÉGOIRE laid the foundations of Byzantine epigraphy and the discovery that Byzantine art had an appeal, against what Byzantines themselves may have intended, established a continuing field. By 1915 a combination of an exhibition of the mosaics of Ravenna and an edition of Liudprand of Cremona may lie behind W. B. Yeats's and many others' poetic conception of Byzantium. DIEHL's *Manuel* of 1925 was the first scholarly compendium of Byzantine art.

The birth of the Sixth, or Modern, Age may be dated precisely: to 1924 when at the First International Byzantine Congress in Bucharest its founding fathers, including Diehl, Grégoire, N. Kondakov, Millet, Ramsay and N. IORGA, proclaimed their testament anew. It confirmed that Byzantine Studies (rather than Byzantine history alone) were an identifiable and coherent international discipline, to which continental Europe was giving expression through research institutions (often linked with Modern Greek) and their periodicals (still a marked form of Byzantine publishing), usually associated with a formidable scholar-founder. The sequence began with Karl Krumbacher (1856–1909) and the Munich institute and journal, the *Byzantinische Zeitschrift*, in 1892. In 1894 St Petersburg Byzantinists such as Vasilievsky and Uspensky sponsored the *Vizantysky Vremennik*. The Russians also ran an outstation and journal in Constantinople, where a largely French Assumptionist order founded the *Échos d'Orient* in 1897. The order moved to Bucharest in 1937 and Paris in 1947; their title is now the Institut Français des Études Byzantines and their journal the *Revue des Études Byzantines*. The first world war brought dispersal from Russia (the *Vremennik* was suspended from 1927 to 47). The *Seminarium Kondakovianum* found a home in Prague from 1927 until its destruction in 1940, but *Byzantinoslavica* of 1929 survives there. Grégoire's *Byzantion*, founded as a direct response to the 1924 Congress, was transplanted to the United States in 1940 for the duration of the war.

BYZANTINE HISTORIOGRAPHY

The coincidental endowment of Dumbarton Oaks to Harvard as an American centre for Byzantine Studies was stimulated by a migration of European scholars such as A. Vasiliev and F. Dvornik: art and archaeology were early strengths. *Dumbarton Oaks Papers* followed and an annual American Byzantine Studies Conference first met in 1975. Australia's sequence of national conferences began in 1981.

Post-war Byzantinists became aware that the approaches, interests and problems of western medieval colleagues were not so different. They turned from chronicles to documents (charters, seals, coins), and from sad stories of the death of kings to *volksliteratur*, historical geography, demography, anthropology and prosopography; women's historians found fresh fields in the labours of the Bollandists. Until he moved to Dumbarton Oaks in 1979 Alexander Kazhdan disseminated a version of the ANNALES SCHOOL in Moscow. The European centres established the Association Internationale des Études Byzantines (AIEB) in 1948, with numerous international projects. From that year OSTROGORSKY headed the Belgrade institute and the pattern was followed by Thessaloniki's centre and journal, *Byzantina*, in 1969. The post-war decades were dominated by three European centres. In Paris Paul Lemerle took up the *Acts* of Athos, founding *Travaux et Mémoires* in 1965. In Munich Hans-Georg Beck, and in Vienna Herbert Hunger, turned to literature; the Austrian *Jahrbuch* began in 1951 and its *Tabula Imperii Byzantini* in 1976.

Typically, British Byzantinists had worked alone: BURY, BAYNES and RUNCIMAN are examples. True, two chairs of Byzantine and Modern Greek were set up: the Koraes at King's College London in 1919 (resigned by TOYNBEE in acrimony), and the Bywater and Sotheby at Oxford soon after (first held by the egregious R. M. Dawkins). But their epigoni were not research students. Only ten British higher degrees in the subject were awarded between 1912 and 1950 (beginning with R. E. M. Wheeler's London MA), by contrast with one hundred (mostly doctorates) in the decade 1976–85. This explosion came despite a decline in the traditional conversion of classicists to Byzantium, and through a local adaptation of the continental model. The British National Committee of the AIEB was established to hold the Byzantine Congress in Oxford in 1966; by 1983 its qualified members were so numerous as to found the Society for the Promotion of Byzantine Studies. An annual spring symposium of Byzantine Studies first met in Birmingham in 1965, where a research centre was established. *Byzantine and Modern Greek Studies* was founded in 1975. By 1986, the centenary of the Byzantine work of the British School at Athens, there were fourteen British universities and colleges collaborating in teaching the subject, and the British Academy's *Prosopography of the Byzantine Empire* was announced. The Seventh Age of Byzantine history must await notice in future editions of this dictionary.   AAMB

Reading

There is no history of Byzantine historiography, but for reflections on it, see:

Beck, H. G.: *Das byzantinische Jahrtausend* (Munich: C. H. Beck, 1978).

Biskupski, L.: *L'Institut Français d'études Byzantines et son activité scientifique et littéraire 1895–1970* (Istanbul, 1970).

Bulletin d'information et de coordination of the AIEB, 1964– .

Bulletin of British Byzantine Studies, 1975– .

Clogg, R.: *Politics and the Academy: Arnold Toynbee and the Koraes Chair* (London: Cass, 1986).

Kazhdan, A. and Constable, G.: *People and Power in Byzantium: an Introduction to Modern Byzantine Studies* (Washington DC: Dumbarton Oaks, 1982).

Lemerle, P.: *Byzantine Humanism*, trans. H. Lindsay and A. Moffatt (Canberra: 1986).

C

Caesar, Gaius Julius (b.100 BC, d.44 BC).
Born into an ancient but undistinguished
patrician family which claimed descent from
Aeneas the Trojan, Caesar grew up in a time
of civil war and political strife, and at one time
was even in danger of arrest and execution
under the dictatorship of Sulla (82 BC). His
political career was consistently *popularis*, as
he supported reformist tribunes against the
Sullan 'establishment' in the Senate, and
eventually won the consulship (59 BC) in the
teeth of bitter conservative opposition.

One of the reforms Caesar forced through
was the introduction of a published record of
the Senate's proceedings, and it is quite possibly to this concern for 'open government' that
we owe his historiographical masterpiece, the
Commentaries on the Gallic War. He received
his special five-year command in Gaul by the
vote of the Roman citizen assembly (overturning the Senate's attempt to fob him off with a
trivial policing job in Italy), and the regular
reports of 'the people's general' at the end of
each season of victory and conquest not only
repaid the citizen body for its confidence in
him but also helped its political leaders in their
continuing conflict with the senatorial Right.

Caesar completed seven successive campaign commentaries on the years 58–52 BC,
culminating in the defeat of the great revolt
under Vercingetorix. The illusion of objectivity is achieved by third-person narrative and a
spare, unadorned style. In theory, 'commentaries' were only factual summaries which provided historians with material to write up in
more elaborate form, but as Cicero pointed
out, only a fool would try to prettify the
muscular elegance of Caesar's prose. He did

however allow himself certain features of
elaborated historiography, such as geographical digressions (in books V and VI) and
invented speeches (in book VII).

By marching into Italy in 49 BC Caesar
precipitated a civil war. ('I ask you', he told the
men of the Thirteenth Legion, 'to defend my
reputation and standing against the assaults of
my enemies.') The war lasted four years, but
the three books of Caesar's *Commentaries on
the Civil War* cover only the period from January 49 to the autumn of 48 BC. It is not known
when they were written, or why they were not
completed; but as sole ruler of Rome after his
victory Caesar was preoccupied with more
urgent matters, and perhaps also less concerned about presenting his own version of
events. His comrade in arms Asinius Pollio,
also a historian, was probably referring to the
Civil War books when he complained that
Caesar's comentaries were careless and inaccurate, and suggested that Caesar himself
would have revised them.

Caesar wrote many other works – a tragedy
(*Oedipus*) in his youth, political speeches in the
70s and 60s BC, a two-volume treatise on
Latin grammar dedicated to Cicero (from
which survives the characteristic advice 'Avoid
the rare and unusual word as a sailor avoids
the rocks'), a political critique of his enemy
Cato, and a poem *The Journey* written on his
way to put down the revolt of Pompey's sons in
Spain late in 46. He received the title 'Dicta-
tor for life' in 44 BC and was murdered on 15
March of that year by a group of senators who
hoped thereby to restore republican government.

Shortly after Caesar's death one of his ex-officers, Aulus Hirtius, wrote an eighth book of the *Gallic War*, to cover the years 51−50 BC, and completed the civil war narrative as well. Of the surviving pseudo-Caesarian commentaries, *The Alexandrian War* may perhaps be Hirtius' work, but *The African War* and *The Spanish War* are certainly not.   TPW

Main writings

Commentarii de bello Gallico; *Commentarii de bello civili* Cambridge Mass.: Loeb Classical Library, Harvard University Press, 1914−17).

Reading

Adcock, F.: *Caesar as Man of Letters* (Cambridge: Cambridge University Press, 1956).

Gelzer, M.: *Caesar, Politician and Statesman*, trans. Peter Needham (Oxford: Blackwell, 1968).

Mutschler, F.-M.: *Erzählstil und Propaganda in Caesars Kommentarien* (Heidelberg: Winter, 1975).

Calmette, Joseph-Louis (b.1873, d.1952) Born at Perpignan, Calmette studied at the École des Chartes, writing a thesis on Franco-Aragonese relations under Louis XI (1900). He became professor at Montpellier (1903), Dijon (1905) and Toulouse (1911), working largely on fifteenth-century history, especially that of Southern France and Burgundy. But his expertise extended to the study of Anglo-French relations, on which he produced (with J. Périnelle) *Louis XI et l'Angleterre* (1930), and of Spanish history, for example *La Formation de l'unité espagnole* (1946). He is perhaps best known for his general book (with E. Deprez) *L'Europe occidentale de la fin du xive siècle aux guerres d'Italie* (2 vols. 1937−9), and to English-speaking readers for his *Golden Age of Burgundy*, an English translation (1962) by G. Weightmann of his *Les Grands ducs de Bourgogne* (1949). Calmette also collaborated with G. Derville on the most widely used modern edition of Philippe DE COMMYNES's *Mémoires* (2 vols, 1924−5).

He was a good example of the French historical scholarship of his time, rooted primarily in political and diplomatic history, yet geographically broadly based. Signs of changing preoccupations and of the early impact of the *Annales* can be found, however, in his work on feudal society where he criticized the use of the term 'feudal' as anachronistic. He contri-

buted a fervent defence of Joan of Arc to the series *Que sais-je?* (1946) and wrote short works tracing the origins of contemporary issues, for example *L'Europe et le péril allemand, 843−1945*.   MGAV

Main publications

With J. Périnelle, *Louis XI et l'Angleterre* (Paris: Picard, 1930; with E. Déprez), *L'Europe occidentale de la fin du xive siècle aux guerres d'Italie*, 2 vols (Paris: Presses Universitaires de France, 1937−9); *Jeanne d'Arc* (Paris: Presses Universitaires de France, 1946); *La Formation de l'unité espagnole* (Paris: Flammarion, 1946); *The Golden Age of Burgundy* (1949) (London: Weidenfeld & Nicholson, 1962).

Camden, William (b.1551, d.1623) For more than twenty years Camden was a master at Westminster School before his appointment as Clarenceux king-of-arms in 1597 gave him better opportunities to pursue his historical interests. Through two great volumes, *Britannia*, first published in 1586 in Latin, and *Annals of Queen Elizabeth*, also published in Latin in 1615, Camden made major contributions to British historical scholarship. He was a keen exponent of what was known as 'civil history', which repudiated providential explanations and offered rational and secular interpretations. In many ways, he was a direct contrast to his great contemporary Walter RALEGH.

Britannia was a grand topographical and historical survey of Britain, undertaken at the suggestion of Ortelius. In Camden's scheme, the counties were grouped according to the British tribes who had lived there, Oxfordshire appearing under *Dobuni* and Shropshire under *Cornavii*. He spent much time touring, calculating Roman itineraries and towns, and collecting evidence of ruins, coins and local traditions. He made considerable use of Leland's work and had access to his notes. *Britannia* was an outstanding success and Camden augmented it in successive editions. The first English translation appeared in 1610.

The *Annals* were begun at the behest of Lord Burghley, who lent Camden letters and documents. Camden took the records as far as the execution of Mary Queen of Scots: the continuation was not published until after his death, in 1625. The emphasis on the use of records was significant and Camden expressly repudiated the tradition of inserting appropriate speeches and orations: 'I have not meddled withal, much less coined them out of mine own head.' Camden succeeded in establishing the interpretation of Elizabeth's reign as a *via media* and the Queen herself as an arch-balancer. He founded the first chair in history at Oxford, the university which he had attended. JAC

Main publications

Britannia (1586); *Annales Rerum Anglicarum et Hibernicarum regnante Elizabetha* (1615).

Reading

Kendrick, T. D.: *British Antiquity* (London: Methuen, 1950).

Levy, F. J.: *Tudor Historical Thought* (San Marino, Calif.: Huntington Library, 1967).

Piggott, S.: *William Camden and the Britannia* (London: Camberlege, 1953).

Trevor-Roper, H.: *Queen Elizabeth's first historian*, Neale lecture (London: Cape, 1971).

Canadian historiography The writing of history is a highly developed art in Canada both in the English- and French-speaking communities, and a politically influential one. Though most Canadian historians are professional academics with doctorates, the most widely read and best-known are not: for example, Pierre Berton, Christina McCall, Sandra Gwyn, James Gray and Robert Rumilly.

The intention of the first Canadian historians was primarily to inform readers in France and Britain about events in their colonies in North America. A Jesuit, F. X. Charleroix, published his *Histoire et déscription générale de la nouvelle France* in 1744, a well-documented account of political, military and religious events. A few years later, in 1749, there appeared in London *A Geographical History of Nova Scotia* by an anonymous author. Eighty years later T. C. Haliburton, best known as a humorist and man of letters, published *An Historical and Statistical Account of Nova Scotia* to inform the British public of what British emigrants were doing across the Atlantic.

History by Canadians for Canadians developed in the nineteenth century as an effort to make sense of political events and particularly of the response of the French- and English-speaking communities to the policies of the British crown. *Histoire du Canada*, by F. X. Garneau, first published in Quebec in 1844, was concerned to assert the reality of French-speaking Canada as a criticism of the assumptions of Lord Durham in his *Report* that French Canadians could and should be made into British North Americans. In Ontario by contrast English-speaking historians such as J. M. McMullen, J. C. Dent and William Kingsford stressed the value of representative and responsible government under the British crown, and the material progress which, they argued, flowed from local self-government.

In 1872 the Public Archives of Canada were established. Between this date and the first world war the teaching of Canadian history in universities and schools developed, and scholars trained in British, American and European universities began to introduce a more rigorous treatment of documentary evidence in the analysis and presentation of political history. The culmination of such study was, perhaps, the work of an Irish scholar of Trinity College, Dublin, trained in European universities and for many years a professor in the University of Toronto, W. P. M. Kennedy. *The Constitution of Canada* and *Statutes, Treaties and Documents of the Canadian Constitution* established a rigorous standard of scholarship which has never been seriously challenged.

A pioneer in the exploration and explanation of the dynamics of Canadian society, which studies of constitutional development did not reveal, was H. A. INNIS. His *The Fur Trade in Canada* (1930), although concerned with a particular aspect of early economic development, established some general propositions about the relationship of cost-effective production in relation to world markets. A number of historians, either collaborators of Innis or inspired by him, for example, A. R. M. Lower, D. G. Creighton and, less directly, Ferdinand Ouellet, amplified the political implications of Innis's work. Between 1937, when he published *The Commercial Empire of the St. Lawrence*, and 1970, Creighton made a substantial contribution in the field of political analysis including an impressive life of Sir John A. Macdonald.

Since 1945 the number of Canadian academic historians has increased enormously, and the public appetite for the reading of history has grown with the increase in the proportion of Canadians having a secondary and tertiary education. International relations, labour relations, business enterprises, provincial politics, regional and urban problems, the native races, immigrant minorities and social problems have all been studied by historians. There have been many biographies of leading politicians and business and labour leaders, and a few of bureaucrats and scientists. One of the most impressive and recent of these is P. B. Waite's life of Sir John Thompson, *The Man from Halifax* (1985). Conrad Black, an international business tycoon with a doctorate, has written a life of Maurice Duplessis which deserves more attention than it has received from the academic professionals.

Historical study itself has been put under scrutiny by Carl Berger in *The Writing of Canadian History* (1976). Canadian history tends to be of absorbing interest to Canadians, but of little interest to other peoples. The net effect of this proliferation of historical inquiry and public interest in Canadian history seems to be a self-awareness which has helped Canadians, if not to solve all their problems, at least to live with them and to eschew crippling political discord.   HSF

Reading

A History of Canada, 19 vols, ed. W. L. Morton, D. G. Creighton, Ramsay Cook et al. (The Canadian Centenary Series, 1960–).
Bothwell, R., Drummond, I. and English, J.: *Canada since 1945: Power Politics and Provincialism* (Toronto: University of Toronto Press, 1981).
Clarke, S. D.: *The Developing Canadian Community* (Toronto: University of Toronto Press, 1963).
Eayrs, James: *In Defence of Canada*, 3 vols (Toronto: University of Toronto Press, 1964–72).
Ferns, H. S. and Ostry, B.: *The Age of Mackenzie King* (London and Toronto: Heinemann, 1975; Toronto: Lorimer, 1976).
Marr, W. L. and Paterson, D. G.: *Canada: an Economic History* (Toronto: Macmillan, 1979).
McNaught, K. W.: *The Pelican History of Canada* (Harmondsworth: Penguin, 1982).

Ouellet, E.: *Histoire économique et sociale du Québec, 1760–1850* (Montreal and Paris: FIDES, 1966).
Wade, Mason: *The French Canadians, 1760–1945* (London: Macmillan, 1955).

Capistrano de Abreu, João (b.1853, d.1927) Educated in Fortaleza and Recife, Capistrano de Abreu moved to Rio de Janeiro, where he taught, worked in the national library and wrote for newspapers. An autodidact, his fundamental ideas derived from English and French positivists and he was influenced by RANKE, whom he took as his model. From 1883 to 1889, he held the chair of history of Brazil in the Colégio Dom Pedro II, resigning to protest against a ministerial decision to annex the teaching of the history of Brazil to the teaching of universal history.

Capistrano de Abreu dedicated his life to research and writing and gave new direction to historical studies in Brazil by emphasizing the importance of archival research, of critical editions, and of an interdisciplinary approach, and by stressing the popular rather than the heroic. His studies of exploration and settlement of the interior led to comparisons with Frederick Jackson TURNER. He was the first Brazilian historian to integrate people (Indians and Portuguese), geography, economy, transportation and cultural factors, in the move to the west. He expressed the view, revolutionary for the 1870s, that the 'real' Brazil lay in the interior and that coastal settlements were but extensions of European civilization. He saw in the *sertão* the locus for independent thought and action, rejection of colonialism, and embryonic Brazilian nationalism. Capistrano de Abreu compiled grammars, texts and vocabularies of Indian languages. He translated Wappaeus, Sellin and Kirchhoff, annotated VARNHAGEN's *História Geral*, and produced critical editions of writings by early Jesuits and of inquisition records.   AJRR-W

Main publications

O Descobrimento do Brasil e seu Desenvolvimento no Século XVI (Rio de Janeiro: Typ. de G. Leuzinger, 1883); *Capítulos de História Colonial* (Rio de Janeiro: M. Orosco, 1907); *Os Caminhos Antigos e o Povoamento do Brasil* (Rio de Janeiro: Briguiet, 1930).

Reading

Fringer, Katherine: The Contribution of Capistrano de Abreu to Brazilian historiography. *Journal of Inter-American Studies* 13.2 (1971) 258–78.

Rodrigues, José Honório: Capistrano de Abreu and Brazilian historiography. In *Perspectives on Brazilian History*, ed. E. Bradford Burns, (New York and London: Columbia University Press, 1967) pp. 156–80.

Carlyle, Thomas, (b.1795, d.1881) Born at Ecclefechan in Annandale, Scotland, the son of a dissenting stonemason, Carlyle made historical writing a stepping-stone to literary success in an age when historical studies lacked professional leadership. He could not stand his original profession of 'schoolmastering', and could never attain the urbanity of his cultural hero, Goethe. He hardly coveted a place in the pantheon of historical scholarship, but could not easily exercise his chosen vocation as a secular prophet, thundering against humbug, without an historical reference. His early translations of *Wilhelm Meister*, his *Life of Schiller* and the preposterously tortuous *Sartor Resartus* brought little success.

The rapidly written, and even more rapidly rewritten, *French Revolution* (1833–42) (the sole manuscript of the first volume was used as kindling by John Stuart Mill's maid) sold slowly at first, but became tremendously successful, and continued to sell for more than a generation. The theme was a good one for Carlyle's prophetic purpose of denouncing conservatism, Enlightenment and democracy at the same time. Starting with a brief sketch of the declining repute of monarchy under Louis XV, Carlyle presents the royal government immediately as humbug about to be swept away by a volcanic eruption from below 'leaving only a smell of sulphur', and creates the opening for a narrative couched in his most self-indulgently explosive prose. The book did not advance historical knowledge or acquaintance with sources, but underlined a moral: 'Shams are burnt up; nay what as yet is the peculiarity of France, the very Cant of them is burnt up. The new Realities are not yet come: ah no, only Phantasms, Paper models, tentative Prefigurements of such!'

Carlyle's public, however, was being more intensively harrowed by doctrinaires than at any other time in its history; though scoffed at by MACAULAY and LINGARD, and entirely unable to dent the sales of the conservative Alison, Carlyle found a market of his own, was eagerly cultivated in the twentieth century by dissenters to whom his style of rhetoric became a way of life, and forty years ago was included by J. M. Thompson in his catalogue of the fifty best books on the French Revolution.

Carlyle declined offers of history chairs in Scotland, but exploited a well-deserved reputation as a public lecturer, and developed his own brand of pamphleteering with an historical reference in *Chartism* (1839), *Heroes and Hero-Worship* (1841) and *Past and Present* (1843). Paradoxically, Carlyle's next essay in history, his abortive attempt to write a biography of Cromwell, resulted in a work of enduring value to history teachers and their students, *Oliver Cromwell's Letters and Speeches* (1845). Again Carlyle's defects in scholarship were numerous, but he caught a tide of opinion. The issues concerning the church establishment and its critics had returned to English politics with a vigour they had not had since Cromwell's day, and the contestants on both sides sought refreshing draughts from seventeenth-century springs. To Carlyle, Puritanism was 'the last of all our Heroisms', and Cromwell was the hero who had given it disciplined power to act, untrammelled by old royal shams and new paper constitutions. For this doctrine there was an enduring market; for scholarly and teaching purposes Carlyle's compilation, however defective, was an immense convenience; and it went on being reprinted, re-edited and imitated into the present century.

Cromwell had been among Carlyle's *Heroes*; another, discovered only later, was Frederick the Great, to whose biography six volumes were devoted (1858–65), though the last twenty-three years of the reign were despatched in half a volume. The attraction of the subject had been the young Frederick II, staging a bravura performance in Silesia, but Carlyle found himself fascinated by the hero's father, the unheroic, cautious, prudent Frederick William I, who disdained even his son's modest bow in the direction of music and culture. By the end Carlyle loathed Frederick II as vigorously as had Frederick William. Nevertheless, two visits to German battlefields splendidly equipped Carlyle as a narrator of battles. The Austro- and Franco-Prussian wars gave an unrivalled actuality to his theme, and in 1870 he was awarded Frederick's own medal, 'Pour le Mérite'. Carlyle's work was used for the education of German officers until the German General Staff put together an official version of their own, and the best recent *Life* of Frederick by Theodor Schieder (1986) lists it as a standard authority.

Carlyle's marriage with Jane Welsh, a woman as independent as himself, and originally devoted to his friend Irvine, constitutes one of the classic conflict-stories of nineteenth-century literary history. Carlyle's vehemence, dyspepsia, absorption in work and general selfishness made him a trying companion; her ill-health, sharp tongue and attempts to form a circle of her own created other difficulties. Only after she died in 1866 did Carlyle, reading her private diaries, discover the depth of her unhappiness, and of his own responsibility for it. He then wrote the sad memoir of her which appeared in his *Reminiscences*, published by Froude in 1881. The humbug of the prophet had been exposed by an historical document. WRW

Main publications

Carlyle's works have been frequently collected but may still be best consulted in H. D. Traill's Centenary edition of 1896–99 (repr. New York: AMS Press, 1969, 1974).

Reading

Cobban, A.: Carlyle's 'French' Revolution. *History* 48 (1963) 306–16.
Ben-Israel, Hevda: *English Historians on the French Revolution* (Cambridge: Cambridge University Press, 1968).
Froude, J. A.: *Thomas Carlyle: a history of the first forty years of his Life* (1882; repr: Ohio State University, Press, 1979).
——: *Thomas Carlyle: a history of his life* (1884; repr. Ohio State University Press, 1979).
Kaplan, F.: *Thomas Carlyle: a biography* (Ithaca, NY: Cornell University Press, 1983).
Sanders, C. R.: *The Collected Letters of Thomas and Jane Welsh Carlyle* (Durham, NC: Duke University Press, 1970–81).
Wilson, D. A.: *Carlyle* (London: Kegan Paul, 1923–34).

Carr, Edward Hallet (b.1892, d.1982) Eldest son in a comfortable middle-class family living in Highgate, Carr was educated at Merchant Taylors' School, London, and at Trinity College, Cambridge, where he took a double first in classics in 1916. He mastered a variety of vocations. From 1916 to 1936 he served in the British Foreign Office, rising to the rank of first secretary. While a second secretary in Riga in the 1920s, he began to study Russian literature and culture, and between 1931 and 1937 he published a brilliant series of biographies on Russian themes. In 1936 he was appointed Woodrow Wilson professor of international politics at the University College of Wales, Aberystwyth; his subsequent books on international relations between the wars are generally regarded as the first attempt to create a science of international politics. During the second world war he was assistant editor on *The Times* under Barrington-Ward, and exercised a considerable influence on its policy. His career as a serious historian did not begin until he embarked on his *History of Soviet Russia* in the last winter of the war at the age of 52; he completed its final fourteenth volume 33 years later in 1977.

In his youth Carr enthusiastically identified himself with the political outlook of his father, who was a reformist Liberal of the Lloyd George variety. But in the 1920s and the 1930s he became a profound critic of western capitalist society under the influence of the upheaval of the first world war, the persuasive scepticism of nineteenth-century Russian intellectuals about western liberal moralism, and the devastating impact of the world economic crisis of the 1930s. Like many other intellectuals, Carr became convinced that capitalism was doomed and that it must be replaced by a new social order based on a planned economy and adapted to a world of mass democracy. These convictions Carr retained until the end of his life: 'in recent years', he wrote shortly before he died, 'I have increasingly come to see myself, and to be seen, as an intellectual dissident.'

Carr's view of the western world and its future explains his fascination with the Soviet experience. He believed that the Bolshevik revolution was the starting point for the creation of a new society; but he was also fully aware that the establishment of a socialist regime in an autocratic and largely peasant country modified and distorted its development. In this context his *History of Soviet Russia*, covering the first twelve years (1917–29) of Soviet development, traced with a wealth of detail the transformation of the Communist Party into Stalin's monolith, the triumph of central planning and the subordination of the Communist International and Soviet foreign policy to the needs of an emerging world power. In Carr's concept this formed the basis for the transformation of the Soviet Union under the direction of the political decisions of a ruling group, and for the emergence of a society which was in some sense socialist but acquired new shapes not foreseen by the makers of the revolution. The *History* was, however, by no means a linear account of progress via revolution and mixed economy to state socialism. It gave full weight to the convolutions of the economic transition, and to the local and personal factors which confused and complicated political developments. The combination in Carr's *History* of a firm grasp of the main threads of development with an open-minded and judicious handling of the evidence was one of its great strengths.

Carr's iconoclasm about western society was extended to the profession of history. In his most popular and controversial book, *What is History?*, he argued that history is the product of the historian, and the historian the product of his own society, and castigated those who deny the relativity of historical knowledge: 'study the historian', Carr wrote, 'before you begin to study the facts.' But he also believed that historians would surmount the limited vision of their own time, and use their understanding of the past for a better insight into the future. Although Carr was strongly critical of the narrowness of view of many British historians, he was a convincing advocate of the value of historical knowledge.

Carr was a fellow of Trinity College, Cambridge from 1955 until his death. A quiet and slightly aloof man, he did not suffer muddle-headedness gladly. But he formed long-standing friendships with many scholars and public figures of his own generation, and he took great pains to advise, help and encourage younger scholars.   RWD

Main publications

(Published by Macmillan, London, unless otherwise stated.)
The Romantic Exiles: a Nineteenth-Century Portrait Gallery (London: Gollancz, 1933); *International Relations since the Peace Treaties* (1937, new edn 1940); *The Twenty Years Crisis, 1918–38: an Introduction to the Study of International Relations* (1939, new edn 1946); *The Soviet Impact on the Western World* (1946); *A History of Soviet Russia*, 14 vols (vols 9–10 with R. W. Davies) (1950–78); *The New Society* (1951); *What is History? The George Macaulay Trevelyan Lectures delivered in the University of Cambridge January–March 1961* (1961, new edn 1986); *1917: Before and After* (1969); *From Napoleon to Stalin* (1980); *The Twilight of Comintern 1930–1935* (1982).

Reading

Davies, R. W.: Edward Hallett Carr 1892–1982. *Proceedings of the British Academy* 69 (1983) 473–511.

Deutscher, Tamara: E. H. Carr – a personal memoir. *New Left Review* 137 (1983) 78–86.

Palla, Marco: La via alla storia di Edward Hallett Carr. *Passato e presente* 1 (1982) 115–44.

Cassiodorus (b.*c.*485, d.*c.*580) Born in Italy, Cassiodorus entered the service of the Ostrogothic king Theodoric, becoming consul in 514. He was secretary to successive kings. His official letters from that period and his *Chronicle*, survive, but the twelve books of his *Gothic History* are extant only in the abridgement made in the mid-sixth century by Jordanes. He retired to a monastery *c.* 555, and there wrote a number of works, including an Ecclesiastical History.   EFJ

Reading

O'Donnell, J. J.: *Cassiodorus* (Berkeley: University of California Press, 1979).

Cassirer, Ernst (b.1874, d.1945) More of a philosopher than a historian, Cassirer was a philosopher for whom history was something more than a hobby. Born in Breslau (now Wrocław) of an upper middle-class Jewish family, Cassirer was appointed professor at the university of Hamburg just after the first world war. He became friends with Aby Warburg and Erwin Panofsky, and owed a good deal to their influence. He left Germany for Sweden in 1933 before settling in the United States.

Cassirer was a leading philosopher of the neo-Kantian school, who believed that the mind works with concepts or categories which are not derived from experience and that these categories change over time. His most famous book, the three-volume *Philosophy of Symbolic Forms* (1923−31), is concerned with the evolution of human thought over the long term from myth to science. In the more strictly historical field he produced some important articles and three major books, one on the fifteenth century, one on the seventeenth century, and one on the eighteenth century. *Individual and Cosmos in Renaissance Philosophy* (1927), was a study of freedom and necessity, subject and object, with special reference to the neoplatonist Nicholas of Cusa, who is presented as the first modern thinker. *The Platonic Renaissance in England* (1932) is a study of the Cambridge Platonists and their twin concerns, religion and science. *The Philosophy of the Enlightenment* (1932) is a more general study which takes in psychology, history, law, aesthetics, and culminates in Kant.

Cassirer is one of the outstanding exponents of *Geistesgeschichte*, a style of intellectual history focused on major texts which are viewed as expressions of intellectual forces, such as puritanism or empiricism, which are virtually personified. The style now seems dated, but Cassirer's work remains impressive for its philosophical acuity, its fluency, and its amazing breadth.   UPB

Main publications

Philosophy of Symbolic Forms (1923−31) (New Haven, CT: Yale University Press, 1958−66); *Individuum und Cosmos in die Philosophie der Renaissance* (1927) (Oxford: Blackwell, 1963); *Die platonische Renaissance in England und die Schule von Cambridge* (1932) (Edinburgh: Nelson, 1953); *Die Philosophie der Aufklärung* (1932) (Princeton, NJ: Princeton University Press, 1951).

Reading

Ferretti, S.: *Il demone della memoria: simbolo e tempo storico in Warburg, Cassirer, Panofsky* (Casale: 1984).

Cassius Dio   See DIO.

Castro, Américo (b.1885, d.1972) A Spaniard born in Brazil, Andalusian by upbringing and early education, philosophy student in Paris, faculty member of the Institución Libre de Enseñanza, a founder, with MENÉNDEZ PIDAL, of the Centro de Estudios Históricos, and professor (1915) of the history of the Spanish language at the University of Madrid, Castro lived his entire life in a state of creative dissatisfaction with learning, the Spanish professoriate, thought, writing, and public affairs as he found them, and all these fields of endeavour felt the effects of his intellectual activism. He moved easily as an equal in the most distinguished intellectual circles of Europe, where some had been his teachers, others his pupils, and where he enjoyed many friendships, sometimes strained by the severe demands he placed upon them. He was bent upon restoring Spain to a position of dignity in the realm of culture, and from the columns of the great liberal newspaper *El Sol* he struck out at abuses needing correction, at personalities whose utterances he found in need of rebuke, and in favour of reforms he thought urgent in education. With the outbreak of civil war in 1936, Castro went into exile in the Americas, eventually (1940) finding an academic home at Princeton University. Passing to emeritus status in 1953, he taught at various other American universities. He returned to Spain in 1969, and died there while swimming in the Mediterranean.

The tranquillity of Princeton allowed Castro to reflect on Spain's many fratricidal conflicts and her difficulty in coming to terms with European modernity, and from his reflections issued a series of works that thrust this intellectual activist, whose fame till then rested upon epoch-making studies of the Spanish language, Cervantes and Lope de Vega, into the centre of Spanish historiography: *España en su historia* and its numerous sequels − *La realidad histórica de España (The Structure of Spanish History)*, several partial, revised versions of the same work (one translated as *The Spaniards*), *Santiago de España*, etc. Spanish history had been seen traditionally as a main stream of Ibero-Christian events starting at some indeterminate point in the remote past and suffering various more or less considerable influences, especially of the Moors and Jews. Castro, deliberately rejecting the notion of influence, saw rather a process in which the social entity Spain came into being through the cultural symbiosis of Christians, Moors and Jews in the first centuries of the so-called Reconquest, and, through an accumulating legacy of linguistic, religious, social, political and artistic monuments, acquired the sense of what he called a 'historical We', inhabitants of the Spanish '*morada vital*' (vital, i.e., existential, dwelling place), a structure of values created by the 'historical We' and providing the terms of reference which enabled the Spaniards to affirm their collective identity as the subject-agents of their history. Earlier scholars had grossly misjudged the significance of Muslim and especially Jewish roles in the structuring of Spanish history because every social bias (fomented inevitably and not least by ex-Jewish Christians) in the emergent life of Catholic Spain had thickened the cloak of secrecy and mendacity surrounding Hispano-Jewishness. Castro's pre-history, as he sometimes called it, has the weaknesses inherent in all-encompassing generalization, but even those averse to accepting his total reconception of the collective identity we call Spaniards have felt obliged to acknowledge his dismantling of this secrecy as an extraordinary contribution to the methods and content of Spanish historiography.   ELK

Main publications

El pensamiento de Cervantes (Madrid: Hernando, 1925); *La peculiaridad lingüística rioplatense y su sentido histórico* (Buenos Aires: Losada, 1941); *España en su historia* (Losada, 1948); *La realidad histórica de España* (English trans., 1954; Princeton, NJ: Princeton University Press, 1954; different trans.: Berkeley:University of California Press, 1971); *De la edad conflictiva* (Madrid: Taurus, 1961); *Sobre el nombre y el quién de los españoles* (Taurus, 1973); *An Idea of History* (selected essays in English trans.) Columbus: Ohio State University Press, 1977).

Reading

Araya, G.: *El pensamiento de Américo Castro* (Madrid: Alianza, 1983).

King, E. L.: Américo Castro and the theory and practice of history. In *Collected Essays in Honour of Américo Castro's Eightieth Year*, ed. M. P. Hornik (Oxford:Lincombe Lodge Research Library, 1965).

Chadwick, William Owen (b.1916) A Cambridge rugby blue 1936–8, Chadwick emerged as an ascetic and dedicated scholar only after his return to Cambridge in 1947. At home equally in the history of religious institutions and ideas, he gave a new impetus to narrative history in a staccato style accessible to scholars and a broader public. The range of his achievement led to the regius chair of modern history in Cambridge (1968–83) and the presidency of the British Academy (1981). Chadwick became chancellor of the University of East Anglia in 1985.   WRW

Main publications

From Bossuet to Newman (Cambridge: Cambridge University Press, 1957); *The Victorian Church* (London: A. & C. Black, 1966–70); *The Secularization of the European Mind in the Nineteenth Century* (Cambridge University Press, 1975); *The Popes and European Revolution* (Oxford: Oxford University Press, 1981).

Reading

Best, Geoffrey: Owen Chadwick and his work. In *History, Society and the Churches: Essays in Honour of Owen Chadwick*, ed. D. Beales and D. Best (Cambridge: Cambridge University Press, 1985).

Chandler, Alfred D. Jr (b.1918) By far the world's most widely cited historian of business, Chandler has been an influence in several disciplines, among them history, economics, sociology and management science, and upon a generation of scholars in many countries besides his native United States. Influenced in his own early years by the works of Max Weber, Joseph Schumpeter and Talcott Parsons, Chandler has brought a distinctively sociological approach to the study of business organizations. He is the author of three books which are landmarks in business history: *Strategy and Structure: Chapters in the History of the American Industrial Enterprise* (1962); *The Visible Hand: the Managerial Revolution in American Business* (1977); and *Scale and Scope* (1989). This trilogy totals approximately 1,500 pages of pathbreaking scholarship on the evolution of big business between about 1850 and 1945. The first two books each won the Thomas Newcomen award, given for the best work on the history of business published during the preceding three years; *The Visible Hand* also won the Pulitzer prize and the Bancroft prize. The third book, *Scale and Scope*, is a major comparative study of the rise of what Chandler calls 'managerial capitalism' in Britain, West Germany, and the United States. In nearly all of his books and articles, Chandler has focused on the internal workings of the large industrial corporation: its strategic moves toward vertical integration: its systematic diversification, rooted in research and development; and its direction by hierarchical teams of top, middle and lower managers.

Although Chandler has written two full-scale biographies (*Henry Varnum Poor*, published in 1956, and *Pierre S. du Pont*, which appeared in 1971), individuals are seldom prominent in his writings. When he has written about them at all he has celebrated the rational organization-builder over the perhaps eccentric genius. Beyond the charge of an excessive rationalism bordering on technological determinism, other criticisms of his work have dwelt on his relative de-emphasis on the human impact of industrialization, his neglect of the role of labour, and his implicit argument that the political state has played only a minor role in the rise of industrial capitalism. Chandler's salient traits in all his personal relations have been an abiding and sometimes obsessive intellectual curiosity, and, despite his patrician origins, a pronounced lack of pretentiousness. TKMc

Main publications

Strategy and Structure: Chapters in the History of the American Industrial Enterprise (Cambridge, Mass.: MIT Press, 1962); *The Visible Hand: the Managerial Revolution in American Business* (Cambridge, Mass.: Harvard University Press, 1977); *Scale and Scope* (Cambridge, Mass.: Harvard University Press, 1989).

Reading

Duboff, Richard B. and Herman, Edward S.: Alfred Chandler's new business history: a review. *Politics and Society* 10 (1980) 87–110.
McCraw, Thomas K. ed.: *The Essential Alfred Chandler* (Boston, Mass.: Harvard Business School Press, 1988).

Chaunu, Pierre (b.1923)   A pupil of Ernest Labrousse, Chaunu taught in lycées while writing his doctoral thesis. He then became professor at the university of Caen, and has been at the University of Paris-Sorbonne since 1970. He is a man of enormous energy, whose boast it is to write a book in six weeks; a Protestant (whose personal work ethic is an argument in favour of the 'Weber thesis'); a vigorous crusader against birth control; and a member of the Institute.

Chaunu is one of the leading members of the ANNALES SCHOOL. He began as a specialist on early modern Spain, and his doctoral thesis, which at 7,343 pages must be among the longest ever written, dealt with the trade between Spain and the New World in the sixteenth and seventeenth centuries, calculating the tonnage of goods transported and constructing a series of economic cycles on this basis. It was at once an adventurous application to transatlantic trade of a method developed by Chaunu's master LABROUSSE for the study of the economy of eighteenth-century France, and a challenge to BRAUDEL. It dealt with a vast ocean in a correspondingly vast book and dwarfed by comparison both *La Méditerranée* and the Mediterranean.

Chaunu continued for some years to write on Spain, America, and European expansion, but his interests have gradually moved from economic to general history, especially historical method and the history of religion, and from Spain and her empire to France. He continues to be fascinated by quantitative methods, the study of continuities and discontinuities by means of a series of similar data extending over a long period, but he is particularly concerned with this 'serial history' (a phrase which he launched) at the 'third level', in other words in the history of *mentalités*. An example of this kind of history is the research on changing attitudes to death in Paris from the sixteenth and seventeenth centuries, based essentially on the study of thousands of wills, conducted by a team of young historians under Chaunu's direction. Dynamic, impatient, often inaccurate on points of detail, Chaunu is bursting with ideas. He will probably be remembered as much for a handful of important articles (on Jansenism, on Philip II, and on serial history) as for a shelf of weighty books.   UPB

Main publications

Séville et l'Atlantique, 12 vols (Paris: SEVPEN, 1955–60); *L'Amérique et les Amériques* (Paris: Colin, 1964); *La civilisation de l'Europe classique* (Paris: Arthaud, 1966); *L'expansion européenne du 12e au 15e siècle* (1969) (Amsterdam: 1979); *L'Espagne de Charles V*, 2 vols (Paris: SEDES, 1973); *Histoire, science sociale* (Paris: SEDES, 1974); *L'État, histoire economique et sociale de la France*, vol. 1, ed. P. Chaunu and R. Gascon (Paris: Presses Universitaires de France, 1977) pp. 9–228; *Histoire quantitative, histoire sérielle* (Paris: Colin, 1978); *La mort à Paris* (Paris: Fayard, 1978); *Église, culture et société: essais sur reforme et contre-reforme, 1517–1620* (Paris: SEDES, 1980); *La France: histoire de la sensibilité des français à la France* (Paris: Laffont, 1982).

Cheney, Christopher Robert (b.1906, d.1987) Apart from brief but stimulating spells teaching in Cairo and London, Cheney's career has been divided between Oxford, Manchester and Cambridge. He graduated at Wadham College, Oxford, and was later university reader in diplomatic at Oxford (1937–45) and fellow of Magdalen College (1938–45); he was Bishop Fraser lecturer in ecclesiastical history at Manchester from 1933 to 1937, and professor of medieval history there (1945–55). In 1955 he was elected professor of medieval history at Cambridge. He retired in 1972. He was a fellow of Corpus Christi College, Cambridge, from 1955, fellow of the British Academy from 1951, and honorary fellow of Wadham from 1968. He died on 19 June 1987.

The early inspiration of Sir Maurice Powicke helped to bring Cheney to his lifelong study of the records of the medieval English church: though Powicke founded *Councils and Synods* to replace the *Concilia* of David Wilkins (1737), the 1,450 pages of volume II are essentially Cheney's work; distinguished by a remarkable mingling of technical skill and common sense, it is one of the supreme monuments of English scholarship of its age. Another is the British Academy's project for editing *Episcopal Acta*, founded and inspired by Cheney himself, who edited volumes 2 and 3. He was a profound student of documents and their making, as *English Bishops' Chanceries* (1950) and *Notaries Public in England* (1972) witness – the latter a characteristically modest expression of learning ranging over much of western Christendom. But his concern for documents always had a practical aim in view. Thus in his Ford lectures *From Becket to Langton* he used them to show exactly how the English church worked. *Pope Innocent III and England* similarly exploited his work on the text of Innocent's letters.

In his editorial work on Innocent, his wife Mary Cheney was his colleague, and their home a centre to which pupils and friends came for advice and friendship, and where they found generous, unstinting help.   CNLB

Main publications

Episcopal Visitation of Monasteries in the Thirteenth Century (Manchester: Manchester University Press, 1931); *Handbook of Dates* (London: Royal Historical Society, 1945; corr. repr. 1981); *English Bishops' Chanceries, 1100–1250* (Manchester University Press, 1950); *From Becket to Langton* (Manchester UP, 1956); ed. with F. M. Powicke, *Councils and Synods with other documents relating to the English Church*, II, *AD 1205–1313*, 2 parts (Oxford: Clarendon Press, 1964); ed. with M. G. Cheney, *The Letters of Pope Innocent III . . . concerning England and Wales* (Clarendon Press, 1967); *Notaries Public in England in the Thirteenth and Fourteenth Centuries* (Oxford, Clarendon Press, 1972); *Pope Innocent III and England* (Stuttgart 1976); ed., *English Episcopal Acta* II and III, *Canterbury 1162–1205* (London: British Academy, 1986).

Reading

Brooke, C. N. L.: C. R. Cheney. *Proceedings of the British Academy* 74 (1988).

Childe, Vere Gordon (b.1892, d.1957) After obtaining a first in classics from Sydney University, Childe migrated from Australia to England and Queen's College, Oxford where he gained a first in Greats and B. Litt., 1916–17. An interest in Indo-European philology led to prehistoric archaeology and Childe became the first holder of the Abercromby chair of archaeology at the University of Edinburgh in 1927; in 1946 he left to hold the directorship and chair of European prehistoric archaeology in the Institute of Archaeology at the University of London. A lonely and inaccessible figure, he retired in 1956, returned to Australia, and committed suicide in the Blue Mountains of New South Wales in 1957.

Childe was the first archaeologist in Britain to see and present European prehistory as an entity and his early books from 1925 were internationally recognized as masterpieces of synthesis based on an unique knowledge of the evidence from the literature and museums of every European country: he was an inveterate traveller and accomplished linguist. Left-wing in politics since youth, he became increasingly sympathetic to the communist world and developed a personal form of Marxist historical theory in a series of archaeological and sociological presentations of the ancient world which gained great popularity and have increasingly contributed to such thinking today.   SP

Main publications

The Dawn of European Civilization (London: Kegan Paul, 1925; 6th edn, 1957); *The Danube in Prehistory* (Oxford: Clarendon Press, 1929); *Man makes Himself* (London: Watts, 1936; many reprints; *What Happened in History* (Harmondsworth: Penguin, 1942; many reprints).

Reading

Green, Sally: *Prehistorian: a Biography of V. Gordon Childe* (Bradford-on-Avon: Moonraker Press, 1981).
McNairn, Barbara: *The Method and Theory of V. G. Childe* (Edinburgh: Edinburgh University Press, 1980).

Chinese historiography For Confucius (b.*c.*551 BC, d.479 BC) the ideal society had existed in the recent Chinese past, so to preserve what remained of its legacy and recreate its lost order became the prime task of his followers. This gave pre-modern Chinese thought a markedly secular and historically minded slant, perceptible both in historical writing and in the three other divisions of Chinese bibliography: belles-lettres, philosophy and classics (*ching*). This last term covers works deemed to constitute the surviving textual reflection of the Golden Age. Two are historical works: the *Shu Ching*, a collection of documents associated with early rulers (some mythical), and the *Ch'un-ch'iu*, a terse court chronicle from Confucius' native state.

The *Ch'un-ch'iu* is said to have been edited by Confucius so as to reveal the sage's moral evaluation of his materials through a subtle use of terminology. This belief proved a mixed blessing: history writing remained a prestigious activity, but many historians took a high moral tone or, more insidiously, edited their material to emphasize norms over realities. At least recognition of the key role of the historian led to considerable concern over historiographic matters.

For about the past millennium there has been a tension between the Neo-Confucian philosopher, anxious to dismiss the recent past in favour of a revival of the pristine values of antiquity, and the historian, who was often a gradualist, ready to change and improve society only on the basis of a thorough knowledge of what China had become over the centuries. The former camp attracted the moralist; the latter drew strength from a longstanding connection between historiography and bureaucracy. Some have seen this as just as pernicious as Confucian moralizing, since it dictated a view of history strictly in accordance with the interests of the ruling group, but in return bureaucratic insistence on the careful organization of materials has left us copious, well-ordered sources the like of which no other Chinese (Buddhist monk-historians, for example) managed to transmit.

The father of this historiography was Ssuma Ch'ien (*c.*145−85 BC). His masterpiece, the *Shih Chi*, ran to over half a million characters and covered all history down to his own times. But an annalistic account of the *Ch'un-ch'iu* type forms only the first section of the *Shih Chi*, which also incorporates tables of kings and high office holders for quick reference and treatises on irrigation, the calendar and other topics of interest to officials. The bulk of the work, however, consists of a series of narratives covering the histories of famous individuals, and also some groups such as foreign peoples, millionaires, swordsmen, entertainers. Moralistic evaluations are appended − the *Tso Chuan*, a narrative chronicle used as a commentary on the *Ch'un-ch'iu*, may have had an influence on this part of the *Shih Chi* — but these sometimes contrast weakly with the broad sympathies evident in Ssu-ma's writing.

His successor Pan Ku (AD 32—92) followed his pattern of organization but adopted a narrow perspective, writing (under imperial patronage) only of the Former Han dynasty. In time it became the practice for each dynasty to compile historical materials for its successor to put into the composite form of the *Shih Chi*, though many of these 25 'standard histories' far exceed the *Shih Chi* in size. The format would appear to emphasize panoramic completeness at the expense of causality, but westerners can rarely have read such works the way their authors intended, as an ensemble, and none has been translated in full.

Official history certainly did not escape criticism in China. In AD 629 a permanent history office was established for editing materials based on court diaries, official obituaries and so on into provisional drafts for a full-scale dynastic history, but soon a former employee, Liu Chih-chi (661—721), incorporated in his *Shih-t'ung* a spirited defence of the individual historian as part of a trenchant review of over a millennium of historiographic practice.

Liu had much to say about the chronicle form, which survived in opposition to the composite standard histories and grew in complexity, though it was not until the *Tzu-chih t'ung-chien* of Ssu-ma Kuang (1019—1086) that it reached its apogee. Ssu-ma's magisterial survey of almost 14 centuries down to his own dynasty wove together over three hundred sources, adding reasons for his choice of authority where they conflicted. This outstandingly objective work was too good for the moralists to leave alone: the philosopher Chu Hsi (1130—1200) charged his disciples with producing a summary, the *T'ung-chien kang-mu*, injecting much discussion of 'praise and blame'. Sadly, this travesty of Ssu-ma Kuang became established as the best-known history textbook in China.

This triumph for didacticism was, however, followed by a triumph for bureaucratic history in the *Wen-hsien t'ung-k'ao* of Ma Tuan-lin (1254—1324/5), a compilation of materials on institutional history half as long again as the *Tzu-chih t'ung-chien*. Books of this type, already pioneered by a son of Liu Chih-chi, clearly involved much straightforward scissors-and-paste work, but Ma and his predecessors were no mere pedants: their editorial comments frequently demonstrated a keen eye for processes of social change spanning many centuries. The ready availability of compilations like this and the other histories, thanks to the invention of printing, gave Chinese scholars a detailed historical knowledge fully apparent in their works.

This holds particularly good for the seventeenth century, a time of broad critical reassessment within the Chinese tradition. By the eighteenth, reassessment had narrowed to an attempt to retrieve the classics from the antihistorical constructions of Neo-Confucian philosophy — though even here a historical sense would sometimes surface. Ts'ui Shu (1740—1816), for example, though he did not doubt the classics themselves, perceived that much of the traditional image of high antiquity had been created by early waves of idealization. One enthusiastic, even cantankerous, defender of all historical studies in this age of classical scholarship was Chang Hsüeh-ch'eng (1738—1801), a man who prompts inevitable comparison with VICO. Both Ts'ui and Chang were little known in their own day: Chang had one book published, but it is not listed among the 2,136 works on history in the imperial library in 1782.

Their posthumous publications and surviving manuscripts were, however, taken up with a vengeance in the early twentieth century by Chinese historians looking for indigenous anticipations of modern thought. Ku Chieh-kang (1893—1980) and others pushed Ts'ui's scepticism further to question the classics, at the same time as they broke through the confines of bureaucratic history through participation in the 'folk studies' movement. With the establishment of the People's Republic in 1949 traditional historiographic values were completely reversed, as peasant rebels formerly execrated as villains became heroes. Yet the long-established practice of conducting veiled discussions of contemporary events through historical analogies made research difficult, and in the perfervid atmosphere of the Cultural Revolution (1966–76) impossible. Since then a revival of historical studies has shown a renewed concern for archival material: central government archives date back to the fourteenth century; earlier documents exist in some local archives. Similar material on Taiwan has received increased attention from local and American scholars.

Until the 1930s most western historical writing on China aped the elderly Chinese tutor's interest in the classical period or exhibited a narcissistic interest in Sino-western relations, ignoring a large chunk (almost two millennia) in the middle. Subsequently a number of historians of China with a knowledge of Japanese acquired during the second world war entered the field, which led to an awareness of the lively debates over the period conducted in Japan by scholars anxious to repudiate or modify the theories of earlier pioneers such as Naitō Konan (1866–1934) too closely identified with Japan's pre-war policies. But such stimuli have been felt mainly in American universities; with one or two honourable exceptions, British interest in the historical experience of this lavishly documented quarter of mankind has been nugatory, even though Chinese historiography has influenced Japanese, Korean and Vietnamese historians and (via the Jesuits) European chronologists too.   THB

Reading

Beasley, W. G. and Pulleyblank, E. G. eds: *Historians of China and Japan* (London: Oxford University Press, 1961).

Nivison, David S.: *The Life and Thought of Chang Hsüeh-ch'eng (1738–1801)* (Stanford, Calif.: Stanford University Press, 1966).

Schneider, Laurence A.: *Ku Chieh-kang and China's New History* (Berkeley and Los Angeles: University of California Press, 1971).

Watson, Burton: *Ssu-ma Ch'ien: Grand Historian of China* (New York: Columbia University Press, 1958).

chronicles and annals   Attempts to define various pieces of medieval western historiography as either chronicles or annals have not been particularly successful, for a desire to systematize the way in which people in the middle ages thought about their past has often led to exercises based upon criteria alien to the society responsible for the works under consideration. It was not until the fourteenth century that a clear distinction was made between chronicles, annals and histories. By then, it had already been recognized that the distinction was inapplicable to many contemporary and previous writings. Yet, despite this cautious approach on the part of their predecessors, modern commentators have often been so insistent upon processes of definition that they have disregarded matters of more fundamental significance in the works they have studied and have failed to note just how much compositions 'peripheral to the established traditions of chronicles and annals', can tell us of the kinds of imaginative reconstruction of the past which medieval writers sought to produce. It is therefore necessary to consider the medieval chronicle not as a narrowly defined genre but as a narrative form which can only be examined at one and the same time as those other forms like the *historia*, the *gesta*, the *genealogia* and the *annales* from which it has often been arbitrarily separated.

It is within this less specific perception of the medieval chronicle that the particular genre of what might be called the universal and local *chronica* must be studied. There are a number of works which can be placed in this subsection essentially because they share certain characteristics in the ways in which they attempt to reach back to a distant past; to cover earlier periods by compiling material taken from older writings; to pay close attention to chronological methods; and to deal either with a world history based on their own particular definition of the extent of that world, or with a more localized history based on the fortunes of an individual community. The Latin tradition of world *chronica* is based on Jerome's *Eusebii Pamphili chronici canones* and incorporates Prosper of Aquitaine's *Chronicon*, Isidore of Seville's *Chronica majora*, Bede's *Chronicon de sex aetatibus mundi* and the works of Regino of Prüm, Herman of Reichenau, Marianus Scotus, Sigebert of Gembloux, Otto of Freising, Robert of Auxerre, Matthew Paris and Ranulf Higden. World chronicles in the vernacular begin in the thirteenth century with

Die Sächsische weltchronik. Representative of the local *chronica* are the *Chronicon Centulense* centred on the abbey of Saint-Riquier, the *Chronicon Hanoniense* centred on Hainault, the *Primera crónica general de España*, the first chronicle in Spanish, and the later *städte-chroniken* of such cities as Lübeck, Mainz and Magdeburg.

The genre of the *historia*, despite its more obvious references to divine influence in the explanation of the historical process, is clearly related to that of the *chronica* and similarly operates on both a world and regional basis. At the universal level, EUSEBIUS again provided an important model and source through the Latin translation and continuation of his *Historia ecclesiastica* but the works of Epiphanius Scholasticus, Suplicius Severus and Paulus OROSIUS also had considerable influence upon the content and spirit of later western historiography. The *Historia ecclesiastica* of ORDERIC VITALIS, which commenced as a history of the abbey of Saint-Evroult but eventually embraced the activities of the Normans throughout Europe, may be compared with the national histories of Jordanes, GREGORY OF TOURS, Isidore of Seville, BEDE, Paul the Deacon, WIDUKIND, SAXO 'GRAMMATICUS' and WILLIAM OF MALMESBURY. Such national histories share many characteristics with those *gesta* which concern themselves with the deeds of particular lines of churchmen or princes, for the *gesta*, although cast within a superficially biographical framework, are also essentially chronicles. The most famous of the *gesta* is the *Liber pontificalis* of the popes of which the oldest part dates from the sixth century. Later, in works produced both north and south of the Alps, the histories of many bishoprics and abbeys were written as *gesta*. In the ninth century, Agnellus produced the *Liber pontificalis ecclesiae Ravennatis*. In the late eleventh century, ADAM OF BREMEN compiled that work which has become such an important source for the history of northern Europe, the *Gesta Hammaburgensis ecclesiae pontificum*. A comparison of ROGER OF HOWDEN's *Gesta* and *Chronica* only serves to demonstrate how closely a particular *gesta* can parallel a *chronica*. The *Flandria generosa*, composed in the twelfth century, similarly evidences how a work,

which is in many senses a *genealogia* and therefore related to documents which are sometimes little more than straightforward lists of names, can develop into a regional chronicle. The same sort of tranformation occurs in the case of annals which were fundamentally uncomplicated historical notes produced in annual succession and had their origins in the margins and between the lines of Easter tables. A primitive type of year book was still produced in the later middle ages, but collections of entries such as the *Royal Frankish Annals*, the *Annals of Ulster* and the *Anglo-Saxon Chronicle*, while retaining their original format, again took on characteristics normally associated with chronicles.

The general tradition of the medieval chronicle therefore came to influence and be influenced by developments in a whole series of interrelated genres. As such, it derived its strength not from classical authors like Tacitus but from the historical writings of Christian authors of the late empire. As a result of the renaissances of the middle ages, more direct antique influence eventually found a place in medieval historiography in works such as those of EINHARD, Otto of Freising and Leonardo Bruni. It is, however, significant that while a greater knowledge of classical literature had a clear impact upon both the stylistic and critical approaches of many medieval historians, it did not greatly affect the dominant forms of historical writing which had been established earlier in the middle ages.   DJC

Reading

Caenegem, R. C. van: *Guide to the Sources of Medieval History* (Amsterdam: North-Holland, 1977), pp. 17–54.

Guenée, Bernard: *Histoire et culture historique dans l'occident médiéval* (Paris: Aubier, 1980).

Poole, R. L.: *Chronicles and Annals* (Oxford: Clarendon Press, 1926).

Churchill, Winston Spencer (b.1874, d.1965)   Statesman and British prime minister, created Knight of the Garter in 1953. Churchill was a prolific writer, principally of newspaper and magazine articles on political, historical and personal themes. But he was also the author of several books which, while centring on his personal activities and reminiscences in five wars, contained substantial historical materials and analysis, and he wrote three entirely historical works: a biography of his father Lord Randolph Churchill; a biography of his ancestor Marlborough, *His Life and Times* and *A History of the English-Speaking Peoples*.

For each of his historical works, Churchill employed research assistants to assemble the documents, often over several years. He then wove the documents together, sometimes with short linking passages, sometimes with considerable analysis and comment. His principal themes were the emergence and preservation of parliamentary democracy, the dangers of military weakness, and the influence of individual decisions on the course of events.

A remarkable feature of Churchill's preparation of his historical works was the extent to which he enlisted the critical help of experts. These included the principal participants in the events themselves, and historians who had been most closely involved in research. For his *History of the English-Speaking Peoples* he sought the advice and made copious use of the notes provided for him by authorities such as Keith Feiling, G. M. Young and D. W. Brogan. Among those whose views he sought for his biography of Marlborough was Lewis Namier, who criticized the imaginary conversations to which Churchill had resorted in the first volume. 'I felt at the time they were a weak indulgence on my part,' Churchill replied, 'but they sometimes make the ordinary reader realize the position. I hope to avoid them altogether in volume two.' To Namier's request that he introduce more of his own experiences of politics into his historical works, Churchill replied: 'I certainly propose to apply my experience in military and political affairs to the episodes. One of the most misleading factors in history is the practice of historians to build a story exclusively out of the records which have come down to them. These records in many cases are a very small part of what took place, and to fill in the picture one has to visualize the daily life – the constant discussions between Ministers, the friendly dinners, the many days when nothing happened worthy of record, but during which

events were nevertheless proceeding.' He made no pretence at impartiality. Reflecting on his father's career, he wrote in 1948: 'I should have thought the biography I have written proved the reverence with which I regarded him.'

In setting down guidelines for his helpers, Churchill twice expressed his philosophy on the writing of history. In 1929, in a letter to Maurice Ashley, his research assistant from 1929 to 1935, he wrote of the *Marlborough* biography: 'Broadly speaking my method will probably be not to attempt to "defend" or "vindicate" my subject, but to tell the tale with close adherence to chronology in such a way and in such proportions and with such emphasis as will produce upon the mind of the reader the impersonation I wish to give. I have first of all to visualize this extraordinary personality. This I can only do gradually as my knowledge increases. One has got to find out what the rules of the age were – there certainly were rules.'

In a second letter to Ashley ten years later, setting out the concept of the work on *A History of the English-Speaking Peoples*, Churchill wrote: 'In the main the theme is emerging of the growth of freedom and law, of the rights of the individual, of the subordination of the State to the fundamental and moral conceptions of an ever-comprehending community. Of these ideas the English-speaking peoples were the authors, then the trustees, and must now become the armed champions. Thus I condemn tyranny in whatever guise and from whatever quarter it presents itself. All this of course has a current application.' It is interesting to note that Ashley wrote to Churchill when the first volume of *The Second World War* (for which Churchill was awarded the Nobel Prize for literature) was published in 1948: 'I shall always remember with gratitude that I learned more of the art of writing history from working for you than I did from my Oxford professors.'

As a statesman who spent more than fifty years at the centre of events, Churchill was conscious both of the weaknesses of historical reconstruction and of the contribution which history could make to the philosophy of future generations. As he told the House of Commons during his obituary of Neville Chamberlain in 1940: 'In one phase men seem to have been right, in another they seem to have been wrong. Then again, a few years later, when the perspective of time has lengthened, all stands in a different setting. There is a new proportion. There is another scale of values. History with its flickering lamp stumbles along the trail of the past, trying to reconstruct its scenes, to revive its echoes, and kindle with pale gleams the passions of former days.'

In his private letters and writings Churchill made frequent references to the concept and uses of history. For example, learning that General Eisenhower was to write his memoirs, Churchill told him: 'I am very glad you are not leaving it to history to write the account of your conduct of these great events.' But he was fully aware that his own history of the second world war was a personal and interim judgement. Setting out his view of some of its controversial episodes, he told Eisenhower: 'However, these are matters on which only another generation can pronounce.' And again, in a private message to Stalin in 1945, Churchill warned that a quarrel between the Communist states and the English-speaking nations 'would tear the world to pieces and that all of us leading men on either side who had anything to do with that would be shamed before history'. Churchill frequently referred to history as the ultimate weapon. Once, speaking of Neville Chamberlain, he said: 'History will judge him harshly; I know, because I shall write it.' He also had confidence, and justly so, in his readability as an historian: 'I have no doubt', he wrote to one of his assistants when embarking on his four-volume biography of Marlborough, 'that I shall be able to tell this famous tale from a modern point of view that will rivet attention.'

Nevertheless Churchill did not exaggerate his historical talents or contribution; indeed he sometimes underrated them. Perhaps his contribution is best summed up in his own words in the preface to the first volume of *The Second World War*: 'I do not describe it as history, for that belongs to another generation. But I claim with confidence that it is a contribution to history which will be of service to the future.'   MG

Main publications

The Story of the Malakand Field Force (London: Longmans Green, 1898); *The River War*, 2 vols (Longmans Green, 1899); *Ian Hamilton's March* (Longmans Green, 1900); *London to Ladysmith* (Longmans Green, 1900); *Lord Randolph Churchill*, 2 vols (London: Macmillan, 1906); *The World Crisis*, 6 vols (London: Thornton Butterworth, 1923–31); *Thoughts and Adventures* (Thornton Butterworth, 1932); *Marlborough, His Life and Times*, 4 vols (London: Harrap, 1933–5); *Great Contemporaries* (Thornton Butterworth, 1937); *Step by Step* (Harrap, 1939); *The Second World War*, 6 vols (London: Cassell, 1948–54); *A History of the English-Speaking Peoples*, 4 vols (Cassell, 1956–8).

Cicero, M. Tullius See CLASSICAL HISTORIOGRAPHY.

Clapham, John Harold (b.1873, d.1946) Born in Salford, Lancashire, and educated at the Leys School, Cambridge, Clapham won a history exhibition to King's College, Cambridge, and took a first class in the historical tripos in 1895. Apart from six years as professor of economics at the Yorkshire College, University of Leeds, from 1902 to 1908, he spent most of his academic life at King's, holding a fellowship until his death. In 1928 he was elected to the newly created chair of economic history at Cambridge.

Clapham was much influenced in his early career by Lord ACTON. This is clear from *The Abbé Sieyès: an Essay in the Politics of the French Revolution* (1912), a study of the revolutionary and Napoleonic period in the light of the kind of political science being taught in Cambridge in the Edwardian period. However, his major contribution to historical scholarship was in the economic rather than the political field. In 1897 the economist Alfred Marshall suggested to Acton that Clapham was the man to write a 'tolerable account of the economic development of England in the last century and a half'. The fruits of this seed were to ripen from Clapham's days at Leeds, where he took the opportunity to study local industry and as a result published *The Woollen and Worsted Industries* (1907). After his return to Cambridge in 1908 he moved to a broader canvas with *The Economic Development of France and Germany, 1815–1914* (1921), and then with his magisterial survey *An Economic History of Modern Britain* (3 vols, 1926–38). In its day this latter study, covering the period 1820–1914, was regarded as the most important book in the whole field of British economic history, and it amply fulfilled Marshall's prediction. Clapham dedicated the first volume to Marshall and to William CUNNINGHAM, from whom he had first learned economic history. After his retirement from the Cambridge chair in 1938, Clapham went on to edit the first volume of the *Cambridge Economic History of Europe* (1941), and to complete another major study, on the history of the Bank of England.

Clapham was awarded the CBE in 1918 after serving in the Board of Trade during the first world war. In 1928 he was elected to a fellowship, and in 1940 to the presidency, of the British Academy; he also served as president of the Economic History Society. Clapham was knighted in 1943.   JVB

Main publications

(All published by Cambridge University Press, Cambridge.)
The Economic Development of France and Germany, 1815–1914 (1921); *An Economic History of Modern Britain*. Vol. 1, *The Early Railway Age* (1926), Vol. 2, *Free Trade and Steel* (1932), Vol. 3, *Machine and National Rivalries* (1938); *The Bank of England: A History*, 2 vols (1944).

Reading

Clark, G. N.: Sir John Harold Clapham. *Proceedings of the British Academy* 32 (1946) pp. 339–52.
Postan, M. M.: Sir John Clapham. *Economic History Review* 16 (1946) pp. 56–9.

Clarendon, Edward Hyde (b.1609, d.1674) Success in politics and greatness as a historian are virtually incompatible. Edward Hyde, first Earl of Clarendon, is one of the very few people to have been outstanding in the public affairs of his age and to have left a full-scale history of it. Yet the rule holds, for his work as a historian corresponded precisely with periods of exile following failure as a politician. It is his combination of marvellous style and personal insight, experience and need for self-justification that makes his writing so readable, so important and so untrustworthy to posterity.

Born of Wiltshire gentry stock, Hyde rose like many ambitious young men of his time through the practice of law. The common law nevertheless interested him much less than history, literature and current affairs, and his career was decisively altered by his election to parliament in 1640. He became a royalist in 1642; during the Civil War he was knighted, and made a privy councillor and Chancellor of the Exchequer. For two years after the war he lived quietly in Jersey, where he began his *History of the Rebellion*. This was interrupted by his return to active service in the royalist cause in 1648. At the Restoration of 1660 he was created Earl of Clarendon and became the most important member of the new government. His daughter married Charles's heir James, and his granddaughters became queens. Yet from 1662 his influence with the king waned and in 1667 he was dismissed as scapegoat for the disastrous Dutch war. His refusal to retire from politics led to his impeachment by a furious monarch and he was banished for life. Living in France in his old age, he was able to complete the *History* and to write a brief autobiography, coupled with an extension of the *History* covering his career under the restored monarchy. He died at Rouen.

Throughout his life Clarendon remained devoted to monarchy and episcopacy as guarantors of an orderly and harmonious society, though he always recognized the right of parliament to correct the policies of an erring monarch and to punish bad ministers. He also remained convinced that doctrinal differences among Christians were fundamentally unimportant. Hence he participated in several attempts to win presbyterians back to the episcopalian church, and was disinclined to persecute them. By the same token he opposed the toleration of Catholics, and vehemently hated Quakers because of the political and social implications of their beliefs. He detested republicanism and behaved harshly towards individual republicans including a former friend, after the Restoration. He instinctively disliked foreigners, including the Scots and Irish, and made only a partial exception for the French, among whom he died.

As a public man Clarendon's greatest assets were his political loyalty and his remarkable industry. The latter was not merely a devotion to administration, for as soon as he found himself in private life he set himself the arduous task of writing his *History*. For this compulsion to labour he neglected both his wife and his health, and the collection of manuscripts which he left behind represents one of the greatest archives for his age. He was notably brave, and both a loyal friend and an implacable enemy. His vices were conceit, overt ambition, self-righteousness and insensitivity. He was equally maladroit when dealing with a foreign minister or a landlady. He suspected men with new ideas, and treated political rivals with childish spite. His friends were few, and even they sometimes found him thoughtless. He was an eloquent speaker and tenacious debater, though with increasing importance he became less inclined to tolerate disagreement. His nature was always passionate, and he disliked subtle and self-controlled people as much as he distrusted brilliance.

These beliefs and qualities are crucial to an understanding of his masterpiece, the *History of the Rebellion*. This was first published in 1702–4, as ammunition for the Tory party in its struggle with the Whigs, and as such was initially treated with a healthy scepticism which has since largely vanished. It is a fairly detailed account of British history from 1640 to 1660, with an introduction covering the 1630s. The style is lucid and elegant, a measured narrative enlivened by philosophical parallels, anecdotes and vivid character-sketches. It is a splendid story for any reader, and contains material of interest to the political, constitutional, military, diplomatic and social historian. As a whole, it is the finest account that any British statesman has left of his times, assembled carefully from the huge number of lesser memoirs and documents which he amassed. But as with Clarendon himself, its defects are equally obvious. It is uneven in quality, Scottish and Irish events and those of the 1650s being treated relatively thinly and with some confusion. His portrait of war-time parliamentarian and republican politics has always been recognized as less valuable than that of the early Long Parliament and the royalist party. But it is precisely when Clarendon is most detailed and plausible that he is most unreliable. His work is not an objective

chronicle, but a gigantic vindication of himself, his friends and his political allies. To this end he repeatedly distorts the truth in a manner which, given the sources from which he worked, must usually have been conscious. If he grants virtues to enemies, this is generally to damn them the more credibly. If he weaves much objective fact into his narrative, this is to make its political purpose less obvious. The most detailed portion of the whole work, covering events in the west of England in 1645–6, was designed specifically to relieve himself of blame for the loss of the region by accusing others. In sum, the *History* can be employed as a source only if it is corroborated by others, not as a substitute for alternative information.

Clarendon rivals Caesar as the author of the greatest political apology ever written, and takes his place with Bolingbroke and Burke as a philosopher of the early Tory party.   RH

Main publications

The History of the Rebellion and Civil War in England, ed. W. Dunn Macray (Oxford: Clarendon Press, 1888); *The Life of Edward, Earl of Clarendon.* (Clarendon Press, 1827).

Reading

Trevor-Roper, Hugh: *Edward Hyde, Earl of Clarendon.* (Oxford: Clarendon Press, 1975).
Roebuck, Graham: *Clarendon and Cultural Continuity.* (London: Garland, 1981).
Harris, R. W.: *Clarendon and the English Revolution.* (London: Chatto & Windus, 1983).

Clark, George Norman (b.1890, d.1979) The son of a Halifax businessman, Clark chose Anglo-Dutch relations in the seventeenth century as his first research topic, at the suggestion of Sir Charles FIRTH, regius professor of modern history at Oxford, and he was able to pursue this in Dutch archives after being paroled from a German prisoner-of-war camp to neutral Holland in April 1918. As a result his first publications were in this field, and he retained a life-long interest in Dutch history; his work on war and trade, and other economic topics, led eventually to his election to the first Chichele chair of economic history at Oxford in 1931. But his interests were wider ranging. *The Seventeenth Century* rejected chronological narrative and compartments of national history in favour of a discussion of various aspects of society and thought, in a manner less usual at that date than now. Some of the topics were taken up in *Science and Social Welfare in the Age of Newton*. His best known work, *The Later Stuarts, 1660–1714*, was the first volume to appear in the Oxford History of England series, which he edited, and to which he added his own stamp by including chapters on intellectual and economic tendencies, literature and thought, and the arts and social life. Regius professor at Cambridge from 1943 to 1947, Clark was a natural choice for another major editorial task, that of planning the New Cambridge Modern History series. His credo as a historian may be found in his general introduction to the first volume which, in its disbelief in the possibility of definitive history, forms the basis for contrast and comparison with the aims of ACTON and his colleagues in an earlier generation. Much of Clark's writing – always clear, unpretentious, and revealing a broad perspective – was based on the widest reading of printed works in several languages, rather than on the direct use of manuscript sources. Clark was knighted in 1953.   KHDH

Main publications

(All published by Clarendon Press, Oxford.)
The Seventeenth Century (1929; 2nd edn, 1947); *The Later Stuarts, 1660–1714* (1934; 2nd edn, 1955); *Science and Social Welfare in the Age of Newton* (1937; 2nd edn, 1949).

Reading

Parker, Geoffrey: Memoir: *Proceedings of the British Academy* 66 (1980) 407–22.

classical historiography It is accepted by all but the most gullible of modern scholars that Greek and Roman historians put invented speeches into the mouths of the characters whose exploits they were describing. This practice, symptomatic of the widespread ancient belief that a work of history should be as elaborate and full-scale as possible, is generally seen as having no significance beyond itself; yet it in fact denotes something fundamental about the nature of classical historiography. Since that which had not happened was thereby represented as though it had, it follows that

historians had a quite different conception of 'historical truth' from our own.

To statements of this sort scholars often object that historians in their prefaces regularly promised to tell 'the truth', the implication being that they had a theoretical commitment from which they may nevertheless have deviated in practice. Yet almost all such promises are so phrased as to make it clear that the commitment is not precisely to truth but to the impartiality with which the individuals of history should be treated. While expressions of this commitment may read strangely today, they were entirely natural in an honour-based society which was more than usually sensitive to envy and in which most forms of literature were regarded as vehicles of encomium or censure.

Classical historiography is ultimately derived from Greek epic poetry, from which it gains its exclusively narrative aspect, its preference for themes of war, its moral dimension, and its liking for set speeches. Each of these elements is present in the twin founders of historiography, HERODOTUS and THUCYDIDES, who in prose set out expressly to rival Homer. Though Aristotle in the fourth century BC famously drew a distinction between poetry and historiography, the two genres continued to be described in terms of each other until at least the sixth century AD, as the rhetorician Quintilian and historian Agathias both testify. With the rise of oratorical prose in fifth-century BC Greece, however, historiography came also to be seen in terms of oratory, as is clear from Aristotle's contemporary, the historian Ephorus, and from DIONYSIUS of HALICARNASSUS. It is therefore hardly surprising that an author in the second century AD, Aristides, said that historians 'fall between orators and poets'. Such was the view throughout classical antiquity. But what are its implications?

Unfortunately, no work of historiographical theory has survived earlier than that of LUCIAN (*c*. AD 120–180). But CICERO deals with the subject in two key passages written in 55 BC, which are all the more valuable as they almost certainly reflect earlier Hellenistic theory. In the first of these, a letter written to a historian called Lucceius (*Letters to his Friends*, 5.12), Cicero stresses that historiography should rouse the emotions of its readers. It is often alleged that these remarks relate to a separate and rather disreputable category of historiography which has been variously labelled 'tragic', 'Peripatetic' or 'Hellenistic'; but since they are strikingly similar to other passages where Cicero offers advice on oratory (for example *On invention*, 1.27; *Divisions of oratory*, 31–2, 72–3), and since Cicero elsewhere consistently describes historiography in terms of oratory, it seems that emotional writing was a standard element in mainstream classical historiography.

The second key passage occurs in Cicero's *On the Orator* and is generally accepted as being applicable to the works of most classical historians. Having complained (2.53–4) that Roman historians had hitherto failed to elaborate (*ornare*) their hard core of facts (*monumenta*), Cicero defines historiography as an orator's task, which he describes in detail by means of a building metaphor (2.62–4). It comprises foundations (*fundamenta*) and superstructure (*exaedificatio*). The former consists of two laws (the historian should neither dare to say anything false nor be afraid to say anything true), which he explains by saying that even the suspicion of bias or prejudice should be avoided. The sequence of thought is confirmed by the letter mentioned above, in which Cicero uses precisely the same phraseology; but in any case he quickly dismisses these foundations in order to concentrate on the superstructure of historiography.

The superstructure also consists of two elements: content (*res*) and style (*verba*). Cicero devotes his attention almost exclusively to content. On style he says merely that it should be smooth and flowing; but for content he lists a number of requirements: chronological order of events, geographical descriptions, the author's views on the intentions which lay behind actions, an explanation of how events unfolded and how speeches were made, and an account both of the causes of events – whether they result from chance or some human consideration – and of the characters of individual protagonists. Now each of these items was also a standard requirement for that part of a forensic speech which was known as the *narratio* or 'statement of the case'. This is

clear from the fact that Cicero describes them in almost identical phraseology to that which he uses for the *narratio* in his other rhetorical works. It thus follows, in view of his earlier definition of historiography as an orator's task, that Cicero has simply transposed the same items from the oratorical *narratio* to historical narrative. The implications of this transposition are momentous.

An orator was expected to fulfil the requirements of the *narratio* by resorting to the familiar rhetorical process of *inventio*, by which is meant 'the devising of material true or lifelike which will make a case appear convincing' (Cicero, *On Invention*, 1.9). It follows that in Cicero's opinion the process was equally applicable to historiography: historians were expected to elaborate (*ornare*) their hard core of facts (*monumenta*) with a superstructure (*exaedificatio*) of rhetorical material (*res*). This material might derive from literature or from life. It is notable that the second-century BC historian POLYBIUS, famous for an allegedly superior type of historiography which he called 'pragmatic', seems more concerned with whether a history is 'realistic' than with whether it reflects 'what really happened': the account of a battle will be better if the historian has experienced a battle himself, but it need not be the same battle as the one he is required to describe in his history. Verisimilitude was the minimal criterion; and since verisimilitude is by definition almost indistinguishable from truth, modern readers of classical historiography are presented with narratives whose genuine historicity cannot often be determined. This way of writing history may seem astonishing, but only if we assume that everyone else's historiography, regardless of period or cultural environment, must be the same as our own.

Of course there were occasionally historians such as VELLEIUS or FLORUS who preferred small-scale works, and summary histories or *breviaria* became particularly fashionable in the fourth century AD (see EUTROPIUS, FESTUS). But classical historiography in general was an elaborate medium which, it will be clear, has rather more in common with today's historical novel than with modern works of specialist history. Certainly there is ample evidence (including statements in Thucydides, Cicero and TACITUS) that one of its principal functions was thought to be the entertainment of its readers. Of how many modern histories can the same be said? AJW

Reading

Fornara, C.W.: *The Nature of History in Ancient Greece and Rome* (Berkeley, Los Angeles, and London: University of California Press, 1983).

Herkommer, E.: *Die Topoi in den Proömien der römischen Geschichtswerke* (Topoi [Commonplaces] in the Prefaces of Roman Historians) (Diss. Tübingen: Polyfoto Stuttgart, 1968).

Jerome, T.S.: *Aspects of the Study of Roman History* (New York and London: G.P. Putnam's Sons, The Knickerbocker Press, 1923).

Momigliano, A: Greek historiography. *History & Theory* 17 (1978) 1–28.

Wiseman, T.P.: *Clio's Cosmetics: Three Studies in Greco-Roman Literature* (Leicester: Leicester University Press, 1979).

Woodman, A. J.: *Rhetoric in Classical Historiography* (London and Portland: Croom Helm and Areopagitica Press, 1988).

cliometrics A form of interdisciplinary history which emerged in the United States and Europe during the late 1950s and early 1960s. Cliometricians are primarily trained in and employed by economics departments, and most teach economic history within economics, although many of them have joint appointments with history departments. Cliometrics is primarily interested in economic history, but it has extended the boundaries of that field to its logical limits. It has dealt extensively with issues in demographic history, political and social history, family and social history. Cliometricians have recently become interested in human biology and medical history, and inter-family social relations.

Cliometrics is defined by the tools used by its practitioners rather than by the subject material or the methodology. The tools fall into two broad categories: quantitative methods and explicit theory. A cliometrician is a historian who uses at least one of these in his research.

The quantitative tools which cliometricians have used come primarily from econometrics and social science statistical methods. More recently, advanced methods in statistical demography have also become increasingly popular. The use of statistical techniques serves two purposes. First, it allows the manipulation of large sets of often highly deficient and inaccurate data, generating new quantitative historical information. Second, it allows the investigator to carry out rigorous statistical hypothesis testing. This means in effect that the cliometrician, when searching for causal sequences in history, can distinguish between the possible and the probable. While cliometricians cannot be sure about logical relations between historical events any more than other historians, he can sometimes set some limit on the chances of being wrong.

By using explicit theory cliometricians have been able to approach many historical issues anew. Much of the theory has been modern, neo-classical economic theory which deals with the allocation of resources by markets or by market-type mechanisms. Within standard economics cliometricians have used almost any type of theory: price theory, international trade, partial and general equilibrium, monetary and macroeconomics, growth theory, game theory, portfolio theory and financial economics. Some cliometricians, however, have wandered beyond the standard fares of economics departments, using Ricardian and Marxian dynamic models, models of institutional change, social choice theory and political economy among others. Some of these models involve a fair amount of (usually simple) mathematics, but it is incorrect to view the use of mathematics *per se* as the characteristic feature of cliometrics.

The subject matter of cliometrics has spanned large segments of economic history, primarily the economic history of North America and Europe. Cliometricians have been involved in many lively debates with more traditional historians and often even more lively debates with each other. Among the issues debated are the causes and consequences of the American Revolution, the economics of American slavery, the divergence between the North and South before and after the Civil War, the economics of American industrialization, business cycles in the US economy including the Great Depression, changes in the distribution of income, the impact of changes in transportation, and many others. In European economic history, most research has been done on the British isles where cliometricians have done much work on the economics of the Industrial Revolution and the subsequent decline in the British economy, changes in British agriculture, the impact of Britain on the international economy, the demographic revolution and others. In the past decade, cliometricians have also began making inroads in the economic history of other European economies, particularly those of France, West Germany, the Low Countries, Spain and Italy. Some work on Russia and Japan also falls within the realm of cliometrics. The issues here have been above all comparative economic performance and the interaction between political changes and economic changes.

Cliometricians in North America meet once a year at the annual Cliometrics Conference, funded by the National Science Foundation. Similar conferences on a smaller scale are held in Canada and Britain. The first International Cliometrics Conference met in May 1985 in Evanston, Illinois. Papers are also presented at the annual meetings of the Economic History Association the American Economic Association, and the Social Science History Association. Cliometricians publish in many different journals, though the cliometrics journal *par excellence* is *Explorations in Economic History*. JM

Reading

(Textbooks and readings incl. cliometrics.)

Floud, R. and McCloskey, D.N. eds: *The Economic History of Britain since 1700* (Cambridge: Cambridge University Press, 1981).

Hughes, J.R.T.: *American Economic History* (Glenview, Ill.: Scott-Foreman, 1986).

Lee, S.P and Passell, P.: *A New Economic View of American History* (New York: Norton, 1979).

Mokyr, J. ed.: *The Economics of the Industrial Revolution* (Totowa, NJ: Rowman & Allanheld, 1985).

(Methodology and achievements of cliometrics.)

Fogel, R.W.: Scientific history and traditonal history. In *Which Road to the Past?* ed. R.W. Fogel and G. R. Elton (New Haven, Conn: Yale University Press, 1983).

McCloskey, D.N.: Does the past have a useful economics?: *Journal of Economic Literature* 14.2 (1976) 432–61.

Cobb, Richard Charles (b.1917) Education at Shrewsbury School and Merton College, Oxford left Cobb with a fierce dislike of all forms of authority and regimentation. After service in the second world war he lived for several years in Paris before returning to England to teach at the universities of Aberystwyth, Leeds and finally Oxford, where he ended his career as a professor. Cobb is the Ancient Mariner of British historians: he waylays the wedding guests on their way to a jolly seminar on social control, and grips them with his strange and timeless tales of love and violence, life and death – usually death. Writing history is as compulsive for him as reading what he writes is for others. It is essentially a matter of reassurance, a word that recurs continually throughout his work. He finds in the annals of the poor, in periods of great cruelty and violence, the confirmation that tenderness, regard for others and civilized values can survive against all the odds.

Cobb has produced only one piece of sustained historical writing, his monumental *Armées Révolutionnaires*, which quite typically dismissed its subject as of no great importance and went on to present a masterly account of what the Terror was actually like to those who implemented it or had it inflicted upon them. His many other books, even the acute *Police and the People*, are mostly collections of essays. These have evolved with time from celebrating the limitations of all government, even the ferocious dictatorship of the Committee of Public Safety, to more general studies of resistance to the dehumanizing influences of poverty and political fanaticism, most strikingly exemplified in his *Death in Paris*. His concern is with people, less as individuals than as figures in a landscape, shaped by their environment and their reactions to it. Despite his formidable historical erudition, his approach is that of the novelist or Impressionist painter, communicating, always with compassion and a total absence of solemnity, what history did to ordinary people and how they managed to survive it. NH

COBBAN, ALFRED

Main publications

(Published by Oxford University Press, Oxford, unless otherwise stated.)
Les Armées Révolutionnaires (Paris: Mouton, 1961–3); *The Police and the People* (1970); *Reactions to the French Revolution* (1972); *Paris and its Provinces* (1975); *Death in Paris* (1978); *French and Germans, Germans and French* (Hanover, NH: University Press of New England, 1983).

Reading

Cobb, R.C.: *Still Life* (London: Chatto & Windus, 1983) [an autobiography].

Cobban, Alfred (b.1901, d.1968) Born and educated in London, Cobban was for seven years scholar and then research student at Gonville and Caius College, Cambridge, before appointment to a lectureship at the University College in Newcastle upon Tyne in 1926. In 1937 he returned to London as reader in French history at University College, where he spent the rest of his career apart from visiting professorships at Chicago (1947) and Harvard (1959). In 1953 he became professor of French history.

He wrote prolifically, and although nobody did more by his writings to introduce English-speaking contemporaries to French history and its problems, his first books were about political theory. *Edmund Burke and the Revolt against the Eighteenth Century* (1929) and *Rousseau and the Modern State* (1934) are still read as convenient and sensible introductions to their subjects. With the onset of the second world war Cobban turned to contemporary problems such as dictatorship and national self-determination, revealing a robust, left of centre, but above all libertarian outlook. A valuable anthology of *The Debate on the French Revolution* in British public life followed in 1950, while *Ambassadors and Secret Agents* (1954) was a detailed study of British diplomacy in the Netherlands in the 1780s. Between 1957 and 1965 he produced a three-volume paperback *History of Modern France* which still sells extremely well; and in 1960 he reverted to earlier interests with *In Search of Humanity: the Role of the Enlightenment in Modern History.* Throughout his career he also wrote frequent learned articles, and between 1956 and 1967 was editor of *History.*

Ironically, Cobban's own forays into French archives were limited. He was chiefly effective as a critic of received historical ideas, and his inaugural lecture of 1954, 'The myth of the French Revolution', started a controversy that was still raging at his death and eventually led to comprehensive scholarly reappraisal of the Revolution and its significance. The myth he attacked was the Marxist picture of the Revolution as the overthrow of feudalism by the capitalist bourgeoisie. By analysing the membership of the governing assemblies, he showed that the bourgeois revolutionaries were not capitalists, but mainly lawyers and office holders. In the Wiles lectures in Belfast in 1962, published as *The Social Interpretation of the French Revolution*, he argued (like TREVOR-ROPER in the 'gentry' controversy) that the men of 1789 were a declining, not a rising group, forced to destroy what was called feudalism against their will, under peasant pressure. The Revolution was also a clash of country against town, and poor against rich, and in the end proved economically retarding and a triumph for the conservative, landowning classes. Ignored or denounced initially in France, these ideas provoked widespread discussion in the English-speaking world by the 1970s, and the validity of Cobban's criticisms was broadly accepted. Eventually the French were also forced to take notice, and *The Social Interpretation* was translated. But few of Cobban's more positive suggestions have stood the test of time. Though anti-Marxist, he still believed in a social interpretation, scorning the view that the Enlightenment was a major cause of the Revolution. Increasing numbers of scholars, however, have followed the lead of G. V. TAYLOR and abandoned the social approach. Cobban's views on the pre-revolutionary nobility and their politics have also been superseded; but as the animator of an immensely fruitful historical debate his reputation is secure.   WD

Main publications

A History of Modern France, 3 vols (Harmondsworth: Penguin, 1957–65); *The Social Interpretation of the French Revolution* (Cambridge: Cambridge University, Press, 1964); *Aspects of the French Revolution* (London: Cape, 1968) [collected papers, including 'The myth of the French Revolution'].

Reading

Bosher, J. F. ed.: *French Government and Society 1500–1850: Essays in Memory of Alfred Cobban* (London: Athlone, 1973).

Doyle, W.: *Origins of the French Revolution* (Oxford: Oxford University Press, 1980).

Cole, George Douglas Howard (b.1989, d.1959)   Educated at St Paul's School and Balliol College, Oxford, where in his first term he founded the *Oxford Socialist*, Cole remained a committed socialist all his life. He was greatly influenced in his younger days by the guild socialist movement; worked for the labour research department during the first world war; and began his academic career at Oxford University in 1925. He became Chichele professor of social and political theory in 1944, and retired in 1957.

Cole wrote voluminously on a wide range of contemporary issues, often in collaboration with his wife Margaret (née Postgate). Cole's historical writings were mostly concerned with the British labour movement and before 1939 he was one of the very few academics who worked in this field. He wrote always for the educated lay public especially for those in the Workers' Educational Association, and never for his fellow historians. His writing was lucid and fluent, and he was largely unconcerned with interpretation except that which followed from his radical point of view. He did pioneering work in labour history, and while little of his historical writing is likely to survive, in his day he was a considerable educator of liberal and socialist opinion. The text which has probably been most influential, in terms of size of readership, is the volume he wrote jointly with Raymond Postgate, *The Common People*.   JS

Main publications

The World of Labour (London: Bell, 1913); *Short History of the British Working Class Movement*, 3 vols (London: Allen & Unwin, 1925–7; many later edns); *Chartist Portraits* (London: Macmillan, 1941); *History of Socialist Thought*, 5 vols (London: Macmillan, 1953–60).

Reading

Briggs, A. and Saville, J. eds: Recollections. In *Essays in Labour History* (London: Macmillan, 1960).

Wright A.W.; *G.D.H. Cole and Social Democracy* (Oxford: Clarendon Press, 1979).

Collingwood, Robin George (b.1889, d.1943)   Born at Coniston in Lancashire, the son of W. G. Collingwood, a talented archaeological artist and illustrator, the friend, secretary and biographer of Ruskin, R. G. Collingwood was educated at Rugby and University College, Oxford. He graduated in 1912 with first class honours in classical moderations and Litt. Hum., and was at once elected to a tutorial fellowship at Pembroke College where he taught both philosophy and ancient history until his appointment to the Wayneflete professorship of metaphysical philosophy in 1934 with a fellowship at Magdalen College. He retired in 1941. He became a fellow of both the British Academy and the Society of Antiquaries, the latter in recognition of his preeminence in Romano-British studies after the death of F. J. Haverfield who had pioneered the subject in its modern form.

In his prime, Collingwood was a first-rate lecturer and tutor in both philosophy and ancient history. His clear-cut, precise and meticulous presentation of topics in either subject, however complex, reflected, as did all his writing, the clarity, speed and eloquence of an exceptionally gifted and well-organized mind. These qualities appeared at their most creative and effective in furthering Romano-British studies, especially in his promotion and organization of the project, still unfinished in his lifetime, for a complete Corpus of Roman inscriptions in Britain (RIB), in preparing the illustrations for which his beautiful draughtsmanship found full scope. But Collingwood himself regarded all his historical and archaeological work as ancillary to the development of his philosophical thought: 'the right way of investigating mind', he wrote, 'is by the methods of history.' His continuously evolving views on the relationship of history and philosophy are best studied in the posthumously published assemblage of his lectures and papers edited by T. M. Knox as *The Idea of History* (1946).

This is not the place to attempt an evaluation of Collingwood's controversial status as a professional philosopher, but it must be recognized that his aims and methods of study and exposition as a historian and archaeologist were profoundly affected by the continuous stream of his philosophical thought. Philosophers moreover, whether agreeing with his views or not, have recognized the impact of his historical thinking on their own discipline: one of them has written, for example, 'after his books English philosophers will be able to continue ignoring history only by burying their heads in the sand'.

Collingwood's philosophical thinking led him to strong, and sometimes severe, though not always consistent, views on the nature of historical evidence. He could maintain that 'genuine history has no room for the ... probable ... or the possible ... all it permits the historian to assert is what the evidence obliges him to assert', a point of view not very far from that of those whom he elsewhere derides as mere 'scissors-and-paste' historians. Nor in his own historical writing did he always prevent his agile and questing mind from pursuing far beyond the bounds of proof, or even of probability, ideas on the course of historical events that appealed to his powerful imagination. The classic instance of this weakness is the Arthurian fantasy with which, in spite of earnest warnings from his best friends, he insisted on concluding *Roman Britain*, the first volume of the Oxford History of England series. Such a romantic *jeu d'esprit*, appropriate enough for an airing in a periodical article, has led many astray and caused endless confusion from its appearance in the magisterial context of the Oxford History. As Collingwood himself wrote elsewhere, 'the attempt to know what we have no means of knowing is an infallible way to generate illusions'.

As already noted Collingwood took a major part in amplifying and systematizing existing knowledge of Roman Britain, especially of Hadrian's Wall and the military areas of the north familiar to him from childhood. Here his use of small-scale excavation to settle specific points of structure or dating is reminiscent of the philosopher's method of advancing knowledge by question and answer, as in Plato's dialogues. But it could be much less rewarding when attempted on large-scale

excavations. As Collingwood soon found, large sites are not only often reluctant to answer pre-arranged questions: they are much more likely to throw up new questions on matters that were not expected to arise. Several of Collingwood's digs on Roman forts in the north were unsatisfactory not only because they failed to answer the questions he was asking, but because he did not fully exploit the answers which they were prepared to provide to questions which he had not asked.

Collingwood's last years were saddened by mental exhaustion and a breakdown in physical health. He knew that he had too little time to complete the projects that his tireless mental energy continued to conceive. After 1939 he turned away from purely historical subjects towards political philosophy, his thoughts increasingly dominated by the war and its possible consequences for the democratic way of western life. His last major work, *The New Leviathan* (1942), an extraordinary performance for one in his condition, appeared in the year before his death, and not without signs of his declining powers. JNLM

Main publications

(All published by Clarendon Press, Oxford.)
Roman Britain. Vol. 1, *Oxford History of England* (1936); *An Autobiography* (1939); *The New Leviathan* (1942); *The Idea of History* ed. T. M. Knox (1946); *Proceedings of the British Academy* 19 (1944) 462–85 [incl. full bibliography].

Reading

Knox, T. M.: Introduction to *The Idea of History* (see above).
Richmond, I. A.: *Antiquaries Journal* 23 (1943) 84–5.

Commynes, Philippe de (b.1447, d.1511) French diplomat and memorialist. Born at Renescure in Flanders of a noble family that had long served the counts, and orphaned at six, Commynes received a traditional upbringing for a cadet, and entered the household of Charles of Charolais, heir to Burgundy (1464). He fought at Montlhéry (1465) during the War of the Public Weal. After further armed service against Dinant and Liège, he was appointed chamberlain and councillor and helped to negotiate peace with Louis XI at

Péronne (1468). Thereafter he played an increasing role in diplomatic affairs. But personal differences as well as dissent over Charles's brutal burnt-earth policy led Commynes to desert to Louis XI, whose pensioner he had already become (1472). He was loaded with further favours – lands, titles and marriage to a wealthy heiress, Hélène de Chambes – to compensate for his lost patrimony. Fully informed about all matters Burgundian, from 1472 to 1477 Commynes was a close confidant in Louis's struggle with Charles. But after the latter's death disputes arose over reconquering Burgundy, which led to temporary disgrace. Sent to assure Lorenzo de' Medici of French support following the Pazzi conspiracy (1478), Commynes subsequently became an expert on Italian affairs. But he did not now enjoy the king's confidence as on his first arrival in France, though he was present at Louis's deathbed (1483). Alienated by the regents of Charles VIII, he joined the rebel Duke of Orléans and was eventually arrested (January 1487). He spent six months in an iron cage at Loches and eighteen in prison at Paris before banishment to his estates, a sentence lifted finally in December 1489. It was then that he first began to compile the *Mémoires*, on which his reputation as a historian depends. With the Italian wars he returned to favour, representing France at Venice (1494–5). But outmanoeuvred by rival ambassadors he rejoined Charles VIII and fought bravely at Fornovo. Sent back to Venice, he finally returned home empty-handed (December 1495). Consulted occasionally, he ceased to have any real influence, even when Orléans succeeded as Louis XII, though Commynes accompanied him to Milan again in 1507. A touchy and mercenary man, his last years were spent in acrimonious disputes, regulating family affairs.

No autograph manuscript of the *Mémoires* survives, nor any that can be dated to the author's lifetime. Ostensibly started to provide materials for a history of Louis XI which Angelo Cato, archbishop of Vienne, intended to write, and occupying Commynes in a period of disgrace, it is clear that they were composed with a wider audience (especially of rulers and their advisers) in mind. They are divided into eight books: I–VI cover Louis's reign and were written in 1489–90 (I–V) and 1492–3 (VI) and published in 1524; VII and VIII date from 1495–8, deal with Charles VIII and Italy, and were published in 1528. The first full edition appeared in 1552. Since then the *Mémoires* have been universally recognized as marking, after the chivalric form popularized by FROISSART, a new departure in political history, together with the work of MACHIAVELLI. Essentially narrative, they provide shrewd analysis and reflections on the role and motives of the politicians of Commynes' day in a refreshingly direct style, displaying realism and psychological insight. Commynes thereby gained a reputation as an acute, honest, impartial and deeply informed writer. This survived until modern reassessment (especially by Jean Dufournet) suggested a radically different interpretation. As a result it is now recognized that the *Mémoires*, far from being the dispassionate account of a respected elder statesman, are deliberately conceived, highly selective in their treatment of events, and nuanced, even vindictive, in their judgements, hence essentially the embittered reflections of a talented but disappointed and unsuccessful man. In its most developed form this hypercritical thesis has not won complete acceptance, but a fuller appreciation of the circumstances and intentions of the author has emerged which must be reflected now in any reading of the *Mémoires*, for so long a major guide to late medieval French (indeed western European) history. MCEJ

Main writings

Mémoires, ed. B. de Mandrot, 2 vols (Paris: Société de l'histoire de France, 1901–3); ed. J. Calmette and G. Durville, 3 vols (Paris, Les Belles Lettres, 1924–5); *The Memoirs of Philippe de Commynes*, ed. and trans. S. Kinser and I. Cazeaux, 2 vols (Columbia: South Carolina University Press, 1969–73); *Memoirs: The Reign of Louis XI, 1461–1483*, trans. Michael Jones (Harmondsworth: Penguin, 1972).

Reading

Bittmann, K.: *Ludwig XI, und Karl der Kühne: die Memorien des Philippe de Commynes als historische Quelle, 3 vols* (Göttingen: Vandenhoeck & Rupprecht, 1964–70).

Dufournet, J.: *La destruction des mythes dans les*

Mémoires de Philippe de Commynes (Geneva: Droz, 1966).

Liniger, J: *Philippe de Commynes: un Machiavel en douceur* (Paris: Perrin, 1978).

Comte, Isidore Auguste Marie François Xavier (b.1798, d.1857) A precocious rebel from a royalist family in Montpellier, Comte attended the École Polytechnique before becoming secretary to Henri Saint-Simon, against whom after seven years his independent genius revolted. Systematically ordering the sciences, then embracing an authoritarian religiosity, he proclaimed himself high priest of humanity, proselytizing princes and meeting humbler members of his Positivist Society. He lectured to both scholars and workmen, and elaborated in multi-volumed treatises a philosophy of history and prospectus for mankind that ranks with the greatest attempts to decipher the universe and construct utopia.

Founder of POSITIVISM, perhaps also of systematic sociology and the history of science, Comte announced three stages in the development of mind (he believed he had directly experienced them) and their corresponding historical epochs: the theological-military (ancient), the metaphysical-legalistic (medieval) and the final positive, scientific-industrial. Although crises occurred in the transitional periods (for example, the French Revolution), a morally and materially superior outcome was certain in a utopia where women, though dependent on men, would guarantee the loving, harmonious nature of a world free of hard labour and want, in unity with the Great Being of transcendent humanity. An original, authoritarian, Eurocentric prophecy and interpretation of history, induced by the conjunction of the Enlightenment, political upheaval in the west and the awakening of historical consciousness, Comte's brilliant analysis did not appeal to workaday historians. Ill-founded, if not wholly imaginary, his work testified to a titanic ambition in his generation to show unity where most historians saw diversity, and scientifically to demonstrate the laws of collective progress.

Mathematician and École polytechnique examiner, frequently ill, suffering breakdown in 1826, perpetually soliciting funds from the benefactors he had a gift for alienating, the monomaniacal Comte drove out his own long-suffering wife and, after her death, worshipped another's as his 'virgin mother'. Unstable, isolated and ridiculed, ever optimistic, he died in 1857 in his celebrated rooms at 10 rue Monsieur-le-Prince. He remains a commanding presence at the crossroads of history and sociology. JCC

Main publications

Cours de philosophie positive, 6 vols (Paris, 1830–42) (English trans., London: John Chapman, 1853); *Système de politique positive ou Traité de sociologie instituant la religion de l'humanité*, 4 vols (Paris, 1851–4) (English trans., London: Longmans, Green, 1875–7); *Cathéchisme positiviste, ou Sommaire exposition de la religion universelle en onze entretiens systematiques entre une femme et un prêtre de l'humanité* (Paris, 1852) (English trans., London: John Chapman, 1858).

Reading

Manuel, Frank E.: *The Prophets of Paris* (Cambridge, Mass: Harvard University Press, 1962), pp. 249–96.

Simon, W. M.: *European Positivism in the Nineteenth Century: an essay in intellectual history* (Ithaca, N. Y.: Cornell University Press, 1963).

Condorcet, Jean Antoine Nicolas de Caritat, Marquis de (b.1743, d.1794) Mathematician and polymath, Condorcet was one of the few *philosophes* of the Englightenment to live to see the French Revolution. Although a nobleman of old stock, he embraced the Revolution with enthusiasm and threw himself into its politics from the outset. Elected to the Convention in 1792, he escaped the purge in June 1793 of the Girondins with whom he was identified, but went into hiding soon afterwards and was outlawed in March 1794. He died in captivity later that month, reputedly by his own hand. Whilst in hiding he wrote his only work of history, *Esquisse d'un tableau historique des progrès de l'esprit humain* (1795). It was the last great statement of Enlightenment optimism about the progressive evolution of human history. His faith in the improvement of humanity undimmed by the strife and bloodshed of the French Revolution, Condorcet looked forward, on the evidence of the past, to a steady and inexorable improvement in the human condition as the management of affairs became more rational and scientific. These perspectives did much to inspire the positivist thinking of Saint-Simon and COMTE in the next century.   WD

Main publications

Esquisse d'un tableau historique des progrès de l'esprit humain, ed. M. and F. Hincker (Paris: 1966).

Reading

Baker, K. M.: *Condorcet: from Natural Philosophy to Social Mathematics* (Chicago: Chicago University Press, 1975).

constitutional history, British The systematic study of 'the British constitution' from a historical viewpoint might be said to have derived from the politics of the seventeenth century and the academic needs of the nineteenth. Certainly the struggles between the king and various parliamentarians led a number of lawyers, such as Sir Edward Coke, to a more systematic study of what were claimed to be the fundamental documents of the English constitution, in an attempt to find justification for opposition to the claims by the crown. Those seeking to limit the king's prerogative found their hope in antiquarian studies. The problems of the Civil War, of the years of the later Stuarts and the Glorious Revolution, even those of various political conflicts of the eighteenth and early nineteenth centuries, continued the process whereby appeals were made to some historical process under which the structure and theory of government could be related to known historical events rather than to general philosophy. Thus, an appeal to 'known' history could be made to seem more appropriate (and more relevant) to contemporary political controversy than an appeal to abstract constitutional theory or 'constitutionalism'.

The seventeenth century saw the study of the historical development of the constitution as part of a political struggle; many works fall into a category of political polemic rather than of historical analysis. Many dealt with ways in which the 'constitution' or the 'state' might originally have been established: others concerned relations between king and parliament and above all their respective powers. Even the

eighteenth century saw a continuation of many such disputes. Lawyers such as Blackstone, political theorists such as HUME, and politicians such as BOLINGBROKE, all played a prominent part in analysing the theory and practice of the state; while foreigners, such as De Lolme and MONTESQUIEU, were anxious to discover the underlying principles of the English state in order to comment on the weaknesses of their own. Political controversy at the end of the century as well as growing pressure for parliamentary reform once again caused attention to be drawn to the alleged 'roots' of the constitution, those most eager for change being the most vociferous in their claims that the original constitution had been perverted by malpractice in succeeding generations. Thus Oldfield, a radical, was anxious to analyse the structure of constituencies in order to prove the need for their reform.

The rise of 'professional historians' in the middle of the nineteenth century saw the removal of constitutional history from the usually polemical into a largely academic study. Growing differences of opinion about the relative desirability of records as distinct from chronicles which made themselves manifest in the attitudes of FREEMAN and ROUND, as well as the desire to find Anglo-Saxon origins for many of England's institutions, led to an increasing interest in discovering documents from which these institutions could be said to have originated. STUBBS was probably the founder − certainly he was its clearest expounder − of this branch of history, and in the introduction to his *Select Charters* as well as in the span of documents which he included there ('from the earliest times to the reign of Edward I') he made its scope most obvious: 'essentially a tracing of causes and consequence; the examination of a distinct growth from a well-defined germ to full maturity ... It is of the greatest importance that this study should become a recognised part of a regular English education.'

It was as a result of the success of Stubbs's *Charters* that it became practicable to envisage parallel collections of documents, claiming to throw light upon the 'constitutional conflicts' of the Tudors or of the seventeenth century, or purporting to illustrate the development of the constitution from its 'origins' up to most recent times. The popularity of various collections of documents edited by GARDINER, PROTHERO, or Tanner reflected at once the interest being displayed in those respective periods of history and the feeling that the subject could only be 'academically respectable' if accompanied by the detailed study of a collection of documents. The growth of large numbers of such collections too often reflected the idiosyncracies of individual teachers.

The institution most usually chosen for detailed study was parliament and the aspect most often examined was the growth of 'parliamentary government'. But as the 'modern state' began to develop in the twentieth century this aspect of constitutional history began itself to be replaced by the study of individual institutions of the state, and to emerge as administrative history, whose principal exponent was T. F. TOUT. He would be for twentieth-century historiography what Stubbs had been earlier. The growth of administrative history, combining as it did the study of individual institutions with the individuals who were responsible for it, was in its turn to have an impact upon the older branch of study, so that in their various ways such persons as B. Wilkinson, with his *Constitutional History of England, 1216–1399*, or L. B. NAMIER equally reflect these newer ideas. It was to be particularly striking that the decision to launch an 'official' *History of Parliament* (really a biographical dictionary of the House of Commons) should have had its origins in a select committee of the House of Commons chaired by one of the last of the radicals, Colonel Josiah Wedgwood, and advised by such modernists as J. E. NEALE and L. B. Namier. Equally striking was that in studying such institutions, and by inference in studying constitutional history itself, there developed an emphasis on looking at the events accompanying changes in them rather than in concentrating narrowly on institutions themselves.

Modern historical studies have tended to be less interested in such comparatively narrow concepts which would differentiate between 'constitutional' history and the political or economic and social changes which often lie behind it. Many works claiming to be constitutional history in practice cover a much wider spectrum.

AN

Reading

In addition to the histories of the constitution and collections of documents cited in the text, see also:

Burrow, J. W.: *Liberal Descent: Victorian Historians and the English Past* (Cambridge: Cambridge University Press, 1981).

Elton, G. E.: *Practice of History* (London: Fontana, 1987).

Kenyon, J.: *The History Men* (London: Weidenfeld & Nicolson, 1983).

Plumb, J. H. ed.: *Crisis in the Humanities* (Harmondsworth: Pelican, 1964).

Coulton, George Gordon (b.1858, d.1947) A very individual, enthusiastic and controversial medievalist, Coulton only got an *aegrotat* at Cambridge, and had to earn his living as a schoolteacher and crammer. He used all his available leisure to produce *From St. Francis to Dante* (1906) (which introduced the English to Salimbene) and *Chaucer and his England* (1908). Appointed Birkbeck lecturer for a year in 1910 he moved to Cambridge and set up, in the manner of a medieval schoolman, as a free-lance lecturer and coach. In 1919, aged 61, he was elected the university's lecturer in English and a fellow of St John's College. He then produced a whole string of books of which the most remarkable were *Five Centuries of Religion* (1923–50) and *Art and the Reformation* (1928). He was extremely widely read in the sources of medieval history and had a great knowledge of medieval art and architecture, especially in its byways. (His valuable collection of medieval masons' marks is now at the *Centre international de recherches cryptographiques* at Braine-le-Château, Belgium.) A passionate anti-Catholic, he expended much energy in denouncing the errors of Cardinal Gasquet. He was also a persistent advocate of military conscription. These controversies made him seem extremely severe, but his friends (of whom I was proud to be one) found that even on these matters he could be very tolerant.

RHCD

Main publications

From St. Francis to Dante (London: David Nutt, 1906); *Chaucer and his England* (1908); *Five Cen-*

turies of Religion, 4 vols (Cambridge University Press, 1923–50); *Art and the Reformation* (Oxford: Blackwell, 1928).

Reading

Coulton, G. G.: *Fourscore Years, an Autobiography* (Cambridge: Cambridge University Press, 1944).

Campian, S.: *Father* (London: Michael Joseph, 1948).

Creighton, Mandell (b.1843, d.1901) Born in Carlisle, Creighton was educated at Durham Grammar School and Merton College, Oxford, where he took a first in Greats and was elected fellow in 1866. In 1868 he was appointed tutor and began a short but influential career as a teacher of history. In 1870 however he was ordained and five years later left Oxford for a remote rural living in the parish of Embleton, Northumberland. He returned to academic life in 1884 when elected to the newly established Dixie chair of ecclesiastical history at Cambridge. In that capacity he became the first editor of the *English Historical Review* in 1886, but resigned both posts in 1891 on his translation to the see of Peterborough. He became Bishop of London in 1897 and died four years later.

When reading Creighton's *Life and Letters* one is struck by the immense force of his character. His energy was such that no single career could offer adequate fulfilment. As a churchman he wrote history and involved himself in educational questions; as a historian he continued to preach and to take an active part in church affairs. But Creighton was never seriously torn between the spiritual and the temporal life. The qualities that raised him to episcopal rank and made him among the most respected and influential churchmen of his day were those that determined the direction and tendency of his historical writing. Creighton was drawn to pastoral work for two reasons. First, he had a deep, abiding concern for people. He was interested in them as individuals. Second, he was a man of affairs. He liked to get things done. But progress in the world of affairs, he believed, lay through an understanding of people. Character was the most potent of all social forces. The motives and actions of men were the moving causes of great events. It was in this manner that he interpreted history. 'My view of history', he said to R. L. Poole in 1887, 'is not to approach things with any preconceived ideas, but with all the natural *pietas* and sympathy which I try to feel towards all men who do and try to do great things. *Mentem mortalia tangunt* is my motto. I try to put myself in their place: to see their limitations, and leave the course of events to pronounce the verdict upon systems and men alike.'

These views are expressed in all of Creighton's historical writings but emerge most clearly in his major work of scholarship, *A History of the Papacy During the Period of the Reformation*, published in five weighty volumes between 1882 and 1894. The book examines the role of the papacy in European affairs from the Great Schism to the Council of Trent. Compiled from printed sources and transcripts the work is written in a clear, if dull style with a high level of portraiture. In its marked concentration on diplomatic relations and the secrets of the council chamber it tends more to uncritical narrative than to reflection and explanation, but it is most conspicuous for its impartiality. This dismayed Lord Acton who remarked bitterly that Creighton 'is not striving to prove a case or burrowing towards a conclusion, but wishes to pass through scenes of raging controversy and passion with serene curiosity, a suspended judgement, a divided jury and a pair of white gloves.' The charge is just. But Creighton's insistence that history was not a 'moral science' and that its aim was 'to give off light without heat' is his greatest contribution to the growth of historical scholarship in Britain.   PRHS

Main publications

A History of the Papacy During the Period of the Reformation, 5 vols (London: Longmans, Green, 1882–94).

Reading

Chadwick, Owen: *Creighton on Luther: an Inaugural Lecture delivered in the University of Cambridge on 3 November 1958* (Cambridge: Cambridge University Press, 1959).

Creighton, L.: *Life and Letters of Mandell Creighton*, 2 vols (London: Longmans, Green, 1904).

Croce, Benedetto (b.1866, d.1952) Born in the Abruzzi, Croce came from a well-to-do family of conservative landowners. Following the death of his parents in an earthquake in 1883 he went to live with his cousin, the statesman and philosopher of the 'Historical Right', Silvio Spaventa. Croce was much influenced by his guardian's circle, and later developed in a comprehensive way the ideas of the Neapolitan Hegelian tradition to which he belonged.

Croce's prodigious literary output exerted a powerful influence over Italian culture for the next 50 years. His works included the four-volume *Philosophy of Spirit* (1902–15), intended as a secular religion encompassing all aspects of human life under the four headings of the Beautiful (the *Aesthetic*, 1902), the True (the *Logic*, 2nd edn, 1909), the Good and, Croce's addition to the classical triad, the Useful (the *Philosophy of Practice*, 1909). History, however, was at the centre of his philosophy, since these four concepts lacked any determinate content beyond that supplied by Spirit's dialectical development through human activity in history (the *Theory and History of Historiography*, 1915). He illustrated this thesis in innumerable historical works, ranging from a multi-volume study of Italian literature since unification to books on his two philosophical mentors, Vico and Hegel, a history of nineteenth-century Italian historiography and his four major histories, examined below. These all first appeared in instalments, together with numerous other essays and reviews, in his periodical *La Critica*. A conservative liberal, he was minister of education under Giolitti in 1921–2. Despite initial support for Mussolini, he became a prominent opponent of fascism, portraying his philosophy as a 'religion of liberty' (*History as the Story of Liberty*, 1938). After the war he was briefly a minister in 1944 and president of the ill-fated Liberal party.

Croce first turned to historical writing as a relief from the tragic loss of his family, burying himself in the Neapolitan archives. This period culminated in his study of the Naples revolution of 1799, still the best available, and his massive history of the Neapolitan theatre between 1500 and 1870. Although he later wrote that this last work gave him his fill of erudition and drove him to philosophy, he frequently returned to this area of research, publishing three further volumes of essays. All these studies sought to show the diverse ways human creativity, in art, philosophy and political activity broadly conceived, endowed human existence with meaning.

Croce argued in his later philosophical works that all history is 'contemporary history', that we could only understand past acts by imaginatively re-enacting them in order to recover the intentions and meaning they had for the persons concerned. History which lacked this understanding was 'chronicle'. The historian was not called upon to criticize the past, 'historical judgement' entailed simply recording the role played by individuals in determinate circumstances and leaving moral appraisal to the turn of events. This argument seemed to countenance passive acquiescence and the belief that might is right, and indeed Croce had an almost religious faith in the ultimate benevolence of history, an attitude forcefully expressed during the first world war. However, fascism led him to revise this thesis by stressing the distinction between ethical actions, which aim to increase the liberty of human action through the transformation of nature and society, and economic actions, which have largely a utilitarian character.

His four 'ethico-political' histories served to illustrate this theme in various ways. The *History of the Kingdom of Naples* (1924) attacked the notion, common to contemporary positivist historians, that the backwardness of the south was determined by the enervating effects of its climate and poor agriculture. Croce praised the Enlightenment and Risorgimento liberals for striving to overcome these difficuties. *The History of the Baroque Era in Italy* (1925), in many respects a thinly disguised critique of the fascist regime, counterposed the stultifying effects of the Counter-Reformation to the spirit of the Renaissance — a drama epitomized by Galileo's clash with the church. The *History of Italy 1871–1915* (1927), the most controversial of his works, challenged the thesis that fascism had simply 'revealed' the inadequacies of the liberal era. Finally his *History of Europe in the Nineteenth Century* (1932) attempted to re-examine the cultural and political values of the period of bourgeois ascendancy and in modified form to argue for their continued validity in spite of the catastrophe of the first world war.

Croce's historical writing inspired a large following in Italy, although perhaps only his British follower R. G. COLLINGWOOD could emulate his command of both philosophy and history. Though few could accept his metaphysics or ideals today, his ideas remain of interest to both historians and philosophers.   RPB

Main publications

The *Opere Complete* 67 vols (Bari: Laterza, last edn 1965); *Filosofia—Poesia—Storia* [selection by Croce] (Milan and Naples: Riccardi 1951), trans. Cecil Sprigge as *Philosophy, Poetry, History* (Oxford: Oxford University Press, 1966); *Autobiography* (1915), trans. R. G. Collingwood (Oxford University Press, 1927).

Reading

Bellamy, R. P.: *Modern Italian Social Theory* (Cambridge: Polity, 1987), pp. 72–99.
Collingwood, R. G.: Croce's philosophy of history. *Hibbert Journal* 19 (1921) 263–78.

Cunningham, William (b.1849, d.1919) More by accident than design, Cunningham became one of the earliest teachers of economic history in Britain and author of a pioneer textbook on the subject. He is remembered as much nowadays for his clash with the distinguished economist, Alfred Marshall, over the nature of the subject as for his own contribution to it.

Born into a devout, middle-class family in Edinburgh, where his father was a lawyer, he was educated at home, school and, from 1865, at the university there. He went on to Cambridge at the age of 19 to read moral sciences. In 1872 he, and his friend F. W. MAITLAND, became scholars of Trinity College and, later that year, the two were bracketed top of the list in the tripos examination. He was ordained priest in 1874 and much of his subsequent life was devoted to his calling as Anglican clergyman. His various writings were concerned with religion, philosophy and politics, but until 1882 not with history. Having failed to gain a

teaching post at Cambridge he became, from 1874, organizer of Cambridge University extension courses in the north-west, based in Liverpool, returning to Cambridge four years later as assistant to the organizer of the Local Lectures Syndicate. He stood in on occasion for the Knightsbridge professor of moral philosophy in 1879, and then volunteered to teach for the paper on political economy and economic history in the recently established history tripos, for (to quote his daughter's biography) 'there was no one else in residence who professed to teach with a view to this paper ... It seemed he drifted from force of circumstances into spending much of his life on a subject which did not specially attract him'. He nevertheless threw himself into the new field with great enthusiasm and produced in 1882 the first, slender, edition of *The Growth of English Trade and Commerce*, which filled a gap in the textbook market and, with the later expanded editions, made him well known among generations of students. He became a university lecturer in history in 1884, though history, economic or otherwise, never became his exclusive concern. He served as chaplain of Trinity from 1880 until he became fellow there in 1891, and was curate of Great St Mary's Church, Cambridge, from 1879 to 1887 when he became vicar, an onerous preaching and pastoral position which he held until 1908, having been appointed archdeacon of Ely the year before.

In preparing his lectures for the history tripos he was, according to his biographer, 'led to the view that Economic History was concerned with growth rather than with mechanism and that the appropriate conceptions were not to be drawn from the mechanical but from the biological sciences'. Understanding of the past was, he believed, to be discovered from original historical sources, not from modern economic theory. As long as Henry Fawcett remained professor of political economy, Cunningham was given a free rein; but when Alfred Marshall succeeded to the chair in 1884, he saw to it that one term of Cunningham's three-term course should be devoted to political economy, even though Cunningham believed that (to quote his biographer once more) formal political economy, 'far from being a help, was a definite hindrance to the apprehension of early Economic History'. When Marshall came to deal with historical topics in his *Principles of Economics* (1890), Cunningham seized his opportunity, addressed the Royal Historical Society on the 'Perversion of economic history' and had his views published in the *Economic Journal*. Marshall, for his part, was more charitably disposed towards Cunningham's views, on paper if not in his lectures. He recognized the contribution made by the later, two-volume edition of Cunningham's textbook which, he believed, showed 'a powerful grasp and great breadth of philosophic thought, combined with much judgement and discretion and [a backhander here] not without strong signs of an aptitude for economic analysis'. Although Cunningham received no academic promotion at Cambridge, he was appointed, with Marshall's blessing, to the Tooke chair of economics and statistics at the Anglican King's College, London (1891–7) and became one of the first fellows of the British Academy.

Cunningham inclined towards the support of state intervention in economic affairs. His textbook did not stretch beyond the repeal of the corn laws and he became a firm supporter of tariff reform in the early twentieth century. He found time to write books on various economic history topics, such as *Alien Immigrants to England* (1897). His influence lived on through his admiring students, particularly Lilian Tomn who helped him with later editions of the textbook. Better known under her married name, Lilian Knowles, she pioneered the study and teaching of economic history at the new London School of Economics and became the second person in Britain to be appointed to a chair in the subject, at the University of London in 1921.   TCB

Main publications

(All published by Cambridge University Press, Cambridge unless otherwise stated.)
The Growth of English Trade and Commerce, 2 vols (1882; 2nd edn, 2 vols 1890–92; 3rd edn, 2 vols 1896–1903; 4th edn, 2 vols 1905–7); *Modern Civilisation in some of its Economic Aspects* (London: Methuen, 1896); *Alien Immigrants in England* (London: Swann Sonnenschein, 1897; repr. London: Cass, 1969); *An Essay on Western Civilisation in its Economic Aspects: Medieval and Modern Times* (1897); *Western Civilisation in its Economic Aspects in Ancient Times*, 2 vols (1898, 1900).

Reading

Cunningham, Audrey: *William Cunningham, Teacher and Priest* (London: Society for Promoting Christian Knowledge, 1950) incl. full bibliography.

Curtin, Philip D. (b.1922) Following his doctorate (1953) in British imperial history from Harvard, Curtin made his way through Caribbean and Latin American history to found the African Studies Program at the University of Wisconsin in 1961. An originator of Africanist scholarship in America, he presided over the African Studies Association in 1970–1 and introduced economic history to Africa. He also explored comparative methods in search of a broadly global vision of the past, achieving appropriately wide recognition as Herbert Baxter Adams professor at the Johns Hopkins University, fellow of the American Academy of Arts and Sciences, president of the American Historical Association (1983), and MacArthur fellow. His principal monographs (listed below) chart his range, his diverse technical skills, and his consistently seminal vision. Curtin's current work on the demographic and medical history of blacks in Africa and the Americas continues his major accomplishment: drawing the once novel and unknown field of African history into the mainstream of the historical discipline.   JCM

Main publications

Two Jamaicas (Cambridge, Mass.: 1955); *The Image of Africa* (Madison: 1964); *The Atlantic Slave Trade: a Census* (Madison: 1969); *Economic Change in Precolonial Africa* (Madison: 1974); *Cross-Cultural Trade in World History* (New York: 1984).

Curtius Rufus The Latin *History of Alexander* enjoyed considerable popularity during the Renaissance. The many surviving manuscripts give as its author Quintus Curtius Rufus. But, since there is not one single reference to the work throughout antiquity, the identity and date of Curtius Rufus are likely to remain a matter of unending scholarly controversy. Some seek to identify the author with either a first century AD rhetorician mentioned by SUETONIUS or the Curtius Rufus who rose to the consulship under Claudius (Tacitus, *Annals* 11.20). Of the ten books the first two and parts of others are missing. The author concentrates on incidents which enable him to display to the full his vivid, highly rhetorical and emotive style and his penchant for moralizing. The work's importance for historians of Alexander the Great is heightened by the fact that none of the contemporary accounts of that monarch survives (cf. ARRIAN). JJP

Main Writings

The History of Alexander, trans. John Yardley (Harmondsworth: Penguin, 1984).

Reading

Atkinson, J. E.: *A Commentary on Q. Curtius Rufus' Historiae Alexandri Magni Books 3 and 4* (Amsterdam: J. C. Giebern, 1980).

McQueen, E. I.: Quintus Curtius Rufus. In *Latin Biography*, ed. T. A. Dorey (London: Routledge & Kegan Paul, 1967).

D

Darby, H. C. See HISTORICAL GEOGRAPHY.

Davis, David Brian (b.1927) Born in Denver, Colorado, and educated at Dartmouth and Harvard, Davis has achieved an international reputation as a cultural and intellectual historian with a particular interest in slavery. *The Problem of Slavery in Western Culture* (1966) and *The Problem of Slavery in the Age of Revolution, 1770–1823* (1975) are the forebears of a final book that is still gestating: *The Problem of Slavery in the Age of Emancipation, 1815–1890*. Among the many awards won by the earlier volumes the most noteworthy are the Pulitzer in 1967 and the National Book Award in 1976. *Slavery and Human Progress*, which appeared in 1984, reflects Davis's penchant for broad themes and his immense erudition in world history.

At Cornell and now at Yale where he is Sterling professor of history, Davis has also written and edited influential works focusing on nineteenth-century American culture, for example *Antebellum Reform* (1967), *The Slave Power Conspiracy* (1969), *Fear of Conspiracy* (1971). LS

Main publications

The Problem of Slavery in Western Culture (Ithaca, NY: Cornell University Press, 1966); *Antebellum Reform* (1967); *The Slave Power Conspiracy and the Paranoid Style* (Baton Rouge: Louisiana State University Press, 1969); editor, *Fear of Conspiracy* (Cornell University Press, 1971) *The Problem of Slavery in the Age of Revolution, 1770–1823* (Cornell University Press, 1975): *Slavery and Human Progress* (New York: Oxford University Press, 1984); *From Homicide to Slavery, Studies in American Slavery* (Oxford University Press, 1987).

Davis, Henry William Carless (b.1874, d.1928) A brilliant academic, Davis's career was cut short by an early death. Born in Gloucestershire and educated at Balliol College, Oxford, he was elected a fellow of All Souls in 1895. He remained at Oxford until 1921, when he moved to a chair at Manchester, but returned to Oxford in 1925 as FIRTH'S successor in the regius chair of modern history.

Davis was one of the few historians to be equally at home in the medieval and modern periods. His text book *England under the Normans and Angevins* (1905) remained a standard work for many years and was reprinted as late as 1949. After the first world war, Davis published a history of the blockade, based upon his wartime work, and when he moved to Manchester he produced a valuable piece on early Lancashire reformers. For the Ford lectures of 1924/5 he took *The Age of Grey and Peel*, which remains a classic. He died unexpectedly of pneumonia in June 1928. JAC

Main publications

Balliol College (London: 1899); *England under the Normans and Angevins* (London: Methuen, 1905); *Medieval Europe* (London: Williams & Norgate, 1911); *Regesta regum Anglo-Normannorum, 1066–1154* (Oxford: Clarendon Press, 1913); *History of the Blockade* (London: 1921); *Lancashire Reformers, 1816–17* (Manchester: Manchester University Press, 1926); *The Age of Grey and Peel* (Oxford: Clarendon Press, 1929).

Reading

Powicke F. M.: *English Historical Review* (1928).
Weaver, J. R. H. and Poole A. L.: *H. W. C. Davis, a memoir* (London: Constable, 1933).

Delisle, Léopold (b.1826, d.1910) A historian with a knowledge of manuscripts unrivalled in the Europe of his day, Delisle played a leading part in promoting the classification and scientific study of medieval books and records, particularly those relating to Normandy. His formal education was in a small Catholic college at his birthplace, Valognes, and at the École des Chartes; his informal training came from antiquarian friends at home, notably Charles Duhérissier de Gerville, and archivists in the libraries of Paris. From de Gerville he learned to transcribe the cartularies and other manuscripts rescued from suppressed monasteries, and became keenly interested in charters and in the mortuary roll of Vitalis of Savigny, a palaeographical treasure containing over two hundred entries in different hands. His life-long interest in the work of ORDERIC VITALIS began when in 1851 he was entrusted with the completion of Auguste le Prévost's edition of the *Ecclesiastical History*, to which he contributed a remarkable introduction. During his student years he collected Norman charters in libraries and archives; one immediate product of this research was his monograph on the rural classes in medieval Normandy, a seminal work of great importance for social and economic history.

Delisle's studies took a somewhat new direction when, in 1852, B. Guérard brought him into the Department of Manuscripts in the Imperial Library (the later Bibliothèque Nationale), and he remained in the service of the library until his retirement in 1905, becoming administrator-general in 1874. He was responsible for cataloguing the manuscripts, then in a state of great disorder, and embarked on the immense but congenial task of tracing the history of the various collections. The *Cabinet des Manuscrits*, produced in the course of this work, was his most substantial publication; but he was frustrated by being required for political reasons to begin the history of the collections with Charlemagne, whereas the real germ of the library was the collection of Charles V. After his retirement he remodelled the first volume and published it as *Recherches sur la librairie de Charles V*.

For 53 years Delisle devoted himself to the duties of his office, travelling in France and England to examine manuscripts and recover those that had been removed from Paris. He received invaluable assistance from his wife, Laure Burnouf, who was herself an excellent Latin scholar and became the inseparable companion of all his work until her death in 1905. His output of texts and studies was prodigious; the bibliography of his works compiled by Paul Lacombe enumerates over two thousand distinct publications. His most lasting achievements were in the field of PALAEOGRAPHY AND DIPLOMATIC. His critical study of charters bore fruit in a catalogue of the acts of Philip Augustus, a memoir on the acts of Innocent III which was the most important contribution to the study of documents from the papal chancery since the work of the eighteenth-century Benedictines, and an introduction to the Norman acts of Henry II. He had begun to collect these in the libraries of Paris and the departmental archives of Normandy and Anjou between 1845 and 1852, and added to them largely through photographs which included many from English repositories. After his retirement he began to prepare his portfolios for publication, and brought out an introductory volume which provided a critical analysis of the charters and discussed their dates. The edition was completed posthumously by his pupil E. Berger. Delisle also did pioneer work on Sacramentaries, on the liturgical commemoration of the dead, and on the scriptoria of Carolingian Gaul.

Delisle took an active part in fostering the École des Chartes as a training ground for scholars. A man of great dignity and serenity, he gave to scholars working in the Bibliothèque Nationale, however young and obscure, the same courteous guidance he had himself received from an earlier generation of distinguished antiquarians. His pre-eminence in manuscript studies was recognized by his election as Membre de l'Institut in 1857, and as a Corresponding Fellow of the British Academy in 1907.   MMC

Main publications

Études sur la condition de la classe agricole et l'état de l'agriculture en Normandie au moyen âge (Évreux:

1851); *Catalogue des actes de Philippe Auguste* (Paris: 1856); *Rouleaux des morts du ixe au xve siècle* (Paris; 1866); *Chronique de Robert de Torigni* (2 vols, Rouen: [Société de l'Histoire de Normandie,] 1872–3); with E. Berger, *Recueil des actes de Henri II*, (4 vols, Paris: [Chartes et diplômes relatifs à l'histoire de France,] 1909–27; See also Paul Lacombe: *Bibliographie des travaux de M. Léopold Delisle* (Paris, 1902); *Supplément 1902–10* (Paris, 1911).

Reading

Delisle, Léopold: Souvenirs de jeunesse. In *Recherches sur la librairie de Charles V* (Paris, 1907).

Poole, R.L.: Memoir: Léopold Delisle. *Proceedings of the British Academy* 5 (1911–12) 203–21.

Delumeau, Jean (b.1923) Born at Nantes, Delumeau was educated at schools in the south of France and Paris, and at the École Normale Supérieure. He spent two years at the French School at Rome (1948–50) before returning to Brittany, where in 1957 he began teaching at the University of Rennes. In 1970 he moved to the Sorbonne, and in 1974 was appointed to a chair at the Collège de France. He has acknowledged his debt to the work of Fernand BRAUDEL, and the influence of *Annales* is reflected in his concern with the history of the 'average Christian' and in his interest in the contribution of other disciplines to the study of the past. But he has drawn too on his own background as a Breton Catholic, and insists on the need for both quantitative and qualitative research. His own books demonstrate an acute awareness of the problems involved in historical interpretation.

His doctoral research on the economic and social history of Rome in the sixteenth century was published in 1957–9. This study opens with a Braudelian examination of the city's communications, roads, and food and water supplies, and concludes with an analysis of papal finance. It was followed by a study of Rome's alum trade, which pointed to the importance of Brittany in international trade. At Rennes, he supervised student dissertations on Breton history, and edited the important *Histoire de la Bretagne*. But it was clear that his interests were already moving away from economic history to the history of attitudes, for the accompanying volume of texts contained sections on denominational relations, popular beliefs, 'christianization' and fear.

A new phase in his career was therefore marked by the twin volumes of 1965 and 1971 on the Reformation and Counter-Reformation. Approaching Protestantism from his own Catholicism, he became convinced that the two reformations had the same origins, used the same methods, and faced the same problems. The books argue that for the majority of the population, the middle ages were not Christian at all, and that Protestant and Catholic reformers were obliged to embark on a campaign of 'christianization'. This term was criticized, however, because it suggested that only the clergy's formulation of the religion deserved the name 'Christian'; and in response, Delumeau has since argued that both the official religion and popular religion were distortions of the faith, because both were based on fear. This theory forms the main theme of his most recent books, in which he has sought to explain the apparent 'dechristianization' of the modern world: the churches, he suggests, have repelled the laity from the true Gospel by teaching a religion based on power and repression, which has added to, and not responded to, the existential fears inseparable from the human condition.

Delumeau has thus moved from the history of commodities to the history of the human psyche, and his writing has in consequence become more autobiographical. He insists, however, that historians can retain their objectivity even when they cannot claim neutrality; no historians can in fact absent themselves from their own subject. His work has received many prizes, including three from the Académie française, and he is a Chevalier of the Légion d'honneur.   NSD

Main publications

Vie économique et sociale de Rome dans la seconde moitié du XVIe siècle (Paris: E. de Boccard, 1957–9); *L'Alun de Rome, XVe–XIXe siècle* (Paris: SEVPEN, 1962); *Naissance et affirmation de la réforme* (Paris: PUF, 1965); *Le mouvement du port de Saint Malo 1681–1720: bilan statistique* (Paris: C. Klincksieck, 1966); *Documents de l'histoire de la Bretagne* (Toulouse: Edouard Privat, 1971); *L'Italie de Botticelli à Bonaparte* (Paris: A. Colin, 1974); *La mort des pays de Cocagne: comportements collectifs de la Renaissance à l'âge classique* (Paris: Publications de la Sorbonne, 1976); *Le Catholicisme entre Luther et Voltaire* (1971) trans. as *Catholicism between Luther and Voltaire:*

a New View of the Counter-Reformation (London: Burns & Oates, 1977); *La Peur en Occident (XIVe–XVIIIe siècles): Une cité assiégée* (Paris: Fayard, 1978); *Le péché et la peur: la culpabilisation en Occident (XIIIe–XVIIIe siècles)* (Paris: Fayard, 1983).

demographic history Though an interest in past populations is as old as history itself, the emergence of demographic history as a sub-discipline has been a recent phenomenon. In part this reflects the wider quantitative revolution in history, but it is also attributable to a few key innovations in methodology and research made during the last 35 years. A clear definition of what constitutes demographic history is made elusive by the fuzzy frontiers that separate it from the wider fields of social history and economic history. Moreover, there is no clear demarcation between demographic and family history.

One feature that sets demographic history aside from other areas of research is the distinctiveness of its data sources and the methods used to analyse them. While sources of the kind more conventionally used by historians (for example, diaries, published materials) are sometimes used to supplement numerical work, the core of demographic research remains quantitative analysis. Researchers working on periods since the later nineteenth century are able to make use of modern registration and census material; earlier studies, however, rely on sources which were not created with the demographer or historian in mind. Parish registers, a particularly valuable source, are a case in point: they record religious ceremonies (baptism and burial) rather than the associated demographic events (birth and death). Nevertheless, historians have been highly inventive in exploiting them.

Early research on parish registers presented simple counts of births and deaths to gain basic information on the growth of populations. Aggregative approaches have become much more sophisticated in recent years. Time-series analysis and other statistical techniques are often employed, and WRIGLEY and Schofield (1981) have used aggregative methods to attempt a vast reconstruction of English demographic history back to the mid-sixteenth century. So elaborate a task would

have been unthinkable without the extensive use of computers.

A different approach to the exploitation of parish registers is family reconstitution, a form of record linkage which reorganizes the data they contain into family histories, enabling a wide array of demographic measures to be calculated. The technique was first developed in France and is particularly associated with Louis HENRY. Registers suitable for reconstitution exist in most of western Europe and in some former colonies, notably in North America. Consequently reconstitution has been widely employed. It was first used on English material by E. A. Wrigley in his study of the Devon village of Colyton, has been extensively used in Scandinavia and Germany, and a group at the University of Montreal is attempting to reconstitute the entire population of colonial French Canada.

An area of overlap between demographic and family history lies in the exploitation of a further source of data: nominative listings. These are census-like documents listing the inhabitants of specific communities, often collected for reasons largely unrelated to the enumeration of population: tax gathering or the assessment of military manpower, for example. A pioneer in the analysis of listings was Peter LASLETT, whose early work on England aroused considerable controversy and stimulated similar research in many countries.

Beyond Europe and its former colonies, the existence of usable demographic records is rare; only Japan appears to have data of analogous quality – particularly the nominative listings of the Shumon-aratame-cho (see Hanley 1974). In areas and periods devoid of documentary sources the techniques of palaeodemography, closely linked to physical anthropology and archaeology are, of necessity, employed.

The results of historical demography have often overturned earlier preconceptions of the nature of historical societies. In a pioneering study of nineteenth-century census material Hajnal (1965) was able to demonstrate that pre-industrial western Europe was characterized by uniquely low nuptiality, high proportions of women never marrying and those who did doing so at a relatively late age. Laslett (1972) found from household analysis that the nuclear family had been typical of England and many other parts of Europe since the sixteenth century. The notion of uniformly high fertility in earlier centuries has also been refuted. Different studies demonstrate large variations in fertility even in the absence of any family limitation, the variation being linked closely to the duration of breastfeeding undertaken by mothers. The picture of a largely immobile peasantry fixed to the land has also been shown to be false, at least for England and the more economically developed areas of continental Europe. In addition to these revelations of pre-industrial times, research on the decline of fertility in nineteenth-century Europe has caused major revisions of previous orthodoxy since the supposedly axiomatic relationships between social and economic development and fertility decline cannot be proved (Knodel and van de Walle, 1979).

The consideration of such varied results has led to new concepts of population change and its place in a wider social, economic and cultural setting. This has given rise to many problems. First, many results from historical studies are based on small populations, and are difficult to generalize. Second, few historical studies are able to present detailed non-demographic data on the populations they study, especially at the level of individual analysis. In spite of these problems, a number of conceptual frameworks linking population to other variables have been adduced. One influential concept is that of the homoeostatic regime. This suggests that pre-industrial societies were marked by the existence of relationships between their demographic characteristics and their socio-economic circumstances such that any move away from an initial position of equilibrium tends to bring about changes elsewhere in the system that restore the original state (Scott Smith, 1977; Wrigley and Schofield, 1981, ch. 11).   CW

Reading

Fleury, M. and Henry, L.: *Nouveau manuel de dépouillement et d'exploitation de l'état civil ancien* (Paris: Institut National d'Etudes Démographiques, 1965).

Hajnal, J.: European marriage patterns in perspective, in *Population and History*, ed. D. V. Glass and D. E. C. Eversley (London: Edward Arnold; Chicago: Aldine Atherton, 1965), pp. 101–43.

Hanley, S. B.: Fertility, mortality and life expectancy in pre-modern Japan. *Population Studies* 28 (1974) 127–42.

Knodel, J. and van de Walle, E.: Lessons from the past: policy implications of historical fertility studies. *Population and Development Review* 5 (1979) 217–45.

Laslett, P.: Introduction. In *Household and Family in Past Time*, ed. P. Laslett and R. Wall (London and New York: Cambridge University Press, 1972).

Scott Smith, D.: A homeostatic demographic regime: patterns in west European family reconstitution studies. In *Population patterns in the past*, ed. R. D. Lee (London and New York: Academic Press, 1977).

Willigan, J. D. and Lynch, K. A.: *Sources and Methods of Historical Demography* (New York and London: Academic Press, 1983).

Wrigley, E. A. and Schofield, R. S.: *The Population History of England 1541–1871: a Reconstruction* (London: Edward Arnold; Cambridge, Mass.: Harvard University Press, 1981).

Denis, Ernest (b.1849, d.1921) A French historian of central Europe, Denis studied in Prague during the 1870s, where he was welcomed by Czech historians, including their doyen, PALACKÝ. This, together with his Huguenot background and anti-German sentiments, influenced his first work, a highly sympathetic treatment of the Hussite movement, and led him to undertake a broader interpretation of the last centuries of the old Bohemian kingdom, which drew heavily on Palacký's thesis of national decay under German pressure. Denis then moved to the modern, post-1620 history of Bohemia, and produced his *chef d'oeuvre*, a masterly study of the 'years of darkness' and especially of the national revival, which, for all its imbalance, has never been superseded. He also produced three books on German history between 1789 and 1871, which remained scholarly, despite his distaste for the evolution they described. During the first world war Denis's political commitment culminated in a major propaganda campaign in favour of an independent Czechoslovakia. A founder of the journal *Le Monde Slave*, he also established the Institut des Études Slaves in Paris in 1920. Heavily indebted to the Czech national school (enthusiasm for him after 1918 in Czechoslovakia even extended to naming a railway station in his honour) Denis was never an archival historian, and his gifts lay in the depiction of atmosphere and psychology: much corroborative detail was supplied by J. Vančura in his Czech translations. Yet Denis's sense of historical relevance, crisp judgements and stylistic grace have earned him a permanent reputation as the outstanding foreign historian of Bohemia. RJWE

Main publications

Huss et la guerre des hussites (Paris: 1878); *Fin de l'indépendence bohême*, 2 vols (Paris: 1889–90); *La Bohême depuis la Montagne-Blanche*, 2 vols (Paris: 1901–3).

Reading

Eisenmann, L: In *Revue des Études Slaves* 1 (1921) 138–70.

Appreciations and polemics from the Czech side by: Goll, J.: Arnošt Denis. In *Česky Časopis Historický* 10 (1904) 69–78, 153–78.

Kybal, V.: *Arnošt Denis a Bílá Hora* [Ernest Denis and the Battle of the White Mountain] (Prague: J. Pelcl, 1912).

Vančura, J.: Arnošt Denis (Prague: Zlal'oroh, 1923).

Deutscher, Isaac (b.1907, d.1967) Born near Cracow, Poland, Deutscher had a mixed education and was employed, from 1924 to 1939, as a journalist, economist and literary critic. He joined the Polish Communist party in 1926 but was expelled six years later for activities as leader of the anti-Stalin faction. He emigrated to England in 1939 and, until shortly after the second world war, was a member of the editorial staff, and later chief European correspondent, of *The Economist* and *The Observer*. Subsequently, he lectured and broadcast on television and radio while continuing to pursue his historical interests. In 1966–7 he was the Trevelyan lecturer at Cambridge.

A leading Marxist writer, Deutscher believed that there was nothing intellectually or politically superior to Marxism as a method for analysing world history: only a Marxist analysis could place the Soviet case within its true historical perspective. His biographies of TROTSKY and Stalin attempted an analysis of the Russian Revolution and some of its key personalities. This theme was continued in his work on the later figures of Khrushchev and Kosygin whose policies were seen as further developments of the earlier Soviet experience. *The Unfinished Revolution* (his Trevelyan Lectures) provides the key to Deutscher's view of Soviet history. The USSR, he believed, was not totalitarian, nor was it developing towards western-style capitalism: the contemporary Soviet Union could only be properly understood through a Marxist appreciation of the difficulties which had beset the nascent socialist state. It was in this context, he maintained, that the Soviet Union today had still to complete the tasks established by the Bolsheviks in 1917. JCh

Main publications

(All published by Oxford University Press, Oxford.) *Stalin: a Political Biography* (1949); *The Prophet Armed* (1954); *The Prophet Unarmed* (1959); *The Prophet Outcast* (1963); *The Unfinished Revolution* (1967).

Reading

Carr, E. H.: Isaac Deutscher: an obituary. *Cambridge Review*, 14 (Oct. 1967).

Labedz, Leopold: Deutscher as historian and prophet. *Survey* (April 1962) 121–44.

—— : Deutscher as historian and prophet – II. *Survey* 23.3 (summer 1977–8) pp. 146–64.

Diehl, Charles (b.1859, d.1944) During his most influential days at the Sorbonne in the 1920s Diehl was widely acclaimed as the grand old *maître* of French Byzantine Studies, but his academic work from the period has survived less well. The most substantial belongs to his time at the university of Nancy, beginning with his thesis on the exarchate of Ravenna (published 1888), from which developed studies on the origins of the *themata* (Byzantine military provinces), on Byzantine Africa (1896) and, finally, on Justinian (1901). Diehl was a cultural as well as institutional historian. A classical archaeologist in origin, his travels based on the French Schools in Rome and Athens from 1880–1914 brought studies of Byzantine monuments in Italy (Venice, Sicily and especially Ravenna), Greece (Hosios Loukas and Salonica), Anatolia and North Africa, which culminated in an encyclopaedic *Manuel d'art Byzantin*. From 1919 he tended towards works of *haute vulgarisation* (the private life of empresses was a favourite topic), which lacked backbone or index. During this stage it would be misleading to call Diehl a *salon* Byzantinist: he was an animator of the First International Byzantine Congress at Bucharest in 1924. But *salons* he enjoyed, and his dapper figure, sociable company and lively lectures were appreciated in many countries. As late as 1940, asked for the subject of a public lecture in Pau, Diehl replied, 'Mais naturellement, l'impératrice Théodora.' But in the last year of his life the old Diehl returned to publish a trenchant formulation of ten major '*grands problèmes*' which still face Byzantinists. Theodora seems not to figure in it, but without an index it is difficult to be sure.   AAMB

Main publications

Manuel d'art Byzantin (Paris: Picard, 1925); besides this, it is not wayward to propose only Diehl's first and last essays as being now of more than antiquarian interest: *Études sur l'administration Byzantin dans l'exarchat de Ravenne (568−751)* (Paris: Thorin, 1888), and *Les grands problèmes de l'histoire Byzantine* (Paris: Leclerc, 1943); see also bibliography of 317 items in *Mélanges Charles Diehl* (see below).

Reading

Articles in his Festschrift, *Mélanges Charles Diehl*, 2 vols (Paris: Ernest Leroux, 1930) [incl, bibliography].
Byzantion 4 (1927−28) [an appreciation]. *Byzantion* 17 (1944−45) [an appreciation].

Dilthey, Wilhelm (b.1833, d.1911) German philosopher. Dilthey held chairs of philosophy at Basel, Kiel and Breslau before moving to Berlin University in 1882. He ranged widely over many aspects of philosophy, biography, literary criticism, the history of ideas and particularly philosophy of history, to which he increasingly devoted his efforts. His intended critique of historical reason was designed to do for history what Kant's critique of pure reason had done for knowledge of the physical world; that is, to define its categories or principles. Like most of Dilthey's writings, however, it remained uncompleted. His influence, especially in Germany, has nevertheless been considerable, not only on historical

thinking but also on epistemology, educational theory and sociology, in which Max Weber adopted his concept of understanding.

Dilthey reacted against the positivist ideal of assimilating history to the natural sciences. He saw history's distinctiveness less in its concern for the particular, which he acknowledged, than in having mankind for its subject: it was here that the division between the sciences of nature and human studies lay. That difference in subject involved a different method of understanding, which in the 'human studies' consisted in recognizing the meaning behind the diverse forms of human expression, both natural ones such as laughter and tears as expressions of joy and sorrow, and social and cultural ones such as codes of law, modes of society, economic activity, literature, art and so on. They all denoted human experience, and the object of the human studies was to identify that experience in terms of the feelings and intentions of its subjects. To that extent all the human studies were interrelated in being concerned with what Dilthey called mind-affected reality, as the products or objectifications of human purposes and values. They provided the meaning and categories of human, as opposed to natural, experience which, Dilthey held, it was the aim of the philosopher to identify.

Applied to history that meant reliving the experiences of the past through the expressions of the past, as Luther's religious experience could be relived from his letters by imaginatively transposing ourselves into his position, what Dilthey called 'rediscovering the I in thou'. It was made possible by a common humanity which enabled those in the present to share the experiences to be found in every culture. Once that was achieved, their meaning could be reached by hermeneutics on the pattern developed by the new biblical criticism in Germany during the nineteenth century, of systematic interpretation of a text both by textual analysis and by reference to its context. The historian thereby works back from outward expressions to inner states and the meanings which they held at the time. All human understanding is an inseparable combination of those three elements.

The importance of history in the attainment

of that understanding was precisely that for Dilthey, in contrast to Kant, it was acquired empirically, from human experience, and not by pure reasoning. It was therefore to be gained most completely from history as the totality of recorded human experience, as memory is the repository of individual experience. Hence history must serve as the basis for the other human studies, on which they draw for their own generalizations. To that extent Dilthey, like the positivists, regarded the study of man as an empirical activity and himself as an empiricist; unlike the positivists and like Kant, he found that that study required its own special categories which, he agreed with Hegel, could only be grasped historically as the expressions of mind: but a human mind, not an absolute spirit, and existing entirely within this world. Dilthey accordingly stood at the convergence of three different traditions, and if he did not succeed in integrating them into a new system, he nonetheless used them to give new direction to the PHILOSOPHY OF HISTORY.   GL

Main publications

Gesammelte Schriften, 12 vols (Leipzig and Berlin: 1914–1936, 2nd edn Stuttgart and Gottingen: Tuebner, 1957–60).

Reading

Hodges, H. A.: *Wilhelm Dilthey : An Introduction* (London: Routledge and Kegan Paul, 1944).
——: *The Philosophy of Wilhelm Dilthey* (London: Routledge and Kegan Paul, 1952).
Rickman, H. P.: *Meaning in History* Dilthey's Thought On History and Society (London: Allen & Unwin 1961).

Dio (b.*c.*164, d. after 229)   Claudius Cassius Dio Cocceianus (that 'Claudius' was part of his nomenclature was revealed for the first time in a recently published inscription) came from the Greek aristocracy of Nicaea, one of the leading cities of Bithynia in north-west Asia Minor. His father, Marcus Cassius Apronianus, had become a Roman senator of some distinction, holding the consulship and a variety of provincial appointments. Dio's own career and writings reveal how far Greeks like himself had been assimilated into the world of Rome. He was at home in Italy, both in Rome

to which he came in his teens, and in the country round the Bay of Naples to which, whenever the public business of Rome permitted, he retired for peace and quiet and to write his history. In his writings he identified totally with Rome and its past.

Dio followed in his father's footsteps and, as the son of a senator, sought to hold the normal Roman magistracies in due order. He was in Rome in the traumatic year AD 193 and was designated praetor by Pertinax, who reigned for a few brief months in that year. Dio actually held the praetorship in 194 or 195 under the eventual victor in the imperial stakes, Septimius Severus. In the normal way Dio could have expected to have held the consulship soon after 205 and there is no reason to suppose that he did not (a later date *c.*222 has been suggested, but has nothing to commend it). He became a 'friend of the emperor', a member of his entourage and of his council and continued in this capacity for Septimius' son, Caracalla – a fact that does not suggest that he fell out of favour, even though he held no offices during these years. Then suddenly his career took off again. Under Caracalla's short-lived successor, Macrinus, Dio was appointed to supervise the affairs of Smyrna and Pergamum in Asia Minor. After a period of recuperation from illness in his home city of Nicaea he was sent as proconsul to Africa. From there, after a brief visit to Italy, he was appointed governor of Dalmatia (Yugoslavia), where his father had served many years before, and then on to govern Pannonia Superior (Hungary), where he formed a low opinion of the native people. This was the only post in Dio's career which gave him command of troops. His attempt to impose stern discipline led to protests. Nevertheless he was honoured with a second consulship, held with the emperor Severus Alexander as his colleague in AD 229. Then an ailment which afflicted his feet forced him to retire to Nicaea. There is no means of knowing how long he survived there.

It was most probably in 193 that Dio presented the new emperor, Septimius Severus, with a pamphlet which described the dreams and portents which had inspired Septimius to aim at the empire. This was an astute move.

Septimius had little in the way of legitimate claim to the throne and a work which revealed the signs of heaven's favour for him was bound to be welcomed. Dio (72.23) tells us that after receiving a long complimentary letter from the emperor, he went to bed and dreamed that his guardian spirit commanded him to write history. Scepticism should not be accepted too readily: many in that age took dreams very seriously. Dio's own interest is manifest throughout his work. On this occasion his initial response was to compose a history of the civil wars and campaigns of the early years of Septimius' reign. When this also got a good reception, he decided to incorporate it in a history of the Roman people from their origins to his own day. He claimed to have spent 10 years collecting material and another 12 writing it. The original intention was to end with the death of Septimius in 211; however another dream inspired him to continue the work through the succeeding years, eventually closing with Dio's second consulship. The 80 books of Dio's *Roman History* represent the last attempt to write a full-scale history of Rome. Only books 36–54 (covering 68–10 BC), much of 55–60 (9 BC–AD 46) and part of 79–80 (from the death of Caracalla into the reign of Elagabalus) survive. But a large number of excerpts were preserved in the collection of historical material ordered by Constantine Porphyrogenitus in the tenth century and in two brief versions of parts of Dio's text written by Ioannes Xiphilinus (eleventh century) and by Ioannes Zonaras (early twelfth century).

The first 50 books cover the Roman republic. What survives of them reads like a reasonable undergraduate essay: strong on narrative, weak on analysis, reflecting inconsistently the viewpoints of his various sources, with rhetorical antithesis and homely platitude serving for a sense of judgement. But Dio did not understand the republic. It was a system of government which had long before given way, inevitably as Dio would have it, to the imperial principate. Here he was on stronger ground. He had had experience of the empire and in his narrative he was careful to point out and to analyse the most important features of this system of government. He also knew how difficult it was to find out how decisions were arrived at in a world where so much of the real debate took place behind closed doors among the emperor's entourage. Like most other classical historians, Dio made frequent use of set-piece speeches put in the mouths of historical characters. In part these were rhetorical showcases; in part a way of commenting on the narrative. The most famous speech, by Maecenas a counsellor of Augustus (52.14), is a vehicle for Dio's own prescription for an ideal imperial system. It reveals that he had learned from his own experience and had much practical advice to offer his contemporaries. Only in advocating a role of increased importance for the senate was Dio looking back to a time which was long past, a sentimental idea that had little to do with the tough military autocracy that the principate was turning into in his own lifetime.   JJP

Main Writings

Roman History [principal edition] ed. U. P. Boissevain, 5 vols (Berlin: Teubner 1895–1931); *Roman History* [text and translation] ed. E Cary, 9 vols (Cambridge, Mass.: Loeb, 1914–27).

Reading

Barnes, T. D.: The composition of Cassius Dio's *Roman History. Phoenix* 38 (1984) 240ff.

Millar, Fergus: *A Study of Cassius Dio* (Oxford: Clarendon Press, 1964).

Diodorus (*fl.* second half of first century BC) Usually known as Diodorus Siculus, the Sicilian, and from Agyrium in Sicily. Diodorus composed in Greek a 'Bibliotheke', a library of history in 40 books, of which 15 are preserved with many fragments of the others. This example of the genre of universal history covered the whole of history down to 59 BC. He has been frequently dismissed as a mere compiler; but recent reassessments suggest that he at least put more of himself into his history than has been thought.   JJP

Main Writings

Bibliotheke, trans. C. H. Oldfather et al. In *Diodorus of Sicily*, vols 1–12 (Cambridge, Mass.: Loeb, 1933–67).

Dionysius of Halicarnassus (b. *c.* 55, d. after 7 BC)   A Greek from Asia Minor, Dionysius settled at Rome *c.* 29 BC, and pursued a literary career in the Augustan period. He taught and wrote on rhetorical theory and literary criticism, but his main work was the *Roman Antiquities*, a history of early Rome, written in Greek. Ten books plus substantial extracts still survive from the original twenty. Dionysius learnt Latin, and did preparatory work on chronology; the main labour was to read other historians, both Greek and Roman. He traced Roman history from the first settlement of their legendary Greek and Trojan ancestors, through the foundation of Rome by Romulus, the regal and early republican periods, and concluded in 265 BC. Although he adopted the traditional annalistic framework from the foundation of the republic onwards, he skimmed over many uneventful years and treated significant episodes at length in a carefully structured fashion.

The argument of the first book is that the Romans were really Greek by origin: this is 'proved' by quotations from over 50 named writers. This citation of sources disappears in the rest of the work, where Dionysius had to rely largely on the full but fictionalized Roman historiographical tradition. He preferred the detailed accounts of the first century BC annalists, which he then reworked to suit his theme.

Dionysius showed how the Romans developed a constitution analysed as 'mixed' in terms of Greek political thought: for him, despite recurrent civil strife, concord was preserved thanks to political debate. Many long speeches purport to relate the arguments used: in reality these do not go back to contemporary evidence but were composed by Dionysius following famous models according to the rules of rhetoric. The content draws on ideas derived from his sources, reflecting the political struggles of the late republic.

Dionysius presents a moral success story: the Romans achieved internal stability and external power through concession and compromise; their institutions formed and expressed the Roman character; chance played no part in Rome's rise to power. This interpretation was intended both for Greeks and for an upper-class Roman audience, for whom there was an implied message: that the restored political balance could be maintained by following the example of their ancestors.   CES

Main writings

The Roman Antiquities of Dionysius of Halicarnassus, ed. E. Cary (London and Cambridge, Mass.: Loeb, 1937–50).

Reading

Gabba, E.: La 'Storia di Roma arcaica' di Dionigi d'Alicarnasso. In *Aufstieg und Niedergang der römischen Welt* II.30.1, ed. H. Temporini and W. Haase (Berlin and New York: de Gruyter, 1982) pp. 719–816 [incl. bibliography].

diplomatic history The study of diplomacy in the past: that is to say the study of formal political relations between sovereign states, the alliances which they made, the origins of the wars which they fought and the negotiation of the peace treaties which concluded these conflicts. Diplomacy, in the sense of continuous political contacts between states and the peaceful management of international relations, had its origins in the Italian peninsula during the second half of the fifteenth century. During the next 250 years a network of embassies developed which connected the major European states and this was accompanied by the evolution of many of the institutions and practices which have characterized modern diplomacy during the past two centuries.

The study of diplomatic history has been central to the development of modern historical scholarship. Its origins are to be found in the emergence of scientific history during the nineteenth century. For Leopold von Ranke the history of Europe was the history of its great powers and their relations with each other. Diplomatic history took on its classic form in the writings of Ranke and his disciples. These scholars assumed that the conduct of foreign policy was the principal function of nation states (*Primat der Aussenpolitik*) and that the essential context and mainspring of history was provided by the negotiations, alliances, wars and peace settlements in which they engaged. The development of diplomatic history was powerfully assisted by the kind of sources on which nineteenth-century historians came to depend. Scientific history was founded on the doctrine that reliable manuscript evidence was the principal and even only source on which historical narrative should be based. Since one of the main functions of the modern state had been the conduct of diplomacy, vast numbers of the documents which it produced and preserved in its archives were concerned with foreign affairs. As a result, when European governments gradually began to open their archives during the nineteenth century, the sources which became available were weighted heavily towards the history of diplomacy. This reinforced the established emphasis on the study of international relations, as did the subsequent publication of important treaty series and other diplomatic documents.

These developments together ensured that classic diplomatic history was pre-eminent as a subject for study by modern historians until 1914, and remained important at least until 1939, especially because of the rush by governments to publish documents to justify their conduct in the crisis which led up to the first world war. But even during its heyday its deficiencies were apparent. Foremost among these was the intellectual aridity which characterized some diplomatic history. The sheer unimportance of many embassies or alliances, together with the massive detail in which these were often studied, inevitably cast doubt on the validity of the discipline, as did the narrow perspective which it embodied. These criticisms were most memorably formulated in G. M. Young's famous complaint that 'the greater part of what passes for diplomatic history is little more than the record of what one clerk said to another clerk'. Another problem was that the thinking which lay behind foreign policy remained elusive, hidden behind the veil of secrecy which traditionally surrounded high policy, when the conduct of foreign affairs was the responsibility of a tiny elite. While the content of diplomacy could usually be studied in detail, the forces which shaped policy could only be glimpsed in outline, if at all, and this remains an important limitation on diplomatic history, though most true for centuries before the twentieth.

Diplomatic history was a casualty of the shift in historical fashions during the twentieth century. The reaction against political history in all its forms, in favour of the study of social, economic, cultural and intellectual developments, contributed to the decline of diplomatic history, especially after the second world war.

Particularly important in this respect was the rise of the ANNALES SCHOOL in France and the enormous influence which they came to have. The new kind of history championed by Marc Bloch and Lucien Febvre embodied an abiding contempt for political history in general (*histoire événementielle*) and diplomatic history in particular, and this hostility does most to explain the undoubted and continuing decline of scholarly interest in diplomatic history, particularly during the past generation.

At the same time, however, as the subject seemed to become so unfashionable, the study of diplomatic history was being renewed and its intellectual limitations recognized and overcome. In the first place, the twentieth century has seen the evolution of a distinct discipline of international relations and foreign policy analysis. This examines modern and contemporary diplomacy, though from the perspective of the social scientist and with a language and set of intellectual assumptions very different from those of the historian. More important has been the evolution of the discipline of diplomatic history itself. During the first half of the twentieth century a handful of scholars, conscious of the deficiencies of classic diplomatic history, had sought to widen its focus and to examine not merely the conduct of a state's external relations but the domestic influences on foreign policy and, in particular, the military and economic factors which influenced the policy-makers. Though at first these men appeared to be voices in the wilderness, they prepared the way for the emergence of a more modern form of diplomatic history during the generation after the second world war.

Central to this development has been the FISCHER controversy during the 1960s and 1970s. The publication by the West German historian Fritz Fischer of a major study of Germany's responsibility for the outbreak of war in 1914, with its emphasis on the primacy of domestic and colonial factors, stimulated a bitter and enduring controversy. One important result of this has been a growing appreciation that strategic, ideological, social, economic and internal political considerations could all influence a state's external policy. Its very sophistication makes this new diplomatic history difficult to write for centuries before the twentieth, where sources are much less abundant and also shed a narrower beam of light. Equally the current emphasis in German historical writing on the supremacy of such domestic considerations in the making of foreign policy (*Primat der Innenpolitik*) seems exaggerated, a case of throwing out the baby with the bathwater. But if such excesses can be avoided, there is no doubt that diplomatic history can be immeasurably strengthened by the appreciation that domestic developments can exert an important and occasionally decisive influence on a state's foreign policy. The recent revival of interest owes something to the carousel of historical fashion, but it also reflects the important contribution which the study of war and peace can make to an understanding of the past.   HMS

Reading

Hinsley, F. H. *Power and the Pursuit of Peace* (Cambridge: Cambridge University Press, 1963).
Watt, D. C. et al.: What is diplomatic history? *History Today* 35 (1985) 33–42.

Douglas, David Charles (b.1898, d.1982) A graduate of Keble College, Oxford, Douglas became lecturer at Glasgow University (1923–34) and professor at Exeter (1934–9), Leeds (1939–45) and Bristol (1945–63). Always a medievalist, he started research under Vinogradoff and produced the *Social Structure of Medieval East Anglia* (1927) and *Feudal Documents from the Abbey of Bury St. Edmunds* (1932). During the 1930s he also contributed to Domesday studies, and in the 1940s and 1950s did much pioneer work on the history of Normandy, culminating in his life of *William the Conqueror* (1964) which had a deserved success as a work of literature as well as history. His most fascinating and most original work, however, was his *English Scholars* (1939) which introduced both medievalists and the public generally to the seventeenth-century scholars who had made the study of English medieval history possible.   RHCD

Main publications

Social Structure of Medieval East Anglia (Oxford: Oxford University Press, 1927); *Feudal Documents*

from the Abbey of Bury St. Edmunds (London: British Academy, 1932); *English Scholars* (London: Jonathan Cape, 1939); *William the Conqueror* (London: Eyre & Spottiswoode, 1964).

Reading

Obituary in *Proceedings of the British Academy* 69 (1983) 513–42 [incl. bibliography].

Droysen, Johan Gustav (b.1808, d.1884) Starting his career as a classical philologist Droysen translated plays of Aeschylus and Aristophanes before proceeding to the study of Alexander the Great. His *Geschichte der Hellenismus* (1836–43) broke new ground in its account of Hellenistic civilization as an amalgam of east and west; a French translation was issued in 1883–5, and it is still used. In 1848 he was a member of the Frankfurt parliament and secretary of its constitutional committee, but resigned from politics when Frederick William IV refused the German crown. Turning to modern history Droysen wrote on the German war of independence, of which he had childhood memories; *The Policy of Denmark towards Schleswig Holstein* (English translation, 1850); a life of York von Wartenburg (3 vols, Berlin, 1851–2); various aspects of the Thirty Years' War, and his *Geschichte der Preussischen Politik* (1855–86) which had reached 1756 by the time of his death. He was an ardent Prussian and an ardent liberal (a combination which did not always win him favour). His *Grundriss der Historik* (1858) on the theory of history was important and remains so in Europe.   RHCD

Main publications

Geschichte der Hellenismus, 2 vols (Hamburg: 1836–43); *Das Leben der Feldmarschalls Grafen York von Wartenburg*, 3 vols (Berlin: 1851–2); *Geschichte der Preussischen Politik*, 14 vols (Berlin: 1855–86); *Grundriss der Historik* (Jena: 1858).

Reading

Bravo, Benedetto: *Philologie, histoire, philosophie de l'histoire: Étude sur J. G. Droysen, historien de l'antiquité* (Wrocław: Zakład Narodowy im ossolińskich, Wydawnictivo Polskrej Akademii, Nauk, 1968).
Spieler, K. H.: *Untersuchungen zu Johann Gustav Droysens 'Historik'* (Berlin: Draker und Humblot, 1970).

Du Bois, William Edward Burghardt (b.1868, d.1963) Born in Great Barrington, Massachusetts, of African, French and Dutch ancestry, this Afro-American scholar took his first degree in 1888 at Fisk University, Tennessee, where he was made sharply aware of the difference between the liberalism of New England and the racial segregation of the South in the United States. Du Bois went on to do graduate work at Harvard and Berlin universities between 1892 and 1896; his doctoral thesis on the suppression of the African slave trade to the United States was the first volume to be published in the Harvard Historical Series. Du Bois's formal academic career centred mainly on Atlanta University, Georgia, where he taught sociology, history and economics during two influential periods: 1897–1910 and 1934–44. Out of the first of his Atlanta periods came fifteen seminal sociological studies on the Negro in the United States, which Du Bois edited with masterly skill. Du Bois's most famous work, *The Souls of Black Folk*, first published in 1903 and extensively reprinted, while not strictly historical writing, has influenced profoundly the historical approach to the study of the black experience in the United States. His *Black Reconstruction* (1939) has affected all subsequent writing on the changes in the American South between 1865 and 1877.

During Du Bois's long life, academic history and sociology competed for his allegiance with politics against white supremacy in America and Pan-African activities overseas; and he did not always finish his projected writings, particularly his book on black soldiers in the first world war. Nevertheless, he published many books and articles, increasingly influenced by Marxism, which are indispensable for the study of the people of African descent in the United States and the African Diaspora.

Increasingly alienated from American life after the end of the second world war, Du Bois joined the Communist Party of the United States in 1961 and emigrated to Ghana as Director of his long-cherished *Encyclopedia Africana* project. He died in 1963 in Accra, where he was given a state funeral by Kwame Nkrumah's government.   GS

Main publications

The Suppression of the African Slave Trade to the United States, 1863–1870 (New York: Longmans, Green, 1896); *The Philadelphia Negro* (Philadelphia: University of Pennsylvania, 1899); *The Souls of Black Folk* (Chicago: McClurg, 1903); *The Negro* (New York: Home University Library, Holt, 1915): The African Roots of the War. *Atlantic Monthly* (May 1915); *Black Reconstruction in America, 1860–1880* (New York: Harcourt Brace, 1939); *Black Folk, Then and Now* (New York: Holt, 1939); *The World and Africa* (New York: Viking, 1947). *See also* Paul G. Partington, ed. *W. E. B. Du Bois: a bibliography of his published writings* (Whittier, Calif.: Paul G. Partington, 1977).

Reading

Aptheker, Herbert ed.: *The Correspondence of W. E. B. Du Bois, 1877–1968*, 3 vols (Amherst: University of Massachusetts Press, 1973, 1976, 1978).

Du Bois, Shirley Graham: *W. E. B. Du Bois* (Chicago: Johnson, 1978).

Huggins, Nathan I. ed.: *W. E. B. Du Bois: Writings*. (New York: Library of America, 1987).

Logan, Rayford W. and Winston, Michael: Du Bois. In *Dictionary of American Negro Biography*, ed. Logan and Winston (New York: Norton, 1982) pp. 193–9.

Rampersad, Arnold: *The Art and Imagination of W. E. B. Du Bois* (Cambridge, Mass.: Harvard University Press, 1976).

Duby, Georges Michel Claude (b.1919) After schooling at Mâcon and university studies in Lyons, Duby became an *assistant* there in 1944, taught medieval history at Besançon (1950) and from 1951 at Aix, where he became professor in 1953. In 1970 he was reluctantly also persuaded to take a chair in the Collège de France, Paris. An affable, mildly unconventional man, he retains a strong attachment to Provence where for preference he resides with his family.

As a follower ('*nourri de ses écrits*'), but not pupil, of BLOCH, hence originally a close associate rather than strict member of the ANNALES SCHOOL, Duby was initially attracted to study a limited area with abundant documentation in order to reconstitute the totality of social relations. *La Société aux XIe et XIIe siècles dans la région mâconnaise* (1953) was immediately recognized as an outstanding contribution to knowledge of feudal society, integrating economic analysis with a study of both institutions and ideology. A notable feature was the particularly close attention paid to vocabulary and its evolution in record sources, thus helping to plot exactly not only changes in meaning but also in substance. The practical implications of the coalescence of early medieval notions of nobility with those of knighthood and the consequent social rise of the knights has been a leitmotif of much of his work. His example has been followed in many subsequent detailed regional studies which have created a much more complex, chronologically exact and subtle view of the development of society in medieval Europe at large.

Though he has kept an abiding interest in agrarian history, from 1953 his field of study began to encompass western Europe as a whole with 'a systematic exploration of the material culture upon which the organization of this fundamentally agrarian society was based'. By the early 1960s Duby turned his attention 'to other phenomena less easy to explain and too long left to the historians of ideas' — mental attitudes and the ideological forms by which social behaviour is governed. Though his preferred period of study was still the tenth—twelfth centuries, excursions into other periods were not lacking. Social classification, kinship and marriage, the precise role of the nobility and knighthood, are but a few of his major areas of concern. A constant stream of books (several winning literary prizes) as well as scholarly acclaim have publicized his interpretation of the evolution of society in the west and of the specific role of France. Although sometimes criticized, especially in English-speaking countries, for the increasingly abstract content of some recent work (for instance, *Les Trois Ordres ou l'imaginaire du féodalisme*, 1978), Duby continues to provoke and illuminate by extensive writings. He has attracted and inspired a whole generation of medieval economic historians through his influential seminars, as director of the Centre d'Études des Sociétés Méditerranéennes, editor of *Études rurales* and of an impressive, lavishly illustrated series of collaborative histories. As a widely recognized academic and man of letters — acquainted with television and other means of publicity — he has helped to bring the very latest research to the attention of a large audience.   MCEJ

Main publications

La Société au XIe et XIIe siècles dans la région mâconnaise (Paris: École Pratique des Hautes Études, 1953); *L'Économie rurale et la vie des campagnes dans l'Occident médiéval* (Paris: Arbier, 1962; trans. London: Edward Arnold, 1968); *L'An Mil* (Paris: Gallimard, 1967); *Guerriers et paysans, VIIe— XIIe siècles, essai sur la première croissance économique de l'Europe* (1973, trans. *The Early Growth of the European Economy*, London: Weidenfeld & Nicolson, 1973); *Le Dimanche de Bouvines (27 juillet 1214)* (Paris: Gallimard, 1973); *Saint Bernard: L'Art cistercien* (Paris: Arts et Métiers Graphiques, 1976); *Les Trois Ordres ou l'imaginaire du féodalisme* (1978, trans. Chicago: University of Chicago Press, 1980); *Le Chevalier, la femme et le prêtre* (1981, trans. Harmondsworth: Allen Lane, 1984).

Reading

Moore, R. I.: Duby's Eleventh Century. *History* 69 (1984) 36—49.

Ducange, C. See MAURISTS.

Duchesne, Louis-Marie-Olivier (b.1843, d.1922) Duchesne was of predominantly Breton stock and background. His studies for the secular priesthood took him to Rome, and he undertook palaeographical investigations in Greece and Asia Minor. In 1877 he received his first major academic appointment as professor of church history at the Institut Catholique in Paris, newly founded as a Christian counterpart to the secular state universities. He rapidly developed one of his lifelong interests — the study of the topography of Rome. In 1880 he began the *Bulletin critique de littérature, d'histoire et de théologie*, which he described as a 'revue absolument orthodoxe et inexorablement scientifique'. He thereby epitomized his own salient characteristics as a scholar; though he also once declared that a scholar should be 'just a little in love with' his subject, and he was a master of lucid exposition. Though Duchesne was an inspiration of Alfred Loisy, he opposed the Modernism with which the Institut Catholique became associated. His own lectures on the development of pre-Nicene Christian doctrine and his study of the early history of the ancient churches of France nevertheless excited criticism, and in 1885 he resigned. From 1885

until 1895 he held a chair at the École Supérieure des Lettres; from 1895 until his death he
was director of the École Française at Rome.

Duchesne published critical editions of two
prime sources for papal history: the *Liber
pontificalis*, a collection of papal biographies
issued in a series of 'editions' from the sixth
century up to 1464, which is the main single
source for the history of the early popes; and
(with P. Fabre) the *Liber censuum*, compiled in
the 1190s, which recorded the dues (*census*)
owed throughout the Catholic Church to the
see of Rome. In a definitive work Duchesne
listed the bishops of French churches from
the beginnings to the end of the ninth century.
He wrote (as he put it) a 'description and explanation of the chief ceremonies of Catholic
worship as they have been performed in the
Latin churches of the West from the fourth to
the ninth century', and a study of the early
development of the papal state. His history
of the early church, published at the height
of the Modernist crisis, at first received the
Imprimatur but in 1912 was consigned to
the Index. 'As a faithful son of the church',
Duchesne commented, 'I must submit to
her decision.' A further, uncompleted volume, on the sixth-century church, appeared
posthumously. The young Duchesne had
been admired and employed by Pope Leo
XIII; after his experiences under the anti-
Modernist Pius X he lived to acclaim in 1922
the election of his friend Pius XI.   HEJC

Main publications

Le 'Liber pontificalis': texte, introduction et commentaire
2 vols (Paris: Thorin, 1886, 1892); *Origines du culte
chrétien: étude sur la liturgie avant Charlemagne* (Paris:
Thorin 1889) trans. M. L. McClure, *Christian
Worship* (London: SPCK, 1903); *Fastes épiscopaux
de l'ancienne Gaule*, 3 vols (Paris: Thorin, 1894,
1900, 1915); *Les Premiers temps de l'état pontifical
(754–1073)* (Paris: Fontemoing, 1898) trans. A. H.
Matthew, *The Beginnings of the Temporal Sovereignty
of the Popes, AD 754–1073* (London: Kegan Paul,
1908); *Histoire ancienne de l'église*, 3 vols (Paris:
Fontemoing 1906, 1907, 1910) trans. *Early History
of the Christian Church*, 3 vols (London: Murray,
1909–14); with P. Fabre, *Le 'Liber censuum' de
l'Église romaine*, 2 vols (Paris: De Boccard, 1926);
*Scripta minora: études de topographie romaine et
de géographie ecclésiastique* (Rome: École française,
1973).

Reading

*Monseigneur Duchesne et son temps: actes du colloque
organisé par l'École française de Rome, 1973* (Rome:
École française, 1975).

D'Espezel, P.: Duchesne, Louis Marie Olivier. In
Dictionnaire d'histoire et de géographie ecclésiastiques
14 (1960) cols. 965–84.

Leclercq, H. Monsignor Duchesne. In *Dictionnaire
d'archéologie chrétienne et de liturgie* 6 (1925) cols.
2680–735.

Dutch historiography See LOW COUN-
TRIES, HISTORIOGRAPHY OF.

Dyos, Harold James (b.1921, d.1978)
After war service in the Royal Artillery Dyos
read economic history at the London School
of Economics, graduating in 1949. He spent
all his academic career at Leicester University,
becoming professor of urban history in 1971.
Though in earlier life a Christian Scientist,
Dyos later became well known for his wit,
ebullience and the breadth of his interest.
A staunch supporter of conservation, he was
elected chairman of the Victorian Society
shortly before his death. His initial research
was on transport history but from the 1960s he
became an enthusiastic and increasingly influential exponent of urban history. A highly
effective organizer Dyos founded the British
Urban History Group in 1962 and edited the
Urban History Newsletter and, later, the *Urban
History Yearbook.* The international urban
history conference that Dyos arranged at
Leicester in 1967 set the agenda for British
urban historians for more than a decade.

Dyos saw urban history as a multidisciplinary
field mobilizing the diverse methodological
resources of historians, geographers, sociologists and others in a systematic examination
of urban development. Under his auspices
interdisciplinary co-operation flourished
(evinced by *The Victorian City*, edited jointly
with Michael Wolff in 1973). Though his
main interest was in the nineteenth century
Dyos also encouraged the revival of interest
in urban development in the pre-industrial
period. His output was small but influential,
his principal research work being on Victorian
London. His study of nineteenth-century
Camberwell, examining the mechanisms of

suburban growth, led to a wave of research on the building process in major urban centres. It might be argued that Dyos was intellectually overcommitted to the great cities of the nineteenth century and their social and other problems, and failed to see them in a sufficiently broad temporal and spatial context. It is also true that the momentum of interdisciplinary research which he fostered has slowed since his death, but he undoubtedly left a powerful imprint on the shape of modern urban history in Britain.   PAC

Main publications

Victorian Suburb: a Study of the Growth of Camberwell (Leicester: Leicester University Press 1961; 2nd edn, 1986); ed., *The Study of Urban History* (London: Edward Arnold, 1968); ed. with M. Wolff, *The Victorian City: Images and Realities* (London: Routledge & Kegan Paul, 1973).

Reading

Cannadine, D. and Reeder, D. eds: *Exploring the Urban Past: Essays in Urban History by H. J. Dyos* (Cambridge: Cambridge University Press, 1982) [See Introduction and conclusion].

E

ecclesiastical historiography Emerging early as a specialized discipline within the historical sciences, ecclesiastical historiography has a long pedigree. It originated as a tool to aid theological understanding and has often been written for theological rather than historical purposes. Indeed, its eventual appearance as an academic discipline was within theology faculties. Before that, however, church history had long played a central part in religious apologetic and progress in the subject, particularly during the period following the Reformation, was often stimulated by religious controversy.

The dissolution of Christianity into a variety of churches and sects often required the examination of ecclesiastical systems themselves, not only in the light of scripture but also in the mist of history. The work undertaken in the course of such apologetics was often bedevilled by denominational prejudices but, nevertheless, laid the foundation for the central role which ecclesiastical history was to play in the development of academic history. This took place in the nineteenth and early twentieth centuries when the problem of the relationship of church and state was of great political importance and exercised the minds of some of the best historians of the day. More recently the comparative work of sociologists and anthropologists has been taken up, and historians such as Gabriel LE BRAS have seen the need to place ecclesiastical history within a wider social and cultural context, borrowing and exchanging concepts and techniques from other disciplines which have concerned themselves with the study of religion. Thus in the last generation ecclesiastical historians have added the study of religious practice and belief to their more traditional concerns with theological systems and ecclesiastical organization. This addition has brought with it, in the work of DELUMEAU and others, a comparative dimension to the history of religion which reflects the ecumenical spirit within Christian churches, whose particular problems are seen by many as secondary to the general problem of the dramatic decline of religious practice in the west.

The origin of ecclesiastical history lies in JEWISH HISTORIOGRAPHY, and early Christian writers of the first century adopted the Jewish approach of placing sacred truth within a historical context. It is with the fourth-century *Ecclesiastical History* of EUSEBIUS, however, that Christian historiography can be said to begin. Though placed firmly in the context of Christian apologetic, the work demonstrated source criticism in a way that the tradition of HAGIOGRAPHY, also established at that time, was soon to ignore. In the following century OROSIUS produced the first comparative writing on church history, but his influence was probably less than that of his master St Augustine, whose vision of the conflict between the worldly and the heavenly cities was to have a profound effect on subsequent writers of church history.

Hagiography continued, but the writing of general ecclesiastical history did not develop until the eleventh century, though some writers, such as BEDE, produced localized histories as well as *Lives of the Saints*. General church history, incorporating the whole history of God's relations with his people, was continued in the work of ORDERIC VITALIS, but by the end of the twelfth century the subject began to be identified more closely with the clergy and the institution in works such as the *Historia Pontificalis* of John of Salisbury. Much later medieval church history was either of this sort or was apocalyptic in approach. Nicholas of Cusa produced an apocalyptic scheme in which one year of Christ's life represented 50 in that of the church, so that by about 1450 the Age of the Spirit would begin.

What was well under way by that date was the revival of humanistic scholarship which, though not directly engaged in ecclesiastical historiography, by means of philological study recast biblical scholarship and exposed some of the central sources of the medieval church. In this way VALLA and others profoundly altered the course of ecclesiastical history, for it was humanist biblical scholarship which influenced Luther. Protestant writers based their claims on scripture, but found in Eusebius's martyrology and Augustine's heavenly city both a method and a conceptual framework which could bridge the gap between the primitive church and the sixteenth century. John FOXE took this up on the Protestant side, while Augustine's view of church history as the story of man's salvation was most fully expressed on the Catholic side by Bossuet. Although controversial in intention, ecclesiastical historians such as SARPI inherited the humanist concern for proper source citation, while both the BOLLANDISTS and MAURISTS made significant advances in source criticism and the ancillary science of PALAEOGRAPHY. By the mid-eighteenth century, when the impetus of the Reformation conflicts had abated, ecclesiastical history had established itself as part of the theological curriculum in Protestant universities on the continent of Europe, the first chair being created at Helmstedt in 1650. Protestant historiography removed the supernatural from church history and, in the words of Johann Lorenz von Mosheim (1694–1755), made its central concern 'all external and internal events in the society of men which takes its name from Christ'. Thus ecclesiastical history as understood today was established. Catholic scholarship soon followed suit, as the study of 'spiritual history' was made compul-

sory throughout the Habsburg territories in 1752.

Church history was, therefore, ready to benefit from the advances made within academic history in the nineteenth century. The opening of public archives, including those of the Vatican in 1884, led to great series of editions of texts, such as the *Monumenta Germanica Historia* and the Rolls Series, which revived scholarly interest in the medieval church. Multivolume histories based on archival sources were produced by writers such as PASTOR and CREIGHTON who was the first holder of the Dixie chair of ecclesiastical history at Cambridge in 1884. This was one of several such chairs created during this period, which also saw the appearance of specialist journals such as *Zeitschrift für Kirchengeschichte* (1876) and *Revue d'Histoire Ecclésiastique* (1900). The specialist studies in such journals have been incorporated into multivolume collaborative histories of the church, edited by FLICHE and Martin in France and Henry and Owen CHADWICK in Britain.

More recently ecclesiastical history has proved a fertile arena for interdisciplinary exchange. The comparative approach of Troeltsch and WEBER encouraged an International Association for the History of Religion which adopted a non-theological stance. Anthropological studies of non-christian religion and the phenomenological approach of Rudolf Otto's *Das Heilige* (*The Idea of the Holy*), published in 1917, have influenced historians like Peter Brown and Jean Delumeau. This multicultural and multidisciplinary approach to religious history is identified with the Chicago school and, in particular, with Mircea Eliade whose study *The Sacred and the Profane* (1961) owes much to the psychologist C. J. Jung. At present ecclesiastical historiography reflects the pluralistic society in which it is now written, combining traditional historical skills in Owen CHADWICK and techniques from newer disciplines in Eliade. What they have in common is a concern to understand the religious experiences of groups and individuals in the past, but whether general rules about such behaviour can be established remains a contentious issue.   WJS

117

ECONOMIC HISTORY

Reading

Chadwick, Owen: *Catholicism and History* (Cambridge: Cambridge University Press, 1978).

Davis, R. H. C. and Wallace-Hadrill, J. M.: *The Writing of History in the Middle Ages* (Oxford: Clarendon Press, 1981).

Jedin, H. and Dolan, J.: *Handbook of Church History* (London: Burns & Oates, 1965).

Knowles, D. M.: *Great Historical Enterprises* (London: Nelson, 1963).

Smart, N. *Religion and the Western Mind* (London: Macmillan, 1987).

economic history As a separate discipline economic history has its roots in the nineteenth century. Late in the century, under the influence of TOYNBEE, CUNNINGHAM and ASHLEY, the subject developed a distinctiveness which drew it away from traditional history. The first chair in economic history was established at Harvard in 1892 and was held by an Englishman, Ashley. UNWIN was appointed to the first chair in Britain which was established at Manchester in 1910. Formal division between history and economic history did not occur until 1926 when the Economic History Society was founded in Cambridge. Among the Society's early luminaries were Ashley, Scott, CLAPHAM, TAWNEY, POSTAN and Lipson. In the early years the subject retained its close links with history.

By 1937 there were still only three chairs but after the second world war the discipline expanded rapidly and by 1958 this had grown to eight, and by 1970 there were 30 chairs. This expansion was in line with the development of the social sciences, and owed much to economics which provided conceptual and theoretical frameworks which enabled economic historians to approach a whole range of historical problems in new and exciting ways. At the same time separate departments of economic history were established (often combined with social history); there was a corresponding increase in publication.

In the early years there had been both considerable need and opportunity simply to get the record straight, since in most political histories the economic factor in historical change was acknowledged but left as something of an empty box; unless, that is, it impinged directly on high politics as in the debate over the repeal of the Corn Laws in the 1840s. Well before 1939, however, a more modern approach, with a strong emphasis on primary research, was discernible and was exemplified by the first two of Clapham's majestic volumes, *An Economic History of Modern Britain* (1931 and 1932), and by such classic monographs as G. Unwin, *Samuel Oldknow and the Arkwrights* (1924), A. Redford, *Labour Migration in England 1800–1850* (1926), G. C. Allen, *The Industrial Development of Birmingham and the Black Country* (1929) and W. H. B. Court, *The Rise of the Midland Industries, 1600–1838* (1938).

During the 1940s new techniques of national income accounting, the rapid development of economic theory and the primary importance which economic growth was assuming in contemporary politics, provided an enormous stimulus to the investigation of the historical process of economic growth. One of the outstanding studies to make its appearance at this time was I. Svennilson's *Growth and Stagnation in the European Economy* (1954); and T. S. ASHTON's little study, *The Industrial Revolution* (1948) was a landmark of the new approach in the UK. Capital formation, agricultural and industrial expansion, population growth and the nature of technical change became particular objects of study. By the early 1960s these developments had coalesced into a more comprehensive analysis of industrialization: the most stimulating and perceptive work in this field was A. Gerschenkron, *Economic Backwardness in Historical Perspective* (1962).

While a macro-economic approach was in the ascendant (in line with the heavy concentration on growth theory in economics) the micro, mainly institutional side of the subject was not neglected. The official history of the war contains some notable volumes on economic history, especially on war production and finance. But the rising star in this area was business history, heralded by the publication of Charles WILSON's *Unilever* (1954). This book was the first independent study in the UK of big business and it marked the beginning of proper scholarly investigation into one of the central areas of the political economy of the twentieth century. Business history also became a major focus of research in the USA though it took on a somewhat different form, with much greater emphasis on the study of corporate structure and development. The seminal work was A. D. Chandler, *Strategy and Structure: Chapters in the History of Industrial Enterprise* (1962).

A quite new, some might say startling, methodology emerged in the late 1950s and came to be known as cliometric, or econometric history. It involved a combination of formal neo-classical economic theory, regression analysis and counter-factual hypotheses. The new-fangled product made its most dramatic appearance in 1962 with the publication of R. FOGEL's *American Railroads*. Fogel posed the question whether the railroads made a significant contribution to American economic growth. By constructing a hypothetical world (with hypothetical canals and roads among other things) the provocative conclusion of 'not much' was arrived at. Although this book has not stood the test of time, it stimulated similar if less ambitious work in a variety of fields. However, the influence of econometric history was felt far less in Britain and Europe than in the United States. But even in the USA enthusiasm for these new methods became much more constrained by the mid-1970s because the degree of abstraction they forced on historical evidence, especially when they were applied to economy-wide issues, was judged unacceptable. Nevertheless, econometric history has had a permanent and beneficial influence on the subject. It has encouraged the use of more sophisticated statistical techniques and more precise specification of theoretical assumptions.

While economic history flourished most in Britain and the USA, it developed noticeably in most major countries after the war. The first international congress of economic history was held in Stockholm in 1960 following an initiative from Postan and BRAUDEL. In France a great deal of economic history was swept into the majestic caravan of *le science de l'homme* under the leadership of Braudel. In this form, however, the subject lacked the theoretical rigour of its Anglo-Saxon counterpart, though outside it much important work

was done in the fields of business and financial history. In very recent years, probably the most rapid expansion of the subject has been in Japan.

The nature of research in economic history has been influenced by the availability of public funding. While much of this activity has been on a fairly modest scale compared with other branches of the social sciences (and certainly so in comparison with the natural sciences) it has made possible a number of team projects.

The study of economic history, in common with most branches of history, reflects contemporary preoccupations and to some extent this accounts for the growing emphasis on work on the period post-1700 and, in very recent years, on the twentieth century. In the 1950s and 1960s the theme of economic growth held sway. Since the 1970s, with the appearance of the ugly and suitably named affliction of stagflation, attention has increasingly focused on the formulation of economic policy in the twentieth century, a development which has been greatly facilitated by easier access to official records. Such work has drawn heavily on statistical techniques devised in the 1950s and 1960s to measure the factors determining economic performance as a means to explaining differences between nations. In Britain, in particular, there has been intense interest in the historical reasons for the economy's comparatively poor economic performance in international terms; indeed, it is perhaps one of the country's few growth industries.

More generally, the crisis in economic theory – most evident in the fierce debate between Keynesians and monetarists – has correspondingly altered perceptions among economic historians. A feature of this has been a growing interest in the possibility of a more theoretical analysis of institutional change than has existed to date. One example centres on the idea that economic growth in twentieth-century Britain has been retarded by the strength and resistance to change of such institutions as the civil service and the educational system; another is provided by work being done on the nature of property rights over the ages. Some of this work may

119

well lead to the revival of the older links between economic history and sociology.

At the end of the twentieth century the study of economic history is a very different creature from what it was when the Economic History Society was founded in 1926. The influence of economics on the subject has been paramount and permanent but the ties with its other parent, history, remain strong; current developments in research indicate that the balance of these influences may well become more even in the future than it has been in the past.　　　　　　　　　　BWEA

Reading

Barker, T. C.: The beginnings of the Economic History Society. *Economic History Review* 30 (1977) 1–19.
Coleman, D. C.: *What Has Happened to Economic History?* (Cambridge: Cambridge University Press, 1972).
Harte, N. B.: *The Study of Economic History* (London: Cass, 1971).
Harte, N. B. Trends in publications in the economic and social history of Great Britain and Ireland, 1925–74. *Economic History Review* 30 (1977) 20–41.
McClelland, P. D.: *Causal Explanation and Model Building in History, Economics and the New Economic History* (Ithaca, NY: Cornell University Press, 1975).

Einhard (b.*c.*775, d.840) Born in the Main valley, and educated at the monastery of Fulda, Einhard was resident at Charlemagne's court from *c.*795. He was sent on missions for the emperor, and was also closely associated with Louis the Pious and Lothar. He may have been associated with the writing of the Royal Frankish Annals, and between 819 and 831 he wrote his *Life of Charlemagne* which was the first medieval secular biography, modelled closely on SUETONIUS. This often intimate portrait was very influential in establishing Charlemagne as the image of an ideal ruler.　　　　　　　　　　EFJ

Main writings

Vita Caroli, ed. L. Halphen (Paris: Les Belles Lettres, 1938); trans. L. Thorpe in *Two Lives of Charlemagne* (Harmondsworth: Penguin, 1969).

Reading

Ganshof, F. L.: Einhard, biographer of Charlemagne. In *The Carolingians and the Frankish Monarchy*, ed. Ganshof (London: Longman, 1971).

Eisenmann, Louis (b.1869, d.1937) Of Alsatian Jewish extraction, Eisenmann followed in the footsteps of other nineteenth-century French scholars in pursuing the history of east-central Europe. Years of study in the Habsburg lands yielded a magisterial doctoral thesis on the genesis and consequences of the Austro-Hungarian Compromise of 1867, a book revealingly described by A. J. P. Taylor as 'a work of superlative genius than which no greater work of history has been written in this century'. Eisenmann immersed himself in Hungarian culture and history, but he turned increasingly to sympathy for the Slavs, cooperating with DENIS during the first world war, then taking over from him at the Sorbonne, the Institut des Études Slaves, and as editor of *Le Monde Slave*. Eisenmann never recaptured the superb qualities of his first work, with its breadth of vision and universal sympathies, its finely balanced assessment of Habsburg constitutional issues, its beautifully pointed and incisive style.　　　　　　RJWE

Main publications

Le Compromis austro-hongrois de 1867: Étude sur le dualisme (Paris: Société Nouvelle de Librairie et d'Édition, 1904).

Elias, Norbert (b.1897) Despite the fact that he is not a historian by profession, Elias's work is of great importance for the writing of history in our time, although it only belatedly came to be recognized. Elias was born in Breslau (now Wrocław), and studied sociology with Karl Mannheim. When Hitler came to power Elias left Germany. He was professor of sociology at the University of Leicester, 1954–62, where he did all he could to make sociologists more historically minded.

Elias's reputation rests principally on one book, published – in German but outside Germany – in 1939 but not translated into English for another 40 years: *The Civilizing Process*. The first part deals with the history of manners, more especially table manners, in western Europe from the end of the middle ages onwards; the second part deals with the decline of feudalism and the rise of the centralized state. What links these two very different parts is Elias's theory of the process of 'civilization', defined as 'the social constraint towards self-constraint'. His theory, which owes something to Freud and something to WEBER but remains distinctively his own, is that it was the centralizing process that led to the civilizing process, the rise of self-control, the raising of what Elias calls the 'threshold of embarrassment'. Years before BRAUDEL (in his work on material culture) and ARIÈS (in his essay on childhood), Elias made it clear that apparently trivial, antiquarian details like the history of the fork and the handkerchief were in fact quite closely linked to major political and social trends such as the rise of courts and absolute monarchies. Now that systematic research on some of the topics he discusses has at last begun, it is possible to fault Elias on matters of detail, and after 50 years his book is beginning to look dated, notably in its almost exclusive concern with the west at the expense of the self-control systems of China, Japan and elsewhere. All the same, as is shown by recent work on social and cultural history published in France, the Netherlands, Germany, the United States and elsewhere, it has not lost its power to stimulate the imagination of historians.

Elias's second book, *The Court Society*, was first published in German in 1969, although an inspection of its footnotes suggests that it too was worked out in the 1930s. It is a kind of appendix to the larger work, looking in more detail at early modern courts (especially in France) and at the way of life of the monarchs and aristocrats, more especially at ritual and patterns of consumption. Among its important points is one about the rationality in this social system of conspicuous consumption by aristocrats of magnificent clothes, houses and so on. Another concerns the political utility to Louis XIV of the ceremonial system which was at its most visible in Versailles; or, to use the concept which Elias prefers to that of 'system', the pattern of relationships or 'figuration'. This concept helps him to relate structure to change

more closely than historians or sociologists have generally managed to do.   UPB

Main publications

Über den Prozess der Zivilisation, 2 vols (Basle: Haus zum Falken, 1939) (English trans., Oxford: Blackwell, 1978–82); *Die höfische Gesellschaft* (Darmstadt and Neuwied: Luchterhand, 1969) (English trans., Oxford: Blackwell, 1983).

Reading

Chartier, R: *Prozess* et *Figuration*: une lecture de Norbert Elias, Preface to French translation of Elias's *La société de cour* (Paris: Flammarion, 1985). Gleichmann, P. Goudblom, J. and Kortel, H. eds: *Human Figurations* (Amsterdam: Sociologisch Tijdschrift, 1977).

Elkins, Stanley, M. (b.1925) Born in Boston, Massachusetts, Elkins graduated from Harvard in 1949, obtained an MA from Columbia University in 1951 and received his doctorate, also from Columbia, in 1959. He taught at school in New York City from 1951 to 1954 and joined the history faculty at the University of Chicago in 1955; since 1960 he has been professor of history at Smith College.

The contributions of Elkins to the writing of history have been more suggestive than definitive. Either alone or in collaboration with others he has sketched hypotheses which he has not himself tested thoroughly but which have influenced the work of other historians. The best known examples include an article, written in collaboration with Eric McKitrick, which essayed the hypothesis that the struggle over the American Constitution in 1787/8 can best be understood, not as involving ideology or economic interests but as pitting energetic *young* Federalists against inertia-prone older statesmen; and his more substantial work, *Slavery: a Problem in American Institutional and Intellectual Life* (1959). The latter book shaped more than a decade of writing about slavery. Unfortunately, neither the article on the Constitution, nor the book on slavery, have withstood the investigations and critical analysis of other historians.

Slavery challenged existing interpretations of the institution by asking new questions. Its approach was explicitly psychological and involved an attempt to gauge the impact of

121

slavery upon the psyche of blacks by comparing their fate with that of the concentration camp victims of Nazi Germany. It prompted many studies which sought to describe more fully than ever before the lives of slaves and the extent to which they were able to control their own environment and develop as people. Judging from successive editions of *Slavery*, Elkins has not been persuaded by his critics but few, if any, other historians can still accept his postulates as descriptive of the realities of slave life and culture. *Slavery* is, none the less, a historiographical landmark and much subsequent writing cannot be understood without reference to it. For many years it generated fertile debate although its categories are now dated. DMacl

Main publications

With Eric McKitrick, The Founding Fathers: young men of the revolution. *Political Science Quarterly* 72 (1961) 181–216; *Slavery: a Problem in American Institutional and Intellectual Life*, 3rd edn (Chicago, Ill.: University of Chicago Press, 1976).

Reading

Lane, Ann J., ed.: *The Debate over Slavery: Stanley Elkins and his Critics* (Urbana: University of Illinois Press, 1971).

Elliott, John Huxtable (b.1929) Educated at Eton and then at Cambridge, Elliott was elected a Fellow of Trinity (1954–67), moving on thereafter to a chair at Kings College, London and then to the Institute for Advanced Studies at Princeton in 1973. There had been little serious interest in England in the history of early modern Spain, and his doctoral thesis, published as *The Revolt of the Catalans*, made its mark as the first substantial English contribution in a field where all the major English-language works had been by Americans. This first book was followed almost immediately by a general survey of the period, *Imperial Spain*, which established itself as a standard work for college use both in the Anglo-Saxon world and in Spain itself. Elliott was one of the first members of the editorial board of *Past and Present*, adding a touch of pragmatism to the otherwise largely Marxist tendency of the journal. His work is not methodologically innovative; his success has arisen from a combination of balanced analysis, clarity of exposition and good literary style. Perhaps his most significant contribution to historical studies has been his direction of a generation of research students, mainly American, who have in their turn added significantly to our knowledge of early Habsburg Spain. He was invited to give the Wiles Lectures at Belfast and the Trevelyan Lectures at Cambridge. At Princeton he devoted his time to research on the central object of his interest, the Count-Duke of Olivares, of whom he published a substantial biography in 1986. His historical work has received wide recognition, and he was elected to the British Academy in 1972. HK

Main publications

The Revolt of the Catalans (Cambridge: Cambridge University Press, 1963); *Imperial Spain, 1469–1716* (London: Edward Arnold, 1963); (the Wiles Lectures) *The Old World and the New 1492–1650* (Cambridge University Press, 1970); (the Trevelyan Lectures) *Richelieu and Olivares* (Cambridge University Press, 1984); *The Count-Duke of Olivares* (London: Yale University Press, 1986).

Elton, Geoffrey Rudolph (b.1921) Born in Germany, the son of the ancient historian Victor Ehrenberg (and a more distant relative of the Richard Ehrenberg who wrote *The Age of the Fuggers*), Elton studied at the University of Prague before coming to England. He changed his name during the second world war, in which he served in the Intelligence Corps. He has taught at Cambridge since 1949, becoming a fellow of Clare College in 1954 and regius professor of history in 1983. He was knighted in 1986.

Elton's first published article dealt with Julius Caesar, but he made his reputation in 1953 with the publication of his doctoral thesis on what he called the 'Tudor Revolution in Government' which he associated with the 1530s and in particular with Thomas Cromwell. He has continued to write on administrative history ever since, and to specialize on the decade of the 1530s, the subject of numerous articles and of two major books: *Policy and Police*, a study of 'the enforcement of the Reformation', and *Reform and Renewal*. He has also produced a best-selling textbook, *England under the Tudors*. He has edited several series and supervised an army of research students.

An early riser and a hard worker, Elton is a man of strong opinions who has never shunned controversy. His battles with John Cooper (over the policies of Henry VII), and with Lawrence Stone (over the policies of Henry VIII), raised a good deal of dust, and revealed Elton as more English than the English in the sense of being more willing than his opponents to defend both monarchs. In *The Practice of History* and occasional writings, he has shown himself to be both a vigorous defender of the study of political history (English political history in particular), and from time to time an aggressive critic of his colleagues.   UPB

Main publications

The Tudor Revolution in Government (Cambridge: Cambridge University Press, 1953); *England under the Tudors* (London: Methuen, 1955); *The Practice of History* (London: Collins, 1967); *Policy and Police* (Cambridge University Press, 1972); *Reform and Renewal* (Cambridge University Press, 1973); *Studies in Tudor and Stuart Politics*, 2 vols (Cambridge University Press, 1974).

Reading

Kenyon, J.: *The History Men* (London: Weidenfeld & Nicolson, 1983).

Engels, Friedrich (b.1820, d.1895) Born the eldest son of a well-to-do textile manufacturer in the Ruhr, Engels quickly abandoned his early pietistic beliefs and became a communist. After the failure of the 1848 revolutions, he settled in his father's firm in Manchester where he continued the active collaboration with Marx which had begun in 1844. On his retirement in 1870 Engels moved to London and, particularly after Marx's death in 1883, became the leading exponent of his friend's ideas.

Engels was a lucid and prolific writer whose talents found their fullest expression in the writing of history. His gift for powerful description, combined with his linguistic skills and his flexibililty in using the Marxist framework made him an influential historian. He produced an immense number of articles on a wide range of topics and earned himself the nickname 'General' by becoming one of the very few civilian experts in the specialist field of military history. His major contributions are three: his analysis of the English working class in the mid-1840s; his research into pre-history; and his attempts to systematize the principles of historical materialism.

Engels's study in contemporary history entitled *The Condition of the Working Class in England* (1845) drew on his own experiences in the north of England to produce an extended account of the social impact of industrialization at its most advanced point. Although marred by a penchant for over-hasty prediction, the book made a strong impact through its descriptive passages, and its excellent use of government publications and statistics confirmed it as a pioneering work in the relatively modern fields of urban geography and sociology.

Towards the end of his life Engels turned his attention to research into primitive societies and produced *The Origin of the Family, Private Property and the State* (1884). The book suffered from too heavy a reliance on the Darwinist evolutionary perspective of Lewis Morgan's *Ancient Society* which had appeared in 1877. But the *Origin* was strikingly original in drawing the attention of socialists to the possibility that sexual and production relations had in some respect been superior in primitive societies.

In his elucidation of the general principles of historical materialism, Engels allowed that elements of the superstructure – ideologies, for example, or legal arrangements – did have a relative or circumscribed independence and could substantially influence the economic basis which nevertheless retained its role as determinant in the last instance.   DTM

Main publications

Selected Works (Moscow: Foreign Languages Publishing House, 1962); *Selected Writings*, ed. W. O. Henderson (Harmondsworth: Penguin, 1967); *Collected Works* (London: Lawrence & Wishart, 1975).

Reading

Carver, T.: *Engels* (Oxford: Oxford University Press, 1981).

Henderson, W. O.: *The Life of Friedrich Engels* (London: Frank Cass, 1976).

McLellan, D.: *Engels* (Glasgow: Fontana/Collins, 1977).

Erdmann, Carl (b.1898, d.1945) The posthumous son of a professor of jurisprudence at Dorpat, Erdmann was a medievalist outstanding alike for his scholarship and for his sense of an historian's wider responsibilities. His career was unusual. Never physically robust and therefore exempt from military service in the first world war, he trained in Berlin for the Lutheran pastorate, but withdrew because of doubts about the worth not only of theology but of any academic as opposed to practical calling. In 1920 he attended under family pressure, a single semester of historical study at Munich; he afterwards regarded Paul Joachimsen as his sole historical teacher. The following year he went to Portugal as private tutor to a German family; in 1925 he returned for two further semesters at Würzburg University.

Erdmann's prolonged stay in Portugal was decisive for his future. He spent a great deal of time in libraries, particularly studying Portugal and the Crusades. In 1926 his exemplary edition of early papal charters for Portugal was commissioned for P. F. Kehr's *Papsturkunden*; this work left Erdmann reassured about the value of historical study. Kehr forthwith made him an assistant at the Prussian Historical Institute in Rome, where he not only pursued archival studies but extended his interest in crusading origins from Portugal throughout western Europe. In 1932 he obtained a doctorate at Berlin where he then settled. In 1934 he became an assistant of the *Monumenta Germaniae Historica*.

The years 1932–43 were a period of dedicated study and phenomenal productivity. As a Monumentist Erdmann worked extensively on letter collections, especially towards an edition of the Hanover letter collection and other eleventh-century material which appeared posthumously (1950). A complementary monograph (1938) added a new dimension to the study of German history by making letter collections usable as never before alongside hard-worked chronicles. In addition Erdmann paid much attention to the phenomenon of rulership in tenth-century Germany. Again, the full range of his studies became posthumously apparent in his collected papers (1951) together with a reprinting of his *Otto-*

nische Studien (1968) — mostly about Henry the Fowler. Above all, Erdmann is remembered for his masterly monograph on the origin of the crusading idea (1935), which he believed to have lain in western notions of holy war as waged by an emerging knighthood summoned to the military service of the church. Erdmann dedicated this book 'with unshaken faith in the future of the German spirit', making clear his detestation of the Nazi regime. He forfeited his university employment; when belatedly offered a professorship he spurned it. In 1943 he was conscripted for service in the Balkans as an interpreter in a war that he saw as unjust and as leading Germany into inevitable catastrophe. He did not expect to escape it. In 1944 he wrote home from Tirana, a town near the Via Egnatia along which in 1096 Crusaders had cheerfully passed to their holy war, that 'surely, as a true humanist one must be able to welcome life's end and know how to die *en philosophe*'. On 5 March 1945 he died, probably of typhus, while serving in a prisoner-of-war camp at Zagreb.   HEJC

Main publications

Die Entstehung des Kreuzzugsgedankens (Stuttgart: Kohlhammer, 1935, trans. M. W. Baldwin and W. Goffart, *The Origin of the Idea of Crusade* (Princeton, NJ: Princeton University Press, 1977); *Studien zur Briefliteratur Deutschlands im elften Jahrhundert* (Leipzig: Hiersemann, 1938); with N. Fickermann, *Briefsammlungen der Zeit Heinrichs IV; MGH, Die Briefe der Deutschen Kaiserzeit* 5 (Weimar: Hermann Böhlaus Nachfolger, 1950); *Forschungen zur politischen Ideenwelt des Frühmittelalters*, ed. F. Baethgen (Berlin: Akademie-Verlag, 1951); *Ottonische Studien*, ed. H. Beumann (Darmstadt: Wissenschaftliche Buchgesellschaft, 1968).

Reading

Baethgen, F.: Memoir: Carl Erdmann. In Erdmann 1951 [see above].

Eusebius (b.c.260, d.339/40) Metropolitan of Palestinian Caesarea from c.313, best known for his *Ecclesiastical History* (*HE*) tracing the course and controversies of 'a new nation', the Christian community, from Christ to the time of Constantine the Great, Eusebius was pupil of the scholar Pamphilus, whose name he added to his own in acknowledgement of indebtedness. During Diocletian's persecution of 303 Eusebius shared a prison-cell with Pamphilus until his teacher was martyred. Extant manuscripts record their dependence on models corrected in prison by the two scholars. Pamphilus taught Eusebius to admire and write in defence of Origen (d.254), to apply to the biblical text philological techniques applied to Homer by Alexandrian scholars, and to move among books of pagan learning as a confident Christian scholar of proper standing. Variant readings and historical allusions make it certain that the *HE*, probably first drafted in seven books before 303, was enlarged to ten books and further revised in Constantine's reign, receiving three or four editions. Eusebius possessed neither elegance of style nor gifts of incisive, coherent narrative, but he was self-consciously a pioneer in telling the church's story, for which the Caesarea library gathered by Pamphilus offered excellent materials. Unlike classical historians, Eusebius put no speeches into his characters' mouths. Distrust of oral tradition led him to give many lengthy quotations from documents and writings, despite the disruptive effect upon the flow of his narrative. Since many citations are from works otherwise lost, the *HE*'s value is obviously very great, but Eusebius wrote in the manner of an archivist gathering materials rather than as a historian with a message in the tradition of Thucydides or Polybius. The work contains relatively little about the western church, but is structured around annalistic notices of the succession of bishops in principal sees, among which Rome is important to him as the see of Peter and Paul (occasionally as just the see of Peter). He recorded earlier opinions about the limits of the New Testament canon, a subject on which general agreement had not been reached by the early fourth century. He highlighted prominent theologians and defenders of orthodoxy, with lists of their chief works; the long and idealizing biography of Origen in book 6 marks an evident climax. Eusebius was interested in refuting pagan intellectuals who scorned not only the historical reliability of the gospel tradition but also the general level of education in the Christian community. Above all, Eusebius was concerned to mark the providential preservation of the orthodox

community-tradition against its vocal and muscular adversaries among Jews, heretics and pagans. The pagan attacks had again become physical in 303. Eusebius wrote a moving account of *The Martyrs of Palestine*, first issued as an appendix to book 8 in one edition of the *HE*, then enlarged to make an independent piece, extant entire only in Syriac. Throughout the *HE* martyrdom is an important theme, linked to the vindication of integrity. The whole work is written, accordingly, with a powerful sense of the church's self-identity and distinctiveness, embattled with opponents whether prejudiced or misinformed, preserved in the truth especially through its succession of bishops and wise teachers, finally attaining an unexpected triumph with Constantine, whose conversion dismantled the barriers between the people of God and the hitherto alien, secular order of government. Therefore, Eusebius presupposed, in the designs of providence, the destinies of church and Roman empire were bound together.

This theme was not original with Eusebius, but went back beyond Origen to Justin Martyr in the mid-second century, or in embryo even to St Luke in the Acts of the Apostles. Eusebius saw the divine mission of the gospel vindicated not only by the wonderful works of Jesus, not only by the fulfilment of prophecy, but as a living event before his eyes in the establishment of Christianity at the citadel of power on the emperor's throne. God's fishermen had overcome the fury of all the opposition. In his last work, the panegyric 'On the life of Constantine', Eusebius again followed the method of long quotations of letters and documents; their authenticity, once doubted, is now generally accepted. The panegyric presents the Christian emperor as the earthly representative of the divine Word, with a mission to unite a divided, warring empire (and a not much less quarrelsome church), to begin the process of dismantling pagan polytheism and to support the welfare-work for the poor undertaken by bishops.

Other major works include his *Chronicle* (the scaffolding for the *HE*); *Praeparatio Evangelica* (again with long and valuable quotations from pagan writers); *Demonstratio Evangelica*; *Contra*

Hieroclem (replying to a pagan critic of Christianity); *Onomastikon* (the only extant part of a longer work on biblical topography, composed as a help for the Bible student: it was adapted for Latin readers by Jerome). The *HE* was translated into Latin in 402 by Rufinus of Aquileia, and, on the basis of a work in Greek by Gelasius of Caesarea, extended to Theodosius (395); it also survives in Syriac and Armenian. It became the model for later church historians, Socrates, Sozomen, Theodoret and Evagrius.   HC

Main writings

Critical edition of principal works in the Berlin Academy series, *Die griechische christliche Schriftsteller*, especially the *HE* by E. Schwartz, and Rufinus's translation by T. Mommsen; English trans. of the *HE* by H. J. Lawlor and J. E. L. Oulton with commentary (London: 1927–8) and by K. Lake and J. E. L. Oulton (London: Loeb, 1926–32).

Reading

Barnes, T. D.: *Constantine and Eusebius* (Harvard: 1981).

Berkhof, H.: *Die Theologie des Eusebius von Caesarea* (Amsterdam: 1939);

Croke, B. and Emmett, A. M.: *History and Historians in Late Antiquity* (Oxford: Pergamon, 1983).

Grant, R. M.: *Eusebius as Church Historian* (Oxford: 1980).

Markus, Robert: *From Augustine to Gregory the Great* (London: Variorum, 1983), ch. 2. [A perspective survey of Eusebius' place in early Christian historiography.]

Mosshammer, A.: *The Chronicle of Eusebius and Greek Chronographic Tradition* (London: 1979).

Lawlor, H. J.: *Eusebiana* (Oxford: 1912).

Wallace-Handrill, D. S.: *Eusebius of Caesarea* (London: 1960).

Eutropius (*fl.* fourth century AD). A high official of the Roman empire, Eutropius rose to the praetorian prefecture (380–1) and became consul in 387. He composed a Latin *Breviarium* (Short Account) of Roman history, a type of historical writing much in vogue in his age. This work, in ten books, dedicated to the emperor Valens, sparsely surveyed the period from the foundation of the city to the year 364 AD.   EDH

Main writings

Eutropius ed. C. Santini (Stuttgart: Bibliotheca Teubneriana, 1979).

F

Fairbank, John King (b.1907) Born in South Dakota, educated at Exeter, Harvard and Oxford, Fairbank taught modern Chinese history at Harvard from 1936 to 1977. His tall, commanding appearance perfectly symbolized his position of unchallenged leadership in western studies of modern China, as this field became more sophisticated in the post second world war era.

Fairbank's basic monographic work dealt with Sino—western relations in the early and mid-nineteenth century. Beginning in the late 1950s, he embarked on a series of editorial projects on a broad range of topics including traditional East Asian diplomatic relations, traditional Chinese thought, Chinese military techniques, China's intellectual response to western expansion, the western missionary effort and the Chinese communist movement. His major theoretical contributions include analyses of China's Sino-centric world order, of 'synarchy' (joint Sino—foreign administration) under the unequal treaties, and of China's difficulty in grafting foreign material progress (*yung*) onto a Confucian moral base (*t'i*).

Apart from his own research Fairbank established the field through setting standards for language training, designing curricula, writing textbooks, compiling bibliographies, training teachers and overseeing Harvard's energetic programme of publication in East Asian history. Most recently he has served as co-editor of the monumental *Cambridge History of China*. Throughout these years Fairbank has been probably the most important influence on American public opinion (and, informally, on American policy) towards China. He was an early and vocal advocate of normalization of relations with the People's Republic.

Fairbank's vision of modern Chinese history has recently been criticized for its unduly narrow focus on the problem of response to the west, and for its implications of stagnation within the indigenous society. Nevertheless the work of subsequent scholars who have rejected these approaches has itself built upon Fairbank's central legacy: his insistence that modern China is not an inferior comic-opera version of the west, but a unique and extraordinarily complex society with its own highly developed socio-political institutions.   WTR

Main publications

(Published by Harvard University Press, Cambridge, Mass., unless otherwise stated.)
The United States and China (1948; 4th rev. edn, 1979): *Trade and Diplomacy on the China Coast* (1953); with Ssu-yu Teng, *China's Response to the West* (1958); *The Chinese World Order* (1968); with Denis Twitchett, ed., *The Cambridge History of China*, projected 16 vols (Cambridge: Cambridge University Press).

family history   See DEMOGRAPHIC HISTORY.

Febvre, Lucien (b.1878, d.1956) Febvre acquired a good interdisciplinary education at the École Normale before teaching at the university of Dijon (1912—14). After the first world war he taught at the new French university of Strasburg (1919—33), in company with Marc BLOCH, with whom he founded the journal ANNALES in 1929 as a mouthpiece for their new kind of history. He moved to the Collège de France in 1933, and after the second world war became president of the

Sixième (historical) section of the multidisciplinary École Pratique des Hautes Études en Sciences Sociales.

Febvre began his historical career with an important piece of research on his native Franche-Comté in the age of Philip II, an innovative piece of social history which concentrated on the conflict between a declining nobility and a rising bourgeoisie of merchants and lawyers, and might be taken (ironically enough, given the author's religious and political views), for the work of a Marxist. He followed this up with a general essay on historical geography in the manner of his master Paul Vidal de la Blache, attacking the geographical determinism of the German geopolitical school (a determinism now associated with Febvre's intellectual son, BRAUDEL), and emphasizing human freedom to shape the environment as well as to react to it in various ways. It was perhaps this concern with freedom which led him to abandon social for intellectual history.

After the war Febvre transformed himself into a specialist in religious history, beginning with a study of Luther (1928), most remarkable for its exploration of the relationship between the founder and his followers, and then turning to the French reformation, clearing the ground with a famous article on the problem of its origins as 'a question wrongly put', and continuing with studies of individuals, notably Marguerite de Navarre, François Rabelais, and the humanists Des Périers and Dolet. These studies were not concerned with ecclesiastical history in the institutional sense, but with the history of religious attitudes, sentiments, or *mentalités*: Febvre's own favourite term was *outillage mental*, which might perhaps be rendered as 'intellectual apparatus'. In the most famous of these studies, on the religion of Rabelais, he discussed the 'problem of unbelief': in other words, whether it was possible to be an atheist in the sixteenth century. He concluded that it was not, approaching the problem with characteristic verve by a sort of *via negativa*, noting the words lacking in the philosophical vocabulary of the period and concluding that they marked limits to thought. At the end of his life he was working on two important new projects which he left to be finished by his collaborators: a history of European books in the century or so after the invention of printing, written with H. J. Martin, and an essay on the social psychology of the early modern French, completed by Robert Mandrou and published under the latter's name.

Although Febvre's work did not travel as well as that of his friend and colleague Bloch, it was immensely influential in France between the 1940s and the 1960s. One reason for this influence is that Febvre was a gifted and tireless *animateur*, who spread the gospel of his movement for the renewal of historical studies by means of his many polemical book reviews in support of 'our' kind of history (problem-oriented, wide-ranging, ill at ease within disciplinary boundaries), and against its opponents. Some of these reviews and programmatic essays have been collected into the appropriately-named *Combats pour l'histoire*. Febvre also cultivated a close relationship with leaders in other disciplines such as geography, linguistics, and social psychology. A formidable academic politician, he managed to take over the French historical establishment after the war, and to pass on his commanding position to the heir he designated, Fernand Braudel.   UPB

Main publications

Philippe II et la Franche-Comté (Paris: 1912); *La terre et l'évolution humaine* (1922); trans. as *Geographical Introduction to History* (London: Kegan Paul, 1925); *Un destin, Martin Luther* (1928); trans. as *Martin Luther* (London: Dent, 1930); *Le problème de l'incroyance au 16e siècle: la religion de Rabelais* (1942); trans. as *The Problem of Unbelief in The 16th Century: the Religion of Rabelais* (Cambridge, Mass., 1983); *Combats pour l'histoire* (Paris: Colin, 1953); *Au coeur religieux du 16e siècle* (Paris: Colin, 1956); (with H.−J. Martin) *L'apparition du livre* (1958); trans. as *The Coming of the Book* (London: New Left Books, 1976).

Reading

Fenlon, D: Encore une question: Lucien Febvre, the Reformation and the School of *Annales*. *Historical Studies* 9 (1974) 65−81.

Hughes, H. S.: *The Obstructed Path* (New York: 1969).

Mann, H.−D.: *Lucien Febvre* (Paris: Colin, 1971).

feminist historiography   Though the term is modern, feminist historiography should not be seen simply as a product of the late twentieth century: a politically committed identification both with past heroines and with the history of women's condition, also characterized many earlier writers. In the late nineteenth and early twentieth centuries a number of distinguished historians and writers, sympathetic to or associated with feminist causes, looked to the past with a new awareness. They wrote of the emergence of feminism itself; for example, in England, Ray Strachey's still unchallenged *The Cause: a Short History of the Women's Movement in Great Britain* (1928), and in the United States the collective authors of the six-volume *History of Woman Suffrage* (1881–1922). Social and economic historians such as Julia Cherry Spruill (*Women's Life and Work in the Southern Colonies*, 1938), Alice Clark and Ivy Pinchbeck showed new insight into the strength of women's involvement in productive activities. Clark's *Working Life of Women in the Seventeenth Century* (1919) and Pinchbeck's *Women Workers and the Industrial Revolution* (1930) have not yet been superseded as fundamental starting points for the study of women's work. Despite such outstanding pieces of historical writing and research, the teaching of history in schools and universities was hardly affected. Even in the 1960s few students studied the history of women.

Since 1970, however, in the United States and Britain feminist historians have had an increasing impact upon the historical record. This movement, emerging from broader political and social concerns, coincided with a more general recovery in the writing of SOCIAL HISTORY – but the two cannot be identified. Early contributors such as Gerda Lerner and Sheila Rowbotham had noted both their consciousness of the absence of women from the historical record, and, at the same time, their sense of continuity with the work of feminist predecessors. In the United States the strength of the women's movement in the late 1960s and during the 1970s undoubtedly contributed to the emergence of a lively and active field of women's history, with an institutional base. Distinguished scholars included Gerda Lerner, Nancy Cott, Martha Vicinus and Linda Gordon. In Britain there were few feminist historians in universities or colleges;

inspiration came from the radical History Workshop and from those writing outside formal academic institutions, and, in particular, the early work of Sheila Rowbotham. Leonore Davidoff at Essex University was a pioneer. By the early 1980s, though feminist history had a stronger foundation, it had still won less acceptance in Britain than in the United States.

Feminist history has focused on the experience of women: historians have illustrated the distance between prescriptive writings on women's role and the realities of their lives. Feminist historians have argued that those realities involved a consideration of topics previously outside the historical record: the history of domestic labour, for example, previously undervalued and dismissed. Leonore Davidoff's work has pointed to the inadequacy of definitions of women's work which follow census categories in England, omitting the many ways in which married women particularly might undertake casual or paid household labour (in *Fit Work for Women*, ed. S. Burman, 1979). Ellen Ross has pointed to the importance of female networks often based on collectively undertaken domestic and household labour in late nineteenth-century London (*Feminist Studies* 8 (1982); *History Workshop* 15 (1983)). Lillian Faderman has illustrated how changing notions of sexuality have altered perspectives on female friendships (*Surpassing the Love of Men: Romantic Friendship between Women from the Renaissance to the Present*, 1981); and Martha Vicinus has traced the history of female communities of middle-class women in the late nineteenth century (*Independent Women: Work and Community for Single Women, 1850–1920*, 1985). Such arguments raise questions about the very definition of historical categories. Feminist historians in the 1970s and 1980s have been united by commitment to the social construction of gender roles, and rejection of any 'natural' sexual division of labour. A new approach to the gender boundaries of particular societies has brought a radical shift. The outstanding work of Barbara Taylor in *Eve and the New Jerusalem: Socialism and Feminism in the Nineteenth Century* (1983) has both recovered the careers of women active in the nineteenth-century

Owenite movement, and set that movement in the context of changing gender relations in a period of early industrialization. The periodical *History Workshop Journal* offers a range of work by socialist and feminist historians committed to the awareness of gender differences, and of the roles of women and men constructed through concepts of femininity and of masculinity.

The writing of an earlier generation tended to emphasize simply the recovery of women's past. Today, most feminist historians would identify themes which entail a new approach to history itself. Feminist history has been attacked for being 'victim-oriented', for leaning too strongly on the theme of women's oppression by men. The term 'patriarchy', implying a universal pattern of male sexual hierarchy as a historical constant, has been a controversial one. While the near universality of sexual inequality can hardly be challenged, it has been suggested that such a framework for historical explanation must incorporate other variables – of class, race, religion – and that neither women's own active experience and consciousness, nor historical shifts in gender relations, should be excluded. The dangers of an exclusive focus on 'women's history', without a full understanding of the distinctive historical context and of the corresponding male worlds, have been increasingly discussed. Feminist history aims to incorporate the implications of gender not only into the study of women's history, but also into a more radical challenge to the male perspective of most existing historical work. As an aspiration this has as yet been more often expressed than achieved: relatively few feminist historians in Great Britain have, for instance, entered into areas of work before the eighteenth century. Though the demand for a history which expresses the realities of the past experience of women as well as of men is by now an established one, it may still be said to have more appeal outside the historical profession than within it.   JR

Reading

Alexander, S.: Women, class and sexual difference in the 1830s and 1840s: some reflections on the writing of a feminist history. *History Workshop* 17 (1984).

—— and Taylor, B.: In defence of patriarchy. In *People's History and Socialist Theory* (London: Routledge & Kegan Paul, 1981).

Carroll, B. ed.: *Liberating Women's History: Theoretical and Critical Essays.* (Urbana, Ill.: University of Illinois Press, 1976).

Clark, Alice: *Working Life of Women in the Seventeenth Century* (Routledge & Kegan Paul, 1982).

Dubois, E., Buhle, M.–J., Kaplan, T., Lerner, G. and Smith-Rosenberg, C.: Politics and culture in women's history: a symposium. *Feminist Studies* 6 (1980).

Harrison, B. and McMillan, J. F.: Some feminist betrayals of women's history. *Historical Journal* 26 (1983).

Kelly, J.: *Women, History and Theory. the Essays of Joan Kelly.* Chicago: University of Chicago Press, 1984).

Lerner, G.: *The Majority Finds its Past: Placing Women in History.* New York: Oxford University Press, 1979).

Pinchbeck, Ivy: *Women Workers and the Industrial Revolution* (London: Virago, 1981).

Rowbotham, S. The trouble with patriarchy. In *Dreams and Dilemmas* (Virago, 1983).

Smith-Rosenberg, C.: Hearing women's words: a feminist reconstruction of history. In *Disorderly Conduct: Visions of Gender in Victorian America* (New York: Knopf, 1985).

Fénelon, François de Salignac de La Mothe

(b.1651, d.1715) Fénelon became one of the most eminent ecclesiastics of his era, famous for his work educating converted Protestant women, for his role in the education of the duke of Burgundy and for his quarrel with Bossuet over quietism. To posterity he has been more celebrated as a political theorist and critic of Louis XIV.

As a member of the circle of the duke of Burgundy he elaborated a critique of the divine right monarchy of Louis XIV which was to have considerable influence on writers during the eighteenth century. As with Bossuet, the basis of his criticisms was Christian but his deep interest in history gave his writings a statesmanlike awareness of the developments undergone by the monarchical state in the seventeenth century and led to the proposal of reforms whose practical nature was partly a result of his historical studies.

His contribution to historiography is to be found in a brief section in the *Lettre à l'Académie*, of which he was a member. Here he suggests that history should be analytical, written in a straightforward style explaining the chain of cause and effect, avoiding superfluous detail and taking great care to portray events in their appropriate historical context. History was to be a source of example supplementing our experience and contributing to our educational and moral development.   PRC

Main publications

Les aventures de Télémaque (1699) 2 vols, ed. A. Cahen (Paris: Hachette, 1927); *Ecrits et lettres politiques*, ed. Charles Urbain (Paris: Bossard, 1920); *Lettre à l'Académie* (1716) ed. E. Caldarini (Geneva: Droz, 1970).

Reading

Chérel, A.: *Fénelon au XVIIIᵉ siècle en France* (Geneva: Slatkine, 1970).

Davis, J. H.: *Fénelon* (Boston: Twayne, 1979).

Festus (d. AD 380)   Like his contemporary EUTROPIUS, Festus was a senior Roman official (proconsul of Asia 372–8) who dedicated to the emperor Valens *c.*369 a *Breviarium* (Short Account) of Roman history, a type of historical writing popular at that time. In a mere thirty chapters he attempted to embrace the entire span from the foundation of Rome to the year AD 364.   EDH

Main writings

The Breviarium of Festus, ed. J. W. Eadie (London: Athlone, 1967).

Finley, Moses I. (b.1912, d.1986)   Born in New York, Finley graduated from Syracuse University at the age of 15 and completed his education at Columbia University. A victim of McCarthyism, he was dismissed from an assistant professorship at Rutgers University in 1952. The rest of his academic life was spent at the University of Cambridge, where he took up a lectureship in 1955. He was professor of ancient history from 1970 to 1979 and Master of Darwin College from 1976 to 1982. He became a British citizen in 1962 and was knighted in 1979.

Finley was a great lecturer and teacher and a prolific and influential writer, principally in the field of Greek society, economy and politics. He was exceptional in the size and range of his audience. He had a large following outside the English-speaking world, won the attention and respect of historians of other periods and of social scientists, and stimulated interest in the classical world among intelligent laymen.

Finley's intellectual formation at Columbia provided him with the basis for an individual approach to ancient history. A training in history and law as distinct from classical literature and philology, close association with the expatriate Frankfurt Institute for Social Research (from 1934) and later with the Hungarian exile Karl Polanyi (from 1946) gave him experience in a wide range of intellectual disciplines, including anthropology, economic history and social theory (Marx and Weber were abiding influences), and a broad, detached view of classical antiquity.

Finley had difficulty in coming to terms with the limitations of the ancient sources and conventional source-based historical scholarship. He held that qualitative deficiencies, inadequate coverage and limited interests of the sources severely circumscribe the subject matter of ancient history. His solution was to employ models, Weber's 'ideal types', to encapsulate the essential features of a society and encourage cross-societal comparison. Finley stressed the uniqueness of ancient societies, the 'primitive' level of their social and economic development, and was highly critical of historians (Marxist and non-Marxist) who blurred the distinctions between ancient and modern.

Finley was a provocateur. His polemic was offensive to some, especially those whose methods and assumptions he attacked. Others were attracted by his iconoclasm, breadth of learning and interest, personal accessibility and success in bringing ancient history alive.   PDAG

Main publications

(Published by Chatto & Windus, London, unless otherwise stated.)
Studies in Law and Credit in Ancient Athens, 500–200 BC (New Brunswick, NJ: Rutgers University Press, 1952); *The World of Odysseus* (New York: Viking, 1954); *The Ancient Greeks* (1963); *Ancient Sicily to the Arab Conquest* (1968); *Aspects of Antiquity* (1968); *Early Greece: The Bronze and Archaic Ages*

(1970); *Democracy Ancient and Modern* (1973); *The Ancient Economy* (1973); *Use and Abuse of History* (1975); *Ancient Slavery and Modern Ideology* (1980); *Economy and Society in Ancient Greece*, ed. B. D. Shaw and R. P. Saller (1981); *Politics in the Ancient World* (Cambridge: Cambridge University Press, 1983); *Ancient History: Evidence and Models* (1985).

Reading

De Sanctis, G.: Moses I. Finley. Note per una Biografia intellettuale. *Quaderni di Storia* 10 (1979) 3–37.

Shaw, B. D. and Saller, R. P. eds.: Introduction to *Economy and Society in Ancient Greece* (London: Chatto & Windus, 1981).

Vidal-Naquet, P.: l'économie et société dans la Grèce ancienne: l'oeuvre de Moses I. Finley. *Archives Européennes de Sociologie* 6 (1965) 111–48.

Firth, Charles Harding (b.1857, d.1936) Born in Sheffield and educated at Clifton College, Firth entered New College, Oxford, as a commoner in 1875. In the following year he won the prestigious Brackenbury scholarship and migrated to Balliol, then the undisputed centre of Oxford historical study. The move was propitious. Among his contemporaries were R. L. POOLE, J. H. ROUND, T. F. TOUT, Sidney LEE, W. J. ASHLEY and Richard Lodge. But more significantly he was taught by STUBBS, and learned from him how history was written. The lessons were soon put to good effect. In 1877 Firth won the Stanhope essay prize and a year later graduated with first class honours in modern history. He travelled to Germany, lectured at his uncle's collegiate foundation in Sheffield, and for a time considered a career in politics. But in 1883, his mind made up, he returned to Oxford to begin what he called 'the steady jog-trot of the professional historian'.

Firth was never popular in Oxford. This, said some, was hardly surprising, for he was burdened with the triple disadvantages of ill-health, private wealth, and a special subject. Unlike most of the tutorial body (whose number he swelled but briefly as a tutorial fellow of Pembroke College between 1887 and 1893) Firth did not have to rely on teaching or the collegiate system for a living. As a teacher he was unbending. He simply refused to undertake survey 'hack work'. As a historian he

eschewed the generalism of his tutorial colleagues and began a deep, intensive study of the seventeenth century. While others wrote school textbooks Firth, inspired by the work and friendship of S. R. GARDINER, dug deep into the history of the Protectorate. His first concern was the discovery, evaluation and publication of sources. For 15 years his work was divided between editing texts, among them: *Memoirs of the Life of Colonel Hutchison* (1885), *The Life of William Cavendish* (1886) and the *Memoirs of Edmund Ludlow* (1894), and contributing extensively to the *Dictionary of National Biography*. But *The Clark Papers*, edited in four volumes between 1891 and 1901, were the turning point. They provided the spur to Firth's two great narrative studies: *Oliver Cromwell and the Rule of the Puritans in England* (1900) and *Cromwell's Army* (1902). The latter, resulting from his Ford Lectures of 1900–1 was a pioneering work among virgin archives which explained how the New Model Army was recruited, equipped, paid, disciplined and fed. It is Firth's most enduring work and still repays study.

In 1902 Firth was elected to only the second research fellowship at All Souls. It was his intention to extend Gardiner's history to the Restoration. But the task was beyond him. *The Last Years of the Protectorate* (1909) covering only the events of the two years 1656–8, filled two massive volumes. Firth was simply incapable of narrowing his focus sufficiently to make an extended narrative possible. Whereas Gardiner limited his study to political, constitutional and religious issues, Firth was also drawn to social, economic and cultural aspects of the age and made numerous notable contributions to literary and art history. Further, in 1904 Firth succeeded York Powell as regius professor of modern history at Oxford. A year earlier Maitland had refused to consider the Cambridge chair because he feared that the holder was 'expected to speak to the world at large'. Firth, a man of strong opinions about the proper place and purpose of higher education, took the office seriously. From 1904 his scholastic output, though by no means negligible, slowed in proportion to the breadth of his administrative concerns. He conducted almost single-handedly an acrimonious but only moderately successful campaign to introduce a compulsory element of research training into the history syllabus. He backed the introduction of the school of medieval and modern languages, the study of geography and the education of women. He served for ten years on the Royal Commission for Public Records (1910–19) and for 20 years as a trustee of the National Portrait Gallery. He was president of the Royal Historical Society from 1913 to 1917 and of the Historical Association from 1906 to 1910 and 1918 to 1920.

Recognition of Firth's services to historical scholarhip and to the machinery growing up to support it was universal. He was elected a fellow of the British Academy in 1903, received honorary doctorates from the universities of Aberdeen, Durham, Cambridge, Sheffield, Manchester, and Oxford and was knighted in 1922. He died on 19 February 1936 aged 78.   PRHS

Main publications

Editor, *The Clark Papers*, 4 vols (London: for the Camden Society, 1891–1901); *Cromwell's Army: a History of the English Soldier during the Civil Wars, the Commonwealth and the Protectorate* (London: Methuen, 1902); *English History in English Poetry from the French Revolution to the Death of Queen Anne* (London: H. Marshall, 1911); *A Plea for the Historical Teaching of History* (Oxford: Clarendon Press, 1904).

Reading

Davies, Godfrey: Sir Charles Harding Firth. *Proceedings of the British Academy* 22 (1936) 380–400.
Slee, Peter R. H.: *Learning and a Liberal Education: History as a Discipline in the Universities of Oxford, Cambridge and Manchester 1800–1914* (Manchester: Manchester University Press, 1986).

Fischer, Fritz (b.1908) It is given to few historians to have their name inseparably connected with a particular historical issue. Of these Fischer is one, though his early career would not have prepared the academic world for such an outcome. Born in Ludwigstadt, he studied at Erlangen and Berlin, where his initial interest was in eighteenth- and nineteenth-century religious history. Ironically, in the light of his later sharp criticism of the German Chancellor in 1914, he wrote an important study of Moritz August von Beth-

mann Hollweg and the Protestantism of his era. Fischer became professor at Hamburg in 1948 and remained at that university for the rest of his career, becoming emeritus in 1973. Nothing he wrote in the dozen years after 1945 brought his name to the attention of his academic colleagues. However, he was steadily amassing material for the large study of German war aims in the first world war − *Griff nach der Weltmacht* − which appeared in 1961 and immediately caused a major controversy within Germany, extending beyond academic circles. The 'Fischer controversy' was born. It continues, in attenuated form, into the present, though in Germany the most acute phase of the debate was in the early 1960s, particularly at the historical congress held in West Berlin in 1964.

The book was weighty in its documentary foundations but not methodologically innovative. The uproar it caused can only be explained by relating its message to the condition of West German society at that time. Drawing on no significant memory of 1914, Fischer's approach was more clinical than that of older established historians. More than that however the thrust of his case upset the consensus which most West Germans appeared to have reached about their twentieth-century past. Although not specifically about war origins, the examination of Bethmann Hollweg's September 1914 *Memorandum* appeared to Fischer to suggest that the aims it disclosed had existed before the war. Civilian politicians, no less than military leaders, were not only willing to risk war, but were actively prepared for it. The Nazi period, it was implied, was not so exceptional after all. Fischer's book forced Germans to re-evaluate their recent past just at the point when they thought that they had found a way of explaining it. There was too an iconoclastic stridency about Fischer's opinions which sprang from the circumstances of the early 1960s, not least from the structural tensions within German universities and within the historical profession.

Throughout the subsequent quarter of a century, Fischer has continued to write both substantial treatises and polemical pieces on this topic. *Weltmacht oder Niedergang* (1965) emphasized strongly his contention that war aims could not be divorced from social analysis. Expansion was designed to defend the existing social structure against pressure from below. *Krieg der Illusionen* (1969) made this point even more explicit, as it probed the activities of individuals and pressure groups between 1911 and 1914. However, other historians have not accepted that the mere existence of the forces Fischer describes leads inexorably to the conclusion that Germany did not engage in 'preventive' war in 1914. Fischer himself has remained unmoved by his critics and has recently reviewed the controversies in which he has been involved in a short survey *Juli 1914: Wir sind nicht hineingeschlittert* (July 1914: we did not stumble into it) (1983).

The recipient of honorary degrees from several British universities, Fischer's work certainly injected fresh vigour into the perennial controversies surrounding the first world war. It has not however brought them to an end. KGR

Main publications

Moritz August von Bethmann Hollweg und der Protestantismus (Berlin: Ebering, 1937); *Ludwig Nicolovius: Rokoko, Reform, Restauration* (Stuttgart: Kohlhammer 1939); *Griff nach der Weltmacht* (1961) trans. as *Germany's Aims in the First World War* (New York: Norton; London: Chatto & Windus, 1967); *Weltmacht oder Niedergang?* (1965) (New York: Norton, 1974); *Krieg der Illusionen* (1969) trans. M. Jackson *War of Illusions: German Policies from 1911 to 1914*, Intro. Alan Bullock (New York: Norton; London: Chatto & Windus, 1975).

Reading

Joll, J.: The 1914 Debate Continues: Fritz Fischer and his critics. *Past and present* 34 (1966) 100–13.
Nelson, K. L. and Olin, S. C.: *Why War? Ideology, Theory and History* (Berkeley & London: University of California Press, 1979).

Flach, Geoffroi-Jacques (b.1846, d.1919) Descended from an old legal family in Strasburg, Flach moved to Paris in 1872 in order to preserve his nationality. Starting as a lawyer with a chair in the School of Architecture, he advanced through comparative law to the origins of feudalism and (eventually) a chair at the Collège de France. Always something of an 'outsider' in Paris, he ignored contemporary teaching and concentrated on sources. His great work, *Les Origines de l'ancienne France* (1886–1917) was based on charters (many of them unpublished), *chansons de geste* and saints' lives (later known as *les mentalités collectifs*). Its main theme, that Aquitaine, Normandy, France and Burgundy did not become 'feudatories' of the French crown till the reign of Philip Augustus, found little support and was convincingly rebutted by F. LOT (1904). His work none the less retains much valuable detail and has exercised more influence (direct or indirect) than is usually acknowledged. RHCD

Main publications

Les Origines de l'ancienne France, vol. 1, *La Régime seigneuriale* (1886), vol. 2, *Les Origines communales et la chevalerie* (1893), vol. 3, *La Renaissance de l'Etat* (1904), vol. 4, *Les Nationalités régionales et leur rapport a la couronne de France* (1917).

Reading

Adams, G. B., in *American History Review* 9 (1903–4) 777–82.
Halphen, L., in *Revue historique* 85 (1904) 271–85 and 129 (1918), 90–6: 5.

Fliche, Marie Joseph Henri Savinien Augustin (b.1884, d.1951) Fliche was the son of a lawyer at Montpellier, where he spent most of his academic career. He studied at Paris under such distinguished medievalists as C. DIEHL, F. LOT, É. MÂLE, and C. Pfister. In 1912 his early studies bore fruit in published theses on the reign of the Capetian king Philip I (1060–1108) and on the life of St Savinien of Sens. From 1906 he was teaching at Bordeaux; in 1919 he became professor of medieval history at Montpellier where he remained for the rest of his life.

Fliche's major achievement was centred upon the Investiture Contest and especially upon Pope Gregory VII (1073–85). As early as 1920 he published a brief biography of this pope; it was the harbinger of the three large volumes on the Gregorian reform that appeared over a period of 13 years: that on the formation of Gregorian ideas in 1924; that on Gregory himself in 1926; and that on the anti-Gregorian opposition in 1937. Fliche was a devout Catholic who regarded all his work as part of the Christian apostolate. He laid great stress upon the religious character of the

Gregorian reform and upon Gregory VII's pontificate as a turning point in the history of the church. In his eyes, the Cluniac reform was primarily monastic and world-renouncing, and as a cure for the church's ills the imperial reform of Henry III (1039–56) was worse than the disease. Gregory vindicated *le gouvernement sacerdotal*; when Henry IV did penance at Canossa in 1077 he displayed the apotheosis of his priestly role. Fliche was, nevertheless, careful not to concentrate exclusively on the figure of Gregory, and was aware of the complexity of the Gregorian reform.

In the first half of his work at Montpellier, Fliche wrote two broad surveys of the medieval west: one on the years AD 395–1254 in the series Histoire du monde (1929), and the other covering AD 888–1125 in G. Glotz's Histoire générale (1930). Thereafter he was the director, together with Victor Martin, of the 21-volume *Histoire de l'église depuis les origines jusqu'à nos jours* (1934–52). Its declared aim was to implement the desire of Pope Leo XIII (1878–1903), who opened the Vatican archives to all scholars, for a universal ecclesiastical history that would offer a conspectus, critical and synthetic, of the whole achievement of modern scholarship.

Fliche was also much concerned with local history. In 1924 he founded a Fédération historique du Languedoc méditerranéen, and over the years he wrote monographs on and guides to towns as widely dispersed as Louvain (1921), Aigues-Mortes and Saint-Gilles (1925), and Montpellier (1935).

Since Fliche, no historian has succeeded in offering a comparable synthesis of the period to which he gave the title The Gregorian Reform. Many of his presuppositions were deeply challenged and modified by the thinking of the Second Vatican Council, and most of his major historical judgements must now be regarded as insecure. But the intellectual force and scholarly depth of his work continue to command close attention and respect. HEJC

Main publications

La Règne de Philippe Iᵉʳ, roi de France (1060–1108) (Paris: Société française d'imprimerie et de librairie, 1912); *Les Vies de Saint Savinien, premier évêque de Sens* (Paris: Société française d'imprimerie et de librairie, (1912); *La Réforme grégorienne*, 3 vols (Louvain: 'Spicilegium sacrum Lovaniense' and Paris: Honoré Champion, 1924–37); *La Chrétienté médiévale 395–1254)*, Histoire du monde, VII/2 (Paris: E. le Boccard, 1929); *L'Europe occidentale de 888 à 1125*, Histoire générale, ed. G. Glotz: Histoire du moyen âge, II (Paris: Les Presses Universitaires de France, 1930); *La Réforme grégorienne et la Reconquête chrétienne (1057–1123)*, with R. Foreville and J. Rousset, *Du premier Concile du Latran à l'avènement d'Innocent III (1123–1198)*, with C. Thouzellier and Y. Azais, *La Chrétienté romaine (1198–1274)*, Histoire de l'église, 8, 9/1, 10 (Paris: Bloud et Gay, 1946, 1948, 1950).

Reading

Jarry, E.: *Dictionnaire d'histoire et de géographie ecclésiastiques* 17 (1968–71) cols 490–2.

Palanque, L.: L'oeuvre historique d'A. Fliche. *La Vie intellectuelle* (June 1953) 139–53.

Flinn, Michael Walter (b.1917, d.1983) Flinn did not obtain a permanent university post until he was 41, but then, helped by his earlier experiences in business, the army and schoolteaching, rapidly established a reputation as one of the most outstanding economic historians of his generation. Born into a large, comfortable, middle-class family in Manchester, he joined a firm of cotton exporters at the age of 18, immediately after leaving William Hulme's Grammar School. He volunteered for the armed forces in 1939, served throughout the war and returned briefly to the cotton industry but, not encouraged by its prospects, he took a history degree at Manchester, specializing in economic history, followed by a diploma in education. He became a teacher, first at Grangefield Grammar School, Stockton, and then, after a brief interval as research fellow at Aberdeen, at Isleworth Grammar School. During a busy teaching career he managed to write a master's thesis on iron-ore mining between 1870 and 1914, and articles on the iron industry, culminating in two books on the Crowley iron business: a critical edition of the law book of the Crowley ironworks (1957) and *Men of Iron: the Crowleys and the Early Iron Industry* (1962).

In 1959 Flinn was invited to join the small, growing and soon to be very impressive teaching staff in economic history at Edinburgh University. There he specialized in the social aspects of the subject, writing and editing a 73-page introduction to Edwin Chadwick's 1842 *Report on the Sanitary Condition of the Labouring Population of Great Britain* (1965), and paying particular attention to the social and intellectual features of the Industrial Revolution's origins in a small book published the following year. Edinburgh awarded him a D. Litt. in 1965 and created for him a personal chair of social history two years later. Population history then came to attract him particularly, as did the movement of real wages in the controversial period between 1750 and 1850. His last years, after early retirement, were taken up with writing the history of the British coal industry between 1700 and 1830, the second volume in a five-volume series commissioned by the National Coal Board and the first to appear. It was a meticulously researched and most readable study which showed how improvements in coal-mining technology enabled growing quantities of cheap fuel to be made available to assist the nation's accelerated economic growth.

Michael Flinn's schoolteaching experience was put to good use in two very successful textbooks published after he had joined the university staff. He then devised a series of pamphlets on specific economic and social history topics and persuaded his publisher, Macmillan, to handle them. These little paperbacks, each written and carefully edited by a specialist on behalf of the Economic History Society and then made quickly available to a wide audience – and particularly to examination candidates and their teachers – were the fruits of the latest scholarship and sold in their thousands. He dealt with 24 titles before handing *Studies in Economic and Social History* to another editor.

A very keen musician who played the viola and was married to a professional pianist, Flinn became chairman of the music panel of the Scottish Arts Council. Between 1980 and 1983 he served as president of the Economic History Society. His very sudden and totally unexpected death at the age of 65 robbed the profession of a generous, warm-hearted and outstanding scholar.   TCB

Main publications

An Economic and Social History of Britain, 1066–1939 (London: Macmillan, 1961); *Men of Iron: the Crowleys in the Early Iron Industry* (Edinburgh: Edinburgh University Press, 1962); *An Economic and Social History of Britain since 1700* (London: Macmillan, 1963); editor, Edwin Chadwick's *Report on the Sanitary Condition of the Labouring Population of Great Britain, 1842* (Edinburgh: Edinburgh University Press, 1965); *The Origins of the Industrial Revolution* (London: Longman, 1966); *British Population Growth 1700–1850* (London: Macmillan/Economic History Society, 1970); editor and co-author, *Scottish Population History from the Seventeenth Century to the 1930s* (Cambridge: Cambridge University Press, 1977); The History of the British Coal Industry, vol. II, *1700–1830: the Industrial Revolution* (Oxford: Clarendon Press, 1984).

Reading

Economic History Review, 38.1 (February 1984); *The Times*, 5 October 1983. Smout, T. C.: *Biographical Introduction to the Search for Wealth and Stability: Essays in Economic and Social History presented to M. W. Flinn* (London: Macmillan, 1979).

Florus (*fl.* first half of 2nd century) The author of a short history of Rome down to the age of Augustus, which concentrated on the wars. Were it not for the fact that his work enjoyed remarkable and widespread popularity until the seventeenth century, Florus would scarcely merit an entry in such a dictionary as this, because nothing is known about him. Even the name appears in the MSS as either L. Annaeus Florus or Julius Florus. Only a bold scholar would stake much on identifying him with either the author of a dialogue on Virgil or the cheeky poet of the court of Hadrian, simply on the basis of some similarity of name. The historian himself says only that he was writing not much less than two hundred years after Augustus. His work bears the title in some MSS of *Epitome of Livy*; but this is misleading both because Florus clearly used a wide range of sources in addition to Livy and because the work bears much more resemblance to the type of brief history which VELLEIUS PATERCULUS wrote than it does to the epitomes composed in the late Empire. The forced rhetoric of Florus' style and his many inaccuracies have not brought him favour in the modern period. Nevertheless, he preserves important and detailed information on some of his subject matter.   JJP

Main writings

Epitome of Livy, main edns: H. Malcovati (Rome: Istituto Poligrafico, 1972); P. Jal (Paris: Budé, 1967); with English trans. by E. S. Forster (Cambridge, Mass.: Loeb Classical Library, 1929).

Reading

den Boer, W.: *Some Minor Roman Historians* (Leiden: E. J. Brill, 1972) pp. 1–18.

Fogel, Robert William (b.1926) Fogel is the chief exponent of the 'new economic history', or CLIOMETRICS. He has held a number of academic posts, beginning with an instructorship at The Johns Hopkins University where he received his doctorate in economics in 1963. He subsequently held positions at the University of Rochester and at the University of Chicago where since 1981 he has been the Charles R. Walgreen professor of American institutions. With the publication of *The Union Pacific Railroad* (1960) and *Railroads and American Economic Growth* (1964) Fogel began to recast the way in which economic history was studied and written. His efforts attracted interdisciplinary attention with the appearance of *Time on the Cross* (1974), written with Stanley Engerman, which won the Bancroft prize in American history in 1975. Fogel is currently at work on an extensive study of North American mortality.   PFP

Main publications

The Union Pacific Railroad: a Case in Premature Enterprise (Baltimore: Johns Hopkins University Press, 1960); *Railroads and American Economic Growth: Essays in Econometric History* (Baltimore: Johns Hopkins University Press, 1964); (and Stanley Engerman) *Time on the Cross* (Boston: Little, Brown, 1974).

Foucault, Michel (b.1926, d.1984) Foucault was born in Poitiers, France. He studied philosophy at the École Normale Supérieure and subsequently undertook research in psychology. He was appointed in 1964 to a professorship in philosophy at the University of Clermont-Ferrand. In 1970 he became 'professor of the history of systems of thought' at the Collège de France, a title of his own contrivance, designed to distinguish his work from conventional history of ideas.

Foucault was a controversial and deliberately provocative thinker, sometimes abrasive and arrogant, whose ideas offered a fundamental challenge to prevailing intellectual activity. It is not altogether surprising, therefore, that his work has met with exasperation and even ridicule, as well as acclaim and sometimes reverence. His writing cannot be placed within conventional disciplinary categories – indeed to attempt to do so would be contrary to the fundamental nature of Foucault's project. In so far as he wrote *histories*, they were histories of the present; attempts to chart the emergence and character of modern forms of rationality, to explore the ways received truths in the human sciences have become established historically. As Foucault's work developed, the key to this undertaking became increasingly the relationship between knowledge and power.

Foucault's conception of power is not that conventionally encountered in historical or sociological writing. He conceived power not as something exerted from above by a sovereign, a state, or a dominant class, but rather as something that permeates society through the linguistic conventions and the conceptual categories which shape and (crucially for Foucault) constrain our existence. His most persuasive and accessible presentation of these ideas was in his studies of therapeutic and coercive institutions, such as the asylum and the prison (in particular, *Surveiller et punir: naissance de la prison*). But institutions of this sort remained, for Foucault, an epiphenomenon of a wider conceptual and semantic coercion. All knowledge, all assertions of truth, however they might be embodied institutionally, represented, for Foucault, claims to power and routes to power. His project was not to establish the truth or otherwise of particular forms of knowlege, but to consider them as strategies, to ask what they *did*.

Foucault's histories are, therefore, histories without linear development, evolution, or progress. He acknowledges that the definitions and discourses through which phenomena such as criminality or madness or sexuality are constituted have undergone radical and important historical shifts but, however they have been transformed, they remain strategies of power and coercion. His histories are also histories without agency — the coercive power he explores is certainly not in any straightforward sense exercised by a ruling individual, group, or class. Indeed, Foucault offers no general theory of power or of historical change at all. There are no over-arching conclusions. Rather he offers a method and a set of questions, both of which are worked out (and are best understood) in the context of particular studies.

Inevitably Foucault's work evoked enormous hostility. He was attacked for the manifest empirical shortcomings of his histories, for their moral relativism (particularly their questioning of humanistic values), for their attacks on scientific objectivity, and for their failure to grapple with economic power and the nature of the modern state. He is a difficult and at times impenetrable writer. But his insights into the relationship between knowledge and power are challenging and important. Whether they can be successfully incorporated into the conventional practice of history is more doubtful.   JAS

Main publications

Folie et déraison: histoire de la folie à l'âge classique (1961) trans. as *Madness and Civilisation: A History of Insanity in the Age of Reason* (London: Tavistock, 1967); *Naissance de la clinique: une archéologie du regard médical* trans. as *The Birth of the Clinic: An Archaeology of Medical Perception* (1963) (London: Tavistock, 1973); *Les mots et les choses: une archéologie des sciences humaines* (1966) trans. as *The Order of Things: An Archaeology of the Human Sciences* (London: Tavistock, 1974); *L'archéologie du savoir* trans. as *The Archaeology of Knowledge* (1969) (London: Tavistock, 1977); with others, *Moi, Pierre Rivière, ayant égorgé ma mère, ma soeur et mon frère* (1973) trans. as *I, Pierre Rivière, having Slanghtered my Mother, my Sister and my Brother* (Harmondsworth: Penguin, 1978); *Surveiller et punir: naissance de la prison* (1975) trans. as *Discipline and Punish: The Birth of the Prison* (London: Allen Lane, 1977); *Histoire de la sexualité*, vol. 1 (1976) trans. as *History of Sexuality*, vol. 1 (London: Allen Lane, 1979)

Reading

Donzelot, J.: *The Policing of Families: Welfare versus the State* (London: Hutchinson, 1980).

Dreyfus, H. L. and Rabinow, P.: *Michel Foucault: Beyond Structuralism and Hermeneutics* (Brighton: Harvester, 1982).

Poster, M.: *Foucault, Marxism and History: Mode of Production versus Mode of Information* (Cambridge: Polity, 1984).

Fournier, Paul (b.1853, d.1935) Fournier was professor of Roman law at Grenoble between 1880 and 1914, and in 1921 first holder of the chair of canon law at Paris. His writing demonstrated his wide-ranging knowledge of canonical (and other) sources in manuscript and his imagination in recreating the mental world of medieval canonists.   JHD

Main publications

The kingdom of Burgundy or Arles. In *Cambridge Medieval History* vol. 8 (Cambridge: Cambridge University Press, 1936); with Gabriel Le Bras, *Histoire des collections canoniques en occident depuis les fausses décrétales jusqu'au Décret de Gratien* (Paris: Sirey, 1931, 1932); contributions in *Histoire littéraire de la France*, vols 35, 36, 37 (Paris: Imprimerie Nationale, 1921–37).

Foxe, John (b.1517, d.1577) Foxe was educated at Brasenose and Magdalen colleges, Oxford, becoming a fellow of the latter in 1538 and gaining an MA in 1544. A Protestant, he declined ordination and married in 1547. His work as a tutor took him to the household of the duchess of Richmond in London and he was ordained deacon in 1550. His historical work had begun when, during Mary's reign, he chose exile, settling finally at Basle among fellow Protestants such as the future archbishop, Edmund Grindal.

In 1554 Foxe published his *Commentarii Rerum in Ecclesia Gestarum* at Strasburg, expanding the Latin text in the 1559 edition. This incomplete work dealt with Protestant historiography in a European rather than a national context, but Foxe's fame rested on his achievement in chronicling the sufferings of English Protestants in his *Actes and Monumentes*, published in 1563. This volume, based on research in diocesan records and on eyewitness accounts, was expanded to *The Ecclesiasticall History* in 1570, which took the story of persecution back to the primitive church. Like contemporary continental European writers, such as Johan Sleidan, Foxe set his account in the context of the universal struggle between Christ and anti-Christ and, so far as

Protestantism was concerned, his history was irenic in purpose. His career reflected those values: he refused office within the Elizabethan church, published sermons, and mediated between the bishops and the Puritans. However, the powerful imagery of the persecutions recorded by Foxe, often illustrated with woodcuts, produced a response among popular readership which obscured his more subtle historical lesson. Popularly known as the *Book of Martyrs*, Foxe's work went through many and varied editions, was revived in the 1800s, and became the historical work most influential on popular religious attitudes in English-speaking Protestantism.   WJS

Main publications

Commentarii Rerum in Ecclesia Gestarum (Strasburg: 1554); *Rerum in Ecclesia Gestarum* (Basle: 1559); *Actes and Monumentes of these Latter and Perillous Dayes* (London: 1563); *The Ecclesiasticall History . . . from the Primitive Tyme till the Reigne of K. Henry VIII* (London: 1570).

Reading

Haller, W.: *Foxe's Book of Martyrs and the Elect Nation* (London: Cape, 1963).

Mozley, J. F.: *John Foxe and His Book* (London: SPCK, 1940).

Norskov Olsen, V.: *John Foxe and the Elizabethan Church* (London: University of California Press, 1973).

Freeman, Edward Augustus (b.1823, d.1892) A private scholar of wide range, enormous industry, large production and strong feelings, Freeman was born at Harborne, the only son in a prosperous Birmingham family. Freeman enjoyed a considerable private income. He was educated in schools at Northampton and Cheam and then privately. Among his acquaintances as a child was Hannah More, and he spent much of his early life in the company of older people. Among signs of precocity was his knowledge of Latin at the age of seven. At Trinity College, Oxford (1841–5), he showed an extraordinary appetite for reading and for historical writing, in many areas and periods; he gained a fellowship, vacated on marriage (1847). From a very early age he went on many rambles in England, though he did not visit the European continent until 1856; he developed a considerable interest in architecture

(he was made Hon. FRIBA); and displayed a skill in sketching, exhibited in *Sketches of Travel in Normandy and Maine* (1897). He was early convinced of the importance of geography, and published a two-volume *Historical Geography of Europe* in 1881.

In childhood Freeman lived at Weston-super-Mare; after his marriage he owned country residences with small adjacent properties at Oaklands, near Dursley (1848–55), Lanrhymney near Cardiff (1855–60), and Somerleaze, near Wells (1860–92). These houses, all in the south-west, symbolized and furthered his interest in the West Saxons; his interest in the Norman Conquest began with his unsuccessful English prize essay on 'The effects of the conquest of England by the Normans' (1846), and reviews of PALGRAVE. He began his history of *The Norman Conquest of England* on 7 December 1865. The time was ripe: the narrative sources were in print, and Kemble's *Codex Diplomaticus* had been completed in 1854. The work was completed in six volumes including an index (1867–79), and was continued in *The Reign of William Rufus and the Accession of Henry the First* (two vols., 1882).

Freeman was adept at the long weighty articles called for by major periodicals of the day, and many of these essays, as well as lighter and slighter ones in the *Saturday Review*, were reprinted in his four series of *Historical Essays* (1871–92) and elsewhere. Freeman's *English Towns and Districts* (1883) often show him at his best. He could meet the demands of regular journalism, contributing 723 articles to the *Saturday Review* between 1860 and 1869; but his main works were the result of labour and thought over a long period, and he usually had several enterprises afoot simultaneously. He completed his *History of Architecture* (1849) and his *History of Sicily* (4 vols, 1891–4), but not *The History of Federal Government* (1 vol. only, 1863). A High Churchman of Liberal sympathies in politics Freeman four times stood for parliament but twice withdrew before the poll. He espoused causes enthusiastically, not to say provocatively: his early classical studies made him an ardent philhellene, strongly interested in nineteenth-century Greece.

FREYRE, GILBERTO DE MELLO

Freeman was a friend of STUBBS, whose dislike of Napoleon III ('the wild beast of Paris') he shared, and of J. R. GREEN, but not of J. H. ROUND, who destroyed Freeman's reputation for accuracy and as a Conservative found Freeman's politics distasteful. Though several times a candidate, Freeman held a chair only for the last eight years of his life, during which he was regius professor of modern history at Oxford; but he much regretted the need for absence from his beloved Somerleaze, and though conscientious, made little impact on the Oxford history school. His *Norman Conquest* remains valuable for its many appendices which bring together information from all the known written sources, even though his valuation of them must often be questioned. Freeman had a well-stocked but at times erratic and insufficiently selective mind with a firm grasp of topography. His thesis of the continuity of Anglo-Saxon institutions in spite of the Norman Conquest has received much support, notably from Sir Frank STENTON.   JFAM

Main publications

The Norman Conquest of England, 6 vols (1867–79), ed. J. W. Burrows (Chicago, Ill.: University of Chicago Press, 1974).

Reading

Cronne, H. A.: Edward Augustus Freeman, 1823–1892. *History* n.s. 28 (1943) 48–92.

Freyre, Gilberto de Mello (b.1900, d.1987) After secondary education in Pernambuco, Freyre's studies at Baylor and Columbia were decisive in his intellectual formation. A prime influence was the anthropologist Franz Boas and a nucleus of social scientists including Giddings and Seligmann. Freyre was part of a circle of artists and intellectuals that included Amy Lowell, W. B. Yeats, and H. L. Mencken. A study trip to Europe preceded his return to Brazil in 1923, where he inspired a group of young intellectuals by his emphasis on regionalism, his search for the cultural and historical riches of the north-east, and his focus on indigenous and African contributions to Brazil.

Freyre ranged across history, anthropology, sociology, ethnology, linguistics, economics, psychology, and literature. Highly influential was his trilogy tracing the creation, rise and decline of the patriarchal family associated with the sugar industry, and subsequent formation of an urban bourgeoisie. Freyre was a pioneer in promoting a culturalist interpretation of history. The distinction between race and culture informs much of his work on the family. For Freyre, it is not church or state but family which is the foundation for Brazilian civilization. By arguing that miscegenation was a positive contribution to the evolution of Brazil, Freyre freed Brazilians from self-perceptions of cultural inferiority, and this lesson applied beyond Brazil. The social amalgam of his 'new world in the tropics', central to which was the thesis of 'luso-tropicalism', was the adaptation of the Portuguese to the tropics and the importance of ecology as a conditioning factor. Freyre attributed to the Portuguese 'racial democracy', derived from prior exposure to non-Caucasians, and refers to oriental influences on Brazil. His impact on Brazilian self-perception and scholarship was profound.

Freyre gave intellectual respectability to Afro-Brazilian studies, stressed the importance of regional studies, brought US sociology and anthropology to Brazil, and emphasized interdisciplinary approaches. He promoted studies of folklore, myths, popular beliefs, traditions, and material cultures. His methodologically innovative use of advertisements for runaways made possible an ethnographic reconstitution of slave life in nineteenth-century Brazil. He opened new horizons for the study of intimacy. Freyre emphasized the role of Amerindian women and asserted the validity of studies of children. He was a keen analyst of the universal human experience and neither chronological development nor spatial context were of great import; rare were individuals or events. His interpretations, especially as regards race relations and the patriarchal family, and his methodologies have not gone unchallenged, but his contributions to understanding of plantation societies, of slavocratic regimes, and of race relations have been seminal. Freyre is recognized as a major force in the intellectual life of Brazil and a voice for the understanding of the third world.

AJRR-W

Main publications

Casa-Grande e Senzala (Rio de Janeiro: Maia e Schmidt, 1933); *Sobrados e Mucambos* (São Paulo: Editora Nacional, 1936); *Nordeste* (Rio de Janeiro: José Olympio, 1937); *O Mundo que o Portugues Criou* (Rio de Janeiro: José Olympio, 1940); *New World in the Tropics* (New York: Knopf, 1959); *Ordem e Progresso* (Rio de Janeiro, José Olympio, 1959).

Reading

Melo Menezes, Diogo de: *Gilberto Freyre* (Rio de Janeiro: Casa do Estudante, 1944).
——: *Gilberto Freyre, Sua Ciencia, Sua Filosofia, Sua Arte* (Rio de Janeiro: José Olympio, 1962).

Friedjung, Heinrich (b.1851, d.1920) One of numerous talented Moravian Jews to settle in nineteenth-century Vienna, Friedjung became a journalist and politician in the German-national and radical-liberal interest (he was the main author of the Linz Programme of 1882). After losing his job as a teacher, Friedjung held no academic position, but he later broke with the pan-German nationalists, who had turned increasingly anti-Semitic, and gained the status of an establishment figure. He wrote chiefly on the history of the Habsburg Empire after 1848, his studies of the diplomatic, political and military struggle between Austria and Germany in the 1860s remaining unsurpassed, while his uncompleted account of Austrian history between 1848 and 1860 retains much of its value. Friedjung's professional reputation suffered as a result of the notorious Zagreb trial in 1909, when it transpired that his newspaper accusations against certain South Slav politicians in the Monarchy rested on forged documents. Yet his scholarly work displays great breadth and clarity, and a notable balanced understanding of the workings of that old-Austrian state whose progressive dissolution clouded his later years.

RJWE

Main publications

Der Kampf um die Vorherrschaft in Deutschland, 1859–66, 2 vols (1897–8) abridged trans. *The Struggle for Supremacy in Germany* (London: Macmillan, 1935); *Benedeks nachgelassene Papiere* (Leipzig: Grübel & Sommerlatte, 1901); *Österreich von* *1848 bis 1860*, 2 vols (Stuttgart/Berlin: Cotta, 1908–12); *Historische Aufsätze* (Stuttgart/Berlin: Cotta, 1919); *Das Zeitalter des Imperialismus, 1884–1914*, 3 vols (Berlin: Neufeld & Henius, 1919–22).

Reading

Taylor, A. J. P.: Preface to *The Struggle for Supremacy in Germany* (London: Macmillan, 1935).

Froissart, Jean (*fl.*1337–1404) French chronicler. Born at Valenciennes, probably of humble bourgeois stock, Froissart entered princely service at an early age, possibly with Margaret of Hainault, widow of Emperor Lewis IV or her uncle, Jean de Beaumont, though he first properly emerges as a clerk in the household of Margaret's sister, Philippa, Queen of England, whom he joined in 1361. In the next few years he was able to visit Scotland (1365) and Gascony (1366–7) and accompany Philippa's son Lionel, duke of Clarence on his journey to marry Yolanda Visconti in Milan (1368). Also in the duke's retinue was Geoffrey Chaucer, and the marriage was attended by Petrarch. Froissart then visited Ferrara, Bologna and Rome, but on learning of Philippa's death he returned to Hainault. Here he was taken up by her nephew, Robert of Namur, Wenceslas, duke of Brabant (d.1383) and, most importantly, by Guy de Châtillon, count of Blois (d.1397), grandson of Jean de Beaumont, with whom he more or less constantly lived until the 1390s. Taking clerical orders, Froissart was provided with a living at Lestinnes-au-Mont near Binche (1373), became Châtillon's private chaplain and a canon of Chimay (1383). Most of his time was subsequently spent either in the Low Countries or at Blois.

At first Froissart's reputation as a writer was based on poetry and romance, but between the mid-1360s and early 1370s he produced a first version of the *Chroniques* on which his lasting fame is based. In the 1380s Châtillon and other noble patrons encouraged him to revise and expand this work. He undertook journeys specifically to collect material (largely in the form of reminiscences from old soldiers). His visit to the court of Gaston Fébus, count of Foix (1388–9) and to Middelburg where he met the Portuguese Juan Fernando Pacheco (1389) gave him much additional colourful material. He was able to attend the Anglo-French peace talks at Amiens in 1392 and in July 1395 he once more visited England to present some of his work to Richard II. Though received in friendly fashion by the king, he found virtually all his former acquaintances dead and the court much changed. He returned home sorrowfully and his whole account of Richard's reign reflects his disappointment. He spent his remaining years in Valenciennes. The final book (IV) of the *Chroniques* breaks off abruptly in its account of the year 1401, but revisions to earlier texts suggest that Froissart was still living in 1404.

After suffering neglect, the quality of Froissart's lyric and narrative poetry has recently been more sympathetically appraised. His one major verse romance in Arthurian style, *Méliador*, runs to over 30,000 lines of octosyllabic couplets and was read to a delighted audience at the court of Foix. But already in his own lifetime, Froissart was known as *the* chronicler of chivalry. With a shrewd eye for the aristocratic market, he fashioned a vast panoramic history of western Europe from 1325 to 1400, eventually divided into four books. In a first version of Book I, completed probably in the early 1370s, he plagiarized Jean le Bel's chronicle for the period to 1356, but he reshaped this several times, lastly in a third major redaction shortly after 1400 dealing with the period 1325–50. As a separate work that was eventually incorporated into Book II (of which there are two versions), he also wrote a *Chronique de Flandre* covering 1378–87. Book III was completed in 1390 and Book IV in 1400. Both exist in only one version.

Deliberately glorifying chivalry with the intent of leaving a memorial for knights in future ages, Froissart generally displays little sympathy for other classes. Although he was conscientious in seeking out those who participated in the events he recounted and occasionally had recourse to documents, he has been well described as the first journalist. This should not detract from an acknowledgement of his growing technical skill as a writer. He revised the *Chroniques* (often in line with the political stance of his patrons) and moved from an early pro-English view of the wars with France that form the basis of the work to a more impartial or even noticeably French outlook. It is fashionable to underline his shortcomings as a historian, but his account should never be neglected because of his range of important contacts and his ear for rumour, while as the spokesman of aristocratic, martial values, his vivid descriptions of all sides of warfare catch incomparably the concerns of an age in which chivalry held her lance on high.

MCEJ

Main writings

Oeuvres complètes de Froissart, ed. Baron J. Kervyn de Lettenhove and A. Scheler, 28 vols (Brussels: 1867–77); *Chroniques de Jean Froissart*, ed. S. Luce, G. Raynaud, L. and A. Mirot, 15 vols continuing (Paris, Société de l'histoire de France, 1869); *Chronicles* trans. G. Brereton (Harmondsworth: Penguin, 1968); *Chroniques: dernière rédaction du premier livre*, ed. George T. Diller (Geneva and Paris: Droz, 1972); *Méliador*, ed. A. Longnon, 3 vols (Paris, Société des anciens textes français, 1895–9).

Reading

Dembowski, Peter F.: *Jean Froissart and his Méliador: Context Craft and Sense* (The Edward C. Armstrong monographs on medieval literature 2) (Lexington, KY: French Forum, 1983).

Palmer, J. J. N. ed.: *Froissart: Historian* (Woodbridge, Suffolk: Boydell), 1981.

Shears, F. C.: *Froissart: Chronicler and Poet* (London, G. Routledge & Sons, 1930).

Froude, James Anthony (b.1818, d.1894) Born in Devon, Froude went up to Oriel College, Oxford, in 1835. He took a second in Greats in 1840, won the Chancellor's Prize and was elected to a fellowship at Exeter College in 1842. It was a difficult time for him. He passed through a deep spiritual crisis which he described in *The Nemesis of Faith*, an autobiographical novel published in 1849. A powerful condemnation of the High Church Movement, the book caused a furore in Oxford. It was publicly burned by Sewell, the Rector of Exeter College and Froude was obliged to resign his fellowship. He determined to earn his living by writing and turned to history as the most interesting, congenial and lucrative outlet for his already considerable literary talents.

Published between 1856 and 1870

Froude's 12 volume *History of England from the Fall of Wolsey to the Defeat of the Spanish Armada* was a bestseller. It went into a seventh edition within his own lifetime, and it is easy to see why. No contemporary ever matched the quality of Froude's prose. Among historians only MACAULAY was his equal as narrator, dramatist and portrait painter. But revered by the reading public, Froude was reviled by his fellow historians. STUBBS, GREEN, CREIGHTON, SEELEY, Pauli, RANKE and above all FREEMAN denied his work any credence as scholarly history. Their charge was simple. Froude had transgressed the two inviolable rules of the nascent historical profession: his work was inaccurate and it was biased. Their claims are not without substance.

Froude was careless. And he was the first to admit it. He made errors in transcribing documents, and he was lax in checking printers' proofs. He was undoubtedly biased. But he never denied it. Indeed, he made the grounds of his prejudice perfectly clear. The purpose of his history, he said, was 'nothing more and nothing less than to clear the English Reformation and the fathers of the Anglican Church from the stains which have been allowed to gather on them.' He wrote to counter the views of LINGARD and Newman.

The mud, thrown by FREEMAN in particular, has stuck. Today Froude is not generally regarded as a serious 'front-line' historian. But there is scope for a more balanced view. Froude's was the first, and indeed for many years the only substantial work in English on the Reformation. Unlike many of his detractors he worked from manuscript sources for which he hunted not only in the British Museum, Rolls House and the Bodleian, but also in Vienna, Brussels, Paris, and in Simencas, where he was the first English scholar ever to visit the archives. POLLARD maintained that no previous history had ever incorporated so much unpublished material. Under these circumstances some errors of transcription were inevitable. Few of Froude's were misleading, and he cannot be charged with intellectual dishonesty. Further, Froude believed the 'scientific' history of which his critics spoke to be impossible. 'Ordinary history, except mere annals', he said, 'is all more or less

fictitious, that is, the facts are related, not as they really happened, but as they appear to the writer.' Value-free history was a chimera. The historian must explain the grounds of his own interpretation, provide evidence for it and argue accordingly. He was faithful to this belief and his work should be judged in that light.   PRHS

Main publications

The History of England from the Fall of Wolsey to the Defeat of the Spanish Armada, 12 vols (London: J. W. Parker, 1856–70); *The Science of History: a lecture delivered at the Royal Institution Feb. 5 1864* (New York and London: G. P. Putnam, n.d.).

Reading

Dunn, W. H.: *James Anthony Froude: a biography*, 2 vols (Oxford: Oxford University Press, 1961–3).

Furet, François (b.1927) Furet moved from the Centre National de la Recherche Scientifique to the École Pratique des Hautes Études, of which he eventually became director. Both the pattern of his career and his own convictions distanced him from the 'Marxism' that was entrenched at the Sorbonne. He made his mark with the two-volume history of the French Revolution, published with Denis Richet in 1965. This asserted that the radical phase of the revolution and notably the Terror, which Marxist historians were inclined to present as its culmination, when Robespierre and his allies tried to transcend the limitations of what had hitherto been a bourgeois movement, was actually both a digression and an aberration. Furet developed this argument further in 1978 in *Penser la Révolution*. Accepting TOCQUEVILLE's thesis that the most lasting consequence of the revolution was to accelerate a trend towards bureaucratic centralization that was well under way before 1789, Furet saw that this made the extreme violence of the Terror incomprehensible unless some other factor had been involved. This had been identified by a somewhat neglected historian, Cochin, who had perhaps derived it from TAINE. Following their lead, Furet saw the revolution as a period when normal political institutions failed to function and political power passed to ideologists, acting through what Cochin had called *sociétés de pensée*, of which the most important were political clubs. The ideology of the revolutionaries, whether they knew it or not, was mainly derived from Rousseau and it became the basis of what Furet rather confusingly called 'democracy'. Like TALMON, he therefore saw the revolution as the source of a conception of democracy that was to permeate subsequent history. Furet has been reproached by his critics for a tendency to brood over secondary sources rather than to undertake archival research. This is not entirely just and, to the extent that it is true, is a source of both strength and weakness. He never loses the wood for the trees – even if he sometimes loses his reader in the thickets of his elusive prose – but he allows little room for contingency, for accident and for the influence of individuals. In this respect his approach is similar to that of the ANNALES SCHOOL of French historians. This was apparent in *Lire et écrire: l'alphabétisation des Français de Calvin à Jules Ferry*, published with Jacques Ozouf in 1977, which dealt with the phenomenon of literacy over a long period of time and with particular reference to regional variations. It also tended to emphasize the relative unimportance of political action in the promotion of literacy. Where Furet differs from most of the members of the Annales school is in the importance that he attaches to ideology. Furet is now turning towards the study of the history of ideas in the nineteenth century, beginning with an investigation into what Marx actually wrote about the French revolution.   NH

Main publications

La Révolution Française (1965; English trans. London: Weidenfeld & Nicolson, 1970); *Penser la Révolution* (1978; trans. as *Interpreting the French Revolution*, Cambridge: Cambridge University Press, 1981); *Lire et écrire, l'alphabétisation des Français de Calvin à Jules Ferry* (1977; English trans. Cambridge: Cambridge University Press, 1982).

Fustel de Coulanges, Numa-Denis (b.1830, d.1889)

Born in Paris, Fustel was left an orphan at an early age. He entered the École Normale in 1850, and read widely, above all in history: he particularly admired GUIZOT. In 1853 he studied at the French School in Athens, excavating on Chios, and publishing a history of the island in 1856 which caused some controversy at the time since he unfashionably praised the Turkish administration. When he returned to France he taught history at a *lycée* in Amiens, and defended his doctoral theses in Paris in 1858. His thesis in French was on POLYBIUS, while his Latin thesis on the cult of Vesta formed the foundation for his best-known book.

In 1860 Fustel became professor of history at Strasburg. He continued his work on Roman religion, and in 1864, failing to find a publisher, he published at his own expense *La cité antique*. It was not long before it was recognized as a classic in its innovations and its literary merits. Fustel argued that religion in pagan antiquity was a social force, binding together both the family and the state. The decline of religious belief in the late Republic had led to a moral crisis which resulted in the Empire, the end of the antique city and, ultimately, the triumph of Christianity and the emergence of theological wrangling. Fustel's attempt to explain political developments in the ancient world by means of underlying religious and social developments was very influential, and he continued this method of analysis in his works on the post-Roman world.

Fustel did not like provincial life, and in early 1870, having been offered a post at the École Normale, he moved to Paris, just before its siege by the Germans and the Commune. During the siege he demonstrated his belief in the contemporary relevance of history by writing a number of pamphlets, on Alsace, 'est-elle allemande ou française?', and on military institutions in Roman and modern times. He also began planning a series of articles on the significance of the German invasions of the fifth century AD.

Fustel taught at the École Normale until 1875, when he moved to a chair of ancient history at the Sorbonne. In the same year he took Guizot's place in the Académie des Sciences Morales. In 1878 a chair in medieval history was created for him at the Sorbonne; in 1880 he reluctantly accepted the directorship of the École Normale. But most of the time between 1872 and his death in 1889 he was working on his great *Histoire des institutions politiques de l'ancienne France*. He had intended to write one volume on the Germanic invasions, a second on feudalism, a third on the later middle ages and the last on the ancien régime. But the reaction to the first volume by German critics and also by French historians such as Havet and ARBOIS DE JUBAINVILLE, upset those plans. He argued that the Germanic invasions were not so destructive as had been portrayed; the Frankish takeover of Gaul was not an invasion but a gradual infiltration into the Roman system. The roots of feudalism were already present in the ancient world; the institutions of Merovingian Gaul owed much more to the Romans than to the Germans. These ideas are all now accepted by historians but they seemed revolutionary at the time, and to some seemed merely the response of French patriotism to German chauvinism. Fustel was keen to demonstrate that his theories rested on accurate analysis of the texts rather than on prejudice, and he spent the next 15 years of his life producing carefully researched studies of the Roman colonate, Lex Salica, privileges of immunity, and so on, to buttress them. These writings were collected together, some of them posthumously, by his pupil Camille Jullian, in the final six volumes of the *Histoire des institutions politiques*.

Fustel de Coulanges died in 1889, at Massy (Seine-et-Oise), where he had moved some years earlier to gain the peace he needed for his studies. Although not a believer he asked in his will that his funeral be accompanied by a church service: 'Patriotism demands that if one does not think like one's ancestors then one at least respects what they believed.'   EFJ

Main publications

La cité antique: étude sur le culte, le droit, les institutions de la Grèce et de Rôme, 2nd edn (Paris: Hachette, 1866); *The Ancient City* (Boston: Lee & Shepard, 1874); *Histoire des institutions politiques de l'ancienne France*: vol. I (1874) expanded to form the first 3 of 6 vols (Paris: Hachette): *La Gaule romaine* (1891); *L'invasion germanique et la fin de l'Empire* (1891); *La Monarchie franque* (1888); *L'Alleu et le domaine rural pendant l'époque mérovingienne* (1889); *Les Origines du système féodal: le bénéfice et le patronat pendant l'époque mérovingienne* (1890); and *Les Transformations de la royauté pendant l'époque carolingienne* (1892). Other articles collected by C. Jullian as *Questions historiques* (Paris: Hachette, 1893).

Reading

Champion, E.: *Les Idées politiques et religieuses de Fustel de Coulanges* (Paris: Champion, 1903).

Guiraud, P.: *Fustel de Coulanges* (Paris: Hachette, 1896).

Leclercq, H.: Fustel de Coulanges. In *Dictionnaire d'archéologie chrétienne et de liturgie*, ed. Cabrol and Leclercq, vol. V (Paris: 1923).

G

Gairdner, James (b.1828, d.1912)   The son and nephew of Edinburgh physicians, Gairdner was born and educated in his native city. He did not attend university, and at the age of eighteen left for London, where he obtained employment as a clerk in the Public Record Office. He remained at the PRO for the whole of his working life, becoming an assistant keeper in 1859 and retiring after 47 years service in 1893. In spite of his Presbyterian background, or perhaps because of it, he became in later life a High Anglican of increasingly Anglo-Catholic sympathies, a commitment which undoubtedly affected his historical judgement.

In his own lifetime, Gairdner was overshadowed by a galaxy of great historians – Stubbs, Froude, Freeman, S. R. Gardiner and others – and was regarded primarily as an archivist. He was an immensely industrious and productive scholar, and his editorial work has stood the test of time far better than his writings. This is particularly true of his main life's work, the *Letters and Papers, foreign and domestic, of the reign of Henry VIII*. This immense undertaking was launched by J. S. Brewer in 1862, and Brewer had published four volumes by the time of his death in 1879; Gairdner, who had been assisting Brewer for some time, assumed full responsibility for volume V. He extended the scope of the work to include material from outside the Public Record Office, and wrote lengthy and meticulous prefaces. He remained responsible for the enterprise until its completion, in twenty-one volumes, in 1910. Volumes V to XIII are entirely his work, and volumes XIV to XXI in collaboration with R. H. Brodie. Although more recent scholars have frequently found fault with the *Letters and Papers*, identifying many mistaken datings and criticizing Gairdner's somewhat arbitrary methods of calendaring, it remains an indispensable tool for the study of the period, and a great monument to the industry and skill of its principal editor.

At an earlier stage in his career Gairdner had gained much valuable experience in the techniques of scholarly editing by producing the *Memorials of Henry VII* (1858) and *Letters and papers...of the reigns of Richard III and Henry VII* (1861–3) for the Rolls Series. He was also responsible for two editions of the *Paston Letters*, in 1872–5 and in 1896, the latter remaining a standard work for many years. For a man who was technically an amateur, he was also a prolific historical writer, contributing nearly eighty notices to the *Dictionary of National Biography*, and producing between 1878 and his death five major monographs in addition to numerous articles and lesser works. Gairdner's literary style won him few admirers, either at the time or since, and as the author of his *Times* obituary felt constrained to point out, 'he had not the gift of popular exposition, he was not a great writer; and he produced no history on the grand scale.' Unfortunately much of the motivation which fuelled his exceptional productivity came from a missionary zeal on behalf of the pre-reformation church. 'For the historical period in which circumstances led him to specialize he felt a profound distaste,' as his obituary put it. William Hunt, completing Gairdner's four-volume *Lollardy and the Reformation in England* in accordance with his wishes, after his death, although sympathetic, was entirely frank: 'He felt constrained to publish the results of his labours, for he considered that much error was current on these matters...and that too little account was taken of the wrongs inflicted on catholics and of the tyranny, greed and irreverence, the robbery of God and his church, which in his view disgraced the reformation in England.' It was perhaps for this reason that recognition was slow to come to Gairdner. He had already retired four years when the university of Edinburgh conferred upon him the honorary degree of LLD. He became a CB in 1900 and an honorary D.Litt of Oxford in 1910. There can be no doubt about his standing as a scholar, and in the words of another judicious contemporary 'his services to the scientific study of historical materials were second to none'. DML

Main publications

Letters and Papers Illustrative of the reigns of Richard III and Henry VII (Rolls Series, 1861−3); *Memorials of Henry VII* (Rolls Series, 1858); *The Paston Letters* (1872−5, and 1896); *The Houses of Lancaster and York* (1874); *Richard III* (1878; 2nd edn, 1898); *Letters and Papers, foreign and domestic, of the reign of Henry VIII* (1880−1910); *Henry VII* (1889); *The English Church in the sixteenth century* (1902); *Lollardy and the Reformation in England* (1908−13); with Charles Spedding, *Studies in English History* (1881).

Reading

Hunt, William: Preface to *Lollardy and the Reformation*, vol. IV, 1913.
The Times, 6 November 1912 [obituary].

Galbraith, Vivian Hunter (b.1889, d.1976) One of the most influential, and certainly the most lively English medievalist of his age. Galbraith was educated at Manchester University where he fell under the spell of T. F. TOUT, and at Balliol College, Oxford, where his tutor was H. W. C. DAVIS. Originally the shyest of men, the first world war in which he served with distinction, turned him into a complete extrovert. He was successively an Assistant Keeper of the Public Record Office (1921−28), fellow and tutor of Balliol College, Oxford, and university reader in diplomatic (1928−37), professor at Edinburgh (1937−44), director of the Institute of Historical Research in London (1944−7) and regius professor at Oxford (1947−57).

At first a late medievalist, he edited *The Anominalle Chronicle, 1333−1387* (1927) and *The St. Albans Chronicle, 1406−1420* (1937), but his greatest enthusiasm was always for records. His *Introduction to the Use of the Public Records* (1934) is unsurpassed, and he entitled his Ford lectures *Studies in the Public Records* (1948). Above all was his work on Domesday Book. Starting with an article in the *English Historical Review* (1942), he dismantled much of the work of J. H. Round and pointed Domesday studies in a new direction, focusing on 'Exon Domesday' and 'Little Domesday', the circuit-returns for the five South-Western and three East Anglian counties respectively. He demonstrated that the intention had always been to produce a Feudal Book (or tenural survey) and that it had indeed been completed in 1086, the administrative machinery being far more sophisticated than had previously been thought. See *The making of Domesday Book* (1961) and *Domesday Book: its place in Administrative History* (1976). The glee with which he pricked and deflated academic pomposity endeared him to the unpretentious, and his fearless and outspoken defence of scholarly causes earned him innumerable friends. RHCD

Main publications

Editor, *The Anominalle Chronicle, 1333−1387* (Manchester: Manchester University Press, 1927); editor, *The St. Albans Chronicle, 1406−1420* (Oxford: Clarendon Press, 1937); *Introduction to the Use of the Public Records* (Clarendon Press, 1934); *Studies in the Public Records* (London: Nelson, 1948); *The Making of Domesday Book* (Clarendon Press, 1961); *Domesday Book: its place in Administrative History* (Clarendon Press, 1974).

Reading

Bishop, T. A. M. and Chaplais, P.: *Facsimiles of English Writs to AD 1100* presented to V. H. Galbraith (Oxford: Clarendon Press, 1957) [incl. bibliography to 1957].
Southern, R. W.: Obituary. *Proceedings of the British Academy* 64 (1978) 397−425 [incl. bibliography from 1958].

Gallagher, John Andrew (b.1919, d.1980) After graduating from Trinity College, Cambridge, where his studies were interrupted by war service in the Royal Tank Regiment,

Gallagher spent most of his working life in Cambridge, although from 1963 to 1970 he was the Beit professor of the history of the British commonwealth in Oxford. In 1971 he returned to Cambridge as Vere Harmsworth professor of imperial and naval history.

He will be best remembered for two publications in collaboration with professor R. E. Robinson. First came an article, 'The imperialism of free trade', in which they argued for the essential continuity of the British empire in the nineteenth century, rejecting the conventional idea of a 'separatist' period, succeeded by renewed interest in expansion. Secondly, there was a substantial book, *Africa and the Victorians*, in which they contended that Britain's participation in the nineteenth-century scramble for Africa could be explained in political and diplomatic terms, rather than by the economic determinism favoured by Marxist writers. The primary consideration was the protection of Britain's Indian empire, not the acquisition of a new empire in Africa. They published a summary of this in the revised *Cambridge Modern History* vol. 11 (1962), in which they maintained that the causes of the 'new imperialism' were not all in Europe but should be sought in non-European societies too.

Their views attracted much discussion and, while not entirely accepted, permanently influenced interpretations of British imperialism. Gallagher delivered the Ford lectures at Oxford in 1973–4. Ill health prevented him from preparing them for publication, but they were edited by Anil Seal and published, together with other collected papers, in 1982.

MEC

Main publications

With R. E. Robinson, The imperialism of free trade, *Economic History Review* 6, 2nd ser. (1953) 1–15; *Africa and the Victorians: the Official Mind of Imperialism* (London: Macmillan, 1961).

Reading

Gallagher, J. A. ed. A. Seal:*The Decline, Revival and Fall of the British Empire* (Cambridge: Cambridge University Press, 1982).

Louis, Wm Roger, ed.: *Imperialism: the Robinson and Gallagher Controversy* (New York: New Viewpoints, 1976).

Ganshof, François-Louis (b.1895, d.1980) One of the most illustrious students of Henri PIRENNE, Ganshof studied at the Athénée Royal before going on to the University of Ghent. After the first world war he served as attaché in the Belgian delegation to the Peace of Paris Congress before continuing his studies. He obtained a D. Phil. et lettres in 1921, a doctorate of law in 1922 and spent a year in Paris at the feet of Ferdinand LOT. Ganshof practised law as a solicitor in Brussels for a year before moving to the University of Ghent in 1923. He succeeded Pirenne in 1930 (when the latter left Ghent as a result of the enforcement of Flemish as the language of instruction), and remained professor of medieval history there until his retirement in 1961.

During the 1920s Ganshof was still overshadowed by Pirenne. He produced a study of the *ministeriales* of Flanders and Lotharingia in 1926, but a number of his early articles, especially that on the *tractoria* and the law of the king's lodging, revealed his developing predilection for the study of medieval law and institutions. By the early 1930s he had begun research on the Carolingian period and in particular on narrative sources, Einhard, and the institution of vassalage. His contributions to national history remained substantial, with collaboration on an historical atlas of Belgium and work on the histories of Flanders and Brabant, and on the topography of towns. The period immediately following his succession to the chair at Ghent saw a flurry of books and articles on Flanders, its judicial institutions and its towns, culminating in 1943 in *La Flandre sous les premiers comtes*. Only occasionally thereafter, in 1951, 1957 and the 1960s, did he again turn his attention to urban history.

Ganshof wrote few syntheses. Much of his prodigious output was in the form of articles, but exceptions to this were his book on the history of international relations in the middle ages, his survey of barbarian Europe (*Les Destinées de l'Empire en occident de 395 à 888*), written in collaboration with Ferdinand Lot, a substantial chapter on the evolution of rural society for the *Cambridge Economic History of Europe* and, perhaps his best-known, though not his most important, work *Qu'est-ce que la féodalité?*

Ganshof's middle years in the 1940s and 1950s saw his most original and powerful work, in which his intellectual acumen and unparalleled mastery of the sources were combined to produce a fundamental series of papers on the political history of Charlemagne and his son Louis the Pious. It is in these that his greatness as a historian is most apparent, with his magisterial study of the capitulary legislation and his exposition of Carolingian administrative and judicial institutions. It was a natural development from his preoccupation with Frankish institutions for Ganshof to focus increasingly after 1965 on historiography and on the history of the law, with such seminal articles as 'Le statut de la Femme dans la monarchie franque' and 'La preuve dans le droit franc'. In the last years of his life he turned increasingly to the rural history of the early middle ages. This bore fruit in his work on the polyptych, or estate inventory, of the monastery of St Bertin and his last work, *Die Entwicklung von Wirtschaft und Gesellschaft in den Europäischen Regionen 8. Das fränkische Reich*, which was published soon after his death.

Ganshof's fame as an historian rests more on his remarkable erudition, which gave a secure foundation to everything he wrote and made of it a substantial contribution to knowledge, than on the striking originality of his ideas or the creativity of his thinking. He was a cautious scholar in his reading of texts, rarely going beyond his facts to speculate. His analysis of his evidence was at all times acute and his interpretation interesting and convincing. His range of examples and corroborative material, packed into his long and discursive footnotes, was ever impressive.

An honorary doctor of many universities, including Glasgow, London and Cambridge, and member of many of the leading historical societies of Britain and Europe, Ganshof enjoyed an international reputation. Many of his works were translated into several languages; Ganshof himself often produced both Flemish and French versions. He was a patriot and royalist, and a loyal supporter of his Flemish university. A modest man, he had, neverthe-

less, a forceful personality which expressed itself most notably in his writing.   RMcK

Main publications

Recherches sur les tribunaux de châtellenie en Flandre avant le milieu du XIIIe siècle (Antwerp and Paris: 1932); *Les Destinées de L'Empire en occident de 395 à 888* (Paris: Presses Universitaires de France, 1934; 2nd edn, 1941); *Qu'est-ce que la féodalité?* (Brussels: Lebegue, 1944); *Feudalism*, (London: Longmans, Green, 1952); 3rd edn, London: Longmans, Green; New York: Harper Torchbooks, 1964; *Histoire des relations internationales*, I: *Le Moyen Age* (Paris: Hachette, 1953); *Wat waren de capitularia?* (Brussels: 1955; French edn, Paris: Sirey, 1958; German edn, Darmstadt: Wissenschäftliche Buchgesellschaft, 1961); *Frankish Institutions under Charlemagne* (Providence, RI: Brown University Press, 1968); *L'historiographie dans la monarchie franque sous les Merovingiens et les Carolingiens*, in *Settimane di Studio del Centro Italiano di studi sull'alto medioevo* 17 (Spoleto: 1970); *The Carolingians and the Frankish Monarchy* (London: Longman, 1971) [incl. select bibliography] with F. Godding-Ganshof and A. de Smet, *Le Polyptyque de l'abbaye de Saint-Bertin (844–849). Édition critique et commentaire* (Paris: Imprimérie Nationale et Klinksieck, 1975).

Reading

Bibliographie des travaux historiques de François-Louis Ganshof (Wetteren: Imprimerie De Meester, 1946).
Verhulst, A: François-Louis Ganshof (1895–1980). *Le Moyen Age* 86 (1980) 523–38.

Gardiner, Samuel Rawson (b.1829, d.1902) Between 1863 and 1901 Gardiner produced a monumental history of England beginning with the accession of James I and working steadily onwards to 1656. Gardiner intended to go on to the death of Cromwell in 1658, but his own death cut short the work. The great enterprise produced many by-products in the form of editions of the documents consulted. They included 12 volumes for the Camden Society of which Gardiner was director from 1869 until 1897, two for the Navy Records Society and one for the Scottish History Society. He was editor of the *English Historical Review* from 1891 until his death. On another level, his *Constitutional Documents of the Puritan Revolution* did for students of the early seventeenth century what Stubbs's *Charters* had done for students of the middle ages. In 1896 Gardiner delivered without a note the first Ford Lectures, subsequently published as *Cromwell's Place in History*. These by-products

149

alone would have given him an important place among English historical writers, but it was his great *History of England* which eventually established his reputation as an outstanding scholar and as 'a historian's historian'.

Gardiner presents a fascinating illustration of what can be done through self-help by a man who is convinced that he has a vocation to write a particular historical work but who cannot count on the income or the leisure which an Oxford fellowship would have given him. He was born at Ropley near Alresford in Hampshire on 4 March 1829 and was descended from Cromwell's eldest daughter Bridget and her husband Henry Ireton. He went to Winchester College and Christ Church, Oxford, where he read *literae humaniores* and was awarded a first in 1851. He might have continued at Oxford and eventually become a fellow of a college but for theological difficulties. He settled in London and in 1856 married his first wife, Isabella, youngest daughter of Edward Irving, founder of the Irvingite or Catholic and Apostolic Church in which Gardiner was for many years a deacon.

In order to get a living while pursuing his life's work, Gardiner held various teaching posts, including a mastership in an academy for young ladies. He taught at Bedford College, London, and became a lecturer and then a professor at King's College, London. He also wrote textbooks and popular histories which sold well. In 1882 Gladstone gave him a Civil List pension of £150 a year, and in 1884, at the age of 55, he was given a research fellowship at All Souls, Oxford. When this ran out, Merton College, Oxford, gave him a fellowship which he held until his death. In 1894 he was offered the regius professorship of modern history at Oxford. He declined, since it would have made it more difficult for him to finish his great work.

Gardiner had a long and hard struggle to win recognition. He began work in the British Museum library in 1856 and in the Public Record Office in 1858; the first two volumes of his *History* appeared in 1863. They were a disastrous failure. The reading public liked history with plenty of colour, and according to one reviewer, Gardiner's careful, detailed and scholarly work made it impossible for the

reader to keep awake. Nevertheless, Gardiner pressed on, and as more and more volumes appeared, he gradually established his reputation. He brought to his task an unusually wide knowledge of foreign languages and he wrote at a time when the Public Record Office and the Historical Manuscripts Commission were making available a vast amount of new material. He wrote a chronological account, consciously seeking, when describing motives and events, to suppress his own knowledge of what happened later. In practice, of course, he could not avoid being influenced by hindsight. The range of his knowledge was remarkable, and his narrative of religious and political events as a factual account has stood the test of time. Christopher Hill has remarked: 'We all stand on his shoulders' and Conrad Russell has commented 'technically he was probably the finest scholar who has ever worked on this period.'

By the late nineteenth century Gardiner's *History* was the orthodoxy for all reputable historians, and after him Sir Charles FIRTH, G. M. TREVELYAN and Godfrey Davies carried on the Great Tradition which Gardiner himself had inherited from the Whig historians. In a simplified form, this meant that the Stuarts were wrong and parliament, which represented the English nation, was right. In the great struggle of the seventeenth century, the English nation continued its triumphant progress towards the nearly perfect constitution of the nineteenth century, fortified by its love of liberty and guided by the puritan spirit.

For 40 years there was little criticism of Gardiner's orthodoxy by English historians, and although an American, Roland Usher, in 1915 produced a devastating attack entitled *A Critical Study of the Historical Method of Samuel Rawson Gardiner*, it made little impact in England.

Just before the outbreak of the second world war, Gardiner's interpretation began to be challenged by Marxist historians who substituted a bourgeois revolution for Gardiner's puritan revolution. In the last 40 years Marxist criticism has continued, and Gardiner's views have also been challenged by historians of many shades of opinion asking different questions and stressing economic and social issues as well as regional variations. In 1902, when Gardiner died, historians were in great measure agreed on what the Civil War was all about. In 1987 there are almost as many different interpretations as there are historians writing about the period. Many of Gardiner's assumptions are no longer tenable, but it is right to pay tribute to the major scholarly contribution he made in his own time and to be grateful for the amazingly detailed and accurate account he produced of political and religious affairs in one of the most crowded and confused periods of British history.   PVM

Main publications

History of England from the accession of James I to the Outbreak of the Civil War, 10 vols (1883–4); *History of the Great Civil War*, 3 vols (1886–1891); *History of the Commonwealth and Protectorate*, 3 vols (1894–1901).

Reading

Shaw, W. A. ed.: *A Bibliography of the Historical Works of . . . S. R. Gardiner* (Royal Historical Society, 1903).
Usher, Roland: A critical study of the historical method of Samuel Rawson Gardiner. *Washington University Studies*, vol. 3, pt. 2.1 (1915).

Gaxotte, Pierre (b.1895, d.1982) A Lorrainer, Gaxotte had a brilliant student career at the École Normale Supérieure, and was first in the History *agrégation* competition of 1920. After several years of school teaching he became a journalist, and lived the rest of his life by his pen. He was elected to the Académie Française in 1953, largely on his reputation as a popular historian. Between the wars he was an open supporter of the right-wing monarchist Action Française movement, and his books on Louis XIV, Louis XV and the French Revolution extol the historical record of the monarchy and denigrate its opponents, its enemies, and the movement which eventually destroyed it. His influence on twentieth-century French interpretations of the *ancien régime* has been persistent, and even genuine scholars, such as Michel Antoine or François Bluche, openly acknowledge it.   WD

Main publications

The French Revolution (Paris: 1929), English trans. W. A. Phillips (London: Scribner, 1932); *Louis the Fifteenth and his Times* (Paris: 1933), English trans.

J. L. May (London: Cape, 1934); *The Age of Louis XIV* (Paris: 1946), English trans. M. Shaw (New York: 1970).

Reading

Weber, E.: *Action Française: Royalism and Reaction in Twentieth Century France* (Stanford, Calif.: Stanford University Press, 1962).

Gay, Peter (b.1923) Born in Berlin, Gay went to the USA in 1941 after a stay in Havana, and was educated in Denver, Colorado, and at Columbia University in New York. After a doctorate in political theory supervised by Franz Neumann he became a professor of history at Columbia in 1962, and Durfee professor at Yale University in 1970. Energetic, witty, urbane and hard working, his principal focus has been on cultural movements, ideas and creative experiences.

Characteristic of Gay's early work are the books on the life and thought of Eduard Bernstein and of Voltaire, two magisterial volumes on the Enlightenment, and an essay on what it meant to be a German during the Weimar years. In the 1970s Gay came to consider Freud's thought as constituting not just one among others but the major interpretive framework able to offer insight into bourgeois society, sexuality and individual autonomy in the nineteenth century. He underwent almost seven years of psychoanalytic training in his quest for understanding all the possibilities of contemporary Freudianism. A biography of Freud is near completion. Freud, through his rigorous commitment to science, humanity and the destruction of myth, is for Gay the great modern exponent of the Enlightenment.
                                                                OR

Main publications

Voltaire's Politics: the Poet as Realist (Princeton, NJ: Princeton University Press, 1959); *The Enlightenment: an Interpretation* (New York: Knopf, 1966); *The Enlightenment: the Science of Freedom* (New York: Knopf, 1969); *The Bourgeois Experience: Victoria to Freud*, vol. 1, *Education of the Senses* (New York: Oxford University Press, 1984), and vol. 2, *The Tender Passion* (1986).

genealogy Information on genealogy is often among the earliest records of a people or society. Divine descent is frequently claimed; for example, Bede tells us that Hengist and

Horsa derived from Woden. After the advent of Christianity monks invented names to carry pedigrees back to Adam.

Much work has been done on Roman families under the early emperors, notably by Sir Ronald Syme. But the collapse of the Roman empire still presents the genealogist with an impenetrable barrier. A good deal is known also about later Roman families; it stands to reason that many landowners must have continued to occupy their estates in Gaul and Italy, but evidence is lacking to bridge the period of the barbarian invasions. From the Merovingian dynasty only problematical descents through daughters survive. The line of Charlemagne (crowned AD 800) can be traced with confidence to St Arnulf, bishop of Metz (d.AD 640). His male issue is extinct; a conservative estimate gave him one thousand descendants by the twelfth century and he may have twenty million today. Such calculations are complicated by the possible existence in all generations of illegitimate children, acknowledged or unacknowledged.

With the advent in AD 987 of the Capetian dynasty (still extant in the male line and occupying two European thrones) in France, and of the Saxon and other successor dynasties from AD 919 in Germany, it becomes possible to identify with more assurance the emergence of new aristocracies. The school of G. TELLENBACH in Germany stressed the need of each ruler to find support in a loyal nobility, often linked by marriage (königsnähe). Ecclesiastical records, not least the *libri memoriales*, are of value, and episcopal appointments often helped to establish a noble house. From the eleventh century the acquisition of a castle frequently furnished a family name. Great reliance is placed on recurrence of Christian names. Some enduring descents emerge. Rainier I, count of Hainault (d. *c*.916), was progenitor of the dukes of Brabant and the rulers of Hesse: from him the Mountbatten family in England derives its unbroken male line.

In England the Norman conquest resulted in a tenurial revolution, and Norman adventurers soon passed into Scotland and Ireland. The number of newcomers was however relatively small, despite the popularity of claims to ancestors who came over with the Conqueror. In sober historical fact we know the names of less than two-score persons who can reasonably be shown to have been on William's side at Hastings. As time passed, families of Saxon origin rose to prominence again, for example Berkeley, Neville, Stanley and Fitzwilliam.

In the fifteenth century matters of armory and genealogy were increasingly entrusted to the heralds, first incorporated as the College of Arms in 1484. From 1530 until 1686 the heralds carried out a series of visitations, county by county, which collectively form a wonderful corpus of English family history. They also included among their number distinguished scholars such as William CAMDEN and Sir William Dugdale (1605–1684). Dugdale was an outstanding example of the best type of officer of arms. In his youth he was associated with the circle of Sir Christopher Hatton and Sir Robert Cotton who foresaw the coming storm and sought to place vulnerable documents and monuments on record. In the early stages of the Civil War he fulfilled the more medieval role of summoning parliamentary garrisons to surrender. With the king at Oxford, Dugdale was already working on both his *Baronage* (finally published 1675–6) and his *Antiquities of Warwickshire* (1656). The *Monasticon*, of which the first volume was produced with Roger Dodsworth in 1655 and the second in 1661, was a third massive labour of scholarship. A remarkable feature of his research is the extent to which original sources are cited in the marginal notes.

In 1660 Dugdale was appointed Norroy King of Arms which gave him authority over the counties north of the river Trent. Between 1662 and 1670 he carried out visitations of all of them with exemplary thoroughness. In each county he would move from hundred to hundred, calling all who claimed a coat of arms to wait upon him. He carried a supply of summonses and also blank forms on which a successful applicant could have a copy of his armorial bearings for a suitable fee. On his return to London, the results of his peregrination were written up in a sumptuous, rubricated format with the shield at the head of the page. At the end of the volume were noted 'disclaimers', those who had unsuccessfully claimed arms, and a valuable section on monumental inscriptions which he and his staff had noted. Many of the heralds were not as conscientious in writing up their work as Dugdale, but the bulk of their labours can be read in the publications of the Harleian Society. In 1676 he was appointed Garter principal King of Arms and knighted; but in his old age Dugdale stayed much of the time in Warwickshire acting through his son in London. His *Baronage* gave a historical account of the English nobility which was not equalled until the publication of the fourteen volumes of *The Complete Peerage*, re-edited by Vicary Gibbs and others (1910–59), which is a work of rich authority and scholarship.

Not all the genealogical work in this country reached Dugdale's high level. Many pedigrees were produced claiming a Conquest descent with little justification and sometimes with positive falsification. At the end of the nineteenth century a more critical attitude to genealogy, based on original manuscript sources, was headed by J. H. ROUND. In our times the science of genealogy has been much enriched by the works of Sir Anthony Wagner. It is probably true to say that England, spared the hazards of revolution and invasion, has a richer collection of records to aid the researcher into pedigrees at all levels than any other state or society. Grateful allusion should however be made to the 'International Genealogical Index', compiled in this century by the Mormons.

A hundred years ago almost every sovereign court had its heralds and some sort of heraldic office, though conditions varied enormously. In Russia, for example, the aristocracy combined a new nobility of service, largely created by Peter the Great, with princely descendants of Rurik (d. AD 879). The end of the Holy Roman Empire in 1807 left the German-speaking area less well organized between the various kingdoms, electorates and principalities. Today it is almost only in countries which remain monarchical that some form of heraldic and/or genealogical authority is to be found. No other realm had so thorough a system as the English visitations.

More attention is paid in European continental genealogy to descents other than through the father. For some orders, noble descent of all 16 great-great-grandparents was required (*seize quartiers*). This is at least a salutary reminder that the genetic inheritance of an individual does not derive exclusively from his or her father and father's father, but from the chromosomes of all the ancestors. Equally, concentration on male ascending lines is likely to conceal the vast number of ancestors which we all are calculated to possess. In fact, the same ancestor must be common to many, many people. Granted the limited mobility of the population for much of history, this is scarcely surprising. If there were no duplication of ancestors, each individual living today should have over 34,000 million individual ancestors at the time of Charlemagne, 36 generations ago. In fact the total population of the world at that date was perhaps of the order of 200 million persons. Marriage within clans and kindreds must frequently have been extensive.

On the other hand, it does not take long for the blood of an outsider to be distributed widely. Alfonso VI of Castile (1072–1109) married a daughter of Mahomet II, king of Seville (who himself claimed descent from the Prophet); their blood has passed to every royal family of Europe. Analogous events must have occurred at various dates and every level of society: racial purity is largely a myth. MM

Reading

Boschetti, A. F.: *I cataloghi dell' opera di Pompeo Litta 'Famiglie celebr. Italiani'* (Arnaldo Forni Editore, 1977) [an index to Litta's works – see below].

Chaffanjou, Arnaud: *Grandes familles de l'histoire de France* (Paris: Editions Albatros, 1980).

Filby, P. William: *American and British Genealogy and Heraldry* (Chicago: American Library Association, 1970).

Forst de Battaglia, Otto: *Traité de Généalogie* (Lausanne: Editions Spes, 1949).

Goodwin, A. ed.: *The European Nobility in the Eighteenth Century* (London: Adam & Charles Black, 1953).

Hamilton-Edwards, G.: *In Search of Ancestry* (Chichester: Phillimore, 1974).

Hueck, Walter von, ed.: *Genealogisches Handbuch des Adels*, 90 vols (Limburg an der Lahn: C. A. Starke Verlag, 1951–).

Jougla de Morenas, Henri: *Grand Armorial de France*, 7 vols (Paris: Les Éditions Héraldiques, 1934–52).

Litta, Pompeo: *Famiglie celebri Italiane* 9 vols (Milan: Litta [author]; Florence and London: Mofini, 1819–83).

Reuter, Timothy ed.: *The Medieval Nobility* (Amsterdam: North-Holland, 1978).

Steel, D. J.: *Sources for Scottish Genealogy and Family History* (Chichester: Phillimore, 1970).

Wagner, Anthony: *English Genealogy*, 2nd edn (Oxford: Clarendon Press, 1972).

Genovese, Eugene Dominic (b.1930)   The son of an Italian–American family in Brooklyn, Genovese has become one of the major historians of American slavery, and perhaps the most prominent Marxist historian in the United States. With degrees from Brooklyn College and Columbia University, he has taught at Rutgers University, where he resigned to avoid further embarrassment after President Nixon had called for his removal because of his anti-Vietnam-war activities, then briefly at Sir George Williams University, Montreal, and since 1969 at the University of Rochester. He has served on the executive council of the American Historical Association and was president of the Organization of American Historians in 1978–79.

Although until recently he has never lived in the south, he has written about southern slave society with exceptional insight and understanding. His early work, notably *The Political Economy of Slavery (1965)*, was more uncompromisingly Marxist than his *magnum opus*, *Roll, Jordan, Roll* (1974) which won him the Bancroft prize. The book painted a vivid and detailed picture of slave life, and of the delicate balance of accommodation and resistance in the slaves' response to the authority of the master. In some of his essays, and in *From Rebellion to Revolution* (1979), a comparative study of slavery in the western hemisphere, he reverts to something closer to his earlier, more assertive, Marxist stance.

Genovese is passionate and combative in his intellectual commitment, and insists that the socialist historian can and must do his political and public duty through his work. He has engaged in numerous controversies with left-wing dogmatists and 'vulgar Marxists'. Heavily influenced by Antonio Gramsci, he speaks of his own pessimism of the intellect and optimism of the will.   PJP

Main publications

(Published by Pantheon, New York, unless otherwise stated.)
The Political Economy of Slavery (1965); *The World the Slaveholders Made* (1969); *In Red and Black: Marxian Explorations in Southern and Afro-American History* (1971); *Roll, Jordan, Roll: the World the Slaves Made* (1974); *From Rebellion to Revolution: Afro-American Slave Revolts in the Modern World* (Baton Rouge: Louisiana State University Press, 1979).

Reading

King, R. H.: Marxism and the slave south. *American Quarterly* 29 (1977) 117–31.

Geoffrey of Monmouth (*fl*.1100–1155)   The author of *The History of the Kings of Britain* is included in this dictionary in spite of the fact that what he wrote was fiction based on legend, because a large number of Britons still like to believe that King Arthur was a real person. The Arthurian legend was already in existence when Geoffrey wrote, but the *History* was such an immediate success that he may be said to be the person who really launched it. He claimed to have found his information (which included the story of the Trojan Brutus, grandson of Aeneas, fixing his capital at 'New Troy' or Trinovantum on the site of London) from a book given to him by Walter Archdeacon of Oxford, who was indeed a real person. One might almost think that he wrote his books in order to tease academics. He probably spent many years at Oxford where, under the name of 'Geoffrey Arthur', he was a canon of St George's-in-the-Castle. He was consecrated bishop of Llandaff in 1153 but probably did not take up residence. His parentage is unknown, but it is thought that he was a Breton who was brought up in Wales.   RHCD

Main writings

Historia Regum Britanniae, ed. Neil Wright (Cambridge: Cambridge University Press, 1986); trans. by Lewis Thorpe (Harmondsworth: Penguin, 1966).

Reading

Barber, Richard, ed.: *Arthurian Literature*, vol. 5 (Woodbridge, Suffolk: Boydell & Brewer, 1985) [pp. 1–36 and 164–71 incl. alphabetical list of the 211 known manuscripts].

Chambers, E. K.: *Arthur of Britain* (London: Sidgwick & Jackson, 1927).

Dumville, David: Sub-Roman Britain: history and legend. *History* 2 (1977) 173–92.

Geoffrey of Villehardouin (b. *c.*1150, d.1212/17) Geoffrey's early career was at the court of Champagne, where he became marshal. In 1190–4 he probably took part in the third crusade, and in 1199 he enlisted with count Theobald of Champagne for the fourth. He was prominent in its planning and was a member of its directing council. After the crusade captured Constantinople Geoffrey was influential in the Latin Empire created there, becoming its marshal and apparently remaining in the east until his death. His history of the expedition, *La Conquête de Constantinople*, was finished in 1207. It is one of the first major French prose works and seems to have been in considerable demand in France.

Geoffrey's chronicle is the most authoritative account of the fourth crusade. In its diversion to Constantinople, he saw the work of God's providence, manifested in a sequence of events which could not have been planned by man. Historians who believe that providence received a helping hand from the ambitions of the leaders have seen him as an official historian engaged in whitewashing the affair, while his admirers have defended him as a diarist of remarkable accuracy. In reality he seems to have been a capable soldier who delighted to describe, as if in a real-life epic, the wonderful events he had seen. Unfair to his enemies, inclined to forget things which were not to the credit of the crusade, he nevertheless wrote an outstanding, and very readable, eye-witness history.　　CM

Main writings

Villehardouin: la conquête de Constantinople, ed. E. Faral, 2 vols (Paris: 1938); *Joinville and Villehardouin: Chronicles of the Crusades*, trans. M. R. B. Shaw (Harmondsworth: Penguin, 1963).

Reading

Beer, J. M. A.: *Villehardouin: Epic Historian* (Geneva: Droz, 1968).

Dufournet, J.: *Les écrivains de la IVe croisade* (Paris: Société d' Édition d'Enseignement Supérieure, 1973).

Longnon, J.: *Recherches sur la vie de Geoffroy de Villehardouin* (Paris: Champion, 1939).

Queller, D. E.: *The Fourth Crusade* (Leicester: Leicester University Press, 1978).

Gerald of Wales See GIRALDUS CAMBRENSIS.

Geyl, Pieter (b.1887, d.1966) After studying Dutch at the University of Leiden, Geyl proceeded to a doctorate in history in 1913. He was a schoolteacher for a brief period, then became London correspondent of the Nieuwe Rotterdamsche Courant in 1913. What he experienced as his exile continued when he was appointed initially reader (1919) then professor of Dutch History and Institutions at University College, London. In 1936 he was appointed to the chair in modern history at the University of Utrecht, despite official fears that his involvement with Flemish nationalism would lead to political difficulties with Belgium, and, apparently, despite initial opposition from Queen Wilhelmina who regarded him as hostile to the house of Orange. During the second world war he was held hostage by the Germans for over three years and dismissed from his post. After the war he was restored to his Utrecht chair, where he remained until his retirement in 1958.

Throughout his life Geyl was an indefatigable worker and a prolific writer, particularly of articles and essays where his most characteristic and possibly his best scholarly work is to be found. His historical writings were fiercely revisionist, successfully challenging established attitudes and interpretations over a wide range of issues in Dutch history. From his student days he had been a passionate supporter of the Flemish nationalist movement, and he became one of its most prominent Dutch advocates in the 1920s and 1930s. His regret at the political division in the Low Countries which divided Dutch speakers in the south from those in the north, led him to challenge the established view that the division between the Netherlands and Belgium had been historically inevitable. He argued that the split between an independent north and a Spanish-controlled south which emerged in the course of the Dutch Revolt was rather a tragic historical accident than the result of fundamental differences in national character. However, while successfully attacking one myth, his assumption of the natural unity of all Dutch speakers (and his exclusion of the French-speaking Walloons) seems suspiciously like an equally unhistorical myth. Similarly, his attempt to write a history of the Dutch-speaking people began to look forced by the time he reached the seventeenth century, and had to face the very real differences in the historical experiences of the Dutch and the Flemings. He struggled on to the end of the eighteenth century, but took the work no further. Similarly, he has forced a reconsideration of the republican and Orangist traditions in Dutch history, through his attacks on the policies of the princes of Orange in the seventeenth and eighteenth centuries, which he argued were more in the interests of the dynasty than of the country; and, more positively, through his favourable reassessment of the character and achievements of the seventeenth-century republican regime, and his attempted rehabilitation of the Patriots of the late eighteenth century.

After the war much of Geyl's best work came in essays commenting on contemporary and past historians, most notoriously in his polemic with TOYNBEE, but perhaps his elegant and thoughtful discussions of the nineteenth-century masters will prove of more lasting interest.

Geyl was from the very start almost exclusively a political historian, and does not seem to have been influenced much, if at all, by the new ideas and methods which were transforming history during his lifetime. Moreover, the greater part of his work grew out of disagreement with interpretations of Dutch history which have since been very largely discarded, to a great extent as a result of his writings. Thus, partly as a consequence of his own success, many of his writings now seem dated. Also, outside the Netherlands the extent of his achievement has rarely been appreciated,

and individual works have been misinterpreted, through ignorance of the historiographical context. JLP

Main publications

Christofforo Suriano, Resident van de Serenissime Republiek van Venetië in Den Haag (1616–1623) (The Hague: Martinus Nijhoff, 1913); *Willem IV en Engeland tot 1748* (The Hague: 1924); *Geschiedenis van de Nederlandse Stam*, 1930–59, partly trans. as *The Revolt of the Netherlands* (London: Williams & Norgate, 1932) and *The Netherlands in the Seventeenth Century*, 2 vols (London: Benn 1961–64); *Oranje en Stuart, 1641–1672* (1939) (London: 1969); *Napoleon. Voor en tegen in de Franse geschiedschriüving* (1946) (London: 1949); *De Patriottenbeweging, 1780–1787* (1947); *Debates with Historians* (Groningen: J. B. Wolters, 1955); *Studies en Strijdschriften* (J. B. Wolters, 1958); *Encounters in History* (London: Collins, 1963); *Pennestrijd over Staat en Historie* (Groningen: Wolters-Noordhoff, 1971).

Reading

Dunk, H. W. von der: Pieter Geyl. History as a form of self-expression. In *Clio's Mirror. Historiography in Britain and the Netherlands* (Zutphen: De Walburg Pers, 1985).

Rogier, L. J.: *Herdenking van P. Geyl* (Amsterdam: Noord-Hollandsche Uitgevers Maatschppij, 1967).

Giannone, Pietro (b.1676, d.1748) Having made a successful career as a lawyer in Naples, Giannone won European fame through his *Civil History of the Kingdom of Naples*, published in 1723. The main argument of this work was that the Roman Catholic church – the ever-growing lands, wealth and abuses of its priests, monks and nuns, and the mounting claims of its popes – had progressively undermined the development of the Neapolitan state and people. The book became noted not only for its anti-papalism and anti-clericalism but also for its glorification of the Neapolitan 'nation'. Its publication led to the author's exile, first in Vienna, where Giannone became acquainted with the more radical and critical currents of northern Catholicism and even with Protestant and deist thinkers.

Giannone began work on a vast, broad study of the history of religions known as the *Triregno* (Triple crown), in which he argued that Christianity was vastly superior to other religions, but only in its primitive form, stripped of the excrescences of wealth, dogma, theology, superstition and, above all, papalism which had become attached to it since the time of Christ. He never finished this book, and it was not published in his lifetime. He left Vienna in 1734 and, after being hounded from state to state in northern Italy and settling in Geneva, was kidnapped and imprisoned by the king of Sardinia. Although he recanted some of his views, he was kept in prison for the rest of his life. Some of his later works were discovered and printed during the battle between church and state over the Jesuits in the 1760s, and in the late nineteenth and the twentieth century his moving autobiography and other writings have been published; but many of his letters and some of his books remain in manuscript.   DEDB

Main publications

A Civil History of the Kingdom of Naples, 2 vols, trans. James Ogilvie (London: 1729–31); *Opere*, ed. L. Panzini, 14 vols (Milan: Classici Italiani, 1823–4).

Reading

Ajello, Raffaelle, ed.: *Pietro Giannone e il suo tempo*, 2 vols (Naples: Jovene, 1980).

Chadwick, Owen: *The Popes and European Revolution* (Oxford: Oxford University Press, 1981), pp. 403–7.

Croce, Benedetto: *History of the Kingdom of Naples* (Chicago, Ill.: University of Chicago Press, 1970).

Giannone, Pietro: *Vita scritta da lui medesimo*, ed. Sergio Bertelli (Milan: Feltrinelli, 1960).

Venturi, Franco: History and reform in the middle of the eighteenth century. In *The Diversity of History*, ed. J. H. Elliott and H. G. Koenigsberger (London: Routledge & Kegan Paul, 1970), pp. 223–44.

Gibbon, Edward (b. 1737, d.1794) After minimal schooling but a great deal of self-directed reading, Gibbon entered Magdalen College, Oxford, shortly before his sixteenth birthday, in April 1752. He was not impressed by the standard of teaching he received there, and his studies were in any case brought to an abrupt end after little more than a year by his conversion to Roman Catholicism. The conversion was short-lived (he returned to the Protestant faith at Christmas 1754), but it led to his being sent to Lausanne, where he spent five of the most important and formative years of his life. He became fluent in French, read widely in French and Latin, learned Greek,

and became clear in his own mind that the life he wanted was that of a scholar and writer. At this stage his interests were as much literary and philosophical as historical, and his first published work, which appeared in 1761, was the *Essai sur l'étude de la littérature*. By this time he had returned to England and was midway through a period of service (May 1760–December 1762) in the Hampshire Militia. From 1763 to 1765 he was on the Grand Tour in France and Italy, arriving in Rome for the first time in October 1764 and receiving there the profound impressions which were to result eventually in the *Decline and Fall of the Roman Empire*. This was still some years in the future, however, and his first attempt at a strictly historical subject, begun in 1768 and soon abandoned, was a *History of the Liberty of the Swiss*. With the death of his father in 1770 he became financially independent, though certainly not rich, and his position was made more secure when he was elected to parliament in 1774, holding a minor government post and acquiring a small additional income. He began writing the *Decline and Fall* in February 1773; the first volume was published three years later in 1776; volumes II and III appeared in 1781; and volumes IV, V and VI in 1788. Having returned to Lausanne, Gibbon was now wealthy and famous. He went back to London in May 1793, the last year of his life, in order to be with his friend Lord Sheffield, whose wife had died a month before. While in England he suffered a recurrence of an old and largely neglected illness, and died at the age of 57 in January 1794. In the latter part of his life he had produced several drafts of an autobiography; the first version was published by Lord Sheffield in 1796.

The *Decline and Fall* is very much the product of the man and of his age. The voracious, indiscriminate reading of the young Gibbon in his grandfather's library was to be the basis of that mastery of source material and of earlier scholarship which was to characterize the finished work. The long period of residence in Lausanne, and the resulting acquisition of French to the point of bilingualism, led to major and fruitful influences on Gibbon's work from such writers as Montesquieu, Bayle and Voltaire, complementing the more native influences of Hume, Robertson and Locke. An early interest in theology – an interest which was to have a very real effect on his own life – contributed to his very distinctive (and at the time highly controversial) treatment of Christianity. From the Roman writers themselves he conceived, or confirmed, an admiration for the classic virtues of courage, steadfastness and personal dignity, and for the traditional values of the senatorial order; with the same writers he shared a view of civilization as opposed to barbarism and of the historian's moral role. But in many of his interests, presuppositions and prejudices he was typical of the eighteenth-century Enlightenment of which he was a part. His civilization, his liberty, were those of the prosperous intellectual, who by his benevolent employment of wealth and power would ensure the well-being of the population at large. His lofty objectivity, his impatience with the irrational in any of its forms, his apparent lack of the more tender feelings (all of these belied, to some extent, by his letters and autobiographical writings) are in keeping with the intellectualism of the age. In the history of historiography he stands as the blender and reconciler of two historical traditions: the antiquarian and the philosophical. On the one hand, in his concern for primary sources and in his interest in such things as 'medals' and inscriptions, he is the successor of the *érudits*, the scholars of the Renaissance and seventeenth century; and on the other, in his belief in the broader patterns and deeper meanings behind events, he was in the tradition of Montesquieu's *Esprit des lois* or Voltaire's *Essai sur les moeurs*. The programme, indeed, which he outlined and advocated in his own *Essai* of 1761 was to be triumphantly followed and perfected in the *Decline and Fall*. It is this, together of course with his technical skill in the handling of so vast a subject and his unrivalled mastery of the English language, that gives the work its permanent value.   JP

Main publications

The History of the Decline and Fall of the Roman Empire (1776–88) ed. J. B. Bury (London: Methuen, 1896–1900, Everyman edn, London: Dent 1910, repr. 1978); *Memoirs of my Life and Writings* (1827) ed. Betty Radice (Harmondsworth:

Penguin, 1984); *The Miscellaneous Works of Edward Gibbon*, ed. Lord Sheffield (London: 1796, additional vol. 1815).

Reading

Bowersock, G. W. et al. eds: *Edward Gibbon and the Fall of the Roman Empire* (Cambridge, Mass.: Harvard University Press, 1977).
Burrow, J. W.: *Gibbon* (Oxford: Oxford University Press, 1985).
Low, D. M.: *Edward Gibbon* (London: Chatto & Windus, 1937).
Momigliano, A.: Gibbon's contribution to historical method. In *Studies in Historiography* (London: Weidenfeld & Nicolson, 1966).
Norton,, J. E.: *A Bibliography of the Works of Edward Gibbon* (Oxford: Oxford University Press, 1970).

Gibson, Charles (b.1920, d.1985) Expanding institutional history to encompass culture as a whole, Gibson made the lasting conflict of civilizations a central theme in Latin American history. He has been accused of sustaining the Black Legend with *The Aztecs under Spanish Rule*, a classic account of colonial exploitation, but Gibson's impressive scholarship and elegant syntheses gave his work an importance outlasting the Hispanist-Indianist debate.   ATB

Main publications

Tlaxcala in the Sixteenth Century (New Haven, Conn: Yale University Press, 1952); *The Aztecs under Spanish Rule: a History of the Indians of the Valley of Mexico, 1519–1810* (Stanford, Calif.: Stanford University Press, 1964); *Spain in America* (New York: Harper & Row, 1966).

Giesebrecht, Wilhelm von (b.1814, d.1889) From a Prussian intellectual family, Giesebrecht's immediate ancestors and relatives were writers, pastors and schoolteachers (see the entries he wrote on them for the *Allgemeine Deutsche Biographie*, ix. 156–62). He studied at Berlin in the Hegel era and prepared himself for a career as a schoolteacher, though not before an early flirtation with the stage. From 1836 to 1854 he taught at the Joachimsthaler Gymnasium in Berlin, while continuing his historical work. Together with WAITZ, SYBEL and others he was among the first members of RANKE's seminar and learnt from Ranke the application of critical method to the sources of history. A striking example of this was displayed in his early (1841) reconstruction of the then supposedly lost annals of Altaich from later sources which had made use of them; the discovery in 1867 of a sixteenth-century transcript of the annals confirmed the accuracy of his reconstruction in all except a few minor details. From 1843 to 1845 he was financed by the Prussian government to visit archives and libraries in Austria and Italy, a journey which produced a substantial monograph, *De literarum studiis apud Italos primis medii aevi saeculis*.

The revolution of 1848 found Giesebrecht on the side of authority; he was on the executive committee of the Patriotic Society and drafted statements on behalf of the federation of constitutional monarchic societies. The events of 1848 left him with a deep aversion to democracy and republicanism (and hence to France, which he refused to visit), but also marked the end of any active political involvement. In 1855 Giesebrecht published the first volume of what was to be a six-volume survey of German history in the high middle ages, his *Geschichte der Deutschen Kaiserzeit*. The work was a remarkable success, combining a deep familiarity with the narrative sources for the period with a distinguished style and an ideology easily acceptable to Giesebrecht's public. He offered a brilliant picture of that period in European history when, in his own words, 'our people, strong and united, achieved the greatest extent of its power and determined not only its own future but that of other nations; when the German man counted for most in the world and the German name was famous'. This was not so much a prophetic anticipation of Wilhelmine imperialism – Giesebrecht was indeed a nationalist, but a conservative and Christian one – but rather reflected the interest in the middle ages characteristic of German romanticism. It was also an expression of the disappointment felt by many German intellectuals at the failure of the 1848 revolution to bring about unification of Germany. Nevertheless, Giesebrecht's work, concentrating as it did on personalities and showing sympathy only for the rulers of Germany and the empire in the high middle ages and not for those who opposed them, helped

to prepare the ground for the adulation of the emperor and the state which became fashionable after 1871 and still more after 1890. It was however this excessive veneration of the ruler as much as the implicit *Großdeutsch* tendency of Giesebrecht's which provoked Sybel's courteous polemic of 1859, and hence the beginnings of the dispute among German medievalists about whether the imperial title had been a blessing or a curse for Germany.

Following the appearance of the first volume of his *Geschichte*, Giesebrecht was appointed to a chair in Königsberg in 1857, and in 1862 he accepted the personal invitation of Maximilian II of Bavaria to succeed Heinrich von Sybel at Munich. Here he remained until his death in 1889. He continued a productive scholarly activity: new and revised volumes of the *Deutsche Kaiserzeit* appeared regularly, and were accompanied by numerous articles. Increasingly, however, he became an academic manager, a rare phenomenon in the nineteenth century. He succeeded in having history adopted as a subject in its own right in Bavarian schools on the Prussian model (though not in having its teaching restricted to specialists), and the first curriculum issued in 1874 was probably drafted by him. He was also highly influential as the secretary of the *Historische Kommission*, founded in 1858 to coordinate the publication of the sources for German history; after Ranke ceased to attend its meetings from 1873 onwards he was effectively its president. TAR

Main publications

Geschichte der deutschen Kaiserzeit, 6 vols (many editions; final volume completed by Giesebrecht's pupil B. von Simson) (Leipzig: Dunckler & Humblot, 1855–88).

Reading

Almanach der bayerischen Akademie der Wissenchaften für das Jahr 1884, pp. 377–80, [incl. bibliography to 1884].

Heimpel, H.: Friedrich Wilhelm Benjamin von Giesebrecht. *Neue Deutsche Biographie* 6 (1964) 379–82.

Riezler, S.: Wilhelm von Giesebrecht: *Allgemeine Deutsche Biographie* 49 (1904) 341–9.

Gildas (*fl.* first half of the sixth century) Gildas was a cleric living in western Britain, who wrote an attack on the sins of the British of his day, the *De Excidio Britanniae*. Nothing reliable is known of his life or even of where he lived. His work includes a number of historical chapters which contain almost all that we know historically about the end of Roman Britain and the origins of Anglo-Saxon England. Regrettably Gildas was not a historian: his work is remarkably devoid of hard fact and has consequently occasioned much (as yet) inconclusive debate.   EFJ

Main writings

Gildas: The Ruin of Britain, ed. and trans. M. Winterbottom (Chichester: Phillimore, 1978).

Reading

Lapidge, M. and Dumbille D. M. eds: *Gildas: New Approaches* (Woodbridge, Sussex: Boydell, 1984).

Gindely, Anton See SLAVONIC HISTORIOGRAPHY.

Gipson, Lawrence (b.1880, d.1971) Born in the American West, Gipson in 1904 was among the first Americans to become a Rhodes Scholar at Oxford. Later, he studied at Yale under Charles M. ANDREWS. Gipson is said to have been the only student Andrews ever permitted to write a doctoral thesis on a biographical subject, a study of the Connecticut loyalist Jared Ingersoll. If so, he repaid this indulgence in full measure when, upon moving to Lehigh University in Pennsylvania in 1924, he set himself to write a history of the worldwide British empire in the years immediately before the outbreak of the War of Independence. The project dominated the rest of his long life: the first three volumes appeared in 1936 and the final volume a year before his death.

Gipson's life work merits comparison with Andrews's magisterial *The Colonial Period of American History*, both for its scope and its focus upon political and institutional history. More truly 'imperial' in its coverage of all Britain's colonial possessions, it is also less analytical in style and less compelling in its handling of other than British sources. From the first, too, reviewers coupled admiration for Gipson's breadth of vision with criticism of his

sometimes acerbic comparisons of London's solicititude for its empire with the colonist's provincial behaviour. This perspective, particularly evident in his widely read text, *The Coming of the Revolution, 1763—1775*, made Gipson's writings more honoured than accepted amid American post-war nationalism. None the less, his achievement was significant: in form looking back to the great multi-volume treatments of an earlier age of American historiography, it prefigured the transatlantic perspective and wide-ranging research that now inform the best writings in early American political and intellectual history.   RJ

Main publications

Jared Ingersoll: a Study of American Loyalism in Relation to British Colonial Government (New Haven, Conn: Yale University Press, 1920); *The British Empire Before the American Revolution*, 15 vols (New York: Knopf, 1936—1970); *The Coming of the Revolution, 1763—1775* (New York: Harper, 1954).

Reading

Main, Jackson T.: Lawrence Henry Gipson: historian. *Pennsylvania History* 36 (1969) 22—48.
Morris, Richard B.: The spacious empire of Lawrence Henry Gipson. *William and Mary Quarterly*, 3rd ser. 24 (1967) 169—89.

Giraldus Cambrensis (b.1146, d.1223) Born in southern Pembroke of mixed Norman-Welsh ancestry, Gerald of Wales, as he is also known, was educated at Gloucester, Paris and Lincoln. An archdeacon by the age of 30 and a royal clerk by the 1180s he seemed set fair for rapid promotion in church and state. But in the 1190s his career faltered badly and irreversibly: he fell out with the king's court and his attempt (1198—1203) to secure the see (and, as he hoped, the archbishopric) of St Davids for himself was likewise thwarted. Deeply embittered by his failures, by the lack of respect shown to his family and by the irresoluble dilemma of his own national identity (he complained bitterly that he was acceptable neither to the Welsh nor the Normans), Gerald took refuge in his writings and in the prospect of literary immortality.

He was a prolific writer on a wide range of topics, moral, ecclesiastical, hagiographical and political (including a bitter diatribe against the Angevin family in *The Instruction of the*

Prince (1190–1217)). A self-conscious stylist, his writings are often opinionated and vitriolic in tone and incurably egocentric in substance; but they are redeemed by his insatiable curiosity about places and peoples and by his keen powers of observation. His qualities are shown to best effect in his books on Ireland and Wales. His *Conquest of Ireland* (1189) is a vivid, well-organized and perceptive narrative of the Anglo-Norman conquest of Ireland which by its concentration on many of Gerald's own kinsfolk becomes a virtual family epic. His *Journey through Wales* (1191) is an entertaining if rambling travelogue, based on his tour of the country in the retinue of Archbishop Baldwin of Canterbury in 1188. But Gerald's greatest claim to fame are his ethnographic works, *The Topography of Ireland* (1188) and, above all, *The Description of Wales* (1194). In them he anatomized the habits, manners, virtues and vices of the Welsh and Irish with consummate skill and presented a remarkable, if somewhat stylized, view of their societies as organic wholes. So successful was he that his descriptions have been given more credence than they deserve. Nevertheless they fully vindicate his own claim to be a 'diligent inquirer into natural history'.

RRD

Main writings

Giraldi Cambrensis Opera, ed. J. S. Brewer et. al., Rolls Series, 8 vols, (1861–91); *The Journey through Wales and the Description of Wales*, trans. and ed. L. Thorpe (Harmondsworth: Penguin, 1978); *The Conquest of Ireland*, trans. and ed. A. B. Scott and F. X. Martin (Dublin: Royal Irish Academy, 1978); *The History and Topography of Ireland*, trans. and ed. J. J. O'Meara (Penguin: 1978).

Reading

Bartlett, R.: *Gerald of Wales 1146–1223* (Oxford: Clarendon Press, 1982).

Richter, M.: *Giraldus Cambrensis: The Growth of the Welsh Nation* (Aberystwyth : National Library of Wales, 1978)

Roberts, B. F. *Gerald of Wales* (Cardiff: University of Wales Press, 1982).

Godechot, Jacques (b.1907) Born in Lunéville and attending school and university in Nancy, Godechot completed his studies at the Sorbonne and taught in schools between 1930 and 1940. In 1945 he joined the Faculté

des lettres of Toulouse, where he spent the rest of his career, serving as doyen, 1961–71. His first published work (1938) was on military administration under the Directory, and most of his subsequent writings were to be devoted to the French revolutionary period. His second book, however, a history of the Atlantic (1947), signalled wider interests, and in the 1950s and 1960s he became known as the chief French proponent of the idea of an 'Atlantic', 'western' or 'democratic' revolution sweeping the wider European world in the late eighteenth century, a concept launched in English-speaking countries by R. R. PALMER. Meanwhile he had also written the standard handbook on French institutions between 1789 and 1815 (1952), and major surveys of French revolutionary expansion (1956) and counter-revolution (1961) as well as reviewing extensively and stimulating and co-ordinating much important research on western Languedoc in the eighteenth century. Elected president of the Société des Études Robespierristes in 1959, he became a tireless defender of established French interpretations of the Revolution as these came under increasing attack from English-speaking scholars in the subsequent decades. Following the publication of a survey of the Revolution's historiography (1974) he became president in 1975 of the International Commission for the History of the French Revolution. WD

Main publications

Les Institutions de la France sous la révolution et l'empire (Paris: Presses Universitaires de France, 1952); *La Grande nation*, 2 vols (Paris: Aubier, 1956); *The Counter-Revolution: Doctrine and Action 1789–1804* (1961) (London: Routledge & Kegan Paul, 1972); *France and the Atlantic Revolution of the Eighteenth Century, 1770–1799* (1963) (London: Macmillan, 1965); *Un Jury pour la révolution* (Paris: Robert Laffont, 1974).

Goldziher, Ignaz (b.1850, d.1921) With a few of his contemporaries, Goldziher established the study of Islam on a truly historical basis. His work stressed the complex relationship between the essential driving ideas of a religion and the historical circumstances in which they develop.

Born at Székesfehérvár (Stuhlweissenburg) in Hungary, Goldziher was a child prodigy, reading the Hebrew Bible at the age of five, the Aramaic Talmud at eight, and publishing (in German) a monograph on a Jewish prayer at 12. As a teenager and while still at school, he studied oriental languages in Budapest with Arminius Vambéry. Subsequent study in Germany, where he completed at Leipzig his doctorate on an Arabic Jewish commentary on the Old Testament, inclined him to Arabic and Islamic studies. His only substantial visit to the Middle East was in 1873–4, when he was the first non-Muslim to be accepted as a student at al-Azhar, the great centre of Muslim learning in Cairo. Although he achieved international recognition and was offered chairs at Cambridge and other universities, he was unwilling or unable to abandon his family commitments. In Hungary, during a time of strong anti-Semitism, his academic achievement was relatively unrewarded. It was only in 1904 that he was appointed professor of semitics at the University of Budapest (ten years after turning down the offer from Cambridge): until then, he had depended on his job as secretary to the Jewish community. His published diaries (*Tagebuch*, Leiden, 1978) reveal an unhappy and often bitter man, although his many friends and colleagues testified to his humanity and kindness.

The bulk of Goldziher's work is monographic. He wrote over 700 articles and five substantial books, only one of which attempted a general account of Islam. His sources were the vast literature of Islamic civilization, and the focus of his attention was religion and culture rather than political history. His work is characterized by an outstanding erudition and analytical incisiveness, but expressed sometimes in a German which is tortuous.

Goldziher was a committed but undogmatic Jew and his own religion illumined his study of Islam. He seems to have been particularly attracted by the Muslim conception of a God remote from and incomprehensible to mankind, and his work combines a knowledge and sympathy which are far removed from the prejudices of many of his predecessors and, sadly, some of his successors.   GRHt

Main publications

Die Zahiriten: Ihr Lehrsystem und ihre Geschichte (1884), trans. *The Zahiris, their Doctrine and their*

History (Leiden: Brill, 1971); *Muhammedanische Studien*, 2 vols (1889–90), trans. *Muslim Studies*, 2 vols (London: George Allen & Unwin, 1967–71); *Vorlesungen über den Islam* (1910), trans. *Introduction to Islamic Theology and Law* (Princeton: Princeton University Press, 1981); *Die Richtungen der islamischen Koranauslegung* (Leiden: Brill, 1920); *Gesammelte Schriften*, ed. J. Somogyi, 6 vols (Hildesheim: Georg Olms, 1967–73).

Reading

Lewis, B.: Introduction. In *Introduction to Islamic Theology and Law* (Princeton: Princeton University Press, 1981).
Somogyi, J. de: Ignace Goldziher. *Muslim World* 41 (1951) 199–208.
Waardenburg, J.–J.: *L'Islam dans le miroir de l'occident* (Paris/The Hague: Mouton, 1963).

Gooch, George Peabody (b.1873, d.1968) Gooch was one of the foremost gentleman-scholars of his generation. Educated at Eton, and then at King's College, London, and Trinity College, Cambridge, he subsequently studied at the universities of Berlin and Paris; but after his failure to be elected a fellow of Trinity College in 1897 Gooch abandoned further thought of a formal academic career. Instead historical scholarship came to occupy only one part of a crowded public life. He was Liberal MP for Bath between 1906 and 1910 and was active in peace movements for many years, serving as president of the National Peace Council in the 1930s.

Gooch produced a series of historical works of remarkable range and diversity. They fall into three broad categories and reflect his own preoccupations at different periods. In his early publications ACTON's influence is clearly identifiable. Gooch contributed to the *Cambridge Modern History*; he wrote a study of seventeenth-century English political thought and then a pioneering investigation of the Rankean historical revolution, which was first published in 1913. During the inter-war period his concern with peace and international affairs was reflected in a series of important publications on DIPLOMATIC HISTORY. He was joint editor and a major contributor to the *Cambridge History of British Foreign Policy* (1922–3); he also edited and had a decisive influence upon the great documentary series on pre-1914 diplomacy, *British Documents on the Origins of* the War (1927 onwards); and he produced two volumes of essays on the origins of the first world war, *Before the War* (1936 and 1938). Finally Gooch turned to eighteenth-century history, producing several attractive and lightly-written studies of its rulers, beginning with a portrait of *Frederick the Great* (1947).

Gooch's historical works were deservedly popular, combining readability with sound scholarship. His most enduring contribution to scholarship, however, was probably his influence on the publication of *British Documents on the Origins of the War.*   HMS

Main publications

(Published by Longmans, Green, London, unless otherwise stated.)
The History of English Democratic Ideas in the Seventeenth Century (Cambridge: Cambridge University Press, 1898); *History and Historians in the Nineteenth Century* (1913, 2nd edn, 1952); *Germany and the French Revolution* (1920, repr. London: Cass, 1965); ed. with A. W. Ward, *The Cambridge History of British Foreign Policy* (Cambridge University Press, 1922–3); ed. with Harold Temperley, *British Documents on the Origins of the War*, 11 vols (London: HMSO, 1927–38); *Before the War: Studies in Diplomacy*, 2 vols (1936–38); *Frederick the Great* (1947); *Maria Theresa and other studies* (1951); *Catherine the Great and other studies* (1954); *Louis XV: the Monarchy in Decline* (1956, repr. London: Greenwood, 1976).

Reading

Butterfield, Herbert: George Peabody Gooch. *Proceedings of the British Academy* 55 (1969) 311–38.
Eyck, Frank: *G. P. Gooch: a Study in History and Politics* (London: Macmillan, 1982).

Goubert, Pierre (b.1915)   Born in Saumur, Goubert was educated at the École Normale des Instituteurs, Angers, and subsequently at the École Normale Supérieure of Saint-Cloud. Between 1937 and 1951 he taught in schools, moving to the Centre National de la Recherche Scientifique in 1951. A director of studies at the École Pratique des Hautes Études from 1955, he was successively professor at Rennes (1958), Nanterre (1965) and the Sorbonne (1969).

His doctoral thesis, published as *Beauvais et le Beauvaisis* (1960) was the first product on a regional scale of techniques of DEMOGRAPHIC HISTORY evolved in the middle of the century.

It was produced not by a single scholar working alone but depended for its findings on teams of assistants gathering serial evidence under the author's direction. But Goubert wrote stylishly, and the result was a memorable picture of a provincial society wracked by the demographic crises of the 'tragic' seventeenth century which in economic and social reality only ended around 1730. His findings were much drawn upon in general studies of seventeenth-century France, and indeed Europe, although he was careful to emphasize the peculiarity of individual regions and the importance of their individual characteristics. Subsequently he turned to general themes himself, with an influential study of Louis XIV's reign (1966) and a two volume students' introduction to the ancien régime (1969–73), which were both translated, wholly or partially, into English. A leading figure in the second generation of the ANNALES SCHOOL, Goubert's robust common sense, unpretentious but readable style and warm humanity mark him out from more fanciful and fashion-conscious members of the group into whose shadow he unjustly fell during the 1960s and 1970s.   WD

Main publications

Familles marchandes sous l'ancien régime. Les danse et les motte (Paris: SEVPEN, 1959); *Beauvais et le Beauvaisis de 1600 à 1730. Contribution à l'histoire sociale de la France du XVIIe siècle* (Paris: SEVPEN, 1960); *Louis XIV et 20 millions de français* (Paris: Fayard, 1966); *L'ancien régime*, 2 vols (Paris: A. Colin, 1969–73).

Gramsci, Antonio   (b.1891,   d.1937) Gramsci acquired fame posthumously. His tormented life and political failures make his eventual apotheosis somewhat unexpected but strangely comforting. He was born in Sardinia, which also produced two other leaders of the Communist party in Italy, Togliatti and Berlinguer. His father was a minor official whose imprisonment for embezzlement dealt a devastating financial and psychological blow to the family. In addition Gramsci suffered all the pains of a hunchback and was continually plagued by chronic illness. Not surprisingly, his health failed to improve during his last ten years as a prisoner of fascism, but he occupied himself by writing copious notes on all aspects of history, politics, culture and religion. He never wrote a book. Apart from newspaper articles, his reputation as an ideologue rests on these prison notebooks.

From 1911 to 1914 Gramsci was a student in Turin, a city soon to be hailed as 'the Petrograd of the Italian revolution'. It was therefore perhaps unavoidable that he should become a political activist. He began writing for the socialist press, helped to launch *L'Ordine Nuovo* in 1919 and became increasingly involved in party affairs and Marxist ideology. A crucial episode was his participation in the factory council movement which culminated in the workers' occupation of the factories in September 1920. When the socialist party split, Gramsci became a central committee member of the new Communist party. In the summer of 1922 he left for Moscow to join the executive committee of the Comintern. Abroad for two years, he missed Mussolini's march on Rome. When he returned he had been elected to parliament and, with Moscow's backing, became effective leader of the party. He fought a courageous but losing battle against fascism. Arrested in 1926, he remained in fascist prisons or clinics until his fatal cerebral haemorrhage in April 1937. His Russian wife and two sons (one of whom he never saw) continued to live in the Soviet Union. Alive, he had become an embarrassment to Togliatti and the communists because of his growing disenchantment with Stalinism; dead he could become an invaluable martyr to the cause. His ideas, always firmly rooted in history, could later be used to justify an 'Italian road to socialism'.

As a Sardinian suddenly transported to industrial Turin, Gramsci had become aware of the stark contrast between city and countryside, proletarian and peasant, North and South. It led him to explore the Risorgimento, the role of intellectuals and the continuing divisions in Italian society. Like CROCE he shared in the revived enthusiasm for VICO with his view of the all-embracing nature of history and, in what James Joll has called his perpetual 'dialogue with Croce', he scrutinized the thought of HEGEL and MARX. Pareto alerted him to the importance of ruling elites and of the political party, or 'Modern Prince' as

Gramsci described it because it must perform the functions which MACHIAVELLI ascribed to the Renaissance leaders. Involvement in the factory councils prompted him to analyse the relationship between leaders and led, and to advocate the active participation of the masses in the socialist movement. In Moscow he personally witnessed some of the implications of bolshevism after the death of Lenin and in Rome he was confronted by Mussolini's fascism. From these experiences and from his omnivorous reading he began to outline theories which not only revealed the crudity of orthodox historical materialism but also attempted to provide a practical Marxist alternative to that dialectical process which had resulted in Stalinism. It was an alternative which would appeal even to non-Marxists and his analysis was so sophisticated that Croce himself, acting as the spokesman for all intellectuals, would reluctantly proclaim that 'Gramsci was one of us'.

In a way reminiscent of Marx's repudiation of Weitling for condoning ignorance, Gramsci constantly urged socialists and workers to study hard, to acquire knowledge and understanding not for its own sake but because it would lead to the transformation of society. He laid great stress on 'hegemony', the replacement of the prevalent ideas which justified the existing political and social system by a new climate of opinion which would produce *l'ordine nuovo*, the new era. The role of ideas, of individual will, of intellectuals and of the whole cultural establishment were vitally significant, as were political parties and other institutions like the church acting as agents of change or resistance. Where orthodox Marxists saw the political and ideological superstructure as being determined by its economic base, Gramsci emphasized the interrelationship between the two. Surveying Italian and European history, he became convinced that ideas need not necessarily have economic origins, that his kind of 'cultural revolution' relying on the persuasive erosion of the old beliefs and values should replace traditional revolutionary theories. In the formation of this new consensus it was imperative to convince the masses as well as the intellectual elite. The pursuit of this goal has, to a large extent, been the inspiration of Italian communism since 1944 and indeed of all movements influenced by Gramsci's writings. He could not solve the problem of reconciling order and spontaneity or of combining the need for discipline from above with the active participation of the masses. Few people have. But his flexible and humane variant of Marxism, his undogmatic approach to the past, the present and the future cannot be ignored by any student of history.   JRW

Main publications

Selections from the Prison Notebooks, ed. Q. Hoare and G. N. Smith (London: Lawrence & Wishart, New York: International, 1979); *Antonio Gramsci: Letters from Prison*, ed. L. Lawner (London: Cape, 1975).

Reading

Clark, M.: *Antonio Gramsci and the Revolution that Failed* (London and New Haven, Conn.: Yale University Press, 1977).

Joll, J.: *Gramsci* (London: Fontana, 1977).

Green, John Richard (b.1837, d.1883) Green was a son of Oxford whose early local studies paved the way for later new departures. At Magdalen College School (then held in the college precincts) and Jesus College (1855−9) he led a solitary life and studied zealously the antiquities of Oxford and district. After ordination (1860) he served in three London parishes where he was a popular preacher and caring pastor; but tuberculosis (following overwork) and the transformation of his earlier fervent high churchmanship into a liberal outlook led him to abandon a career in the church, and he became librarian of Lambeth Palace Library. He was a contributor to *The Saturday Review*. In youth he had been drawn to history by reading GIBBON and by the influence of A. P. Stanley, Canon of Christ Church. In 1859−60 he wrote for *The Oxford Chronicle* articles on 'Oxford in the eighteenth century', which were reprinted as *Studies in Oxford History* (1901) by the Oxford Historical Society (in the formation of which, as of *The English Historical Review*, he took a leading part). Ill-health led him to concentrate on his *Short History of the English People* (1874), which was intended for English readers 'of a general

class' and was an instant success, the greatest since Macaulay; it was frequently reprinted.

Sustained by his marriage to Alice Stopford (1877), and by a supreme effort of will, Green continued to write. He took up again plans for a scholarly history to 1066, which had been interrupted by the *Short History*, but completed only *The Making of England* (1883) on the period before Egbert, written 'under the shadow of death'. He took into account 'physical geography', 'incidental facts' from Bede, and the findings of archaeology; he provided long chapters on 'The settlement of the conquerors' and 'The church and the kingdoms'. *The Conquest of England* (1883, posthumous), revised and as far as possible completed by his widow, continued the story to 1066.

Green was a brilliant talker and fine literary stylist, but ill-health restricted his opportunities and limited his output. He had a keen eye for turning points and landmarks, and showed great skill in weaving together strands of history that had been kept separate. He was a friend of STUBBS, FREEMAN and BRYCE, one of the first historians to be attracted by the study of Oxford itself, and a writer who widened the scope of history; he traced the history of a people rather than of a state and its politicians.   JFAM

Main publications

The Conquest of England (London: Macmillan, 1883); *The Short History of the English People* (London: Macmillan, 1874; new edn, 1884; rev. edn enlarged, 1916); *Stray Studies from England and Italy* (London: Macmillan, 1876) and 2nd ser. (1903); *Letters of J. R. Green*, ed. Leslie Stephen (London: Macmillan, 1901).

Reading

Bryce, J.: *Studies in Contemporary Biography* (1904), pp. 131−69.

Green, A.: Preface (by Green's widow) in *The Short History of the English People* (1888) and in *The Conquest of England*.

Grégoire, Henri (b.1881, d.1964) Belgian patriot and a founder of modern Byzantine studies, Grégoire's protean life is best demonstrated by two of the journals which he founded and edited until his death: *Le Flambeau*, first circulated as a clandestine resistance sheet during the German occupation of

1914–18 and later a political and cultural periodical similar to *Encounter*, and from 1924 the then scholarly *Byzantion*.

By upbringing Grégoire was liberal and Walloon; his education was classical and philological. His Liège University doctorate of 1902 was followed by the secretaryship of a commission of inquiry into Leopold II's misgovernment of the Belgian Congo. His critical report was not well received by the king, with the happy result that the young Grégoire left for Athens and a series of expeditions in the Balkans, Anatolia and to Mount Sinai. Already working on HAGIOGRAPHY, these travels turned the classicist into a Byzantine historical geographer and enthusiast of the live modern Greek, Slav and Islamic cultures. In 1909 Grégoire returned to Belgium to create a Byzantine course (which he also taught extramurally) at the Université Libre of Brussels, where he remained, with teaching breaks in Cairo in the 1920s and California in the 1930s. He was among the founding fathers who proclaimed the new discipline at the First International Byzantine Congress at Bucharest: *Byzantion* followed. In 1932 he helped to establish his university's Institut de Philologie et d'Histoire Orientales et Slaves, with its formidable Byzantine research seminar (Nicholas Adontz, Ernest Stein, Ernst Honigmann and Paul Wittek among them).

By the 1930s, Grégoire's work on the epigraphy and archaeology of Cappadocia had developed into research on its Byzantine epic hero, Digenis. He was perhaps over-zealous in applying one to the other, but Digenis led to an exploration of heroic poetry elsewhere, from Roland and the Nibelung to Prince Igor and Seyyid Battal Gazi. At a time when the nature of orality was being discussed, Grégoire was more concerned with the historicity of such heroes.

Grégoire rose to the challenge of the second world war. When on 10 May 1940 *Le Flambeau* was temporarily extinguished, he managed successfully to transplant *Byzantion* to New York until 1946. Here, with de Gaulle's acclaim, Grégoire helped gather French and Belgian refugee scholars into a 'New School'. American Byzantinists have vivid memories of the polymath 'quiz pro-fessor' and his seminar. They date the real establishment of Byzantine studies in the United States to the academic impetus of this wartime migration, which coincided with the endowment of Dumbarton Oaks to Harvard University as a centre in 1940.

As an epigraphist Grégoire was supreme. His interpretation of texts was more fallible. Always ingenious, his creation of a whole new thirteenth-century emirate out of a two-acre island on the basis of four letters of a Konyan inscription, or his advocacy of a Bulgarian origin for Shakespeare's *The Tempest*, have not caught on. Grégoire's bibliography of 753 items is a curiosity. It includes no work of synthesis or any 'book' independent of a series or journal. He translated extensively, for example George OSTROGORSKY, and ancient Greek, medieval Slav and modern Russian poetry. To most French readers Gregoire remains best known for his pleasing translations of Russian literature (including Lermontov and Chekhov) – and for *Le Flambeau*. Grégoire's scale was large, for it embraced whole series and journals which he partly wrote. His faithful collaborator on *Byzantion* and *Le Flambeau* was P. Orgels, but Grégoire also controlled his institute's *Annuaire* as well as *Renaissance*. His archaeological reports can be found in *Studia Pontica* and the *Bulletin de Correspondance Hellénique*. To historians Grégoire's Anatolian (especially Pontic) archaeological papers are considered immutable.

AAMB

Reading

Byzantina Metabyzantina 1 (1946) [bibliography and appreciation].
Byzantion 35 (1965) [bibliography and memoir].
Festschrift. *Mélanges Henri Grégoire*, 4 vols (Brussels: Annuaire de l'Institut de Philologie et d'Histoire Orientales et Slaves, vols 9–12, 1949–52).

Gregorovius, Ferdinand (b.1821, d.1891) Of Polish stock in East Prussia, Gregorovius studied at Königsberg; in the 1840s he wrote romances and studies of Polish and Hungarian popular literature. In 1852 he went to Italy and until 1874 lived in Rome, with a wide and cosmopolitan circle of acquaintance; he was made an honorary citizen in 1876. His

Wanderjahre in Italien gave expression to his love for the songs, folklore and especially the evocative significance of the country's monuments and landscape. He also wrote on Capri and Corsica, translated Italian dialect poets and was a prodigious journalist, diarist and correspondent.

Gregorovius's greatest work, *Geschichte der Stadt Rom*, coincided with a revival of historical writing on Rome and with the political and ideological implications of resurgent national consciousness in the Europe of Bismarck and Pio Nono, of the relationship of the ecclesiastical and municipal in the city's history and future, and of the long association of Italy and Germany. A Protestant liberal of strong romantic and poetic instinct, he was drawn to the historic grandeur of the papacy, the medieval empire and the commune, as the revival of the most ancient municipal law, that of the Roman Republic, set against the *immobile saxum* of St. Peter. These issues also run through his Roman diaries, covering the years of his residence in the city.

As a historian his major assets are his great sense of the physical and literary monuments and his vivid and engaging style; these, and translation into several languages, explain his continuing, entertaining and still justified *magisterium* in a complex field.   PABLI

Main publications

Wanderjahre in Italien (1856–77, latest edn Munich: Beck, 1967; trans. Italian 1906–11; French 1911); *Geschichte der Stadt Rom im Mittelalter vom V bis zum XV Jahrhundert* (Stuttgart; 1859–73; latest edn Munich: Beck, 1978; trans. Italian 1872–6; English 1894–1902, repr. New York: American Historical Society, 1967; Dutch, 1927–8); *Romische Tagebucher*, ed. F. Althaus (Stuttgart, 1892; trans. Italian 1895; English *The Roman Journals of Ferdinand Gregorovius 1852–1874*, 1907.

Reading

Hönig, J. *Ferdinand Gregorovius: Eine Biographie* (Stuttgart: Cotta, pp. 411–18.
Falco, G.: Storia e storici di Roma medievale. *Romana* I (1937).
Forni, A.: *La Questione di Roma Medioevale. Una Polemica tra Gregorovius e Reumont* (Rome: Istituto Storico per il Medio Evo; Studi Storici, fast 150–1, 1985).

Gregory of Tours (b. *c.*539, d.594) Georgius Florentius was probably born in Auvergne, in the diocese of Clermont. His parents were of Roman senatorial descent, with close connections with the church. His paternal uncle Gallus had been bishop of Clermont; his maternal uncle Tetricus had been bishop of Langres, succeeding his father St Gregory, whose name Georgius Florentius took on entering the church as a young boy. Initially Gregory lived in the household of his great-uncle Nicetius (later bishop of Lyons). Then he studied under Archdeacon Avitus at Clermont. After that he seems to have served as a deacon with Bishop Nicetius; at this time he made a pilgrimage to the shrine of St Martin at Tours, whom he was later to celebrate in four books of miracle stories. He may have served as a priest in Brioude (Auvergne); later he wrote a book on the martyrdom and miracles of St Julian of Brioude. In 573 the Frankish king, Sigibert I, appointed him to the bishopric of Tours, in succession to his mother's cousin Eufronius. To those in Tours who opposed the appointment of this foreigner from Clermont he retorted that all but five of the bishops of Tours had belonged to his family. He remained bishop until his death.

Gregory's reputation as a historian rests on the *Decem Libri Historiarum*, which since the eighth century have generally been known, misleadingly, as the *History of the Franks*. The first book begins with Adam and Eve, and continues until the death of Martin of Tours in 397. The second book takes events up to the death of the Frankish king Clovis in 511, and includes much valuable information about the early Franks, some of it drawn from now lost Roman historians. By the end of book IV he had reached the time of his own appointment as bishop, and thereafter the work became more detailed and more reliant upon his personal experience. He may have finished the first six books by 584 or soon after; a seventh-century manuscript survives of the first draft. He revised these books, inserting much more information about bishops and holy men, and making the work conform better to the model of an ecclesiastical history such as that by EUSEBIUS. The last four books deal with the

167

events of fewer than eight years, ending in 591.

Gregory of Tours is the only source for much of the history of Gaul in the sixth century, which makes historical analysis of his work difficult. He often relies on hearsay and rumour, and on occasion can be caught out twisting the facts to suit the lessons which he wished his readers to draw: the rewards due to good men, on earth and in heaven, and the evil deaths which lie in wait for those responsible for civil war and brutal violence. He is a passionate supporter of religious orthodoxy and of those who uphold it, such as St Martin of Tours and the other saints who are the heroes of all his works. Yet at times his own clear delight in telling a good story gets the better even of these interests, as can be seen in the relish with which he recounts the cunning deeds of the barbarous King Clovis. The anecdotal style developed by Gregory for his miracle stories is used to perfection in the *Histories*. The resulting work is an original and unique mixture of genres, drawing on both historiographical and hagiographical traditions. Gregory's stories are told in a Latin which (as he well knew) was poor by classical standards; but it was colloquial and even racy, and admirably suited for its purpose. Gregory is consequently the most entertaining of all early medieval historians, and has been widely read since at least the eighth century.   EFJ

Main writings

Scriptores Rerum Merovingicarum I, ed. B. Krusch, in *Monumenta Germaniae Historica*. In *History of the Franks*, trans. O. M. Dalton (Oxford: Oxford University Press, 1926) and trans. L. Thorpe (Harmondsworth: Penguin, 1974); *Life of the Fathers*, trans. E. James (Liverpool: Liverpool University Press, 1985).

Reading

Oldoni, M.: Gregorio di Tours e i Libri Historiarum. *Studi medievali* 13 (1972) 563–700.
Wallace-Hadrill, J. M.: The work of Gregory of Tours in the light of modern research. In *The Long-Haired Kings* (London: Methuen, 1962).

Grote, George, (b.1794, d.1871) Banker, historian of classical Greece and archetypal Victorian committee man, Grote's numerous family was German and Huguenot in origin. In 1810 Grote's supposedly tyrannical father drove the Charterhouse schoolboy into the family firm, where he took refuge in philosophy (he was an early Kantian), among other distractions. In fact he seems to have been a rather good banker. But other distractions included 'advanced liberal' politics (he was a champion and member of the reformed Commons from 1832) and association with James Mill, Jeremy Bentham, J. S. Mill and the Utilitarians, which made him an important young member of the circle which founded the future University of London and its University College in 1826–30. Typically, he resigned from this committee over the appointment of a cleric to the chair of philosophy of mind and logic, but was back to fight the same issue when it recurred in 1866. Grote (who served as both vice-chancellor and president of University College London) ended by endowing the chair on condition that it was held by a layman, uncommitted to sectarian beliefs.

The calculated turning points came when Grote left parliament in 1841 and his bank in 1843. The ethos of his new university demanded a new classical scholarship: rational, accessible, canonical. The first-fruits of Grote's first retirement were twelve volumes of his *History of Greece* (London, 1846–56), on which he may have been working since 1823. Besides its Thucydidean narrative, an attraction of the work is its discussion of myth and philosophy. Grote went on to major studies of Plato (1865) and, more congenial to him, Aristotle (posthumously published in 1880). At second hand this corpus helped create what may be termed the 'fifth-century' or 'public school' view of the efficacy of the study of classics; but for Grote the relevance of ancient Greece to his French radical friends, or of its city states to the fate of contemporary Swiss cantons, was more immediate. He evinced no interest in the fate of contemporary Greece. The authority and influence of Grote's *History* was unchallenged in England until this century. To London he left his brain (weight 49.75 oz), the Grote chair at University College (still in lay hands) and, less happily, much of the university's tangle of government – with which he also wrestled. He refused a peerage from Gladstone, but could not stop them burying him in Westminster Abbey.

AAMB

Main publications

As cited above; none now in print.

Reading

Grote, Harriet: *Personal Life of George Grote* (London: 1873). [Against his father's wishes, Grote's courtship of, and secret marriage to, the remarkable Harriet Lewin (1792–1878) brought him his biographer.]

Toynbee, A. J.: *A Study of History*, X (London: 1954). [A quaint comparison of Grote's career and working methods with those of Rashīd-ad-Dīn al-Hamadānī.]

Grundmann, Herbert (b.1902, d.1970) It was by no means clear from the beginning that Grundmann would choose history as a career; he had originally studied accountancy and management with the intention of taking over his father's paper factory. After this collapsed in the inflation of 1923 and a scholarly career became necessary, his interests lay at first in literary history. Though his contributions to handbooks showed that he could treat political history with sensitivity and insight, he was more interested in the history of ideas and feelings – what the ANNALES SCHOOL called *mentalités*, though Grundmann's approach was rather different. This was reflected in his work from his two earliest books, on Joachim of Flora and on religious movements of the high middle ages, through his editorship of the *Archiv für Kulturgeschichte* up to the publications of his last years. Grundmann was professor at Münster from 1945 to 1959, and from 1959 until his death president of the *Monumenta Germaniae Historica*. He gave the *Monumenta* new impulses, not least by widening its classical definition of 'historical sources' to include works of importance for the history of ideas. TAR

Main publications

Studien über Joachim von Floris (Berlin: Teubner 1927); *Religiöse Bewegungen im Mittelalter* (Berlin: Ebering, 1935); *Ausgewählte Aufsätze*, 3 vols (Stuttgart: Hiersemann, 1976–8).

Reading

Borst, A.: Herbert Grundmann. In Grundmann,

Ausgewählte Aufsätze, vol. 1, pp. 1–25 [incl. bibliography pp. 26–37].

Guicciardini, Francesco (b.1483, d.1540) Guicciardini came from a distinguished patrician family of Florence. He studied law at the universities of Ferrara and Padua, and was sent to Spain as Florentine ambassador in 1511. He served the Medici popes, Leo X and Clement VII, as governor of the cities of Modena, Reggio and Parma, and as president of the Romagna. He was an adviser to Alessandro de'Medici, the ruler of Florence, but Alessandro's successor Cosimo had no use for his services and he retired to his country villa in 1537 to write his memoirs, 'in imitation of Caesar', as he put it (no one could accuse Guicciardini of underestimating his own abilities). These memoirs turned into the *Storia d'Italia* (1561–4).

Though he published nothing in his lifetime, as early as 1508–9 when he was in his mid-twenties, Guicciardini wrote *Storie fiorentine* (from 1378 to the present), which he left unfinished. When he came to write down his reminiscences of the 1520s, the period of his deepest involvement in politics, he found that he could not explain what was happening without going back to 1492, when the death of Lorenzo de Medici destroyed what Guicciardini was the first to call the 'balance' of power and led to the French invasion of Italy two years later. Guicciardini also discovered that it was impossible to write about Florence or the states of the church without making constant reference to affairs in other parts of the peninsula. In this way he was led to break with the Italian tradition of histories of individual city-states and to look at Italy as a whole, with some discussion of the rest of Europe and the occasional reference to the world beyond it, from the Ottoman Empire to the Americas.

Guicciardini's work is an example of historical writing in the grand manner, the manner of the ancients, notably LIVY, whose history he reread in preparation for his own. He wanted to conform to the literary 'laws' of historical writing and submitted his work to a humanist friend for stylistic criticism. Like the ancient historians and their humanist imitators in

169

fifteenth-century Italy (Leonardo Bruni, for example), Guicciardini devoted much of his space to formulaic literary set-pieces such as character-sketches, the description of battles, and speeches (sometimes invented) in favour of or against a particular course of action. The speeches were much appreciated by contemporaries, as their appearance in anthologies demonstrates. Like Tacitus, Guicciardini places great emphasis on simulation and dissimulation, presenting ideals as masks for ambition, greed and other forms of self-interest (Montaigne found him too cynical to be credible). In a less precise manner Guicciardini's sense of tragic irony and the power of fate or 'fortune', his stress on the way in which actions turn out to have consequences which are the very opposite of the actor's intentions – all this, however closely it fits the author's own political experiences, is also reminiscent of the conventions of Greek tragedy, perhaps mediated through Thucydides.

Guicciardini was no slavish imitator of the classics. The *Storia d'Italia* has some claim to be regarded as the masterpiece of humanist history, but in some respects it breaks out of the genre altogether. Unlike many of his contemporaries, including his friend Machiavelli, Guicciardini thought it foolish to attempt to imitate the Romans or 'govern oneself by examples', because history did not repeat itself. He criticized Machiavelli for his simplifications, and his own awareness of the complexity of history and the difficulty of discovering the truth is revealed in his explanations, frequently couched in terms of 'either...or'. In a remarkable 'digression', as he called it, on the states of the church (a passage eliminated from the first edition by the censors), Guicciardini brought the history of institutions into contact with the history of events. A bureaucrat for most of his working life, he made considerable use of official documents in his history, though not sufficiently to escape the criticisms of Ranke.   UPB

Main writings

Storia d'Italia (1561–4, London: 1579); *Le cose fiorentine* (Florence: 1945); *Storie fiorentine*, partial trans. in *Guicciardini*, ed. J. R. Hale (New York: Washington Square Press, 1964); *Considerazioni intorno ai Discorsi di Machiavelli*, trans. in *Guicciardini:*

Selected Writings, ed. C. Grayson (London: Oxford University Press, 1965).

Reading

Gilbert, F.: *Machiavelli and Guicciardini* (Princeton: Princeton University Press, 1965).
Hale, J. R.: Introduction. In *Guicciardini: History of Italy and History of Florence* (New York: Washington Square Press, 1964).
Phillips, M.: *Francesco Guicciardini: the Historian's Craft.* (Manchester: Manchester University Press, 1977).
Ridolfi, R.: *Vita di Francesco Guicciardini* (trans. London: Routledge & Kegan Paul, 1960).

Guizot, François Pierre Guillaume (b.1787, d.1874) Guizot was to say of himself that he had three careers, one political, one literary and one religious (this last arose out of his Protestantism). Throughout the period from 1815 to 1848 political activity absorbed his time and he held high office during the reign of Louis Philippe. He had already made his mark as an historian. As early as 1812 (after translating and editing Gibbon) he became professor of history in Paris, and during the 1820s he achieved considerable fame as a lecturer at the Sorbonne. He lectured on the history of representative government and on the history of civilization, both in Europe and in France. These lectures were remarkable for their analytical qualities. Guizot always tried to determine and to describe the fundamental characteristic of a particular stage of historical development and he therefore established a degree of determinism, which had its effect upon Marx among others. He discussed the influence of class and of generation in history; he believed that the individual intellectual was isolated in France, and that this isolation could stem from a reluctance to indulge in generalizations and to associate the past with the present. In this sense he was often described as the leader of the '*école fataliste*' in historical writing. But he was also an accomplished writer of narration, who published at the same time two volumes of a history of the English revolution devoted to Charles I, which he completed when the revolution of 1848 ousted him from political office. Guizot was a great historian whose determination that history should make sense was linked to an understanding of the importance of documents.   DJ

Main publications

Histoire des origines du gouvernement représentatif en Europe (Paris: 1821–2); *Essais sur l'histoire de la France* (Paris: 1823); *Histoire générale de la civilisation en Europe* (Paris: 1828); *Histoire de la civilisation en France* (Paris: 1829–32); *Histoire de la révolution d'Angleterre*, 6 vols (Paris: 1826–56); *Mémoires pour servir à l'histoire de mon temps*, 9 vols (Paris: 1858–68).

Reading

Johnson, Douglas: *Guizot: Aspects of French History 1787 – 1874* (London and Toronto: Routledge, 1964).
Mellon, Stanley; *The Political Uses of History* (Stanford: Stanford University Press, 1958).
Rosanvallon, Pierre: *Le moment Guizot* (Paris: Gallimard, 1985).

Gutman, Herbert George (b.1928, d.1985)
A New Yorker who became very much a part of his native city's radical intellectual tradition, Gutman helped to redraw the map of at least two key areas of American social history. A graduate of Queen's College, Columbia University and the University of Wisconsin, he taught at a number of other universities before returning to New York city in 1972 as professor at City College and at the Graduate Center of the City University of New York.

The main emphasis of Gutman's work was on the history of ordinary working people, whether wage-earners or slaves, in nineteenth-century America. The essays in his *Work, Culture and Society in Industrializing America* (1976) shifted the focus of labour history from the institutional history of unions to the problems, attitudes, and life-styles of working men and women themselves. In his last years, he was engaged in a large-scale study of factory workers and managers, and also oversaw the American Social History Project at the Graduate Center.

Gutman's powerful critique of *Time on the Cross*, the controversial work on slavery by Robert W. FOGEL and Stanley L. Engerman, did much to undermine its methodology and its conclusions. Gutman's own major work in the field was *The Black Family in Slavery and Freedom, 1750–1925*, a densely packed and often difficult book which put new emphasis on the central importance of the family in slave society and culture. Determined to counter the Moynihan Report which ascribed to slavery much of the responsibility for the deterioration of modern black family life, Gutman claimed rather too much for the slave family, but his book broke important new ground.   PJP

Main publications

Slavery and the Numbers Game: a critique of 'Time on the Cross' (Urbana: University of Illinois Press, 1975); *Reckoning with Slavery*, ed. Paul A. David, Herbert G. Gutman et al. (New York: Oxford University Press, 1976); *Work, Culture and Society in Industrializing America* (New York: Knopf, 1976); *The Black Family in Slavery and Freedom, 1750–1925* (New York: Pantheon, 1976).

Reading

Meier, A. and Rudwick, E.: *Black History and the Historical Profession, 1915–1980* (Urbana: University of Illinois Press, 1986).

H

Habakkuk, Hrothgar John (b.1915) Of Welsh parentage, John Habakkuk began his academic career at Cambridge and moved to Oxford as Chichele professor of economic history in 1950, later becoming principal of Jesus College (1967–84) and vice-chancellor of the University (1973–7). He was knighted in 1976.

A historian widely respected for the originality of his ideas, the intellectual quality of his argument and the clarity of his writing, Habakkuk made a contribution to historical understanding in three distinct fields: English landownership in the later seventeenth and eighteenth centuries, the growth of English population in the eighteenth century, and the pace and nature of technological change in the nineteenth century. In all three areas he propounded theses which, even when they attracted criticism, had a profound effect on subsequent scholarship. In particular virtually all literature on English landownership after 1660 which has appeared since the publication of his seminal article of 1940 has been devoted either to confirming, modifying, or overturning 'the Habakkuk thesis'. His writings on this subject continue to appear. Much of Habakkuk's most influential work has appeared in scholarly periodicals; he had (to 1988) written only two short books.　　　　CC

Main publications

English landownership, 1680–1740, *Economic History Review*, 1st ser., vol. X, (1940) 2–17; *American and British Technology in the Nineteenth Century* (London: Cambridge University Press, 1962); *Population Growth and Economic Development since 1750* (Leicester: Leicester University Press, 1971).

Habsburg historiography See AUSTRIAN HISTORIOGRAPHY.

hagiography The earliest hagiographical texts are naturally accounts of martyrdoms. A few of these, such as those concerning Polycarp of Smyrna and Cyprian of Carthage, are more or less contemporary with the martyrs in question and can even take the form of records of the trial or eye-witness accounts of the trial and execution. Many, however, were written long periods after the martyrdom and contain much legendary material. From the fourth century persons other than martyrs came to be regarded as saints, and hagiographers began to produce lives of them which developed into a recognizable literary genre. Particularly influential in this process were the lives of the Egyptian hermit St Anthony (d. 356) by Athanasius and the account of the Frankish bishop St Martin of Tours (d. 397) by Sulpicius Severus. Other important early medieval hagiographers included GREGORY OF TOURS, Pope Gregory the Great and BEDE. Saints' lives were frequently collected into series and this practice continued into the later middle ages, a notable example being the *Golden Legend* of Jacobus de Voragine. Bede seems to have initiated the practice of assembling summaries of saints' lives in calendar order and his compilation was amplified by ninth-century Carolingian scholars, most fully by Usuard. Texts of this sort, which H. Quentin has termed 'historical martyrologies', are also represented by the ninth-century *Old English Martyrology* and the official *Roman Martyrology* (published 1584). The compilation of accounts

172

of the posthumous miracles of saints is mentioned by Augustine of Hippo, and many such miracle-books have been preserved. Among the earliest are those compiled by Gregory of Tours, among the largest are the *Miracles of St Benedict* (ninth−twelfth centuries). Accounts of translations of relics date at least from the fifth century, although their development as a genre really belongs to the eighth and ninth centuries with the composition of texts such as Adrevald's description of the translation of St Benedict from Monte Cassino to St Benoît-sur-Loire and Einhard's description of the translation of Sts Marcellinus and Petrus to Frankia.

The study of these materials from a historical viewpoint has proved complex. The BOLLANDISTS, whose original aim was to establish the canon of saints who had a real existence and an early cult, strove to derive from hagiographical and liturgical sources what were for them the vital pieces of information − the feast-day of the saint and the place of veneration (the 'hagiographic co-ordinates' as the Bollandist Delehaye called them). Many passions and lives were rightly seen as unreliable sources of information about saints as historical figures, for, although some texts were written soon after the saint's death, many were composed long afterwards and contain a considerable quantity of evidently legendary material and descriptions of miracles. These features are often to be found even in near-contemporary accounts and Delehaye attributed them to the irrational demands of the 'masses' on the hagiographer. Accepting this view, some scholars have explored the possibility of using hagiographical narratives as a source for folk-traditions and even pagan survivals. This approach has some potential, for example with regard to Irish texts, but doubt has been cast on it, notably by F. Graus, partly because very few elements of hagiography can be shown to be genuinely 'popular', partly because the narrative texts are now seen as belonging to a sophisticated literary genre. Many indeed are based directly − sometimes verbatim − on earlier lives, not out of plagiarism but rather out of a wish to demonstrate the uniform working of the Holy Spirit in all the saints. A similar motive lies behind the practice of explicitly comparing a saint's miracles with those of other saints or with those described in the Bible. Studying the literary influence of particular saints' lives on others can provide evidence for the cultural contacts of the churches where the lives were written. For example, the fact that the Lindisfarne version of the life of St Cuthbert is influenced by the life of St Martin of Tours may point to a greater continental influence at Lindisfarne than appears from Bede's account of that church. In terms of content, hagiographical narratives are often valuable sources for social history. This is especially true of miracle collections which often deal with the life of people who rarely figure so fully in other texts, describing for example peasant social mobility and the actual working of legal cases.

The priorities and preocupations of those who wrote, read or listened to hagiographical texts can also be studied by examining the 'ideal of sanctity' which these texts project. Thus the late Roman saint tends to appear as a great patron such as dominated late Roman society while the saint of the feudal period is presented as a warlord defending his church by *force majeure* and well-connected to a noble lineage. Controversy has raged around the hagiography devoted to royal saints: some have seen it as an attempt to christianize concepts of sacral kingship but others have argued that it expressed the church's support for kingship or at least for particular ways of exercising it. In more general terms, hagiographical texts have provided the basis for attempts to establish a sociology of sanctity with regard to the social class and lifestyle of saints. Finally, scholars such as the Bollandist Baudouin de Gaiffier (d.1984), have gained considerable historical insight from defining the precise functions of various hagiographical texts. It is known that some were used from at least the eighth century for liturgical readings and this may in part account for the frequent practice of revising them with regard to their literary style rather than their content. Private devotional reading, for which metrical texts were very suitable, and preaching to the laity especially on feast-days were other uses to which they were put. Hagiography can also be viewed as in part a means by which the church brought influence to bear on contemporary society. Certainly many texts, expecially miracle-stories, relate to the miraculous punishment of those damaging ecclesiastical property or rights, and some seem to have been linked with the fabrication of charters, itself almost a form of propaganda in defence of a church's interests. DWR

Reading

Aigrain, R. 1953: *L'hagiographie: ses sources, ses méthodes, son histoire* (Paris: Bloud & Gay).

Brown, P. *The Cult of the Saints: Its Rise and Function in Latin Christianity* (London: SCM Press, 1981).

Delehaye, H. *The Legends of the Saints* (1917; repr. London: Chapman, 1962).

Folz, R. *Les saints rois du moyen âge en occident (VIe–XIIIe siècles)* (Brussels: Society of Bollandists, 1984).

Gaiffier, B. de. *Études critiques d'hagiographie et d'iconologie* (Brussels: Society of Bollandists, 1967).

Gerould, G. H. *Saints' Legends* (Boston: Houghton Mifflin, 1916; repr. Folcroft: Folcroft Library Editions, 1980).

Graus, F. *Volk, Herrscher und Heiliger im Reich der Merowinger: Studien zur Hagiographie der Merowingerzeit* (Prague: Nakladatelstvi Cekoslovenske akademie ved, 1965).

Heinzelmann, M. *Translationsberichte und andere Quellen des Reliquienkultes* (Turnhout: Brepols, 1979).

Quentin, H. *Les martyrologes historiques du moyen âge* (Paris: J. Gabalda, 1908; repr. Aalen: Scientia Verlag, 1969).

Weinstein, D. and Bell, M. R. *Saints and Society: The Two Worlds of Western Christendom, 1000–1700* (Chicago, Ill.: University of Chicago Press, 1982).

Zoepf, L. *Das Heiligenleben im 10. Jahrhundert* (Leipzig: Teubner, 1908).

Halévy, Élie (b.1870, d.1937) Born at Étretat in France and educated at the École Normale Supérieure, Halévy came to history through the study of philosophy, and his volume *La formation du radicalisme philosophique en Angleterre* (1901) combined both interests. He visited England at the age of 22, became an admirer, and set out to explain its peaceful modern development. From 1898 onwards he lectured on British political ideas at the École des Sciences Politiques.

The fruits of his enquiries began to appear from 1912 onwards with the publication in Paris of the first volume of *Histoire du peuple Anglais au XIXe siècle*, in which he attempted to relate political history to social, economic, religious and cultural factors. Nineteenth-century English stability he explained by the intensity of religious feeling and, particularly, by the influence of Methodism. Halévy's grand design was never completed and there followed a confusing sequence of books. The second and third volumes, carrying the narrative to 1841, appeared in 1922, but Halévy then jumped to the late Victorian and Edwardian period, publishing an epilogue as volume five, in two parts. He was concerned to evaluate the situation when the religious sanctions, that had operated so strongly, had begun to weaken. The first English translation of volume 1 appeared in 1924 and the second part of the epilogue in 1934. Its publication in the Pelican series gave the book a wide readership. Though it is now generally accepted that his emphasis on Methodism as a conservative force was excessive, Halévy's work attained classic status. It was republished in France in the 1970s and a new English edition, with a foreword by Asa BRIGGS, came out in 1987. JAC

Main publications

La théorie platonicienne des sciences (Paris: 1896); *La formation du radicalisme philosophique en Angleterre* (Paris: 1901); *L'Angleterre et son Empire* (Paris: 1905); *Histoire du peuple Anglais au XIXe siècle* (Paris: 1912–32); *L'Ère des tyrannies* (Paris: 1938); *Histoire du socialisme Européen* (Paris: 1948).

Reading

Barker, E.: Élie Halévy, *English Historical Review* 209 (January 1938) 79–87.

Gillespie, C. C.: The work of Élie Halévy: a critical appreciation. *Journal of Modern History* (March 1950) 232–49.

Semmel, B.: Introduction, Halévy, Elie: *The birth of Methodism in England*, ed. B. Semmel (Chicago: University of Chicago Press, 1971).

Richter, M.: In *International Encyclopedia of the Social Sciences*, vol. 6, ed. D. L. Sills (New York: Macmillan/Free Press, 1968) pp. 307–10.

Hall, Edward (b.1496/7, d.1547) Hall has the rare and, happily for him, the posthumous distinction of having had his works burned by the public hangman. This was under Mary I who was incensed by the anticlerical and antipapal tone of his *Chronicle* — or to give it the full title under which it was published in 1548 by Richard Grafton his 'literary executor' (Hall never married): *The Vnion of the Two Noble and Illustre Fameiles of LANCASTRE & YORKE beeyng long in continual discension for the croune of this noble realme, with all the actes done in bothe the tymes of the princes, bothe of the one linage and of the other, BEGINNYNG AT THE TYME OF KYNG HENRY THE FOWERTH, the first aucthor of this deuision, and so successiuely proceadyng to the reigne of the high and prudent prince KYNG HENRY THE EIGHT, the vndubitate flower and very heire of both the sayd linages.*

To rehearse the original title given to Hall's work — he only called it a 'chronicle lately made' — is to show immediately how familiar his approach to English history is. And what makes it familiar is that it is the history we find in Shakespeare; some chapter headings might be almost subtitles for his plays: 'the vnquiet tyme of kyng Henry the Fowerth'; 'the victorious actes of kyng Henry the v'; 'the troubleous season of kyng Henry the vj'. Hall, it is true, took much of his interpretation and much of his pre-1509 material from Polydore VERGIL while Shakespeare probably relied less on Hall directly than on HOLINSHED's later reworking, but Hall is the key transmitter of an interpretation which, immortalized on stage, has become the standard popular history of the period — and will remain so, however scholars try to modify it.

A Gray's Inn lawyer, educated at Eton and King's College, Cambridge, Hall was a Londoner through and through, born in the merchant community and practising in the courts of the City and at Westminster. The climax to his career was appointment (at royal request) first as common serjeant of London in 1533 (the year in which he gave his first reading at Gray's Inn) and then (in 1535) as undersheriff and thus judge in the sheriffs' court, a post which he held to his death.

Hall's London identity comes out again and again in his writing which is based on personal enquiry and observation from about 1518, but he rises above the mere municipal chronicler for two reasons. First, even if indebted to Vergil, Hall produced what was the first period history in English in anything like the new

renaissance manner in which an author imposed a conscious form and meaning on the past. Secondly (and this gives him his continuing importance), Hall's standing in London, and later with Thomas Cromwell and Henry VIII himself, brought opportunities to observe national events at first hand. In particular, Hall's frequent membership of the Commons where he was in later years a valued supporter of Thomas Cromwell (with whom he shared a taste for map-collecting), has left us unique accounts of several episodes.

Hall had a connection with an earlier chronicler, Robert Fabian, and his link with Grafton and the next generation created a sort of apostolic succession of London historians, but his own formed narrative — adulatory of Henry and bitter against the clergy — only goes to 1532. The rest was assembled by Grafton from Hall's notes and drafts. However, what we have is all of a piece and fully congruent with the man we know from other sources, an evangelical (but not a radical) and Erastian to the core.

Hall's point of observation enabled him to offer a compelling narrative full of great set pieces, but only as seen from the outer circle of power. Equally the king dazzled him, and when anything such as the fall of Anne Boleyn threatened his panegyric, Hall found it easier to say as little as possible. Nevertheless his new-style vernacular narrative is far and away the best contemporary history of Henry VIII's reign and, on frequent occasions, a primary source of great significance.   EWI

Main publications

The Union of the Two Noble and Illustre Fameiles of Lancaster and York ... (London: Richard Grafton, 1548), standard edn by Henry Ellis (London: J. Johnson, 1809).

Reading

Bindoff, S. T. ed.: *The House of Commons, 1509–58*, Vol. II (London: History of Parliament Trust, 1982) pp. 279–82.

Campbell, Lily B.: *Shakespeare's 'Histories': Mirrors of Elizabethan Policy* (San Marino, Calif.: Huntington Library, 1947) pp. 67–72.

Hallam, Henry (b.1777, d.1859)   The son of a well-read dean of Bristol, Hallam showed some literary talent at Eton, and graduated at

Christ Church in 1799 in the days before modern examinations. He first practised as a barrister on the Oxford circuit, but his appointment as Commissioner of Stamps in 1806 (an office he held until 1827) and the inheritance of his father's Lincolnshire estates in 1812, enabled him to devote himself to historical reading, the fruits of which he gathered in three major studies. The first, a *View of the State of Europe during the Middle Ages* (1818), a remarkable survey in itself, prepared the way for the later works. It offered 'a comprehensive survey of the chief circumstances that can interest a philosophical inquirer' (always Hallam's chief concern), and included major thematic treatments of 'the state of society in Europe during the Middle Ages', and the English constitution, a topic 'less fully dwelt upon in former works of this description'. In Hallam's most influential work, *The Constitutional History of England from the Accession of Henry VII to the Death of George II* (1827), the latter theme was developed into a full-scale challenge to the popular Tory perspective on British history created by Hume. Hallam insisted that the Stuarts had tried to break the English constitution; but he was a very conservative Whig who disapproved of the Reform Bill, sustained a law-court approach to historical evidence and understood that the principles of both parties were 'mingled ... in the complex mass of the English nation'. Though Southey treated him as a partisan, Macaulay wrote of his 'cold, rigid justice'. In his final work, a four-volume *Introduction to the Literature of Europe in the Fifteenth, sixteenth and seventeenth centuries* (1837–39), Hallam struck out boldly into territory too rarely explored by British historians, and, though himself an insular Protestant lawyer, mobilized a wealth of sources on an international, interdisciplinary and interconfessional basis, avoiding the short-cuts offered by the German system-makers.   WRW

Main Publications

The Constitutional History of England (1827) (London: Garland, 1978); *Views of the State of Europe* (1818) (Darby, Pa.: Arden Library, 1979); *Introduction to the Literature of Europe* (1837–9) (London: Johnson, 1970).

Reading

Gooch, G. P.: *History and Historians in the Nineteenth Century* (London: Longmans, Green, 1913, and later edns).

Hale, J. R.: *The Evolution of British Historiography* (London: Macmillan, 1967).

Kenyon, J.: *The History Men* (London: Weidenfeld & Nicolson, 1983)

Halphen, Louis (b.1880, d.1950) Like many of his contemporary French medievalists, Halphen was a pupil at the École des Chartes in Paris. From 1910 to 1928 he taught at the University of Bordeaux; he then returned to Paris, first to the École des Hautes Études, and then, in 1937, to the Sorbonne. He was unable to teach in the occupied zone, and in 1941 moved to a university post in Grenoble. When the Germans occupied the town in 1943 he went into hiding until, in September 1944, he could return to Paris and the Sorbonne. A meticulous scholar, he was also a skilled teacher and popularizer, and in pursuit of that he founded two influential series: 'Les Classiques de l'histoire de France au Moyen Age' (texts with translations) and 'Peuples et civilisations'; to the first he contributed *Eginhard: vie de Charlemagne* (1938) and to the second *Les barbares des grandes invasions aux conquêtes turques* (1926) and *L'essor de l'Europe (XIᵉ–XIIIᵉ siècles)* (1932).   EFJ

Main publications

Le comté d'Anjou au XIᵉ siècle (Paris: Picard, 1906); *Études sur l'administration de Rome au Moyen Age* (Paris: Champion, 1907); *Études critiques sur l'histoire de Charlemagne* (Paris: Alcan, 1921); *Charlemagne et l'Empire carolingien* (Paris: Michel, 1947, English trans. Amsterdam: North-Holland, 1977); *A travers l'histoire du moyen âge*, collected essays (Paris: Presses Universitaires de France, 1950).

Reading

Perrin, Ch.-E.: Preface to *Mélanges Louis Halphen* (Paris: Presses Universitaires de France, 1951).

Hamilton, Earl Jefferson (b.1899) After doing his postgraduate thesis (1928) at Harvard, Hamilton was appointed to a post at Duke University, with which he thereafter remained associated. Following in the footsteps of Thorold ROGERS for England and d'Avenel for France, Hamilton set out to compile a definitive series of data for commodity prices, wages and monetary values in the Spanish peninsula during the sixteenth and seventeenth centuries. Eventually he published the results in his fundamental study on *American Treasure and the Price Revolution in Spain, 1501–1650*. It was a fully joint effort: his wife collected much of the manuscript data and, as he says, 'Mrs Hamilton and I have spent more than six years on the present study, working jointly about 30,750 hours.' The skills they learnt in this massive exercise they put to further use in the compilation of other major studies on prices in medieval Aragon (1936) and in eighteenth-century Spain (1947). Hamilton's work has stood the test of time very well: modern criticism is directed at defects in the type of sources he used (institutional records) and at some incorrect conclusions, but his base data remain unquestioned.

HK

Main publications

American Treasure and the Price Revolution in Spain, 1501–1650 (Cambridge, Mass.: Harvard University Press, 1934).

Hammond, John Lawrence Le Breton (b.1872, d.1949) and **Barbara** (b.1873, d.1961) Lawrence Hammond was born into a middle-class liberal family. After Oxford, he pursued a career in journalism, and for most of his life he was associated with the *Manchester Guardian*. He and his wife, who were married in 1901, were pro-Boer, and both remained radical-minded liberals all their working lives. They were much influenced by the dedicated group of liberals with whom they closely associated: L. T. Hobhouse, F. W. Hirst, J. A. Hobson, Graham Wallas and Gilbert Murray. The Hammonds' historical writing emerged from their political concerns. The land question was a major issue with liberal radical circles from the 1870s onwards, and together with the growing awareness of mass poverty in the closing decades of the nineteenth century, liberal intellectuals were provided with many of the issues for their historical studies. Barbara Hammond undertook most of the original research for their books at the Public Record

Office and the British Museum, and put the great mass of fact which accumulated into coherent order, which Lawrence then transformed into a subtle and evocative style that was immensely compelling and readable. The Hammonds were not socialists; the capitalism they analysed so acutely and sharply was the unrestrained capitalism of the early decades of British industrialization.

The first manuscript completed by the Hammonds was so long that it had to be issued as two volumes. *The Village Labourer* (1911) was the first to be published; *The Town Labourer* followed a few years later. *The Village Labourer* was a searing indictment of the policies of government and the landlord classes which destroyed the pre-industrial village. It was a pioneering work of great importance and was one of a spate of volumes from a number of historians in the years before 1914 which analysed the changes in rural England in the previous four centuries. *The Town Labourer*, which took a pessimistic view of the social consequences of industrialization in the growing urban areas, led to a famous controversy between the Hammonds and J. H. CLAPHAM over the problem of living standards. This was in the 1930s, but the debate was revived again after 1957, and still continues.

Nothing the Hammonds wrote subsequently to these two volumes achieved the same classic quality. *The Skilled Labourer* (1919) contained much original material, and it was followed by a series of volumes which extended their pessimistic view of Britain before 1850. These later works were written with their customary lucidity and careful marshalling of facts, and for many years were used as texts in schools and for the growing adult education movement. The Hammonds were among the great educators of their day – especially in the years between the wars – and their first two books are still read by undergraduates. Lawrence Hammond's last work, *Gladstone and the Irish Nation*, published in 1938, was intended to be his *magnum opus*. It was a detailed and elaborate vindication of Gladstone and remains essential reading for the specialist, but it never achieved the status that was hoped for.

During the second world war Lawrence

Hammond wrote leaders for the *Manchester Guardian*, and for the years of war Manchester was their home. Within a few weeks of peace they returned to their house in Hertfordshire where Lawrence died in 1949. Barbara, increasingly lonely and sad, disillusioned with the post-war world, gradually lost her memory in the last years of the fifties and died in 1961.

JS

Main publications

(All published by Longmans, Green, London.)
The Village Labourer, 1760–1832. A Study in the government of England before the Reform bill (1911); *The Town Labourer, 1760–1832. The New Civilisation* (1917); *The Age of the Chartists, 1832–54. A study in discontent* (1930).

Reading

Clarke, P. F.: *Liberals and Social Democrats* (Cambridge: Cambridge University Press, 1978).

Hampe, Karl (b.1869, d.1936) Hampe studied history under Paul Scheffer-Boichorst in Bonn. After working at the Monumenta Germaniae Historica between 1893 and 1897 he held chairs first at Bonn and then at Heidelberg until his death. His scholarly work consisted mainly of investigation of the sources for medieval history, especially in regard to Italy. His major works on the other hand were narratives for an educated lay audience: history as fine writing, without a conscious interpretation either of the past or the present. During the first world war he worked for the German government in the Belgian archives and sought to provide historical justification for the German treatment of Belgium in 1914; at the very end of his life he edited a collection of eight essays by prominent German medievalists entitled *Karl der Gross oder Charlemagne?*, which was a quiet polemic against Nazi attacks on Charlemagne as a man who had corrupted the Germanic tribes by subjecting them to foreign, Romanic influences. Both these activities were expressions of the consistent if unreflective conservative nationalism found also in his large-scale writings.

TAR

Main publications

Deutsche Kaisergeschichte in der Zeit der Salier und Staufer (Leipzig: Queller & Meyer, 1909; last rev. edn, 1937); *Herrschergestalten des deutschen Mittelalters* (Leipzig: Queller & Mayer, 1927); *Das Hochmittelalter. Geschichte des Abendlandes von 900–1250* (Berlin: Propyläen Verlag, 1932).

Reading

Baethgen, F: Karl Hampe. *Archiv für Kulturgeschichte* 27 (1937) 1–32.

——: Karl Ludwig Hampe. *Neue Deutsche Biographie* 7, (1966) 598–9.

Hancock, William Keith (b.1898) An Australian, born in Melbourne, Hancock was a professor in the University of Adelaide (1924–33) and returned to Australia as professor of history in the National University at Canberra (1957–65), but most of his working life was spent in Britain. He was a fellow of All Souls, Oxford, from 1924; professor of history at the University of Birmingham (1934–44); Chichele professor of economic history at Oxford (1944–9); and director of the Institute of Commonwealth Studies at the University of London (1949–56). Hancock was knighted in 1953 for his services to history.

His first interest was in Italian history and he published a study of Ricasoli in 1926; but he was best known for his writings on the British commonwealth. He was responsible for the monumental *Survey of British Commonwealth Affairs*, 1937, 1940 and 1942. His Marshall Lectures in Cambridge in 1949 (Wealth of Colonies) did much to provoke a lively debate on the relative importance of economic and political factors in the nineteenth-century European acquisition of empires. He was joint author, with M. M. Gowing, of *British War Economy* in the official *History of the Second World War*. But he returned to commonwealth themes in his two volumes on the career of Smuts. He had written a vigorous history of Australia, with an economic slant, in 1930 and in 1972 he again took up the topic of Australian development in *Discovering Monaro*. A son of the vicarage, Hancock was always concerned with the problem of how the historian should treat moral questions – an interest further provoked by the tragedies of two world wars. He published a number of occasional papers on this, some of the early ones inspired by his study of Machiavelli. Some of these were republished in 1947 under the title *Politics in Pitcairn*. Historiography also fascinated him and late in life he published *Professing History* (1976) and *Perspective on History* (1982).   MEC

Main publications

Australia (London: Benn, 1930); *Survey of British Commonwealth Affairs* (Oxford: Oxford University Press, 1937, 1940, 1942); *Politics in Pitcairn* (London: Macmillan, 1947); with M. M. Gowing, *British War Economy* (London: HMSO, 1949); *Smuts*, 2 vols (Cambridge: Cambridge University Press, 1962, 1968); *Discovering Monaro: a study of Man's Impact on his Environment* (Cambridge University Press, 1972).

Hartung, Fritz (b.1883, d.1967)   The son of a Prussian bureaucrat, Hartung enjoyed the best education imperial Germany had to offer, counting among his illustrious teachers at the universities of Berlin and Heidelberg Otto HINTZE, Gustav Schmoller and Wilhelm DILTHEY. Of these, Hintze proved the most influential, directing Hartung's attention, first to the constitutional history of Prussia and then to the Holy Roman Empire. In 1922 Hartung was elected to the chair of modern history at Kiel, from which he moved in the following year to succeed Hintze at Berlin. Given his conservative political views, it was odd that Hartung remained in (East) Berlin after 1945. He resigned his chair in 1949 after a row over academic freedom but remained a member of the Academy.

Hartung's best-known and most durable work has been his constitutional history of Germany from the fifteenth to the twentieth centuries, first published in 1914 and re-issued several times. His most original work, however, is to be found in the numerous papers and articles which testify to his remarkable chronological range. His main achievement in terms of methodology was finally to liberate constitutional history from jurisprudence and to establish its independence. Although prepared to utilize the work of economic and legal historians, he was less open to the history of ideas or of political theory.   TCWB

Main publications

Deutsche Verfassungsgeschichte vom 15. Jahrhundert bis zur Gegenwart, 8th edn (Stuttgart: Koehler, 1964); *Volk und Staat in der deutschen Geschichte: Gesammelte Abhandlungen* (Leipzig: Koehler & Amelang, 1940); *Staatsbildende Kräfte der Neuzeit* (Berlin: Duncker & Humblot, 1961).

Reading

Dietrich, R.: Fritz Hartung. *Historische Zeitschrift* 206 (1968) 525–8.

Faulenbach, B.: *Ideologie des deutschen Weges* (Munich: Beck, 1980).

Hartz, Louis (b.1919, d.1986)   Born in Youngstown, Ohio, Hartz graduated from Harvard in 1940 and received his doctorate in 1946. His whole teaching career, which began in 1945, was spent at Harvard. From 1955 to 1958 he was chairman of the Commission on American Civilization.

Hartz has written about the nature of economic policy at the state level, especially with respect to Pennsylvania, but his major contribution has been to the consensus school of American historiography which emphasizes the uniqueness of the American experience. In *The Liberal Tradition in America* he argued that the United States had been shaped by the absence of a feudal tradition and by the importation of European liberal thought. The broad liberal consensus was embodied in a common constitutional understanding which cut across lines of conflict; indeed, Hartz greatly plays down even such conflicts as the Civil War, insisting that what united Americans was more significant than that which divided them.   DMacl

Main publications

The Liberal Tradition in America (New York: 1955); *Economic Policy and Democratic Thought: Pennsylvania, 1776–1860* (Cambridge, Mass.: 1948).

Haskins, Charles Homer (b.1870, d.1937) One of a small group who initiated the study of medieval history in America, Haskins opened new fields for both American and European scholars. A pioneer in archival research, he systematically scoured the European repositories for documentary records. The 'Haskins Thesis' of medieval renaissance, his most renowned theory, excited new inquiries, re-examinations of old materials, and a continuing search for new evidence. He focused attention anew on pre-Conquest Norman sources for English institutions, and the Normans as a separate force in Europe. His work in medieval science initiated its study. He co-founded the Medieval Academy of America, the History of Science Society and its journal *Isis*, and the American Council of Learned Societies, serving as head of each, as also of the fledgeling American Historical Association. As dean of the Harvard Graduate School, 1908–24, he was a prime architect of American secondary, undergraduate and graduate education.

Haskins also served government at the highest level. He helped to plan American policy for the Paris Peace Conference at Versailles, 1918–19, where he was President Woodrow Wilson's adviser and interpreter. He subsequently wrote (with R. H. Lord) an important eyewitness account of the conference (*Some Problems of the Peace Conference*, 1920).

Haskins was a man of great charm, wit and vitality. He welcomed students of talent and ability from all backgrounds to Harvard, freely giving them his time, expertise and affection. His twinkling eye and subtle humour endeared him to audiences. His final years were marred by Parkinson's disease, which he endured with great courage.   SNV

Main publications

Norman Institutions (Cambridge, Mass.: Harvard University Press, 1918); *Studies in the History of Medieval Science* (Harvard University Press, 1924); *Studies in Medieval Culture* (Oxford: Clarendon Press, 1929); of general interest are *The Normans in European History* (Boston and New York: Houghton Mifflin, 1915); *The Renaissance of the Twelfth Century* (Harvard University Press, 1927).

Reading

Powicke, F. M.: Charles Homer Haskins. *English Historical Review* 52 (1937) 649–656.

Vaughn, Sally N.: Charles Homer Haskins. In *Dictionary of Literary Biography* vol. 47: *American Historians, 1866–1912*, ed. Clyde N. Wilson (Detroit: Gale Research Bruccoli Clark, 1986) pp. 122–45:

Hauck, Albert (b.1845, d.1918) Always a deeply committed Lutheran, in the mid-1860s

Hauck studied theology, Christian archaeology, and history at the universities of Erlangen and Berlin, where Leopold von RANKE became his lifelong ideal as a historian though current Prussian politics disturbed him. He completed his studies for the Lutheran pastorate at Munich. While he was a pastor in rural Bavaria amicable contacts with Catholicism widened his mental horizons. He held chairs at Erlangen (1878–89) and thereafter at Leipzig until his death in 1918. His five-volume masterpiece, *Kirchengeschichte Deutschlands*, appeared in stages from 1887. Beginning with urban Christianity in the second-century Roman Rhineland, he intended to conclude with the peace of Augsburg (1555) but the final part, which H. Boehmer completed, breaks off with the council of Basel (1437). Hauck skilfully blended religious with political and social history, and was a master of lucid and epigrammatic exposition. He was also editor, at first jointly with J. J. Herzog but for long solely, of the *Realencyclopädie für protestantische Theologie und Kirche*, to which he made substantial contributions.   HEJC

Main publications

Kirchengeschichte Deutschlands (Leipzig: J. C. Hinrichs'sche Buchhandlung, 1887–1920); *Realencyclopädie für protestantische Theologie und Kirche*, 3rd edn, 21 vols (1898–1908, plus *Register* 1909, and *Ergänzungen und Nachträge*, 2 vols, 1913).

Reading

Heimpel, H.: Albert Hauck. *Neue Deutsche Biographie* 8 (1969) 75–6.

Hays, Samuel Pfrimmer (b.1921) Hays is a pioneering practitioner of social scientific history. Influenced by the *Gestalt* or situational school of psychology, he developed the concept of the 'social analysis' of American political history. Using quantitative methods and behavioural theory, he considers voting behaviour and political life generally as expressions of social, religious, or ethnocultural group norms and values. Individuals act politically on the basis of group beliefs and perceptions. Hays thus stresses group conformity or hegemony goals, and tends to dismiss individual ideas as mere rhetoric.

A recognized author and master teacher, Hays significantly reshaped the history discipline in the 1960s and 1970s. He has authored some 20 books and major articles. His followers belong to the 'ethnocultural school' of historiography.

Hays was born into an ambitious sixth generation Scots-Irish family in southern Indiana. He graduated from Swarthmore College (1948) and earned his doctorate in history at Harvard (1953). He taught at the State University of Iowa until 1960 and then at the University of Pittsburgh, where he presently is distinguished service professor of history. In 1982 he was Harmsworth visiting professor of history at the Queen's College, Oxford.   RPS

Main publications

The Response to Industrialism (Chicago, Ill: University of Chicago Press, 1957); *Conservation and the Gospel of Efficiency* (Cambridge, Mass.: Harvard University Press, 1958); *American Political History is Social Analysis* (Knoxville: University of Tennessee Press, 1980) [collection of essays].

Reading

Kousser, J. Morgan: History as past sociology in the work of Samuel P. Hays. *Historical Methods.* 14 (1981) 181–86.
Stave, Bruce M.: A conversation with Samuel P. Hays. *Journal of Urban History* 2 (1975) 88–124.

Hazard, Paul (b.1878, d.1944) Descended from a Flemish family, Hazard was educated in France, where he pursued a distinguished academic career that took him from the École Normale Supérieure to the Sorbonne, the Collège de France and eventually to the French Academy in 1940. Although most of his work was on French literature, he is best known in England for his writing on the history of ideas. *La Crise de la conscience européenne* of 1935 was a pioneering work on the intellectual consequences of the scientific revolution of the late seventeenth century. This was followed by *La Pensée européenne de Montesquieu à Lessing* which came out posthumously in 1946 and surveyed the whole range of the rationalist phase of the Enlightenment, stopping short of the cult of sensibility that preceded the French Revolution. This he intended to explore in a third volume that was never written. Hazard saw the Enlightenment as an attempt to substitute reason, science and progress for classicism, religion and stability. As a unifying force it failed since its insights, which he respected, pointed in divergent directions. Its search for peace and unity was therefore to prove an illusion, but for Hazard, as for Goethe's Faust, everything was redeemed by the commitment to what he called 'truth'.   NH

Main publications

La Crise de la conscience européene (1935) trans. *The European Mind* (London: Hollis & Carter, 1953); *La Pensée européenne de Montesquieu à Lessing* (1946) trans. *European Thought in the Eighteenth Century* (London: Hollis & Carter, 1954).

Heckscher, Eli Filip (b.1879, d.1952) Heckscher was largely responsible for securing the recognition of economic history as an independent academic discipline in Sweden and for establishing the country's reputation in the subject. Born in Stockholm, he received his higher education at the University of Uppsala, where he was strongly influenced by both the political historian Harald Hjärne and the economist David Davidson. His doctoral dissertation on the impact of the railway on Sweden's economic development (1907) demonstrated a belief in the importance of economic theory for the interpretation of economic history which remained a leading characteristic of all his work. In 1909 he was appointed professor of economics and statistics in the recently founded Stockholm Business School.

While he never attached himself to any particular political party, he always took a lively interest in current economic and political problems: in 1911 he helped to found the journal *Svensk tidskrift*, of which he became an editor; and at the end of the first world war he became chairman of the National Mobilization Commission. Economic conditions during the war undoubtedly influenced the choice of subject for his first major work on economic history, a study of the Napoleonic continental system. He had already proclaimed his attachment to laissez-faire economic policy and his deep suspicion of attempts by the state to play more than a minimal role in economic life. Throughout the interwar period he strongly defended orthodox government financing, although he combined this with support for a positive social policy. In 1929 he was appointed to a personal chair in economic history as director of the Institute of Economic History in Stockholm. Two years after this appeared his great two-volume study of mercantilism, which, after Schmoller and CUNNINGHAM, he interpreted in terms of the pursuit of power and national unification. He has been criticized for trying to make mercantilism conform to a consistent and uniform system and for not paying enough attention to the influence of peculiar national political and social conditions; but the work as a whole has not been superseded.

The remainder of Heckscher's life was largely taken up with his magisterial economic history of Sweden from the early sixteenth century onwards. This was planned to reach to the 1930s, but at the time of his death he had completed only the four volumes to 1815. Meanwhile, however, he composed a single-volume economic history of Sweden, posthumously translated into English. In all his later works on Swedish history he made full use of the particularly rich statistical evidence available in Swedish archives. Heckscher was a prolific writer. A bibliography of his works, published in 1950, lists no fewer than 1,148 items, not including the regular contributions which he made to the liberal daily *Dagens Nyheter* from the first world war until his death. SPO

Main publications

Kontinentalsystemet. En ekonomisk-historisk studie (1918) trans. as *The Continental System: an Economic Interpretation* (Oxford: Clarendon Press, 1922; *Merkantilismen* (1931) (London: Allen & Unwin, 1935, rev. edn, 1955); *Sveriges ekonomiska historia från Gustav Vasa* (Sweden's economic history from Gustav Vasa) (Stockholm: Bonniers, 1935–49); *Svenskt arbete och liv från Medeltiden till Nutiden* (1941) trans. Göran Ohlin *An Economic History of Sweden* (Cambridge, Mass.: Harvard University Press, 1954).

Reading

Coleman, Donald C.: Eli Heckscher and the idea of mercantilism. *Scandinavian Economic History Review* 5. 1 (1957) 3–25.

Gerschenkron, Alexander A.: Eli F. Heckscher. In *An Economic History of Sweden*, trans. Göran Ohlin (Cambridge, Mass.: Harvard University Press, 1954), pp. xiii–xlii.

Ohlin, Göran: Heckscher, Eli. *International Encyclopedia of the Social Sciences*, vol. 6, ed. D. L. Sills (New York: Macmillan/Free Press, 1968) pp. 339–41.

Hegel, Georg Wilhelm Friedrich (b.1770, d.1831) Son of a tax official in Stuttgart, Hegel attended the theological seminary at Tübingen, where he was influenced by the works of Rousseau and Kant. He obtained his first university post at Jena, reputedly taking the proofs of his *Phenomenology of Spirit* to the printer during the battle in 1806. As a result of Napoleon's victory, which he welcomed, Hegel lost his job and had to work as an editor and later a headmaster before taking a chair at Heidelberg in 1816. In 1818 he succeeded Fichte at Berlin, where he remained until succumbing to cholera in 1831. He married in 1811, having earlier fathered an illegitimate son, whom his wife accepted into the family.

Hegel was at Berlin during the Prussian national revival and the post-Waterloo reaction. He was consequently attacked as a time-serving apologist for authority by Schopenhauer and, in the present century, as a precursor of totalitarianism by Popper. But he always celebrated Bastille day, as well as admiring Napoleon as a progressive force, a 'world historical individual'.

Apart from some discussion of types of historical writing and the delimitation of history's subject matter, Hegel had little interest in historical practice. He was thus less an 'analytical' than a 'speculative' philosopher of history, devoting his *Lectures on the Philosophy of History* (delivered in the 1820s, but published posthumously) to outlining the developmental pattern of world history. This is only one phase of the grand metaphysical scheme of the *Phenomenology* of 1807, according to which both physical and social reality are seen as manifestations of spirit or mind, developing according to its inner logic – the dialectic. Reality is thus rational and intelligible. In particular, beneath history's surface confusion of events and actions, follies and vices, can be seen the evolution of the idea of freedom and its progressive embodiment in institutions. This seems to amount to the thesis that the scope of freedom, in the sense of autonomy and individual fulfilment in society, is enlarged as the Oriental world (China, India and Persia) is succeeded first by Greece and Rome and later by the 'Germanic' world of modern, western Europe. (The remarkably wide use of 'Germanic' should be noted.) In the Orient only *one*, the despot, was free; in the slaveholding societies of Greece and Rome *some*, the citizens, were free; only in the constitutional monarchies of Hegel's own day, with the complex history of church and empire, renaissance and reformation behind them, was there the institutional possibility of *all* being free.

Running through Hegel's development is a fall and salvation theme: in Greece the individual was 'at home', harmoniously identified with his city; this unity disappears as the soulless empires take over, and the consequently alienated individual is driven to seek consolation in other-worldly faith and personal morality. The thesis of external law and the antithesis of inner morality are transcended in the synthesis of Hegel's ethical state. In such a complex, plural society (unlike Rousseau, Hegel can accommodate churches and other self-subsistent institutions in his state) mankind is once more at home. Hegel was worried by class divisions, but did not see them as unbridgeable. The nation state is the largest social unit that Hegel recognized. Like the later Rousseau, he did not regard humanity at large as a society and had no time for Kantian-style confederalism in the interests of peace. Warfare, inescapable in a world of nation-states, is not seen as a threat to civilization, but as ethically progressive, raising people from the selfish particularism of civil society to the 'universal'. Private morality is rightly overridden for reasons of state, and especially by world historical Caesars and Napoleons. Anti-totalitarian critics naturally fasten upon such sentiments, though Hegel is arguably mainly over-compensating for the extreme individualism of bourgeois culture and Enlightenment moral philosophy.

Hegel has been immensely influential, not least for bequeathing the dialectic and the division of history into a few great epochs to MARX. He was, moreover, not really 'idealistic' in the sense Marx condemned. The ideas he concerned himself with are conceived as embodied in institutions and, though he did not regard the economic as primary, he certainly saw the political as but one aspect of social structure. Beyond this, though, there is much in Hegel that is bound to offend the practising historian, who will suspect him of imposing an *a priori* structure on the imperfectly grasped detail of history. Not only did Hegel give exclusive emphasis to a narrow thread of development, he had the presumption to represent it as *necessary*, as if the philosopher, without the pain of actual enquiry, were qualified both to explain the past and predict the future.

Yet Hegel expressly disclaimed any power of prediction; and his selective vision of the past arguably derives only from focusing on elements that were reflected in the consciousness of his own day. Of course the Orient and South America had their history, but it is not implausible to hold that it had little effect on Hegel's Europe. No mind can encompass the whole of the past: history cannot be written from no point of view. It may be granted that Hegel's viewpoint is legitimate; but it is doubtful whether Hegel would have conceded that others are so too.   RFA

Main publications

Phänomenologie des Geistes (1807) trans. A.V. Miller (Oxford: Clarendon Press, 1977); *Philosophie des Rechts* (1821) trans. T. M. Knox (Oxford: Oxford University Press, 1942); *Vorlesungen über die Philosophie der Weltgeschichte* (1837), trans. J. Sibree, (New York: Dover NY, 1956), trans. H. B. Nisbet (Cambridge: Cambridge University Press, 1975).

Reading

Dray, W. H.: *Philosophy of History* (Englewood Cliffs, NJ: Prentice-Hall, 1964) ch.6.

O'Brien, G. D.: *Hegel on Reason and History* (Chicago, Ill.: University of Chicago Press, 1975).

Walsh, W. H.: *An Introduction to Philosophy of History*, ch.7 (London: Hutchinson, 1951).

Wilkins, B. T.: *Hegel's Philosophy of History* (New York: Cornell University Press, 1974).

Henry of Huntingdon (b. *c.*1080, d. after 1154) Son of Nicholas, archdeacon of Cambridge, Hertford and Huntingdon, Henry entered the household of Robert Bloet bishop of Lincoln in 1093, becoming archdeacon of

Huntingdon and Hertford in 1110 after his father's death. When Bishop Robert died in 1123 Henry served his successor Alexander, nephew of Roger bishop of Salisbury, who commissioned Henry's great historical work *Historia Anglorum* (1129–1133).

The most ambitious work of Stephen's reign, the *Historia* covered English history from the earliest times, drawing upon both classical and English historians such as EUTROPIUS, AURELIUS VICTOR, NENNIUS, GILDAS and BEDE. Yet Henry wrote within the Anglo-Norman historical tradition, paralleling Malmesbury and ORDERIC, quoting documents and first- or second-hand eyewitness accounts.

The work enjoyed wide popularity: twenty-five manuscript copies survive, perhaps eight from the twelfth century, in both Normandy and England. Henry revised the *Historia* in 1135, 1145 and 1154, adding books, reorganizing chapters, and including letters to King Henry I detailing royal and imperial successions; to Warin, 'a Briton', concerning British kings, drawn from GEOFFREY OF MONMOUTH; and to Walter, probably archdeacon of Leicester, on *De contemptu mundi*, one of Henry's major themes. Henry avoided recounting miracles in the text but put them all together in one added chapter.

Henry directly influenced the Norman historian Robert of Torigny, to whom he personally presented his history on a visit to Bec in 1139; he received in return a copy of Geoffrey of Monmouth's history, which subsequently influenced his next revision. Henry intended a final revision to include the reign of Henry II, but died before its completion.   SNV

Main writings

Henrici Archidiaconi Huntendunensis Historia Anglorum, ed. Thomas Arnold (London: Royal Society, 1879); for an English trans. see *The Chronicle of Henry of Huntingdon*, ed. and trans. T. Forester (London: 1853).

Reading

Clanchy, M. T.: *From Memory to Written Record: England, 1066–1307* (Cambridge, Mass.: Harvard University Press, 1979).

Gransden, Antonia: *Historical Writing in England c.550 to c.1307*, (London: Routledge & Kegan Paul, 1974) pp. 193–201.

Partner, Nancy: *Serious Entertainments: the Writing of History in Twelfth Century England* (Chicago: University of Chicago Press, 1977).

Henry, Louis (b.1911)   Though principally a demographer, Henry has played a major role in the development of demographic history. Unquestionably his largest contribution has been the development of the technique of family reconstitution. This form of record linkage allows the baptisms, marriages and burials recorded in parish registers to be assembled into genealogies or life histories and detailed demographic measures to be calculated. The technique opened up a vast data source (registers were kept in most European countries from the seventeenth or eighteenth centuries) to penetrating, quantitative analysis. In a string of works in the 1950s and 1960s Henry devised the necessary methodology, demonstrated its use in two highly perceptive case studies and (with Michel Fleury) codified the procedures to permit their wider use. The technique was enthusiastically adopted by historians all over Europe; in England its use was pioneered by E. A. WRIGLEY.

Throughout his career Henry's main interest has been the study of fertility; his original intention in studying past populations was to obtain information on societies whose members did not employ deliberate birth control. Such a strategy of reproduction was termed 'natural fertility' by Henry and his approach to the subject has been widely copied. Historical sources are, indeed, excellent for Henry's purpose and his studies, and those following his example, have produced many new insights into childbearing in the past. As a part of his research on fertility, Henry organized the reconstitution of some 40 French parishes (approximately 1 in 1000) for the period down to 1830. The results of this survey have been crucial in demonstrating the early and widespread use of birth control in France.

A product of the École Polytechnique, Henry originally embarked upon a military career, but his ambitions in this regard were curtailed by the second world war. Working thereafter in the Institut National d'Études Demographiques, his work has always retained the style of a technocrat rather than an academic.   CW

Main publications

(Published by Institut National d'Étude Démographique, Paris, unless otherwise stated.)
Anciennes familles genèvoises: étude démographique XVIe−XXe siècle (1956); with E. Gautier, *La Population de Crulai, paroisse normande: étude historique* (1958); *Eugenics Quarterly* 8 (1961) 81−91 [incl. data on natural fertility]; with M. Fleury, *Nouveau manuel de dépouillement et d'exploitation de l'état civil ancien* (1965); *Manuel de démographie historique* (Geneva and Paris: Droz, 1967); *Techniques d'analyse en démographie historique* (1980).

Herodian (*fl.* 178−248) A Greek from the eastern provinces of the Roman empire, though precise place of origin is unknown, Herodian served as a minor public official. His surviving *Roman History* in eight books covers the period of his own lifetime, from the death of the emperor Marcus Aurelius in 180 to the accession of Gordian III (238), and was probably completed within the subsequent decade. As was conventional among historians of the Roman empire, Herodian focused attention almost exclusively on imperial politics, for which he claimed rich interest in his period, given the large number of those who occupied the throne. The dying Marcus Aurelius may be said to be the 'hero' of the work, the exemplar of an ideal of Roman rule which was to be perverted by the tyranny of some of his successors. Herodian's work is overshadowed by that of his more illustrious contemporary DIO, with whom he has often been unfavourably compared. Yet Herodian preserves some authentic detail not to be found in Dio and offers an alternative viewpoint on the history of his own time. His failings are those which he shares with other classical historians: vagueness of chronology, the omission of significant evidence, stereotyped characterization, and the pervasive influence of the rhetoric which was central to the culture of his age.   EDH

Main writings

Herodian, 2 vols, ed. and trans. C. R. Whittaker (London: Heinemann, 1969−70).

Herodotus of Halicarnassus (*fl.*430 BC) The only certain fact about Herodotus' life is that he became a citizen of Thurii in southern Italy at some time after its foundation by the Athenians *c.*443 BC. Later Hellenistic speculative biography produced Halicarnassus as his native city and *c.*484 BC as the year of his birth: neither suggestion is certain.

Herodotus wrote his *Histories* (more accurately, *Researches*) at some time during, or immediately after, the long and destructive Peloponnesian War between the oligarchic Spartan alliance and expansionist, democratic Athens (431−404 BC). There is significant disagreement about the precise date of the work's composition with suggestions ranging from *c.*426 BC through *c.*415 BC to as late as the 390s BC.

In his work Herodotus claimed to have travelled widely to Egypt, the Black Sea, Phoenicia and Mesopotamia, as well as throughout the Greek world, and much of his work is devoted to detailed descriptions of barbarian (i.e. non-Greek) peoples and places. Despite justified doubt of the truth of at least some of these claims to extensive travel, they have been used to construct an artificial scheme of Herodotus' intellectual development from geographer and ethnographer to historian with the change in emphasis ('the creation of Western historiography') occurring during his stay in Egypt or Athens. In fact empirical and rational inquiry into both geography and history is found possibly as much as a century before Herodotus in the partially preserved works of Hecataeus of Miletus (*c.*500 BC).

Herodotus' announced purpose at the beginning of his work is to preserve the memory of past human history, to ensure the future fame of the great deeds of the Greeks and barbarians in the past, and in particular to explain the cause of the conflict between them. He disdainfully rejects the tradition about the Trojan War, which had earlier concerned Hecataeus, as incredible and unverifiable and begins with Croesus of Lydia (*c.*560−546 BC), the first man whom Herodotus definitely *knew* to have attempted the subjection of the Greeks. The work then proceeds from Croesus to Cyrus, founder of the Persian empire (559−529 BC), and on through Cambyses (530−522 BC) and Darius (521−486 BC) to Xerxes (486−465 BC) and the failure of his invasion of Greece in 480−479 BC. Within this simple but clear chronological structure the first half of the work (books 1–4) is marked by long ethnological digressions on the barbarian victims of Persian expansionism, for example the Lydians, Egyptians, Scythians and Libyans, as well as shorter historical digressions on similarly subjected or threatened Greek communities, especially the Ionians in Asia and the Spartans and the Athenians on the Greek mainland. In the second half of the work (books 5–9) the narrative moves through a detailed description of the Ionian revolt (499–494 BC) and the subsequent battle of Marathon (490 BC) to a developed account of the battles of Thermopylae, Artemisium, Salamis (480 BC), Plataea and Mycale (479 BC).

Despite clearly creative writing in a storied narrative, dramatized through direct dialogue and speeches in the long-established poetic tradition of Homeric epic, Herodotus' insistence on the importance of empirical inquiry, his frequent citation of sources and his concern with the rational evaluation of evidence have all recommended him to some modern historians as the founder of modern positivist historiography. In fact his overriding concern is, through selective and seductively detailed descriptions of foreign customs and past history, to demonstrate general, rather than particular, truths concerning the interrelationship between divine and human in human affairs, the importance of traditional behavioural norms (*nomoi*) in different human societies, the causes of war within and between social groups, and the necessary pattern ('rise and fall') of imperialist expansionism. He worked within an intellectual environment conditioned by a new faith in the ability of human reason to investigate, understand and control all aspects of the human condition. His own researches, although within the earlier Ionian tradition of Hecataeus, were determined by this contemporary 'sophistic' movement; Herodotus employed its methodology to undermine its central faith. According to him the past showed not the ability but the inability of human reason to control a divinely determined order realized through the principal vehicles of divine will, oracles and dreams. All human efforts to transcend, particularly through imperial expansionism, the limits of this moral and political order were, and are, in vain.

In his presentation of past Persian imperialism and its failure, Herodotus is demonstrably influenced by his own experience of contemporary imperial Athens; for instance, the debate at the Persian court as it appears in Herodotus before Xerxes' invasion of Greece is strikingly similar to the debate at Athens which, according to the contemporary Athenian historian, Thucydides, preceded the Athenian expedition to Sicily in 415 BC. The consensus of modern scholarship is that Herodotus was writing before the massive Athenian failure in Sicily in 413 BC and certainly before Athens' final defeat by Sparta in 404 BC. However it could be argued that the whole tenor of his work is best explained if he was writing some time later, in the aftermath of Athenian failure and perhaps as late as the 390s BC. The 'Ionian question', i.e. the problem of the Greek presence in Asia and whether it should be preserved, abandoned or extended, receives significant structural emphasis at the beginning, middle and end of the *Histories*. It first came into prominence in the 390s BC when many Greeks, especially the poor and dispossessed, favoured an expansionist war against Persia. Herodotus reflected the concerns of his conservative and propertied readership in opposing such expansionism. In fact, it is precisely the attitudes evident in the work, and not the 'facts' its author supposedly narrates, which make Herodotus' *Histories* so useful, not to the military and political historian of the Persian Wars, but to the intellectual historian interested in the complex ideology of the emergent bourgeoisie of the Greek world at the end of the fifth century BC.   JDS

Main writings

The Histories, trans. A. de Sélincourt (Harmondsworth: Penguin, 1971).

Reading

Drews, Robert: *The Greek Accounts of Eastern History* (Cambridge, Mass: Harvard University Press, 1973).

Fornara, Charles W.: *Herodotus: An Interpretative Essay* (Oxford: Clarendon Press, 1971).

Hunter, Virginia: *Past and Process in Herodotus and Thucydides* (Princeton, NJ: Princeton University Press, 1982).

Immerwahr, H.R.: *Form and Thought in Herodotus* (Cleveland: Western Reserve University Press, 1966).

Hexter, J. H. (b.1910) Jack Hexter's fame rests less upon his performance as a scholar than as a reviewer, in the greatest and broadest sense. He would examine a notable work of history or controversy between historians, and then use the information gained from this analysis to go beyond it and to suggest a new framework of explanation. In his later years he developed this habit into a general interest in the theoretical nature of the past, and became arguably the premier American philosopher of history.

Hexter's progress to fame was slow. Brought up in Ohio, he took his first degree at Cincinnati and second at Harvard, and taught at Queen's College and Washington University (St Louis) for most of his career. He published some respected monographs, but was already forty when he seized international attention with his essay 'The myth of the middle class in Tudor England'. His great chain of analytical writings followed, and in 1964 he took charge of the history department at Yale. In 1978 he retired from this to an honorary appointment in his old workplace at Washington University.

Hexter conducted relatively little archival research, but was a voracious reader of published sources and secondary material in a wide field. During his forties he would teach all morning and then study and write until midnight. His literary style was informal and exuberant. He loved to coin neologisms, one of which, 'tunnel history', may have taken on permanent currency. To make abstract points about the historical process he culled images from the baseball pitch and the yacht club, and drew upon anecdotes from peoples as scattered as Polish Jewry and American small-town-dwellers. His mind lent itself to tabulation and quantification: only Hexter would draw a map showing the international origins of contributors to a *Festschrift*, or calculate the precise percentage of a famous work which could be skipped over without loss. He liked the thought of being the funniest historian of his age, and at times he probably was.

He had the zeal of a true inconoclast, his mission being in his own words 'to pelt the children of light, the historians à la mode'. His especial hatred was for attempts to reduce human action to anonymous causes, such as economic changes: he was therefore a natural foe of Marxists. In later life, as he became a 'child of light' himself, he found new opponents in historians who emphasized short-term causes and the role of accident in political developments. Suddenly it became obvious that behind his dislike for Marxism lay not only the scholarly rigour of Harvard but a Midwestern passion for the American Dream. He spoke of 'the central importance of liberty and the rule of law in the ordering of human affairs', and the man who had seemed the prophet of the restoration of politics to the centre of historical action became known as the last Whig historian. In truth he is *sui generis*, as much an individual in his opinions as in his literary style.   RH

Main publications

The Reign of King Pym (Cambridge, Mass.: Harvard University Press, 1941); *More's Utopia* (Princeton, NJ: Princeton University Press, 1952); *Reappraisals in History* (London: Longmans, Green, 1961); *The Judaeo-Christian Tradition* (New York: Harper & Row, 1966); *Doing History* (Bloomington: Indiana University Press, 1971); *The History Primer* (New York: Basic, 1971); *The Vision of Politics on the Eve of the Reformation* (Basic, 1973); *On Historians* (Harvard University Press, 1978).

Higden, Ranulf (d.1363/4) A monk of St Werburgh's Abbey at Chester, Higden composed the *Polychronicon*, the fullest universal history written in England during the middle ages. Unusually, he devotes the whole of the first book to a physical geography of the world. Higden was not original, nor over-critical, in the history he related, yet he did present a coherent and detailed history from a medieval Christian standpoint. When the *Polychronicon* was translated into English by John Trevisa in the 1380s, Higden's history outstripped the works of BEDE and GEOFFREY OF MONMOUTH in popularity because of its monumental scale and range of reference.   MTC

HIGHAM, JOHN

Main publications

Polychronicon Ranulphi Higden monachi Cestrensis, 9 vols, ed. C. Babington and J. R. Lumby (Rolls Series, 1865–86).

Reading

Gransden, A. *Historical Writing in England*, vol. 2 (London; Routledge, 1982).

Taylor, J.: *The Universal Chronicle of Ranulf Higden* (Oxford: Clarendon Press, 1966).

——: *English Historical Literature in the Fourteenth Century* (Oxford: Clarendon Press, 1987).

Higham, John (b.1920) Higham made his name with *Strangers in the Land* (1955), a study of American nativism, in which he analysed three main strands: fear of Catholicism, fear of radicalism, and a sense of Anglo-Saxon racial superiority. While maintaining his interest in questions of ethnic relations, anti-Semitism for example, he has also written on historiography, on cultural history with emphasis on its concealed assumptions and on 'the ambiguity of American experience'. He taught at UCLA, Rutgers and the University of Michigan before returning in 1971 to his Alma Mater, Johns Hopkins.   AEC

Main publications

Strangers in the Land: Patterns of American Nativism, 1860–1925 (New Brunswick, NJ: Rutgers University Press, 1955); with L. Krieger and F. Gilbert, *History* (Englewood Cliffs, NJ: Prentice-Hall, 1965); *From Boundlessness to Consolidation: the Transformation of American Culture, 1848–1860* (Ann Arbor: University of Michigan Press, 1969); *Writing American History* (Bloomington, Ind.: Indiana University Press, 1970); *Projects in History: A Guide for Students* (Edinburgh: 1974); *Send These to Me, Immigrants in Urban America* (Baltimore, MD: Johns Hopkins University Press, 1975).

Hill, John Edward Christopher (b.1912) Christopher Hill's career was formed by a curious dichotomy. In one sense he was an outsider, brought up in the north of England and from a Methodist family. He was converted to Marxism at college and remained a member of the Communist party for twenty years, an association which resulted in his being passed over for a chair and rejected by some publishers. He made his way by exceptional industry. The favourite part of his childhood home was the seat where he read, he fainted in his final undergraduate term from overwork, and in one decade, his fifties, he wrote seven books, twenty-eight essays and 125 reviews. On the other hand, his progress was relatively comfortable. His parents were wealthy and lived in York, not the industrial north. A Balliol don drove there especially to persuade young Christopher to study at his college. He duly won a top 'first' and an All Souls fellowship. When others of his age and views were going to die in Spain, he accepted an invitation to teach at Cardiff, on the assumption that he would soon return to Oxford. He did so after two years, to Balliol, where he eventually became Master. The large revenue from his books ensured him an affluent retirement, enlivened by an appointment at the Open University. The size of his output was eased by the fact that he rarely read manuscripts and (some thought) unconsciously selected evidence which supported his case regardless of context.

Hill's preoccupations as a historian derived directly from his parentage and politics: religious and political nonconformity. His first significant publication, in 1940, was a crude interpretation of the English civil war as an economic struggle. His first widely-admired work came in 1956, *Economic Problems of the Church*, which readjusted perceptions of the Reformation permanently. His textbook *The Century of Revolution* (1961) was a very sophisticated Marxist history linking social, economic and political issues in a manner new to school-teaching. There followed his great sequence of writings upon Puritanism and more radical dissent culminating in *The World Turned Upside Down* (1972). These received much praise and little serious criticism, for they stood apart from constitutional and narrative history rather than challenged them. They made him a hero to young radicals in the campus activism of 1968–72.

Such relative lack of trouble in his career combined with his nature to make Hill one of the most engaging of academics. He took remarkable trouble over pupils, colleagues and his public and was a tremendous holder of entertainments. He would cross a room to befriend somebody who seemed isolated at a party. He was modest about his achievements and a gentle critic.

This happy world crashed suddenly in late 1975, when J. H. HEXTER made his fundamental attack upon Hill's method of writing history. This was followed closely by the 'revisionist' school of seventeenth-century historians, who rejected his view of the period. This rain of blows provoked some equally intemperate defenders: one academic announced publicly that in English letters only Shakespeare and Hill deserved respect. Caught in this storm, Hill was forced into the novel role of controversialist. His reviews became more acerbic, and he produced a number of essays against the 'revisionist' case. The exchange goes on, and so a man who was born in the lifetime of Franz-Josef continues to play a lively part in the academic world of the late 1980s.   RH

Main publications

Economic Problems of the Church, from Archbishop Whitgift to the Long Parliament (Oxford: Oxford University Press, 1956); *Puritanism and Revolution* (London: Secker & Warburg, 1958); *The Century of Revolution* (Edinburgh: Nelson, 1961); *Society and Puritanism in Pre-Revolutionary England* (Secker & Warburg, 1964); *Intellectual Origins of the English Revolution* (Oxford: Clarendon Press, 1965); *Reformation to Industrial Revolution* (London: Weidenfeld & Nicolson, 1967); *God's Englishman* (Weidenfeld & Nicolson, 1970); *The World Turned Upside Down* (London: Temple Smith, 1972); *Change and Continuity in Seventeenth-Century England* (Weidenfeld & Nicolson, 1974); *Milton and the English Revolution* (London: Faber & Faber, 1977); *Collected Essays*, 3 vols (Brighton: Harvester, 1985).

Reading

Kaye, H. J.: *The British Marxist Historians* (Cambridge: Polity Press, 1984).

Hilton, Rodney Howard (b.1916) From a radical background, Hilton studied at Oxford in the thirties, and after war service became a lecturer at Birmingham University where he held a chair of medieval social history from 1963 until 1982. His researches into medieval society have been informed by Marxist perspectives. One of his concerns has been to explain the totality of past societies, achieved through exploration of a single English region, the West Midlands, which culminated in a

book inspired by French regional studies. In his social analysis he argues that the peasantry formed a self-conscious class, capable of struggle against feudal lordship from the early middle ages, which culminated in the movement of 1381. His belief that the peasants' struggle achieved some success is linked with the idea of general crisis, that is, the process by which internal pressure built up until the social system went through a great upheaval in the fourteenth century. Thus changes in the structure of society resulted from a combination of rebellion and economic trends. He has questioned many orthodox ideas about the origins of capitalism, recognizing medieval towns not as precocious novelties but as integral features of feudal society. He has combined theoretical perspectives, especially those deriving from social scientists, with a strong concern for evidence, so he has edited texts, sponsored excavations, and sought social meaning from literature. His international reputation rests on his writings, many published abroad, and his role in the journal *Past and Present* of which he was chairman of the editorial board for many years.   CCD

Main publications

A Medieval Society: The West Midlands at the End of the Thirteenth Century (London: Weidenfeld & Nicolson, 1966); *Bond Men Made Free: Medieval Peasant Movements and the English Rising of 1381* (London: Temple Smith, 1973); *The English Peasantry in the Later Middle Ages* (Oxford: Oxford University Press, 1975).

Reading

Kaye, H. J.: *The British Marxist Historians* (Cambridge: Polity Press, 1984).

Hintze, Otto (b.1861, d.1940) After two years at Greifswald university Hintze was a student, research student and professor (1899–1920) at Berlin university. Schmoller set him to work in 1888 for the *Acta Borussica* on the silk industry, and in 1901–10 he edited six volumes of documents on the Prussian constitution and administration, 1740–56, for this series. He was editor of volumes 10–25 (1897–1913) of the *Forschungen zur brandenburgischen und preussischen Geschichte*. His work ranged from the seventeenth to the twentieth century and his own research was published in many learned journals and in the Proceedings of the Prussian *Akadamie der Wissenschaften*. Hintze believed that because Prussia was a military state and socially divided its constitutional development was unique, but he made constant comparisons with other countries. He was interested in sociological explanations and the dynamics of institutional development. He published nothing after 1933. A general comparative constitutional history in manuscript was lost in 1945–6.　　　AR

Main publications

Die Epochen des evangelischen Kirchenregiments in Preussen. *Historische Zeitschrift* 97 (1906) 67–118; Die monarchische Prinzip und die konstitutionelle Verfassung. *Preussische Jahrbücher* 144 (1911) 381–412; *Die Hohenzollern und ihr Werk* (Berlin: 1916).

Reading

Hartung, F.: Einleitung to Otto Hintze. In *Gesammelte Abhandlungen zur allgemeinen Verfassungsgeschichte* 3 vols (Göttingen: Vandenhoek & Rupprecht, 1962) [incl. complete bibliography].

Hispanic historiography Though Spain has a tradition of history writing as long as that of any other European nation, the most formative influences date principally from the early twentieth century, with the inspirational studies produced by Marcelino Menéndez y Pelayo, and Ramón Menéndez Pidal whose scheme for a multivolume *History of Spain* made available to a wide readership the findings of previous scholarship. These and other scholars of their generation – in ancient history one must note the work of P. Bosch-Gimpera – were heavily influenced by foreign, especially German, historiography; and subsequent research methods in the peninsula have continued to be profoundly inspired by foreigners, who continued, as in E. Lévi-Provençal's work on Muslim Spain, to make fundamental contributions to knowledge. The period chosen for study tended to be late medieval or the dawn of the modern age; this choice of themes was, in the wake of the imperial defeats of 1898, dictated by a nostalgia for the ages of success. The unbroken dominance of Catholic thinking meant that much writing continued to be on religious subjects; only occasionally, as with the pioneering work of Padre Fidel Fita, did exploration involve the rigorous use of archival documentation.

The Spanish Civil War (1936–9) and the subsequent Franco regime marked a watershed in historical studies. Under Franco academics were persecuted and only one type of history – right-wing, Catholic, and inspired by a mythological view of the reign of Ferdinand and Isabella – favoured; archives (many of them destroyed by the Republicans) were gradually restored but the documents were seldom catalogued and their use was not fostered. It was no accident that most prominent historians, the scholar and diplomat Salvador de Madariaga, for example, emigrated and produced their work abroad: among the notable studies written in exile were those by Américo Castro and Claudio Sánchez-Albornoz, both medievalists; modern history, hitherto neglected, remained so among the exiles, and was cultivated within Spain by very few, notably Ramón Carande (1943). This left the way open for a revival of interest in the Iberian past among non-Spaniards, and the appearance of Bataillon's study of Erasmus (1937) and of BRAUDEL's on the Mediterranean (1949) helped to give leadership to foreigners in the study of Spain's modern history. The two phenomena of emigration and foreign scholarship helped to depress further the state of historical studies, while the regime's suppression of any informed research into contemporary themes converted the twentieth century and much of the nineteenth into a historical desert.

Key importance must be given to the date 1950, when the Catalan historian Jaume VICENS VIVES, holder of the chair of history in Barcelona since 1948, attended a historical conference at Paris and returned to Spain convinced that the methodological horizons opened up by the ANNALES SCHOOL should be used to give a new direction to peninsular historiography. The rapid shift of Vicens in the 1950s to socio-economic history and contemporary themes, began a trend among Spanish historians; it now became possible to use tools of analysis that did not require straying into the still dangerous terrain of political history. French influences became important among historians such as Vicens's many pupils (notably Nadal and Giralt), and the political radicalism of some French scholars (such as the Marxist Pierre Vilar) appealed to students in the peninsula; in practice, French methodology was seldom put into effect, partly because of the undeveloped state of the university system and the lack of financial support for research. Despite important work done in the 1950s, then, by Vicens and other scholars (one may single out the pioneering anthropological work of Julio Caro Baroja, the seventeenth-century researches of Antonio Domínguez Ortiz, and the later modern studies of Miguel Artola), the most innovative research was being undertaken outside the country. American scholars had periodically made fundamental contributions to Hispanic studies, for example Henry Charles LEA's great work on the Inquisition (1906) and R. B. Merriman's multivolume survey of early modern Spain (1918); on the eighteenth century important work was subsequently done (1958) by Richard Herr. In England probably the most influential of the early contributions was Gerald Brenan's *Spanish Labyrinth* (1943). French scholars, however, maintained their leadership in research, notably with Jean Sarrailh's work on the eighteenth century (1954) and Pierre Vilar's on Catalonia (1962).

As the Franco epoch neared its end, interest in contemporary affairs spawned a wealth of new work, instanced by the study of the American, Gabriel Jackson, on the Civil War (1965), and that of Raymond Carr (1966) on the nineteenth century; the work of the latter represents incontestably the most important contribution made by any English historian to Hispanic studies in this century. At the same time a newer generation, both Spanish and foreign, was at last producing substantive research: for the earlier period the outstanding work was Bennassar's thesis on the city of *Valladolid* (1967); for the later period there were major contributions by Americans such as Stanley Payne and Edward Malefakis, and Spaniards such as Gonzalo Anés. The works of all these historians stimulated younger scholars to explore the archives, and from about 1970 the Spanish market began to be inundated by the piecemeal and often disordered results of original research; as a result, progress has been rich in quantity but unsystematic, and major areas of study remain superficially explored. On balance, historical writing within Spain seems to have liberated itself from its past reliance on foreign scholarship, and numerous scholars, such as Ladero Quesada on the Catholic monarchs and Pere Molas on the eighteenth century, have through their careful use of documentation and synthesis helped to give Spanish historiography a value and distinction that it lacked during the dictatorship years.   HK

historical geography The methodology and subject matter of historical geography have changed over the past century, but its central concerns remain with the interaction of people and the environment during the past, and with the resolution of questions asked about differences between places in the past.

From its nineteenth-century origins in historical atlases and a concern with 'geographical' influences on 'history', historical geography emerged in the English-speaking world with a new emphasis in 1936 with the publication of *An Historical Geography of England before AD 1800* edited by H. C. Darby. This presented a series of reconstructions of past geographies in the form of a sequence of cross-sections describing the economy and society of England at successive periods before 1800. At the same time, in America C.O. Sauer was forging another new identity for historical geography with a series of regional studies with strong anthropological overtones which he and his students developed as a form of 'cultural geography'.

By the early 1960s four main approaches were prevalent: *geographies of the past* characterized by cross-sectional studies; the *description of changing landscapes* with longitudinal studies considering man's influence on the environment; investigations of *the past in the present* in which relict landscapes were mapped and analysed; and *geographical history* concerned with the influence of geographical considerations on the course of history. Of these, it was

191

the cross-sectional approaches, concerned with the mapping and elucidation of specific historical sources, that were most common, the archetypal example being found in the Domesday geographies of England, which mapped and described the evidence of Domesday Book in a series of regional volumes produced under Darby's direction.

The increased use of quantitative techniques, and the implicit adoption of the tenets of logical positivism within much of geography in the 1960s, found little favour among historical geographers and by 1970 the subject found itself in something of a backwater. Two broad strands can nevertheless be identified within historical geographical research at this time. On the one hand were the increasing number of detailed analyses of historical sources (Baker et al; 1970), and on the other were investigations of settlement morphology and field systems (Baker and Butlin, 1973). The advances that had taken place within historical geography since 1936 were illustrated by the publication in 1973 of Darby's edited volume *A New Historical Geography of England*. This combined both the horizontal and vertical approaches to the subject, and consisted of a series of cross-sections based mainly on historical sources such as Domesday Book, the 1334 Lay Subsidy and the 1801 census, interspersed with longitudinal accounts of the economic and social forces giving rise to changes in the landscape.

During the 1970s dissatisfaction with the descriptive nature of much writing in historical geography and increased awareness of the sterility of logical positivism led a younger generation of historical geographers to turn to idealism, phenomenology, and structuralism (Gregory, 1978) in their search for new modes of explanation, and a wider dialogue was opened with other social scientists. This theoretical reappraisal was also associated with a shift of emphasis in the subject matter of historical geography, with increased attention being paid to the nineteenth century and changes in industry, agriculture and urban life associated with the emergence of capitalist relations of production. The development of a more interpretative approach to the past was reflected in Dodgshon and Butlin's

Historical Geography of England and Wales (1978). Themes being explored by historical geographers in the 1980s include a renewed interest in the ideological landscape, refinements in the techniques of historical demography, and a new concern with a revivified regional geography of the past (Dennis, 1984, 1985).   PTHU

References

Baker, A. R. H. and Butlin, R. A.: *Studies of Field Systems in the British Isles* (Cambridge: Cambridge University Press, 1973).

Baker, A. R. H., Hamshere, J. D. and Langton, J. eds: *Geographical Interpretations of Historical Sources* (Newton Abbot: David & Charles, 1970).

Darby, H. C., ed.: *An Historical Geography of England before AD 1800* (Cambridge University Press, 1936).

——: Historical geography. In *Approaches to History*, ed. H. P. R. Finberg (London: Routledge & Kegan Paul, 1962) pp. 127–56.

Dennis, R.: Historical geography: theory and progress. *Progress in Human Geography* 8 (1984) 536–44.

——: Historical geography: landscape with figures. *Progress in Human Geography* 9 (1985) 575–84.

Gregory, D.: The discourse of the past: phenomenology, structuralism and historical geography. *Journal of Historical Geography* 3 (1978) 55–67.

Reading

Baker, A. R. H. ed. *Progress in Historical Geography* (Newton Abbott: David & Charles, 1972).

Baker, A. R. H. and Billinge, M., eds. *Period and Place: Research Methods in Historical Geography* (Cambridge: Cambridge University Press, 1982).

Darby, H. C. ed.: *A New Historical Geography of England* (Cambridge University Press, 1973).

Dodgshon, R. A. and Butlin, R. A., eds.: *An Historical Geography of England and Wales* (London: Academic, 1978).

Journal of Historical Geography 1975—(quarterly).

historical materialism See MARXIST INTERPRETATION OF HISTORY.

historicism A confused and confusing word, which should be abandoned, since it obscures more than it illuminates. In origin, it was a translation of the German *historismus*, an assertion of the paramount importance of historical explanation. But this comparatively neutral technique developed, in the course of time, certain tendencies which, in the eyes of some critics, became heresies to be extirpated. First, the emphasis on the importance of understanding the historical context made for relativism and fell foul of writers who were anxious to maintain absolute and unchanging moral standards: the desire to understand the past in its own terms slid easily into a defence of or justification for the past. Secondly, growing confidence in their techniques for explaining the past tempted certain thinkers, particularly Marx and his followers, into the conviction that they could, by extrapolation, predict the future. Thirdly, it became increasingly clear that if historical circumstances greatly influenced or even dictated human attitudes, this must also apply to the historian, who could not shake off his or her own assumptions and presuppositions. This removed historians from their lofty positions as umpires and brought them into the historical arena itself.

Although the period of the Enlightenment saw much distinguished historical work, the prevailing tone was by no means historical. Religious revelation, empirical science or pure reason were still preferred methods of enquiry. History was relegated to a comparatively inferior role. It was, ironically, one of the greatest of eighteenth-century historians, Edward GIBBON, who dismissed history as 'little more than the register of the crimes, follies and misfortunes of mankind'. VOLTAIRE, another celebrated historian, agreed with him: it was 'no more than the portrayal of crimes and misfortunes'. From such a subject amusement might be had, distaste or disgust engendered, and a few telling examples exhibited, but it was scarcely a repository of wisdom. Nor, despite MONTESQUIEU, was there much sense of the role of history in explaining different cultures and societies. David HUME remarked that 'mankind is so much the same, in all times and places, that history informs us of nothing new in this particular. Its chief use is only to discover the constant and universal principles of human nature' (*Enquiry Concerning Human Understanding*).

The work of enthroning historical study as one of the most important methods available to the human mind was begun by Edmund Burke and German writers such as Herder and Wilhelm von Humboldt, reacting against what they regarded as the arid rationality of the French Revolution. The coincidence of this reaction with a significant rise in national feeling in many parts of Europe meant that, in the early nineteenth century, there was renewed interest in the study of the past. The work of RANKE placed German historians in the vanguard and, particularly after the establishment of the German Empire in 1871, historians in many countries modelled themselves upon German methods. By the end of the century, history as a discipline appeared to have achieved both a firm theoretical foundation and, in most countries, a secure institutional base in the universities. Ranke's much-quoted and often misunderstood dictum, that one should write history *wie es eigentlich gewesen* — as it really happened — seemed to invest the findings of historical study with rock-like certainty. Friedrich MEINECKE, tracing the evolution of German historical writing, called it, with some exaggeration, 'the greatest spiritual revolution which occidental thought has undergone'.

In the nineteenth century, the study of history had emerged as a conservative intellectual force to be directed against rash and doctrinaire reformers. In the course of time, there was a change of front. In the view of MARX and ENGELS, historical understanding was a weapon of the class struggle and their followers were assured of ultimate and inevitable victory. After the Bolshevik revolution of 1917, the struggle against Marxist history ceased to be a theoretical matter and became a pressing political need. This change was signalled by a significant shift in the meaning attached to historicism. The translation of the German *historismus* as 'historism' increasingly gave way to 'historicism', and the new term rapidly acquired pejorative undertones, hinting at defects and extravagancies. In the 1918 edition of the *Dictionary of Philosophy and Psychology*, the term 'historism' was still employed, but by 1942, in the *Dictionary of Philosophy*, 'historicism' had ousted it.

The new term became a means of belabouring left-wing or 'presentist' historians. In 1938 Raymond Aron in *Introduction à la philosophie de l'histoire* denied that history could be either scientific or predictive. Aron's book was not translated into English until 1961. In 1944 the publication of Karl Popper's *The Poverty of Historicism* gave a boost to the employment of the term. Popper was greatly concerned to contest the Marxist claim that historians could predict the future and dedicated his book to 'countless men and women' who had fallen victim to communist or fascist belief in historical destiny. Popper's motives, however admirable, were, therefore, as political as those of his adversaries, and he was in the common position of believing that everyone was biased save himself. As a political broadside, the book had some success, but it wrecked whatever chance was left of preserving historicism as a useful word. Indeed, Popper seems to have brought it into the title largely to make a piquant reflection of Marx's *The Poverty of Philosophy*. His introduction was particularly disturbing:

I have deliberately chosen the somewhat unfamiliar label 'historicism'. By introducing it I hope I shall avoid merely verbal quibbles: for nobody, I hope, will be tempted to question whether any of the arguments here discussed really or properly or essentially belong to historicism, or what the word 'historicism' really or properly or essentially means.

That was cavalier in the extreme. It is true that the arguments for and against historical prediction apply whether we call that practice 'historicism' or not. But it is a strange philosopher who regards definition as 'mere verbal quibbles' and one could hardly imagine a more disastrous start to what was necessarily a complex discussion.

Historicism, like a dragon, has been slain again and again. Four years after Popper's work was published in book form, E. H. CARR gave the 1961 Trevelyan lectures on *What is History?* and took the opportunity to complain that Popper had emptied the term of any precise meaning: 'Professor Popper uses the word 'historicism' as a catch-all for any opinion he dislikes.' That, indeed, is the trouble with the word now. Few, if any, historians admit to being historicists and it has became a mere term of abuse. Subsequent articles and even conferences to get the word

back on to its legs have merely served to confirm that it should be buried.   JAC

Reading

Aron, R.: *Introduction à la philosophie de l'histoire* (Paris: 1938).

History and Theory Suppl. 14 (1975) on Historicism.

Iggers, G. G.: Historicism, In *Dictionary of the History of Ideas*, ed. P. P. Wiener (New York: Scribner, 1973).

Lee, D. E. and Beck, R. N.: The meaning of 'historicism'. *American Historical Review* (April 1954) 568–79.

Meinecke, F.: *Die Entstehung des Historismus* (Munich and Berlin: 1936).

Momigliano, A.: Historicism revisited, In *Essays in Ancient and Modern Historiography* (1977).

Popper, K.: *The Poverty of Historicism* (London: Routledge & Kegan Paul, 1957).

Hobsbawm, Eric (b.1917)   The best-known Marxist historian of his generation, Eric Hobsbawm spent his early childhood in Vienna and Berlin; he has lived in England since 1932, but has kept the cosmopolitan interests and facility for languages which set him apart from most British historians. After Cambridge and war service, Hobsbawm returned to research and in 1947 moved to Birkbeck College, London, where he taught for the rest of his career. He became a fellow of the British Academy in 1976 and has received many honorary degrees.

Hobsbawm has a reputation in three fields: in the history of the nineteenth and twentieth centuries; in modern European politics; and in jazz. Superficially distinct, these fields are linked for him by his abiding interest in the history and future of the working class. His early research on the Fabians led him in the 1950s to study the impact of the industrial revolution on the British working class; this was followed by study of the upper working class, the aristocracy of labour. Meanwhile he was a founder member of *Past and Present*.

More recently, his work has embraced popular protest especially in Italy and Latin America; particularly influential have been his studies of *Bandits*. He has never glorified working class culture, seeing it as a reflection of poverty and oppression; bourgeois culture, too, is seen in context and illuminated, as in his three *Age of . . .* books, by astonishingly wide knowledge, or gently debunked, as in *The Invention of Tradition*.

History and working-class culture came together again in jazz criticism under the pseudonym of Francis Newton. But since the 1970s Hobsbawm's non-historical writing has been dominated by the emergence of Euro-communism in Italy and France and by the travails of the British left. A lifelong communist, he has preached the need for unity on the left; his political writing, like his history, is based on unemotional analysis and scholarship but expressed with fervour and passion.   RCF

Main publications

(Published by Weidenfeld & Nicolson, London, unless otherwise stated.)
The Jazz Scene (London: MacGibbon & Kee, 1959); *The Age of Revolution* (1962); *Labouring Men* (1964); *Industry and Empire* (1968); with G. Rude, *Captain Swing* (London: Lawrence & Wishart, 1970); *Primitive Rebels* (Manchester: Manchester University Press, 1971); *Bandits* (Harmondsworth: Penguin, 1972); *The Age of Capital* (1975); with T. Ranger, *The Invention of Tradition* (Cambridge: Cambridge University Press, 1983); *The Age of Empire* (1987).

Reading

Genovese, E. D.: The politics of class struggle in the history of society: an appraisal of the work of Eric Hobsbawm. In *The Power of the Past*, ed. P. Thane, G. Crossick and R. Floud (Cambridge: Cambridge University Press, 1984).

McClelland, K.: Bibliography of the writings of Eric Hobsbawm. In *Culture, Ideology and Politics*, ed. R. Samuel and G. Stedman Jones (London: Routledge, 1982).

Hodgkin, Thomas (b.1831, d.1913) Banker, historian of late-Antique and early-Medieval Italy. Hodgkin was born at Tottenham into a comfortable middle-class, traditionally Quaker, family. Excluded by his faith from the older English universities, he attended University College, London, where he wrote a prize-winning essay on 'The Study of History with special reference to Herodotus and Tacitus' and graduated BA with Classical Honours in 1851. Originally intended for the Bar, because of doubtful health he instead went into country banking with fellow-Quakers, and eventually settled at Newcastle upon Tyne, then the centre of a vigorous provincial culture. Unsurprisingly Hodgkin was a Gladstonian Liberal, although he later broke with the party on Irish Home Rule; he acclaimed the Italian kingdom's political achievements in the 1860s, while doubting whether it was rejecting Papacy energetically enough. On visiting Italy for the first time in the winter of 1868, Hodgkin wrote that he could now understand 'why Kings and Emperors . . . flung away whole realms of dim transalpine regions to secure one bright duchy or county on the sunny side of the Great Wall'; and next year he lectured in Newcastle on thirteenth- to sixteenth-century Italy. He subsequently planned a 9-volume history of the Peninsula to 1860. But a growing interest in the transition from 'Roman' to 'Germanic' Europe, reflected in his first book (on Claudian) and involvement in early scientific excavations of Hadrian's Wall, suggested a more restricted theme. Free from his banking duties only on Fridays and in summer holidays, Hodgkin published, between 1880 and 1899, the eight volumes (nearly 4000 pages!) of *Italy and her Invaders* (to 814). The work was written throughout in a vigorous if sometimes wordy prose, with trenchant judgements and showing an unusual sensitivity to the topographical settings of the events he described. T. F. TOUT, who like Hodgkin was a founding Fellow of the British Academy, correctly described the work as 'good old-fashioned narrative history of the best sort, scholarly but not too technical, literary yet precise', but criticized it for its lack of source-criticism and unfamiliarity with recent scholarly literature. Neither of these criticisms is justified. Only since the 1950s has Hodgkin's treatment of controversial aspects of the period he covers been largely superseded by international scholarship: and a comparable work of synthesis on the grand scale is still lacking.   DAB

Reading

Bullough, D. A.: *Italy and her Invaders* (Nottingham: University of Nottingham Press, 1968) [incl. brief survey of complex publishing history of Hodgkin's *Italy and her Invaders*].
Creighton, Louise: *Life and Letters of Thomas Hodgkin* (London: 1917).

Hoetink, Harry (b.1931) Harmannus (known as Harry) Hoetink was born in Groningen, the Netherlands, on 7 January 1931, and was educated at the University of Amsterdam, where he studied sociology and history. Between 1953 and 1977 he served in a number of teaching positions in Curaçao, Puerto Rico and the Netherlands. In 1977 he accepted the position of professor of anthropology and comparative sociology of Latin America and the Caribbean area at the Rijksuniversiteit at Utrecht.

Apart from Hoetink's formal academic duties, he served as a member of the commission investigating the Curaçao riots of 1969, and wrote a report on health insurance in the Netherland Antilles in 1971. He has been a member of the Foundation for Cultural Co-operation as well as the Foundation for Academic Research in the Tropics. He has served on the editorial boards of *Christoffel, Nieuwe West-Indische Gids, Boletin de Estudios Latinoamericanos y del Caribe, Caribbean Review,* and *Plantation Society.* He was also the editor of the Encyclopedia of the Netherlands Antilles, published in 1969.

A prolific, intellectually provocative writer, Hoetink has published extensively in English, Spanish and Dutch. His *Two Variants in Caribbean Race Relations* introduced the concept of the 'somatic norm image' as a basis of social differentiation, and made a major theoretical contribution to American ethnic studies. *The Dominican People, 1850–1900* brilliantly combined several disciplines and provided a model of historical reconstruction; *Slavery and Race Relations: a Study of their Nature and Nexus* destroyed the notion that conditions of slavery provided a good indicator of subsequent race relations in a free society.   FWK

Main publications

De Gespleten Samleving in Het Caribisch Gebied (1962) trans. as *Two Variants in Caribbean Race Relations* (London: Institute of Race Relations, 1967); *Caribbean Race Relations: a Study of Two Variants* (New York: Oxford University Press, 1971); *El Pueblo Dominicano, 1850–1900* (1971) trans. as *The Dominican People, 1850–1900* (Baltimore, MD: Johns Hopkins University Press, 1982); *Slavery and Race Relations: a Study of their Nature and Nexus* (New York: Oxford University Press, 1973).

Hofstadter, Richard (b.1916, d.1970) One of the most distinguished historians of his generation, Hofstadter emphasized complexity, ambiguity and irony in his wide-ranging examinations of American history and culture. He shaped his work in resistance to the economic determinism of the progressive generation of historians who had preceded him − Charles BEARD, Vernon PARRINGTON − but he shared with them an engagement with the present. His work was marked by extraordinary literary skill; by scorn for single causes; and by an interaction with modernist social science, psychoanalytic thought and literary criticism.

Hofstadter was born in Buffalo, in upstate New York. He attended the University of Buffalo where he found his friends among left-wing students and radical political organizations. His father was a Polish-born Jewish immigrant; his mother an American-born Episcopalian of German ancestry who died when he was ten. Although brought up a Protestant, when Hofstadter reached adulthood he identified himself as Jewish. The identification was strengthened when he married Felice Swados in 1936 and by his response to world politics in the era of war and holocaust.

After a brief attempt at law school, Hofstadter enrolled at Columbia University, where he received an MA in 1938 and a doctorate four years later. He spent the next four years as a member of the faculty at the University of Maryland. While he was there his son Dan was born and his young wife − whose politics and researches had deeply influenced his own − died. In 1946 he returned to Columbia, and remained there for the rest of his career.

In the first decade of his career Hofstadter published three important books in quick succession, offering his readers an intellectual history located in the realm of social history, and treating the transformation of ideas into ideologies that shaped the ways people thought about the possibilities of their society and culture. Against the patriotic hagiography of the cold war, *The American Political Tradition and the Men Who Made It* (1948) offered scepticism and the insistence that the American liberal consensus was grounded in capitalist culture and selfish ambition. In *The Age of Reform* (1955), Hofstadter showed that 'political culture', rather than narrowly defined partisan politics, could be the historian's subject. Subjecting political language to close scrutiny, he found in political myth, symbolism and language guides to the psychic needs which political campaigns served, guides even more revealing than considerations of simple economic self-interest. He advanced the hypothesis that the energy of reformers derived in large part from a sense of alienation and from anxiety about threats to social status.

Hofstadter often found the key to significant issues in the quirky and the marginal. Sentimentalizing neither the masses nor the reformers, he valued the independent intellectual, who was also vulnerable and marginal. In modern times such a person was likely to be found within the university, and Hofstadter — who was a member of the first generation of Jewish men to achieve faculty appointments at major American universities — displayed a long-standing concern for the conditions of intellectual and academic freedom. In his essays of the 1950s and 1960s, Hofstadter responded to McCarthyism by treating the radical right as 'pseudo-conservatives', and placing them as one among many long-standing American political traditions.

Although Hofstadter identified himself simply as a historian, his work was congruent with interdisciplinary approaches being developed in American studies. He was perplexed when he was linked with the consensus historians of the cold-war decade, accurately believing his work too marked by irony to be appropriated in that way; even when he drifted towards the centre at the end of his life — especially in his Columbia University commencement address of 1968, delivered in the context of the Vietnam war and a student revolt — he located himself as a critic on the left. His last books were suffused by a sense of tragedy as well as irony. In *The Progressive Historians* he returned to the men whose work he had begun his career by criticizing, now setting each historian in the context of his own times. *The Idea of a Party System* supplemented the scepticism of *The American Political Tradition* by admiration for the Founders' successor

generation for developing the strategies for a loyal opposition which made democratic politics possible.

The characteristic elements of Hofstadter's work were clear early in his career: a focus on ideology; an approach which stressed synthesis based on a fresh reading of sources already in print (rather than archival research); and the essay as his principal form. The least doctrinaire of academics, his students were permitted the freedom to go their own ways, and their work displays a wide variety of subjects and strategies of research. Hofstadter insisted throughout his life that his work as historian be consequential, not antiquarian; that it connect with the politics and argumentation of his own time. Along with Lionel Trilling and C. Wright Mills, he defined a career for the modern intellectual which was made both within and outside the academy.

LKK

Main publications

(Published by Knopf, New York, unless otherwise stated.)
Social Darwinism in American Thought, 1860–1915 (Philadelphia: University of Pennsylvania Press; London: Oxford University Press, 1944); *The American Political Tradition and the Men Who Made It* (1948): *The Development of Academic Freedom in the United States*, part 1 (New York: Columbia University Press, 1955); *The Age of Reform: from Bryan to F. D. R* (1955); *Anti-Intellectualism in American Life* (1963); *The Paranoid Style in American Politics and Other Essays* (1965); *The Progressive Historians: Turner, Beard, Parrington* (1968); *The Idea of a Party System: the Rise of Legitimate Opposition in the United States, 1780–1840* (Berkeley: University of California Press, 1969); *America at 1750: a Social Portrait* (1971).

Reading

Baker, S. S.: *Radical Beginnings: Richard Hofstadter and the 1930's* (Westport, Conn.: Greenwood, 1985).

Elkins, S. and McKitrick, E.: Richard Hofstadter: a progress. In *The Hofstadter Aegis: a Memorial* (New York: Knopf, 1974), pp. 300–67.

Fass, P. S.: Richard Hofstadter. In *Dictionary of Literary Biography: Twentieth Century Historians* 17 (1983) 211–30.

Singal, D. J.: Beyond consensus: Richard Hofstadter and American historiography. *American Historical Review* 89 (1984) 976–1004.

Holinshed, Raphael (*fl.* 1560–1580) Little is known of the author and editor (he was both) of *The Chronicles of England, Scotlande and Irelande* (1577). Holinshed worked for the printer Reyner Wolfe who had embarked on a collection which would have included maps and covered the histories of all nations. When Wolfe died in 1573 the work (much reduced in size and restricted to the nations of Britain) came out for the first time in 1577. The form of *The Chronicles* was basically the traditional town chronicle of London, which had greatly evolved since its first beginning in the thirteenth and fourteenth centuries. But for the early Tudors such chronicles were of considerable amplitude, reaching their culmination in works like those of Fabyan and Edward HALL, the latter of whom absorbed the recent humanist works of More and Polydore Vergil. These works also influenced Holinshed, independently of his use of earlier chronicles. The publication history of the work that goes under Holinshed's name is extremely complicated. When a second edition came out in 1586 it was coordinated by John Vowell (or Hooker, d.1601) and had many additions as well as coming down to the dangerous contemporary scene. This edition was accordingly heavily censored by the Privy Council. It was, however, Vowell's edition which was widely read by the Elizabethan dramatists and from which Shakespeare in particular derived his plots for the fifteenth-century historical plays as well as for *Macbeth*, *King Lear* and *Cymbeline*. 'Holinshed' in this way was to lay his imprint on generations of Englishmen's view of their past. Shakespeare in particular was greatly influenced not only by the facts in Holinshed's *Chronicles* but often adopted the words before him. The second edition was reprinted by a consortium of London booksellers in six volumes in 1807–8, including the matter suppressed in the edition of 1586.　　　　　　　　　　　　DH

Main publications

The Chronicles of England, Scotlande and Irelande (London: 1577).

Reading

Boswell Stone, W. G.: *Shakespeare's Holinshed* (1896).
Levy, F. J.: *Tudor Historical Thought* (San Marino: The Huntingdon Library, 1967) ch. 5.

Holtzmann, Robert (b.1873, d.1946)　After studying history under Harry Bresslau and Paul Scheffer-Boichorst, Holtzmann held chairs successively at Giessen, Breslau (Wrocław), Halle and Berlin. He became emeritus in 1939; after the end of the war he had intended to resume his work as a university teacher but he died before he could do so. His major contribution to historical scholarship lay in the field of bibliography and works of reference. He was active between the wars as a member of the Comité international des sciences historiques; he edited the seventh edition of Gebhardt's *Handbuch der deutschen Geschichte* and revised the standard guide to the narrative sources of German medieval history so extensively that his edition is essentially a new work. His other major interest was the German colonization of eastern Europe, which led to a major edition of Thietmar of Merseburg's *Chronicle* and a history of Germany under the Saxon emperors. The latter is one of the last works in the long tradition of German historical writing which drew political inspiration for Germany's present from the supposedly most glorious and united period of her past.　　TAR

Main publications

Französische Verfassungsgeschichte (Munich: Oldenbourg, 1910); W. Wattenbach, *Deutschlands Geschichtsquellen im Mittelalter*, 7th edn rev. R. Holtzmann (Berlin: Ebering, 1938–43); *Die Chronik des Bischofs Thietmar von Merseburg und ihre Korveier Überarbeitung*. Monumenta Germaniae Historica, Scriptores rerum Germanicarum n. 9, Berlin: Weidmann, 1935); *Geschichte der sächsischen Kaiserzeit* (München: Callwey, 1941).

Homans, George Caspar (b.1910)　From a patrician New England background Homans went to Harvard to study literature and became interested in sociology in the early 1930s. His historical research into the thirteenth-century English peasantry arose from his admiration for Pareto's theories of social systems, and he was also influenced by Mayo's psychological and anthropological teachings. His achievement as a historian was to recognize that medieval manorial court records allowed the investigation of family relationships, marriage customs and retirement arrangements. He was able to define regional differences in family structures, though he took little note of social change. His conservative and traditional outlook made it natural for him to study the roots of New England in the old world, and his emphasis on Germanic origins led him in the 1950s and 1960s to expound an unfashionable ethnic interpretation of medieval society. By this time historical writing had become a sideline for him and he was best known as a sociologist. CCD

Main publications

English Villagers of the Thirteenth Century (Cambridge, Mass.: Harvard University Press, 1941).

Reading

Homans, G. C.: *Coming to My Senses: The Autobiography of a Sociologist* (New Brunswick, NJ: Transaction Books, 1984).

Hoskins, W. G. See LOCAL HISTORY, ENGLISH.

Huizinga, Johan (b.1872, d.1945) Included among the greatest historians of this century, Huizinga's place is based largely upon his famous book, *The Waning of the Middle Ages* (1919). But he also deserves a prominent position among historians for his perceptive book on *Erasmus of Rotterdam* (1924), his many essays and articles such as 'Renaissance and Realism' (1920), 'Dutch civilization in the seventeenth century' (1932), and the other papers gathered together in such collections as *Men and Ideas*. Huizinga was above all a cultural historian. His 'path to history', as he called it in an autobiographical essay, was unconventional. Beginning as a highly promising Sanskrit scholar and philologist with a doctoral thesis (1897) on the role of the jester in Indian drama, he did not turn towards medieval and Renaissance history until after 1902. The exhibition of early Netherlandish painting held at Bruges in that year stimulated him to look afresh at northern civilization in the later middle ages. Although he continued to teach and write as an Orientalist until 1904, he became professor of general history at Groningen in 1905, taking the chair of history at Leiden in 1915. During the 1930s he became increasingly concerned by contemporary

issues and published a number of polemical and topical works, especially *In the Shadow of Tomorrow* (1936) which dealt with western cultural decline and the forces which he felt were undermining western civilization. Huizinga died in the food shortage in Holland during the winter of 1944–5 after imprisonment by the Nazis.

Huizinga's approach to history could be described as essentially aesthetic. 'A feeling of immediate contact with the past', he wrote, 'is a sensation as deep as the purest enjoyment of art.' As far as he had a philosophy of history at all, it was based upon Hegelian dialectic and is perhaps best expressed in *The Waning of the Middle Ages*. In that book he saw the later middle ages 'as the dying of the past rather than the announcement of the future' and he attempted to re-interpret the art of the Van Eycks and their contemporaries, seeing it as a reflection of other manifestations of their times. This kind of unitary or holistic interpretation of a civilization clearly owed much to Hegel, but also reflected some of the aesthetic movements of the 1890s. By the 1930s Huizinga was more concerned with such questions as the means whereby both overt and latent violence in human society could be contained and by the relationship between play and seriousness in culture. *Homo Ludens: a Study of the Play-Element of Culture* (1949) drew upon a wide range of historical examples to illustrate his views. Although much criticized, there can be no doubt of his standing among the great cultural historians of the past century. His vision of 'the forms of life, thought and art in France and the Netherlands in the fourteenth and fifteenth centuries', as he sub-titled *The Waning of the Middle Ages*, bears comparison with that of BURCKHARDT. His influence on historical scholarship has been subtle and indirect, and he founded no 'school'. With characteristic modesty he singled out his biography of his friend the painter Jan Veth (1927) and his history of Groningen university (1914) as his best work. But his readers would undoubtedly choose *The Waning of the Middle Ages*, with all its faults, as the masterpiece which shows him at the height of his powers as a historian. MV

HUME, DAVID

Main publications

The Waning of the Middle Ages (1919) (Harmondsworth: Penguin, 1955); *Erasmus of Rotterdam* (1924) (London: Phaidon Press, 1952):, *Homo Ludens* (1944) (London: Paladin, 1970); *Dutch Civilization in the Seventeenth Century and Other Essays*, ed. P. Geyl and F. W. N. Hugenholtz (London: Collins, 1968); *Men and Ideas*, ed. J. S. Holmes and H. Van Marle (New York and London: Harper & Row, 1970).

Reading

Colie, R. L.: Johan Huizinga and the task of cultural history. *American Historical Review* 69 (1964) pp. 607–30.

Geyl, Pieter: Huizinga as an accuser of his age. In *Encounters in History* (London: Collins, 1963).

Gombrich, E. H.: Huizinga's *Homo Ludens*. In Koops et al. (1973) pp. 133–54.

Hugenholtz, F. W. N. 1973: The Fame of a Masterwork. In Koops et al. (1973) pp. 91–103.

Jacob, E. F.: Huizinga and the Autumn of the Middle Ages. In *Essays in Later Medieval History* (Manchester: Manchester University Press, 1968), pp. 141–53.

Keen, M. H.: Huizinga, Kilgour and the Decline of Chivalry. *Medievalia et Humanistica* 7 (1977) 1–20.

Koops, W. R. H., Kossmann, E. H. and Van der Plaat, G.: *Johan Huizinga 1872–1972* (The Hague: Martinus Nijhof, 1973).

Vale, M.: *War and Chivalry* (London: Duckworth, 1981), pp. 1–13.

Hume, David (b.1711, d.1777) The younger son of Joseph Hume of Ninewells, from a small Berwickshire estate, Hume was educated at the University of Edinburgh from 1722 to 1725/6. He then studied privately, with three years in France from 1734. In his early years Hume was pre-eminently a moral philosopher, though his greatest works, including the *Treatise on Human Nature* (1739) received a disappointing reception. He failed in 1744 to secure the chair of moral philosophy at Edinburgh, at least partly because of his reputation for scepticism. By 1751, after several temporary posts, he had decided to settle in Edinburgh and in 1752 was made keeper of the Advocates Library. He became a leading member of the Edinburgh 'literati' in the most creative period of the Scottish Enlightenment, though he could still be attacked, as he was by the General Assembly of the Church of Scotland in 1755. As his historical and political writing gained international recognition after 1752, he began to look for a wider stage. In Paris from 1763 to 1767, as secretary to Lord Hertford at the British Embassy, he was lionized for his historical writing. In 1767 he returned as a senior civil servant to London, and in 1769 moved back to Edinburgh, where he was most at home in the society of his friends.

Hume wrote a number of essays on historical and political topics, published from 1741 to 1758. His major historical work was the *History of England* (1754–62); the first volume covered the period 1603–49 and was followed by volumes taking the *History* on to 1688, those covering the sixteenth century, and finally two covering the period from Julius Caesar to Henry VII. Hume, and most later readers, found the first volume the best. The *History* was greeted with acclaim and established Hume's reputation much more surely than his philosophical writings had done. The complete work was subject to a number of revised editions in his lifetime. Hume ridiculed the practice of research as merely the collection of tedious uninteresting facts, and insisted that the proper work of the historian was the orderly and methodical perception of the general lessons which history offers to humanity. Nowhere however did Hume systematically discuss his philosophy of history; it can only be pieced together as a part of a much wider project for a 'science of man'. Yet at the same time he was also greatly concerned with readability and entertainment; his preoccupation with style is impressive and the pace of his narrative speedy.

Hume's historical writing was in many ways rooted in his moral philosophy. He recognized the imperfect condition of human nature, the power of the passions and of the irrational motives which the study of psychology revealed. Custom, not reason, tended to guide individual behaviour; but strong passions, including religious 'enthusiasm', could stimulate violent innovation. Such disruptive forces could be moderated only through the slow growth of a civilization which brought with it common agreement on basic principles of legislation and co-existence, learnt through education, through social sympathies, through national awareness. The test for governments lay in the extent to which they advanced that process of civilization. In his discussion, for instance, of the House of Commons in 1641, Hume stressed how a new kind of passion for liberty in the Commons created a novel, revolutionary situation. But Charles I had reacted arrogantly and thoughtlessly, without that wisdom and moderation which might have preserved the political fabric.

Hume was also one (though not the most representative) of a group of Scottish historians, including ROBERTSON and SMITH, who were committed to the study of human societies in a methodical and comparative way. Their aim was to trace human development through certain common stages of progress from barbarism to refinement. There was agreement on the constant human desire for improvement in the economy, politics and society. Yet stress on the material context of change led to the view that progress was not a matter of conscious planning or legislation, but often came about accidentally or through the clash of opposed interests. Hume was profoundly interested in social and economic change, though for him, unlike Smith, the proper criterion of progress lay ultimately in the degree of political civilization reached. Still, in his essays he tackled such themes as the relationship between growing material wealth and political liberty. For him the roots of seventeenth-century conflict lay in the expansion of the sixteenth-century world — in navigation, wealth, commerce and exploration. Nevertheless, his *History* can be criticized for its relegation of social and economic affairs to the appendices; its strength lay in the force of its political narrative, which powerfully conveyed that irreconcilable clash of opposing interests which had accidentally generated that British constitution so much admired in his own century.

In his political essays there is much that can be learned of Hume's outlook on contemporary British politics. He rejected Whig claims to the existence of an original contract and Tory justifications of divine right and passive obedience. He prided himself on his detachment and distance from any party, compared with other historians such as the Huguenot RAPIN-THOYRAS: he attempted to root the political phenomena of his own day in human behaviour and social change. Similarly the style of the *History* is judicious and balanced, and he attempts to weigh praise and blame in, for example, his treatment of James I. Nevertheless he was accused of Tory sympathies: the charge had some foundation, since in his treatment of the 1640s his attacks on the fanaticism of Independency left little doubt that his sympathies by this stage were with the monarchy. Recent interpretation of Hume, especially by Duncan Forbes, has stressed the way in which, though claiming impartiality, the *History* was rooted in mid-eighteenth century political preoccupations, and particularly the need to defend the principle of authority in the shape of the Whig establishment.

JR

Main publications

The History of England from the Invasion of Julius Caesar to the Revolution in 1688 ..., 8 vols (London: 1763); *Essays Moral, Political and Literary.* In *The Philosophical Works of David Hume*, vol. 3 ed. T. H. Green and T. H. Grose (London: Longmans, Green, 1874–5).

Reading

Forbes, D.: *Hume's Philosophical Politics* (Cambridge: Cambridge University Press, 1975).
Miller, D.: *Philosophy and Ideology in Hume's Political Thought* (Oxford: Clarendon Press, 1981).
Mossner, E. C.: An apology for David Hume, historian. *Publications of the Modern Languages Association of America*, 56 (1941) 657–90.
——: *The Life of David Hume* (Clarendon Press, 1954).

I

Ibn Khaldun (b.1332, d.1406)   Certainly the most remarkable and original historical thinker to be produced by the civilization of medieval Islam, Ibn Khaldun may be regarded as a historian, a philosopher of history, and a proto-sociologist. His great work is the *Muqaddima*, the introduction to his universal history, the *Kitab al-'ibar*. In this he expounded his understanding of the causes of change in the social and political organization of mankind. The effect of the ideas to be found in the *Muqaddima* was not great in Ibn Khaldun's own day, but they have come into their own in more recent times, and they continue to exercise a considerable influence on the thought of contemporary writers such as Ernest Gellner.

Ibn Khaldun's education was the conventional one of a Muslim man of letters, encompassing the Koran, Muslim traditions (*hadith*), Islamic jurisprudence and philosophy. He was born in Tunis, and played a part in the turbulent politics of the north African states until, in 1382, he went to Egypt. There too he enjoyed high office, being several times appointed by the Mamluk sultan to the office of chief judge (*qadi*) of the Malikites (one of the four schools of Sunni Islamic law mutually recognized as orthodox). In 1401 he met the central Asian conqueror Tamerlane, who was then besieging Damascus, and he left in his autobiography a vivid account of their discussions.

During a three-year period beginning in 1375, Ibn Khaldun withdrew from active politics and lived in the castle of Qal'at Ibn Salama. There he completed his *Muqaddima* in which he presented a cyclical view of history. Commencing with a consideration of man's physical environment, he concludes that man is a political being who needs to associate with others. Hence he sees the state as a natural growth — a most unusual point of view for an Islamic political theorist. He regards urban civilization as the highest form of political organization. For the formation and perpetuation of a state, kingship is necessary to impose order and restrain conflict among people. But state formation cannot come from within urban civilization, which lacks the essential ingredient, *'asabiyya*.

'Asabiyya, 'natural solidarity' or 'group feeling', is found in the more primitive kind of social structure, that of the nomads and semi-nomads, since the conditions under which life is lived outside the cities require tribal organization. *'Asabiyya* is founded on the blood ties, the alliances and the relationships of clientage which exist in tribal society. Within each nomadic community there will be a ruling family, normally that whose *'asabiyya* is the strongest. The nomads possess strength, courage and endurance, as well as *'asabiyya*, to a far higher degree than the more 'civilized' townspeople. Consequently they have the capability to conquer an existing civilized state, or to create a new one. For such a creation one further binding element is required: religion. The classic example is that of the early Muslim conquests. The Arabs, united under the rule of the Prophet and his successors by both a strong *'asabiyya* and a divinely revealed religion, were invincible. Beginning as no more than unconsidered Arabian tribes, they were able to set up the urban civilization of the caliphate.

The state, once established, proceeds

through a natural sequence of growth, maturity, decline, and fall. Ibn Khaldun's opinion was that no dynasty could expect to survive for more than three or at most four generations. Civilization inevitably erodes tribal *'asabiyya*. The ruler becomes an absolute monarch rather than a tribal chief, and begins to rely on a paid army and bureaucracy, and no longer on his virile tribesmen. Luxury and leisure become the aims of life; the state enjoys economic prosperity. Comfort is conducive to physical weakness and moral degeneration. Decline sets in. Loss of military effectiveness is revealed when either a civilized state at an earlier stage of development, or an outside tribal grouping, attacks the state. It falls; the conqueror becomes the ruler, and the cycle begins again.

This powerful and persuasive theoretical framework is illustrated in the *Muqaddima* by many examples. It has been said in criticism of Ibn Khaldun that although his scheme fits well enough the circumstances of north Africa in his own day, it is not of such universal application, even within the world of Islam, as he seems to have supposed. Another criticism is that having in the introduction to the *Kitab al-'ibar* propounded an exciting new way of writing history, he then went on, in the remainder of his book, not to write it. Nevertheless the author of the *Muqaddima* remains in a class of his own. (See ISLAMIC HISTORIOGRAPHY). DOM

Main writings

Muqaddima, 3 vols, trans. F. Rosenthal, (London: Routledge, 1958); one-volume abridgement by N. J. Dawood (London: Routledge, 1967); selections trans. C. Issawi: *An Arab Philosophy of History* (London: John Murray, 1950); *Ibn Khaldun and Tamerlane: their Historic Meeting in Damascus, 1401 AD (803 AH)*, trans. W. J. Fischel (Berkeley and Los Angeles: University of California Press, 1952).

Reading

Lambton, A. K. S.: *State and Government in Medieval Islam* (Oxford: Oxford University Press, 1981) ch 10.
Mahdi, M.: *Ibn Khaldun's Philosophy of History* (London: Allen & Unwin, 1957).

idealism See CROCE; HEGEL; MOORE.

imperial historiography The word imperialism only became naturalized in the English language in the late nineteenth century. It was at first a derogatory term, associated with Bonapartism and especially the meretricious empire of Napoleon III. In 1869 *The Times* could speak contemptuously of 'Imperialism, or, indeed any worse form of despotism'. But by the end of the century it had became a laudatory term, signifying what Lord Rosebery called 'that greater pride in empire, which is called Imperialism and is a larger patriotism'. Changing attitudes to empire were associated with Social Darwinism; the unscientific application of ideas of evolution to human history and the belief that Charles Darwin's theory of the 'survival of the fittest' meant the natural dominance of the strongest and most aggressive. The Great Powers came to believe that they were working out their necessary destiny in carving up the rest of the world between themselves.

Not all interpretations were quite so crude. Classical education still dominated the nineteenth century and people looked back to the empires of Greece and Rome for precedents. One of the great proconsuls, Lord Cromer, when he became president of the Classical Association in 1910, delivered his presidential address on 'Ancient and modern imperialism'. In preparing it, he consulted many of the leading scholars of the time, including Gilbert Murray and J. B. BURY. It worried Cromer that the British empire had not succeeded in assimilating its colonial subjects as the Roman empire had done. His correspondents, who later included A. J. Balfour and James BRYCE, almost all held that colour-consciousness was a recent development and that there was little evidence for it in the ancient world.

Although Bryce had already published (1901) an essay on 'The Roman empire and the British empire in India', many thought that the British empire, at least in the white colonies of settlement, more closely resembled the Greek, or Hellenistic, empire of loosely associated trading colonies. The highly organized and centralized French empire, above all others, had modelled itself on the Roman empire. Even when governing non-European peoples, the British tended to resort to the device of 'indirect rule' and tried to leave foreign cultures intact.

The classical empires provided exemplars for later empires but, in recent years, the searching criticisms to which the latter have been subjected have also been applied to the former. Scholars have asked how far they were 'accidental', 'defensive' or 'exploitative'. A product of the Cambridge classical seminar, *Imperialism in the Ancient World* (eds P. D. A. Garnsey and C. R. Whittaker) provides an excellent introduction to this inquiry; J. de Romilly, *Thucydides and Athenian Imperialism*, is also important.

Nowadays 'imperialism' is usually taken to mean the rule of one people over other peoples but it has an alternative meaning of a system of government under an emperor. Understood in this sense the Roman empire had two successors, the Byzantine and the Holy Roman empires. The Byzantine, or Eastern, empire was a theocracy held together by allegiance to the Orthodox Church and incorporating many different peoples. The Holy Roman, or Western, empire, which nominally lasted from the coronation of Charlemagne in AD 800 to its destruction by Napoleon in 1806, represented, especially in the high middle ages, a secular alternative to the domination of the papacy. A good modern discussion of its nature can be found in R. Folz, *The Concept of Empire in Western Europe*; but Bryce's classic, *Holy Roman Empire* (1864), with its sense of both a classical and a modern dimension, has never been completely superseded.

The Byzantine empire was taken over by the Ottoman Turkish empire in 1453 – a useful reminder that empires are not a purely European phenomenon. The greatest non-European empires included the Chinese and Persian empires, the Mogul empire in India and the Aztec and Inca empires in America. As historical studies become less Eurocentric, all have attracted scholars and popularizers. A good example of the latter is Bamber Gascoigne's *The Great Mughals* (London, 1971).

The western Roman empire fell apart to allow the emergence of the national states of modern Europe. Competition between them, the confidence engendered by the Renaissance and the religious quarrels of the Reformation led to the first wave of overseas expansion, well chronicled by J. H. Parry in *Europe and a Wider World, 1415–1715* (1949). The discrediting of mercantilist theories of national self-sufficiency in the early nineteenth century seemed to destroy the *raison d'être* for these empires, but very little colonial territory was actually relinquished (see J. A. GALLAGHER). The last quarter of the nineteenth century saw another great scramble for empire, during which the whole of Africa and much of Asia (apart from India which had already been appropriated by Britain) was carved up between the European powers.

At the time both advocates of imperialism, such as Joseph Chamberlain, and severe critics, such as J. A. Hobson, believed the motives to be mainly economic. This line of argument was endorsed by Marxists, notably by Lenin himself in *Imperialism: the highest stage of capitalism* (1916), in which he identified imperialism with the monopoly stage of capitalism. Lenin believed that imperialism had led to the first world war which would, in turn, lead to the revolution of the proletariat and the overthrow of capitalism. With some notable exceptions, such as W. L. Langer or J. S. Schumpeter who preferred diplomatic or social explanations, historians between the wars, even if they were not Marxists, accepted the essentially economic nature of imperialism. This view was challenged by Sir Keith HANCOCK in 1949, who pointed out that the European scramble for colonies preceded the emergence of monopoly capitalism, which Lenin himself had placed about 1900. There ensued a very important debate on the motives for European imperialism. Among the leading contributors were professors Robinson and Gallagher, Fieldhouse and Platt.

Marxist historians were now on the defensive, not least because the European empires were being dissolved and the revolution of the proletariat had still not arrived. This led in turn to a reassessment of what Lenin had meant by 'imperialism' and the conclusion that Lenin had used the term to describe a particular form of capitalism, which was only loosely linked to the acquisition of overseas territories. In fact, Lenin's use of the word seems to have been ambiguous. The clearest exposition of the issues is by a non-Marxist historian, Eric Stokes, in his article 'Late nineteenth-century colonial expansion and the attack on the theory of economic imperialism: a case of mistaken identity?', *The Historical Journal* 12 (1969) 285–301. The debate led to a series of seminars in Oxford in which Marxists and non-Marxists tried to arrive at common definitions. They failed, but the attempt led to interesting papers by the leading protagonists, published under the editorship of R. Owen and B. Sutcliffe.

The debate on the motives for European imperialism continues. There are important suggestions in H.-U. Wehler, *Bismarck und der Imperialismus* (Berlin, 1969); W. Baumgart, *Imperialism: the Idea and Reality of British and French Colonial Expansion, 1880–1914* (1975) (Oxford, 1982); and in the early chapters of F. Fischer, *Germany's Aims in the First World War* (1961) (New York, 1967). But academic interest has begun to turn to the decolonization of the European empires and the relations between the advanced industrialized nations and what is now called the Third World. American scholars have been prominent in this. Interesting contributions to the debate include W. R. Louis, *Imperialism at Bay: the United States and the Decolonization of the British Empire, 1941–1945* (Oxford, 1977), and P. Gifford and W. R. Louis, eds, *The Transfer of Power in Africa: Decolonization 1940–1960* (Hartford, Conn., 1982).   MEC

Reading

De Romilly, J.:*Thucydides and Athenian Imperialism* (1947) (Oxford: Blackwell, 1963).

Fieldhouse, D. K.: *Economics and Empire 1830–1914* (London: Weidenfeld & Nicolson, 1973).

Folz, Robert: *The Concept of Empire in Western Europe from the Fifth to the Fourteenth Century* (1953) (London: Edward Arnold, 1969).

Garnsey, P. D. A. and Whittaker, C. R. eds, *Imperialism in the Ancient World* (Cambridge: Cambridge University Press, 1978).

Hobson, J. A.: *Imperialism: a Study* (1902) (London: Unwin Hyam, 1988).

Koebner, Richard: *Empire* (Cambridge University Press, 1961).

Koebner, Richard and Schmidt, H. D.: *Imperialism: a Political Word 1840–1960* (Cambridge University Press, 1964).

Lenin, V. I.: *Imperialism: the Highest Stage of Capitalism* (1916).

Owen, R. and Sutcliffe, B.: *Studies in the Theory of Imperialism* (London: Longman, 1972).

Parry, J. H.: *Europe and a Wider World, 1415–1715* (London: Hutchinson, 1949).

Platt, D. C. M.: *Finance, Trade, and Politics: British Foreign Policy, 1815–1914* (Oxford: Clarendon Press, 1968).

Robinson, R. & Gallagher, J.: *Africa and the Victorians: the official mind of imperialism* (London: Macmillan, 1961)

Thornton, A. P.: *The Imperial Idea and its Enemies* (Macmillan, 1963).

——: *Doctrines of Imperialism* (New York: Wiley, 1965).

Indian historiography   Historical writing was one of the least developed areas of ancient Indian culture. The mythological texts, the Puranas, did however include dynastic lists which contained rudimentary material for political history. A few Sanskrit texts from the Hindu 'middle ages' also record the achievements of individual monarchs or the history of regional dynasties. Kalhana's *Rajatarangini*, a history of Kashmir, is the best known among these works.

Systematic chronicles of political events, especially wars, conquests, succession of dynasties and the like, really begin with the Muslim chroniclers, who were often historians at the courts of the Turko-Afghan rulers (thirteenth to early sixteenth century) of the Delhi-based empires and the various provincial kingdoms. While concerned primarily with the rise and fall of dynasties, these chronicles, usually written in Persian, the language of court and culture, often contain valuable data on the administrative system, socio-economic conditions and topography. Amir Khusrau, the most famous poet of medieval India, and Ziauddin Barani, a contemporary of the eccentric yet highly innovative fourteenth-century ruler, Muhammad bin Tughluq, are reckoned the finest historians of the Turko-Afghan era.

The court historians of the Mughal empire, established in 1526, added copiously to this particular genre of historical writing. There are several extant accounts for virtually every major ruler of the dynasty. In addition, two of the emperors, Babur and Jahangir, have left behind their memoirs. The historiography for the reign of Akbar is particularly rich, especially because it includes the doctrinally eclectic minister Abul Fazl's admiring account of his patron and friend, the *Akbarnamah*, and the more critical and fundamentalist chronicle written by his rival in court, Badauni. The Mughal period also witnessed the development of regional historiographies, the *bakhars* of Maharashtra in western India and the *buranjis* of Assam in north-east India. Orissa had her own chronicle of events, the *Madlafanji*. The twilight of the Mughal successor state in Bengal, technically a province of the empire, and the foundation of the English East India Company's rule in the region is described in a remarkably objective Persian chronicle, Ghulam Hussain Tabatabai's *Siyar-ul-Mutaqqherin*.

The transition to modern historical writing on India has a twofold origin. It begins with the linguistic studies of the late eighteenth century, especially the pioneering work of Sir William Jones, which explored the affinities between ancient Sanskrit and other Indo-Aryan languages. Indological studies with their investigation of ancient Indian philosophy, literature, legal texts and later archaeology laid the foundation for the writing of the country's cultural history. British, and later German, Indologists were the pioneers in the field. Among the early Indian pioneers was the antiquarian Rajendralal Mitra. A second source of modern historiography was the accounts of the English East India Company's rise to power and, in that context, some very scholarly accounts of the indigenous states and peoples with whom the British came into conflict. An early classic, James Mill's *History of the British Rule in India*, describes the rise of British power down to the second decade of the nineteenth century. This fairly straightforward narrative however is informed by the emerging pattern of racial attitudes: a profound contempt for the society and civilization of India. MACAULAY's historical essays on India, including the one on Clive, are further examples of this emerging attitude. Grant-Duff's *A History of the Mahrattas* belongs to a different genre. It is the first serious attempt to reconstruct the history of an Indian people. Despite its predominantly political focus and narrative method, it has insightful accounts of Mahratta society and administration. James Tod's *Annals and Antiquities of Rajasthan*, based on ballads and folk traditions, offered by contrast a highly romanticized and inaccurate 'history' of the Rajput principalities and a misleading description of their society based on clans as an Asian version of Europe's feudalism.

The narrative tradition has long dominated the writing of Indian history. In the early years of this century V. A. Smith tried to reconstruct an inclusive structure of Indian history, following partly in the footsteps of his nineteenth-century predecessor, Elphinstone, and supplemented his basically political narrative with descriptions of administration, culture and society emphasizing India's 'unity in diversity'. He drew upon the accumulated Indological and Indo-Islamic scholarship — works such as the dynastic lists prepared by Pargiter, Max Müller's studies of Vedic literature, R. G. Bhandarkar's monographs, the epigraphic and archaeological studies under the auspices of the Archaeological Survey of India and the translations of Persian chronicles published by the Asiatic Society — to build up his work of survey. Around his time and in the decades that followed, a large number of Indian scholars began to produce monographic works based on detailed analysis of original source material. Sir Jadunath Sarkar's multi-volumed *A History of Aurangzeb*, Sardesai's *History of the Marathas*, H. C. Raychaudhuri's *A Political History of Ancient India*, Nilakantha Sastri's *The Cholas* are some of the outstanding examples of this new scholarship. Concerned with factual accuracy, these studies too were primarily focused on narration and description, but the social and administrative systems as well as cultural achievements began to feature prominently in some of them. Despite the effort at objectivity, much of this work was nationalist in inspiration. The attempts of K. P. Jaiswal to discover democratic governments in the tribal oligarchies of ancient India and R. C. Majumdar's description of the south-east Asian archipelago in ancient times as 'Greater India' are instances in point.

An essentially political debate on the economic consequences of the colonial rule generated a historical controversy. The anti-colonial position emphasizing the thesis of exploitation and impoverishment was projected most powerfully in R. C. Dutt's two volumes on the economic history of British India. The projection of a more positive assessment of the British impact on India's economy is the central concern of works by Theodor Morisson, Vera Anstey, Knowles and others. Moreland's writings on the economy of Mughal India — works of great scholarship and considerable analytical skill — also drew attention to the relative excellence of British rule.

The debate on the nature of the colonial impact grew sharper in the period after the second world war. Monographic research on agriculture, trade and regional economies, based on archival sources, now dealt with the themes of exploitation and impoverishment and alternatively with growth and structural reasons for poverty. Marxist historical analysis became a prominent feature of Indian historiography. At the other end of the spectrum, studies of indigenous politics explored the networks of self-interest questioning the centrality of ideology in Indian nationalism. A new 'school' of 'subaltern' studies is concerned to establish the autonomy and importance of underprivileged elements in society as a factor in the political and cultural processes. Quantitative methods have had their impact on the study of trade history. Most recent work draws attention to the relevance of ecological factors, the Braudelian concepts of historical time, and comparison with the historical experiences of other traditional cultures.   TRi

Reading

Case, M. H.: *South Asian History: a Guide to Periodicals, Dissertations and Newspapers* (Princeton, NJ: Princeton University Press, 1968).

Philips, C. H. ed.: *Historians of India, Pakistan and Ceylon* (Oxford: Oxford University Press, repr. 1962).

Sarkar, Sumit: *History of Modern India* (London: Macmillan, 1984).

Innis, Harold A. (b.1894, d.1952) A Canadian, Innis developed the 'staple thesis' which was an important theoretical tool for the analysis of the development in communities of 'recent settlement' in the Americas, Australasia and parts of Africa. Innis never stated his argument in abstract theoretical terms but deduced it from his study of the Canadian fur trade published in 1930. The 'staple thesis' explains how commercial capitalists/entrepreneurs developed the large-scale production of natural resources — at first furs and fish, then timber, agricultural and mineral products — for sale in the markets of more populous and industrialized societies. The secondary consequences of this commercial activity were manifested in the establishment of transport networks, cities, financial institutions and the industrial and agricultural activities necessary to sustain the world-wide trade in natural resources. The trade in staples was the major factor in the development of the United States (until the Civil War), Canada, Australia, New Zealand, Brazil and Argentina.

Innis tended to take a pessimistic view of the outcome of the 'staple thesis'. The exploitation of natural resources created communities and produced wealth in abundance, but this did not necessarily lead to the development of mature, well-balanced societies as was the case in the United States. Dependence on the trade in staples exposed communities to the hazards of world markets and changes in consumer demand, over which nations born of the staple trade had only limited powers of control.

In his last years Innis developed an interest in information and the techniques for its diffusion, as fundamental factors in social, intellectual and political change. His *Empire and Communication*, published in 1950, is a seminal work the implications of which have not yet been fully explored.   HSF

Main publications

(Published by the University of Toronto Press, Toronto, unless otherwise stated.)

A History of the Canadian Pacific Railway (1923); *The Fur Trade* (1930); *The Cod Fisheries* (New Haven Conn.: Yale University Press, 1940); 'Minerva's Owl', presidential address to the Royal Society of Canada: Transactions and Proceedings of the Royal Society of Canada (Ottawa: 1947); *Empire and Communications* (Oxford: Clarendon Press, 1950); *The Bias of Communication* (1951); *Changing Concepts* of Time (1952); *Essays in Canadian Economic History*, ed. Mary Quale Innis (1956).

Iorga, Nicolae (b.1871, d.1940) Romanian historian, statesman, journalist, dramatist and poet. Iorga was the son of a lawyer. He studied at the universities of Iasi, Paris and Berlin. In 1893, having previously graduated from the École des Hautes Études, he took his doctorate at Leipzig under the supervision of Karl Lamprecht. In 1894 he won the Bucharest chair of universal history, medieval and modern, which he held until 1940. Iorga early revealed a formidable power of research as editor of numerous documents on Romanian history at a time when a great deal of it was obscure. This activity fed his aspiration to render past life in its 'fullness', thus following the examples of RANKE and MICHELET. Having acquired from LANGLOIS and MONOD the best training in scholarship his time could offer, he revolted against the lack of critical spirit then prevalent among his senior colleagues.

Teaching at a new university, in a country which had enjoyed an independent existence only since 1877, and belonging to a nation which had not yet achieved political unity, Iorga felt himself called to the roles of ruler of the academic establishment, reformer of the Romanian society and political leader. He created three historical journals and supplied them with materials: *Revista istorica*, (1915–1946); *Bulletin de l'Institut pour l'étude de l'Europe sud-orientale* (1914–1923); *Revue historique du Sud-Est européen* (1924–1946). He wrote several literary reviews, founded three Institutes (for south east European studies in 1914, for Byzantine studies in 1935, for universal history in 1938), undertook the task of preserving the historical monuments of his country and initiated educational reform whilst in office as prime minister (1931).

Increasingly involved in political life after 1906, Iorga stressed the importance of tradition, seeing in monarchy the best protection against revolutionary movements (rightist and leftist) and he came to regard the parliamentary system with distrust. But his professional integrity was not lessened by his commitment to a political creed which coupled culture-oriented nationalism with populism. Before

and during the first world war, he gave legitimacy and impetus to Romanian national sentiment. When a pro-Nazi dictatorship found him a firm opponent, he was shot by the Iron Guard.

Iorga's achievements, taking into account the amazing range of books, pamphlets, learned articles and lectures which constituted his work, show the breadth of his historical interests. To place any Romanian problem in context, he had to investigate the broad area of south east Europe, which he was among the first to identify as a historical unit; this led him to reappraise the Crusades, Byzantium and the Turks. He attempted to assert the totality of history in writing 'historiology' (his own term). Dissatisfied with positivism and with the fragmentation of historical studies Iorga searched for the recurring elements in historical change ('les permanences de l'histoire', as he called them: land, race and idea). A fine stylist in prose and verse, he defended the rights of creative personality in historical interpretation. AP

Main publications

Philippe de Mézières (1327–1405) et la croisade au XIVe siècle (Paris, 1896; London: Variorum Reprints, 1973); *Notes et extraits pour servir à l'histoire des croisades au XVe siècle*, 6 vols (Paris: 1899–1902; Bucharest: 1915–16); *Studii si documente cu privire la istoria românilor*, 31 vols (Bucharest: 1901–16); *Geschichte des Osmanischen Reiches*, 5 vols (Gotha: 1908–13); *Histoire des états balkaniques* (Paris: J. Gamber, 1925); *Essai de synthèse de l'histoire de l'humanité*, 4 vols (Paris: J. Gamber, 1926–9); *Histoire de la vie byzantine*, 3 vols (Bucharest: Édition de l'auteur, 1934); *O viață de om, așa cum a fost* (A human life as it has been) 3 vols (Bucharest 1934); *Byzance après Byzance* (Bucharest: Éditions de l'Institut d'études byzantines, 1935); *Histoire des Roumains et de la romanité orientale*, 10 vols (Bucharest: Imprimerie de l'État, 1937–45); *Études byzantines*, 2 vols (Bucharest: Institut d'études byzantines, 1939–40).

Reading

Campbell, J. C.: Nicolas Iorga. *The Slavonic and East European Review* 26 (1947) 44–59.

Mélanges offerts à M. Nicolas Iorga par ses amis de France (a collection of 60 essays in honour of N. Iorga) (Paris: J. Gamber, 1933).

Pippidi, D. M. ed.: *Nicolas Iorga, l'homme et l'oeuvre* (Bucharest: Editions de l'Académie de la République Socialiste de Roumanie, 1972).

Theodorescu, B.: *Nicolae Iorga* (Bucharest: Editura Militară, 1976 [incl. extensive bibliography].

Irish historiography The disciplined study of Ireland's past is a relatively recent phenomenon. There have long been narrative accounts of events in Ireland (for example, those of GIRALDUS CAMBRENSIS, Edmund Campion, Richard Stanyhurst, Edmund Spenser and Geoffrey Keating) and romantic reconstructions of previous centuries have been based on their visible remains, on written records (legal, religious, and literary) and on a rich oral tradition. Pioneers of scholarly method applied to sources and concerned with accurate presentation, began to emerge during the mid-nineteenth and early twentieth centuries, for example, O'Curry and O'Donovan, Bagwell and LECKY, Dunlop and Wilson, Curtis, Maxwell, O'Brien and MacNeill. The past began to assume an agreed shape, even if it lacked accepted assessment of men and events, let alone a standard analysis of the social and economic forces underlying political, constitutional and cultural activities. But Ireland did not have the stability, the prosperity, or the freedom from alien domination that might have permitted an undisputed past.

It was therefore well into the twentieth century that Irish historians at last gained the experience and the confidence to re-examine their own past and by individual research and joint endeavour to achieve a measure of professionalism. By this time a degree of national independence had been achieved and the discipline of history had developed elsewhere, notably in Britain, with rigorous standards of source-based scholarship by university-based scholars, an accepted historical chronology, academic histories and journals, and professional associations.

It fell to the generation of MOODY, Edwards and Quinn, BECKETT and McCracken, Hayes-McCoy and Williams to establish standards, organize the profession, provide the outlets for systematic publication and usher in a second generation of scholars, among them LYONS and Lydon, Byrne and Corish, Connell and Kearney, Cullen, Green and MacDonagh.

Of the pioneers, Moody and Edwards were the innovators, founding respectively the Ulster Society for Irish Historical Studies and the Irish Historical Society in 1936, and jointly in 1938 the journal *Irish Historical Studies* and the Irish Committee of Historical Sciences. From these developments followed the monograph series 'Studies in Irish History' (1944), the biennial Irish Conference of Historians (1953) with its proceedings published as *Historical Studies* from 1955, the Irish History Students Association (1950), the pioneering Thomas Davis radio lecture series (1953) and in due time the magisterial *New History of Ireland*, first suggested by Moody in 1962, adopted by the Royal Irish Academy in 1968, and with its first multi-contributor volume published in 1976.

The *New History* has not been free of controversy. Its volumes have been slow in appearing, with the result that some contributions have become dated by the time of publication. Its vision nevertheless remains sound: to provide a framework of modern scholarship (backed by ancillary volumes of maps and statistics) to serve as a reference for the contemporary reader and a platform from which future scholars may advance. It bears witness to the vitality of research in all eras, especially the transformation of early and medieval understanding by the application of rigorous linguistic and historical skills, cutting through formalized tracts, genealogies and chronicles, with all their anachronisms and special pleadings, harnessing literary evidence and combing British and continental archives to amplify and correct local sources. The early modern and modern periods too reflect the applied techniques of other disciplines — economics, law, social and political sciences — so that such matters as land settlement and usage, legal innovation, demography, diet, language and culture take their place beside ecclesiastical, constitutional, military and political events.

Happily the work of professional historians has been underpinned by state institutions, the Public Record Office Ireland and the Public Record Office Northern Ireland, and by a new determination in the National Library of Ireland to gather in and make accessible material of Irish interest, in manuscript form or increasingly on microfilm; by the Irish Manuscripts Commission (1928) and, especially in relation to early Irish material, the Dublin Institute for Advanced Studies (1939). An ever-widening service to scholars is still being built up, with the addition of 'Writings in Irish History' (published annually in *Irish Historical Studies*); *Irish Historiography, 1936–70* (ed. T. W. Moody, 1971); *Irish Historiography, 1970–79* (ed. J. Lee, 1981); and such guides as R. Hayes's *Manuscript Sources for the History of Irish Civilization*, and much source material itself reproduced in, for example, *Analecta Hibernica* and *Archivium Hibernicum*.

Concurrently, university departments have expanded throughout the island, including a department of economic and social history at the Queen's University of Belfast. Local historical societies have multiplied and general texts have synthesized the new specialist monographs, notably J. C. Beckett, *The Making of Modern Ireland, 1603–1923*, A. J. Otway-Ruthven, *A History of Medieval Ireland*, F. S. L. Lyons, *Ireland since the Famine*, the paperback series on Irish history published by Gill & Macmillan, Dublin (10 vols, begun in 1972), its Helicon successor (10 vols, begun in 1981) and *The Course of Irish History*, edited by T. W. Moody and F. X. Martin. New societies and journals have carried forward particular enthusiasms: the Dublin Historical Association (founded by T. D. Williams in 1956) initiating a student pamphlet series from 1961; The Irish Society of Archives (formed, with R. D. Edwards its first chairman in 1970); *Irish Economic and Social History*, which began publication in 1974, and *Saothar*, the journal of the Irish Labour History Society, in 1975.

Under the inspiration of Professor L. M. Cullen, bilateral conferences, with Scottish and with French historians, have assumed prominence, while other recent developments include book and pamphlet publishing by historical societies on an increasing scale, more imaginative curriculum development work for schools, north and south, conducted by Education Ministry units and within Teachers' Centres, a project competition for northern schools ('Studying our Past') and an island-wide schools essay competition run by a major

newspaper. An *Irish Dictionary of National Biography* is being discussed, and the possibility of an Irish Institute of Historical Research explored.

This evidence reveals a profession still young and vigorous without smugness or despondency. Written Irish history (as opposed to the mythical versions still, alas, peddled orally in dark places) has come of age. The record is established, analysis and interpretation proceed throughout the island and beyond, notably in Britain, North America and Australia.

Early Ireland may yet lack its full economic and social dimensions but here archaeologist and historian can co-operate, and other fruitful co-operation can help interpret early literary texts, both Latin and Gaelic, to throw light on Christian and pagan interaction, upon continental contact and upon the medieval and early modern Gaelic twilight. The medieval record itself requires development beyond the ecclesiastical world, and here again the call is for economic and social research, though there will be source difficulties. Here it is with geographers that historians have begun to explore such topics as settlement and trading patterns. In the early modern and modern periods the greater volume of research has, as indicated above, involved even greater interdisciplinary activity, though there remains much to be achieved in local history, demography, cultural, intellectual and administrative history, in the early social role of the Catholic church, the agricultural economy before the famine, and in many aspects of social history from leisure activity to the impact of the motor car.   DWH

Reading

Beckett, J. C.: *The Making of Modern Ireland* (London: Faber & Faber, 1966; rev. edn 1981).

Cosgrove, Art ed.: *New History of Ireland*, vol. 2 (Oxford: Oxford University Press, 1987).

Hayes. R.: *Manuscript Sources for the History of Irish Civilization* (Boston: G. K. Hall, 11 vols, 1965; 3 suppl. vols, 1979).

Johnston, Edith: *Irish history: a select bibliography* (Historical Association, 1969).

Lee, J. ed.: *1970–79* (Cork: ICHS, 1981).

Lyons, F. S. L.: *Ireland since the Famine* (London:

Weidenfeld & Nicolson, 1971; rev. edn London: Fontana, 1973).

Moody, T. W. ed.: *Irish Historiography, 1936–70* (Dublin: Irish Committee of Historical Sciences, 1971).

Moody, T. W. and Martin, F. X. eds: *The Course of Irish History* (Cork: Mercier, 1967).

Moody, T. W. and Vaughan, W. E. eds: *New History of Ireland*, vol. 4 (Oxford University Press, 1986).

Moody, T. W., Martin, F. X. and Byrne, F. J.: *New History of Ireland*, vol. 3 (Oxford University Press, 1976).

Otway-Ruthven, A. J.: *A History of Medieval Ireland* (London: Ernest Benn, 1968).

Islamic historiography *Ta'rikh* in Arabic means the organization of material by date and hence, by extension, 'history'. The first histories (in the sense of sustained narratives of important political events) were written in the ninth century. They drew on biblical models and possibly on pre-Islamic Sassanian histories of the Persian kings as well as on orally transmitted information about the genealogies and warfare of the tribes of the Arab peninsula. Above all they drew on *hadith*, orally transmitted recollections of the sayings and deeds of the Prophet Muhammad. In the first two centuries of Islam there was some hostility in scholarly-clerical circles towards the writing down of *hadith* and still more to their use in syntheses, such as Ibn Ishaq's *Sira* (or 'Life of the Prophet', as it survives in Ibn Hisham's ninth-century recension) which attempted to reconstruct the origins of Islam from such data. More generally, though it had no official place in the syllabus of higher education in the medieval Islamic lands (any more than in the medieval west), history was for a long time conceived of as a handmaid of Quranic and *hadith* studies. The earliest Islamic historians all wrote in Arabic even though some of the most important and eloquent, such as Baladhuri (d.892) or TABARI (d.923), were Persians.

Biographical dictionaries also began to appear in the ninth century. At first the main subjects of such compilations were contemporaries of the Prophet and his immediate successors who passed on traditions concerning that time. These dictionaries provided a means of checking the reliability of the *hadith* which played such a large part in directing religious practice and the development of law. However biographical dictionaries soon broadened their coverage and aims. Ibn Khallikan (1211–82), for example, produced a biographical dictionary which covered not only the pious and the scholarly but also statesmen, soldiers, merchants and women, producing a mosaic of Islamic society as the product of the achievement of its individual members. Panegyrics of rulers and dynasties written by civil servants or courtiers first appeared at the Ghaznavid and Buyid courts in the tenth century and then spread to the western Islamic lands. As politicians and court scribes began to take a hand in history writing it became common to insert transcriptions of official documents into the chronicles. A knowledge of history came to be regarded as a desirable part of the literary formation (*adab*) of state functionaries and an important source for improving table talk among the educated elite generally. The sheer bulk of information provided by Islamic annals and biographical dictionaries cannot be matched by European history writing in the pre-modern period.

Generalizing (perhaps rather wildly), Muslim history writing tended to reconstruct events from discrete pieces of testimony, to interpret events in terms of individual actions and to portray individuals through telling anecdotes and striking sayings. Unless the modern reader is very skilled at reading between the lines, the narrative of events comes over as rather atomistic and the historical personalities, however vivid the illustrative material, driven by stereotyped (if not downright enigmatic) motives. The North African historian and philosopher IBN KHALDUN (1332–1406) appears to be an astounding and almost unique exception to this general tendency. In the *Muqaddima*, a lengthy methodological preface to his 'world' history, the *Kitab al-Ibar*, Ibn Khaldun studied the general laws of historical development and examined the role of environment, economy and social solidarity bonds in determining the cyclical rise and fall of Islamic and other dynasties. Ibn Khaldun had little influence on his immediate successors though his pupil, Maqrizi, pursued Ibn Khaldun's interest in economic and demographic factors. Indeed very few coherent narratives of events were written in Arabic between the Ottoman conquest of the Arab lands in the early sixteenth century and the revival of history writing by the Egyptian, Jabarti, at the end of the eighteenth century. However, Ibn Khaldun was studied with enthusiasm by Turkish Ottoman historians in the seventeenth century and, in the twentieth century, historians and sociologists in the east and west have not only praised his achievement but continue to find his insights fruitful. Even Ibn Khaldun had relatively little information about or interest in the world beyond the frontiers of Islam. In this he was more typical of his age, though Juwayni (1226–83) and RASHID AL-DIN (c.1247–1318), Persian historians working under Mongol overlordship, had wider horizons than most.

In the seventeenth century European historians for the first time had access to Arab histories through a translation into Latin of a general history by al-Makin (an Arab Christian of the thirteenth century, but one writing within the conventions of Islamic historiography). Unfortunately this was a relatively late compilation, and the tendency to select copious but late and on the whole unoriginal compendia, such as those of Abu'l-Fida and Maqrizi, for editing and translation in the west continued until the late nineteenth century. In the 1890s Ignace GOLDZIHER (1850–1921) and Julius Wellhausen (1844–1918) pioneered more critical approaches to specifically early Islamic sources. Wellhausen applied techniques first developed for Old Testament source criticism to the first two centuries of Islamic history. Goldziher called

into question the authenticity of many of the *hadith* and their supporting literary materials. Since then, as western research has progressed, less and less can confidently be said about the Prophet and his immediate successors. Much more recently, since the 1960s source critical techniques have been patchily applied to the vast quantity of late medieval chronicle writing. Ulrich Haarmann's concentration on such matters as the nature of the audience for these works and the appearance of literary and folklore elements in them seems particularly promising. In the first half of the twentieth century in Europe, two visions of the past and future destiny of the Islamic community have been particularly influential, those of Louis Massignon (1883–1962), a mystic Catholic with a strong sympathy for Sufism and an important polemicist against European colonialism, and of Hamilton Gibb (1895–1971), a skilful interpreter particularly of the role of the scholarly-clerical elite in defining Islam's self-image, but perhaps better known for his studies of Saladin's career. Bernard LEWIS studied with both these men and did much to develop and popularize their ideas.   RGI

Reading

Haarmann, Ulrich: *Quellenstudien zur frühen Mamlukenzeit* (Freiburg im Breisgau: Klaus Schwarz, 1970).

Hourani, Albert: *Europe and the Middle East* (London: Macmillan, 1980).

Lewis, Bernard and Holt, P. M. eds: *Historians of the Middle East* (London: Oxford University Press, 1962).

Rosenthal, Franz: *A History of Muslim Historiography* (Leyden: Brills, 1952).

J

James, Francis Godwin (b.1913) A graduate student under Wallace Notestein at Yale, 'Jeff' James spent much of his career at Tulane University, New Orleans; he retired in 1979. As befitted the son of an episcopalian minister, his first book, *North Country Bishop* (1956), was a study of a cleric, William Nicolson, bishop in turn of Carlisle and Derry in the early eighteenth century. This was a well-rounded biography, particularly strong on its subject's pastoral activities, and in its treatment of national politics soundly based on a traditional, party-oriented interpretation, at that time under attack from James's contemporary, Robert Walcott. When his research interest followed his subject across the Irish Sea, James was transmogrified into a historiographical pioneer. An American of non-Irish extraction working on pre-Union Irish history would have been unusual enough, but James's major work, *Ireland in the Empire 1688–1770*, published in 1973, broke new ground in more significant ways. Its choice of period redressed an imbalance which had afflicted students of eighteenth-century Ireland since W. E. H. Lecky. Secondly, it looked closely at the politics of the Anglo-Irish ascendancy in Ireland, revealing the existence of English-style parties under Queen Anne, and a rapidly maturing patriotism thereafter. Lastly, it anticipated calls for a more integrated approach to the history of the English-speaking Atlantic world by exploring comparisons and connections between Protestant Ireland and colonial America. A decade and a half later, these foundations still wait to be built on.   DWHn

Main publications

North Country Bishop (New Haven, Conn.: Yale University Press, 1956); *Ireland in the Empire 1688–1770* (Cambridge, Mass.: Harvard University Press, 1973).

Japanese historiography Japanese historical writing began with the introduction of the Chinese script, and Chinese dynastic chronicles. From the seventh century Japanese emperors sponsored the compilation of official histories, and the oldest surviving example, the *Kojiki*, appeared in 712. This complex blend of myth, legend and reality describes the origins and achievements of the Imperial Household. The next major history, the *Nihon Shoki* (720), followed the language and form of the Chinese chronicles even more closely, and continued the glorification of the imperial line.

In the eighth, ninth and tenth centuries, palace officials compiled five official histories, but with the weakening of the imperial court unofficial scholarship became a major feature of Japanese historiography. Now both courtiers and Buddhist monks used new forms and methods to reinterpret the Japanese past. Particularly important was the monk Kōen's *Fusō Ryakki* which used temple records and other Buddhist sources to broaden the scope of historical writing. A second innovation was the narrative history which copied the style of the 'literary tale'. The first example of this genre was the *Eiga Monogatari* (*c*.1030) which celebrated the lives and exploits of the rich and powerful Fujiwara family. The greatest work in this style was the *Ōkagami* which surveys the years 850 to 1025. The novelty of this history

213

lay in its use of an imagined dialogue between impossibly old men to describe the decline of imperial power and the glories of the Fujiwara.

As the power of the aristocracy waned and warriors rose to authority, themes of decline and fate increasingly dominated historical writing. Against this background, the distinguished monk Jien wrote the *Gukanshō* (*c*.1220), the first philosophical treatment of Japanese history. In contrast to many earlier works, the *Gukanshō* was written in simple Japanese and explored the rules and cycles of historical development. Jien divided history into seven periods and saw cyclical patterns in the growth of Japan. In contrast to the sophistication of the *Gukanshō*, the popular *Heike Monogatari* was filled with vivid drama. But even this popular epic embodied ideas of transience and decline which were obvious products of Buddhist philosophy.

Although the court never regained its former authority, powerful rulers continued to commission official histories. In the late thirteenth century, officials of the Kamakura shogunate compiled the *Azuma Kagami*. This major history was composed in a special blend of Japanese and Chinese and described the successful establishment of the Kamakura regime.

In the civil wars of the fourteenth and fifteenth centuries, military chronicles became a dominant genre, but with the achievement of national unity the writing of national histories became an important activity. In the seventeenth century the Tokugawa shogun's advisers turned to Chinese historiography for their models, and Hayashi Razan and his son completed the *Honchō Tsugan* (1670). This national history embodied the ethics and accuracy of the best Confucian scholarship. In the Tokugawa period some individual lords also commissioned histories, and in 1657 the ruler of Mito ordered the compilation of a history of Japan, the *Dai Nihon Shi*. This was eventually completed in 1906 and remains a major monument of Japanese scholarship.

Perhaps the most original historian of the seventeenth and eighteenth centuries was Arai Hakuseki (1657–1725), an adviser of the sixth Tokugawa shogun. Although Hakuseki was a Confucian scholar he took a new detached attitude to Japanese and Chinese historical records. In such works as *Dokushi Yoron* he divided earlier centuries into 'early' and 'medieval' periods and attempted the psychological analysis of important historical figures. In exploring such new fields as transport, money and international relations, this remarkable scholar dramatically widened the scope of Japanese historical studies.

In the late eighteenth and early nineteenth centuries, many non-samurai scholars avoided Confucian moralism and developed the pursuit of so-called 'National Learning'. Such writers as Motoori Norinaga (1730–1801) re-evaluated Japan's early literature and chronicles and his 'Commentary on the *Kojiki*' (1798) combined both linguistic and historical analysis. Such writers often criticized the accretion of Buddhist and Confucian thought in Japanese culture and claimed that this had damaged traditional virtues.

Even before the opening of Japan in 1854, scholars of the 'Textual Criticism School' embarked upon the rigorous evaluation of documents and the collection of source materials. However, contact with the west and the creation of the modern state (1868) brought a major transformation of historical studies. In fact German historical method fused with existing textual criticism to produce a new academic tradition.

In 1879 Tokyo University founded its historical section and eight years later von Ranke's student, Ludwig Riess, was invited to become professor of history. Soon after, the Historical Study Society (Shigakkai) began the publication of its prestigious journal, *Shigaku Zasshi*, which remains of major importance.

Although modernization was a stimulus to historical scholarship, the political orthodoxy of the new state soon began to limit intellectual freedom. In 1892, the distinguished scholar Kume Kunitake was expelled from Tokyo University for dismissing emperor-based Shinto as an 'ancient practice'.

This was only the first of a series of conflicts between historians and government which were to continue until 1945. In particular, research which probed the mythology of the imperial household was largely suppressed.

Perhaps the most striking feature of research between the wars was the development of social and economic history, including major works of Marxist analysis. Indeed the most important historical debates of the 1930s were inspired by attempts to fit modern Japanese history into a Marxist framework.

During the war years, nationalist writing was superficially dominant but with Japan's surrender and occupation, Japanese historians experienced unparalleled freedom. Again, Marxism became a major influence on historical writing and it was only in the 1970s that American historiographical methods came to challenge Marxist dominance in many fields.

Although serious western studies of Japanese history were pioneered by British diplomats in the 1860s, large scale research did not develop until the second world war. Some wartime western works, such as E. H. Norman's *Japan's Emergence as a Modern State*, were influenced by Japanese Marxist writing but in the postwar years specialist 'empirical' studies have dominated western publications on Japan.   GD

Reading

Ackroyd, Joyce: *Told Round a Brushwood Fire: the Autobiography of Arai Hakuseki*, translated with an Introduction and Notes (Tokyo: University of Tokyo Press, 1979).

Aston, W. G. transl.: *Nihongi: Chronicles of Japan from the Earliest Times to AD 697* (Repr. of 1896 edn) (Tokyo: Tuttle, 1972).

Brown, Delmer M. and Ishida, Ichirō: *The Future and the Past, A translation and study of the Gukansho, an interpretive history of Japan written in 1219* (Berkeley: University of California Press, 1979).

Brownlee, John S. ed.: *History in the Service of the Japanese Nation* (Toronto: University of Toronto and York University Joint Center on Modern East Asia, 1983).

Dower, John W. ed.: *Origins of the Modern Japanese State – Selected Writings of E. H. Norman* (New York: Pantheon, 1975).

Kitagawa, Hiroshi and Tsuchida, Bruce T. (transl.): *The Tale of the Heike* (University of Tokyo Press, 1975).

Koschmann, J. Victor: *The Mito Ideology, Discourse, Reform and Insurrection in Late Tokugawa Japan, 1798–1864* (University of California Press, 1987).

Matsumoto, Shigeru: *Motoori Norinaga, 1730–1801* (Cambridge, Mass.: Harvard University Press, 1970).

McCullough, Helen Craig: *Okagami, The Great Mirror, Fujiwara Michinaga (996–1027) and his Times: a study and translation* (University of Tokyo Press, 1980).

Philippi, Donald L.: *Kojiki, a translation with an Introduction and Notes* (University of Tokyo Press, 1969).

Shinoda, Minoru: *The Founding of the Kamakura Shogunate, 1180–85, with Selected Translations from the Azuma Kagami* (New York: Columbia University Press, 1960).

Jaurès, Jean (b.1859, d.1914)   Born in the Tarn and educated at the École Normale Supérieure, Jaurès went on to become a deputy and a leading figure in French socialism during the Third Republic. He was assassinated as he campaigned against war in July 1914. Throughout an extremely active political career he managed to read widely, and his known interest in history produced an invitation in 1898 to edit a socialist history of France from 1789. He accepted, and undertook to write the first volumes, on the Revolution, himself. The result, which began to appear in instalments in 1900 and was complete in four volumes by 1902, was *Histoire socialiste de la Révolution française*, dealing with the period from 1789 to 1795. Jaurès's ideological position was clear from the outset, and its Marxist inspiration undisguised. The Revolution represented the seizure of power and overthrow of feudalism by a class of bourgeois enriched by the expanding capitalism of the eighteenth century. It had also opened the way for the proletariat to play a role of increasing importance in national affairs. Although intended as an encouragement to fellow socialists and a celebration of the origins of the French left, the socialist history was far more than a partisan polemic. It was based on wide reading and fresh research, notably in economic sources scarcely tapped by previous historians. Subsequently Jaurès used his influence as a deputy to secure state funding for the publication of a (still appearing) series of economic documents on the history of the Revolution. MATHIEZ acknowledged Jaurès as a major influence, and the economic and social interpretation of the Revolution which he pioneered dominated

215

writing on the subject for more than three generations. WD

Main publication

Histoire socialiste de la Révolution française, 4 vols (Paris: 1901–2).

Reading

Goldberg, H.: *The Life of Jean Jaurès* (Madison: University of Wisconsin Press, 1962).

——: *La Pensée socialiste devant la Révolution française* (Paris: 1966).

Jensen, Merrill (b.1905, d.1980) Brought up in modest circumstances on small farms, Jensen never abandoned his populist concerns. His long scholarly career centred on the University of Wisconsin, from which he received his doctorate in 1934 and where he taught from 1945 to 1976. His work focused upon the period of the American Revolution and argued that internal conflicts of economic interest shaped many major events; that the Revolution promoted internal democracy; and that the Articles of Confederation formed a successful government true to the basic revolutionary principles of democracy and localism. Neglected somewhat by 'consensus' historians during the 1950s, his work again became popular during the 1960s and 1970s as younger historians (many his own pupils) began to reinterpret American history in terms of internal conflict. MDK

Main publications

The Articles of Confederation: an Interpretation of the Social-Constitutional History of the American Revolution, 1774–1781 (Madison: University of Wisconsin Press, 1940); *The New Nation: a History of the United States during the Confederation, 1781–1789* (New York: Knopf, 1950); *The Founding of a Nation: a History of the American Revolution, 1763–1776* (New York: Oxford University Press, 1968); *The American Revolution within America* (New York: New York University Press, 1974).

Reading

Ferguson, E. J.: Merrill Jensen: a personal comment. In *The Human Dimensions of Nation Making: Essays on Colonial and Revolutionary America*, ed. J. K. Martin (Madison: State Historical Society of Wisconsin, 1976),

Martin, J. K.: The human dimensions of nation making: Merrill Jensen's scholarship and the American Revolution, In *The Human Dimensions of Nation Making*.

Stevens, M. E.: Merrill Jensen, *Twentieth-Century American Historians*, ed. C. N. Wilson (Detroit: Gale, 1983) pp. 236–41.

Jewish historiography In modern times Jewish history has emerged almost as a break with the past. Simon Dubnow (1860–1941) pointed to its twin nature: it is intimately intertwined with the history of those non-Jewish societies and cultures in which the Jews have lived and at the same time possesses its own characteristics. To the general problems which face all historians the Jewish historian has the particular task of attempting to define a specific group which seems to have none of the characteristics of a historical entity: no home, no unity, no apparent coherence.

Judaism is a 'historical' religion, in that its basis is a historical memory. Indeed every religious occasion refers to one particular historical event: the Exodus from Egypt. The Bible itself is a historical narrative, and the works of the Old Testament are in varying degrees attributable to a historical background. But the developments of Rabbinic Judaism led to a blurring of that clear concept, so that the liturgical calendar might well retain the memory of individual events without necessarily maintaining either chronology or perspectives of time. Thus in the period after JOSEPHUS strict history tends, in the second century AD, to be replaced by the *Memorbuch* of an individual community or congregation, the listing of the benefactors to the community or the disasters which might have befallen it. What writings there were tended to put contemporary events into a quasi-Messianic format, using Scripture as a way of elucidating the problems of the contemporary world and offering reassurance that delivery was at hand. Rarely would the annalist or the commentator have sought to create a historical work. Not until more modern times has there been any tradition of historical writing or search for any historical continuity.

Such writings begin to appear in the period of the Renaissance, partly as a result of the expulsion of the Jews from Spain and Portugal. Joseph Ha'cohen (1496–1578) proclaimed himself as the first writer of history since Josephus, while it was said of David Gans

(1541–1613) that he was 'the first Jew in Ashkenaz [Germany] to concern himself with professional history' (Kochan 1977, pp. 1, 42). But even Gans tended to the chronological rather than the analytical, listing disasters and martyrdoms. Two hundred years later the first who could be described as a modern Jewish historiographer, Isaac Marcus Jost (1793–1860), lamented that Jewish histories tended to be little more than 'the transmission of rabbinic teaching, martyrologies of the Jews ... chronology and knowledge of places are everywhere confused' (Jost, in Kochan, p. 2).

Modern Jewish historiography begins with the creation of the movement known as *Die Wissenschaft des Judentums* (The science of Judaism), a result of the combination of the emergence of the 'Enlightenment' into Jewish consciousness, the appearance of 'emancipation' as a factor in Jewish thought, and the rise of national feelings at the beginning of the nineteenth century. With the intent of examining Judaism 'scientifically' there was an attempt to put Jewish history under the microscope. One of the problems facing Jewish historians was the contemporary association of history with nationalisms. Leopold Zunz (1794–1886) echoed his colleagues in that movement, with his belief that without a state and a historical unit there could be no history. That did not prevent him from pioneering concepts that were essential for the next generation's understanding of history, above all that could be applied to the ways in which Hebrew literature, sacred and profane alike, could be used as the basis for historical study and analysis. Heinrich Graetz (1817–1891) was the greatest of the *Wissenschaft* scholars, combining a history of thought and ideas with a history of martyrdom and suffering. His 'universalist' history has been criticized as representing a 'lachrymose school of history', while he ran counter in many ways to the various nationalistic fervours of the late nineteenth century. There was too an emphasis on the active spiritual content of Jewish life, which led him to regard the German Jews as being more important than the numerically much greater East European Jewish communities. Despite little attention to demography, social history or economic history,

his *History of the Jews* has been translated into many languages and is still widely read, making him certainly the major Jewish historian of the century.

Simon Dubnow was at once the heir to the Jewish Enlightenment (the *Haskalah*) and to the views of the contemporary Russian intelligentsia. He saw a Jewish national existence, more latterly in Eastern Europe where, as he pointed out, Jews had existed within a group of autonomous communities living inside a state but none the less controlling not merely religious life but social institutions. He proclaimed, 'I occupied myself with the history of the people, not with the history of literature, and history is essentially the development or decline of the national self in relation to the environment' (Davis 1954, p. 27). His greatest work was his ten-volume *World History of the Jewish People*, written in Russian and translated into virtually every language of the western world. His theme was the importance of the Jew in the Diaspora; he died in the Holocaust, that massive onslaught on European Jewry which in itself denied the validity of much of his argumentation.

In 'western' Jewish historical writing the doyen of studies is inevitably Salo Wittmayer Baron (b.1895), one of the truly outstanding figures in the entire history of Jewish historiography. The holder of the first chair in Jewish history at a western secular university (the Miller chair at Columbia, New York), and the teacher of innumerable scholars, he represents possibly the last attempt to create a 'universalist history' combined with a clear understanding of the various processes by which historians of all allegiances have attempted to understand the past. At the age of 88 he published volume 18 of *A Social and Religious History of the Jews* (which has not yet passed 1650); in preparing his material he uses the techniques of the twentieth century, yet his work contains clearly those ideas which run throughout all Jewish historiography: the links which have existed between the people and their religion, links which have enabled a peculiar people to survive millennia of persecution. Baron denied the validity of the 'lachrymose school of history' – indeed it was he who invented the phrase – and it has been

his work which has done most to undermine
it.   AN

Reading

Davis, M.: Jewry east and west: the correspondence
of I. Friedländer and S. Dubnow. *YIVO Annual*
9 (1954) 27 [pub. New York: YIVO Institute].

Jost, I.M.: Geschichte des Judentums and Seiner
Secten (1859). In Kochan.

Kochan, Lionel: *The Jew and his History* (London:
Macmillan, 1977).

Meyer, Michael ・A.: *Ideas of Jewish History* (New
York: Behrman House, 1974).

Yerushalmi, Yosef Hayim: *Zakhor* (Seattle: University of Washington Press, 1982).

Joinville, Jean, Sire de (b.1224/5, d.1319)
Hereditary seneschal of Champagne, Joinville
voluntarily accompanied Louis IX on crusade
to Egypt in 1248 and remained overseas until
1254. In old age he was asked by Jeanne of
Navarre, queen of Philip IV of France, to have
a book written of 'the holy sayings and good
deeds of our king St Louis', who had been
canonized in 1297. Joinville composed a book
which is his own memoirs of the crusade
reinforced by secondary material on Louis's
life. The book was composed in French by
dictation and was intended to be read aloud.
Using direct speech and colourful description
(particularly of clothes), Joinville created a
gripping narrative with strong images of the
king and his nobles. He presents himself —
perhaps unwittingly — as the perfect knight or
prud'homme, more perfect indeed than Louis
himself. Like the author of a *chanson de geste*,
Joinville looks back to a better and nobler
time. The book was not completed until 1309,
when he was 85 years old.   MTC

Main writings

Histoire de St Louis, ed. N. de Wailly (Paris: Societé
de l'histoire de France, 1868); *La Vie de St Louis:
texte du XIVe siécle*, ed. N. L. Corbett (Quebec:
Sherbrooke, 1977); English trans.: Joan Evans
(Oxford: Oxford University Press, 1938), R. Hague
(London: Sheed & Ward, 1955), M. R. B. Shaw
(London: Penguin, 1963).

Jones, Arnold Hugh Martin (b.1904, d.1970)
Jones, whose massive work on the later Roman
empire has been described as 'the greatest
contribution in English to Roman imperial

history since Gibbon', was professor of ancient history at University College, London
(1946—51) and subsequently at Cambridge
(1951—70). After classical 'Mods and Greats'
at New College, Oxford, he was elected to a
fellowship at All Souls (1926—39), then a
lectureship at Wadham College (1939—46);
the war years found him first at the Ministry of
Labour (where his concern with manpower
deployment fuelled his future academic interest in the economic organization of the
Roman empire) and then — like many an
Oxbridge don of his generation — in Intelligence. His Oxford career had already been
interrupted by a period (1929—34) spent
as reader in ancient history at the Egyptian
University of Cairo, which opened up for him
the world of the eastern Roman empire and
led to his first major publications, *Cities of the
Eastern Roman Provinces* and *The Greek City
from Alexander to Justinian*. The latter book,
especially, revealed Jones's hallmark as a
historian: the detailed study of institutions
across a wide geographical area and chronological range, densely packed with information
and yet organized with systematic clarity. It
also showed him departing from the traditional
paths of Oxford ancient history into more
neglected corners of the classical world, the
Hellenistic age and the early Byzantine empire. During his years of teaching in London
and Cambridge he embraced Greek and
Roman history with equal facility. His lectures
made no concessions to feebler minds in his
audiences: they were the basis of classic papers
on the workings of Athenian democracy and
the Roman principate.

It was his increasing preoccupation with
that period of Roman history conventionally
dubbed 'the decline and fall' which was to lead
to the masterpiece of Jones's career: *The Later
Roman Empire AD 284—602: A Social, Economic
and Administrative Survey* appeared in 1964,
presaged during the 1950s by a series of
important articles, chiefly about economic
matters. One reviewer saw the impact of this
book as 'the arrival of a steel plant in a region
that has been given over to light industries',
and it is destined to remain for a long time the
authoritative study of how the late Roman
empire worked. It is evident from his sub-title

that it was not Jones's intention to write a narrative history (although he did include some opening narrative chapters), still less to chart the 'decline': it was, rather, a huge analysis of the structure and organization of late Roman government and society, from its central institutions – administration, finance, army – out to the cities, countryside, and economic life of the empire, and not least its religion and culture. Jones fully appreciated the role of the Christian church in late Roman society. Only when all the evidence had been marshalled and discussed did he allow himself a final, dispassionate chapter on the 'decline'.

Jones's mastery was directed, overwhelmingly, at ancient texts. His knowledge of the classical authors was prodigious (he is credited, for instance, with 'total recall' of the works of Cicero), and extended beyond the traditional corpus to the Roman law codes and the literature of the early church as well as to the multifarious data of the Egyptian papyri. For one who made a point of travelling widely in the former provinces of the Roman empire, he took remarkably little note of archaeological evidence. Notoriously, as his career progressed, Jones paid less and less attention in what he wrote to the work of other scholars: for him the primary sources alone, expertly known and studied, were sufficient to yield all that one could hope to know of the ancient world. This was an approach which characterized the last great project of his life, a three-volume *Prosopography of the Later Roman Empire* which he inspired and instigated, and the first volume of which was in press at the time of his death. While acknowledged as an indispensable tool for the study of late Roman history, this work has aroused criticism for its lack of attention to modern scholarly research. Jones has also been accused of an obsession with institutions at the expense of individuals. It is true that his use of religious texts, for example, was more as a quarry for details of ecclesiastical organization than as a spiritual guide to late antiquity: yet his volume on *Constantine* at least, the best of his smaller books, shows that he was not insensitive to the religious thinking of the first Christian emperor.

Before what was to have been his last year in

the Cambridge chair, Jones took a sabbatical term. He and his wife set off for a spell in Greece, but he died suddenly, on 9 April 1970, at sea between Brindisi and Patras. His body was taken to Athens, where he is buried.   EDH

Main publications

Cities of the Eastern Roman Provinces (Oxford: Oxford University Press, 1937): *The Herods of Judaea* (Oxford University Press, 1938); *The Greek City from Alexander to Justinian* (Oxford University Press, 1940); *Constantine and the Conversion of Europe* (London: Hodder & Stoughton, 1948); *Athenian Democracy* (Oxford: Blackwell, 1957); *Studies in Roman Government and Law* (Blackwell, 1960); *The Later Roman Empire AD 284–602: A Social, Economic and Administrative Survey* (Blackwell, 1964); *Sparta* (Oxford University Press, 1967); *Augustus* (London: Chatto & Windus, 1970); with J. R. Martindale and J. Morris, *The Prosopography of the Later Roman Empire*, vol. I: *AD 260–395* (Cambridge: Cambridge University Press, 1971); *The Criminal Courts of the Roman Republic and Principate* (Blackwell, 1972); *The Roman Economy*, ed. P. A. Brunt (Blackwell, 1974).

Reading

Crook, J.: Arnold Hugh Martin Jones 1904–1970. *Proceedings of the British Academy* 57 (1971), 425–38.

Josephus (b.37, d. after 95) As a historian Josephus has a unique place in the Roman empire: in his person and in his writings he embraced three separate worlds, Jewish, Greek and Roman, and he was close to events of enduring historical significance. He was always a correct Jew, and indeed a priest, but when he left Judea it was as the companion of emperors and as a citizen of Rome. As a writer, he composed almost entirely in Greek, and his target, when writing both of contemporary events and of antiquarian matters, was a wide readership of Greeks, as well as of Greek-speaking Jews. It is no accident that this figure would be best appreciated in time by a Christian audience.

What we know of Josephus' life is essentially what he writes in his own defence. There are therefore problems of interpretation; none the less, the record of the early part is relatively full and the story memorable. The essential feature is that of a promising career interrupted and distorted by the advent of a national catastrophe. Born in AD 37 of a noble family with priestly and royal (Hasmonean) ancestry; a Jerusalem education; a training with each of the three major Jewish sects, of Pharisees, Sadducees and Essenes, as well as with a vegetarian hermit; and moderate political views — these qualified him to represent his country in a special mission to Rome, on the eve of the great Jewish revolt against Roman rule which broke out in AD 66.

On return, though still inexperienced, Josephus was made, together with others of his class, a reluctant 'general' in a rebellion that could not be stopped. Those who deemed him treacherous, and there were many, even in his own lifetime, held that his defence of the Galilee was half-hearted, to say the least. Their distaste was fuelled by his conduct on defeat, when the town of Jotopata fell to a Roman siege: a suicide pact was dodged; close contact was soon established with the Flavian conquerors, Vespasian and Titus; and Josephus' position was secured, it seems, when he proved correct in his famous prediction that the Flavians would succeed Nero to the imperial purple. From these dramatic events came both the possibility and the impulse to become a historian.

Josephus remained with Titus and accompanied him to Rome. There his writing was done, presumably, in the house which had been a gift from Vespasian. And Josephus, son of Mattathias, had become the Roman citizen Flavius Josephus. Continuing attacks from his countrymen called forth imperial protection, so that we may wonder if he ever returned to his homeland where, also through imperial favour, he was an absentee landowner. The rest is obscure, but he refers to various marriages, apparently to Jewish wives. Once, he solemnly protested that he could never contemplate abandoning the laws of his ancestors.

Josephus was a practitioner of several more or less established types of history writing. The *Jewish War* (as the work later came to be entitled) was issued between AD 75 and 79 and is a detailed, 'eye-witness' account of a major war (the greatest ever, it is claimed), in seven books. An earlier version had been done in Aramaic and sent 'beyond the Euphrates'; it is inconceivable that the later work should be a mere translation of that Semitic original, and we may be assured that it is an original Greek history. The *Jewish Antiquities* (or *Archaeology*) was issued after AD 93/4 and is a would-be full history of a people, in 20 books, starting at the beginning. The first half follows the Bible, with many omissions, but turns the various texts into a more-or-less rational and often vivid historical narrative, just as classical historians did with their legends. The later history is drawn where possible from other authors, supplemented by folk-tale, oral evidence and a few documents: again, the mix was learned from Greek historians, but adapted to a very different tradition. As for the minor works, the *Life*, an autobiography of sorts, which was an appendix to the *Antiquities*, shows how closely ancient biography was linked with history; it is a defensive work, as autobiography often is, and much of it is taken up with a second, fuller account of the war in the Galilee, justifying the author's conduct. *Against Apion* was often entitled 'On the antiquity of the Jews', and at its heart is a vigorous historical inquiry about the comparative newness of Greek culture, as against that of Hebrews and other oriental nations.

Such diversity, together with the fortunate survival of Josephus' works, allows the author to claim a position of some importance among later Greek historians, though he is too often omitted from this company because of his alien affiliations. The classical stamp is especially apparent in the use of speeches, sometimes paired, as vehicles for political analysis, for the author's own views, or even just for rhetorical colouring. Pathos, drama and romance are more dubious but influential attributes, in keeping with the historical fashion of the age.

But the classical historian's mode was not incompatible with Jewish theology and interpretation, and it was Josephus' achievement to blend the two. Alexandrian Jewish forerunners had attempted this, to our knowledge, only on the simplest of levels. A traditional theory, of Deuteronomic type, about sin and punishment runs through the *Jewish War*: the fall of the temple was due to the violence and sacrilege of Jewish extremists, who were more to blame than the victorious Romans. In the *Antiquities*, Rabbinic-type exegesis is dressed as history and the Biblical heroes are granted an interesting blend of Jewish and Greek virtues.

Whatever he was writing, Josephus exercised independence: misplaced moral censure and suspicion have often led to his being unjustly derogated as a historian. It is true that imperial support was repaid with lavish eulogy of Titus. But the *Jewish War* is not official history or propaganda for Rome; it is too personal a work for that. The *Antiquities*, in fact, had a different kind of patron, a freedman named Epaphroditus, who had professed a true interest in the subject matter.

While our age has tended to be overly mistrustful of Josephus, opinion was for many centuries uncritically favourable, regarding him as the author who offered contemporary testimony to the life and death of Jesus (in fact, the passage about Jesus is either wholly or partly an interpolation into the text of the *Antiquities*). To Jerome Josephus was the Greek Livy, and in the early medieval period, he was often pronounced 'the most veracious of historians'.   TRK

Main writings

The Jewish War, The Jewish Antiquities, The Life, Against Apion, text and trans, all in *Josephus*, vols 1–9 (Cambridge, Mass.: Loeb Classical Series, 1926–65).

Reading

Rajak, Tessa: *Josephus: the Historian and his Society* (London: Duckworth, 1983; Philadelphia: Fortress Press, 1984).

K

Kantorowicz, Ernst Hartwig (b.1895, d.1963) Kantorowicz had a dual career. As a young man he was a keen devotee of the charismatic poet Stefan George, and his literary skills were recognized when he was charged with the duty of writing a biography of the Hohenstaufen emperor Frederick II. The George circle saw biographies of great men as models for the youth of Weimar, on whom it was incumbent to restore Germany to its former glories; though proudly nationalistic, most members of the circle had little contact with the Nazis, and Kantorowicz himself was an assimilated Prussian Jew. When his life of Frederick II appeared in 1927, therefore, it had already been heralded in the poetry of his master and in the shorter studies of his colleague Wolfram von den Steinen. Kantorowicz's book aroused a wave of adulation followed by a storm of protest; its remarkable literary qualities were said to detract from its accuracy as a picture of one of Germany's most controversial rulers, and the redoubtable Brackmann wrote of the book that 'one can write history neither as a pupil of George nor as a Catholic nor as a Protestant nor as a Marxist, but only as an individual in search of truth'. That Kantorowicz had set out to write a historical epic rich in lessons to a supposedly decadent and disgraced Weimar Germany is clear. A bitter conflict raged in the journals and lecture-halls of Germany as Kantorowicz sought to defend the use of his *imagination créatrice*, demanding that a unifying idea be applied to historical data in order to give a subject shape and coherence. Having left out footnotes in his biography (to the horror of his detractors), Kantorowicz pro-

ceeded to publish an *Ergänzungsband* in 1931, consisting of extremely valuable and thoughtful annotations and commentaries on his main text; it is clear, however, that much of this research was conducted after he had already published the biography. The *Ergänzungsband* marks the transformation of Kantorowicz from a gifted littérateur into a historian.

Kantorowicz received academic recognition and became a professor at Frankfurt-am-Main. But with the rise of Nazism he was banished from his chair; living for the next three years in Berlin he witnessed the start of the destruction of German Jewry, and was unable to publish in his native country. He left to spend a year at New College, Oxford, and then migrated permanently to the United States, serving as professor first in Berkeley (which he left after a dispute over a loyalty oath demanded of Californian professors) and later at the Institute for Advanced Study, Princeton. He retained a strong interest in Frederick II but became especially interested in the idea and symbols of medieval kingship. He addressed a difficult conundrum, expressed in the phrase 'the king is dead; long live the king', in *The King's Two Bodies* (1957) a rich and subtle work that handles with zest art-historical, legal and literary sources as well as more conventional evidence; in *Laudes Regiae* (1946) he looked at the ritual acclamation of medieval kings; and at the end of his life he bacame interested in the symbolism of the Valois court in Burgundy, though his work on this remained unpublished. In America he was known for his passionate interest in cooking. DSHA

Main publications

Kaiser Friedrich der Zweite (Berlin: 1927); *Kaiser Friedrich der Zweite, Ergänzungsband* (Berlin: 1931); *Frederick the Second*, trans. E. O. Lorimer (London: Constable, 1931); *Laudes Regiae* (Los Angeles: Berkeley, 1946 in limited edn of 30 copies, repr. 1958); *The King's Two Bodies* (Princeton, NJ: Princeton University Press, 1957); *Selected Studies* (Locust Valley, NY, 1965) [with full bibliography].

Reading

[For the debate over the biography of Frederick II see the first edition only of G. Wolf, ed. *Stupor Mundi: zur Geschichte Friedrichs II von Hohenstaufen* (Darmstadt: 1966), where many of the key articles are reprinted.]

Abulafia, D. The Elusive Emperor. *Theoretische Geschiedenis* 12 (1985) 204–8.

——: Kantorowicz and Frederick II. *History* 62 (1977) 193–210; repr. with additional note in Abulafia, D.: *Italy, Sicily and the Mediterranean, 1050–1400* (London: 1987).

Grünewald, E.: *Ernst Kantorowicz und Stefan George: Beiträge zur Biographie des Historikers bis zum Jahre 1938 und seinem Jugendwerk 'Kaiser Friedrich der Zweite'* (Frankfurter Historische Abhandlungen 25, Wiesbaden: Steiner, 1982).

Malkiel, Y.: Ernst H. Kantorowicz. In *On Four Modern Humanists: Hofmannsthal, Gundolf, Curtius, Kantorowicz* ed. A. R. Evans (Princeton, NJ: Princeton University Press, 1970) pp. 146–219.

Karamzin, Nikolay Mikhailovich (b.1766, d.1826) Born into the provincial nobility, Karamzin was educated in Moscow at a private school and then at the university. He broadened his outlook through travel in western Europe from the spring of 1789 to the autumn of 1790, and recorded his mixed impressions in *Letters of a Russian Traveller*, first published in 1791–2. While in Paris Karamzin wrote that Russia had a great history, but no historians to compare with Tacitus, Hume, Robertson and Gibbon. Resolving to fill as much of that gap as possible, he moved away from an early approval of some of the ideas of the Enlightenment to a resolute conservative nationalism. After his return to Russia Karamzin was appointed historiographer by Alexander I in 1803. His first major publication in this capacity was his lengthy *Memoir on Ancient and Modern Russia*, submitted to Alexander I in 1811, in which he argued against liberal reform and in favour of the retention of unalloyed autocracy. In 1816 the first volume of his *History of the Russian State* was published; at his death ten years later he was working on the twelfth volume bringing his account up to the year 1611. Pushkin dubbed Karamzin the 'Columbus of Russian History' though censuring his uncritical acceptance of the necessity for autocracy. Fellow historians were soon revealing the many weaknesses of the *History of the Russian State*, but it remained popular and influential throughout much of the nineteenth century.

Karamzin had access to private and state archives, and was able to use some sources destroyed in the Moscow fire of 1812. The voluminous notes accompanying the *History* are therefore of considerable interest in themselves. His approach to the subject was based on that of his eighteenth-century predecessors, but Karamzin surpassed them all in literary style and patriotic passion. While the central, unifying feature of his work is the formation of the state, Karamzin also wrote with enthusiasm about the princes who made major contributions to this glorious end.   PD

Main publications

Istoriia gosudarstva Rossiiskogo, 12 vols (St. Petersburg: 1818–19); *Histoire de l'empire de Russie*, 11 vols (Paris: 1819–1826); *Karamzin's Memoir on Ancient and Modern Russia*, trans. and ed. Richard Pipes (Cambridge, Mass: Harvard University Press, 1959).

Reading

Black, J. L.; *Nicholas Karamzin and Russian Society in the Nineteenth Century: a Study in Russian Political and Historical Thought* (Toronto: Toronto University Press, 1975).

—— ed.: *Essays on Karamzin: Russian Man-of-Letters, Political Thinker, Historian, 1776–1826* (The Hague: Mouton, 1975).

Cross, A. G.: *N. M. Karamzin: a Study of his Literary Career* (Carbondale, Ill.: Southern Illinois University Press, 1971).

Klyuchevsky, Vasily Osipovich (b.1841, d.1911) Originating from a long line of parish priests, Klyuchevsky grew up in a small village where he developed a close acquaintance with the life of the neighbouring peasants. His early education had a pronounced clerical slant, and he was deeply affected by the premature accidental death of his father. Entering the local seminary in 1856, he studied modern history as well as theology and ancient languages. After considerable personal anguish and administrative difficulty, he transferred to the University of Moscow and began an exclusive devotion to the study of history.

His teacher was S. M. Solovyev, then in the middle of a multi-volumed *History of Russia*. Under the sympathetic guidance of this teacher, Klyuchevsky wrote a master's thesis on the *Lives of the Early Russian Saints as a Source of History*, (finally published in 1871). Another early project was *Accounts of Foreigners concerning the Muscovite State*, not published until 1918. Other notable monographs included *The Boyar Council in Early Russia* (1883) and *A History of Social Estates in Russia* (1913). However, Klyuchevsky's most notable work was his five-volume *Course in Russian History* (1904–1921), based on his lectures at Moscow University, where he took over the chair from Solovyev in 1879 and held it until 1911 shortly before his own death. Soviet publication of his work has included *The Study of Sources in History* (1959) as well as a number of other pieces and a new edition of the *Course*.

Klyuchevsky's lectures were allegedly so popular that no others were scheduled for the hour at which they were given. According to Chaliapin (*Pages from my Life*, pp. 194–5), who consulted him on the personality of Boris Godunov, 'An artist in words, and gifted with a most powerful historical imagination, Klyuchevsky was, in addition to being an historian, a most remarkable actor.' Although hampered by a lifelong stammer, he made subject after subject come to life for a wide range of spellbound audiences. The *Course* is a literary as well as scholarly achievement of the highest order, and it remains regrettable that only the volumes dealing with the seventeenth century and the reign of Peter the Great have received a satisfactory translation. Many of his finest pen portraits, of Boris Godunov, Ivan the Terrible and others, can be perceived only dimly through the opaque prose of C. J. Hogarth. However, the *Course* is by no means exclusively concerned with the deeds and misdeeds of those on high. Klyuchevsky gave much attention to the peasant problem in its multifarious manifestations (and devoted a separate essay to the origins of serfdom, emphasizing the part played by peasant indebtedness). More than Solovyev and other predecessors, he was anxious to give full consideration to economic and geographical aspects of his subject. This enabled him to give coherent explanations of such problems as the rise of Muscovy, and to present a well-rounded account of the national development as a whole. For Klyuchevsky, the fundamental reason for the formation of the autocratic state and its chief underpinning, the landowning and military nobility, was the constant necessity to defend ever-widening frontiers.

There are serious omissions from the *Course*: it says very little about international relations, the Mongol invasions, peasant revolts and the non-Russian peoples. Without the romantic patriotism of Karamzin's *History*, it is still essentially an account of the problems faced by central government and the efforts made to overcome them. It steers clear of interpretation that could be called markedly Westerner or Slavophile, attempting for example to give a balanced view of the complex and controversial legacy of Peter the Great:

The reform emerged by itself from the urgent needs of the state and the people, and it was felt instinctively by a towering human being with an acute intellect and a powerful character, with talents harmoniously mixed in one of those exceptionally well formed natures, which for reasons still undiscovered, appear among mankind from time to time. (*Sochineniia*, vol. 4, p. 220)

Klyuchevsky did not bring his general history far into the nineteenth century, and, although politically aware, did not often broach in public subjects of a controversial nature. However, both in his lifetime and posthumously, he has been considered the outstanding historian of his age.   PD

Main publications

Sochineniia, 8 vols (Moscow: 1956–9); *A History of Russia*, 5 vols, trans. C. J. Hogarth (London and New York: Dent, 1911–31); individual vols trans. L. Archibald as *The Rise of the Romanovs* (London: Macmillan, 1970) and *Peter the Great* (Macmillan, 1958).

Reading

Byrnes, R. F.: Nechkina's Kliuchevskii. *Russian Review* 37 (1978) 68−81.

Chaliapin, F. I.: *Pages from my Life* (New York: 1927).

Karpovich, M.: Klyuchevski and recent trends in Russian historiography. *Slavonic Review* 21 (1942−3) 31−9.

Kiesewetter, A.: Klyuchevsky and his *Course of Russian History*. *Slavonic Review* 1 (1922−3) 504−22.

Maklakov, B.: Klyuchevsky. *Slavonic Review* 13 (1934−5) 320−9.

Mazour, A. G.: V. O. Kliuchevsky: the making of a historian. *Russian Review* 31 (1972) 345−59.

Parry, A.: Vasily Osipovich Kliuchevsky. In *Some Historians of Modern Europe*, ed. B. E. Schmitt (Port Washington: Kennikat 1966).

Knowles, Michael Clive, in religion **Dom David** (b.1896, d.1974) David Knowles was a monk and university professor, and the foremost English monastic historian of the twentieth century. When just eighteen he joined the Benedictine community at Downside and he remained a monk for the rest of his life, though from 1939 he lived apart from his community. He read classics at Christ's College, Cambridge (1919−22) and taught classics at Downside for some years: his retentive memory and devotion to literature enabled him to recall passages from Greek and Latin and from English classics all his life, and helped to mould his English style. In 1922−3 he was at Sant' Anselmo at Rome to finish his study of theology, which remained a central interest all his life. But it is as an ecclesiastical historian that he will be remembered: in 1929 he began work on *The Monastic Order in England*, which was published in 1940, and rapidly acclaimed a masterpiece of medieval scholarship. The years over which it was written witnessed a deep crisis in his life: he and a group of younger monks planned a new monastic community in which to pursue their ideals; when the scheme was forbidden at Rome in 1934 all but he accepted the verdict; after a spell at Ealing Priory (1933−9) he felt compelled to leave his community. He was cared for by Dr Elizabeth Kornerup, a devout Swedish doctor, and lived in London. Knowles was formally reconciled to his community in 1952, but 'exclaustrated': that is to say, he had leave to live outside the abbey and was free to pursue his second career. In 1944 he was elected fellow of Peterhouse, Cambridge, and divided his time between London and Cambridge until his retirement in 1963. Meanwhile academic promotion came rapidly: in Cambridge he was professor of medieval history from 1947 and regius professor of modern history from 1954. With promotion came many honours: he was president of the Royal Historical Society (1956−60), fellow of the Society of Antiquaries and of the British Academy (1947); LittD in 1941; and received later honorary doctorates in eight universities, of which the Cambridge DD was one.

As a young monk Knowles met Edmund Bishop, the great liturgical scholar, and lived among a galaxy of scholars; he had also read Macaulay, Gibbon, Grote, Clarendon and other classics of historical literature; *The Monastic Order* is a remarkable combination of rich scholarship and beautifully written historical narrative in the grand manner. He was a prolific writer and published many good books and essays on monastic history − on Thomas Becket and his circle, on the English mystics, and on wider themes of medieval church history. He showed the width of his culture by drawing Erasmus, Macaulay, Motley, Mommsen and many others from Sophocles and Cicero onwards into his service in his inaugural lecture as regius professor (reprinted in *The Historian and Character*, pp. 1−15). But his central achievement remained *The Monastic Order*, in which he reflected with notable objectivity on the central themes of monastic inspiration of the middle ages, while his personal life was torn apart by the same themes in the twentieth. Its three-volume sequel, *The Religious Orders in England*, continued the story to the Reformation; and the third volume gave a sustained narrative of the Dissolution, in which irony and emotion were brilliantly controlled in the service of scholarship.

A notable feature of the first two volumes of *The Religious Orders*, is the emphasis on intellectual history, one of the fields in which Knowles had strong influence on his pupils: for he was a teacher as well as a scholar, with

many devoted pupils and friends. Knowles was a small, courteous and gentle man: 'Human, urbane and humorous; a great historian and master of prose, a professor and teacher of wide influence; an austere and solitary monk; a devout priest ministering to his household and his friends. He was all these things and none of them by halves' (*Proceedings of the British Academy* 61 (1975), 476).
CNLB

Main publications

The Monastic Order in England 940–1216 (Cambridge: Cambridge University Press, 1940; 2nd edn, 1963); *The Religious Orders in England*, 3 vols (Cambridge University Press, 1948–59), vol. 3 abbrev. as *Bare Ruined Choirs* (1976); *The Episcopal Colleagues of Archbishop Thomas Becket* (Cambridge University Press, 1951); with R. N. Hadcock, *Medieval Religious Houses: England and Wales* (London: Longmans, Green, 1953; 2nd edn, 1971; 3rd edn with C. N. L. Brooke and V. C. M., London, 1972); *The English Mystical Tradition* (London: Burnes Oates, 1961); *The Evolution of Medieval Thought* (Longmans, Green, 1962; 2nd edn 1988); collected papers, ed. M. D. Knowles, *The Historian and Character and other essays* (Cambridge University Press, 1963) [incl. bibliography to 1962, pp. 363–73]; *Great Historical Enterprises and problems in monastic history* (London and Edinburgh: Nelson, 1963).

Reading

Brooke, C. N. L. David Knowles. *Proceedings of the British Academy* 61 (1975) 439–77.

Knowles, M. D.: Academic History. *History* 47 (1962) 229–32.

Morey, A.: *David Knowles: a memoir* (London: Darton, Longman & Todd 1979) [incl. bibliography; pp. 155–62].

Stacpoole, A.: The making of a monastic historian. *Ampleforth Journal* 80 (1975) 1, 71–91; 2, 19–38; 3, 48–55 [incl. bibliography from 1963] and 81 (1976) 1, 40 [incl. addit. bibliography].

Koebner, Richard (b.1885, d.1958) In his life and work Koebner exemplified the experience and the fate of the German-Jewish scholars who, expelled from their universities by the Nazi regime, left Germany to rebuild their life and career in their adopted countries, in his case, Palestine-Israel.

Born in the city of Breslau, Koebner studied at the universities of Berlin, Breslau and Geneva. In 1911 he received his doctorate from the University of Breslau where he was appointed Privat Dozent (lecturer) for medieval and modern history in 1920 and Professor-Extraordinarius in 1924. Dismissed as a Jew from his university, he left Germany for Palestine in 1934 to become the Cecil Lyons memorial professor of modern history and chairman of the newly established department of history at the Hebrew University in Jerusalem.

Before leaving Germany Koebner had established a reputation as a scholar of unusual scope in his chosen fields of research. He was a respected authority on medieval economic and social history, in particular on the medieval movement of settlement and urbanization, and he distinguished himself as a most sensitive student of the cultural and intellectual history of medieval and early modern Europe. In medieval history his research focused on the origins of the city of Cologne, as well as on a series of pioneering studies on the urban settlements in the Polish Silesian countries of the Piast dynasties. The results of this work were summed up in the notable synthesis published in the *Cambridge Economic History* as 'Settlement and colonization in Europe'. In the field of culture, intellectual history and political concepts his investigations ranged widely: from the concept of marriage in the late middle ages, to the historical views of James Harrington in the seventeenth century; from the edicts of the curia under Gregorius VII to the brilliant essays on the development of the fundamental concepts of cultural history, published in 1933/4.

The transition from Breslau to Jerusalem meant a total revolution in Koebner's life. A stranger to the Zionist movement and to the world of a vital Jewish culture as well as to the mentality of a new and pioneering society, he had also to acquire a new language, Hebrew, and to build the department to which he had been appointed as chairman. A man of fifty, Koebner accepted the challenge. He became an active member of the academic community and a concerned citizen involved in the grave issues facing his country and the free world. Under his guidance the department of history became a centre of intellectual and scholarly training in the historical disciplines which introduced the student to the main traditions of western civilization and to the formative forces of modern and contemporary history.

By the end of the war a number of important studies had appeared, signifying a new phase in Koebner's work. These were his studies on the concepts of economic imperialism, despotism and western civilization, and the series of essays which preceded his monumental study on the concept of empire and imperialism, published posthumously. Together they form an inquiry into the process by which concepts of historical thought and of the public mind are formed; their impact on ideologies is examined and the influence which generally accepted cultural and historical conceptions have on historical writings is analysed. The results of this work were summed up in an important programmatic essay, 'Semantics and historiography' (1953), in which Koebner explicated his views on the problems of HISTORICISM and objectivity and on the necessity for semantic 'self-analysis' of the historical mind in order to reach cognitive distance from its own historical involvement.

In 1955 Koebner retired from the Hebrew University. He died in England in 1958. Modest in manners and of a true courtesy, Koebner valued friendship and social intercourse. He loved teaching and the intellectual contact with students, and he trained a generation of scholars and teachers not only in history but in almost every field of the humanities and the social sciences. This uncommon influence derived from a rare fusion of a wide humanistic erudition, a close acquaintance with the social sciences, a penetrating intellect controlled by severe standards of scientific training, and a lucid and expressive style. An eminent scholar, Koebner enlarged historical knowledge and insight in every field he touched, and created in the semantic approach to history a new and fruitful method of historical inquiry. Koebner's lifelong interest in the nature of the aesthetic experience was expressed in one of his last books, written together with his wife, Gertrude Koebner.   YA

Main publications

Die Eheauffassung des ausgehenden deutschen Mittelalters (Breslau: Archiv für Kulturgeschichte Bd9, 1911); *Die Anfänge des Gemeinwesen der Stadt Köln* (Bonn: P. Hanstein, 1922); *Zur Begriffsbildung der*

Kulturgeschichte. *Historische Zeitschrift* CXLIX, No. 1 and No. 2 (1933/4); The settlement and colonization of Europe. *Cambridge Economic History* 1 (1941); Semantics and historiography. *The Cambridge Journal* VII (1953); with Gertrude Koebner, *Vom Schönen und seiner Wahrheit* (Berlin: de Gruyter, 1957); *Empire* (Cambridge: Cambridge University Press, 1961) with H. D. Schmidt, *Imperialism: the Story and Significance of a Political Word 1840–1960* (Cambridge: Cambridge University Press, 1964).

Reading

Arieli, Y.: Richard Michael Koebner – in memoriam. *The Richard Michael Koebner Chair of German History* (The Hebrew University of Jerusalem, 1984).

Rothenstreich, N., Prawer, Y. Arieli, Y., Talmon, Y. L.: *In Memory of Richard Koebner* (Jerusalem: Magnes Press, 1955).

Korzon, Tadeusz (b.1839, d.1918) A Pole from Lithuania, Korzon studied law in Moscow and spent six years in internal exile for anti-tsarist activities before being allowed to live in Warsaw in 1869. He emphasized the educational value of history and wrote excellent school textbooks. His research centred on the internal recovery of Poland under her last king, and he led the attack of the Warsaw positivists against the Cracow school's interpretation that the Poles were themselves mostly to blame for the partitions. He wrote extensively on methodology before embarking on a pioneering military history of Poland. An avid polemicist and energetic writer, he did most in this period, in addition to his antagonist BOBRZYŃSKI, to promote the study of history in Poland.   WHZ

Main publications

Wewnętrzne dzieje Polski za Stanisława Augusta (The internal history of Poland under Stanislas Augustus), 2nd edn, 6 vols (Warsaw: 1897–1903); *Kościuszko* (Cracow: 1894).

Reading

Grabski, A. F.: The Warsaw school of history. *Acta Poloniae Historica* 26 (1972) 153–70.

Kula, Witold (b.1916, d.1988) After an education at the University of Warsaw in history and the social sciences, Kula's career was interrupted by the invasion of his native Poland in 1939 and the subsequent upheavals.

KULA, WITOLD

He was involved in the Polish resistance and spent a period in a prisoner-of-war camp. He taught at Łódź University until 1948 and then returned to the University of Warsaw, where he became professor of economic history in 1950. Kula played an active role in the development of his subject notably through the Historical Institute of the Polish Academy of Sciences, and achieved widespread international recognition in the 1960s, serving as president of the International Economic History Association in 1968–70.

Kula worked within the Marxist tradition, using a notably critical and humanistic approach. He combined an emphasis on class struggle and economic systems with a tolerance of human eccentricities. His main interest was in the economic history of the seventeenth to nineteenth centuries, especially in Poland. As his concern was to understand the workings of traditional and feudal society and to show how capitalism developed from such a society, his works have a wide application. His book, *An Economic Theory of the Feudal System*, generalizes on the basis of the well-documented workings of the rural economy of Poland in the seventeenth and eighteenth centuries, and has been influential in the west.   CCD

Main publications

Szkice o manufakturach w Polsce w XVIIIw (Essays on eighteenth-century factories in Poland) 2 vols (Warsaw: PWN, 1956); *Teoria ekonomiczna ustroju feudalnego* (1962) trans. L. Garner *An economic theory of the feudal system* (London: New Left Books, 1976); *Problemy i metody historii gospodarczej* (Problems and methods of economic history) (Warsaw: PWN, 1963); *Miary i ludzie* (1970) (*Measures and Men*, trans. R. Szreter) (Princeton NJ: Princeton University Press, 1986).

L

labour history In Britain labour history has a long pedigree, to be expected in the country which was the first to industrialize. Radicals from the 1790s wrote their memoirs and autobiographies; the Chartist movement found an early historian in R. G. Gammage (1854); and from the 1880s, with the revival of socialism, there developed a growing interest in the origins of the trade union and radical movements. Some of the earliest writing on working-class institutions and movements was by German historians, but the British tradition began in the 1890s with the classic studies of Beatrice and Sidney WEBB, Graham Wallas's biography of Francis Place (1898) and Foxwell's remarkable introduction to Menger's *The Right to the Whole Produce of Labour* (1899). It was pre-1850 radicalism that attracted most attention before 1914, with Chartism as the main focus of interest.

The majority of historians writing about labour history in its broadest sense were radically minded liberals. The HAMMONDS were among the most distinguished, with Max Beer's important *History of British Socialism* (2 vols, 1919–20) coming out of a central European socialist tradition much influenced by Fabian ideas. Between the wars there continued a slow accumulation of materials: memoirs, trade union histories and the first synoptic accounts, especially those by COLE. Most of the writing came from those sympathetic to the mainstream ideas of the labour movement in Britain; the only substantial Marxist study was by Theodore Rothstein, *From Chartism to Labourism*, published in 1929, which had remarkably little influence although it was a serious study based upon a wide reading of original sources.

The revival of writing on labour themes developed fairly slowly in the 1950s and then increased rapidly from about 1960. The subject of labour history was taught at the university level only as part (and usually a small part) of more general historical surveys, although it had for several decades been an important component in adult education classes, especially those organized by the Labour College movement or by the Workers' Education Association. But from the 1960s the subject began to enter the curricula of university history schools. It was now an academic subject and those who wrote were mainly, although not entirely, academic historians. Except for memoirs and autobiographies the tradition of historical writing about the labour movement by working-class militants, while not entirely eliminated, was becoming much diminished. During the past three decades or so the ideological values underlying labour history writing have become varied. Henry Pelling must be counted as a liberal-minded conservative historian whose work has been consistently of a high quality; Asa BRIGGS has been more in the mainstream of labour progressivism; and of the many who work within a Marxist tradition, Edward P. THOMPSON and Eric HOBSBAWM are the outstanding representatives.

These last two are the best known and most influential of all labour historians. Hobsbawm is the more wide-ranging, and his writing has concerned itself with materials from Europe and the Americas: of all the historians in this field, his work has been the most stimulating in its emphasis upon comparative relationships. The most important and influential work in all the English-speaking countries has

229

been Thompson's *The Making of the English Working Class*, first published in 1963 and reprinted with an important postscript in 1968. The book is a study of the first decades of industrialization in Britain and their social consequences, with an emphasis upon the complexity of factors which produced by 1832 a working-class presence, which he argues was 'the most significant factor in British political life'. Thompson's work has generated a large-scale exegesis: in methodology, especially in the discussion of class structure, as well as in certain of his general conclusions concerning social consciousness. No other piece of writing in social history has occasioned such a vigorous debate; and it is far from having ended.

The volume of work in labour history has greatly increased since the early 1960s. One indication of the growing interest in the field was the establishment of the Society for the Study of Labour History in 1960 and the publication of a twice-yearly bulletin which is now an indispensable research source and has a wide international circulation; another has been the publication of a multi-volume *Dictionary of Labour Biography*, edited by J. M. Bellamy and J. Saville, the first volume of which appeared in 1972.

There has been a notable increase in the general sophistication of labour movement studies. The traditional emphasis upon institutional history has now become more complex, much assisted by the parallel growth since the second world war of the disciplines of SOCIAL HISTORY and political sociology. The development of a growing interest in industrial relations has inevitably had its effect upon the writing of trade union histories, and the expansion of psephological studies has greatly influenced the analysis of political parties and their evolution. The recent expansion of studies of the labour process has allowed a more subtle discussion of the variegated strata within the general working-class category, and the rapid growth of FEMINIST HISTORIOGRAPHY has encouraged new dimensions of study of the working-class movement, the potential of which has only begun to be realized.

Labour history has today become an accepted part of general historical studies in most countries. The levels of development, and of political sophistication, vary widely. The countries where industrialization took root in the nineteenth century have all developed thriving schools of teaching and research. Radical and socialist historiography in France and in other European countries also has a strong tradition. There are major archival collections in Europe and the English-speaking countries, with the United States having a number of outstanding depositories of original materials. Access to government sources — an important requirement for the labour historian — varies considerably. The most important collection of documentary sources not yet available are the Comintern archives in Moscow, but many governments, including the British, are still chary of making available some important sections of the materials in their keeping. Labour historians are not alone among historians in facing these kinds of problem, but they suffer especially in certain sensitive areas which concern the relations between labour movements and the state.

JS

Reading

Bellamy, J. and Saville, J. eds: *Dictionary of Labour Biography* (London: Macmillan, 1972–).

Gammage, R. G.: *History of the Chartist Movement, 1837–1854* (1854) (New York: A. M. Kelley, 1969).

Hobsbawm, E. J.: *Labouring Men* (London: Weidenfeld & Nicolson, 1964).

Maitron, J., ed.: *Dictionnaire biographique du mouvement français* (Paris: Éditions Ouvrières, 1964–).

Maitron, J., ed.: *Dictionnaire biographique du mouvement ouvrier international* (Éditions Ouvrières, 1971–).

Menger, A.: *The Right to the Whole Produce of Labour, with an introduction and bibliography by H. S. Foxwell*, (1899) (New York: A. M. Kelley, 1970).

Montgomery, D.: *Workers' Control in America* (Cambridge: Cambridge University Press, 1979).

Palmer, D. J.: *Working Class Experience: The Rise and Reconstitution of Canadian Labour, 1800–1980* (Toronto: Butterworths, 1983).

Thompson, E. P. *The Making of the English Working Class* (London: Gollancz, 1963; 2nd edn revised, Harmondsworth: Penguin, 1968).

Winter, J., ed.: *The Working Class in Modern British History: Essays in honour of Henry Pelling* (Cambridge University Press, 1983).

Journals
Actualité de l'histoire (Paris: 1954−), then *Le Mouvement social* (Paris: 1965−).
Bulletin of the Society for the Study of Labour History (London: 1960−).
International Review of Social History (Amsterdam: 1955−).
Llafur (Swansea: Society for the Study of Welsh labour history, 1973−).
Saothar (Dublin: Irish labour history society, 1975−).

Labrousse, Ernest (b.1895) During his earlier years Labrousse was a committed political activist, a contributor to *L'Humanité* (1919−24) and director of the *Revue socialiste* (1946−51). This, together with the circumstances of the 1930s, encouraged an interest in socio-economic structures and economic cycles. The influence of SIMIAND stimulated the development of a methodology which was analytical, quantitative, and dependent upon the identification and use of sources of quantifiable information. Furthermore, though he rejected a simple Marxist emphasis on the mode of production as the basic motor of history, Labrousse's research was certainly centred upon the relationship between classes, as well as upon an appreciation of the need to examine the complex interrelationships between the economic sphere and social and mental structures. The result is a history which avoids both traditional empiricism and the dehumanizing excesses of the econometricians.

Among Labrousse's many major contributions, the development of a model of the *crise de l'ancien type* must be highlighted. The *crise* was caused by a poor harvest and its impact upon the fundamentally pre-industrial agrarian and mercantile structures which persisted well into the nineteenth century in continental Europe. High food prices reduced the purchasing power of the mass of the population and demand for manufactured goods, thereby causing a generalized crisis throughout the economy. Labrousse also sought to relate the shorter term movement of prices, profits and wages in the periods of recession before the Revolution of 1789 (and also those of 1830 and 1848) to the development of social tension and political conflict.

This approach, taking into account such factors as agricultural productivity and demographic pressures, challenged prevailing monetarist assumptions concerning price movements. It stimulated an awareness of the complexity of processes of historical change, and although it was in turn criticized for its mechanistic explanation of political behaviour in relation to economic phenomena, Labrousse's analysis of price movements and social structures laid the foundation for later work on the *ancien régime* and the French Revolution. The influence of Labrousse's publications was increased by the author's central role as a research supervisor at the École Pratique des Hautes Études. His was the fundamental influence on a generation of young historians, many of whom engaged in 'serial history', reconstructing price, wage, production and trade statistics as the bases for a wider social history. Their frequent adoption of the region as the proper unit for study reflected the prevailing strength of French regional geography and the close links between historians and geographers. Typically, his encouragement of more analytical statistical and socio-professional approaches to the study of the bourgeoisie stimulated the subsequent work of FURET and Daumard on social structures in Paris in the eighteenth and nineteenth centuries. In short, Labrousse's work was probably the most important single influence upon the development of French economic and social history for some three decades after 1950.   RDP

Main publications

Esquisse du mouvement des prix et des revenus en France au XVIII siécle, 2 vols (Paris; Dalloz, 1933); *Crise de l'économie française à la fin de l'ancien régime et au début de la révolution* (Paris: Presses Universitaires de France, 1944); 1848, 1830, 1789: Comment naissent les révolutions. In *Actes du congrès historique du centenaire de la révolution de 1848* (Paris: 1948); Voies nouvelles vers une histoire de la bourgeoisie occidentale aux XVIIIᵉ et XIXᵉ siècles, 1700−1850. *X Congresso Internazionale di Scienze Storiche* (Rome: 1958); editor, Aspects de la crise et de la dépression de l'économie française au milieu du XIX siécle, 1846−51. *Bibliothèque de la Révolution de 1848*, 19 (1956); editor with F. Braudel, *Histoire économique et sociale de la France*, 4 vols, (Presses Universitaires de France, 1970−9).

LANDES, DAVID S.

Reading

Braudel, F. et al. eds: *Conjoncture économique: structures sociales. Hommage à Ernest Labrousse* (Paris: Mouton, 1974).

Landes, David S. (b.1924) Landes was born and grew up in New York City. Between 1943 and 1946 he served in the US Army, ending with the rank of first lieutenant, Signal Corps. After posts in economics at Columbia University, he was appointed professor of history and economics at Berkeley in 1958. In 1964 he returned to Harvard, where he had studied both as an undergraduate and for his PhD.

Landes's major contributions have been to the study of technological change and economic growth, international economic development and entrepreneurial history. His first book, *Bankers and Pashas* (1958), established both the quality of his scholarship and his considerable and rare skills of writing vivid economic history. This book combines broad economic and cultural history with a dramatic study of individual French entrepreneurial endeavour in nineteenth-century Egypt.

Landes achieved major international recognition with his skilful comparative studies of technological change and the spread of industrialization in western Europe, first as a large interpretative essay in *The Cambridge Economic History of Europe* (vol 6, ed. Habakkuk and Postan, 1965), and then expanded in scope as a book, *The Unbound Prometheus* (1969). His ability to explain the nature and significance of technological changes, to integrate these within economic history and to see their impact on the culture of their time is well exemplified in his study of clocks, *Revolution in Time* (1983): a book which again displays considerable literary skills and a certain old-fashioned rhetoric.

CJW

Main publications

Bankers and Pashas (Cambridge, Mass.: Harvard University Press; London: Heinemann, 1958); *The Unbound Prometheus* (Cambridge: Cambridge University Press, 1969); *Revolution in Time* (Harvard University Press, 1983).

Lane, Frederic Chapin (b.1900, d.1984) Lane was born in Michigan and studied in Europe before taking his doctorate at Harvard. He spent most of his working life at The Johns Hopkins University, Baltimore, and applied it to the detailed study of the instruments of early capitalism in medieval and Renaissance Venice. His books and articles were, like himself, direct, vigorous and sensible, eschewing jargon and determined to overcome technical difficulties. They commanded international respect, and he rose to become president of the American Historical Association in 1964. Lane's work ranged over international commerce, shipping, business partnerships, banking, real and ideal moneys, the public debt, the bullion market, and the organization of public enterprises and early industrial concentrations such as the arsenal and the mint. He was better at dealing with specific problems of this nature than at presenting any comprehensive view of the Venetian past. *Venice: a Maritime Republic* (1973) is his most widely read book and valuable for its special insights into economic history, but it tends to treat Venice in unnatural isolation from its possessions on the mainland of Italy.

BSP

Main publications

(Published by The Johns Hopkins University Press, Baltimore except where otherwise stated.)
Venetian Ships and Shipbuilders of the Renaissance (1934), rev. French edn *Navires et constructeurs à Venise pendant la Renaissance* (Paris: SEVPEN, 1965); *Andrea Barbarigo, Merchant of Venice, 1418–1449* (1944); *Venice and History: the Collected Papers of Frederic C. Lane* (1966); *Venice: a Maritime Republic* (1973); (with Reinhold C. Mueller), *Money and Banking in Medieval and Renaissance Venice*. Vol. I, *Coins and Moneys of Account* (1985) vol. II, forthcoming.

Langlois, Charles-Victor (b.1862, d.1929) Like many of his peers, Langlois was an archivist by training, and he emerged as one of the most distinguished medievalists of his generation. He was for many years professor of palaeography and medieval history at the Sorbonne, and his last ten years were spent as director of the Archives Nationales. His most important work was devoted to the reigns of the last Capetian kings of France, above all his definitive volume, *Le Règne de Philippe le Hardi* (1887). He contributed the section on 'St. Louis, Philippe le Bel, les derniers Capétiens directs' to the general *Histoire de France* edited by Lavisse (1901). The institutional bias of his early formation was reflected by such volumes as his *Textes relatifs à l'Histoire du Parlement [de Paris] depuis les origines jusqu'en 1314* (1888), and he made substantial contributions to the reconstitution of the medieval archives of France through his study of inventories and knowledge of lost documents. Langlois wrote many articles, some of them revealing an original cast of mind, such as his advocacy of the comparative method in the study of Anglo-French relations during the middle ages in 'The comparative history of England and France', *EHR* 5 (1890), where he wrote that 'under the Capetians and Plantagenets nearly all elements of French and English society are commensurate'. This was an approach to be taken up by T. F. TOUT and, more recently, John Le Patourel.   MV

Main publications

Le Règne de Philippe le Hardi (Paris: Hachette, 1887); *Textes relatifs à l'histoire du parlement depuis les origines jusqu'en 1314* (Paris: Picard, 1888); *St Louis, Philippe le Bel, les derniers Capétiens directs* (Paris: Hachette, 1901).

Laslett, Thomas Peter Ruffell (b.1915) A fellow of Trinity College and, from 1966 to 1983, reader in politics and the history of social structure in the University of Cambridge, Peter Laslett has left his mark on two fields of historical study. His early work on the seventeenth-century political theorists, Locke and Filmer, has been followed by a stream of articles, books and collaborative volumes of essays on the history of the family and the household which have made him one of the most influential and provocative of social historians. With E. A. WRIGLEY, he founded the Cambridge Group for the History of Population and Social Structure in 1964 and created a vigorous and innovative centre of historical research. Beginning with studies of listings of population in early modern England, and what they reveal about family size and the processes of household formation, his

own work has extended to subjects such as illegitimacy, old age and models of kinship systems. Critics have found his 'historical sociology' limited in its dependence on quantifiable evidence and generalized concepts. But the force and originality of his perceptions, and his success in communicating them to a wide audience, have done much to determine the direction of modern research in social history.   PAS

Main publications

Ed., *John Locke: Two Treatises of Government* (Cambridge: Cambridge University Press, 1960); *The World We Have Lost* (London: Methuen, 1965); ed. with R. Wall, *Household and Family in Past Time* (Cambridge University Press, 1972); *Family Life and Illicit Love in Earlier Generations* (Cambridge University Press, 1977).

Reading

Bonfield, L., Smith, R. and Wrightson, K. eds: *The World We Have Gained: essays presented to Peter Laslett* (Oxford: Blackwell, 1986).

Latin American historiography A historiographical tradition preceded the arrival of Columbus in the New World. Screenfolds of animal skin or bark paper covered with a layer of fine lime plaster on which are painted pictures predated the arrival of Cortés in Mesoamerica. Mayan and Mixtec codices and picture books which used iconographic, ideographic and phonetic symbols, are genealogical or historical in content, describe symbols and events, and discuss cosmogony and cosmology. Immediately post-conquest (1521), a further series of picture books were commissioned by Spaniards and prepared by native artists who used a pictographic system of writing and worked in conjunction with Spanish friars who wrote accompanying commentaries. Such was the *Codex Mendoza*, an Aztec painted manuscript prepared on the authority of viceroy Don Antonio de Mendoza for dispatch to Charles V. Large numbers of manuscripts were destroyed in military action or burnt as 'works of the Devil', but there was also a concerted effort to preserve manuscripts and reconstitute historical information which would otherwise have been lost. Friars primarily collected pre-Cortesian pictorial manuscripts, commissioned new pictorial manuscripts to record pre-conquest events, or themselves compiled compendia of information from native informants. Such sources contain detailed information on calendars, gods, rituals, mores, and events and are invaluable historical and ethnographic sources. The works of Toribio de Benavente Motolinía, Andrés de Olmos, Bernardino de Sahagún, Alonso de Zorita, and Diego Duran are invaluable. There are no pre- or post-first-contact counterparts to these Mesoamerican materials from South America, although some later texts in Andean languages are available, nor was there so strong a historical tradition in an attempt to reconstitute the histories of native peoples.

With the arrival of the Spaniards there came into being a literature of conquest and exploration. Cortés dispatched letters to Charles V; Bernal Diaz del Castillo provided a foot soldier's record of the conquest of Mexico; Alonso de Aguilar gave his own eye-witness account; and Alvar Nuñez Cabeza de la Vaca recorded his travels as the first white person to journey from Florida to the Pacific. The dominican friar Bartolomé de las Casas, known as the 'apostle of the Indies', wrote an early account of the customs and destruction of native peoples. In South America, Garcilaso de la Vega, mestizo offspring of a conquistador and an Incan princess, wrote of the origins of the Incas. For the southern Andes, Geronimo de Bibar accompanied Pedro de Valdivia on his conquest of Chile and wrote of this and further travels in his *Cronica e relación copiosa y verdadera de los reinos de Chile* (1558). Heroic events required epic treatment, and the most outstanding of the genre was Alonso de Ercilla y Zuñiga's *La Araucana* (1569) describing Spanish attacks on the Araucanians. In short, once allowance has been made for variations between regions (the basin of the Rio de la Plata receiving little attention in this period), for Hispanic America, the Caribbean and circum-Caribbean of the sixteenth century, there is great richness of indigenous sources and chronicles by Spanish, mestizos and Indians. These include chronicles, letters, grammars, vocabularies, and screenfolds.

This literature of conquest and early Euro-pean settlement had no Brazilian counterpart. The moving letter (1500) from Pero Vaz de Caminha to Dom Manuel described the first contact with Brazilian Indians, but it was left to missionaries (French as well as Portuguese) and Jesuits such as Manoel da Nóbrega, José de Anchieta and Pero Cardim to describe Brazil to a European readership. Treatises by laymen included those by Gabriel Soares de Sousa (1587) and Pero de Magalhães de Gandavo (1576) for the sixteenth century. More general histories of Brazil were penned in the seventeenth century by the Franciscan Vicente do Salvador (1627) and the Jesuit Simão de Vasconcellos (1663). Sebastião da Rocha Pitta covered the history of Brazil from first contact to 1724 in his *Historia da America Portugueza* (1730).

The nineteenth century witnessed French, German, and British interest in Latin America as an area for historical and scientific enquiry. Robert Southey's *History of Brazil* (3 vols, London: 1810–19) was comprehensive and pioneering. In the United States William H. Prescott's *History of the Conquest of Mexico* (3 vols, New York: 1843) and *History of the Conquest of Peru* (2 vols, London: 1847) built on, and contributed to a shared historical, cultural, and linguistic legacy which was to be coupled with scholarly enquiry into the west, southwest and borderlands and which, by extension, led to an interest in Hispanic America. By 1900 there was in the United States a corps of scholars whose reputations had been made by studies of Spain in America. The 1930s was a decade of 'great names' in Latin American scholarship in the United States and burgeoning pan-American sentiment. Interest in Brazil was slower to develop and at a lower level of scholarly intensity. Since the second world war there has been a surge of interest in Latin America, most apparent in the United States and to a lesser degree in Europe. More recently, aspects of Latin America have become of interest (sometimes for ideological reasons) to scholars in India, Japan, People's Republic of China, Australia, and the USSR where Latin American Centers or Institutes have been established (see, for example, Martin H. Sable, *Latin American Studies in the Non-Western World and Eastern*

Europe, Metuchen, NJ: Scarecrow Press, 1970) and Carmelo Mesa-Largo, *Latin American Studies in Asia* (Pittsburgh: Center for Latin American Studies, 1983).

The historiography of Latin America represents a trajectory away from what had initially been an Europacentric perspective couched in the broader rubrics of the expansion of Europe and colonialism. Increasingly, the historical agenda is being set by Latin Americans, interpretations represent a Latin American perspective, and Latin Americans are writing their own histories. Historical studies have become increasingly professionalized in Latin America. In Mexico the establishment of the Centro de Estudios Historicos, training programmes at the Escuela Nacional de Antropologia e Historia, and the creation of the Instituto de Historia at the National University exemplify this trend toward the creation of institutional frameworks fostering forums for historical research, such as the seminar in the modern history of Mexico. Brazil has witnessed the creation of training programmes for archivists and document librarians and establishment of doctoral programmes in history.

These developments have led to changing emphases on certain themes at different times and with varying intensity depending on regional differences and nationalist concerns. The result has been uneven coverage of countries, periods, and themes. Mexico and Brazil have attracted the bulk of international scholarly attention; Peru and Argentina somewhat less. Social, demographic, economic and political histories have predominated at the expense of histories of ideas, of science, of music, of medicine, and of religion. As regards Latin Americans, their interests and writings have been focused by their own national histories rather than by broader themes. For Argentinians, these are the age of Rosas, the revolutions of 1890 and 1930, and Peron and the post-Peron era; for Brazilians, historical precedents for the Republic, and the Vargas era; for Mexicans, the Reforma, Porfiriato, and revolutions of 1910 and 1940. Meticulously researched monographs based on public and private archives are the norm. Exceptional are the multi-volume histories by the Brazilian

Francisco Adolfo de Varnhagen (*História Geral do Brasil*, 5 vols, 5th edn, São Paulo: 1948), the Chilean Francisco Antonio Encina (*Historia de Chile desde la prehistoria hasta 1891*, 20 vols, Santiago de Chile: 1941–52) and the Peruvian Jorge Basadre (*Historia de la República del Peru desde sus origenes hasta la presente*, 10 vols, 5th edn, Lima: 1961–64).

While pioneering studies of high quality on the colonial period continue to appear, the surge both in scholarly interest and in publications is most apparent for the national and contemporary periods. Early interest in voyages of exploration has declined, the idiom of 'discovery' has been replaced by the language of 'first contacts' between Europeans and the indigenous peoples, and the 'vision of the vanquished' is replacing the earlier drum and trumpet paeans to *conquistadores*. Themes identified in the 1930s still provoke controversy: the *leyenda negra*, the demographic impact on Amerindian populations stemming from the European presence, land usage and formation of the latifundia, labour systems (*encomienda*, *repartimiento*, *mita*), the *hacienda*, American treasure and the rise of capitalism in Europe, and New Spain's 'century of depression'. Institutions of empire, commercial networks and structures, and missionary activities have been well studied.

Although advances are being made in institutional, economic, and political history, the most exciting recent research and writing is in social history. New interpretations and reinterpretations are being made concerning Indian reactions to European intrusions, biomedical history, persons of African descent, manumissions, the role of women, family history, and the inter-relationship between gender, ethnicity, and kinship. Emerging as a subtheme has been the history of the underprivileged (persons of African descent, native Americans, and women). Proto-independence, independence, and revolutionary movements are being reassessed.

From an early date Latin American history has reflected a strong interdisciplinary tradition. There has been cross-fertilization between history, geography, sociology, social anthropology, archaeology, and linguistics. Methodologically, techniques have been borrowed from the quantitative sciences and social sciences. PROSOPOGRAPHY has thrown new light on collectivities, be they merchants, crown judges, planters, conquistadores, or freedmen of colour. Quantitative techniques have opened up new avenues for inquiry on the Middle Passage, demography (natality, fertility, fecundity, mortality, migration), colonial Treasuries, domestic mores (age at first marriage, selection of partners, stability of marriage), and manumission. Comparative studies across time or space within Latin America, or taking Latin America as one point in the comparison, have thrown new light on systems of slavery, plantation societies, economies, systems of government, independence movements, and the transition from colonies to republics. For the colonial period especially, historians are now looking beyond 'official' sources such as royal and gubernatorial edicts and correspondence to notarial and court records and parish archives. The richness of census data and baptismal, marriage, and burial registers for the seventeenth and eighteenth centuries is being exploited by social and demographic historians to study the structure of households and transformation of the family in rural and urban milieux.

The most comprehensive historical overview in English for the whole of Latin America and from the eve of conquest to the present is *The Cambridge History of Latin America (8 vols, Cambridge: Cambridge University Press, 1984—)*. Written by contributors drawn from the Americas and Europe, this multi-volume history comprises a series of highly effective syntheses, incorporating the most recent interpretations and research, on the social, political, intellectual and cultural history of Latin America.   AJRR—W

Reading

Rather than select works on specific themes, the prime purpose of this list is to direct the reader to bibliographic resources.

Carbia, Romulo D.: *Historia critica de la historiografia argentina desde sus origenes en el siglo XVI* (Buenos Aires: 1940).

Cline, Howard F. ed.: *Latin American History. Essays on its Study and Teaching, 1898—1965*, 2 vols

(Austin and London: University of Texas Press, 1974).

Craz, Guillermo Feliu: *Historiografia colonial* (Santiago de Chile: 1958).

Handbook for Latin American Studies (1936—) [provides updated and annotated bibliography].

Gibson, Charles and Keen, Benjamin: Trends of United States studies in Latin American history. *American Historical Review* 62 (1957) 855—77.

Graham, Richard and Smith, Peter H. ed.: *New Approaches to Latin American History* (Austin and London: University of Texas Press, 1974).

Griffin, Charles C. ed.: *Latin America: a Guide to the Historical Literature* (Austin: University of Texas Press, 1971).

Humphreys, Robin A.: *Latin American History. A Guide to the Literature in English* (London: Oxford University Press, 1958).

de Moraes, Rubens Borba: *Bibliographia Brasiliana*, 2 vols, rev. edn (Los Angeles and Rio de Janeiro: 1983).

Rodrigues, Jose Honorio: *Guide to the History of Brazil, 1500—1822. The Literature in English* (Santa Barbara and Oxford: ABC—Clio, 1980).

Sabor, Josefa Emilia: *Manual de fuentes de informacion: obras de referencia* (Buenos Aires: 1957).

Steele, Colin: *English Interpreters of the Iberian New World from Purchas to Stevens, 1603—1726* (Oxford: 1975) [biblio. guide to English trans. of Spanish and Portuguese sources].

Steward, Julian H. ed.: *Handbook of South American Indians*, 6 vols (Washington DC: 1946—50) [provides ethnohistorical material].

Wauchope, Robert ed.: *The Handbook of Middle American Indians*, 16 vols (Austin: University of Texas Press, 1964—76) [incl. surveys of extant indigenous materials and post-conquest ethnohistorical sources, esp. vols 12, 14 and 15].

Wilgas, A. Curtis: *The Historiography of Latin America* (Metuchen, NJ: Scarecrow Press, 1975) [pre-1800 historiography].

——: *Latin America, Spain and Portugal. A Selected and Annotated Bibliographical Guide to Books Published in the United States, 1954—1974* (Metuchan, NJ: Scarecrow Press, 1977).

The following journals are valuable sources of current research and historiographical assessment on regions, subdisciplines, specific themes.

The Americas (1944—).
Hispanic American Historical Review (1918—).
Inter-American Review of Bibliography (1951—).
Journal of Inter-American Studies and World Affairs (1959—).
Journal of Latin American Studies (1969—).
Latin American Research Review (1965—).
Revista de Historia (1950—) [for Brazil].
Revista de Historia [for Spanish America].
Revue de l'Amerique Latiné (1922—).

Lavisse, Ernest (b.1842, d.1922) One of the most influential figures in the history of French education, Lavisse was successively professor at the Sorbonne (1888) and director of the École Normale Supérieure (1904–19). He was elected to the French Academy in 1892. Author of textbooks on a wide variety of subjects (some pseudonymously) at several levels, he was by training a historian. His greatest monuments were the general series he planned and edited: *Histoire générale du IVe siècle à nos jours* (with A. Rambaud) (1893–1900); *Histoire de France depuis les origines jusqu'à la Révolution* (1900–12); and *Histoire contemporaire de la France* (1920–2). Lavisse himself contributed important volumes to these series (for example a volume on Louis XIV in the *Histoire de France*), but they were fundamentally collective works, written by the most distinguished scholars of their day. Though broadly reflecting the official patriotic and secularizing values of the Third Republic, they are packed with information that is still useful, and the volumes for some periods in the *Histoire de France* have yet to be replaced as basic surveys.   WD

Main publications

Ed. with A. Rambaud, *Histoire générale du IVe siècle à nos jours*, 12 vols (1893–1900); ed. *Histoire de France depuis les origines jusqu'à la Révolution*, 10 vols (1900–12); ed. *Histoire contemporaire de la France*, 9 vols (1920–2).

Reading

Lavisse, E.: *Souvenirs* (Calmann-Lévy, 1912).

Lea, Henry Charles (b.1825, d.1909) Lea was born in Philadelphia, of old Quaker stock, but his mother was brought up a Roman Catholic. He worked in his father's publishing business from 1843, and ran it after 1865. During the 1860s and 1870s Lea was active in support of republican causes, and later of municipal reform. He retired when his health broke down in 1880.

Lea's interest turned to history when he read FROISSART in 1849, and became intrigued by the question of his accuracy. His first book, *Superstition and Force* (1866), embodied his abiding conviction that 'the history of jurisprudence is the history of civilization'.

His method, self-taught and clearly displayed in the posthumous *Materials toward a History of Witchcraft*, derived from the strong interest in natural history and science of his youth: before forming any conclusion he painstakingly transcribed and arranged every reference he could find, both in the printed sources which he collected avidly and from the copyists whom he employed in archives all over Europe, especially in Spain. The library which he formed in this way and bequeathed to the University of Pennsylvania with a substantial endowment is his greatest monument, but his books are still to be read for the humanity of their insight as well as the breadth of their learning. The greatest of them, the *History of the Inquisition*, was translated into French at the time of the Dreyfus trial, and circulated in chapters by Belgian and Spanish as well as by French liberals.   RIM

Main publications

(All modern publications, New York.)
Superstition and Force (1866) (B. Blom, 1971); *An Historical Sketch of Sacerdotal Celibacy* (1867) (AMS Press, 1984); *A History of the Inquisition of the Middle Ages* (1888) (AMS Press, 1984); *A History of Auricular Confession and Indulgences* (1896) (Greenwood Press, 1968); *The Moriscos of Spain, their Conversion and Expulsion* (1901) (Burt Franklin, 1968); *A History of the Inquisition of Spain* (1906–7) (AMS Press, 1984); *Materials towards a History of Witchcraft*, ed. A. Howland (1939) (AMS Press, 1984).

Lecky, William Edward Hartpole (b.1838, d.1903) Lecky was one of the last and most distinguished of the great Victorian gentlemen scholars, holding no university appointment but supporting himself by private means and his writing. He was born in County Dublin into a prosperous and well-connected family and educated at Cheltenham and at Trinity College, Dublin, where a statue to him has a place of prominence. As an undergraduate, he was much influenced by BUCKLE's *History of Civilization in England*, which came out in 1857 during his first year in college. He had originally considered taking holy orders but developed religious doubts and decided to pursue a career in letters. This initial difficulty gave an orientation to his whole life since he became convinced of the value of scepticism and traced it in a series of publications.

An early book of poems attracted little attention and his first major book, *Leaders of Public Opinion in Ireland*, published in 1861, was equally unsuccessful. But in 1865 he surveyed the spread of religious toleration and enlightenment in *The Rise and Influence of Rationalism in Europe*. It was well received and established Lecky as a member of the London literary elite, mixing with Leslie STEPHEN, CARLYLE, FROUDE, Browning, Tennyson, Spencer and Huxley. He followed it with a *History of European Morals from Augustus to Charlemagne* (1869), which was, in some respects, a background to the previous book, showing how religious orthodoxy had been imposed. He compared paganism with early Christianity, often to the advantage of the former, and was particularly respectful towards Marcus Aurelius, whom he regarded as one of the most humane and far-sighted of rulers.

In 1878 he began the publication of his most substantial work, the *History of England in the Eighteenth Century*, a period which attracted him as an age of reason. It was enormously successful, the eighth and final volume coming out in 1890. Lecky greatly admired the English aristocracy, whose liberality, in contrast to that of their continental European counterparts, had 'probably done more than any other single cause to determine the type and ensure the permanence of English freedom'. Their greatest failure was their treatment of Ireland, to which Lecky accorded, in the view of some critics, disproportionate attention. His final volume, written under the influence of the Home Rule crisis, concluded with a sharp contrast between 'the complete success' with which England had governed India 'and her signal failure in governing a neighbouring island'. The Irish question, in the nineteenth century, had had a baneful effect upon English politics, producing 'apostasies and transformations so flagrant, so rapid and so shameless, that they have sunk the level of public morals ... to a point which had scarcely been touched in England since the evil days of the Restoration or the Revolution'.

Lecky was bitterly opposed to Home Rule and in his later years he turned to politics, representing his own university from 1895 as a Liberal Unionist. Though neither a vigorous speaker nor a ready debater, his wide knowledge gained him a hearing in the House of Commons. In 1896 he added to the considerable number of Victorian publications viewing the advent of democracy with trepidation in *Democracy and Liberty* and his last major work *The Map of Life* (1899) was a rather odd volume of reminiscence, reflection and advice, in which his admiration for stoicism and paganism was still apparent. It remains readable, though the comments are sensible rather than brilliant. Lecky had the good fortune to die in his study, surrounded by his books. JAC

Main publications

All published in London.
Leaders of Public Opinion in Ireland (1861); *The Rise and Influence of Rationalism in Europe* (1865); *History of European Morals from Augustus to Charlemagne* (1869); *The History of England in the Eighteenth Century* (1878–1890); *Democracy and Liberty* (Longman, 1896); *The Map of Life* (Longman, 1899).

Reading

McCartney, D.: Lecky's 'Leaders of public opinion in Ireland', *Irish Historical Studies* 14 (1964–5) 119–41.

Walpole, Spencer: *Proceedings of the British Academy*, 1904, pp. 207–10.

Wyatt, A.: Froude, Lecky and 'the humblest Irishman' *Irish Historical Studies* 19 (1974) 261–85.

Lefebvre, Georges (b.1874, d.1959) The son of a minor employee in the Lille cotton industry, Lefebvre was the personification of the virtues and limitations of the educational system of the Third Republic. It was possible to work one's way to the top without wealth or influence but the way was long and arduous and the struggle left permanent scars. His own outstanding ability and his insatiable passion for hard work eventually took Lefebvre to the Sorbonne chair in French revolutionary and Napoleonic history, but only after he had spent twenty-five years in a *lycée*. He did not present his doctorate thesis until he was fifty. His Spartan habits were perhaps the product of necessity as much as temperament, but they became part of the man. Although his hero was Robespierre, he was himself more like Saint-Just: laconic, inflexible and totally dedicated to a conception of republican *vertu* that left no room for the cultivation of the emotions and the imagination, made no concessions to human frailty and had little time for those to whom the pursuit of history was less than a matter of total dedication. A man of immense erudition, he was brought up in a positivist tradition which encouraged the belief that the only legitimate way to deepen one's understanding of a period was by more research into the primary sources. He took the validity of his assumptions for granted. Jacobin to the core, he identified himself with his revolutionary heroes, and increasingly with Robespierre, sharing their nationalism, their impatience with the multi-coloured muddle of the *ancien régime* and their faith in the regeneration of a unified and disciplined nation by the rigorous enforcement of rational and scientific policies. In his later years he was impatient for the physiologists to produce what he called a 'science of temperaments' that would at last eliminate the unpredictability of human behaviour, so that it could be objectively investigated, explained and predicted.

Lefebvre established his reputation in 1924 with the publication of his massive doctorate thesis, *Les Paysans du Nord*, whose statistical appendices ran to a hundred pages. This at once became a classic, although it has been more praised than read and more read than imitated. To some extent he was to remain the historian of the peasantry, but of a peasantry as seen from the urban perspective of the revolutionaries. This was not unsympathetic, but it insisted on fitting them into a world of aspirations and calculations that was only partially theirs and it had no place for the study of specifically peasant values and attitudes. In 1932 he produced a much more accessible book, the *Grande Peur*, in which he traced the origins and progress of the various alarms that swept the French countryside in July 1789. A splendid example of the kind of patient detective work at which he excelled, it used local archives to establish the precise identity of a nation-wide movement that previous historians had been content to describe in impressionistic terms.

To commemorate the 150th anniversary of the French Revolution Lefebvre published in 1939 the work by which he is best known,

Quatre-vingt-neuf. This was both a more-or-less Marxist interpretation of the immediate causes of the revolution and an appeal to French opinion as a whole to unite in defence of what Lefebvre saw as liberal and democratic values in the face of the totalitarian threat from across the Rhine. The result was a synthesis of such clarity and power that when it was reprinted after the war, most of the original edition having been destroyed by order of the Vichy government, it achieved world-wide acceptance as an authoritative explanation of why the revolution happened, until its interlocking assumptions were challenged, notably by COBBAN and G. V. TAYLOR, in the 1960s. It is no longer possible for any historian, Marxist or otherwise, to accept the book as it stands, but it remains a brilliant example of historical craftsmanship and an enduring memorial to the attitudes of its time.

True to his academic formation, Lefevbre wrote several text-books, on the Thermidoreans, the Directory, and Napoleon. After collaborating in a joint history of the French Revolution, he published a revised version of his own in 1951. These are works in the French pedagogic tradition: erudite, somewhat austere and clinical in their style and concentration on high politics, inevitably communicating a personal point of view but expressing it as though it distilled itself from a scientific scrutiny of the evidence. Lefebvre went on working to the end of his long life, revising a study of Orleans and its surroundings that he had begun forty years earlier, which involved an attempt to determine class structure from a detailed statistical analysis of fiscal documents. When *Études Orléanaises* appeared posthumously in 1962−3 they marked the end of a school of history as well as constituting a memorial to their author.   NH

Main publications

(English translations published by Routledge & Kegan Paul, London, unless otherwise stated.) *Les Paysans du Nord* (Lille: Robbe, 1924); *La Grande Peur de 1789* (1932; trans. London: New Left Books, 1973); *Napoléon* (1935; trans. 1969); *Les Thermidoréans* (1937; trans. 1965); *Quatre-vingt-neuf* (1939; trans. Princeton, NJ: Princeton University Press, 1947); *Le Directoire* (1946; trans. 1965); *La Révolution française* (1951; trans. 1962−4).

LEGAL HISTORY

Reading

Annales historiques de la Révolution française 159 (1960) 1–89 [memorial edn].

Cobb, R. C.: Georges Lefebvre. In *A Second Identity* (Oxford: Oxford University Press, 1969).

legal history The history of legal systems, their content and their operation in practice. Legal history should be kept separate from the history of governments and constitutions though it obviously contributes to them and at times has done great work in these areas. A relatively recent arrival on the historian's agenda, it was intensively studied during the Renaissance and in the nineteenth century, the two periods during which history in general dominated intellectual pursuits. At all times, the need to comprehend the technicalities of the law has tended to remit its history to trained lawyers, more interested in discovering the antecedents of what they practise than in understanding the meaning and impact of laws in the past; nevertheless many practitioners contributed notably to the framing of sound principles in the study of history.

In practice, legal history has chiefly concentrated on two systems of law, that of the Roman or civil law and that of the common law of England. In the Renaissance, the former attracted the main attention. Its study formed an aspect of the general humanist search for the true ancient past behind medieval incrustations. The work began in Italy, with Lorenzo VALLA (1406–57) and his attack on the medieval glossators; it reached an impressive level of historical reconstruction in the hands of Andrea Alciato (1492–1550). The most accomplished practitioners, however, were French. The humanist demand for the use of the ancient law of Rome here encountered varied and entrenched customary laws; the resulting conflict produced that contrast of claims which frequently leads to serious study. The leading names were Guillaume Budé (1468–1540), François Baudouin (1520–73), Jean BODIN (1530–96) and Jacques Cujas (1522–90) who by stages enlarged linguistic and textual criticism into a comprehensive descriptive analysis. Though similar encounters between the canon law of the church and the common law of England initiated tentative beginnings of comparative studies in England also, the overwhelming ascendancy of the latter inhibited such endeavours from bearing much fruit. Its leaders, calling their law immemorial and refusing to recognize any change in its past, created an antihistorical attitude which ruled English lawyers till the nineteenth century.

It was in that century that the history of law, like all history, achieved true maturity. The lead was taken by the German historians of the Roman law, particularly by Friedrich Karl von SAVIGNY (1779–1861) and his school. Initially jurists, they turned to history in an endeavour to understand the correct meaning of the law in the past in order to be able to formulate it more successfully for the present. They concentrated on the post-Roman era of the Roman law and branched forth also into the history of the canon law of the Church, hitherto rather neglected by historians. The successes of this school led other scholars, especially Heinrich Brunner (1840–1915) and Otto Gierke (1841–1921), to apply the new methods to the native law of medieval Germany. Their example inspired similar researches in Italy and Spain, though France, with its law settled in the Napoleonic Code, participated less. More recently, the historical study of civil law has become an international enterprise, as the list of the contributors to a volume presented to Helmut Coing (b. 1912), the leading German practitioner, testifies. Modern attention to the canon law also derived from German inspiration which the dispersal of German scholars transmitted to the English-speaking world through such influential historians as Walter Ullmann (1911–83) and Stefan Kuttner (b. 1907).

The English common law remained stubbornly resistant to the new learning until the trumpet call reached the ears of F. W. MAITLAND (1850–1906) who in twenty-two years of hectic labour erected the major edifice of English legal history. He also founded the Selden Society whose massive publications of legal–historical material contain in their introductions some of the foremost expository work. For a time English legal historians remained stuck in the middle ages, with several scholars carrying on Maitland's work, especially T. F. T. PLUCKNETT (1897–1965), H. G. Richardson (d.1973), G. O. Sayles (b. 1901) and S. E. Thorne (b. 1907). Since 1945 legal history has become an important component of post-medieval history in England and America. It has developed in two branches, each taking up one of the two sides of Maitland's message. One branch continues to concentrate on the law itself; the work of such scholars as S. F. C. Milsom and J. H. Baker has revolutionized our understanding of the common law between 1066 and 1700. The other branch followed Maitland's demonstration that legal history forms one of the best guides to the inwardness of a past society; it studies especially crime as an indicator of social concepts and change. The appearance in the last generation of four new specialist journals underlines the vigorous state of legal history in the English language.

At the same time the expansion of that history has begun to reveal some problems. The great initiators – men such as Alciato, Savigny and Maitland – were originally lawyers. They knew the law, comprehended its language, and had to acquire a similar familiarity with the skills and attitudes of the historian. The first branch of English legal–historical studies continues in that tradition and still occasionally, more commonly in American hands, falls victim to the teleological preferences of lawyers' history. The second attracts trained historians who need to turn themselves into expert lawyers if they are to get what they want from the records of the law. It is for this reason that studies of crime have predominated. Here the law is relatively simple, and the enterprise responds to the sociological prejudices of historians influenced by the French ANNALES SCHOOL. The risks lie in the manifest lack of interest in by far the largest part of the law. However, signs that more wide-ranging matters such as the laws of property, of inheritance or of contract are also being studied for the light they can throw on history in general promise a further renaissance in legal history, and suggest that the common law rather than the offsprings of the law of Rome will profit most from that next stage. GRE

References

Alciato, A.: *De verborum significatione libri quattuor* (Lyons: 1565).

Baker, J. H.: *An Introduction to English Legal History* (London: Butterworth, 1979).

Brunner, H.: *Deutsche Rechtsgeschichte* 2 vols (Berlin: 1887–92).

Coing, H.: *Epochen der Rechtsgeschichte in Deutschland* (Munich: Beck, 1971).

Cujas, J.: *Paratitla in libros quinqeginta Digestorum seu Pandectarum* (Frankfurt: 1615).

Elton, G. R.: *F. W. Maitland* (London: Weidenfeld & Nicolson, 1985; New Haven, Conn.: Yale University Press, 1985).

Kelley, D. R.: *Foundations of Modern Scholarship: Language, Law and History in the French Renaissance* (New York: Columbia University Press, 1970).

Milsom, S. F. C.: *Historical Foundations of the Common Law* (London: Butterworth, 1969).

Lelewel, Joachim (b.1786, d.1861) Lelewel was the son of a Polish lawyer and educational administrator of Swedish-German descent (original surname, Loelhoeffel). Although largely self-taught, Lelewel was also educated by the Piarists in Warsaw and at the university of Vilna (Wilno). He combined his historical research with teaching in the Krzemieniec *lycée* and with a period as a civil servant in Warsaw. After 1815 he lectured in history at Vilna university and on bibliography at Warsaw before receiving the chair of history in Vilna in 1821. An inspired and popular lecturer of strong democratic views, he was removed from his post in 1824 by the Russian authorities and returned to Warsaw. His national and international reputation was established by 1830.

Lelewel was interested in broadening the scope and methodology of history; he wrote on bibliography, and on ancient India, and developed the comparative approach to history in his work on early modern Spain and Poland. His popular history of Poland ran to 20 editions in the nineteenth century. He rejected NARUSZEWICZ's monarchical periodization of Polish history in favour of one based on the progress of popular liberties; his theory of the communal liberties of the pre-Christian Slavs and eulogy of Polish republicanism confirmed the impact of Romanticism on Polish historiography. He inspired many young patriots and radicals, and, as minister of education, represented the 'left wing' of Polish politics in the National Government during the 1830–1 uprising.

After 1831 Lelewel lived in exile, mostly in Brussels. To retain his political independence he declined the chair of history and geography in Brussels and pursued the life of an ascetic scholar. He made a pioneering contribution to the study of medieval numismatics and of medieval historical geography, especially of Arabia. His work on Polish history centred on the struggle of the peasant masses, while his republican and democratic politics brought him in contact with Lafayette, Marx, Engels and later Herzen. His influence on the spread of democratic ideas in Poland was considerable and continued, through his writings, after his death.   WHZ

Main publications

Dzieje Polski potocznym sposobem opowiedziane (Poland's past recounted in a familiar way) (Warsaw: 1829); *Historyczna paralela Hiszpanii z Polską w w. XVI, XVII, XVIII* (The historical parallel between Spain and Poland in the sixteenth, seventeenth, eighteenth centuries) (Warsaw: 1831); *Numismatique du Moyen-Age*, 2 vols (Brussels: 1835); *Géographie du Moyen-Age* (Brussels: 1852–7).

Reading

Rose, W. J.: Lelewel as historian. *Slavonic and East European Review* 15 (1936–7) 649–62.
Serejski, M. H.: Joachim Lelewel, 1786–1861. *Acta Poloniae Historica* 6 (1962) 35–54.

Lemarignier, Jean-François (b.1908, d.1980) An inspiring and enthusiastic teacher as well as a meticulous scholar, Lemarignier was trained in law, diplomatic and palaeography in Paris, served as the *bibliothécaire archiviste* to the Conseil d'État (1934–41), and had a brief period on active service (1939–40). Thereafter he devoted himself to academic life. He was titular professor of law at Lille (1948–58) and Paris (1959–70) and subsequently (1970–9) of 'Les institutions publiques et des faits sociaux' at the University of Paris IV, a post which made the most of his expertise in law and institutional history. Lemarignier's scholarly output concentrated on the tenth, eleventh- and twelfth-century history of France, and

fully exploited his legal and diplomatic training. His early research was on monastic exemptions in Normandy, followed in the 1950s by a series of influential articles tackling many of the key problems in the history of medieval France, such as the growth of public authority, the role of monasticism in the reform of the church, and the development of political and legal institutions. His exposition of royal government under the early Capetian kings, published in 1965, is his major work. His two other syntheses on ecclesiastical institutions and the history of medieval France were more obviously the fruit of his twenty years experience as a university teacher. In 1955 he initiated *Gallia monastica*, a survey of all Benedictine abbeys in France; so far only the first volume, covering the diocese of Rheims, has appeared. His historical scholarship, for which he won a number of major prizes, was of a high calibre, original in both method and conception, rigorous, and copiously documented.   RMcK

Main publications

Étude sur les privilèges d'exemption et de juridiction ecclésiastique des abbayes normandes depuis les origines jusqu'en 1140 (Paris: Archives de la France Monastique 44, 1937); *Recherches sur l'hommage en marche et les frontiers féodales* (Lille: Travaux et memoires de l'Université de Lille, n.s. 24, 1945); 'Les institutions ecclésiastiques en France de la fin du Xe au milieu du XIIe siècle', in *Histoire des institutions françaises au moyen age*. Vol. III; *Institutions ecclésiastiques*, ed. F. Lot and R. Fawtier, (Paris: Presses Universitaires de France, 1962); *Le gouvernement royal aux premiers temps capétiens 987–1108* (Paris: Picard 1965); *La France médiévale; institutions et sociétés* (Paris: Colin, 1970).

Reading

Hubert, M.–C.: Jean-François Lemarignier. *Bibliothèque de l'École des Chartes* 140 (1982) 350–353.

Le Roy Ladurie, Emmanuel Bernard (b.1929) The son of a landowner (who was minister for agriculture under the Vichy regime), Le Roy Ladurie reacted against his father by joining the Communist party. An upper-class Norman, he has spent much of his life in the study of the peasants of the south. His academic career has taken him from a lycée in Montpellier to the École des Hautes

Études and finally, on the retirement of BRAUDEL, to the Collège de France.

Le Roy Ladurie made his reputation in his late thirties with the publication of his massive doctoral thesis, *The Peasants of Languedoc*, covering the period between the late fifteenth and the early eighteenth centuries. It began with a geographical introduction, in the style of Braudel, who supervised the research, and continued with a meticulous analysis of price and population trends in the manner of LABROUSSE. To this history of structures and trends Le Roy Ladurie added a study of the ways in which his peasants perceived and interpreted their world, looking in particular at the Reformation, at witchcraft, and at rural revolt. This study corresponds to the third section in Braudel's *Mediterranean*, but in Le Roy Ladurie's work events and structures were more closely related than in that of Braudel. It is no wonder that Le Roy was nicknamed 'Le Dauphin', the heir to the kingdom of *Annales*.

In 1975 Le Roy Ladurie, as an acknowledged specialist on early modern France suprised the historical world by publishing a large book on the middle ages, or more exactly on a village in fourteenth-century Languedoc, Montaillou. His main source, the records of interrogations of suspected heretics, was well known to specialists and had been printed, but no one seems to have thought of using it as he did, as a means of reconstructing a community and describing its whole material and mental world. Ladurie's account of the material culture and ecology is particularly impressive. Carried along by the Occitan revival as well as by the author's fluent style and his gift for characterization, *Montaillou*, (1975) reached the top of the best-seller lists in France, while the village itself was almost buried under a mass of tourists. Specialists were less impressed, not to say highly critical.

In a third major study, Le Roy Ladurie moved somewhat closer to traditional narrative history, taking an episode discussed in a few pages of *The Peasants of Languedoc*, that of the Carnival of Romans, a small town in Dauphiné, in 1579, and making it the focus of a book. He used the story of a festival which went wrong and turned into a massacre to illuminate the life of a small town during the Wars of Religion.

Le Roy Ladurie is also an accomplished essayist, whether he is writing about the court of Louis XIV, the journal of a country gentleman in sixteenth-century Normandy, or about new methods in historical writing. He combines an interest in social theory — any theory he can use, from Chayanov on the peasant family to Victor Turner on social dramas — with a vivid historical imagination. The standard-bearer of *Annales* in its third generation, he has led the movement away from the quantitative history so prominent in his thesis and towards the new lands of historical anthropology.   UPB

Main publications

The Peasants of Languedoc (1966) (Urbana: Illinois University Press, 1974); *Histoire du climat* (Paris: Flammarion, 1967) (New York: 1971); *The Territory of the Historian* (1973) (Hassocks: Harvester, 1979); *Montaillou* (1975) (London: Scolar Press, 1978); *Carnaval* (1979) (London: Scolar Press, 1980); *L'amour, l'argent et la mort au pays d'Oc* (Paris: Seuil, 1980).

Reading

Le Roy Ladurie, E.: *Paris-Montpellier: PC−PSU 1945−63* (Paris: Gallimard, 1982).

Lévi-Provençal, Évariste (b.1894, d.1956) After graduating in Arabic at the University of his native Algiers in 1913, Lévi-Provençal served in the army and was wounded in the Dardanelles. Posted to Morocco to work for the Office of Native Affairs, he became in 1919 Professor of Arabic at the Institut des hautes études marocaines in Rabat, where he joined several dynamic French orientalists grouped around the periodical *Hespéris*. He wrote several works on Moroccan history, notably his doctoral thesis, *Les historiens des Chorfa* (1922), and became director of the Institut in 1926, and editor of *Hespéris* and of the monumental *Encyclopédie de l'Islam* before moving to a chair at Algiers in 1935.

Lévi-Provençal began to concentrate his researches increasingly on the Almoravid and Almohad dynasties, who had ruled both Morocco and Southern Spain, and to extend

LEVISON, WILHELM

them to Spanish Moslem history. He produced many seminal monographs on the political, economic and administrative activities of both dynasties in Spain and Africa; revised Dozy's elderly classic account of early Moslem Spain (711–1110); and wrote the first version of his own great work of synthesis, on the society and institutions of the Caliphate of Córdoba. More important was his sensational talent for discovering unknown medieval Arabic texts, including chronicles, official letter-collections, geographical surveys, biographical encyclopaedias, manuals of civic administration and one marvellous autobiography (of an eleventh-century king of Granada). He found them in private and public libraries, mosques and monasteries, and edited them in an apparently unending stream until the end of his life.

During the second world war he was dismissed from his chair by the Vichy government, because he was a Jew, and the second of his three marriages broke up; he seems to have done secret war work, as well as writing the first version of his history of Ummayad Spain. In 1945 he moved to a chair of Arabic especially created for him at the Sorbonne, where in 1950 he became the director of its Institut des Études Islamiques and undisputed leader of French Arabism. His last years were spent in incessant lecturing, writing and publishing, in France, Spain, Egypt and elsewhere.

As a historian, Lévi-Provencal's great achievement was the discovery and publication of so many new sources; and his merits included enormous energy and omnivorous reading. His volumes on Ummayad Spain (711–1031) have not been bettered, although they add nothing but extra illustrative facts to the traditional interpretation expounded in the nineteenth century by Conde and Dozy. With so many new texts and so much more information, it is regrettable that Lévi-Provençal did not reassess the value of the sources, ask and answer new questions and produce a new interpretation both of the Ummayad and of later periods. How far his failure to do so is attributable to the marital, political and professional vicissitudes which made him a rather isolated and embittered, though always upright and loyal, man, is impossible to say. DWL

Main publications

Documents inédits d'histoire almohade (Paris: Geuthner, 1928); *Le Kitab al-Bayan al-mugrib d'Ibn Idari al-Marrakusi. Tome III* (Geuthner, 1930); *L'Espagne musulmane au Xe siècle.* (Paris: Larose, 1932); *Les 'Mémoires' de Abd Allah, dernier roi ziride de Grenade,* 2 vols (Madrid: Maestre, 1936–40); *Histoire de l'Espagne musulmane, I: de la conquête à la chute du califat de Cordoue, 710–1031* (Cairo: Institut Français d'Archéologie Orientale, 1944).

Reading

Garcia Gómez, E.: Lévi-Provençal (4 enero 1894–23 marzo 1956). *Al-Andalus* 21 (1956) i–xxiii.

Levison, Wilhelm (b.1876, d.1947) Born in Düsseldorf of a Jewish family, Levison studied from 1894 at the University of Bonn, also spending a term in Berlin. His doctoral thesis was in the field of ancient history and classical philology but in 1898 he published a masterly article on the Frankish king Clovis which led to his appointment as assistant to Bruno Krusch, editing texts for the *Monumenta Germaniae Historica.* Levison's chief work in this capacity was the edition of Merovingian hagiographical texts. His studies led him to familiarize himself with many libraries, not least those of Britain, and one of the fruits of this was his conspectus of hagiographical manuscripts, a model of painstaking scholarship, published as an appendix in the *Monumenta* series. In 1903 at Bonn Levison presented a further dissertation (*Habilitationschrift*) on St Germanus of Auxerre, in which he drew on British Library manuscripts, and at Bonn he became a lecturer (*Privatdozent*). He received the title of professor in 1909 and was established in a full chair of history in 1920.

Besides his continuing work as an editor, Levison published numerous articles on hagiography, on source criticism and on the Rhineland, to which he felt a great attachment. In 1925, for example, he contributed a lecture to the millennial festival of Rhenish history and in 1927 he published his masterly study of the legend of St Ursula of Cologne. His renown as a scholar was equalled by the affection and admiration in which he was held as a teacher: his students included the Bollan-

dist Maurice Coens and the future medievalists P. E. Hübinger, E. Ewig and T. Schieffer.

In 1935 the Nuremberg laws forced Levison as a Jew to resign his chair. For a while he
continued his work in Bonn but in November
1938, in common with other Jews, he was
debarred from the use of libraries. To its great
credit the University of Durham, which had in
1931 awarded Levison a doctorate *honoris
causa*, now offered him an honorary fellowship. In April 1939 he and his wife Elsa
moved to Durham where Levison continued
his research until his death. To that period
belongs his most important work, *England and
the Continent in the Eighth Century*. Based on
the Ford Lectures which he gave in Oxford in
1942, this deals with the English missionaries
to the Continent and the relationship between
England and the Carolingian world especially
in learning and scholarship. In his preface
Levison expressed the hope that his pages
would 'contribute to join again broken links'
and he paid tribute to his *alma mater Bonnensis*
to which, despite pressing invitations, he was
never able to return.

Levison's importance as an historian lies
not in any broad re-interpretations but rather
in his solidly based, meticulous, impartial
approach to medieval history and in the immense weight of learning he brought to bear.
These qualities are clearly seen in the remarkable series of appendices to *England and the
Continent*, above all in his discussion of the
Anglo-Saxon charters. Courteously but firmly
he demonstrated that the early charters of
St Augustine's Abbey, Canterbury, were
eleventh-century forgeries and then – a
typical example of his vast erudition – he was
able from a continental source to identify the
death-bed confession of the man who had
forged them.   DWR

Main publications

Das Werden der Ursula-Legenda (Cologne: Albert
Ahn Verlag, 1928); An Eighth-Century poem on St
Ninian, *Antiquity* 14 (1940) 280–91; St Alban and
St Alban's, *Antiquity* 15 (1941) 337–59; *England
and the Continent in the Eighth Century* (Oxford:
Clarendon Press, 1946); *Aus rheinischer und fränkis-
cher Frühzeit: ausgewählte Aufsätze von Wilhelm Levi-
son* (Dusseldorf: L. Schwann, 1948).

Reading

Hübinger, P. E.: Wilhelm Levison 1876–1947. In
*Bonner Gelerhte: Beiträge zur Geschichte der Wissen-
schaften in Bonn: Geschichtswissenschaften* (Bonn:
Ludwig Röhrscheid, 1968).

Levison, Elsa ed.: *Wilhelm Levison 1876–1947: A
Bibliography* (Oxford: Oxford University Press,
1948).

Schieffer, T. et al.: *In Memoriam Wilhelm Levison
(1876–1947): Reden und Grußbotschaften bei der
Gedenkfeier der Universität zum 100. Geburtstag am
31. Mai 1976* (Cologne and Bonn: Peter Hanstein,
1977).

Lewis, Bernard (b.1916) Lewis studied at
the School of Oriental and African Studies,
London, and at the Sorbonne. His earliest
researches were in the origins of the Isma'ili
Shi'ite movement and its conflicts with mainstream Sunni Islam. The Assassin branch of
the Isma'ilis emerge as the doomed precursors
of the no less futile modern terrorist groups.
But Lewis's extraordinary linguistic competence in Arabic, Persian, Turkish and
Hebrew has allowed him to make contributions in almost all areas of medieval and
modern Islamic history. He is a prolific, stylish
and, at times, polemical writer. In particular,
he has found it a duty and a pleasure to
demonstrate the way in which particular
aspects of the Near Eastern past have been
rewritten by modern scholars (Arabs, Iranians,
and Russians especially) in order to conform
to current preoccupations and cultural self-
images. His popular synthesis *The Arabs in
History*, weighted towards the first six centuries of Islam in which the Arabs were more
or less in control of their empire, has influenced generations of students.   RGI

Main publications

The Arabs in History (London: Hutchinson, 1950);
The Assassins (London: Weidenfeld & Nicolson,
1967); *History: remembered, recovered, invented*
(Princeton, NJ: Princeton University Press, 1975).

Liebermann, Felix (b.1851, d.1925)
Liebermann was from a wealthy and cultivated family of Berlin burghers: his grandfather had told the king of Prussia that he had
driven the English from Europe's calico trade,

and his brother was the painter, Max. Destined for business, he was introduced to England through two years in Manchester cotton, but finally persuaded his father to let him study Germanic history. He was taught by the master 'constitutionalist' Georg Waitz, and by Reinhold Pauli, author of the first scholarly study of King Alfred. He wrote as his doctoral dissertation a seminal *Einleitung in den Dialogus de Scaccario* [Introduction to the dialogue of the Exchequer] (1875), and began a career in scholarship which left few areas of English history between Hengist and Horsa and Henry VIII untouched.

Thanks to private means and a slight speech impediment, Liebermann was never a university teacher or administrator. His was a life of 'pure' scholarship, and few have made better use of such an enviable position. His bibliography runs to 659 items. Most are reviews or notices, but their range extends from Stonehenge to the Versailles treaty, and from Shaw's *St Joan* to Afrikaner bureaucratese. He was a philologist (apparently self-taught) and student of literature as well as a historian; and, as a historian, his interests ran to annals and hagiography as well as law. His early work on the *Monumenta* volumes of excerpts from English sources for German history led to analyses that are still valuable of *Ungedruckte Anglo-Normannische Geschichtsquellen* [Unprinted sources for Anglo-Norman history] (1879) and *Ostenglische Geschichtsquellen* [East Anglian historical sources] (1893). After his legal work, his greatest service to early English studies was probably his edition and discussion of *Die Heiligen Englands* [The Saints of England] (1889), and he long remained the only scholar to see how important it was. But his claim to immortality is his colossal edition and elucidation of the earliest English codes and tracts of law, work to which he was directed by Konrad von Maurer and Heinrich Brunner, and which he signalled in an article for the *Savigny-Zeitschrift* (1884). Before the great edition itself came studies of the 'Anglo-Norman law-books' (1892–1901) which, for the most part, are still the only systematic treatments of these works; but for Liebermann they were mere preludes to the massive symphony of text and subject matter that is *Die Gesetze der Angelsachsen* [The laws of the Anglo-Saxons] (1903–16).

Die Gesetze is an astonishing work, in more ways than one. The first volume, devoted to establishing the texts, is a typographical as well as editorial masterpiece: Liebermann rightly refused to follow his predecessors in search of an *ur-text*, and printed variant versions in parallel columns, committing himself to any one (and then to what he saw as the sense as well as the literal meaning) only in his German translation. The *Wörterbuch* (II.i) remains a huge improvement on anything else available for these matters. But in the *Sachglossar* (II.ii) and the *Erklärungen* (III) there are striking weaknesses as well as great strengths. Apart from a degree of compression which Maitland had already called 'algebraic' – for Liebermann himself, only Maitland could make specialist work 'easy or amusing' – Anglo-Saxon law is seen as a static and coherent system, albeit imperfectly revealed. He never deigned to describe this 'system' as such: all that was needed to bring it out was an exhaustive list of references to legal texts for each aspect of the law, buttressed (though never modified) by charters or narratives. Except occasionally (when influenced by Chadwick), he saw little development; so that though he certainly believed more than Brunner and Maitland in the importance of Anglo-Saxon influence on later English law, he never showed how one could reconcile the Anglo-Saxons' Germanic inheritance with a legacy to the 'common law'. His training in the 'Germanist' view combined with his ivory-tower life to produce an approach that is as much juridical as historical, which explains why the effects on Anglo-Saxon and legal historians predicted by his obituarists have yet to materialize.

Nor is this the only irony of Liebermann's career. He dedicated his third volume, published during the Battle of the Somme, to the memory of Brunner and Maitland.

In the hope that the storm of hate and the sea of blood which drown out the time in which these pages appear will soon be understood as essentially caused by the historical necessity of conflict between the thoughtless claims of a world-empire, used to power, to monopolize sea-travel and trade, and the justified determination of a united German people to share the goods of the earth peacefully and prudently but in strength and freedom, and to expand itself in accordance with its inborn life-force.

It is evident and unsurprising that these words were less than well received by his English readers, and their reaction had a counter-effect in Germany. Of his obituarists, only TOUT even hints at this part of the dedication (which he privately ascribed to 'simple-mindedness'), and Tout was also the first, and almost the only, English scholar to send Liebermann his books after the war. On the other hand, English scholars are significantly absent from his 1921 *Festgabe* (prefaced by what one thinks a characteristic portrait, presumably by his brother), and the blame was laid on the *Ungunst der Zeit* (unfavourable times). From a late-twentieth-century perspective, the episode is more poignant yet: like many great legal historians, Liebermann was a Jew and proud of it.

Post-war inflation deprived Liebermann of most of his livelihood. He was knocked down by a car outside his Berlin home on 7th October 1925, and died shortly afterwards. Yet perhaps he was lucky. Ten years later, his brother died peacefully, but in isolation and disgrace.   PW

Main publications

On the Instituta Cnuti aliorumque regum Anglorum. *Transactions of the Royal Historical Society*, n.s. 7 (1893) 77–107; The text of Henry I's Coronation Charter. *Transactions of the RHS* n.s. 8 (1894), 21–48; King Alfred and Mosaic Law, *Transactions of the Jewish Historical Society of England* 6 (1908–10) 21–31; A contemporary manuscript of the 'Leges Anglorum Londiniis Collectae'. *English Historical Review* 28 (1913) 732–45; *The National Assembly in the Anglo-Saxon Period* (Halle, 1913).

Reading

Davis, H. W. C.: The Anglo-Saxon laws. *English Historical Review* 28 (1913) 417–30.

Hazeltine, H. D.: *Proceedings of the British Academy* 24 (1938) 319–59.

Heymann, E.: *Zeitschrift der Savigny-Stiftung für Rechtsgeschichte, germanistische Abteilung* 46 (1926) xxiii–xxxix.

Kleinschmidt, H.: *Felix Liebermann, 1851–1925: Bibliographie seiner Schriften, 1875–1927* (Stuttgart: 1983).

Torkar, R.: *Eine Altenglische Übersetzung von Alcuins de Virtute et Vitiis Kap 20* (Munchen: 1981), pp. 1–5.

Tout, T. F. T.: *History* n.s. 10 (1926) 311–19.

Lingard, John (b.1771, d.1851) Born in Winchester into a family of humble status and long-standing Roman Catholic allegiance, in 1782 Lingard entered the English college at Douai in France, and proceeded to the school of theology there ten years later. In 1793 the college was closed by the revolutionary government and he returned to England, to be briefly tutor to the eldest son of Lord Stourton, and then in 1794 to rejoin other members of the Douai community who had established themselves at Tudhoe in County Durham, England. Ordained priest in 1795, he became vice-president of the re-constituted college, first at Crook Hall, and, from 1808, at Ushaw, both in County Durham. In 1811 he resigned the vice-presidency and retired to a small mission at Hornby near Lancaster, where his friend Pudsey Dawson was Lord of the Manor.

Lingard remained at Hornby for the rest of his life, having discovered, and enabled himself to pursue, his true vocation as a historian. In 1806 he published the first edition of his *Antiquities of the Anglo-Saxon Church*, and shortly thereafter embarked upon a *History of England* which was to be his main life work. Originally intended as a school primer and a piece of Catholic apologetic, this project grew enormously both in scope and stature as it advanced. In spite of Lingard's other activities as a controversialist, his *History* was remarkable both for its objectivity, and for the manner in which he sought out and employed original sources. In this respect his clerical contacts all over Europe proved to be invaluable; he was the first historian to take full account of diplomatic despatches in writing the history of Tudor England. The first three volumes of the *History*, to 1509, were published in 1819, and the whole work, to 1688, was completed in eight volumes by 1830. Four subsequent and revised editions appeared during his lifetime.

The work was almost universally acclaimed, only extreme protestants and ultra-papalists attacking it. Pope Pius VII conferred doctorates of Divinity, Canon Law and Civil Law on Lingard in 1821, and he received an annuity of £300 from the Privy Purse in 1839. He died at Hornby in 1851. DML

Main publications

The Antiquities of the Anglo-Saxon Church 2 vols (Newcastle, 1806; 2nd edn 1810; 3rd edn Philadelphia, 1841; 5th edn London, 1858); *The History of England*, 8 vols (London, 1819–30); several edns: 1823–31, 1835, 1839, 1849–51 London, 1854, New York, 1915; trans. into French, Italian and German).

Reading

Culkin, G.: 'The making of Lingard's *History*'. *The Month* 192 (1951) 7–18.
——: *New Catholic Encyclopedia* (Washington, D. C.: 1967) 8, 772–3.
Haile, M. and Bonney, E.: *Life and Letters of John Lingard* (London: 1911).
Milburn. D.: *A History of Ushaw College* (Durham: 1964).

literature and history The distinction between literature and history is, in the true meaning of the word, academic. The writings of great historians from Herodotus to Macaulay are works of literature in themselves. The art of narrating the great epics of the past requires considerable literary skill to carry conviction. Gibbon's *Decline and Fall of the Roman Empire* survives as a classic as much for its style as for its scholarship. Schools of literature and history tend to distinguish imaginative authors, who create fictions, from historians, who reconstruct past realities. However, this is not wholly satisfactory. Historical reconstruction requires an imaginative sympathy, while imagined worlds usually have some relationship with the real world; and where do historical novels belong?

There is nevertheless a valid distinction to be drawn between creative literature and other kinds of records for the purpose of evaluating them as historical source material: Shakespeare's history plays are fundamentally a different genre from the chronicles upon which they were based. To be sure, the chronicles were biased, and inclined to special pleading. The evaluation of any historical document requires the subjective element to be taken into account. But the purposes for which they were written, and even the audiences at which they were aimed, differed from those of Shakespeares. How Shakespeare reworked them for his own dramatic purposes is in itself an interesting historical question. Any historian who relied upon Shakespeare's version of the Lancastrian and Yorkist kings however would be led far more seriously astray than one who used the contemporary chronicles.

That creative writing is a dubious source for political history is perhaps obvious. Yet it is often used by social historians to provide colour and 'background' in ways which are just as suspect. Depictions of eighteenth-century country gentlemen, for instance, have drawn on such fictitious characters as Henry Fielding's Squire Western and Tobias Smollett's Matthew Bramble to represent the gentry of Hanoverian England as uneducated, untravelled, hard-drinking boors. The evidence which they themselves left behind paints a rather different picture. Their personal correspondence, diaries and private libraries document a much more educated and civilized country gentleman than the booby squire of Augustan fiction.

The distortions of playwrights, poets and novelists have led many historians to dismiss their works as evidence on the grounds that they are essentially unreliable. Certainly any attempts to establish what was typical about past societies largely from their testimony will be fatally flawed. Creative writing is intuitive and subjective. To document what was normal requires sources which are quantitative and objective. To ascertain the age of marriage in sixteenth-century England, for example, requires recourse to Tudor parish registers rather than to Shakespeare's *Romeo and Juliet*, and the structure of the Victorian family should be established from census schedules and not from Dickens.

Yet the fact that certain forms of documentary evidence provide a more objective source than creative writing raises the questions, why and how does imaginative literature distort reality? The answers to these questions are usually sought by literary critics, but they can be of concern to historians. Of course the range of possible explanations is almost infinite, stretching from literary convention to human psychology. However, one source of bias susceptible to historical explanation is the ideological stance of the writer. Shakespeare's concern to toe the Tudor line on the fifteenth century goes far to explain the distortions of his historical plays. Whig animus against Tory gentry similarly accounts a great deal for the booby squire of Augustan literature.

That an individual author had a political axe to grind does little to enhance the usefulness of his works to the historian. However, when the published writings of whole generations of authors are examined, patterns of thought can emerge which establish the ideological assumptions of their age. Kingsley Amis's contempt for provincial academics in *Lucky Jim*, and Malcolm Bradbury's attack on university sociologists in *The History Man* can be dismissed as subjective quirks reflecting only their own idiosyncratic views. Certainly any historian using the first to document life in redbrick universities in the 1950s, or the second to depict typical lecturers of the 1970s, would scarcely paint an objective picture. Yet the fact that academic life is almost always satirized in recent English fiction has some relationship with a climate of opinion which places a low value on universities in general and social scientists in particular.

The prominence given to certain genres of literature also documents prevalent attitudes. For example the decline of the epic poem in the late seventeenth century, and the rise of the novel in the eighteenth, reflect a transition from an age which saw its religion and politics in heroic terms to one which had a rather more secular outlook on society.

Literature, therefore, can complement history provided the right questions are asked of it. It cannot tell us what society was really like, but it is a unique source for informing us how it was perceived by contemporaries.   WAS

Reading

Literature and History (London: Thames Polytechnic, 2 edns per year).

Livy (b.*c*.64 BC, d.*c.* AD 17)   Of the life of Titus Livius almost nothing is known apart from his place of birth, Padua. From the tone and wording of his preface it can be inferred that he began to write in the mid-thirties BC, while the civil wars between Mark Antony and the future emperor Augustus were still raging. His intention was to write a history of Rome 'from the founding of the city' (*ab urbe condita*) to (almost certainly) the murder of Cicero in 43 BC, an act which symbolized the nadir of the republic. The history was to be a celebration of Rome's growth and imperialism from the eighth to the third centuries, and a Sallustian (see SALLUST) record of her accelerating decline thereafter.

Though only 35 books (1–10, 21–45) now survive of the 120 which he devoted to his theme, an outline of the contents of the lost books can be reconstructed from the brief summaries (*periochae*) which still exist. Though the scale of his narrative increased as such sources as POLYBIUS became available, and as he neared the events of his own time, one striking characteristic of the earlier volumes is their detailed account of events which belong to the 'dark age' of Roman history and about which Livy and his predecessors can have known almost nothing. This phenomenon has been explained in terms of 'the expansion of the past'.

In order to equip Rome with a worthy past, successive generations of Roman historians attributed to the early centuries a series of 'events' which often had little or no intrinsic connection with Rome at all. Livy represents the culmination and ultimate refinement of this process, which can be seen at work in two almost adjacent episodes from his narrative of the fourth century BC in book 7 (9.6–10.4 and 26.1–10). Each episode describes a single combat between a Roman hero and a giant Gaul, and each belongs to a well-known class of folk-tale of which the story of David and Goliath is another example. At some early point in the historiographical tradition the tale was imputed to two heroes, T. Manlius Torquatus and M. Valerius Corvus, to provide retrospective aetiologies of their *cognomina* or 'surnames' ('Collared' and 'Crow' respectively). Since Livy's immediate source for the episodes happens to have survived (Claudius Quadrigarius, fragments 10 and 12), we can see that Livy has: doubled the length of the Torquatus story by introducing direct speech and details of a rationalizing and circumstantial nature; transferred motifs between the two episodes and reinterpreted others; emphasized the national significance of the combats and made their respective morals more explicit; eliminated obsolete archaisms; and transformed Quadrigarius' primitive sentence structure into the smooth and elegant periodic style which is Livy's hallmark. The resulting episodes are not only excellent examples of CLASSICAL HISTORIOGRAPHY in action, they also illustrate Livy's engaging enthusiasm for the past and his remarkable ability to tell dramatic stories. Assuming that countless other episodes of early Roman 'history' were treated in a similar way, we can readily appreciate how Livy was able to write on such a large scale.

Long before his vast project was completed, Livy was overtaken by political events. The defeat of Antony in 31 BC brought about the end of the civil wars, the establishment of the Augustan principate, and the gradual return of stability to the Roman world. In this increasingly optimistic atmosphere Livy eventually decided to extend his history by 34 years (42–9 BC), taking up a further 22 books. Since this decision involved him in describing the first two decades of Augustus' reign, it suggests that he revised his opinion that Rome was declining and came to see the Augustan age as a period of rejuvenation. Though none of these extra volumes has survived, the *periochae* indicate that Livy concentrated on the emperor's military exploits, which could be represented as a return to the glorious days of Rome's imperialist past and of which the German campaigns of 12–9 BC were a triumphant climax.

Livy's patriotic instincts and narrative skill combined to ensure the immediate success of his awesome work, which constituted a challenge that no later Roman historian was able fully to meet. Yet despite his incursion into imperial times, the loss of all but his earlier volumes means that he will forever be identified as the pre-eminent historian of the early Roman republic, who has provided successive generations of readers with their most memorable insight into the world of ancient Rome.

AJW

Main writings

Livy: From the Founding of the City, text, with trans. by B. O. Foster, E. T. Sage and A. C. Schlesinger, vols 1–14 (London and Cambridge, Mass.: Heinemann and Harvard University Press, 1919–59); *A Commentary on Livy Books 1–5*, R. M. Ogilvie (Oxford: Clarendon Press, 1965); *A Commentary on Livy Books 31–33*, J. Briscoe (Clarendon Press, 1973); *A Commentary on Livy Books 34–37*, J. Briscoe (Clarendon Press, 1981).

Reading

Luce, T. J.: *Livy: the Composition of his History* (Princeton, NJ: Princeton University Press, 1977). Walsh, P. G.: *Livy: his Historical Aims and Methods* (Cambridge University Press, 1961).

local history, English As practised by scholars in England today, local history represents the comparatively recent fusion of two older historiographical traditions, both of which had originated during periods of *national* self-enquiry – the sixteenth and the nineteenth centuries respectively.

During the earlier of these two periods, the reign of Elizabeth I in particular was marked not only by 'the discovery of England', but also by what might be described as 'the discovery of the English' in terms of both their language and their earlier polity. Intellectually, it was no accident that the pioneer work of English local history was written by a man who had hoped to write a national survey or that it was illustrated by perhaps the earliest map to be drawn of the Old English 'heptarchy'. In its title and in its compass, however, William Lambarde's *A perambulation of Kent: conteining the description, hystorie, and customes of that shyre* (1576) came to epitomize many of the strands that were subsequently to characterize the writing not of such rare national descriptions as CAMDEN's *Britannia* (1586), but of those regional surveys that were aimed particularly at county audiences of nobility and gentry. In these regional surveys, the emphasis alternated between 'chorography' – the affectionate topographical description of the region, its present institutions and social customary practices (as in

Richard Carew's *Survey of Cornwall*, 1602) — and the 'antiquities' of a district or town (see STOW; URBAN HISTORY). Perfected by Sir William DUGDALE in his *Antiquities of Warwickshire* (1656), which was widely emulated down even to the late nineteenth century on an ever more massive scale, and with ever-increasing quantities of documentation, the overwhelming concerns of this genre were largely to detail, parish by parish, the ancestries of the leading county families, their heraldry, their sepulchral and other physical monuments as well as to allude to conspicuous archaeological remains, or to those rare moments when events of 'national significance' occurred on local soil. If the historical content tended to be deployed sequentially in annalistic form, the descriptive gazetteer format was infinitely flexible. It could range from the 'history' of a single parish, of which the earliest is usually held to have been *Parochial Antiquities attempted in the History of Ambroseden and Other Adjacent Parts* by White Kennett (1695), to attempts to embrace the whole country as Daniel and Samuel Lysons intended in their unfinished *Magna Britannia* (1806–22), or as, in more sophisticated and systematic form, that most ambitious of all such projects, *The Victoria History of the Counties of England*, has sought to do ever since its inception in 1899.

The second great historiographical tradition originated in that scholarly efflorescence which marked the accelerating development of analytical history during the middle to late nineteenth century and, with it, the new urge to explain the origins and peculiar institutions of the English people as a whole, including the most humble. In an age of revolution and of empire abroad, of massive urbanization at home, and in an intellectual climate concerned with the evolution of society from its prehistoric origins (in so far as these might be investigated both through archaeology and through folklore) to the present, the English intelligentsia became obsessed, not only with such matters as the origins of England's cities and boroughs, but also with the problems of freedom, law and political participation as these might be variously reflected in such historical subjects as the so-called 'village community', the manor, or enclosure. These themes found influential expression in Erwin Nasse, *On the Agricultural Community of the Middle Ages, and Inclosures of the Sixteenth Century* (1869 in German, translated by H. A. Ouvrey, London, 1877), and in Frederic SEEBOHM, *The English Village Community Examined in its Relations to the Manorial and Tribal Systems and to the Common or Open-Field System of Husbandry* (1883). From these and from the works of MAITLAND and VINOGRADOFF, among others, there began to emerge on the one hand a view of early medieval agrarian 'community' that reflected an abstract construct — almost a model built up from the documentation — which was thus largely irrespective of region or particular place; and, on the other hand, an equally generalized vision of its disintegration under the impact of enclosure, with all that that meant for the fate of the peasant landholder.

The historiographical gulf between the traditional local gazetteer and the new national mode of generalization however, could only be bridged eventually with the sophistication of certain non-documentary techniques that allowed for the reinstatement of the genius of place: advances in field archaeology, place-name analysis, aerial photography, and the study of maps. It was with this marriage of the visual evidence with the documentary as it was effected, especially in the work of W. G. HOSKINS, H. P. R. Finberg and M. W. Beresford, that the modern analytical study of English local history may be said to have begun. For Hoskins and Finberg, the immediate topographical context of place was seen to be crucial to its understanding, but the central object of study, nevertheless, was in Finberg's words 'the Origins, Growth, Decline and Fall of a local Community' (*The Local Historian and his Theme*, 1954). Within this localized system of chronology, the major themes were socio-economic in character: settlement, survival, or even desertion, but in certain cases they could be pursued comparatively and inclusively to national levels, as in Beresford, *The Lost Villages of England* or *New Towns of the Middle Ages*. Alternatively, fresh insights of potentially wider historical application might be propounded from the microscopically detailed study of single places: the problems of 'continuity' from Roman to Anglo-Saxon England in Finberg, *Roman and Saxon Withington*; or the nature and decline of the peasant farming culture of open-field Wigston Magna in Hoskins, *The Midland Peasant*.

If, more recently, the study of particular rural or urban 'communities' has become both more systematically comparative and ever more rounded — with an increasing emphasis on such matters as kinship, education, religious or political attitudes, popular culture and ritual (for example Hey, *An English Rural Community*; Spufford, *Contrasting Communities*; Phythian-Adams, *Desolation of a City*) — the basic objects of local historical investigation are beginning to change. With Alan Everitt's influential evocation of 'the county community' of gentry during the Great Rebellion; with the elucidation of English farming regions and their social characteristics by Joan Thirsk ('The farming regions of England'); and with their categorization and further refinement by Alan Everitt into a limited number of comparable *pays* (woodland, fenland and the like) which may be regarded as inhabited by distinctive localized societies ('Country, county and town') — English local history is beginning to move towards a new perception of English society, from settlement through to the present day, as a more broadly subdivided whole than once used to be thought to be the case when the focus was mainly restricted to individual villages and towns.   CVP-A

References

Beresford, Maurice: *The Lost Villages of England* (London: Lutterworth, 1954).

——: *New Towns of the Middle Ages: Town Plantation in England, Wales and Gascony* (Lutterworth, 1967).

Everitt, Alan: *The Community of Kent and the Great Rebellion* (Leicester: Leicester University Press, 1966).

——: Country, county and town: patterns of regional evolution in England, *Transactions of the Royal Historical Society* 5.29 (1979) 79–108.

Finberg, H. P. R.: *Roman and Saxon Withington: a study in Continuity* (Leicester: University Dept. of English Local History Occasional Papers, 8, 1955).

Hey, David G.: *An English Rural Community: Myddle under the Tudors and Stuarts* (Leicester: Leicester University Press, 1974).

Hoskins, W. G.: *The Midland Peasant: the Economic*

and Social History of a Leicestershire Village (London: Macmillan, 1957).

Phythian-Adams, Charles: *Desolation of a City: Coventry and the Urban Crisis of the later Middle Ages* (Cambridge: Cambridge University Press, 1979).

Spufford, Margaret: *Contrasting Communities: English Villagers in the Sixteenth and Seventeenth Centuries* (Cambridge University Press, 1974).

Thirsk, Joan: The farming regions of England. In *The Agrarian History of England and Wales, vol. 4, 1500–1640*, ed. Thirsk (Cambridge University Press, 1967) 1–112.

Reading

Dewey, C.: Images of the village community: a study in Anglo-Indian ideology. *Modern Asian Studies* 6 (1972) 291–328.

Finberg, H. P. R.: *The Local Historian and his Theme* (Leicester: University Dept of English Local History Occasional Papers, 1, 1954).

Flower, R.: Laurence Nowell and the discovery of England in Tudor times. *Proceedings of the British Academy* 21 (1935) 47–73.

Phythian-Adams, C. V.: *Rethinking English Local History* (Leicester: University Dept of English Local History Occasional Papers, 4th ser., 1, 1987).

Simmons, J. ed.: *English County Historians*, 1st ser. (Wakefield: E. P. Publishing, 1978).

Lot, Ferdinand (b.1866, d.1952)   Born in Paris, Lot began his medieval studies at the École des Chartes in 1886, attending lectures by FUSTEL DE COULANGES and working under A. Giry for his thesis on the last Carolingian kings (completed in 1890); his doctoral thesis (completed in 1904 for the University of Nancy) carried these researches on into the period of the first Capetians. After leaving the École des Chartes in 1890 he worked for some time as a librarian at the Sorbonne; in 1900, on Giry's death, he returned to a position at the École des Chartes. He began teaching at the Sorbonne in 1909, and despite his public attack in 1912 on the standards and methods of teaching there, was appointed professor in 1920. Lot retired from the Sorbonne in 1937, although he continued teaching at the École des Hautes Études for three more years and remained as active as ever in his writing.

Lot's complete bibliography, published in volume I of his *Recueil* (1968) contains 388 items, including reviews, some scores of articles and nearly forty books. The range of his interests was considerable. He started his career as a fairly conventional product of the École des Chartes, publishing studies of various Carolingian monarchs through their diplomas and charters. But he considered this somewhat of a chore, and even while working on Carolingian history he was following up interests in other periods and in related disciplines. He never took a narrow view of a historian's concerns, and throughout his life kept up other areas of research, notably in medieval literary history and philology. His first published articles on medieval *chansons de geste* were as early as 1890, and from the 1890s too dates his pursuit of the 'Matter of Britain', not just through French medieval literature but also to its Celtic roots across the Channel. He was a great believer in the Celtic, rather than Roman or Germanic, origins of the French people. Unusually perhaps for one of his background, this interest led him to spend some time in England and in Wales, and to publish a number of important studies of early British sources, notably of GILDAS, NENNIUS and GEOFFREY OF MONMOUTH. Nor were his philological interests narrowly Romance; in the 1890s he published articles on Old Irish and Breton philology and on early Breton history. From the historical viewpoint, perhaps his most significant philological contributions were his pioneering studies on place-names, particularly in relation to the history of the Germanic invasions, and on the development of spoken Latin in the early middle ages.

Lot occupied a prominent position in French medieval historical studies for nearly half a century, providing a living link between the pioneering age of Fustel de Coulanges and the followers of BLOCH and FEVBRE in the period after 1945. Although he did not have much sympathy with the ANNALES SCHOOL, believing that it diminished the historical importance of the individual, towards the end of his life he took up an interest in quantitative methods, as applied to urban and military history.   EFJ

Main publications

La Fin du monde antique et le début du Moyen âge (Paris: Renaissance du Livre, 1927; trans. London: Kegan Paul, Trench, Trubner; New York: Knopf, 1931); with C. Pfister and F. L. Ganshof, *Les destinées de l'Empire en Occident de 395 à 888* (Paris:

Presses Universitaires de France, 1928); *L'Art militaire et les armées au moyen âge en Europe et dans le Proche-Orient*, 2 vols (Paris: 1946); *Naissance de la France* (Paris: Fayard, 1948). *Recueil des travaux historiques de Ferdinand Lot*, 3 vols (Geneva: Droz, 1908, 1970, 1973) [vol. 1 incl. full bibliography].

Further Reading

Perrin, Ch.: Ferdinand Lot: l'homme et l'oeuvre. In *Recueil des travaux historiques de Ferdinand Lot*, I, pp. 3–118, (Geneva: Droz).

Lovejoy, Arthur Oncken (b.1873, d.1962) Though trained as a philosopher at Harvard, Lovejoy significantly altered the methodology of intellectual history with the development of the history of ideas. Believing that certain fundamental 'unit-ideas' lay at the basis of western thought, Lovejoy developed methods for tracing those ideas and in *The Great Chain of Being* (1936) provided an exemplar of the method.

Born to an American father and a German mother, Lovejoy had a troubled childhood dominated by the evangelicalism of his father. As a student at the University of California he discovered philosophy and the solidity of reason in a changing world. He did graduate work at Harvard under William James and Josiah Royce. After early appointments in philosophy at Stanford, Washington University (St Louis), the University of Missouri, and Columbia, he was appointed professor of philosophy at The Johns Hopkins University in 1910, where he remained until he retired in 1938.

Despite his training as a philosopher, many of Lovejoy's essays were in the history of ideas. He initially sought in history assurance that a religion of faith had been superseded by a rational religion. As early as 1905 he began to develop the notion of the 'unit-ideas', which formed the core of his method. Unit-ideas were 'persistent dynamic factors, the ideas that produce effects in the history of thought', but Lovejoy nowhere defined more precisely what he meant by this. The closest he came in *The Great Chain of Being* was listing various types of unit-idea: implicit or explicit assumptions, dialectical motives, a susceptibility to metaphysical pathos, or a single key proposition enunciated early in the history of western thought. Having identified a unit-idea, Lovejoy argued that the historian should trace its manifestations across time and disciplines so as to uncover the vicissitudes undergone by the original idea. It was this task that he accomplished most successfully in *The Great Chain of Being* where he traced the ideas of plenitude, continuity, and gradation from their Platonic origins to the early nineteenth century.

Critics have argued that Lovejoy treated ideas as unchanging, fundamental units, as atoms of thought, which remained stable over time. Lovejoy's own language describing the procedure of the history of ideas as 'somewhat analogous to that of analytic chemistry' fostered the image of a historian dealing with solid particles of thought. At his best however as in *The Great Chain of Being*, Lovejoy himself treated ideas as unstable collections held together by the will of the thinker. Idea complexes could be found in realms of thought far from their origins and Lovejoy saw this as a spur to interdisciplinary co-operation. To encourage that co-operation he helped to establish *the Journal of the History of Ideas* in 1940. Lovejoy's work had its greatest influence on literary and intellectual history in the 1920s and 1930s when it helped shatter rigid disciplinary boundaries. Critics since the second world war have found the history of ideas too confining and insufficiently aware of changing social, economic, and cultural contexts. A more careful reading, however, suggests that he avoided many of the pitfalls ascribed to his method.

Lovejoy was not primarily a historian. He saw himself as a philosopher and was a major contributor to the revival of realism in the United States and to the development of a scientifically oriented philosophy. He was an advocate of reason and common sense in philosophy, and many of his writings are concerned with problems of knowledge. He was a dualist believing in mind and matter, and his central problem was developing a theory of knowledge to explain how we could know anything about the real world. His belief that we obtain knowledge of the world mediated through ideas was most fully developed in his Carus lectures, published as *The Revolt Against Dualism* (1930).

Lovejoy was also active in the professionalization of the professoriate by helping to found the American Association of University Professors in 1915, serving as its first secretary and as president in 1919. His work helped to establish firmly the principle of academic freedom in American universities. He was a staunch opponent of the communist influence in universities after the second world war and remained active politically and professionally until blindness and ill-health overtook him in the late 1950s. He never married and lived alone in Baltimore until his death in 1962. DJW

Main publications

(Published by the Johns Hopkins University Press, Baltimore, unless otherwise stated.)
The Revolt Against Dualism (LaSalle, Ill.: Open Court, 1930); *The Great Chain of Being* (Cambridge, Mass.: Harvard University Press, 1936); *Essays in the History of Ideas* (1948); *The Reason, the Understanding and Time* (1961); *Reflections on Human Nature* (1961); *The Thirteen Pragmatisms and Other Essays* (1963).

Reading

Boas, G.: A. O. Lovejoy: reason-in-action. *American Scholar* 29 (1960) 535–42.

Feuer, L. S.: Arthur O. Lovejoy. *American Scholar* 46 (1977) 358–66.

Wilson, Daniel J.: *Arthur O. Lovejoy and the Quest for Intelligibility* (Chapel Hill: University of North Carolina Press, 1980).

Wilson, Daniel J.: *Arthur O. Lovejoy: An Annotated Bibliography* (New York: Garland Publishing, 1982).

Low Countries, historiography of Perhaps the fundamental problem facing historians of the Low Countries has been the difficulty of determining the geographical limits of their subject. The region has no natural boundaries, except the sea, and where the Low Countries ended and France or the Germanic lands began has varied significantly over the centuries. Indeed, for much of its history the area has been divided, nominally at least, between France and the Holy Roman Empire. Moreover, throughout the middle ages the region was divided among a great number of separate political jurisdictions, and its linguistic and economic diversity only added to the lack of homogeneity.

Despite, or perhaps because of, this intractable situation, the states which emerged in the region needed histories, if only to give them a legitimacy which the revolutionary nature of their origins denied them. The Dutch state which emerged from the revolt against Spanish rule at the end of the sixteenth century dealt with the problem of an inconvenient past in two main ways. Firstly, a myth of Batavian liberties was developed, and expressed in elegant Latin for an international public by Grotius. This traced Dutch political liberties back to Roman times, and granted them an uninterrupted history until the Spanish Habsburgs attempted to suppress them. The Dutch republic was thus portrayed as the legitimate continuation of a hallowed tradition. Secondly, a parallel but contrasting religious myth was constructed by, or revealed to, the partisans of the Reformed church: this saw the hand of God in the revolt and thus endowed the new Dutch state with a providential purpose and a specifically religious identity.

This providential interpretation of Dutch history was continued in the nineteenth century, though on a rather more scholarly base, by Calvinists such as Groen van Prinsterer, and still flourishes in the twentieth, at least in the attenuated form of a particular emphasis on the role of religion in the Revolt, and on the historical centrality of Calvinism for Dutch national identity. One effect of the lasting influence of this interpretation of the Dutch past was to stimulate Dutch Catholics to provide their rival version; clearly the calvinist image of the Dutch past was of no use to them, particularly in the late nineteenth and early twentieth century as they strove to win acceptance for themselves as full and equal members of Dutch society. Much of the history that resulted was polemical, but in the work of L. J. Rogier (especially his *Geschiedenis van het katholicisme in Noord-Nederland in de zestiende en zeventiende eeuw*, 1946) [History of Catholicism in the Northern Netherlands in the sixteenth and seventeenth centuries] it reached a maturity greater than that of the committed calvinist scholars, though without losing entirely its apologetic overtones. However, the central historical tradition in the nineteenth century was liberal, but with one curious twist – notable especially in the greatest Dutch historian of the period, Robert Fruin – that it tended to regard the period of the Dutch

republic with more than a little ambiguity. Whereas in the eighteenth century the republican tradition had been strong, and produced at least one outstanding historian, Jan Wagenaar, in the following century Orangism was triumphant in Dutch historiography: the Calvinists had always associated Orange with God, and now the liberals, unable in a confessionally divided land to use religion as a unifying symbol, turned to the monarchy. While recognizing the republic's achievements, they deplored its endemic provincial separatism, and its failure to recognize the princes of Orange as the natural leaders of the country.

The Belgian state was a much later creation but also resulted from a revolt – against union with the north under a Dutch king in 1830. Subsequently, Belgian historians sought to demonstrate that their country was not an artificial modern creation, but the expression of an essential identity which had existed for centuries but had been denied effective political form. It was not something which was easy to achieve with both conviction and scholarship. Romantics such as J. Kervyn de Lettenhove (*Histoire de Flandre*, 1847–50) rhetorically asserted the ancient origins of the Belgian nation, but it was only with the work of Henri PIRENNE (*Histoire de Belqique*, 1900–32) that Belgium was put in possession of a past that satisfied both the demands of patriotism and the highest scholarly standards. Pirenne found the essence of Belgian nationhood in a common economic and social experience, notably through the early importance of towns in the area, and in the creative fusion of Germanic and Romance cultural influences. Primarily a medievalist, he thus achieved a fruitful synthesis of his country's notable penchant for medieval history, marked from at least the eighteenth century, and for works of urban and local piety. The flaw in Pirenne's great work was that it largely ignored the challenge that Flemish nationalism was making even as he wrote. Indeed, the most devastating attack on Pirenne's thesis of the historical inevitability of the Belgian state came from the Dutch historian Pieter GEYL, who in turn was inspired by his passionate interest in the Flemish cause.

The historians on either side of the political divide in the Low Countries were faced with problems of a similar nature from the sixteenth century onwards, but particularly in the later modern period. Both needed to discover a historical justification for somewhat accidental new states. In both countries religion played a large part in the creation of a national identity, in the one Protestant, in the other Catholic, and in both this religious definition of nationality was also challenged by more secular traditions. Most importantly, perhaps, the historiography of the late nineteenth and early twentieth century was faced with the problem that large sections of the population of both countries felt deeply slighted by the dominant historical traditions in their respective states: the Catholics in the north and the Flemings in the south. Despite these common themes it has, however, not proved easy to provide a more integrated history of the region as a whole. The attempts since the second world war to create a more homogeneous history of the Low Countries, specifically in the *Algemene Geschiedenis der Nederlanden* [General history of The Low Countries] (1949–58) and in the new *AGN* (1977–83), have not been very successful. In both works the histories of the north and south have been generally dealt with in separate, almost hermetically sealed, chapters, written by Dutch and Belgian historians respectively. Even the editors of the new *AGN*, whose eccentricity is otherwise remarkable, have not been prepared to challenge the fundamental divide between the Dutch and the Belgian historiographical traditions. JLP

Reading

Arnould, M.-A.: *Le travail historique en Belgique des origines à nos jours* (Brussels: Editorial Office, 1953).

Duke, A. C. and Tamse, C. A.: *Clio's Mirror, Historiography in Britain and the Netherlands* (Zutphen: De Walburg Pers, 1985).

Geurts, P. A. M. and Janssen, A. E. M. eds: *Geschiedschrijving in Nederland*, 2 vols (The Hague: Martinus Nijhoff, 1981).

Houtte, J. A. van, ed.: *Un Quart de siècle de recherche historique en Belgique* (Louvain: Nauwelaerts, 1970).

Mijnhardt, W. W., ed.: *Kantelend Geschiedbeeld. Nederlandse Historiografie sinds 1945* (Utrecht/Antwerp: Het Spectrum, 1983).

Vercauteren, F.: *Cent Ans d'histoire nationale en Belgique* (Brussels: Renaissance du Livre, 1959).

Luchaire, Achille (b.1846, d.1908) A lawyer by training, Luchaire held chairs at Bordeaux (1879) and at the Sorbonne (1889) where he worked upon the history of France under the Capetians. His *Histoire des institutions monarchiques sous les premiers Capétiens directs* (987–1180) appeared in 1883 and soon established itself as a fundamental work of reference in the style of that period. This was followed by two further institutional studies: *Les Communes françaises a l'époque des Capétiens directs* (1890), dealing with urban developments; and *Manuel des institutions françaises: période des Capétiens directs* (1892) which provided a textbook for students of both history and law. Like his younger contemporary, LANGLOIS, he wrote a major chapter in Lavisse's *Histoire de France* (1901) on 'Les premiers Capétiens'. A certain broadening of approach is evident in his last work, *La société française au temps de Philippe Auguste* (1909), translated as *Social France at the time of Philip Augustus* (1912) in which nobles, townsmen and peasants as well as monarchical institutions receive attention. It was from this starting-point that much modern French historical writing on medieval society was to begin. MV

Main publications

Histoire des Institutions monarchiques sous les premiers Capétiens directs (987–1180) (Paris: Imprimerie Nationale, 1883); *Les Communes françaises à l'époque des Capétiens directs* (Paris: Hachette, 1890). *Social France at the Time of Philip Augustus* (1909) (London: John Murray, 1912).

Lucian (b.*c.*120, d.*c.*180) Lucian spent his career in lecturing and writing, and in the administration of Roman Egypt. Famous as the author of (largely satirical) dialogues in Greek, he is also responsible for the one work of historiographical theory which has survived from classical antiquity. No doubt belonging to the same genre as *On Historiography* by Theophrastus (*fl.* 320 BC) and Praxiphanes (*fl.* 250 BC) Lucian's *How to Write History* simultaneously displays his satirical gifts and provides a short but valuable introduction to historiography as it was understood in the classical world. Much of his most biting criticism is concerned with style; and though he anticipated Ranke in stating that 'the one task of the historian is to say how it happened' (ch. 39), it is clear from the immediate context that the reference is not to any modern concept of 'historical truth'. Both here and elsewhere Lucian (like POLYBIUS, with whose programmatic statements his work has much in common) sees truth as equivalent to impartiality. This is confirmed by his later statement (ch. 55) that, preface apart, 'the body of a work of history is simply an extended *diēgēsis*': this was the technical term for that part of a forensic speech known as the 'statement of the case', in which the standard criteria were plausibility and verisimilitude. These were thus the criteria which, along with impartiality, governed historiography also. Such was the usual view in antiquity; it is found more fully expressed by Cicero more than two centuries earlier (see CLASSICAL HISTORIOGRAPHY).   AJW

Main Writings

How to Write History, Greek text, with English trans. by K. Kilburn, *Lucian*, vol. 6 (Loeb Classical Library, London: Heinemann, 1959); *Wie man Geschichte schreiben soll*, Greek text, with German trans. and commentary by H. Homeyer (Munich: Fink Verlag, 1965).

Reading

Avenarius, G: *Lukians Schrift zur Geschichtsschreibung* [Lucian's work on historiography] (Meisenheim am Glan: Verlag Hain, 1956).

Lyons, Francis Stewart Leland (b.1923, d.1983)   The foremost scholar of Irish history of his day, Leland Lyons divided his career between Ireland and Britain. Born in Londonderry, educated at Dover College and at Trinity College, Dublin, where he took first class honours in 1945 and a doctorate in 1947, he then lectured at Hull University before returning to a Trinity College Fellowship in 1951.

In 1964 Lyons became founding professor of modern history at the University of Kent at Canterbury (and master of its Eliot College, in 1969), leaving to return to Trinity College as provost in 1974, the year he was elected a fellow of the British Academy. During seven years as provost and a further two as research

professor at Trinity, Lyons turned down three Oxford college headships, but the completion of his biography of Yeats, cut short by his untimely death, would no doubt have been followed by the acceptance of a fourth offer. He was elected to the chancellorship of The Queen's University of Belfast a matter of days before he died.

Lyons's publications transformed our knowledge of modern Ireland. His biography of Parnell earned him the Heinemann award of the Royal Society of Literature, to which *Culture and Anarchy in Ireland 1890–1939*, based on his 1978 Ford Lectures, added the Ewart Biggs and Wolfson awards. This was evidence of his capacity to span the historical and literary disciplines which his biography of Yeats would surely have crowned.   DWH

Main publications

The Irish Parliamentary Party 1890–1910 (London: Faber, 1951); *The Fall of Parnell* (London: Routledge & Kegan Paul, 1960); *Internationalism in Europe 1815–1914* (Leyden: Sythoff, 1963); *John Dillon, a biography* (Routledge & Kegan Paul, 1968); *Ireland since the Famine* (London: Weidenfeld & Nicolson, 1971); *Charles Stewart Parnell* (London: Collins, 1977); *Culture and Anarchy in Ireland 1890–1939* (Oxford: Clarendon Press, 1979).

Reading

Foster, R. F.: Francis Stewart Leland Lyons 1923–1983. *Proceedings of the British Academy* 52 (1984) 463–79.

Lyte, Henry Churchill Maxwell (b.1848, d.1940)   Deputy keeper of the Public Records, Lyte was born in Devon into a west-country family of which H. F. Lyte, the hymn-writer, was another member. He was educated at Eton and studied history at Christ Church, Oxford, graduating in 1870. Lyte published *A History of Eton College 1440–1875* in 1875, and *A History of the University of Oxford* in 1886. In the intervening years he worked as one of the inspectors of the Royal Commission on Historical Manuscripts, established in 1869 to survey historical records in private hands, and prepared a number of substantial reports, including that on the manuscripts of St Paul's Cathedral (1883).

In 1886, at the age of 38, Lyte was appointed deputy keeper, and with no more

257

knowledge of the institution than his occasional editorial work had given him undertook the direction of the Public Record Office. He held the post until 1926, an active and decisive tenure of 40 years, unmatched by any of his predecessors or successors. He was knighted in 1897.

When Lyte entered the Public Record Office it had developed little since PALGRAVE's day. The records were still being assimilated, and the policy of publication which had been followed under Thomas Duffy Hardy and his brother William had done little to advance their use. Lyte brought a new sense of purpose to the Office. His principal achievement, apart from a general style which was an accomplishment in itself, was to extend the principle of calendaring to the great series of Chancery rolls, charter, patent and close, a policy which transformed the study of medieval England. His own contributions included the *Book of Fees* (1920–3) and *Historical Notes on the Great Seal* (1926), but he concerned himself with every aspect of the operation of the Office, and the work of several generations of historians has testified to his achievements.   GHM

Reading

Reports of the Royal Commission on the Public Records (London: HMSO, 1912–19).

M

Mabillon, Jean See MAURISTS.

Macartney, Carlile Aylmer (b.1895, d.1978)
Macartney pursued a career as journalist,
minor official, semi-freelance author and private scholar, becoming an acknowledged
authority on central Europe and especially on
Hungary, to which he broadcast when Foreign
Office adviser during the second world war.
Frustrated in his practical hopes for the area,
he produced learned work of outstanding
value in four different fields. Between the wars
he concentrated on the problems of ethnic
identity and self-determination in the Danube
basin, while engaged also in pioneering studies
of the early Magyar chroniclers. After 1945 he
completed two *magna opera*: an authoritative
and absorbing account of the political history
of inter-war Hungary, which rests substantially on the reminiscences of those who participated in it; and a monumental general survey
of the later Habsburg Empire, written with
great insight, verve and puckish humour,
which is far the best thing of its kind.   RJWE

Main publications

The Magyars in the Ninth Century (Cambridge: Cambridge University Press, 1931); *National States and
National Minorities* (London: Royal Institute of International Affairs, 1934); *Hungary and her Successors: the Treaty of Trianon and its consequences* (RIIA,
1937); *The Medieval Hungarian Historians* (Cambridge University Press, 1953); *October Fifteenth: a
history of modern Hungary, 1929–45*, 2 vols (Edinburgh: Edinburgh University Press, 1956); *The
Habsburg Empire, 1790–1918* (London: Weidenfeld
& Nicolson, 1968).

Reading

Seton-Watson, H.: Memoir. *Proceedings of the British
Academy* 67 (1981) 411–32.

Macaulay, Thomas Babington (b.1800,
d.1859)   Regularly hailed in his time as the
best contemporary historian Macaulay has
since been called the finest writer of narrative
history who ever lived. His father, Zachary
Macaulay, was a leader of the campaign against
the slave trade, and his moral certitude was
an influence on Macaulay. A precocious child
and a popular Cambridge undergraduate,
Macaulay first took up a career at the bar but
soon made his name as a writer of political and
literary reviews. The excellence of these and
their impeccably Whig sentiments led to a
parliamentary seat, and his oratory led to
government office. He sat on the Supreme
Council of India (and designed its penal code)
and served as secretary-at-war and paymaster-
general. Throughout this period he continued
to write historical essays and epic poetry, and
conceived the project of a *History of England*
concentrating upon the period from 1688 to
1820. At the age of 50 his health collapsed,
and he decided to give up politics in order to
write. Upon his retirement he was raised to
the peerage as Baron Macaulay of Rothley.
But his health continued to deteriorate, partly
through his tendency to overwork, and when
he died the *History* was only completed to the
year 1702.

Thus outlined there is a tragic hue to
Macaulay's life, but he considered both his
own story and that of his nation to have been a
record of spectacular success. He took it for
granted that his *History* would still be read a
thousand years after his death and thought
himself the world's greatest historian since
Thucydides. Lord Melbourne once wished
that he might be as cocksure about anything as
Macaulay was about everything. He revelled in

259

his intellectual powers, exhibiting feats of memory such as the ability to recite the whole of *Paradise Lost*. He remarked that any fool could say his archbishops of Canterbury backwards, and assumed that his readers would recognize a quotation from a minor Italian poet. Throughout his life he took measures to eliminate personal unpleasantness, remaining a bachelor and steadily narrowing his friendships. He assuaged the pain of his greatest blow, the death of a sister, by reading a huge quantity of fiction. The satisfaction with which he contemplated his own achievements was paralleled by that with which he contemplated those of his country and, to a lesser extent, of the human race. He summed up England's story since 1689 as 'eminently the history of physical, of moral and of intellectual improvement'. By this he meant the growth of national power as well as economic and scientific progress, but his test of 'improvement' was the increasing health and wealth of all classes, which he automatically equated with happiness. He believed that progress was natural to his species, and pointed out that although the Spanish and Dutch were no longer great powers, their peoples were considerably better off than in their days of greatness. In most of these attitudes, of course, he was reflecting the mood of early nineteenth-century England: few writers have been so completely in harmony with their place and time.

Inevitably, such a cast of mind filled Macaulay's work with what have since been considered blemishes. Too often he behaved like a headmaster on prize day, handing out praise to people if they had supported what he regarded as progress and administering severe rebukes to others. At times he wrote as advocate rather than judge, notably in his account of the trial of Alice Lisle when he acts as counsel for the defence: James II's adultery is portrayed as a disgusting vice, but William III's as a trivial lapse. He repeatedly warned his readers not to consider the past by the standards of the present, and repeatedly ignored his own advice. He condemned Elizabeth I for not tolerating Catholicism, and caricatured squires, parsons, Covenanters and non-jurors because they offended not only the canons of

his age but of his political party. He pelted opponents (both living and dead) with abuse, calling Laud a 'ridiculous old bigot', describing the verses of Frederick the Great as 'hateful to God and man', and comparing the reading of work by a contemporary historian with the treadmill. At times he distorted the facts appallingly: for example he misrepresented Bacon's political career in order to cry up his gifts as a philosopher. He knew little of the history of Europe and openly despised that of India. His poetry confirms what his historical writings suggest: that he was a humane and cultured Philistine.

Of course, Macaulay had many other, and greater, qualities. In evaluating his worth it is important to distinguish between his essays and his *History*. His essays made little pretence to be objective or dispassionate and were dashed off in weeks. He himself considered many of them to be ephemeral. The *History* was the work which he intended to live for ever, over which he agonized, and which effectively killed him. It reproduces the vices of the essays, but in muted form and as part of an incomparably greater achievement. His preoccupation differed from that of many other historians: whereas they have struggled to ascertain the truth of the past, Macaulay was more concerned with its presentation. It was his expressed fear that narrative history was no longer read by a wide public and his ambition was, in his famous phrase, to replace 'the last fashionable novel upon the tables of young ladies'. He laboured to reconstruct 'the spirit of an age' with 'appropriate images presented in every line'. The result is not so much like a novel as an epic drama: it does not satisfy curiosity about what will happen so much as enable readers to experience events already familiar in outline. It provides a fast-moving narrative while adding an incredible wealth of detail. It hinges upon the struggle between past (James II) and present (William III), but with an enormous complexity of subplots. It embodied with extraordinary skill every prejudice of its novel-reading public: optimism, evangelical morality, superficial piety, common sense, business acumen, sentimentality, patriotism, pageantry and melodrama. The past is both belittled for the sake of the present and enjoyed as an unreal world of emotional adventure. Action is built around a series of individual dilemmas, such as conscience or ambition, bravery or cowardice, Protestant or Catholic, Whig or Tory. The reader is led along by the historian as if by a stern and upright judge, and knows that right will prevail in the end.

In his ambition, he was completely successful. Not only was he a best-seller in England, but most squatter families in the Australian outback during the 1880s possessed his works (together with the Bible and Shakespeare). He was proportionately admired in Europe and America, and the *History* has become a classic. Moreover it is fundamentally accurate. Details have been disproved, but its narrative form and the author's distaste for theorizing have saved it from major error. He dazzled the public as no historian had done before or has since, and misled few colleagues in the process.   RH

Main publications

Critical and Historical Essays (London: Longmans, Green, 1843); *The History of England from the Accession of James II*, 4 vols (London: Longmans, Green, 1855–61).

Reading

Clive, J.: *Macaulay* (London: Secker & Warburg, 1973).

Millgate, Jane: *Macaulay* (London: Routledge, 1973).

Levine, G.: *The Boundaries of Fiction* (Princeton: Princeton University Press, 1968).

McFarlane, Kenneth Bruce (b.1903, d.1966) After a sheltered upbringing and conventional education at Dulwich College and Exeter College, Oxford, McFarlane was elected a fellow by examination at Magdalen College in 1927 and a year later a tutorial fellow, a post which he held for the rest of his life. He remained unmarried, devoting much time to college teaching and (especially during the war) administration, and had considerable influence on successive generations of pupils. A shy and deeply sensitive man, of somewhat fragile health and temperament, he set a high value on personal relationships and was rewarded by the devoted friendship of many in and outside his academic circle.

McFarlane transformed the study of late medieval English history which, at the outset of his career, was still largely written from narrative sources and based on Stubbs's view of constitutional development. McFarlane's search for a broader and more realistic interpretation led him to work on political, social and religious themes, in all of which he utilized new types of evidence and pioneered a new approach. From being the most neglected and incomprehensible period of English history, the fifteenth century became a field of intensive research and seminal methodology.

With Tout's work on the fourteenth century in mind, McFarlane's first inquiry was into the workings of English government in the following century, and was pursued through extensive investigation of the fiscal and administrative records at the Public Record Office. His unrivalled knowledge of the operation of the council, exchequer, and seals imparted a new perspective and significance to his account of 'The Lancastrian Kings' in volume VIII of the *Cambridge Medieval History* (1936). Subsequent detailed articles on the loans of Cardinal Beaufort and others were also drawn from these researches. From government he turned to explore the bonds of political society, characterized in the late medieval indentures of retainer. His two seminal articles on bastard feudalism explored the nature of these and their implications for the relations of lords and gentry, and marked the opening into a wider study of the governing class which became his abiding concern. His researches into the affairs of the English nobility rescued them from a historical stereotype and set them as a class in an intelligible political and social context. Here again it was the extensive research into hitherto unused private archives throughout England which gave his Ford Lectures of 1953 on the late medieval nobility their novel and authoritative quality. But the attempt to encompass so vast a field proved too great and the text of the lectures, with related papers, was left for publication by his pupils.

The diversity of fields in which McFarlane worked (including John Wyclif, the Lollard Knights at the court of Richard II and, in collaboration with Edgar Wind, a revision of the canon of the paintings of Hans Memling) and the authority of his contribution in each attests his great intellectual energy and rigorous and critical scholarship. His achievement in re-shaping the interpretation of the late middle ages and inspiring research into it ranks him among the outstanding English historians of the twentieth century.   GLH

Main publications

The Lancastrian Kings. In *Cambridge Medieval History*. Vol 8, *The Close of the Middle Ages* (Cambridge: Cambridge University Press, 1936); *John Wycliffe and the Beginnings of English Nonconformity* (London: English Universities Press, 1952); *Lancastrian Kings and Lollard Knights* (Oxford: Oxford University Press, 1972); *The Nobility of Later Medieval England* (Oxford University Press, 1973); *England in the Fifteenth Century*, collected essays (London: Hambledon, 1981).

Reading

Leyser K. J.: Memoir: Kenneth Bruce McFarlane. *Proceedings of the British Academy* 62 (1976) 485–506.
Richmond, C. F.: After McFarlane. *History* 68 (1983) 46–60.

Machiavelli, Niccolò (b.1459, d.1527) A Florentine administrator and historian, Machiavelli, who rose in the chancery of Florence, was unlike his more celebrated historian predecessors in writing almost exclusively in the vernacular. He is thus hardly to be described as a humanist; and in other ways, like his contemporary GUICCIARDINI, he belonged to a new type of historian and writer: obsessed by politics he exemplified what is sometimes termed the 'second school' of Florentine historian, as opposed to the first, men such as BRUNI and Poggio Bracciolini. For his characteristics were derived not only from his relatively humble background, but also from his career as an official (later employed in embassies) and his involvement in organizing Florentine warfare: his celebrated advocacy of a 'citizen' army, absurd though it was, was much admired by nineteenth century advocates of democratic government although regarded as somewhat comic in his own day. But what in a sense turned him from being a cog in the machine of Florentine administration to becoming one of the innovators of a new type of political history and theory was the fall of Medici dominance in Florence in 1494. For some years Machiavelli's efforts were devoted to ingratiating himself with the Medici pope (Leo X) who from 1512 was running Florence through minor members of his family. When this collapsed Machiavelli was deprived of a future. Tortured, excluded from office, he turned to digesting his experience in a new type of history, a history which was empirical and sought to turn the lessons of the past into moral aphorisms for the present-day practitioner. The material he absorbed into his analysis was not only derived from his personal experiences: his most elaborate work was a commentary on Livy, *The Discourses* (1513–21), which displays his fundamental adherence to republican government for Florence and, in a sense, for Italy as a whole. This was history in its traditional sense. Alongside it we must place his essay on *The Prince*. This remarkable work (1516) was to earn him his reputation and his infamy ('old Nick') but it failed to secure his re-employment in Florence when the Medici were re-established in 1512. Like Guicciardini he was obsessed by the 'disasters of Italy', the invasions by the French (1494), and tried to turn the catastrophe into political capital. His later reputation was ambiguous. Regarded as an immoral writer (which some of his literary works, the plays, reinforced) he was dismissed by the political realists who digested his lessons but disowned their patronage.   DH

Main writings

Opere, ed. Mario Bonfantini (Milan: Ricciardi, 1950).

Reading

Gilbert, Felix: *Machiavelli and Guicciardini* (Princeton, Princeton University Press, 1965).
Raab, Felix: *The English Face of Machiavelli* (London and Toronto; Routledge, 1964).

McIlwain, Charles Howard (b.1871, d.1968) American constitutional historian and political theorist. McIlwain was educated at the College of New Jersey, later Princeton University, and Harvard University, where he became assistant professor in 1911 and from 1926 to 1946 was Eaton professor of the science of government. He was George Eastman visiting professor of American history at Oxford in 1944 and honorary fellow of Balliol College. McIlwain's main interests were in constitutional history and political theory, especially their relation to law.

The close interconnection of the theory and practice of government treated both historically and contemporarily, was a feature of McIlwain's writings, together with their wide range, extending from classical Greece and Rome to his own age and country. A recurrent theme was the contrast between two different kinds of sovereignty which characterized the middle ages and the post-medieval world respectively. The first kind of sovereignty – the subject of his *Growth of Political Thought in the West* – evolved from a combination of Stoic, Roman, Christian and Germanic conceptions of an independent pre-existent law, which was equally binding upon rulers and ruled and was crystallized in the feudal doctrine of inviolable rights. Medieval rulers accordingly owed their authority to upholding the law and could not override it. That concept of limited authority represented for McIlwain true constitutionalism. It was largely superseded in the seventeenth century by the second kind, of absolute sovereignty, of which Hobbes, in the Anglo-Saxon world, was the main originator. In contrast to the first kind it vested arbitrary authority in the sovereign as the source of all law. It thereby substituted right for might as the basis of a ruler's power. It became enshrined in the act of settlement of 1689 and so inaugurated the modern pretence of popular sovereignty which McIlwain saw as responsible for the growth of intolerance and tyranny, leading, among its other effects, to the revolt of the American colonists and finally to Hitler, against whose threat McIlwain warned in various public addresses during the years before the outbreak of the second world war. He still repays reading.   GL

Main publications

The High Court of Parliament and Its Supremacy (New Haven, Conn.: Yale University Press, 1910); *The American Revolution* (New York: Macmillan, 1923); *The Growth of Political Thought in the West* (1932; repr. New York: Macmillan, 1964); *Constitutionalism and the Changing World* (1939: repr. Cambridge:

Cambridge University Press, 1969); *Constitutionalism Ancient and Modern* (Ilthaca, NY: Cornell University Press, 1960).

Reading

Post, G., Strayers, J. R. and Thorme, S. E.: Memoir, C. H. McIlwain. *Speculum* 44 (1969) 528.

Mackintosh, James (b.1765, d.1832) Educated at Aberdeen and Edinburgh universities, Mackintosh's youthful radical politics rapidly gave way to more conservative Whiggism, in keeping with the *Edinburgh Review* for which he wrote on historical subjects. His major work, the *History of the Revolution in England of 1688*, posthumously edited, embodied extensive research in Britain and in imperial archives accessible in Paris in 1814. MACAULAY used his research, but commented that the *History* contained 'perhaps too much disquisition and too little narrative' (p. 279). Mackintosh's work helped, transitionally, to shape the Whig tradition in that he inherited from his Scottish background the 'philosophical' tradition of historical analysis, but also stressed a political commitment to the defence of liberty, as restored to England by William III.   JR

Main publications

History of the Revolution in England in 1688. Comprising a View of the Reign of James the Second, from his accession to the enterprise of the Prince of Orange . . . and completed to the settlement of the Crown by the Editor (*W. Wallace*) (London: Longmans, Green, 1834).

Reading

Macaulay, T. B.: Sir James Mackintosh's 'History of the Revolution'. In *Critical and Historical Essays*, 2 vols, ed. A. J. Grieve (London: Dent, 1907).
Mackintosh, R. J.: *The Memoirs of the Life of the Right Honourable Sir James Mackintosh* (London: E. Moxon 1835).

McLaughlin, Andrew Cunningham (b.1861, d.1947) After studying with Thomas Cooley, author of *Constitutional Limitations*, at the University of Michigan Law School, McLaughlin taught constitutional history at Michigan and served as managing editor of the *American Historical Review* (1901–6). Publication of his influential reinterpretation of

America's 'critical period', *The Confederation and the Constitution* (1905), led to his appointment as chairman of the history department at the University of Chicago. Long a leading figure in the American Historical Association, McLaughlin was made president in 1914. He received a Pulitzer Prize for his last major work, *The Constitutional History of the United States* (1935).

McLaughlin is best known for arguing that American federalism grew out of the colonial experience in the extended polity of the British Empire. He asserted that the federal Constitution of 1787 solved a 'problem of imperial organization' that had defied the best efforts of British statesmen. Countering the then conventional wisdom, McLaughlin concluded that American revolutionary principles were secured — not betrayed — by constitutional reform. McLaughlin's interest in the historical development of leading principles led him to explore the impact of Puritan conceptions of covenant on the American legal tradition. One of the most important exponents of constitutional history in his day, McLaughlin anticipated and influenced a later generation's rediscovery of the 'ideological origins' of the Revolution (see BAILYN).   PSO

Main publications

The Confederation and the Constitution, 1783–1789 (New York: Harper, 1905; The Background of American Federalism. *American Political Science Review* 12 (1918) 215–40; *Foundations of American Constitutionalism* (New York: New York University Press, 1932); *Constitutional History of the United States* (New York: Appleton, Century, 1935).

McNeill, William Hardy (b.1917) McNeill was born in Vancouver, graduated from the University of Chicago in 1938, and has held a chair there since 1957. He was in Greece with the US Army between November 1944 and June 1946, and apart from several books on Greece, from *The Greek Dilemma. War and Aftermath* (1949) to *The Metamorphosis of Greece since World War II* (1978), the relations between peoples of the mountains and the plains and between nomadic invaders and pastoralists have been among his leading preoccupations. War service also provided a background for *America, Britain and Russia*

(1953), written at the Royal Institute of International Affairs and published as the ninth volume of its history of the war under the editorship of A. J. Toynbee. Its final chapter places the subject matter in the context of world history, foreshadowing McNeill's most distinctive contributions to historiography. *The Rise of the West* (1963) was probably the first serious attempt in many years, by a professional historian, to encapsulate the history of the world in a single volume, and certainly the most successful; the shorter *A World History* appeared four years later.

The chief units of McNeill's history are civilizations, very much as defined and enumerated by TOYNBEE; their destinies are seen as being shaped largely by the belief that 'encounter with bearers of another culture or civilization is sure to change local ways of life' (A defence of world history, p. 78) by inspiring imitation and emulation or, more probably, rejection and resistance. Hence McNeill is less interested in the internal dynamics of civilizations than in the nature and repercussions of contacts between them, whether through tribute, depredation and warfare, commercial and cultural exchange, or technical innovation. That 'this was and remains the main drive wheel of historical change' (A defence of world history, p. 78) is the theme not only of the world histories but of several more specific studies, including *Europe's Steppe Frontier* (1964) and *The Pursuit of Power* (1982). McNeill has recently turned towards biological and environmental perspectives on world history, perhaps most successfully in *Plagues and Peoples* (1976). There he argues that the most dramatic and significant impacts of disease have come at times when disease-bearing micro-organisms have been enabled by trade or conquest to cross the barriers between civilizations formerly isolated from each other, and hurl themselves with devastating vigour on populations which have had no opportunity to build immunity against them. Thus the influenza virus and the cholera bacillus exemplify, in their fashion, McNeill's 'drive wheels of historical change'.

Nobody who ranges so widely could entirely escape whipping by specialists. But the quality of McNeill's scholarship and the freedom of his work from philosophical and ideological presuppositions, as well as the clarity of his prose, the sweep of his vision and the remarkable fertility of his imagination, have made him increasingly influential, and contributed greatly to rescuing WORLD HISTORY from the disrepute into which it had fallen in the first half of the twentieth century.   RIM

Main publications

(Published by Chicago University Press, Chicago, Ill., unless otherwise stated.)
America, Britain and Russia: Their Co-operation and Conflict, 1941–46 (London: Royal Institute of International Affairs, 1953); *The Rise of the West: a History of the Human Community* (1963); *Europe's Steppe Frontier, 1500–1800* (1964); *A World History* (Oxford: Oxford University Press, 1967); *Venice The Hinge of Europe, 1081–1797* (1974); *The Pursuit of Power: Technology, Armed Force and Society since AD 1000* (Oxford: Basil Blackwell, 1982).

Reading

McNeill, W. H.: A defence of world history. *Transactions of the Royal Historical Society*, 5th ser., 32 (1982) 75–89.

Madox, Thomas (b.1666, d.1727)   Little is known of Madox's personal life. His mother was a dissenter and this may account for his prodigious industry and sense of dedication: the writing of history was 'in some sense a religious act; it ought to be undertaken with purity and rectitude of mind'. For his first book, *Formulare Anglicanum*, he said he perused a great number of ancient charters and writings. Likewise in his history of the Exchequer, he pointed out 'the labour besides the expense of resorting often and often to repositories of records in distance places, of enoting and copying memorials from thence, and of perusing a vast number of things for a few comparatively that one collects'. This statement reveals Madox's method of working: first to transcribe the original documents (not copies), and only then to decide upon chapters and headings. These are to be elicited from the materials, instead of being preconceived opinions. Madox consciously set himself as an example to future historians. In *Formulare Anglicanum* he laid down the principles of the science of 'diplomatic' in England. In his history of the Exchequer he established a now

familiar hierarchy of reliability for documents, with 'the public records of the crown' being superior to monastic chronicles. Madox was himself an officer of the crown: first a clerk in the Exchequer and from 1714 Historiographer Royal in succession to RYMER. Madox died at the age of 60 before he could produce his *Feudal History of England*, for which he had accumulated over 90 volumes of transcripts.   MTC

Main publications

Formulare Anglicanum (London: James Tonson, 1702); *History and Antiquities of the Exchequer* (London: John Matthews, 1711); *Firma Burgi* (London: William Bowyer, 1722); *Baronia Anglicana* (London: Robert Gosling, 1736).

Reading

Douglas, D. C.: *English Scholars 1660–1730*, 2nd edn (London: Eyre and Spottiswoode, 1951).

Mahan, Alfred Thayer (b.1840, d.1914) After nearly 30 years of undistinguished and unsatisfying service as a naval officer, Mahan became famous in the 1890s as a historian and apostle of sea power. A graduate of the United States Naval Academy in 1859, Mahan was an aloof and unpopular officer who detested life at sea. But he found solace in history and won a place on the faculty of the Naval War College where he wrote his *Influence of Sea Power upon History* (1890) and established his reputation as a historian. He retired from the navy in 1896 to become a writer (20 books and 137 articles altogether) and an adviser to successive governments of the United States.

Although many of Mahan's histories now seem unsophisticated, they were extraordinarily influential at the turn of the twentieth century. He argued in book after book that the fate of nations – especially of Britain in the eighteenth and nineteenth centuries – depended upon control of the seas, and that control of the seas depended upon superior battle fleets. Such arguments, unencumbered with scholarly qualifications, were very appealing to leaders of nations competing for overseas colonies and commerce and to anyone who was eager to justify building warships. Mahan's histories sold well, and he was honoured by scholars and statesmen of many nations.

IDG

Main publications

(Published by Little, Brown, Boston, Mass.)
The Influence of Sea Power upon History, 1660–1783 (1890); *The Influence of Sea Power upon the French Revolution and Empire, 1793–1812* (1892).

Reading

Seager, R.: *Alfred Thayer Mahan: the Man and his Letters* (Annapolis: Naval Institute Press, 1977).

Maistre, Joseph de (b.1753, d.1821) Savoyard polemicist and diplomat (Sardinian envoy to Russia, 1802–17). De Maistre belongs to the leading ranks of those who promptly denounced the French Revolution, and the Enlightenment that inspired it, as the embodiment of intellectual and moral folly. De Maistre's reputation as an articulate defender of authoritarian Throne and Altar (often too passionately 'ultra' for the comfort even of those whom he sought to champion) was first established with his *Considérations sur la France* (1796), and later consolidated through such works as *Du Pape* (1819) and *Les Soirées de Saint-Pétersbourg* (1821). He assailed the *philosophes* for their optimistic estimation of man's natural sociability, their credulity about the capacity of intellect to restrain instinct, and their belief that the course of history was moulded by human rather than divine will. De Maistre's God weaves, over the very long run, a pattern of redemption. On a more immediate scale, however, history presents scenes of constant carnage that appear to signify only the deity's wrath at the Fall of mankind. 'The whole earth, continually steeped in blood, is nothing but an immense altar on which every living thing must be sacrificed without end, without restraint, without respite, until the consummation of the world, the extinction of evil, the death of death' (*Les Soirées de Saint-Pétersbourg*, seventh dialogue). No modern commentator can go through de Maistre's obsessively sanguinary prose without questioning how far the author's mind was unhinged. Even so, he possessed some historical and psychological insight — perhaps especially into the circumstances under which the mass of men may crave do-

mination or court destruction. Moreover, in repeatedly warning about the chaos which might ensue once a sense of religious awe vanished, de Maistre was addressing himself valuably to the historical theme of secularization and to one of the anxieties that would most insistently recur within nineteenth-century social and moral debate.

MDB

Main publications

The Works of Joseph de Maistre, trans. and intro. J. Lively (London: Allen & Unwin, 1965; New York: Schockem, 1971).

Reading

Berlin, I.: The Counter-Enlightenment. In *Against the Current: Essays in the History of Ideas* (London: Hogarth, 1979).
McClelland, J. S. ed.: *The French Right, from de Maistre to Maurras* (London: Cape, 1970).

Maitland, Frederick William (b.1850, d.1906) Maitland proceeded from Eton to Cambridge and thence to Lincolns Inn, where he was called to the bar in 1876. He was not successful as a barrister and first showed his interest in history in 1881 with a paper on the Welsh law of blood feud. In 1884 his new career was established with his appointment to a Readership at Cambridge and the publication (at his own expense) of *Pleas of the Crown for the County of Gloucester, 1221*. In this his enthusiasm for medieval legal records was manifested: here is 'a picture', he wrote, 'or rather a photograph of English life as it was ... taken from a point of view at which chroniclers too seldom place themselves'. A new sort of history was to be written from such records, not only of English law but of society. In order to do this, however, a substantial amount of transcribing and editing would need to be done. Maitland made his next contribution to this with *Bracton's Notebook* in three volumes (again published at his own expense) in 1887. In 1888 he was elected professor of the laws of England at Downing College where he remained.

Maitland's work is so useful because he was such a productive and lucid editor of texts. Between his first volume for the Selden Society in 1887 and his death in 1906 he saw 21 volumes through the press and edited seven of them himself: plea rolls of the king's courts, seignorial court rolls, lawyers' treatises, and year books. From the start, each text had an English translation in parallel, whereas other record societies left their texts in sometimes incomprehensible Latin. Maitland's most influential single volume was his edition of the records of parliament for 1305, the *Memoranda de Parliamento*, published in 1893. This emphasized, contrary, to the view of STUBBS, that parliament had essentially been a court of law.

On the basis of his decade of work among medieval manuscripts, in 1895 Maitland published his monumental *History of English Law before the time of Edward I*. So uncertain was he of success that he associated the better-known name of Sir Frederick Pollock with his own as co-author; but, of the 1,400 pages, Pollock contributed only 38 (on Anglo-Saxon law). When he saw Pollock's work, Maitland wrote fast to stop him from writing any more. With the success of the *History*, Maitland launched into writing his own books, as well as editing texts. In the two years 1897–8 he published *Domesday Book and Beyond, Township and Borough* (a study of medieval Cambridge), a second and considerably revised edition of the *History*, and another refutation of Stubbs in *Roman Canon Law in the Church of England*. He also wrote articles and reviews for the non-specialist.

Maitland was a victim of Victorian medicine. In 1889 he had been warned that he might have only a year to live. He was obliged to winter in the south and, in consequence, on his voyage to the Canary islands in 1906 he died of pneumonia caught on board ship. His death was such a shock to the academic world that the university of Oxford sent an unprecedented letter of condolence to Cambridge and appreciations of Maitland have kept flowing ever since. In the most recent one from Cambridge, Sir Geoffrey Elton describes him as the 'patron saint' of historians.　　MTC

Main publications

The single most important is with F. Pollock, *The History of English Law before the time of Edward I*, 2nd edn reissued in 2 vols with intro. by S. F. C. Milsom (Cambridge: Cambridge University Press, 1968).

Reading

Bell, H. E.: *Maitland: a Critical Examination and Assessment* (London: A. & C. Black, 1965).

Cameron, J. R.: *F. W. Maitland and the History of English Law* (Norman: University of Oklahoma Press, 1961) [incl. substantial bibliography].

Elton, G. R.: *F. W. Maitland* (London: Weidenfeld, 1985).

Fifoot, C. H. ed.: *The Letters of F. W. Maitland* (London: Selden Society, 1965).

——: *Frederick William Maitland* (Cambridge, Mass.: (Harvard University Press, 1971).

Milsom, S. F. C.: Lecture on a master mind: Maitland, *Proceedings of the British Academy* 66 (1980) 265–281.

Stones, E. L. G. ed.: *F. W. Maitland: Letters to George Neilson* (Glasgow: Glasgow University Press, 1976).

Mâle, Emile　See ART HISTORY.

Mansi, Giovanni Domenico (b.1692, d.1769) Born into a patrician family at Lucca, where he spent most of his life Mansi became archbishop in 1765. Professed as a Clerk Regular of the Mother of God (1710), he initially specialized in moral theology, and published (1724) a study of 'Reserved Cases' (sins where absolution is not delegated to the priest by the bishop). But his fame rests on the 90 folio volumes with his name on the title-page, reprinting works of reference in church history and moral theology. Among these, his greatest achievement is his *Amplissima Collectio*, a vast corpus of the Acts of Church Councils in thirty-one volumes (1759–98). In eight years of toil to 1764 he had prepared the essentials of all volumes. Tome 15 (1769) records his death; tome 19 (1774) includes a memoir by Franceschini with a portrait. The volumes appearing after his death were in the charge of his friend and supporter, the Venetian librarian, Antonio Zatta.

The editing of conciliar acts had proceeded far more slowly than that of individual church fathers. After Merlin (1524), ever larger collections were gathered (for example, Crabbe, 1538; Surius, 1567; Nicolini, 1585; Bini, 1606, with Roman edition 1608, Paris royal edition 1644) until the massive collection in 17 vols by Philippe Labbe SJ (1671–2), published after Labbe's death by G. Cossart, with an important supplement (1683) by E. Baluze. Controversy between Gallicans magnifying conciliar authority and Ultramontanes claiming papal superiority both stimulated and hindered the task. In 1715 the Jesuit J. Hardouin produced the finest of all conciliar editions, but his Ultramontane annotation provoked a Gallican storm. Labbe's work was reissued by the Venetian N. Coleti in 23 volumes (1728–33). To this Mansi produced a six-volume Supplement (1748–52). His *Amplissima* integrated this Supplement into Coleti's re-edition of Labbe.

The value of Mansi's *Amplissima* lies in its near-completeness, not in his critical judgement. He did not correct proofs, and admitted that he never read many of the texts he was reprinting. His occasional claims to be printing major texts for the first time are sometimes correct, sometimes merely due to his ignorance of earlier and better editions by Coustant (for papal letters) or even Crabbe and others. The later volumes take on a jungle-like appearance, with some texts appearing two, three or even four times under various headings. He could have learnt more than he did from the Ballerini's splendid edition of Leo the Great. For English councils he did not understand how superior Wilkins was to Spelman, and for German councils could have made much more use of Hartzmann's collection. Nevertheless he added to Labbe notes of no less than 380 councils of which the Acts do not survive, but which are mentioned by chroniclers. Sometimes his chronological notes represent advance. He had the fortune to have three good canonistic manuscripts in Lucca cathedral library, and above all the great eighth-century Lucca 490, prince of all manuscripts of the *Liber Pontificalis* and basis for the editions by Duchesne and Mommsen. The collection breaks off in the middle of the council of Florence. It is astonishing how much is still most easily to be found through his *Amplissima*.

Contemporary scholars of the 1760s were not deceived about the quality of Mansi's compilations. The *Amplissima* had not rendered Labbe or Coleti superfluous; Mansi

attempted more than one man could do. Moreover, the *Amplissima* was but part of all that he was producing: reprints of Baronius and Raynaldus in 28 volumes (1738–56), Fabricius' *Bibliotheca latina mediae et infimae aetatis* (1754), Aeneas Sylvius (1755), Natalis Alexander's church history (1758–62) and other works. A cardinal's hat would have come his way had he not distressed Clement XIII by a bowdlerized volume of the condemned *Encylopédie* (1759); but he felt no disappointment. All his money went either on books or on alms for the poor. He could not meet the expenses of his installation as archbishop of Lucca four years before his death; his last 18 months were made a misery by a severe stroke. Mansi was not a great scholar, but a man who provided the learned with very useful tools on a scale no meticulous scholar could or would have done.   HC

Main writings

Sacrorum Conciliorum Hora at Amplissima Collectio, 31 vols, folio (Florence: 1759–98); series continued from 1901 by J. B. Martin and L. Petit [incl. *Vatican I* (1870)]; *Acts of Trent (1545–63)* (Görres-Gesellschaft; ongoing); entire Mansi series repr. Graz: 1960–2 [incl. index vol.].

Reading

Quentin, H.: *J. D. Mansi et les grandes collections conciliaires* (Paris: 1900).

Marczali, Henrik (b.1856, d.1940) Hungarian historiography, once established as a discipline separate from AUSTRIAN HISTORIOGRAPHY, was quickly appropriated by the emergent national cause, as in the distinguished but partisan writings of Mihály Horváth, who played a prominent part in the 1848–9 revolution. Its scholarly credentials were set up after 1867, with the founding of the Hungarian Historical Society (Magyar Történelmi Társulat) and its journal *Századok*, and especially by Marczali, a prodigious researcher and author, who rose from the simplest circumstances as a village Jew with no schooling, to become professor at Budapest in 1895. Marczali wrote numerous fluent general accounts, covering almost all aspects of Hungarian history except the sixteenth and seventeenth centuries, as well as guides to the sources and a wealth of detailed studies, all characterized by high professionalism. He is remembered today mainly for an outstanding series of books on the eighteenth century, above all about the reform movement under Joseph II, to which he felt attracted on account of his own liberal sympathies. Marczali's liberal world fell apart after 1918, and he ceased to play a public role in inter-war Hungary; but his academic standards lived on in his pupils, particularly in SZEKFŰ. RJWE

Main publications

Magyarország története II József korában (History of Hungary in the time of Joseph II) 1881−8 3 vols. Vol. I trans. as *Hungary in the Eighteenth Century*, ed. H. W. V. Temperley (Cambridge: Cambridge University Press, 1910); *A legújabb kor története, 1825−80* (History of our times, 1825−80) (Budapest: 1892); *A magyar nemzet története* (History of the Hungarian nation), vols I, II, VIII (Budapest: 1895−8); *A magyar történet kútföinek kézikönyve* (Handbook of the sources for Hungarian history) (Budapest: 1902); *Az 1790−91 országgyülés története*, (History of the Diet of 1790−91), 2 vols (Budapest: 1907); *Ungarische Verfassungsgeschichte* (Constitutional history of Hungary) (Tübingen: 1911).

Reading

Gunst, P.: Introduction to Marczali's *Világtörténelem − magyar történelem* (World history − Hungarian history) (Budapest: Gondolat, 1982).

Várkonyi, A.: *A pozitivista történetszemlélet a magyar történetírásban* (The positivist view of history in Hungarian historiography), 2 vols: (Budapest: Akadémiai Kiadó, 1973).

Marx, Karl (b.1818, d.1883) Marx referred to his view of the world as 'the materialist conception of history'; he nowhere used the expression 'historical materialism', still less 'dialectical materialism'. The central idea of this conception is that the essential element in an understanding of human history is the productive activity of human beings − the way they obtained their means of subsistence by interaction with nature.

Marx expounded this materialist conception of history most fully in *The German Ideology* (1846) in conjunction with Engels. Here he claimed that human beings first distinguished themselves from animals when they began to produce their means of subsistence and enunciated his general thesis as follows:

The way in which men produce their means of subsistence depends first of all on the nature of the actual means of subsistence they find in existence and have to reproduce. This mode of production must not be considered simply as being the reproduction of the physical existence of the individuals. Rather it is a definite form of activity of these individuals, a definite form of expressing their life, a definite *mode of life* on their part. As individuals express their life, so they are. What they are, therefore, coincides with their production, both with *what* they produce and with *how* they produce. The nature of individuals thus depends on the material conditions determining their production.

Marx then pointed to the increasing division of labour as a crucial concomitant of the development of these material conditions of production and showed how the division of labour led to the separation of town and country and then to the separation of industrial from commercial labour and so on. Next he summarized the different stages of ownership that corresponded to the stages in the division of labour: tribal ownership, communal and state ownership, feudal or estate ownership. His general aim was to show how the division of labour, leading to private property, created social inequality, class struggle, and the erection of political structures. Marx also claimed that the tensions involved in the development of the productive forces and the consequent class struggle had, in his own day, reached a point where a revolution was imminent in which the working masses would abolish the division of labour and private property in the means of production − a state of affairs he referred to as communism.

The conception of history outlined in *The German Ideology* is impressionistic and, to some extent, tentative: Marx never revised it for publication. But he did provide a summary of 'the guiding thread' of his studies in the *Preface to a Contribution to the Critique of Political Economy* (1859). Owing to its centrality to most discussions of Marx's theory of history, it deserves lengthy quotation:

In the social production of their life, men enter into definite relations that are indispensable and independent of their will, relations of production which correspond to a definite state of development of their material productive forces. The sum total of

269

these relations of production constitutes the economic structure of society, the real foundation, on which rises a legal and political superstructure and to which correspond definite forms of social consciousness. The mode of production of material life conditions the social, political and intellectual life process in general. It is not the consciousness of men that determines their being, but, on the contrary, their social being that determines their consciousness. At a certain stage of their development, the material productive forces of society come in conflict with the existing relations of production, or — what is but a legal expression for the same thing — with the property relations within which they have been at work hitherto. From forms of development of the productive forces these relations turn into their fetters. Then begins an epoch of social revolution.

Such programmatic statements are heavily qualified by the way in which Marx dealt with more specific questions or periods. For example, when discussing, later in his life, the possibility of revolution in Russia, he modified the seemingly universal laws of historical development of some of his earlier writings. He insisted on the possibility of Russia's bypassing the capitalist stage and criticized those who 'absolutely must metamorphose my historical sketch of the genesis of capitalism in Western Europe into a historico-philosophical theory of the path every people is fated to tread.' Engels once advised a correspondent who had enquired about historical materialism to read Marx's comments on contemporary history such as *The Eighteenth Brumaire* which is a subtle and scintillating account of the social and economic circumstances surrounding Louis Bonaparte's rise to power. In a broader perspective, Marx's account of precapitalist economic formations in the *Grundrisse* and the historical passages in the first volume of *Capital* are impressive examples of historical research.

Given the fragmentary nature of much of Marx's work and the political debate surrounding it, extended controversy over his theory of history has been inevitable. These controversies have centred on two main issues. The first concerns the extent to which Marx's view of history is determinist; some are inclined to read his theory as a fairly straightforward economic determinism while others

prefer to stress Marx's emphasis on social relations and class struggle. The second — not unconnected, of course, with the first — has to do with the scientificity of Marx's work; some see it as basically an empirical theory, while others see a moral, or indeed prophetic, dimension as central. But however much his confidence in rationality, his enthusiasm for schemata of change and development and his optimism about the potentiality of human beings may have been imbued by the spirit of his own age, Marx the historian has also been one of the powerful influences on subsequent generations.   DTM

Main publications

The German Ideology (1846); *The Poverty of Philosophy* (1847); *The Communist Manifesto* (1848); *The Class Struggle in France 1848–50 (1850); Grundrisse* (1857–8); *Preface to a Contribution to the Critique of Political Economy* (1859); *Capital*, vol. I (1867).

Reading

Bober, M.: *Karl Marx's Interpretation of History*, 2nd edn (New York: International Publishers, 1965).

Cohen, G.: *Karl Marx's Theory of History: a Defence* (Oxford: Oxford University Press, 1978).

Elster, J.: *Making Sense of Marx* (Cambridge: Cambridge University Press, 1985).

Evans, M.: *Karl Marx* (London: Allen & Unwin, 1975).

Lichtheim, G.: *Marxism: a Historical and Critical Study* (London: Routledge & Kegan Paul, 1961).

Marx, Karl: *Selected Writings*, ed. D. McLellan (Oxford: Oxford University Press, 1977).

McLellan, D.: *Karl Marx: His Life and Thought* (London: Macmillan, 1974).

Rader, M.: *Marx's Interpretation of History* (New York: Oxford University Press, 1979).

Marxist interpretation of history Referred to by Marx himself as 'the materialist conception of history' and by many of his followers as 'historical materialism', this is an interpretation of history as the result, above all, of the economic development of society, of the consequent division of society into classes, and of the struggle of these classes against each other.

In its classical form, as enunciated by Marx in the 1859 *Preface to a Contribution to the Critique of Political Economy*, Marxism interprets the general course of human history by reference to the development of the productive forces. The growth and demise of different social and economic organizations – the relations of production – corresponds to and is to be understood in terms of the increasing productive capacity of society, or the forces of production. These forces and relations of production combine to form a mode of production. Marx picked out the Asiatic, ancient, feudal and capitalist as successive modes of production. The key to the course of human history lay in the succession of modes of production, often referred to as the 'economic basis' of society, rather than in superstructural elements such as politics and ideology. Marx and Engels insisted that it was possible for superstructural elements to react back upon the economic basis, and even, for a time, to be decisive. And some Marxists have seen the relations and forces of production as together determining rather than attributing any primacy to the productive forces as such. There has also been much dispute as to where and how to draw the line between base and superstructure. But essential to any Marxist interpretation of history is that the economic is, in Engels's classic formulation, dominant 'in the last analysis'.

Two central aspects to the Marxist interpretation of history follow from this. The first is the importance attached to class struggle, of which history is said in the *Communist Manifesto* to consist. Classes are the basic social groups by means of whose conflict society develops in accordance with changes in the forces and relations of production; class membership is determined by certain common material interests that the individual shares with others, typically a relationship of ownership or non-ownership of the means of production. This class position is also held to determine the characteristic world view or consciousness of members of that class. In some versions of Marxism this rather more subjective element is built into the definition of class: a class only exists when it is conscious of itself as such, and this always implies common hostility to another group. But class consciousness and the fate of any particular class is ultimately dependent on its relationship to the development of the productive forces.

The second central aspect is that the legal and political institutions of society are seen as moulded by developments in the economic basis and the concomitant class struggle. This is encapsulated in the Marxist theory of ideology as a body of ideas and practices which serves to preserve the asymmetrical distribution of material resources and power in society. The rights of man for example as proclaimed in the French Revolution and the Constitution of the United States were not eternal truths about the nature of man which happened to be discovered at that particular time, as those who proclaimed them imagined; their significance could be fully understood only if viewed in the context of demands by new commercial groups for the end of feudal restrictions and for free competition in economic affairs. It was this tendency of all political and cultural arrangements to be skewed towards serving particular class interests that gave them their ideological tinge.

The Marxist interpretation of history is at its strongest in dealing with periods of sharp social conflict. The transition from feudalism to capitalism and the phenomenon of European imperialism over the last century have been the subjects of impressive analyses. But Marxists have recently become increasingly critical of the classic base/superstructure model, seeing this metaphor from heavy engineering as too crude a framework. This dissatisfaction is due to two main factors. First, there is the advent of so-called socialist societies such as the Soviet Union which are less obviously patient of being analysed in the conceptual framework of a Marxism designed principally to account for the rise of capitalism in western Europe. Second, most Marxists have held their interpretation of history to contain a predictive quality. But the expected revolution – or at least growth of revolutionary class consciousness – in the heartlands of capitalism has so far failed to materialize. This has led many Marxists to soften their economic determinism and attribute more influence to societal superstructures. In the work of GRAMSCI, for example, the analyses of the role of intellectuals, of the concept of hegemony, and of cultural influences in general represent a much more subtle respect for the superstructure. Again the work of Louis Althusser and his followers, with its strong integration of Durkheimian elements, has produced a neo-structuralist version of Marxism in which determination by the economic is often all but invisible. Still more recently a more sharply analytical version of Marxism has appeared in the Anglo-Saxon world whose aim is to construct a research programme of a conceptual precision hitherto foreign to Marxism. Cohen for example, is concerned to argue for macro-level functional relations between large units of the social structure; Elster's work is intended to found these relations on the study of individual-based micro-processes. How far some of this is describable as Marxism is, of course, a matter of much dispute; but at least it can be said that the inspiration provided by much of the Marxist interpretation of history is still very much alive.   DTM

Reading

Anderson, P.: *Considerations on Western Marxism*, (London: New Left Books, 1976).

Cohen, G.: *Karl Marx's Theory of History: a Defence* (Oxford: Clarendon Press, 1978).

Elster, J.: *Making Sense of Marx* (Cambridge: Cambridge University Press, 1985).

Fleischer, H.: *Marxism and History* (London: Allen Lane, 1973).

Kolakowski, L.: *Main Currents of Marxism*, 3 vols (Oxford: Oxford University Press, 1978).

McLellan, D.: *Marxism After Marx* (London: Macmillan, 1980).

Plamenatz, J.: *German Marxism and Russian Communism* (London: Longmans, Green, 1954).

Mathiez, Albert Xavier Emile (b. 1874, d.1932) Intellectually brilliant, physically robust and violent tempered, Mathiez became one of the greatest authorities on the French Revolution. He wrote extensively about the period and championed its achievements, and in the process identified himself with Maximilien Robespierre, whose character he deeply admired.

Mathiez attributed his academic success to the education he received from the school teachers of the Third Republic. Born into a modest peasant family in rural Franche Comté, he rose through the educational system thanks to his vigorous mind and capacity for hard work. By the time he entered the École normale supérieure in 1894, he had developed into an ardent republican and anti-clerical. Emerging three years later as an *agrégé* in history and geography, he devoted his scholarship almost exclusively to the Revolution. Despite his sharp temper, Mathiez climbed the ranks of the teaching profession from provincial lycées to the universities of Besançon and Dijon, then to the Sorbonne where he remained from 1926 until his death.

In 1904 Mathiez completed his doctoral dissertation on revolutionary religion, written under the direction of his mentor Alphonse AULARD. His subsequent publications examined church–state relations, frequently denouncing Catholic clergy for having impeded the progress of the Revolution. By 1908 Mathiez broke with Aulard for personal and doctrinal reasons and founded his own historical journal, *Annales révolutionnaires*, as well as the Société des études robespierristes. Both enshrined Robespierre as the true hero of the Revolution. Using his detective-like flair to discover new documents in the archives, Mathiez strove to unmask revolutionaries like Georges-Jacques Danton who were corrupted by political power.

During the first world war Mathiez turned his scholarship to defending France against the German invader. Numerous journal articles and newspaper columns recalled how the Committee of Public Safety led by Robespierre had mobilized the nation's resources and won victory on the battlefield in 1793–4. As he examined the economic and social aspects of the Terror for the first time, Mathiez realized that the Revolution was far more than a political and religious phenomenon. Problems such as scarcity, rationing, wage and price controls and popular agitation he explored with fresh understanding. The Russian Revolution of 1917 also provided him with insights into the revolutionary process. He soon came to view the Bolsheviks are neo-Jacobins and Lenin as a latter-day Robespierre.

Mathiez's admiration for Bolshevism and disillusionment with the conservative Republic induced him to join the Communist Party. He considered it the embodiment of France's revolutionary tradition and used its publications to denounce government policies. Although he left the party in 1923 when his intellectual independence was compromised, he retained a Marxist historical outlook. During the 1920s Mathiez produced several major works of synthesis. These popularized his thesis that the Revolution began as a struggle between aristocracy and bourgeoisie, then developed into a conflict that pitted middle classes against labouring classes. The Terror he considered the essential phase of the Revolution, when popular democracy flourished under Robespierre's leadership. By overthrowing this Republic of Virtue, the reactionary Thermidorians prepared Napoleon's rise to power.

Mathiez expounded these ideas in the classroom where he both terrorized and inspired his students. Exhausted by his ceaseless labours, he died from a stroke suffered in a Sorbonne lecture hall. The considerable body of first-rate work that he left behind perpetuated his influence. Based on extensive original research and written in a highly readable style, it succeeded in transcending his fierce partisanship.
JF

Main publications

La Théophilanthropie et le culte décadaire, 1796–1802 (Paris: F. Alcan, 1904); *Les origines des cultes révolutionnaires (1789–1792)* (Paris: Société nouvelle de librairie et d'édition, 1904); *La Révolution et l'église* (Paris: A. Colin, 1910); *La victoire en l'an II* (Paris: F. Alcan, 1916); *Études robespierristes* 2 vols (Paris: A. Colin, 1917–18); *La Révolution et les étrangers* (Paris: La Renaissance du livre, 1918); *Danton et la paix* (La Renaissance du livre, 1919); *Robespierre terroriste* (La Renaissance du livre, 1921); *La Révolution française*, 3 vols (Paris: A. Colin, 1922–7); *La vie chère et le mouvement social sous la terreur* (Paris: Payot, 1927); *La réaction thermidorienne* (Paris: A. Colin, 1929); *Girondins et Montagnards* (Paris: Firmin-Didot, 1930); *Le dix août* (Paris: Hachette, 1931); *Le Directoire* (Paris: A. Colin, 1934).

Reading

Friguglietti, J.: *Albert Mathiez, historien révolutionnaire (1874–1932)* (Paris: Société des études robespierristes, 1974).

Godechot, J.: *Un Jury pour la Révolution* (Paris: Robert Laffont, 1974).

Lefebvre, G.: L'oeuvre historique d'Albert Mathiez. *Annales historiques de la Révolution française* 9 (1932) 193–210.

Maurists The Congregation of St Maurus was founded in 1618 to spread reforming ideals among the French Benedictines. Dom Grégoire Tarrisse when superior-general (1630–48) emphasized the importance of learning in the religious life and the Maurists began to attract vocations from men who were academically gifted, but it should be stressed that only some 200 out of a total of 3,000 professed brethren were engaged in full-time study at any one time. This monastic milieu proved favourable to scholarship. The religious superiors helped to plan the academic work of the Congregation and could direct brethren to assist in areas where their talents were most needed. The Maurists were able to embark on projects which would take decades to complete, secure in the knowledge that time was unimportant and that new monks could always be directed to undertake such work when their older colleagues died. The brethren achieved a great deal because they regarded academic work as a religious activity: Dom Bernard Montfaucon (d.1741) spent at least thirteen hours each day in study.

Though austere in their observance, the Maurists did not live remote from the world. At their Paris headquarters, Saint-Germain-des-Prés, the brethren regularly entertained the intelligentsia of the city, and left the cloister to work in the private libraries of Paris, including that of the king. The Maurists undertook literary journeys through Europe, copying manuscripts and buying books to add to their library which became one of the best in the Christian world. They specialized in editing the works of the church fathers and wrote many theological works, but from the beginning they were interested in history, particularly that of their own Order. Dom Luc d'Achéry (d.1685) published miscellanies of historical texts, which he called *Spicilegium* (The Gleaning [from archives]). He assembled materials for a study of the saints of his Order which was used by his assistant, Jean Mabillon (d.1707), to prepare the *Acta sanctorum ordinis S. Benedicti* (6 vols, 1668–80). In addition to his treatise on historical method, *De Re Diplomatica* (1681), Mabillon also published collections of documents, the *Vetera Analecta* (4 vols, 1675–85), and prepared the

Annales Ordinis S. Benedicti, a major historical work which traced the history of his Order from its inception to the twelfth century. Mabillon's younger contemporary, Dom Edmond Martène (d.1739), with the help of his travelling companion Dom Ursin Durand, produced two large collections of unpublished texts which they had discovered during their literary journeys, while Dom Bernard Montfaucon wrote what long remained the standard work on Greek palaeography and produced a catalogue of the manuscripts to be found in the many western libraries in which he had worked. In 1750 the Maurists produced *L'Art de vérifier les dates*, a pioneering work which became a model for later handbooks of chronology. The fathers also wrote much excellent local and regional history of which the history of Languedoc, by Dom Joseph Vaissette and Dom Claude de Vic, is an outstanding example.

During the eighteenth century the Maurists undertook three monumental projects: the revision of *Gallia Christiana*, a seventeenth-century history of the French church; the completion of A. Du Chesne's *Historiae Francorum scriptores* of 1636; and the production of an *Histoire littéraire de la France*. Thirteen volumes of *Gallia Christiana* were produced in the years 1715–85, containing the histories of the bishoprics and religious houses of France. Dom Martin Bouquet and his successors published thirteen volumes of the *Recueil des historiens des Gaules et de la France* in 1737–86, while twelve volumes of the *Histoire littéraire* appeared in 1733–73. All these projects were incomplete at the time of the Revolution, when the Maurists were suppressed and their superior-general, Dom Ambroise Chevreux (d.1792), executed for refusing to take the constitutional oath. The Institut de France resumed publication of the *Recueil* and of the *Histoire littéraire* and some measure of continuity was provided by the co-operation of the long-lived Dom Michel Brial, who had entered Saint-Germain in 1771, retired into private life at the suppression and lived until 1828. The Maurist Congregation was never refounded, but many of their manuscripts were preserved and are now in the Bibliothèque Nationale.

The Maurists occupy a central place in western historiography because they were responsible for many innovations which became an accepted part of the scholarly tradition: the *Recueil*, for example, was the first major publication of national histories, preceding the *Rolls Series* and the *Monumenta Germaniae Historica* (though not MURATORI) by almost a century. The Maurists are chiefly read now because they transcribed a large number of manuscripts and inscriptions which have since been destroyed, so that their copies have become primary sources. Their unpublished writings remain a rich source of evidence to scholars, but many of their printed texts are also valuable and several of their collections have been photographically reproduced in recent years.

BH

Main publications

J. Mabillon: *De Re Diplomatica libri VI*, 2 pts (Paris: 1681–1704); *Gallia Christiana*, 13 vols (Paris: 1715–85), compl. by B. Hauréau, 3 vols (Paris: 1856–63; repr.: Gregg International, 1970); *Histoire littéraire de la France*, par des religieux ... de Saint-Maur, 12 vols (Paris: 1733–73), continued by the Académie des Inscriptions et Belles Lettres (Paris: 1807– in progress); Martin Bouquet et al.: *Receuil des historiens des Gaules et de la France*, 24 vols (Paris: 1738–1904; repr. Washington, DC: Microcard, 1966). J. Vaissette and Cl. de Vic: *Histoire générale du Languedoc*, 5 vols (Paris: 1730–45), new edn, A. Molinier, 16 vols (Toulouse: 1872–1915; repr. Osnabrück: Otto Zeller, 1973).

Reading

Baudot, J.: Mauristes. In *Dictionnaire de Théologie Catholique*, X (I) (Paris: Librarie Letouzey et Anes, 1928).

Charvin, G. ed.: *E. Martène. Histoire de la Congrégation de Saint-Maur*, 9 vols (Ligugé: 1928–43).

Knowles, D.: The Maurists. In *Great Historical Enterprises* (London: Nelson 1963).

Tassin, R.P.: *Histoire littéraire de la Congrégation de Saint-Maur* (Brussels and Paris: 1770) suppl. U. Robert (Paris: 1881); second suppl. H. Wilhelm, and U. Berlière (Paris: 1908).

Meinecke, Friedrich (b.1862, d.1954) Meinecke's long life coincided with a turbulent period of German history. At the age of nine, he watched the veterans of 1813 participating in the victory parade of 1871; three quarters of a century later the eighty-six-year-old historian witnessed the destruction of

Hitler's Reich. When in the divided city of Berlin the Free University was created, he became its first Rektor. Meinecke's historical writings and letters reflect the changing ideas and reactions of a perceptive member of the educated German *Bürgertum* through these years. His particular contribution to the study of history is that he was one of the founders of intellectual history – *Ideengeschichte*. After 1945, Meinecke occupied a special place of veneration in democratic West Germany, but was bitterly attacked in East Germany as a conservative, imperialist and nationalist. He adapted his historical writings to changing national circumstances; his early emphasis on the importance of the state and the *Volk* has been critically commented on by western historians. He is seen by some of his critics as supporting ideas which prepared the way for national socialist ideologies.

Meinecke served in the Prussian State Archives (1887–1901) where he fell under the spell of the 'Prussian' school of Leopold von RANKE and Heinrich von SYBEL. His first major work, a study of the life of General Field Marshal von Boyen, published between 1896 and 1899, reveals him, however, as a not uncritical admirer of imperial Germany. In Meinecke's view, nothing could remain static; the prime requirement of preserving the power of the state necessitated adaptation and change. He maintained that the people (*Volk*) and the state should not be regarded as in natural opposition but as complementary. His study of Boyen reflected Meinecke's growing disquiet about the alienation of the German working masses from the empire Bismarck had founded. Meinecke's appointment to professorships in Strasbourg (1901) and Freiburg (1906) was followed in 1908 by the publication of *Weltbürgertum und Nationalstaat: Studien zur Genesis des deutschen Nationalstaats* (Cosmopolitanism and the National State). It established Meinecke as one of Germany's leading historians. The theme of the book is how cosmopolitanism, with its universal morality, had to give way to the concept of *Realpolitik*, policies which best served the interest of the state. Meinecke chose the readable biographical form, describing the changing attitudes of influential conservatives in the nineteenth century to the concept of the German state. As a cultural history the book became a model complementing the hitherto predominant political history and the new social and economic history.

In the winter of 1914 Meinecke was appointed to a professorship in Berlin. It was characteristic of his sounder instincts that he opposed extremes in political aims. Just as he sought synthesis in his historical studies, so he pleaded for compromise in the political conflict between the liberals and the moderate left. He also advocated early on a compromise peace.

Defeat in 1918 made a deep impact on Meinecke. Bitter and disillusioned, he did not view the new democratic republic with much warmth. However, he supported it as the most realistic way to preserve and recover the power of the German state. In his most important book, *Die Idee der Staatsräson in der neueren Geschichte* (1924) (published in English as *Machiavellism*) he questioned his own earlier assumptions about the state and traced the spread of the idealization of power from the time of the Medicis to the calamity of 1914. The application of Machiavellism, according to Meinecke, had reached its most dangerous form in Germany.

Communism and national socialism were twin totalitarian dangers against which Meinecke warned his countrymen as late as February 1933. He rejected the crude racial-*Volk* conceptions of the national socialists and under pressure in 1935 gave up the editorship of the *Historische Zeitschrift*, which he had held for thirty-nine years. He continued to write, and published in 1936 his monumental *Entstehung des Historismus* (Origins of historicism). His concern here was principally with the eighteenth century and the beginnings of an historical consciousness, again through the study of individuals, concluding with Goethe.

Meinecke's best-known work, though a less satisfactory study, is *Die deutsche Katastrophe* written in 1945 when he was eighty-three, and published the following year. Meinecke was not heroic in opposition, but had remained an opponent of the national socialist regime, though some of his contemporary letters reveal that Hitler's diplomatic (1935–8) and military victories (1940) had created in his mind moments of uncertainty. In the *German Catastrophe*, Meinecke sought to uncover the causes of Germany's defeat and the reasons for the relapse into Nazi barbarism. From his early veneration for power and the state he turned during the last years of his life to the abiding values of *Kultur* as typified by that other great representative German, Goethe.

Meinecke will remain a controversial figure among German historians, but his influence as a cultural historian was profound. JASG

Main publications

Weltbürgertum und Nationalstaat (Munich: Oldenbourg, 1908); *Die Idee der Staatsräson* (Oldenbourg, 1924/5) trans. as *Machiavellism* (London: Routledge & Kegan Paul, New Haven, Conn.: Yale University Press, 1957); *Die Entstehung des Historismus*, 2 vols (Oldenbourg, 1936) trans. as *Historism: the rise of a new historical outlook* (New York: Herder & Herder, 1972); *Die deutsche katastrophe* (Wiesbaden: Brockhaus, 1949); trans, Sidney Fay (Cambridge, Mass: Harvard University Press, 1950).

Reading

Erbe, M., ed.: *Friedrich Meinecke Heute* (Berlin: Colloquium, 1981).

Pois, R. A.: *Friedrich Meinecke and German Politics in the Twentieth Century* (Berkeley: University of California Press, 1972).

Menéndez Pidal, Ramón (b.1869, d.1968) Menéndez Pidal was born in La Coruña of a family from Asturias, where Spanish dialects are thickest on the ground; after graduating at Madrid University he became a philologist first, and only secondarily a historian of literature, ideas and society. He held the chair of romance philology at Madrid University from 1899 until retirement (1939), devoted his life to teaching and research and was rewarded with innumerable academic honours, as Spain's leading scholar and the world's outstanding Romance philologist. Caught in Madrid by the civil war, he was used for Communist propaganda but escaped to America, returning only after Franco's victory, to be punished by temporary deprivation of his directorship of the Royal Spanish Academy. He continued writing until he died, in Madrid.

With his first published book, on the Lara legend, Menéndez Pidal introduced rigorous Germanic scholarship into the intellectual de-

sert of contemporary Spain, and showed himself the equal of any European philologist, demonstrating how forgotten medieval epics could be recovered from the chronicles in which they had been prosified. He discovered later that medieval ballads were, even today, being learned through oral transmission and sung by ordinary people, and he launched and organized the gigantic task of collecting them wherever in the world Spanish was sung. Lastly, he published innumerable early texts and documents, and used them to write the early history of the Spanish language, and its standard historical grammar.

The most purely historical work produced by Menéndez Pidal was a massive account of the Cid's life and times, supplemented with minor monographs, and based solidly on contemporary chronicles and documents and less solidly on the epic *Poema de Mio Cid* which he edited and unwisely considered historically accurate. Placing the Cid in his historical context, Menéndez Pidal showed him to be not a treacherous mercenary but a genuine Christian hero, fighting for God, his king, Spain and justice. This became the orthodox view, though it perhaps under-rated the king, Alfonso VI; in contrast, Pidal was less convincing when writing about later Spanish imperialism, and its chief critic, Las Casas.

Plain, austere, scrupulously honest, broadminded and stubborn, he consciously stressed in both his scholarly and his numerous popular works certain basic ideas: a populist Castilian nationalism; a tradition, derived from the Visigoths, almost untouched by clerical or learned influence, and surviving among the people even when unrecorded in writing; and an exaltation of historicity and realism, even at the expense of other literary merits. Most students of medieval Spain, anywhere, are now his intellectual debtors, even when disagreeing with him; within Spain itself, for the second half of his life, disagreement was rather difficult. DWL

Main publications

La leyenda de los Infantes de Lara (Madrid: Hijos de Ducazcal, 1896); *Crónicas generales de Expaña* (Madrid: Sucesores de Rivadeneyra, 1898); *Primera Crónica General de España* (Madrid: Bailly-Balliere, 1906); *Cantar de Mio Cid*, 3 vols (Bailly-

Balliere, 1908–11); *Orígenes del español* (Madrid: Hernando, 1926); *La España del Cid*, 2 vols (Madrid: Plutarco, trans. as *The Cid and His Spain* (London: John Murray, 1934); *El imperio hispánico y los cinco reinos* (Madrid: Instituto de Estudios Políticos, 1950); *Romancero hispánico*, 2 vols (Madrid: Espasa-Calpe, 1953); *El Padre Las Casas, su doble personalidad* (Espasa-Calpe, 1963); *Romancero tradicional*, many vols (Madrid: Gredos, 1957–   ).

Reading

Smith, C.: *Ramón Menéndez Pidal, 1869–1968* (London: Hispanic & Luso Brazilian Councils, 1970).

Meuvret, Jean (b.1901, d.1971) Holding the position of director of studies at the École Pratique des Hautes Études, VIe, Meuvret published seminal articles in the years after 1944 which established his reputation as one of the most influential figures in the areas of agrarian and demographic history.

Meuvret was fortunate in having at his disposal an almost unique document in European history in terms of its completeness: the series of grain prices kept by the municipality of Paris. With Mlle Baulant, he co-edited the series for the period from 1520 to 1698. He was the first to demonstrate that there was a great divide between the demographic traumas of Louis XIV's reign and the less dramatic incidents of the eighteenth century.

Yet it will be for his posthumous study of French agriculture that Meuvret will be most remembered. His principal conclusion was that the contemporary obsession with the fear of starvation was a serious obstacle to agrarian progress. Meuvret's analysis of traditional agriculture still merits attention as the crucial link between Marc BLOCH's pioneering work on French rural history in the 1930s and the great outpouring of regional studies (by GOUBERT, LE ROY LADURIE, and others) in the 1960s.   RB

Main publications

Études d'histoire économique. Recueil d'articles (Paris: Cahiers des Annales ESC, 1971); *Le problème des subsistances à l'époque de Louis XIV*. Vol. 1, *La production des céréales dans la France du xviie et xviiie siècle* (Paris/The Hague: Mouton, 1977) vol. 2 *La Production des céréales et la société rurale* (Paris: Éditions de l'École des Hautes Études en Sciences Sociales, 1987).

Michelet, Jules (b.1798, d.1874) The son of a poor but educated Paris printer, Michelet was brought up surrounded by memories of the French Revolution and at the age of 12 visited the Musée des Monuments Français, from which he derived a vivid sense of the past. He always believed that he was destined to write history as no one else had before him, and while he read voraciously and studied philosophers (especially the Italian VICO and the German Herder) as well as historians, he was always moved by documents, buildings and tombstones, since he thought that they put him in direct touch with the past. This sense of dramatizing and personalizing history has caused many to regard him as the greatest of Romantic historians.

He became professor of ancient history at the École Normale Supérieure in 1826, and wrote on both Roman and universal history. But his life's work was his history of France which he wrote when he was also Keeper of the Archives Nationales (from 1831) and professor at the Collège de France (from 1838). By 1843 he had published six volumes of this history, taking the story from the Celtic origins of France to the Renaissance. These contain his famous *Tableaux de France* (volume 2) which describe the different provinces and explain the variations in the French character by their physical and geographical features, as well as a particularly moving study of Joan of Arc (volume 5). During the 1840s Michelet became increasingly influenced by politics, finding that the government of Louis-Philippe (in which his fellow-historian Guizot was the dominant influence) was too conservative and too pacific. He therefore interrupted the chronological order of his history and turned to write *La Révolution française* (1847–1853, 7 volumes), as well as an attack on the influence of the Catholic church, especially the Jesuits (*Du prêtre, de la femme et de la famille*, 1845) and a remarkable essay ('Le Peuple', 1846) which praised the historic role of the peasantry and the industrial workers. Along with his colleagues (Edgar Quinet and Miciewicz) he was banned from lecturing at the Sorbonne and he welcomed the revolution of 1848. He could not accept the Second Empire and since he refused to swear allegiance to Napoleon III he lost all his official posts. He retired to the country, and there completed his history (*Histoire de France*, 1855–67, 11 volumes, taking the story from the Renaissance to the reign of Louis XVI) and wrote a study of the origins and evolution of religious belief (*La Bible de l'humanité*, 1864). He also developed an interest in natural science, writing a series of lyrical works, (*L'Oiseau*, 1856; *L'Insecte*, 1858; *La Mer*, 1861; *La Montagne*, 1861). He kept a journal which, when its publication was started in 1952, surprised many of his admirers, since it showed in his personal life and in his relations with his wife, almost obsessive preoccupations with physical phenomena. This is a sign of one of Michelet's outstanding characteristics, his curiosity about everything that concerned life.

Michelet was a historian of great erudition. It is his style which has often been criticized, becoming at times over-dramatic and declamatory. His love of France, and his celebration of the formation and persistence of France has also, at times, seemed excessive. But in recent years his reputation has revived. He has been recognized as an exponent of total history, using art and architecture, legend and literature, as well as the archives, the charters, the chronicles and the memorialists in which he was steeped. He is also a historian who is concerned with ordinary people and with ordinary things. He admired the Revolution because it was an event without a hero, without proper names, an event which demonstrated the unity of millions. The masses were often held down, oppressed, stunned, rendered senseless. All the more reason then, as Michelet put it, to listen to their silences which were 'les silences de l'histoire'. He often used antithesis as a means of historical explanation. The east is contrasted to the west, the country to the town, the old world to the new, male to female, individual to community, liberty to federality. But out of such antagonisms and conflicts, there emerges the essence of history. For Michelet, this was France.   DJ

Main publications

(Many editions of his numerous works exist); *Oeuvres Complètes* (Paris: Flammarion, ongoing); *Histoire de France (1855–67)*, 40 vols (Flammarion, 1893–8); *Journal 1820–1874*, 4 vols (Paris: Gallimard, 1952–1976).

Reading

Barthes, Roland: *Michelet par lui-même* (Paris: Le Seuil, 1954).

Calo, Jeanne: *La Création de la femme chez Michelet* (Paris: Nizet, 1975).

Monod, Gabriel: *La Vie et la pensée de Jules Michelet* 2 vols (Paris: Champion, 1923).

Rudler, Gustave,: *Michelet historien de Jeanne d'Arc*, 2 vols (Paris: Presses Universitaires de France, 1925–6).

Viallaneix, Paul: *La Voie Royale* (Paris: Delagrave, 1959).

Migne, Jacques-Paul (1800–1875) Born at Saint-Flour in the Auvergne, Migne was educated at the seminary of Orleans and worked as a parish priest for nine years. In 1833, with the consent of his bishop, he became a religious journalist in Paris where three years later he founded a publishing house under the name of the Ateliers Catholiques. He aimed to make Catholic Tradition available to ordinary priests by republishing earlier printed texts at a modest price as a 2,000-volume *Bibliothèque universelle du clergé*. His energy was prodigious and over 1,100 volumes, closely printed in double columns, had appeared by 1868 when the Ateliers burned down. This fire marked the effective end of Migne's career, since he was unable to obtain adequate compensation from his insurance company to rebuild his factory.

Much of Migne's work (for example his 100 volumes of French sermons) is little read today, but his *Patrologia* is highly valued by medieval historians. This consists of 217 volumes of the texts of the Latin Fathers of the church, from Tertullian to Pope Innocent III, and 161 volumes of the Greek Fathers, from St Clement of Rome to the Council of Florence. The Greek texts were printed with parallel Latin translations where those were available. Migne enlisted the help of scholars from all over Europe in preparing the *Patrologia* but his chief collaborator was the distinguished patristic scholar, Jean-Baptiste Pitra, prior of Saint-Germain-des-Prés, who later became Vatican librarian. Pitra supervised the production of all the Latin texts and the first 104 volumes of the Greek texts.

The editors interpreted the term 'Fathers' in a broad sense. The *Patrologia* is not restricted to theological works, but includes many secular histories written by churchmen as well as a large body of secular and ecclesiastical records, while volume 131 of the Greek Fathers is unexpectedly devoted to Anna Comnena's *Alexiad*. In effect the *Patrologia* volumes are an historical miscellany and this makes them useful to modern scholars. Comparatively few libraries contain the original editions of the 3,414 authors whom Migne reprinted, whereas complete sets of the *Patrologia* are readily accessible.

BH

Main publications

Patrologiae Cursus Completus . . . Series Latina, ed. J. P. Migne, 221 vols, incl. 4 vols indices (Paris; 1844–64); *Patrologiae Cursus Completus . . . Series Graeca*, ed. J. P. Migne, 162 vols, index vol. 162 by F. Cavallera (Paris: 1857–1912); *Pour revaloriser Migne: tables rectificatives*, P. Glorieux (Lille: 1952); *Patrologiae Cursus Completus, Series Latina, Supplementum*. 5 vols, Accurante A. Hamman (Paris: Garnier, 1958–74).

Reading

Marchal, L.: Jacques-Paul Migne. In *Dictionnaire de Théologie Catholique* X (2) (Paris: Librairie Letouzey et Ane, 1929).
Sheppard, L. C.: The Abbé Jacques-Paul Migne. *American Benedictine Review* 7 (1956–7) 112–28.

Mignet, Auguste (b.1796, d.1884)   A Provençal born in Aix, Mignet made his name as a journalist under the Restoration. In 1830 he signed the journalists' petition against the repressive policies of Charles X, and after the revolution of that year was made director of the foreign ministry archives, where he served until the revolution of 1848. His best-known work of history was the first general survey of the French Revolution written by someone who had not lived through it (1824). Liberal in tone, it sought to celebrate the Revolution as a national achievement at a time when the official view was growing increasingly hostile. It remained popular throughout the nineteenth century and was translated into English. After becoming an archivist Mignet turned to diplomatic history, producing carefully docu-

mented studies of the Spanish Succession war (1843) and Philip II (1845). Elected to the Académie Française in 1836, his last work was a life of Mary, Queen of Scots (1851).   WD

Main publication

Histoire de la Révolution française (Paris: 1824).

Reading

Mellon, S.: *The Political Uses of History: a Study of Historians of the French Restoration* (New York: Columbia University Press, 1958).

Miller, Perry (b.1905, d.1963)   An intellectual historian, a literary critic, and a historian of American culture, Miller was a towering figure in American intellectual history. Born in Chicago in 1905, he was educated at the Tilton School and Austin High School, and in 1922 enrolled at the University of Chicago. A year later Miller left the university. He travelled first to Colorado, where he rejoiced in the spectacular scenery and company of hoboes and 'wobblies' (Industrial Workers of the World). Then he moved to Greenwich Village in New York city where he wrote 'true-confession' stories for pulp magazines. During this time the theatre drew his attention, and for a time he had occasional parts in plays. The stage, however, did not hold his interest for long, and he went abroad, first as a seaman and later as a worker for an oil company in the Belgian Congo.

While unloading oil drums in the Congo port town of Matadi, Miller experienced a sudden revelation, 'the epiphany at Matadi', as he later described it, which set him in pursuit of what became his lifelong goal and mission: to expound and interpret 'the innermost propulsion' of American history. This vision demanded that he spend his life expounding the nature and meaning of American civilization in the light of the Puritans and the Puritan tradition in America. On returning to the United States, Miller resumed his studies at the University of Chicago, where he received his bachelor's degree in 1928 and a doctorate in 1931. He taught at Harvard from 1931 until his death. In 1946 he became full professor of American literature, and in 1960 Powell M. Cabot professor of American literature.

Believing that an interpretation of the American past ought to begin with an explanation of those traditions that 'have gone into the making of the American mind', Miller was initially drawn to Puritanism because it represents a genuinely rigorous intellectual tradition at the foundation of the American experience. In his view, Puritanism was not merely a historical phenomenon of seventeenth-century New England, but rather a fundamental component underlying the entire American past from its beginning until his own time. Puritanism, according to Miller, became 'one of the continuous factors in American life and thought. Any inventory of the elements that have gone into the making of the "American mind" would have to commence with Puritanism.'

Orthodoxy in Massachusetts, Miller's doctoral dissertation, was published in 1933 and established his reputation in the field of American Puritanism. This book, along with *The Puritans* (2 vols, 1938, edited with T. H. Johnson), and *The New England Mind: the Seventeenth Century* (1939), which became the standard work in the field of American Puritan studies, radically transformed many popular stereotypes about the Puritan tradition in America. Miller's academic career was interrupted by service in the United States Army, 1942–5. He attained his greatest influence as scholar and teacher following the second world war with the publication of works such as the intellectual biography, *Jonathan Edwards* (1949); *The New England Mind: from Colony to Province* (1953), perhaps Miller's finest work; *Roger Williams: his Contribution to the American Tradition* (1953); and *Errand into the Wilderness* (1956), a book of collected essays on American Puritanism.

The uniqueness of Miller's contribution to the study of Puritanism lies in locating it as a major cultural and intellectual movement in the larger context of western civilization. Puritanism, according to Miller, was one of the most important movements in early modern history, radically transforming western culture and mind. This change from a medieval to a modern perspective involved the shift from a theocentric to an anthropocentric position. The errand into the wilderness symbolized for Miller the general evolution of western culture

from the medieval world view into the Enlightenment; namely, 'that no force but the will of man can bring order out of the chaos of human depravity' (1953). Accordingly, Miller interpreted the whole American experience in light of man's relationship to the 'wilderness' of the universe; an existentialist view which stresses human responsibility without an appeal to transcendental support. In this approach Miller was much influenced by the existentialist theology of Reinhold Niebuhr.

Miller's studies of Puritanism signified a turning point in American historiography and soon became the most authoritative works in this field. The uniqueness of Miller's contribution to the study of American Puritanism is twofold. Rooting Puritan religion in the medieval tradition of Ramist logic and typology, he eloquently portrayed the elements of continuity and change between Puritan thought and the medieval world view. Similarly, through his studies of Roger Williams, Jonathan Edwards, Solomon Stoddard and the phenomena of revivalism, he showed the continuing relevance of Puritanism to later American history. In his last work, *The Life of the Mind in America*, a part of a larger projected study which was published posthumously by his widow in 1965 and won the 1966 Pulitzer prize in history, Miller presented an account of the development of the American 'mind' in the new nation, attempting to distinguish the various strands of intellectual experience that went into the establishing of an American identity.
                                                                    AZ

Main publications

Orthodoxy in Massachusetts (Cambridge, Mass: Harvard University Press, 1933); *The New England Mind: the Seventeenth Century* (New York: Macmillan, 1939); *Jonathan Edwards* (New York: Sloane, 1949); *The New England Mind: from Colony to Province* (Harvard University Press, 1953); *Roger Williams: his Contribution to the American Tradition* (New York: Bobbs-Merrill, 1953); *Errand into the Wilderness* (Harvard University Press, 1956); *The Raven and the Whale: the War of Words and Wits in the Era of Poe and Melville* (New York: Harcourt, Brace, 1956); *The American Transcendentalists: their Prose and Poetry* (New York: Doubleday, 1957); *The Life of the Mind in America: from the Revolution to the Civil War* (New York: Harcourt, Brace & World, 1965); *Nature's Nation* (Harvard University Press, 1967).

Reading

Calhoon, Robert M.: Perry Miller. In *Twentieth-Century American Historians*, ed. C. N. Wilson (Detroit: Gale Research Company, 1983) pp. 272–285.

Lynn, Kenneth: Perry Miller. *The American Scholar* vol 52 (Spring 1983) pp. 221–7.

Middlekauff, Robert: Perry Miller. In *Pastmasters: Some Essays on American Historians* ed. Marcus Cunliffe and Robin W. Winks (New York: Harper & Row, 1969) pp. 167–90.

Zakai, Avihu; Epihany at Matadi: Perry Miller's *Orthodoxy in Massachusetts* and the meaning of American history. *Reviews in American History* 13 (December 1985) 627–41.

Milman, Henry Hart (b.1791, d.1868) Educated at Eton and Brasenose College, Oxford, Milman was first known as something of a poet, before becoming a historian, a canon of Westminster Abbey (1835) and dean of St Paul's (1849). His *History of the Jews* (1830) was a remarkable scholarly and modernistic work (it made a most unfavourable impression on John Henry Newman), but his main historical work was his *History of Latin Christianity down to the Death of Pope Nicholas V* (1855). Though little read today it remains one of the best narrative histories of the church and the papacy. It is genuinely learned, wide in its sympathies, and extremely readable. It ran to three editions during his lifetime and was rightly praised by his friends who included LECKY and MACAULAY.   RHCD

Main publications

History of the Jews 3 vols (London: J. Murray, 1829); *History of Latin Christianity down to the Death of Pope Nicholas V* (1855) 9 vols (London: J. Murray, 1840–55; fourth edn, 9 vols, 1867).

Milyukov, Paul (b.1859, d.1943) Son of a Moscow architect, the ambitious Milyukov distinguished himself at school and entered Moscow university in 1877. The professors who most impressed him were Paul VINOGRADOFF and Vasily KLYUCHEVSKY, but the different effects they had on him put him in a quandary. He warmed towards Vinogradoff and found Klyuchevsky somewhat distant, but decided to undertake research in the field of the latter. Like Geoffrey ELTON at a later date,

he believed it was sensible for students of history to focus on sources close to home. Since Vinogradoff worked on western Europe, Milyukov learned what he could from his methods but became a postgraduate in the Russian field dominated by Klyuchevsky. The decision had important consequences. A polyglot and a keen traveller, Milyukov was one of the most sophisticated and cosmopolitan intellectuals of his generation. On hearing him lecture at Liverpool in 1909, Bernard Pares 'wondered whether there was anyone except Oliver Elton in the audience who could have matched the wonderful range of his knowledge of English literature'. Knowledge of foreign cultures was not part of Klyuchevsky's armoury. Supervisor and pupil shared little more than a scrupulous respect for historical evidence. On publishing his first book and submitting it as a dissertation in 1892, Milyukov hoped that it would gain him not only the master's but also the doctoral degree. Such an achievement would not have been unprecedented, but Klyuchevsky was lukewarm and Milyukov began to abandon the idea of making a conventional academic career. He continued writing history, but became increasingly involved in politics. By the time of the Russian Revolution he was the best-known member of the moderate Constitutional Democratic party, and served briefly as foreign minister after the fall of the tsar. During his subsequent long exile in Paris, he edited a Russian newspaper and became a 'historian of his own time' like Burnet and Clarendon.

Despite the relative brevity of his full-time commitment to history, Milyukov produced books which lasted. His dissertation *Russia's State Economy in the First Quarter of the Eighteenth Century and Peter the Great's Reform* greatly extended the debate about Peter I. Before Milyukov, historians had focused on Peter's military and naval achievements and his 'westernization' of Russian culture. Milyukov concentrated on the financial and institutional reforms which supported the more striking changes and tended, by removing the tsar from the centre of the stage, to undermine the widely accepted convention that Peter I had been a 'revolutionary on the throne', whether beneficent or malignant. In his *Outlines of Russian Culture* Milyukov was equally innovative. Having published as his first article a critique of the so-called 'juridical' or 'state' school of nineteenth-century Russian historians, he was anxious to get away from the courses of narrative history which predominated in universities. Convinced of the need to write for the educated layman, keen to relate the past to the present, impressed by GUIZOT's *Histoire de la civilisation en France*, and influenced by the journalistic surveys of contemporary Russia written by the perceptive foreigners Donald Mackenzie Wallace and Anatole Leroy-Beaulieu, he produced a work which diverged markedly from the approach to the past taken by most of his predecessors. A recent Soviet commentator has called the *Outlines* almost 'legal Marxist' in their underlying philosophy; not revolutionary, let alone Leninist, but far closer to the idea of 'history from the bottom up' than to 'history from the top down'. Milyukov would have had difficulty accepting praise of such a kind (and from such a source), but he certainly aimed to create his own niche in the history of historical writing. In academic as well as political life, he was independent to a fault.   DBS

Main publications

Gosudarstvennoe khoziaistvo v Rossii v pervoi chetverti XVIII stoletiia i reforma Petra Velikogo (Russia's state economy in the first quarter of the eighteenth century and Peter the Great's reform) (St Petersburg: 1892); *Glavnye techeniia russkoi istoricheskoi mysli* (Main currents of Russian historical thought) (Moscow: 1897); *Ocherki po istorii russkoi kul'tury* (Outlines of Russian culture) 3 vols (St Petersburg: 1896–1901); *Russia and Its Crisis* (Chicago: 1905); *Vospominaniia* (Memoirs) 2 vols (New York: Chekhov Publishing House, 1955); *Political Memoirs 1905–1917* (Ann Arbor: University of Michigan Press, 1967).

Reading

Riha, T.: *A Russian European: Paul Miliukov in Russian Politics* (Notre Dame and London: University of Notre Dame Press, 1969).
Tsamutali, A. N.: *Bor'ba napravlenii v russkoi istoriografii v period imperializma: istoriograficheskie ocherki* (The conflict of trends in Russian historiography of the imperialist period: historiographical essays) (Leningrad: Nauka, 1986), pp. 155–204.

Mitteis, Heinrich (b.1889, d.1952) The son of a distinguished Romance philologist, Mitteis studied law in Leipzig before the first world war and was appointed to the chair of legal history at Cologne at the age of 32 and then as successor to his supervisor, Hans Fehr, at Heidelberg in 1924. Though he was not dismissed from office by the Nazis, his interventions on behalf of persecuted colleagues led first to a period of exile in Vienna and after 1938 to banishment to the insignificant university of Rostock; from 1945 he taught at Munich. His first major book, *Lehnrecht und Staatsgewalt*, set the pattern for his scholarly work: a wide-ranging comparative approach to legal history. Though he was not wholly free of the tendency of an earlier generation of German legal historians to over-systematize and to confuse past legal prescript with past legal practice, he did much to set the study of legal history on a firmer historical footing. The culmination of his work was the large-scale synthesis *Der Staat des hohen Mittelalters*, which showed how feudal law could be used by medieval rulers to enhance their power as well as by their subjects to evade it.   TAR

Main publications

(Published by Böhlau, Weimar, unless otherwise stated.)
Lehnrecht und Staatsgewalt (Feudal law and state power) (1933); *Die deutsche Königswahl* (The German royal election) (Baden bei Wien: Röhrer, 1938); *Der Staat des hohen Mittelalters* (1940) (The state of the high middle ages (Amsterdam: ET, 1975)); *Die Rechtsidee in der Geschichte. Gesammelte Aufsätze und Vorträge* (The idea of law in history) (1957) [incl. bibliography, pp. 724–31].

Reading

Bader, K.S.: Nachruf auf Heinrich Mitteis. In Mitteis: *Das Rechtsidee*, XIII–XXIX (see above).

Momigliano, Arnaldo Dante (b.1908, d.1987) Momigliano was born at Caraglio (Cuneo) into a well-known Piedmontese family of Jewish intellectuals. He studied at the University of Turin under Gaetano De Sanctis, the foremost Italian historian of classical antiquity, and obtained his degree in 1929 with a dissertation on Thucydides. In 1932 he went to Rome as professor of Greek history, and in 1936 returned to Turin to the chair of Roman history, which he held until 1938 when he was dismissed under Mussolini's race laws. During this time he published a prodigious number of research papers, monographs, textbooks, and encyclopaedia articles on various aspects of Greek and Roman history and the history of Judaism. He also formed a close association with CROCE, whom he had first met as a student in Turin.

In 1939 Momigliano came to England with his wife and small daughter and took up residence in Oxford, where he worked for several years. Meanwhile the war claimed the lives of many of his family and friends, including both his parents, who were murdered in Nazi death camps in 1943.

Momigliano was already well known in England through a translation of his study of Claudius (1934) and three chapters in the *Cambridge Ancient History* (vol. X, 1934). These and other studies of the political, intellectual and religious history of the Roman principate remain important and influential. In 1947 he was appointed to a lectureship at Bristol, and in 1951 became professor of ancient history at University College London. In the liberal atmosphere of Gower Street, where he taught until his retirement in 1975, he was able to redefine his approach to the ancient world and its place in the formation of modern culture. During the 1940s and 1950s he began to produce the studies of ancient and modern historians (Herodotus, Gibbon, Grote, Rostovtzeff, among others) for which he is still best known in the English-speaking world. In 1955 he published the first of his collections of essays, the *Contributi*, of which eight have so far appeared.

Momigliano's interests extended to all periods of ancient history. They included the study of archaic Rome (which in the 1960s and 1970s was being transformed by archaeological research), ancient religions (especially Judaism and Christianity, in their relation both to each other and to Graeco-Roman paganism; at the end of his life he was actively engaged in research on religious developments in the Roman empire), the issues of political, religious and intellectual liberty (especially freedom of speech), and the interaction of cultures (see especially *Alien Wis-*

dom, 1975). The subject matter varied widely, but the method was always the same: analysis of sources, reconstruction of events, and study of historical interpretations were combined within a wider framework of the history of ideas.

In addition to detailed problems of ancient history, Momigliano also studied the history of historiography and the development of historical method, fields in which his learning was unrivalled and in which he was recognized as the leading authority. He consistently stressed that the historian must attempt to account not only for the data at his disposal but also for subsequent interpretations of the data. Historians must continually seek to ask new questions, but will not be able to do so unless they can understand and control the old questions. There is therefore no distinction between history and historiography as objects of study. For Momigliano the task of historical reconstruction had to be accompanied by reflection on method; and his discussions of method proceeded from the precise analysis of historical facts. To suggest, as some have done, that his work on Gibbon, Niebuhr, Droysen and so on is 'mere historiography' is to misunderstand it; he himself was as impatient with researchers who work on Gibbon without knowing or caring about the Roman empire as he was with Roman historians who ignore Gibbon.

Momigliano's interest in the role of the intellectual in history, and in the ways in which historical events and circumstances shape ideas and vice versa, led him to devote much attention to the study of individuals: political figures, poets, philosophers, and above all historians. This distinctive focus led him in two interesting directions. First, he explored the position of the historian in society in periods when history had no recognized place in formal education, and before the development of an institutionalized historical profession; secondly, he investigated the origins and characteristics of biography, and its development as a genre separate from history.

Momigliano's publications, numbering well over 1,000, cover a vast range of subjects and periods. His preferred medium was the short essay, in which analysis of detailed problems could interact with wider questions of historical method. With his light touch and clear style, he was a complete master of this difficult form.

Until the very last weeks of his life, Momigliano showed great physical and intellectual energy; he travelled regularly between England, Italy and the USA, and continued to give lectures and research papers until shortly before his death. Although he and his wife had their home in London, he remained an Italian citizen. He received many international awards and honours, including honorary degrees from more than a dozen leading universities in Europe and America, and was given an honorary KBE in 1974. He died in London after a short illness in September 1987.　TJC

Main publications

Prime linee di storia della tradizione Maccabaica (Outlines of the history of the Maccabaean tradition) (Rome: 1930; 2nd edn, Amsterdam: Hakkert, 1968); *L'opera dell'Imperatore Claudio* (Florence: 1932), *Claudius: the Emperor and his Achievement* (Cambridge: Heffer, 1961); *Filippo il Macedone: saggio sulla storia greca del IV secolo a.C.* (Philip of Macedon: essay on Greek history in the fourth century BC) (Florence: Le Monnier, 1934); editor, *The Conflict between Paganism and Christianity in the fourth century* (Oxford: Clarendon Press, 1963); *Studies in Historiography* (London: Weidenfeld, 1966); *The Development of Greek Biography* (Cambridge, Mass.: Harvard University Press, 1971); *Alien Wisdom: the Limits of Hellenization* (Oxford: Blackwell, 1975); *Essays in Ancient and Modern Historiography* (Blackwell, 1977); *La storiografia greca* (Greek historiography) (Turin: Einaudi, 1982); editor, *Aspetti dell'opera di G. Dumézil* (Aspects of the work of G. Dumézil) (Pisa: Scuola Normale Superiore, 1983); *Sui fondamenti della storia antica* (On the foundations of ancient history) (Turin: Einaudi, 1984); *Tra Storia e Storicismo* (Between history and historicism) (Pisa: Nistri-Lischi, 1985); *Storia e storiografia antica* (Ancient history and historiography) (Bologna: Il Mulino, 1987); Collected papers: *Contributi alla storia degli studi classici (e del mondo antico)* (Contributions to the history of classical studies (and of the ancient world)), vols 1–8 (Rome: Storia e Letteratura, 1955–87) [vols 4, 6 and 8 include (cumulative) bibliography].

Mommsen, Theodor (b.1817, d.1903) Once, it is told, while travelling in Italy, Mommsen was in a party which was held up by robbers. When the chief brigand turned his attention to him, Mommsen indignantly stated, 'Sono Theodoro Mommsen!', whereupon he found himself hailed as a hero. What was it that so impressed this cultivated bandit? Perhaps it was the fierce, nervous energy of this rather slight man, who inspired devotion and fear by turns in his colleagues and pupils; or maybe his impeccable record of unswerving commitment to the causes of nationalism and of liberal ideas. Most likely it was his fame as the author of the *History of Rome* and his indefatigable researches which placed the study of the Roman past on a solid foundation which remains unshaken to this day.

Born the eldest son of a pastor at Garding in Schleswig, Mommsen studied at Kiel from 1838, where his teachers inspired in him an interest in philology and law, which remained central to his work throughout his life. A scholarship took him to Italy from 1844 to 1847, a particularly exciting time for classical research. There was much talk of the need for a definitive collection of inscriptions from Roman Italy. Mommsen's own researches in southern Italy, subsequently published in his *Inscriptions of the Kingdom of Naples* (1852), laid his claim to be in charge of such a project – a claim which after much infighting was recognized by the Berlin Academy. He still found time to carry out philological research and to prepare a study of his collection of Roman coins, which later became a major work. On his return to Germany Mommsen, as a liberal intellectual and editor of the *Schleswig–Holstein Zeitung*, in 1848 found himself deeply involved in the heady days of constitutional reform. He was also appointed to an extraordinary professorship of law at Leipzig. It was inevitable that during the reactionary years which followed Mommsen's views would get him into trouble. His involvement with fellow scholars in disturbances in May 1850 led to a prosecution and his suspension by the senate of the university. He found refuge as professor of Roman law in Zurich in 1852. Two years later he returned as professor at Breslau, and in 1858 he moved to Berlin as editor of the *Corpus Inscriptionum Latinarum*. From 1861 he held the professorship of ancient history at the university of Berlin. From 1873 to 1895 he was perpetual secretary of the Academy. These were years of enormous industry and the organization of vast projects on epigraphy, law and PROSOPOGRAPHY which changed the face of Roman scholarship. Retaining a passionate interest in public affairs, for a number of years Mommsen was a member of the Prussian Chamber of Deputies. His commitment to German nationalism first led him to support Bismarck and then, like many others, to disillusioned opposition which culminated in a court case in 1882 on a charge of slander. Mommsen's liberal stance never wavered. He took a firm stand against the anti-Semitism of the distinguished German historian, TREITSCHKE and his defence of academic freedom from political interference still inspires admiration.

Mommsen's scholarly output was prodigious. Much of it was fundamental research which gave scholars access for the first time to a vast range of new material. There was scarcely any aspect of the study of Rome to which he did not contribute, whether it was the study and editing of texts, philology, epigraphy or Roman law. The work which brought him the widest recognition was his *History of Rome* (1854–6), a vigorous, critical account of the rise of Rome with obvious influences from his own political experience. He saw the unification of Italy under Rome as a model for Germany in his own day and offered vivid and trenchant comments on Roman public figures as though they were his contemporaries. Most notorious was his uncritical praise of Julius Caesar, who is represented as all that Mommsen might have hoped that Bismarck would become. However Mommsen clearly distinguished Caesar from Caesarism. This antipathy to autocracy may explain why only the first three volumes of history, down to Caesar's victory in the civil wars, were ever completed. The imperial period of Rome did not attract attention and of the projected continuation only his *Provinces of the Roman Empire from Caesar to Diocletian* (1885) ever appeared. This important study rested on another of his finest achievements, his editorship of the *Corpus Inscriptionum Latinarum*, a collection of primary evidence of lasting significance. His most influential work was the *Römisches Staatsrecht* (Roman Public Law, 1871–88) with the later addition of the

Römisches Strafrecht (Roman Criminal Law, 1899). Although in these works he was at times too ready to posit a constitutional or legal principle on the flimsiest of evidence, all modern studies of Roman public life cannot but be based upon his work. In one sense Mommsen represented the culmination of the greatest period of German classical scholarship in the eighteenth and nineteenth centuries; yet in another way he represented a new epoch, a decisive move forward. In 1902 he was awarded the Nobel prize for literature.

JJP

Main publications

Römische Geschichte, vols 1–3 (1856) trans. W. P. Dickson, *The History of Rome*, (London: R. Bentley, 1894); editor, *Corpus Inscriptionum Latinarum* (Leipzig and Berlin: Berlin Academy, 1863 onward); *Römisches Staatsrecht*. In J. Marquardt and Th. Mommsen, *Handbuch der römische Alterthümer* (1871–87, repr. Graz, Austria: Akademische Druck- u. Verlagsanstalt, 1969); *Die Provinzen von Caesar bis Diocletian* (1885) (*Römische Geschichte* vol. 5) trans. W. P. Dickson, *The Provinces of the Roman Empire from Caesar to Diocletian* (London: Macmillan, 1909); *Römisches Strafrecht* (*Syst. Hb. der Deutschen Rechtswissenschaft*, vol. 1.4 (1899), repr. Akademische Druck- u. Verlagsanastalt, 1955).

Reading

Heuss, A.: *Theodor Mommsen und das 19. Jahrhundert* (Kiel: Veröffentlichungen des Schleswig-Holsteinischen Universitätsgesellschaft, no. 19, 1956).

Wickert, L.: *Theodor Mommsen, eine Biographie*, vols 1–3 (Frankfurt: Klostermann, 1959–69).

Wucher, A.: *Theodor Mommsen, Geschichtschreibung und Politik* (Göttingen: Göttinger Bausteine zur Geschichtswissenschaft, Band 26, 1956).

Zangmeister, K. and Jacobs, E.: *Th. Mommsen als Schriftsteller: Ein Verzeichnis seiner Schriften* (Berlin: 1905) [incl. a full bibliography].

Monod, Gabriel (b.1844, d.1912) Monod founded the *Revue Historique* in 1876. This review was to promote the 'scientific' study of history on the model of German developments during the period. Monod's method was above all else based upon critical study of the sources and his influence, as director of research at the École Pratique des Hautes Études, was an important one in the shaping of French historical scholarship before the first world war. Although Monod had been profoundly influenced by the institutional studies of FUSTEL DE COULANGES, such as his *Histoire des institutions politiques de l'ancienne France* (1875–89), he envisaged the *Revue historique* as a forum for other approaches and Henri PIRENNE contributed a challenging article on the importance of economic and social issues to the journal in 1897. Monod's own work lay in the field of early Frankish history and his *Études critiques sur les sources de l'histoire mérovingienne* (1872–85) were exercises in method for the study of early written sources. These were followed by his *Bibliographie de l'histoire de France* (1888) and by a historiographical work which discussed three of the greatest figures in French nineteenth-century historical writing: *Les maîtres de l'histoire: Renan, Taine, Michelet* (1894). His career ended with a chair at the Collège de France, to which he was elected in 1905.   MV

Main publications

Études critiques sur les sources de l'histoire mérovingienne (Paris: A. Franck, 1872–85); *Bibliographie de l'Histoire de France* (Paris: Hachette, 1888); *Les Maîtres de l'histoire: Renan, Taine, Michelet* (Paris: C. Levy, 1894).

Montesquieu, Charles-Louis de Secondat (b.1689, d.1755) From a noble family of moderate distinction, the Baron de la Brède et de Montesquieu himself stated: 'My birth is so well suited to my fortune that I should be sorry if either were more distinguished.' The death of his father when he was 24 left Montesquieu in charge of the family estate. Two years later he married a wealthy wife and when he was 27 an uncle left him money, the barony and the office of president, or judge, in the Bordeaux *parlement*. In 1721 he published the *Lettres Persanes*, in which he tried to distinguish between the natural and conventional elements within French society. Written with elegance and irony, this was the first major work of the French Enlightenment and it made Montesquieu's reputation almost overnight. He sold his judicial office and spent much of the rest of his life in Paris. He was elected to the French Academy when he was only thirty-eight. A period of extensive travel in Europe included a long stay in England from 1729 to 1731. After his return to France he published a short book on the reasons for the greatness and decline of the Roman Empire (1734) and began accumulating the material for his most important work, *De l'esprit des lois*, which was published in 1748. In the opinion of Burke it was, after the Bible, the greatest book ever written.

Montesquieu was a reasonable rather than a rational man, who lived by the principle, 'We should accommodate ourselves to this life; it is not up to this life to accommodate itself to us.' He delighted in the complexity of things, in whatever was different or exotic, and he was resolutely cosmopolitan, believing himself to be human by nature but French by accident. Despite his acute sense of the relativity of most things, he believed the pursuit of freedom and justice to be moral absolutes. He combined a conservative temperament, apprehensive about the unpredictability of change, with dissatisfaction about the state of the French monarchy, which he believed Louis XIV to have made despotic. He may reasonably be considered the creator of sociology since he believed that all aspects of a society, including its politics and religion, were determined by the complex interaction of moral and material forces, that could be investigated and, to some extent, brought under the control of human intelligence.

There was a sense in which Montesquieu's vision was profoundly historical since he saw the present as derived from a past that determined how men thought and what goals they chose to pursue: 'The customs of an enslaved people are part of its servitude and those of a free people are part of its liberty.' He saw this historical conditioning as partially conscious and willed, partially unconscious and involuntary. Any attempt to impose upon a society policies — however enlightened in the abstract — that were at variance with its traditions and assumptions, could only be effected by force, which would corrupt what it set out to improve. On the other hand, he shared the sociologist's impatience with the specific and contingent and his analysis of societies tended to be somewhat static. It was not merely that he was uninterested in conventional political narrative; even 'philosophical' history, as practised by men like ROBERTSON and VOLTAIRE, had little appeal for him. His essay on the Roman Empire used its history as a quarry from which to extract the building materials for statements of general principle and universal relevance.

De l'esprit des lois began as a treatise on comparative government. Montesquieu argued that monarchies were sustained and prevented from declining into despotism by the sense of honour of the nobility, which offered the monarch free but conditional service. This was to become the campaigning slogan of the French *parlements* in their opposition to Bourbon absolutism. Rousseau and the more radical of the French revolutionaries were equally influenced by Montesquieu's belief that the classical republics had relied on the generalized practice of *vertu*, the citizen's identification of his own fulfilment with service to the community. In the second part of his book, however, Montesquieu abandoned this descriptive approach for a normative one. He now advocated moderate or restrained government in which the competing interests within a society were each given political representation within a constitution that held them in balance. He saw the British constitution as an almost perfect example of what he had in mind and it was this aspect of his argument that was adopted by the French constitutional monarchists in 1789. The remainder of his book consisted largely of an examination of the kind of interests that existed within a society, the values they generated and the way in which they reacted with each other. By way of conclusion he inserted a study of the way in which French law had evolved to reflect the attitudes and respond to the needs of feudal society. It was, in a sense, the only history that he wrote and it is the part of his work that is least read. As Voltaire wrote of *De l'esprit des lois*, 'This defective work is full of admirable things.' Montesquieu changed his ground as the book progressed; he was more concerned with getting things right than with consistency as an end in itself. Drawing his historical examples from the whole range of world history, he was inclined

to take too much on trust and he became somewhat obsessed with the importance of climate. What unifies and dignifies the work is its consistent humanitarianism, its mistrust of theory carried to the point where it becomes inquisitorial, and its concern to guarantee to individuals a space in which they can be free to work out their own destiny. It can be considered the foundation document of modern liberalism. The peculiar shape of the book also meant that ideas which Montesquieu himself was to reject became slogans for all the French revolutionary factions. He may not have written very much history but he helped to make a great deal.   NH

Main publications

Lettres Persanes (1721); *Considérations sur les causes de la grandeur des Romains et de leur décadence* (1734); *De l'Esprit des lois* (1748).

Reading

Hampson, N.: Montesquieu. In *Will and Circumstance: Montesquieu, Rousseau and the French Revolution* (London: Duckworth, 1983).

Hulliung, M.: *Montesquieu and The Old Regime* (Berkeley: University of California Press, 1976).

Richter, M.: *The Political Theory of Montesquieu* (London: Cambridge University Press, 1977).

Shackleton, R.: *Montesquieu: A Critical Biography* (London: Oxford University Press, 1961).

Moody, Theodore William (b.1907, d.1984) The most influential Irish historian, Theo Moody led the professionalization of Irish historical scholarship. Born and educated in Belfast (at the Academical Institution and The Queen's University), he earned his doctorate in 1934 after studying at the Institute of Historical Research in London (1930–2). He began teaching history at Queen's, Belfast in 1932 and assumed responsibility for Irish history in 1935 (see IRISH HISTORIOGRAPHY). In June 1939 Moody moved to the chair of modern history at Trinity College, Dublin, where he remained a powerful influence as editor of *Irish Historical Studies*, fostering research and publication and initiating historical broadcasting on radio (north and south from 1953) and television (from 1966). The televised *Course of Irish History* (published 1967), to which he contributed, remains a vital school text while the multi-contributor, multi-volume *New History of Ireland* (inaugurated 1968, first volume 1976) of which he was chief editor, will be his monument. On this project and on his biography of Michael Davitt, Moody continued to work after his retirement in 1977. DWH

Main publications

The Londonderry Plantation 1609–41: the city of London and the plantation of Ulster (Belfast: Wm Mullan, 1939); *Thomas Davis 1814–45* (Dublin: Hodges Figgis, 1945); with J. C. Beckett, *Queen's Belfast 1845–1949: the history of a university*, 2 vols (London: Faber & Faber 1959); *The Ulster Question, 1603–1973* (Dublin and Cork: Mercier, 1974); *A Bibliography of Modern History* (Dublin: Dublin University Press, 1977); *Michael Davitt and Irish Revolution, 1846–82* (Oxford: Oxford University Press, 1981).

Reading

Lyons, F. S. L.: T. W. Moody. In *Ireland under the Union: varieties of tension. Essays in honour of T. W. Moody*, ed. F. S. L. Lyons and R. A. J. Hawkins (Oxford: Clarendon Press, 1980).

Mulvey, Helen F.: Theodore William Moody (1907–84): an appreciation. *Irish Historical Studies* 24 (Nov. 1984) 121–30.

Moore, Barrington (b.1913) Since 1951 Moore's academic base has been the Russian Research Center at Harvard University. His doctoral research was in sociology and during the second world war he had appointments as a political analyst with the Office of Strategic Studies and the Department of Justice. Freed by private wealth from the need to pursue a conventional academic career, Moore has acquired a reputation for dogged independence of mind and character. He has developed a critical stance on contemporary western societies which derives from rigorous comparative and historical analysis. His critique is deeply rooted in the values of the Enlightenment.

All Moore's writings have a bearing on the project of using historical knowledge as a means of comprehending the limits within which human beings can influence their own destiny. In his two early books on Russia, Moore asked how the Soviet elite coped with the conflict between ideological goals and political means in the context of a developing industrial society. In *Political Power and Social Theory* (1958) he explored a variety of topics – including pre-industrial totalitarianism and the role of the family – in the course of inquiring which elements of the contemporary industrial social order were unique and necessary to that type of society. In *Social Origins of Dictatorship and Democracy* (1966) Moore asked the question: what forms of modernization in commercialized agrarian societies (for example early modern Britain, revolutionary France, the early American republic, Meiji Japan, Imperial Japan and British India) were most favourable to democratic (as opposed to fascist or communist) outcomes? Paying particular attention to relations among key elites (landed, commercial and state bureaucratic) and classes (the peasantry and their masters), Moore delineated three routes to the modern world. Britain, France and the United States followed the bourgeois democratic route; Japan and Germany experienced authoritarian modernization leading to fascism; Russia and China underwent peasant revolutions which benefited communist regimes.

In *Reflections on the Causes of Human Misery* (1972), Moore again pursued through empirical analysis a major political and moral issue: which aspects of human misery were, strictly speaking, unnecessary and what prospects, in practice, were there for eliminating them? In the course of this analysis Moore developed a model of 'rational political authority' which he later exploited in *Injustice* (1978). In this Moore analysed the development of the German working class from before the 1848 crisis until the rise of the Nazi party. He argued that a social contract specifying norms of reciprocity and justice – and legitimizing outrage or even rebellion in certain circumstances – could be found in all societies. This study of public norms was subsequently complemented by an examination in *Privacy* (1984) of those aspects of private behaviour which were socially acceptable and those which were not.

Moore's most influential work has been *Social Origins* which helped to recreate a favourable climate for comparative and historical approaches among English-speaking social scientists in the 1960s. The offspring of no single academic tradition, Moore is sometimes wrongly described as following a Marxist approach. In fact, he espouses rational analysis of the prospects for the 'truly American' values of liberal democracy.   DS

Main publications

(Published by Harvard University Press, Cambridge, Mass., unless otherwise stated.)
Soviet Politics – the Dilemma of Power (1950); *Terror and Progress USSR: Some Sources of Change and Stability in the Soviet Dictatorship* (1954); *Political Power and Social Theory* (1958); *Social Origins of Dictatorship and Democracy: Lord and Peasant in the Modern World* (Boston: Beacon Press, 1966); *Reflections on the Causes of Human Misery and upon Certain Proposals for Eliminating Them* (Beacon Press, 1972); *Injustice: The Social Bases of Obedience and Revolt* (White Plains, NY: M. E. Sharpe, 1978); *Privacy: Studies in Social and Cultural History* (Armonk, NY: M. E. Sharpe, 1984).

Reading

Smith, Dennis: *Barrington Moore: Violence, Morality and Political Change* (London: Macmillan, 1983).

Morgan, Edmund Sears (b.1916) The son of a distinguished law professor, Morgan was educated at Harvard and taught for most of his career at Brown and at Yale, where he recently retired as Sterling professor of American history. Described accurately but inadequately as a 'counter-progressive' historian, he is better seen as belonging to the line of patriotic and patrician scholars stretching from BANCROFT to MORISON whose main interest has been to understand how early Americans created 'a great nation with great principles of freedom'.

Morgan began his career just before the second world war. He was undoubtedly impressed by the strength and resilience of American institutions at a time when Europe seemed doomed to a totalitarian future. Temperamentally indisposed to regard cynicism as a higher form of wisdom, and trained by Perry MILLER to believe that ideas suffused by passion had the power to shape behaviour, Morgan sought the origins of the American republic in three different areas: New England puritanism, colonial Virginia and the revolutionary era.

Between puritanism and republicanism there ran a twisted road. Puritans faced a dilemma in trying to live in an impure world without becoming tainted. Some, like John Winthrop, surmounted the difficulty but most eventually gave up on the world and retreated into 'tribalism', content if they and their children were saved. Puritanism therefore failed as a religious movement but certain of its values survived in secular form. Morgan identified the 'Puritan ethic' as a complex of ideas, values and principles, chief among which were personal independence and virtue. When imperial policies threatened property, the basis for both virtue and independence, the colonists evoked long-held constitutional principles in their defence. The constitutional argument was not merely a contest of abstract ideas; what was important was the 'enduring human needs' that lay 'behind' the constitutional principles. The Revolution itself transformed those principles by clarifying their implications and broadening their application: it culminated in the Constitution of 1789, a work of genius which has allowed the further expansion of republican values.

Morgan's early work, concentrated as it was on New England, gave only a partial explanation of American republicanism. Eventually, he realized, he would have to shift his focus southward and come to grips with the institution of slavery, the greatest evil of the American past. That he did so during the era of the Vietnam War meant that his subsequent work would be infused with the elements of tragedy. In his greatest and darkest work, *American Slavery, American Freedom* (1975), Morgan argued that the patriot leaders of Virginia were able to espouse the ideals of liberty and equality only because racial slavery had eliminated from political participation almost all of the labouring class. In his latest book, *Inventing the People* (1988), Morgan found that it was the leaders of Virginia who most fully realized that the doctrine of popular sovereignty could be used to justify a political system in which the few ruled the many.

No one today could plausibly say of Morgan's work that it exhibits an uncritical patriotism. Nevertheless Morgan remains much the same historian who began his career nearly 50 years ago. He persists in his belief that the idea of equality has shaped, and will continue to shape American life. He still heeds one of his favourite lines from George Washington: 'It is not the part of a good Citizen to despair of the republic'. JPW

Main publications

With Helen Morgan, *The Stamp Act Crisis* (Chapel Hill: University of North Carolina Press, 1953); *The Birth of the Republic* (Chicago: University of Chicago Press, 1956); *The Puritan Dilemma* (Boston: Little, Brown, 1958); *American Slavery, American Freedom* (New York: Norton, 1975); *Inventing the People* (1988).

Reading

Courtwright, David T.: Fifty years of American History: an interview with Edmund S. Morgan. *William and Mary Quarterly* 44.2 (April 1987).

Hall, D. D., Murrin, J. M. and Tate, T. W. eds: *Saints and Revolutionaries* (New York: Norton, 1984), Preface.

Morgan, *The Challenge of the American Revolution* (New York: Norton, 1976). [Collection of his major essays with prefaces by Morgan].

Morison, Samuel Eliot (b.1887, d.1976) Born in Boston of aristocratic stock, Morison's life as a student and teacher centred on Harvard University (though he began his academic career in 1914 at the University of California, Berkeley). Shy and diffident as a youth, he acquired confidence through learning to sail and to ride: skills that later influenced his choice of historical subjects: Christopher Columbus and George Washington. Morison admired the great nineteenth-century historians of Boston such as Parkman, Prescott and Motley. He wrote in the narrative tradition throughout the period when such a form was in eclipse and various forms of theoretical, statistical, social and ideological history were in fashion. Despite their customary narrative or biographical form, Morison's many books did not lack theoretical assumptions and insights. Among Morison's many honours was his selection as the first Harmsworth professor at Oxford in 1922, an experience which gave rise to the *Oxford History of the United States* (2 vols 1927). He later collaborated with Henry Steele Commager in producing one of the most popular American textbooks, *The Growth of the American Republic* (1st edn 1930). Morison served as president of the American Historical Association in 1950

and used the occasion of his inaugural address to warn against the attempt to put history to the service of some social purpose. Morison's style was graceful, earthy, and tuned to oral expression. Although a devout Episcopalian, his acceptance of the puritan belief that idleness was the most heinous of sins caused him to work with unremitting energy until he had completed, shortly before his death, all the historical tasks he set for himself, of which his 2-volume *European Discovery of America: The Northern Voyages* (1971) and *The Southern Voyages* (1974) were the last. WEW

Main publications

With Henry Steele Commager, *The Growth of the American Republic* (1930), 2 vols (New York: Oxford University Press, 1962); *The Founding of Harvard College* (Cambridge, Mass.: Harvard University Press, 1935); *Three Centuries of Harvard, 1636–1936* (Harvard University Press, 1936); *Harvard College in the Seventeenth Century*, 2 vols (Harvard University Press, 1936; *Admiral of the Ocean Sea: a Life of Christopher Columbus*, 2 vols (1942); *History of US Naval Operations in World War II*, 15 vols (Boston: Little, Brown, 1947–62)) *By Land and Sea: Essays and Addresses by Samuel Eliot Morison* (New York: Knopf, 1953); *Vistas of History* (Knopf, 1964); *The Oxford History of the American People* (New York: Oxford University Press, 1965); *Harrison Gray Otis, 1765–1848: the Urbane Federalist* (Boston: Houghton Mifflin, 1969); *Sailor Historian: the Best of Samuel Eliot Morison*, ed. Emily Morison Beck (Boston: Houghton Mifflin, 1977).

Reading

Bentinck-Smith, William: Samuel Eliot Morison. *Massachusetts Historical Society Proceedings* 88 (1976) 121–2.

Morley, John (b.1838, d.1923) Morley combined a political and literary career. Born in Blackburn and educated at Lincoln College, Oxford, he established himself in London in the 1860s, editing the *Fortnightly Review* and later the *Pall Mall Gazette*. He was on close terms with Leslie STEPHEN, and with Joseph Chamberlain and Charles Dilke formed a radical group in the Liberal party. Elected to parliament in 1883, he was chief secretary for Ireland in Gladstone's administrations of 1886 and 1892. By 1906 he was a Liberal elder statesman, serving as secretary of state for India and as Lord Privy Seal. He went to the Lords in 1908, but resigned from Asquith's cabinet at the outbreak of war in 1914.

Morley's historical work was mainly biography. He produced studies of Burke, Crómwell, Walpole, Cobden, Voltaire and Rousseau, and edited the successful English Men of Letters series. His most celebrated work was the *Life of Gladstone*, which came out in 1903, sold well, and held the field until the tradition of discreet and reverential biographies went out of fashion.   JAC

Main publications

Voltaire (London: Chapman and Hall, 1872); *Rousseau* (London: Chapman and Hall, 1873); *Cobden* (London: Chapman and Hall, 1881); *Burke* (London: Macmillan, 1879); *Walpole* (London: Macmillan, 1888); *Cromwell* (London: Macmillan, 1900); *Life of Gladstone* (London: Macmillan, 1903); *Recollections* (London: Macmillan, 1917).

Reading

Hamer, D. A.: *John Morley, Liberal Intellectual* (Oxford: Clarendon Press, 1968).

Hirst, F. W.: *Early Life and Letters of John Morley* (London: Macmillan, 1927).

Kent, C.: *Brains and Numbers: Elitism, Comtism, and Democracy in mid-Victorian England* (Toronto: University of Toronto, Press, 1978).

Möser, Justus (b.1720, d.1794) A native of Osnabrück and a practising lawyer, Möser was important in the development of HISTORICISM. Sharply critical of the ideas of Voltaire, he believed in the organic growth of national institutions, considering that those of Saxony derived from (pre-Frankish) free democratic communities called *Markgenosschäfte*. This theory, which he expounded in his *Osnabrückische Geschichte* (1768), was well received in the nineteenth century and contributed to the belief that all liberty and democracy emanated from the Germanic or Aryan peoples. This notion, as further developed by Georg von Maurer (1790–1872), had a great influence on William STUBBS, who consequently considered that the *fons et origo* of the English constitution was to be found in the Anglo-Saxon village community.   RHCD

Main publications

Osnabrückische Geschichte, 2 vols (Osnabrück, 1768; 2nd edn, Berlin and Stettin, 1780).

Reading

Meinecke, F.: *Historism: the Rise of a New Historical Outlook*, trans. J. E. Anderson (London: Routledge & Kegan Paul, 1972), ch. 8.

Motley, John Lothrop (b.1814, d.1877) American author, son of a Boston merchant and a Unitarian minister's daughter. Motley wrote of his *Rise of the Dutch Republic* (1856) that 'if ten people in the world hate despotism a little more and love civil and religious liberty a little better in consequence of what I have written, I shall be satisfied' (quoted in Cheyney). He published his book at his own expense, and found to his surprise that on two sides of the Atlantic it sold about thirty thousand copies in a year. His vivid narrative of the dramatic episodes of the Dutch Revolt (then little known in the Anglo-Saxon world), based on a reading of printed and manuscript sources to an extent unusual at that time, and written from a very clear and definite point of view, became the classic account in English for many years. Lionized in Holland itself, and with a circle of friends extending from Bright to Bismarck, Motley later continued the story in further volumes from the death of his hero William the Silent to 1618. But the passionate partisanship which gained him so many readers led twentieth-century scholars to find his account unsatisfactory. His conception of the struggle as between light and darkness – he talked of 'pitching into Alva and Philip to my heart's content' and praised the virtues of Republicanism against the vices of 'superstition and despotism' – made it impossible, in spite of his extensive archival researches, for him to do justice to both sides of the question.   KHDH

Main publications

The Rise of the Dutch Republic, 3 vols (London: Chapman; New York: Harper, 1856); *History of the United Netherlands* [covering period from 1584 to 1609], 4 vols (London: Murray, 1860, 1867; New York: Harper, 1861, 1868); *Life and Death of John of Barneveld, Advocate of Holland*, 2 vols (London: Murray; New York: Harper; 1874); *The Writings of John Lothrop Motley*, 17 vols (New York: AMS Press, 1973).

MOUSNIER, ROLAND

Reading

Curtis, C. W. ed.: *The Correspondence of John Lothrop Motley*, 2 vols (London: Murray; New York: Harper, 1889) (Repr. in the 1973 edn, above).

Geyl, P. C. A.: Motley and his *Rise of the Dutch Republic*. In *Encounters in History* (London: Collins 1963), pp. 107–114.

Mousnier, Roland (b.1907) Mousnier studied at the Sorbonne and passed the *agrégation* in history and geography in 1931. He spent the next 16 years teaching in *lycées*, first in Rouen and then, from 1937, in Paris. In 1945 he completed his *thèse d'état* on venality of office in France under Henri IV and Louis XIII, prepared under the supervision of Georges Pagès. By its combination of local detail drawn from archives in Normandy with the wider perceptions provided by Parisian sources, the thesis represented a move away from drier institutional history towards a more sophisticated recognition of the importance of social attitudes in conditioning the development of institutions. Shortly after its publication Mousnier became a lecturer and then a professor of early modern history at the University of Strasbourg, and from 1949 also lectured at the Institut des Études Politiques in Paris. From 1955 until his retirement in 1977 he was a professor at the Sorbonne, where his lecture courses were popular for their research and precision. In 1958 he created the Centre des Recherches sur l'Histoire de la Civilisation de l'Europe Moderne which has stimulated research in several fields and published more than 20 volumes.

Mousnier has ranged widely within his chosen field, that of the social and political institutions of the absolute monarchy in France, and his publications have been numerous and influential. They embrace institutional history, popular revolts, social stratification and its methodology, the theory and practice of the absolute monarchy, the family, patron-client relationships and the history of Paris. In 1958 he entered the lists against the Soviet historian B. PORSHNEV over the causes of popular revolt in seventeenth-century France. The debate stimulated controversy over social stratification and the relations of social groups to the expanding state. Mousnier published the documentary evidence in the *Lettres et mémoires adressés au Chancelier Seguier* and followed this with a more general and comparative work on peasant uprisings in 1967. He must largely take the credit for the methodological advances made on the problems of social stratification in a specific historical context. A visit to the United States gave him the opportunity to pursue his interest in American sociology. Its theoretical influence can be detected in *Les hiérarchies sociales de 1450 à nos jours* (1969). During the 1970s he continued his research on patronage and clientage, for which he employs the concept of 'fidélités', and further explored notions of social structure, order and class in the *ancien régime*. His most recent major work, a two-volume study of institutions, is at once a manual and a lengthy restatement of – in view of his work on society – a surprisingly orthodox view of the development of the absolute monarchy. Politically conservative, Mousnier represents the traditional school of French historiography. He has exerted a considerable influence over historical studies of the early modern period, both in France and abroad.

PRC

Main publications

(Published by Presses Universitaires de France, Paris, unless otherwise stated.)
La vénalité des offices sous Henri IV et Louis XIII (Rouen: 1945; PUF, 1946); with F. Hartung, Quelques problèmes concernant la monarchie absolue. In *Relazioni del X Congresso Internazionale di Scienze Storiche, IV, Storia Moderna* (Florence) 4 (1955) 1–55; *Lettres et mémoires adressés au Chancelier Séguier, 1633–1649*, 2 vols (1964); *L'assassinat de Henri IV, 14 mai 1610* (Paris: Gallimard, 1964) trans. *The Assassination of Henry IV* (London: Faber, 1973); *Fureurs paysannes* . . . (Paris: Calvrann-Levy, 1967) trans. *Peasant Uprisings* . . . (London: Allen and Unwin, 1971); editor, *Problèmes de stratification sociale* (1968); *Les hiérarchies sociales de 1450 à nos jours* (1969) trans. *Social Hierarchies from 1450 to the Present Day* (London: Croom Helm, 1973); *La plume la faucille et le marteau* (1970); *Les institutions de la France sous la monarchie absolue, 1598–1789*, 2 vols (1974) trans. *The Institutions of the Absolute Monarchy* (Chicago: University of Chicago Press, 1979 and 1984).

Reading

Durand, Y. ed.: *Hommage à Roland Mousnier* (Paris: PUF, 1981).

Muratori, Ludovico Antonio (b.1672, d.1750) Historian of medieval Italy, text-editor and literary critic. Born at Vignola (Modena), Muratori was directed to a career in the Church, having been taught at Modena by the Benedictine, Benedetto Bachini, who introduced him to the recently-developed historico-critical methods of the French MAURISTS. Family pressure encouraged Muratori in the study of canon and civil law, in which he qualified in 1694, although he later recalled how much it bored him. In 1695, the year of his ordination to the priesthood, he was established as *doctor* in the Borromean 'Biblioteca Ambrosiana' at Milan. His five years there, with ready access to a collection of medieval Greek and Latin manuscripts and participation in a congenial intellectual and social circle — reflected not only in his correspondence but also in verse — largely determined the pattern of his scholarly life and his perspective as a historian. Muratori's first publications, two volumes of *Anecdota*, i.e. Greek and Latin texts he had found in the Library (1697/8, two further volumes in 1713), were in a tradition that originated among the late fifteenth-century Humanists. But while Muratori initially deplored the destruction of 'civilization' by the Germanic invaders of Italy and the Roman provinces, he came to recognize that medieval Italy — which he perceived as a single culture with local variations in the peninsula's many political units — had achievements to its credit at least as great as those of other countries which had given more attention to their medieval past; and he deplored the fact that the recent uncovering of Italy's manuscript treasures was the work of itinerant French scholars. In 1699 the extraordinary Apostolo Zeno (a man of letters, opera librettist and diplomat) wrote to Muratori with details of a proposal for the publication of Italy's medieval chronicles. His other activities prevented his giving effect to the plan: Muratori adopted it as his own.

Muratori was recalled to Modena in 1700 to become Librarian of the Ducal library, whose collections included a substantial archive of documents — historical source-material of a type which he had not encountered in Milan although he was aware of the problems it

posed from Mabillon. Legal disputes between the Este family and the Holy See over the ownership of the territory of Comacchio prompted a series of publications (1708, 1711, 1720) based on original documents but polemical, because touching on some of the central ideological and juridical problems of the Italian Middle Ages. Simultaneously he was engaged on biographies and literary-critical studies of recent and older Italian writers including Petrarch (1711), and assembling copies of both the Latin and the vernacular chronicles of the peninsula. The first of 28 volumes of the *Rerum italicarum scriptores* (*RIS*) appeared in 1723, the last in 1738: the new critical editions of the German Monumentists began to replace them in the middle decades of the nineteenth century and a 'new Muratori' was begun in 1900; but for a small number of chronicles the original *RIS* is still the best or most accessible edition.

Muratori journeyed frequently, although uncomfortably, to most parts of the peninsula over more than thirty years and maintained a network of scholarly correspondents among both clergy and laity — reflected in an enormous surviving correspondence. He was simultaneously assembling an impressive collection of documents, the majority unpublished, which would throw light on almost all aspects of Italy's medieval past: institutions and laws, education, sports and daily life. Several hundred of them were printed in full as the supporting evidence for the seventy-five dissertations that constituted the epoch-making *Antiquitates Italicae Medii Aevi* — six folio volumes published from 1738 to 1742. They covered laws and institutions, education and learning, sports and daily life, many still-familiar topics being discussed in a strictly historical way for the first time (for example, the nature of the *arimanni(a)* or the powers of royal *missi*). In his last years Muratori compiled a twelve-volume *Annali d'Italia* from AD 1, based on material already available elsewhere but notable for coming down to 1749 and written with fearless judgement in vigorous prose.

Muratori was indeed as much a man of letters as a historian: he wrote on tragedy and encouraged performances of theoretically-sound plays at Modena; he wrote on the connections between culture and morals, in spite of his avowed distaste for his early training in *morale*. By a natural extension he was openly critical of contemporary human failings in the application of the law, which seemed to him to challenge natural rights and man's humanity. Conversely he wrote a spirited defence of the conduct of the Society of Jesus in Paraguay, as an example of 'the kingdom of virtue' (1743; an English translation already in 1759), which has latterly attracted renewed interest among scholars. But his advocacy of a notable reduction in the days of obligatory holiday, in the interests of the material well-being of the ordinary Catholic, was one of several expressions of a 'rational' religion that prompted attacks from traditionalists. Forced into silence by episcopal authority, he insisted on his death-bed that he had never sought to challenge orthodoxy and that he had always accepted the authority of his church.

GIBBON always regretted that England had 'not yet found her Muratori'. A positivist historian who stood out against Fascist ideological reinterpretation of Italy's past could remark in 1942 that he 'did not have much regard for medievalists who did not read the entire *Antiquitates*', although it would have been equally true to comment that many of them were reluctant to seek out evidence not already known to Muratori. The post-war renaissance in Italian medieval historiography publicly avows a greater debt to CROCE and latterly to MARX than to Muratori: but the importance of the Dissertations in prescribing the main directions, and at times even the methods, of inquiry is widely acknowledged; and in the importance attached to the preparation of critical editions of documents and their simultaneous philological and social-historical analysis, the debt to Muratori is even greater.   DAB

Main publications

The most convenient analysis of the contents of the *Anecdota, Rerum italicarum scriptores*, and the *Antiquitates* (and of the 'new Muratori') is in *Repertorium fontium historiae Medii Aevi* 1 (1962) 509–22.

Reading

There is no extended English language account of Muratori.

Bertelli, S.: *Erudizione e storia in Ludovico Antonio Muratori* (Naples: 1960).

Monaco, M.: *La vita, le opere, il pensiero di L. A. Muratori e la sua concezione della pubblica felicità* (Lecce: 1977).

N

Namier, Lewis Bernstein (b.1888, d.1960) Born into a Jewish family in Polish Russia, Namier came to England in 1908 and was educated at the London School of Economics and at Balliol College Oxford. He spent many years studying history in his spare time, until he amazed the historical world with the publication of his two greatest works, *The Structure of Politics at the Accession of George III* (1929) and *England in the Age of the American Revolution* (1930). These helped him to secure the chair of modern history at the University of Manchester, a post he held for twenty years. During this time he wrote many volumes of essays on eighteenth-century England and on modern European diplomacy. Knighted in 1952, he spent his last years establishing the History of Parliament Trust and editing the volumes on *The House of Commons 1754–1790*.

Many of Namier's conclusions on mid-eighteenth-century English politics are still generally accepted. He demolished the myth that George III was trying to restore royal absolutism; he denied the claim that the political disputes of the 1760s revolved around two organized parties, Whig and Tory; and he played down the amount of political corruption employed by the government and leading aristocrats. Critics have rightly pointed out, however, that Namier went too far in denying that there was anything questionable about George III's conduct. Subsequent research has also clearly demonstrated that party was an important ingredient in the political life of the nation in the decades before and after the 1760s. It is unfair to attack Namier for his interest in the propertied elite, though other scholars have rightly turned their attention to the middle and lower orders of the eighteenth century who were ignored by Namier.

Namier's reputation rests as much upon his methodology as upon his particular conclusions. In trying to understand how the parliamentary system worked, Namier attempted to stop the political machine in order to examine its component parts and its functioning. To support this technique of STRUCTURAL ANALYSIS he adopted a relatively new method of historical inquiry, namely PROSOPOGRAPHY or collective biography. By collecting evidence on the life, career, connections and behaviour of every single MP, Namier acquired quantifiable evidence which he could use to test more stringently than ever before the factors which may have motivated the political actions of an individual or group. He made a detailed investigation of the composition of the House of Commons, a study of the electoral process and an assessment of the impact of ambition, vested interest and personal grievances on the behaviour of ordinary MPs. Though Namier's method has been criticized as myopic and as atomizing history it is capable of producing fruitful results.

Namier was well aware of the complex psychological forces which influenced the actions of men and so the charge that he 'took the mind out of history' hardly stands up to close scrutiny. On the other hand he did rely too much on Freudian psychology and had a very cynical view of human nature. Furthermore his technique of structural analysis inevitably tends to elevate personal ambition, petty intrigue and family connections above political principles, public opinion or party ideology. Namier was certainly guilty of over-emphasizing self-interest as the prime motivating factor in human action and of seeing all ideas as the mere rationalization of selfish conduct: not surprisingly, much recent research has insisted that ideas and ideologies must be put back into any adequate interpretation of eighteenth-century politics.

Namier's professional skills were of the highest order. His sheer intellect and clarity of mind are apparent in all his works. He was a rigorous and demanding scholar who achieved an unrivalled mastery over his sources and who improved the professional standards of his age by his meticulous concern with accuracy. At times he showed rare insight and always wrote beautiful prose. Nevertheless, he did more to demolish the old edifice than to build a new one, and failed to integrate his detailed findings into either a satisfactory narrative or an overall synthesis.

A deeply conservative man, Namier brandished his assumptions in a provocative manner and enjoyed controversy. At times he pushed his arguments to unreasonable lengths and he rode his prejudices hard. On the other hand he could be innocent and lovable, and he enlisted many devoted disciples. Though he received too much praise towards the end of his life, he is too much criticized now. A legend in his own lifetime and a scholar who gave his name to a school of historians and to a historical method, he made a permanent contribution to the study of history.   HTD

Main publications

The structure of Politics at the Accession of George III (London: Macmillan, 1929; New York: St Martin, 1957); *England in the Age of the American Revolution* (London: Macmillan, 1930; New York: St Martin, 1974); *Personalities and Powers* (London: Hamish Hamilton, 1955; Westport, Conn.: Greenwood, 1974); *Crossroads of Power* (London: Hamish Hamilton, 1962; Salem, NH: Ayer, 1962); ed. with John Brooke, *The House of Commons 1754–1790*, 3 vols (London: Oxford University Press, 1964; North Pomfret, Va.: David & Charles, 1985); with John Brooke, *Charles Townshend* (London: Macmillan, 1964; New York: St Martin, 1964).

Reading

Cannon, J. A.: Lewis Bernstein Namier. In *The Historian at Work*, ed. J. A. Cannon (London: Allen & Unwin, 1980).

Namier, Julia : *Lewis Namier: A Biography* (London: Oxford University Press, 1971).
Sutherland, Lucy S.: Sir Lewis Namier. *Proceedings of the British Academy* 18 (1962) 371–85.
Winkler, Henry R.: Sir Lewis Namier. *Journal of Modern History* 35 (1963) 1–19.

Napier, William Francis Patrick (b.1785, d.1860) A member of the distinguished military family, Napier saw active service in the Peninsular War of 1808–14, and his six-volume *History of the War in the Peninsula*, published between 1828 and 1840, established itself as the most influential work in English on the subject. He was knighted in 1848. Combining a flair for narrative on the grand scale with a keen eye for personal detail Napier conveyed something of what it had been like to be under fire, and although he indulged in lengthy and controversial discussions of tactics and strategy he enlivened his account by referring to the experiences of individual soldiers. His main purpose was to defend the reputations of Moore and Wellington, both of whom he admired, and in this he succeeded. But his work contained blemishes which led to heated controversy and which detract from its value. He was grossly partisan in his treatment of British politicians, especially Canning and Perceval whom he detested, and denigrated the Spanish and Portuguese contributions to the defeat of the French, heaping paragraphs of invective on Spanish politicians, generals and guerrillas, and claiming in extravagant language that England liberated the Iberian peninsula virtually unaided. But his flamboyant and rhetorical prose may still be read with pleasure, and at his best Napier created an impression of epic grandeur while communicating masses of information which have enabled later historians to use his work almost as a primary source.   JWD

Main publications

A History of the War in the Peninsula (London: John Murray, 1828–40; *The War in the Peninsula*, ed. B. Connell (London: Folio Society, 1973); *The Conquest of Scinde* (London: Boone, 1845).

Naruszewicz, Adam (b.1733, d.1796) A Polish Jesuit from Lithuania, educated in Vilna (Wilno) and Lyons, Naruszewicz was the leading literary figure of the Polish Enlightenment until Krasicki. His close association with King Stanislas Augustus Poniatowski and his reform policies enabled Naruszewicz to enjoy high office in church and state, and to pursue historical research in some comfort. His *On Writing a National History* (Warsaw, 1775) is considered as the beginning of modern Polish historiography. He urged the collection and critical use of documentary sources, and produced the first scholarly account of medieval Polish history in which he lamented the weakening of monarchical authority. His monarchical periodization of Polish history was later challenged by LELEWEL.   WHZ

Main publications

Historia narodu polskiego (History of the Polish nation), vols. 2–7 (Warsaw: 1780–86), vol. 1 (Warsaw, 1824).

Reading

Rutkowska, N.: *Bishop A. Naruszewicz and his History of the Polish Nation: a Critical Study* (Washington, DC: Catholic University of America Press, 1941).

national record societies Working in parallel with official bodies performing the same task, national record societies are private associations whose primary aim is to publish historical records. In Britain and Ireland, the crown first assigned that task in 1800 to the Record Commission, which between 1802 and 1848 published texts relating to England, Wales and Scotland, while the Irish Record Commission published from 1826 to 1901. In 1856 the Public Record Office began to publish calendars of records (some of which related to Scotland or Ireland), to be followed by the Irish Record Office in 1861, the Scottish Record Office in 1867, and the Public Record Office of Northern Ireland in 1973. Also published under the direction of the Master of the Rolls and therefore known collectively as the *Rolls Series*, though officially called *Rerum Britannicarum Medii Aevi Scriptores* or *Chronicles and Memorials of Great Britain and Ireland*, were 99 titles, mostly CHRONICLES AND ANNALS, issued between 1858 and 1896. From 1870 the Royal Commission on Historical Manuscripts has published reports and calendars, and from 1968 editions of prime ministers' papers.

The first private society for producing historical texts appears to be the Roxburghe Club, which was still surviving in 1988; it was formed in 1812 to celebrate the sale from the library of John, third duke of Roxburghe (d.1804), of the 1471 edition of Boccaccio, and had 24 members who presented to their fellows printed versions of ancient texts, often curiosities or of literary rather than of strictly historical interest. Two less exclusive societies began publishing in 1838: the English Historical Society, which up to 1856 published a limited number of important medieval chronicles, its work being later assumed by the *Rolls Series*; and the Camden Society, which was named after William CAMDEN and had a larger and more varied output. The Camden Society became more predominantly historical when the Early English Text Society began publication in 1864 of texts illustrating the language but including some of strong historical interest, and in 1896 it amalgamated with the Royal Historical Society, which has continued its publication of records in the *Camden Third and Fourth Series*. Between 1844 and 1854 the Caxton Society published under the title *Scriptores Monastici* 16 volumes of editions of medieval chronicles and letters, most of which have been printed again in later editions. The List and Index Society, though not strictly a record society, deserves mention for its extensive continuation, from 1965, of the Public Record Office's series of *Lists and Indexes*, begun in 1892, providing a means of access to unedited public records.

Other record societies have specialized in particular subjects: the Hakluyt Society has from 1847 published records of exploration; the Pipe Roll Society, from 1884, early exchequer records; the Selden Society (named after John SELDEN), from 1888, records of legal history, mostly medieval; the Navy Records Society, from 1894, naval records; and the Harleian Society and the Index Library of the British Record Society Ltd, from 1869 and 1888 respectively, records relating to family history and GENEALOGY, which naturally include many of a wider historical significance.

NATIONAL RECORD SOCIETIES

All those specialist societies remained active in 1988, as did three occasional series published from 1914 onwards by the British Academy on social history and economic history, Anglo-Saxon charters, and English episcopal *acta*. Records of ecclesiastical history and religion have been published by a range of societies: records of liturgy and church furniture by the Alcuin Club from 1899 (though since 1962 the club has published no texts, only essays and monographs), liturgical texts by the Henry Bradshaw Society from 1891, medieval bishops' registers by the Canterbury and York Society from 1907, reformation texts by the Parker Society from 1841 to 1855, and records relating to particular religious groups by the British Society for Franciscan Studies from 1908 to 1937, the Catholic Record Society from 1905, the Hanserd Knollys Society (Baptist) from 1846 to 1854, and the Huguenot Society of London from 1887. The Jewish Historical Society of England has from 1901 published records for Jewish history. For Welsh history the Honourable Society Cymmrodorion published the *Cymmrodorion Record Series* from 1892 to 1936 and occasional texts thereafter in other series, and from 1946 the Historical Society of the Church in Wales has published texts. All the societies named above except the Roxburghe Club, the Early English Text Society, and the List and Index Society are included in E. L. C. Mullins's *Texts and Calendars* parts I and II (Royal Historical Society), which lists their record publications, together with those of official bodies relating to England and Wales.

For Scottish history, on which a series of *Chronicles and Memorials* under the direction of the Lord Clerk Register matched the predominantly English volumes of the *Rolls Series*, Sir Walter SCOTT founded in 1823, on the model of the Roxburghe Club, the Bannatyne Club, which published a valedictory volume in 1867. Similar clubs that survived for some years included the Maitland (publishing 1829–59), Abbotsford (1835–65), and Grampian (1869–91), while others had regional or local interests. In urban history the Scottish Burgh Records Society published from 1868 to 1911, and up to 1967 further volumes were published in conformity with but not as part of that series. The Scottish History Society has from 1887 published texts of Scottish Records generally, the Stair Society has from 1936 published those relating to legal history, and the Scottish Record Society has from 1897 published mostly indexes of records relating to demographic and family history. A full survey, supplementing Mullins's work, is provided by D. and W. B. Stevenson's *Scottish Texts and Calendars* (Royal Historical Society and Scottish History Society). For Irish history, in addition to *Analecta Hibernica* published from 1930 by the Irish Manuscripts Commission established in 1928, there are two series of ecclesiastical record publications: *Archivium Hibernicum* or *Irish Historical Records*, issued by the Catholic Record Society of Ireland from 1912; and *Collectanea Hibernica* or *Sources for Irish History*, issued by the Friars Minor from 1958.

Record publication in Britain and Ireland has had a strong medieval bias. The national record societies have published many volumes of a local nature, and a few of the record societies concerned primarily with local history have issued volumes that are national in scope, such as *Sir Christopher Hatton's Book of Seals* (Northampton Record Society) and *John Constable's Correspondence* (Suffolk Record Society). The last prompts a mention, for historical records of art and architecture, of the Walpole Society (from 1912) and the Wren Society (1924–43).

In mainland Europe national societies have produced large and important record series, supplementing the publications of religious and governmental organizations and of editors of single texts. A few of those societies may be mentioned.

In Germany the Gesellschaft für Ältere Deutsche Geschichtskunde, founded in 1819, sponsored the *Monumenta Germaniae Historica*, a massive series in five sections (*Scriptores*, *Leges*, *Diplomata*, *Epistolae*, and *Antiquitates*) and various subsections, of which the first volume appeared in 1826; the series was taken over by the Königliche Akademie der Wissenschaften of Prussia in 1874 and later by the Reichsinstitut für Ältere Deutsche Geschichtskunde. The first editor was Georg Heinrich PERTZ (1795–1876). Since he served for 50 years (1823–73) and was responsible for the *Scriptores*, that section is sometimes cited as 'Pertz'. His main collaborator, J. F. Böhmer, was closely linked to the *Diplomata*, which he not only edited but also initially financed.

The Société de l'Histoire de France, founded with the encouragement of François GUIZOT as minister of public instruction, began its long series in 1835, the same year as the *Collection de Documents Inédits sur l'Histoire de France*, under the minister's auspices; both carried forward the work done earlier by the MAURISTS and Martin BOUQUET and by the Académie des Inscriptions et Belles Lettres (founded 1663, reorganized 1701). The society in 1927 absorbed the Société d'Histoire Contemporaine, which had been publishing records since 1892.

Succeeding to the tradition of Lodovico MURATORI, whose *Rerum Italicarum Scriptores* (1723–38) was published with the aid of the Società Palatina of Milan, the Istituto Storico Italiano began publishing *Fonti per la Storia d'Italia* in 1885 and *Regesta Chartarum Italiae* in 1907; the institute was expressly 'per il Medio Evo' from 1934, a parallel series of *Fonti* being published from 1935 by the Istituto Storico Italiano per l'Età Moderna e Contemporanea.

There are also series of national record publications for Sweden (published from 1816), Belgium (1836), Spain (1842), Austria (1849), Portugal (1856), Norway (1858), Switzerland (1877), Denmark (1885), and the Netherlands (1905).

See also entries on DEMOGRAPHIC, ECONOMIC, LEGAL, LOCAL, SOCIAL, URBAN HISTORY, and on IRISH, JEWISH, SCOTTISH, WELSH HISTORIOGRAPHY.   CRE

Neale, John Ernest (b.1890, d.1975) Neale was the academic heir of A. F. POLLARD. Beginning in 1914 as Pollard's research student at University College London (having been an undergraduate at Liverpool), Neale joined the staff in 1919 and except for two years as professor at Manchester (1925–7), he remained at University College for the next 35 years, succeeding Pollard in the full-time Astor professorship in 1927. Although not the

'autocrat' of the London History School that his mentor had been (and Pollard remained director of the Institute of Historical Research until 1939, a post Neale never held), Neale was still the dominant figure among the historians of the university. Indeed for many foreigners, especially students from the USA who experienced his Monday postgraduate seminar at the Institute, history at London *was* 'Jimmy' Neale.

Neale's short, rotund frame was topped by a shiny bald head and a face which could light up with good humour and infectious enthusiasm. Many of his numerous research students, as well as benefiting from his rigorous supervision, developed a lasting affection for this Mr. Pickwick among historians. However, to others less in Neale's shadow or debt, such students often seemed the victims of their supervisor's narrow personal obsession with the reign of Elizabeth I and particularly with the relations between the queen and parliament (or to be more correct, the House of Commons). Neale unashamedly directed postgraduates to subjects he wanted studied, and with brief acknowledgement incorporated their findings in his own books. At one public lecture he caused great offence by seeming to imply that this was an appropriate destiny for the second-class student who would then go on to be a schoolteacher.

Having lost his father at the age of five and been forced to leave school at 14, Neale could not have got to the top without this ambition and single-mindedness. Yet the price was not only an absence of interest in much apart from history, and the confining of his own considerable research abilities to a limited range of concerns, but also the exerting of a narrowing and to an extent distorting influence on sixteenth-century studies at London, then still the world capital of Tudor research. That said, Neale's achievement in his chosen field was outstanding. Determination to find and survey every relevant source led to highly important discoveries. He also pioneered significant advances in method, applying to the study of the Elizabethan House of Commons what he and his generation called 'the biographical method', but which later jargon would ignorantly label 'prosopography'.

Neale's reputation rests on four major works. The first, published in 1934, was a highly successful and long-lived biography of Elizabeth which won the James Tait Black memorial prize. Two generations on, the interpretation appears heavily predetermined by the author's eulogistic intuitions about the queen's character (Neale wrote the book, in part, as a counter to Lytton Strachey's *Elizabeth and Essex*). However, the biography remains a monument to Neale's adherence to the principle that the ultimate duty of the historian is to the wider literate public for whom he must make the past live.

What will probably be the most enduring of Neale's books is the second, *The Elizabethan House of Commons* (1949). Not only was this an authoritative exploration of the House as an institution, but it also tried to relate developments there to the broader dimension of Elizabethan society. Indeed one might say that it was Neale who first gave wide currency to the role and importance of faction and patronage in Tudor England. The remaining two books, the successive volumes entitled *Elizabeth and her Parliaments*, were never intended to be a rounded history of parliamentary affairs — that criticism is unjust — but they do suffer from Neale's belief that tension between the Crown and the Commons was normal, from an exaggerated view of what and how important puritanism was, and from a failure to treat the Commons as one element only (and then not the most important) in the overall Elizabethan political machine. Nevertheless they evoke quite brilliantly the relations between the personnel of the Commons and the royal personality Neale had sketched in the earlier biography. Again he achieved his object; his characters 'live'.

Given Neale's specialization, the invitation in 1951 to join the editorial board of the project for a biographical 'history of parliament' was inevitable. It was, however, disastrous. For Neale, as for S. T. Bindoff, his most brilliant appointment to the UCL department and editorship of the volume on early Tudor parliaments was a millstone which drowned all alternative scholarship; neither man in the end was able to complete the vital introductory volume, and in Neale's case what did finally appear for Elizabeth's reign did so without revision by him. Thus, unlike his election to the British Academy in 1948, Neale's knighthood in 1955 marked the effective end of his scholarly productivity; the biographical method was a good tool but a bad master. Neale's diversion from the great work of his retirement on the earl of Essex is a reminder of the new relevance that increasing sophistication in research gives to Voltaire's warning: *Malheur aux détails, c'est une vermine qui tue les grands ouvrages.*   EWI

Main publications

(All published by Jonathan Cape, London.)
Queen Elizabeth (1934); *The Elizabethan House of Commons* (1949); *Elizabeth and her Parliaments, 1559–1581* (1953); *Elizabeth and her Parliaments, 1584–1601* (1957).

Reading

Hurstfield, Joel: *Proceedings of the British Academy* 63 (1977) 403–21.

Needham, Joseph (b.1900)   The foremost historian of Chinese science, Needham lacked formal qualifications both in Chinese (learned in middle age) and the history of science. Needham was the son of parents of disparate temperaments, and his life has been marked by a persistent urge towards synthesis. He arrived in Gonville and Caius, Cambridge, from Oundle, and has been a member ever since, from 1924 as a fellow and from 1966 to 1976 as master. Though work on chemical embryology made him Sir William Dunn reader in biochemistry by 1933, an interest in China aroused by Chinese fellow researchers bore unexpected fruit when he became head of the British scientific mission to China in 1942–6. Thereafter his research turned towards the production of *Science and Civilization in China*, a pioneering (though increasingly collaborative) survey of which 15 separate parts have appeared and a yet greater number are promised.

Had Needham never learned Chinese his name would still be widely known to non-embryologists. He soon developed at Caius a highly individual blend of Christianity and Marxism which found expression in a variety of publications, from *Science, Religion and*

Reality in 1925 to *History is on Our Side* in 1946. The resoluteness of his writings has been matched on occasion in action, too: participation in the International Commission for the Investigation of Charges of Bacteriological Warfare in North China and Korea earned him predictable opprobrium at home and abroad for reporting evidence unfavourable to the United States. Assessments of *Science and Civilization in China* have also been tinged with controversy, but his studies have provided such a mass of information overlooked by earlier historiography that although even close collaborators, such as Nathan Sivin, do not accept some of his most cherished interpretations, the quality of debate over those interpretations has steadily improved, and whatever his shortcomings, the balance sheet now adds up very much in his favour. His remarkably long and productive 'retirement' may lead to Needham being remembered as a somewhat fallible, orientalizing sage in a way that does no justice to earlier enthusiasms, like folk dancing, which the years have forced him to leave behind.   THB

Main publications

Science and Civilization in China (Cambridge: Cambridge University Press, 1954 onward); *The Grand Titration* (London: George Allen & Unwin, 1969).

Reading

Sivin, N. and Nakayama, S.: *Chinese Science* (Cambridge, Mass.: MIT Press, 1973).

Nennius   Some late manuscripts of the *Historia Brittonum* claim that it was written by a certain 'Nennius'; most attribute it, quite wrongly, to GILDAS. The *Historia*, probably written in 829/30 in western Britain, is a miscellany of annals, genealogies and other historical material, mostly concerning Britain and Ireland; it includes the earliest traditions about Arthur.   EFJ

(Attributed) writings

Historia Brittonum: British History, ed. and trans. J. Morris (Chichester: Phillimore, 1980).

Nepos, Cornelius (*fl.* 99–24 BC)   The earliest writer of biography in Latin whose work survives. He came from the region beyond the river Po in north Italy. Although he never undertook a political career, he spent at least some of his life in Rome, where he mixed in literary circles. The poet Catullus, a fellow northerner, dedicated his book of poems to Nepos with a poem which elegantly praised his achievement in producing a three-volume chronological outline history of the world (no longer extant). Nepos corresponded on literary matters with Cicero and dedicated at least some of his biographies to Cicero's close friend, Atticus.

He wrote on a variety of subjects, including geography, but his reputation rests upon his 16 books *De viris illustribus* (Lives of famous men), largely written before the death of Atticus (32 BC), but added to later. The work covered a variety of categories, such as kings and poets; but what survives consists of 23 brief lives of great foreign generals and two lives of Latin historians. He wrote in the tradition developed in Greek biography that claimed that a man's character determined his fortune and therefore his true nature was revealed by his actions. This biographical genre, which was recognized as distinct from history, was much more elaborately developed later by PLUTARCH. Despite their uneven quality, Nepos' *Lives* deserve better than their fate as a source for easy passages for translation for generations of schoolchildren.   JJP

Main writings

Cornelius Nepos, ed. and trans. J. C. Rolfe (Cambridge, Mass.: Loeb Classical Library, Harvard University Press, 1929).

Reading

Jenkinson, E.: Nepos: an introduction to Latin biography. In *Latin Biography* ed. T. A. Dorey (London: Routledge & Kegan Paul, 1967).

Netherlands historiography   See LOW COUNTRIES, HISTORIOGRAPHY OF.

New Zealand historiography   In the conventional sense of written narratives and explanations of aspects of the development of a distinctive society, New Zealand historiography dates from the original exploration and settlement of the country by Europeans.

NEW ZEALAND HISTORIOGRAPHY

There is another sense in which the history of New Zealand is recorded and analysed in the oral tradition of the Maori. Although recent years have seen determined efforts by pakeha (non-Maori New Zealand) authors to incorporate the Maori viewpoint into their analyses of the past, and a little writing in the standard historiographical tradition by Maori historians, the two approaches to the past remain largely distinct.

The European discovery of New Zealand is best regarded as an aspect of European exploration of the Pacific. New Zealand historians found this a convenient link between their isolated location and the mainstream of historical scholarship, and this preoccupation reached its pinnacle in the various works of J. C. Beaglehole (1901–1971), culminating in his posthumously published *The Life of Captain James Cook* (1974). The subject continues to produce some fine scholarship, especially in combination with studies of the European impact on the indigenous peoples of the Pacific, but as archives, researchers and perspective made possible deeper analysis of developments within New Zealand itself, it ceased to be a focus of New Zealand historiography as a whole.

Some early European settlers wrote accounts of their experiences and these constitute the beginning of a narrowly defined New Zealand historiography. They also set a pattern in which apparently dispassionate accounts of New Zealand history contain arguments relating to contemporary issues. Thus E. J. Wakefield, *Adventure in New Zealand, from 1839 to 1844* (1845), is not only a narrative of the excitement of a young man engaged in policy decisions of a kind which would have been reserved to much more experienced people in England, but is a partisan defence of the New Zealand Company which organized some of the settlement of New Zealand. Later books such as G. W. Rusden, *History of New Zealand* (1883), and Alfred Saunders, *History of New Zealand* (1896), continued this pattern; Rusden's work has retained interest primarily because it is unusual to find in one work the jaundiced view of an English Tory and knowledge of what happened in New Zealand (and Australia). The most successful of all such works was William Pember Reeves, *The Long White Cloud* (1898). Reeves was a politician who made his reputation as a youthful radical; he became a cabinet minister and was responsible for the act which set the basic pattern in industrial relations to the present day. Reeves retreated to London, first to become the equivalent of a high commissioner, and then director of the London School of Economics and a bank chairman. His view of New Zealand history was essentially the triumph of progress in a new environment, culminating in successful experiments with new uses of the power of the state. In various textbooks, with a number of different nuances, this account of New Zealand remained dominant for 60 years.

It was only with Keith Sinclair, *A History Of New Zealand* (1959), and W. H. Oliver, *The Story of New Zealand* (1960), that new standard sources displaced Reeves. While both drew on the scholarship which followed Reeves and brought the story and analysis into later years, Sinclair was aggressively nationalistic, while Oliver gave more attention to the European heritage. Over 20 years later, Oliver was co-editor with B. R. Williams of *The Oxford History of New Zealand* (1981). As a multi-authored work, this could be expected to have a less defined theme, but while that is true, the volume has some features which distinguish it from its predecessors. It draws on many more sources, following the flowering of theses, articles and books in the 1960s and 1970s. But even more, it has a less optimistic view of New Zealand history. To some extent, this maintains the pattern of reflecting current issues; in the 1970s, full employment disappeared from New Zealand and so did the widespread satisfaction that a better society had been built in the South Pacific. It also reflected the breakdown of the Reevesian view of progress under the pressure of sustained historical research.

This was clear in the treatment of Maori–pakeha relations. Traditional historiography had not hidden the misunderstanding and conflict between Maori and settlers, but had generally accepted the view that there were no more than a number of unfortunate incidents in an essentially commendable record in which new wealth was brought to the Maori who were permitted to become part of pakeha society when they chose to do so. There remains considerable weight in this view, but recent scholarship has emphasized the insistence of pakeha on setting the rules for contact with Maoris – the theme of Alan Ward, *A Show of Justice: Racial 'Amalgamation' in Nineteenth Century New Zealand* (1973) – and the creative response of Maoridom isolated from 'mainstream' New Zealand life. Sinclair had drawn attention to one aspect of this many years earlier, and the specialist subfield of 'race relations' had developed it, but only with the *Oxford History* did it really become a central theme of New Zealand historiography as a whole.

New Zealand historiography has a rich literature, and specialist areas reflect the sequence of partisan accounts, emphasis on progress and recognition of greater complexity. In economic history, for example, the field was dominated by J. B. Condliffe, *New Zealand in the Making* (1930), partly because he chose the enduring theme of relations between New Zealand and the international economy as his central concern. Later writers, notably C. G. F. Simkin, *The Instability of a Dependent Economy* (1951), added greatly to the content of Condliffe, but only with G. R. Hawke, *The Making of New Zealand* (1985), was there a new account shifting the balance from international price trends to the local response. GRHk

Reading

Beaglehole, J. C.: *The Life of Captain James Cook* (London: A & C. Black, 1974).

Condliffe, J. B. : *New Zealand in the Making* (Chicago: University of Chicago Press, 1930).

Hawke, G. R. *The Making of New Zealand* (Cambridge: Cambridge University Press, 1985).

McLintock, A. H., ed.: *An Encyclopedia of New Zealand* (Wellington: Government Printer, 1966).

Oliver, W. H.: *The Story of New Zealand* (London: Faber, 1960).

Oliver, W. H. and Williams, B. R., eds: *Oxford History of New Zealand* (Wellington: Oxford University Press, 1981).

Reeves, W. P.: *The Long White Cloud* (London: Horace Marshall & Son, 1898).

Rusden, G. W.: *History of New Zealand* (London: Chapman & Hall, 1883).

Saunders, A. C.: *History of New Zealand*, vol. 1 (Christchurch: Whitcombe & Tombs, 1896), vol 2 (Christchurch: Smith, Anthony, Sellars, 1899).

Simkin, C. G. F.: *The Instability of a Dependent Economy* (Oxford: Oxford University Press, 1951).

Sinclair, Keith: *A History of New Zealand* (Harmondsworth: Penguin, 1959).

Wakefield, E. J.: *Adventure in New Zealand, from 1839 to 1844* (London: John Murray, 1845).

Ward, Alan: *A Show of Justice: Racial 'Amalgamation' in Nineteenth Century New Zealand* (Auckland: Auckland University Press, 1973).

Nicolaus of Damascus (*fl.* 64 BC – AD 6) The son of a prominent public figure in his home city, Nicolaus became a tutor to the children of Antony and Cleopatra and a close adviser of King Herod of Judaea. He made three visits to Rome on diplomatic missions. The most important historical work of this voluminous Greek writer was a huge universal history in 144 books, covering the period down to Herod's death in 4 BC; significant fragments have survived in the works of other authors. His panegyrical biography of the emperor Augustus' early life is preserved in fragments in the collection of classical authors ordered by Constantine Porphyrogenitus in the tenth century. JJP

Main writings

Life of Augustus text and trans. with intro. and notes, Jane Bellemore (Bristol: Bristol Classical Press, 1984).

Reading

Bowersock, G. W.: *Augustus and the Greek World* (Oxford: Oxford University Press, 1965).

Niebuhr, Barthold Georg (b.1776, d.1831) Son of Carsten Niebuhr, the noted Danish traveller, Niebuhr was born in Copenhagen, and studied at Kiel and Edinburgh. He joined the civil service first of Denmark and subsequently of Prussia. In 1816–23 he had an unhappy time as Prussian ambassador to the papal court in Rome. He returned to Bonn, where he lectured and published on a wide range of subjects. In 1810 as a member of the Academy he gave a famous series of lectures at the newly founded university of Berlin. From these lectures came his *History of Rome*, a landmark in the development of critical historiography. Niebuhr was extremely sceptical of the historical tradition about early Rome, particularly as found in LIVY. Much of it, according to Niebuhr, was based upon the 'carmina' (lays) which the Elder Cato claimed had been sung at feasts to extol the supposed achievements of the ancestors of the great aristocratic families of Rome. Although Niebuhr only became aware of it after he had published, this theory had already been suggested by the Dutch scholar, Perizònius (1651–1715). By application of logic and source criticism Niebuhr sought 'to place tradition on its proper footing and demonstrate its real dignity'. JJP

Main publications

(Published by Walton & Maberly, London.)
The History of Rome (1811–12, 2nd edn 1827–30) trans. J. C. Hare and C. Thirwall (1855); *Lectures on the History of Rome*, 3rd edn ed. L. Schmitz (1853).

Reading

Momigliano A.: G. C. Lewis, Niebuhr e la critica delle fonti. *Rivista Storica Italiana* 64 (1952) 208ff.
——: Perizonius, Niebuhr and the character of the early roman tradition. *Journal of Roman Studies* 47 (1957) 104ff.

North, Douglass Cecil (b.1920) A leading proponent of CLIOMETRICS, the quantitative and analytical approach to economic history. North analysed in his first book the impact of international and interregional forces upon the development of the US economy between 1790 and 1860. Subsequent books have dealt with the causes and consequences of institutional change, the importance of the allocation of property rights, and the analysis of transactions costs. North received his doctorate from the University of California in 1952. He taught at the University of Washington from 1950 to 1983, when he was appointed Henry R. Luce professor of law and liberty at Washington University (St Louis). He has been president of the Economic History Association (1972–3) and the Western Economic Association (1975–6). SLE

Main publications

The Economic Growth of the United States, 1790–1860. (Englewood Cliffs, NJ: Prentice-Hall, 1961);

with Lance E. Davis, *Institutional Change and American Economic Growth* (Cambridge: Cambridge University Press, 1971); with Robert P. Thomas, *The Rise of the Western World: a New Economic History* (Cambridge University Press, 1973); *Structure and Change in Economic History* (New York: Norton, 1981).

numismatic history Numismatics may be loosely defined as the study of coins and medals, coins being metallic objects used as currency and medals similar but usually more elaborate objects made for commemorative or presentation purposes. The latter originated in Renaissance Italy and because of their artistic qualities and historical interest were collected and studied almost from the first, so that what are still major reference books, such as the huge monographs of G. van Loon (1723–31) and F. van Mieris (1732–5) on the medals of the Low Countries, date from the eighteenth century. Coins were first studied in the fourteenth century, one of the earliest known collectors being Petrarch (d. 1374). These were initially Roman coins, which independently of their beauty and historical interest were recognized as useful for identifying ancient statues and other works of art. The earliest monograph on a medieval series was one of Erasmus van Houwelingen on the coins of the counts of Holland (1597). French coins were studied in the light of archival material in F. le Blanc's *Traité historique des monnoyes de France* (1690), a work still useful to the modern scholar. The serious study of Greek coins did not begin until the eighteenth century, when they first became available to western scholars.

Numismatic scholarship took an enormous leap forward in the 1830s and 1840s, decades which saw the foundation of national numismatic societies in France, England and Belgium, bringing together scholars of similar interests to exchange information and ideas, and the establishment of the major numismatic periodicals, the *Numismatic Chronicle* (1838, preceded 1836–8 by the *Numismatic Journal*), the *Revue numismatique* (1838), and the *Revue belge de numismatique* (1842). Other countries followed suit in the course of the nineteenth century: Austria with the *Numis-*

matische Zeitschrift in 1870; Germany (Berlin) with the *Zeitschrift für Numismatik* in 1874 — this had had predecessors at Weissensee, Hanover, Leipzig, Berlin and elsewhere — and Italy with the *Rivista di numismatica* in 1888.

Numismatic studies in the nineteenth century were still mainly devoted to the collection of material and its proper classification. Since only occasional coin series before the seventeenth century are dated, this was largely done in the light of their stylistic evolution. The outstanding figures were, for antiquity, the eighteenth century Austrian Joseph Eckhel (1737–98), and for the middle ages, the Polish scholar Joachim LELEWEL (1786–1861) who spent the last three decades of his life as an exile in Brussels and published most of his major works in French. Stylistic criteria, in which there is often a strong subjective element, were in due course largely superseded by detailed iconographic and epigraphic studies. These identified die-linkages and interpreted their significance, and in favourable circumstances allowed scholars to trace the wearing out of the dies with which the coins were struck and even that of the punches used in their manufacture. Another important line of study is that of coin finds and hoards, which help to define the areas over which particular coins circulated and over what period, and in the case of hoards contribute greatly to chronology. In recent decades the study of metallic content has come to the fore, for modern methods of non-destructive analysis provide evidence for changes in value (debasement, inflation) and exceptionally can be used to identify sources of metal.   PG

Reading

Babelon, J.: *Traité des monnaies grecques et romaines, 1ere partie: Théorie et doctrine* (Paris, 1901) coll. 66–325.

Clain-Stefanelli, E. E.: *Numismatics: an ancient science. A survey of its history* (Washington DC: Government Printing Office, 1965) repub. in *Bulletin 229, Paper 32* (Washington: Smithsonian Museum/United States National Museums, 1970).

Engel, A. and Serrure, R.: *Traité de numismatique du moyen âge*, I (Paris: 1891) pp. i-xxx.

O

O'Gorman y O'Gorman, Edmundo
(b.1906) After ten years of successfully
practising law, and graduate work in philosophy, Edmundo O'Gorman chose to dedicate
himself to history. He received a doctorate
from the Universidad Nacional Autónoma de
México in 1939 and became one of its leading
professors and scholars. After many years'
work in the Archivo General de la Nación,
in Mexico City, he has retrieved, edited and
meticulously annotated many of Mexico's (indeed many of America's and Europe's) neglected, key documents, publishing most of
them in the *Boletín del Archivo General de la
Nación.*

O'Gorman studied under the exiled Spanish philosopher José Gaos, whose influence
proved lasting, in the years when Spanish
intellectuals who had fled Franco's regime
stimulated a Mexican cultural renewal. They,
and O'Gorman's generation of scholars, rejected the neo-positivist outlook they found
prevailing among writers on Mexican history.
O'Gorman then declared himself a historicist
and continues to present himself as an anti-
essentialist in his approach to history. He rejects predetermination in all historical process.
True to this perspective, his major and recurrent thrust has been to challenge the traditional
point of view embodied in the statement
'Christopher Columbus discovered America'.
Not so, he continues to argue; rather, America
is an invention of European culture.

O'Gorman has taken issue with venerable
works and official history to the point of becoming the established *enfant terrible* of historical studies in Mexico. He sees history as a
revelation, an insight that comes to the his-

torian after long and rigorous research. His
work combines densely-reasoned argument
with creative wide-ranging statement. Evident
in it is his masterful use of language and
knowledge of classical literature, as well as the
lasting influence of his legal background and
philosophical training. It also attests to a fertile
interaction with his country's more recent past
and with its intellectual traditions. Rejecting
positivism, he outdoes its proponents in his
respect for the power of rational and imaginative interpretation. O'Gorman's latest work,
Destierro de Sombras, discusses, the origin of
one of Mexico's remarkable features: its profound devotion to Our Lady of Guadalupe.
Not since the famous nineteenth-century
scholar Joaquín García Icazbalceta, has any
historian dared to point out the lack of historical evidence regarding events alleged to
have occurred in 1531. As O'Gorman's title
suggests, his research attempts to dispel the
dark areas of the venerable Guadalupe tradition in the hope of clarifying its enduring
value to México, explaining its existence as the
product of ordinary human deeds in the 1550s,
and not as a 1531 'miracle'. That it was
accomplished with the utmost respect for a
national cherished tradition, without compro-
mising rigorous scholarship, is one of its many
contributions to the vast Guadalupe historiography.

In craftsmanship, and in attention to archival sources, O'Gorman has set standards
widely acknowledged by students of Mexican
history, to whom he has given a sense of
importance by repeated polemics. He has
argued with Lewis Hanke against a too beneficent evaluation of the personality and ideas of

Bartolomé de Las Casas. He has criticized Silvio Zavala for over-emphasis on documents. He has pressed his insistence with Marcel Bataillon on the Invention of America. He has taken issue with Jacques Lafaye and Georges Baudot over their peculiar way of using sources.

O'Gorman's works include an impressive list of publications which introduce, translate, review, or clarify classical historiographical works by, among others, José de Acosta, Francisco Cervantes de Salazar, José Servando Teresa de Mier, Gonzalo Fernández de Oviedo, Christopher Columbus, Fray Bartolomé de Las Casas, Fray Toribio de Benavente (Motolinía), and Fernando de Alva Ixtlilxochitl. He has also translated into Spanish works of Adam Smith, David Hume, John Locke, R. G. Collingwood, John Neville Figgis, and others.

O'Gorman has received many awards and prizes in Mexico and elsewhere (Premio Nacional de Humanidades, 1974; Premio Universidad Humanidades, 1986). He is currently president of the Academia Nacional de la Historia and professor emeritus of the Universidad Nacional Autónoma de Mexico.

PKL/GJC

Main publications

Breue Historia de las Divisiones Territoriales de México (México D. F.: Editorial Polis, 1937); *Crisis y Porvenir de la Ciencia Histórica* (México D. F.: Imprenta Universitaria, 1947); *La idea del descubrimiento de América* (México: Centro de Estudios Filosoficos, 1951); *La invención de América* (México D. F.: Fondo de Cultura Económica, 1958) [English editions: Bloomington: Indiana University Press, 1961]; *La supervivencia politica novohispana* (México D. F.: Fundación Cultural de Condumex, 1969); *Meditaciones sobre el criollismo* (México D. F.: Centro de Estudios de Historia de México, 1970); *México, el trauma de su historia* (México D. F.: Universidad Nacional Autónoma de México, 1977); *El Heterodoxo Guadalupano* 3 vols (México D. F.: Universidad Nacional Autónoma de México, 1981); La incógnita de la llamada. In *Historia de los Indios de la Nueva España* atribuida a Fray Toribio de Motolinia (México D. F.: Fondo de Cultura Economica, 1982); *DeStierro de Sombras* (México D.F.: Universidad Nacional Autónoma de México, 1987).

Reading

Ortega y Medina J. ed: *Conciencia y autenticidad historica* (México D. F.: Centro de Estudios de Historia de México, 1968).

Discursos en el homenaje a Edmundo O'Gorman en su septuagesimo anniversario (México D. F.: Centro de Estudios de Historia de México, 1977). *La obra de Edmundo O'Gorman* (Mexico: Universidad Nacional Autónoma de México, 1978).

Ogot, Bethwell Allan (b.1929) Born in Gem, western Kenya, Ogot was the son of a teacher. He was educated at local schools and then at Makerere University College, the University of St Andrew's and the School of Oriental and African Studies, London. After receiving his doctorate in 1965 from London, Ogot became chairman of the department of history at the University of Nairobi, a post he held until 1975. In 1966 he founded the Historical Association of Kenya and has served as its chairman since then. Ogot is revered as the father of Kenyan historiography, and has been chairman of the International Scientific Committee steering UNESCO's General History of Africa project.

Ogot's own research moved beyond the orthodox historical training he received in East Africa to the collection and analysis of oral traditions, linguistic materials, and songs. Indeed, he was a pioneer in the use of oral traditions in the reconstruction of the past of a people, the Luo of eastern Africa. He is well known for his enthusiasm for unconventional work in social and cultural history such as the biography of an obscure individual, the close study of a breakaway church, the social history of jiggers, or the collection of farm-workers' songs.

Ogot has frequently found himself called upon to direct major institutions in Kenya, including both the International Louis Leakey Memorial Institute of African Prehistory and Kenya Telecoms, tasks which he has undertaken without sacrificing his intense commitment to researching and teaching the history of Africa. He continues to edit the *Hadith* series of publications of the Historical Association of Kenya.

DWC

Main publications

History of the Southern Luo: Migration and Settlement (Nairobi: East African Publishing House, 1967); *War and Society in Africa* (London: Cass, 1972); *Zamani: A Survey of East African History* (Nairobi:

Longman, 1974); *Kenya in the 19th Century* (Nairobi: Bookwise, 1985).

Oliver, Roland (b.1923)   Born in Srinigar, Kashmir and educated at King's College, Cambridge, Oliver has been a central figure in the establishment of African historical studies. Professor of African history in the University of London since 1963, he was on the staff of the School of Oriental and African Studies, London, from 1948 until his retirement in 1986. Under his direction the SOAS African History Seminar was the premier setting in the world for the presentation of new work on Africa's past. With J. D. Fage Oliver founded the *Journal of African History*; he conceived and was the general editor of the eight-volume *Cambridge History of Africa* and since 1981 has been president of the British Institute in Eastern Africa.

Oliver's first publications focused on the early phase of the European 'scramble for Africa' and drew attention to the ways in which local forces and events reshaped the imperial mission. He directed students and colleagues to local sources, including the oral tradition. To fill the immense gaps in the knowledge of precolonial and colonial periods, Oliver has actively promoted the integration of archaeology and linguistics in the study of Africa's past. Since the early 1960s he has pursued an interest in broad population movements and economic and cultural change over the past three millennia in the region now known as Bantu Africa. Through a series of seminal articles and the supervision of doctoral dissertations, Oliver defined a large, multi-disciplinary programme of research on the Iron Age in Africa, the questions posed being taken up by scholars in Africa, Europe, and North America.   DWC

Main publications

The Missionary Factor in Africa (London: Longmans, Green, 1952); *Sir Harry Johnston and the Scramble for Africa* (London: Chatto & Windus, 1957); with J. D. Fage, *A Short History of Africa* (Harmondsworth: Penguin, 1962); with A. Atmore, *Africa Since 1800* (Cambridge: Cambridge University Press, 1972); with B. M. Fagan, *Africa in the Iron Age* (Cambridge University Press, 1975); with A. Atmore. *The African Middle Ages* (Cambridge University Press, 1981).

Oman, Charles William Chadwick (b.1860, d.1946)   Born in India, educated at Winchester and New College, Oxford, Oman was elected a fellow of All Souls College in 1883 and remained a fellow until his death. From 1905 to 1945 he was also Chichele professor of modern history. He was editor of the Methuen *History of England*. He complained that college tutors did not send undergraduates to his lectures, and indeed the Oxford School of History ignored him. This was partly because his history was narrative, and partly because his range was so wide (through ancient Greek, Roman and medieval history to the nineteenth century) that the dons did not believe he could be a 'real scholar'. This was a mistake, because he was a man of great learning and intelligence, and in his medieval works he sometimes expressed views which, as in his *England before the Norman Conquest* (1910), were out of favour when he wrote them but have since become fashionable. Oman's *Art of War in the Middle Ages* (1884), for all its faults, remained the only work available in English for about 90 years, while *A History of the Peninsular War* in 7 volumes (1902–30) was a major achievement by any standard. None the less the fact that he represented the university in parliament (as a Conservative) from 1919 to 1935, and enjoyed it, only served to confirm those outside All Souls that he was not a serious historian. He was knighted in 1920.

RHCD

Main publications

History of Greece (London: Rivingtons, 1890; 7th edn Longmans, Green, 1901); *The Art of War in the Middle Ages*, 2 vols, (London: Methuen, 1898; 2nd edn revised and enlarged, 1924); *The History of England from the Accession of Richard II to the Death of Richard III, 1377–1485*, vol. 4 of *The Political History of England*, ed. W. Hunt and R. L. Poole (London: Longmans, Green 1905); *England Before the Norman Conquest*, vol. 1 of *A History of England*, ed. C. W. C. Oman (London: Methuen, 1910); *The Art of War in the Sixteenth Century* (London: Methuen, 1937); *A History of the Peninsular War*, 7 vols (Oxford: Clarendon Press, 1902–30).

Reading

Oman, C. W. C.: *Memories of Victorian Oxford* (London: Methuen, 1941) [a biography].
Robertson, C. G.: Memoir. *Proceedings of the British Academy* 32 (1946) pp. 300–6.

oral history The term does not imply a novel kind of history. It describes a particular source of information about the past, distinct from the documentary sources more commonly used by historians. Yet the two are not wholly separate. Numerous medieval documentary 'sources' were not contemporary with the events they describe but were based upon accounts transmitted orally from an earlier generation.

The use of oral sources by historians in relation to a more recent era is the result of their observation of the interviewing techniques of sociologists and anthropologists. Its aim has been to extend historical knowledge in areas where documentary evidence is scarce, one-sided or non-existent.

In Europe this has led mainly to an investigation of the less literate sections of society which have not hitherto been the subject of historical writing except as observed and interpreted from outside. This type of research had an honourable antecedent in the work of T. Fisher Unwin and Jane Cobden Unwin at the beginning of the twentieth century. Their concern was to present historical issues of a social and economic character in a new light. Their method was to publish in the newspaper press letters inviting information, written or oral, from individuals who had experienced the effects of specific government policies. The result was the publication of two books, *The Hungry Forties*, dealing with the difficulties of living under protectionist legislation and the corn tax, and *The Land Hunger*, which reported the experiences of some of those who had rented or bought land, especially small holdings and allotments, and of others who had been ejected from their land without compensation. The weakness of these books was that the evidence upon which they were based, though delivered in an authentic and hitherto unheard voice, was collected in a random fashion from the whole country and was presented without any attempt to discriminate between the situation in different regions.

More recently attention has been deliberately focused upon small groups in which one source of information can be readily tested against others. Notable for its contribution in this field in Britain has been the History Workshop movement which began in the 1960s. This group of socialist historians – not all of them professionals – has drawn upon the experiences of working-class oral informants in town and country to produce, for example, Raphael Samuel's long essay on *Life and Labour in Headington Quarry, 1860–1920* and Jerry White's *Rothschild Buildings: Life in an East End Tenement Block, 1887–1920*.

The disadvantage of using oral sources in this as in other contexts is that the less recent the events or issues under investigation the greater the likelihood that the information has been changed in transmission. The alteration may have been deliberate, with the intention of achieving some objective known only to the informant, or it may have been inadvertent, having resulted from an unconscious change in attitude or emphasis on the part of the transmitter. In consequence, the study of these sources may be more revealing of the dominant ethos or motivation of a particular group than of the events the information purports to describe.

It is in the study of pre-literate societies, notably in Africa, that historians have come to rely most heavily upon oral sources since the second world war. Initially, the discovery that a number of the more centralized African states possessed orally transmitted lists of former rulers and their achievements aroused hopes of extending the knowledge of African history back for several centuries. These hopes were raised still higher when it was learnt that oral traditions were not restricted to states with a strong central government. It soon became clear, however, that although the existence of oral traditions in neighbouring states made a measure of cross-checking possible, the purpose of the traditions was not necessarily to present an account of the past acceptable to professional historians. Not only was the information contained in the traditions increasingly scarce the further back in time it went; not only was its chronology remarkably difficult to pinpoint; but the very existence of the people and events described was often difficult to substantiate.

Other disciplines – archeology and linguistics among them – were called in to verify the oral evidence, but their time-span was too wide to provide the accurate corroboration which historians needed. Even in areas where contemporary documentary evidence existed, external observers were often concerned with issues not dealt with by the oral sources. In most instances the latter were primarily intended to justify the exercise of power or the enjoyment of privileges by specific groups in the present rather than to provide an accurate record of the past.

Without entirely abandoning their earlier hopes, historians began to focus their attention upon a more recent period of history, the colonial era. Here the oral sources were more plentiful and more varied and they could be checked against each other as well as by comparison with written evidence supplied by, among others, colonial administrators. By these methods a new, African dimension has been added to the history of the later nineteenth century and the first half of the twentieth.

Once again investigators have had to be alert to note alterations which may have taken place in the course of the oral transmission of information. To recognize such alterations and to understand the reasons for them calls for an intimate knowledge of the society which has produced them – the sort of understanding which anthropologists seek to achieve through field work. Following this example a number of historians have undertaken projects in the field and not least important among those researchers have been Africans familiar with the language and culture of the societies under investigation and trained in the techniques of historical analysis. (See OGOT; OLIVER.)

Oral sources have more serious limitations for historians than do contemporary documents, but without them African initiatives and African responses to external stimuli in the pre-literate age would have to be ignored. If a more comprehensive view of recent African history is to be obtained, however, it is essential that the fruits of these researches into the history of individual societies – the oral information – should be recorded and edited in greatest detail by those who made them. Without such editing historians unfamiliar with the ethos of those societies would

be incapable of understanding the significance of the texts and still more of comparing the history of one society with that of another. A structuralist approach to oral sources would be disastrous. KI

Reading

Cohen, D. W.: *The Historical Tradition of Busoga*. (Oxford: Clarendon Press, 1972) pp. 28–69.

Hampate Ba, A.: The Living Tradition. In *General History of Africa*, vol. I, ed. J. Ki-Zerbo (Geneva: UNESCO/Heinemann, 1981) pp. 166–203.

Henige, D.: *Oral Historiography* (London: Longman, 1982).

Samuel, R., ed.: *Village Life and Labour* (London: Routledge & Kegan Paul, 1975).

Tosh, J.: *The Pursuit of History* (London: Longman, 1984) pp. 172–91.

Unwin, T. F. and J. C.: *The Land Hunger: Life under Monopoly* (London: T. Fisher Unwin, 1913).

Vansina, J.: (pub. 1961 in French) *Oral Tradition* (London: Routledge & Kegan Paul, 1965).

——: Oral Tradition and its Methodology. In *General History of Africa* , vol. I, ed. J. Ki-Zerbo (Geneva: UNESCO/Heinemann, 1981) pp. 142–165.

——: *Oral Tradition as History* (London: James Currey, Nairobi: Heinemann, 1985).

White, J.: *Rothschild Buildings: Life in an East End Tenement Block, 1887–1920* (London: Routlege & Kegan Paul, 1980).

Orderic Vitalis (b.1075, d.*c.*1142) The most remarkable chronicler of the Anglo-Norman world, Orderic was born in Shropshire on 16 February 1075, the son of an English mother and a French priest in the household of Earl Roger of Montgomery. At the age of ten he was sent as a child oblate to become a Benedictine monk in the Norman abbey of Saint-Évroult, then at the height of its fame as a centre of religion and learning. There he spent the remainder of his life, apart from visits to other monastic houses including Crowland, Worcester and Cluny, and attendance at the 1118 Council of Rheims.

Orderic's interest in history was stimulated by the teaching of his master, John of Rheims, by his reading of the Bible, and by his copying of other historical works in the scriptorium – he was a skilled calligrapher. His principal work, the *Ecclesiastical History*, combined a chronicle from the birth of Christ with a history of his own day, which filled over three-quarters of its thirteen books. Modelled to some extent on the work of EUSEBIUS and BEDE, and making full use of the annals and Norman histories in the library of his abbey, it was nevertheless an intensely personal work, shaped by the sources for the history of great Norman churches and families that were available to him. The patrons of Saint-Évroult were Norman magnates and knights, who placed their sons in the abbey as monks, themselves visited the cloister, and were remembered in the prayers of the community. From them, no less than from visiting abbots and prelates, Orderic learned of events in places as far away as Jerusalem, Sicily, Spain and Scotland.

Orderic's reputation as a reliable historian at one time suffered because long passages from his work, including legends and imaginary speeches, were incorporated in the narrative history of E. A. FREEMAN as if they had been literally true. They must be seen as products of the historical conventions of the twelfth century, which were strongly influenced by rhetoric and oral poetry. Accurate information was mixed with stories embroidered in *chansons de geste*. Moreover, after the first two books Orderic wrote, as Bede had done, thematically rather than strictly chronologically. His history is an unrivalled source for the way of life of the members of the Norman knightly class, which describes their battle tactics no less than their religious aspirations. His mixed birth and knowledge of both England and Normandy enabled him to chart the first seventy-five years of Norman rule in England with understanding of both sides. Character sketches of individual rulers, prelates, and more humble men and women are shrewd and vivid. His work enables us to trace the growth of new concepts, such as the idea of a holy war in the gradual Christian expansion into Spain and the Holy Land before the word 'crusade' had been coined. Among the outstanding passages in his history are the account of the reign of William the Conqueror, given in an imaginary death-bed speech, a treatise on the new monastic orders, the description of the wreck of the *White Ship*, the narrative of a vision of 'Hellequin's

hunt' told him by a parish priest, and the Epilogue in which he recorded his own early life. MMC

Main writings

Orderici Vitalis Ecclesiasticae Historiae Libri tredecim, ed. A. Le Prévost, assisted by L. Delisle, 5 vols (Paris: Société de l'histoire de France, 1838–55); *The Ecclesiastical History of Orderic Vitalis*, ed. and trans. M. Chibnall, 6 vols (Oxford: Oxford University Press, 1968–80).

Reading

Chibnall, M.: *The World of Orderic Vitalis* (Oxford: Oxford University Press, 1984).
Wolter, H.: *Ordericus Vitalis* (Wiesbaden: Franz Steiner, 1955).

Orosius (*fl.* early fifth century AD)   A native of Spain, possibly from Bracara (now Braga in Portugal), Orosius became a follower of St Augustine and St Jerome. His *History against the Pagans*, a seven-book history of the world down to his own day, was designed to demonstrate Augustine's contention that disasters had afflicted men at all times and therefore the current collapse of the Roman empire in the west could not be ascribed to its conversion to Christianity, as pagan historians claimed. Orosius was enormously popular in the middle ages. A version of his work in Old English survives, composed in the time of King Alfred. JJP

Main writings

The Seven Books of the History against the Pagans, trans. R. J. Deferrari (Washington: Catholic University of America Press, 1964).

Reading

Fabbrini, F.: *Paolo Orosio uno storico* (Rome: Edizione di Storia e Lettere, 1979).

Osgood, Herbert Levi (b.1855, d.1918) Born to a yeoman family of puritan stock at Canton, Maine, Osgood was educated at home, village academy and parsonage, and at the Congregational citadel of Amherst College, where he was converted to the new Germanic history by John W. Burgess. The social religion of Osgood's forebears combined with the scientific ethos of the Rankean system to colour and shape all of Osgood's work. In the intervals of secondary school teaching, Osgood studied at Amherst, Yale, Berlin, Columbia and (it was his real alma mater) the Public Record Office. Called thence to Columbia by Burgess in 1896, Osgood helped found the department of history and died in harness in 1918, having almost completed his life work on the political and administrative history of the American colonies from English discovery to the peace of Paris.

Osgood's analysis of 'English institutions, worked by Englishmen, but under new and strange conditions' in America filled seven sizeable volumes. Three were devoted to the seventeenth century, two subtitled 'Self-Government,' the third 'Imperial Control'. Their author concluded that the transition from corporate and proprietary colonies to royal provinces during the restoration was 'the most significant transition in American history previous to the colonial revolt'. Henceforward, the conflict of imperial executives with provincial legislators was 'the central theme of our colonial history'. Because that conflict took its impetus and its issues from the 'intercolonial' wars (1689–1763), Osgood made them the skeletal structure of his four volumes on the eighteenth century. Peacetimes Osgood occupied with chapters on bureaucracy and commerce, Indian relations and the frontier, religious institutions and awakening, European diplomacy and immigration.

Osgood's topical range was greater than is usually recalled, his judgements more penetrating, his Christian idealism more pervasive, and his manuscript scholarship (supported by his students – A. M. Schelesinger Sr, G. L. Beer, W. R. Shepherd, A. C. Flick, S. M. Kingsbury, C. A. Beard, and D. R. Fox, to name only those more famous than their master) more profound. Today's scholars ignore Osgood at the risk of repeating him.

SSW

Main publications

The American Colonies in the Seventeenth Century (New York: Columbia University Press, 1904, 1930; Gloucester, Mass.; Peter Smith, 1957); *The American Colonies In The Eighteenth Century* Columbia University Press, 1924; Peter Smith, 1958).

Reading

Fox, Dixon Ryan: *Herbert Levi Osgood. An American Scholar* (New York: Columbia University Press, 1924).

Ostrogorsky, George (b.1902, d.1976) Born and educated in St Petersburg, Ostrogorsky left Russia with his family after the 1917 revolution. From 1921 to 1924 he read philosophy and then classical archaeology at the University of Heidelberg, where Percy Schramm encouraged him towards Byzantium. Ostrogorsky's Heidelberg thesis of 1925, on *Die ländliche Steuergemeinde des Byzantinisches Reiches im X. Jahrhundert*, established an interest and approach to Byzantine institutions which he developed throughout his life. Study in Paris in 1924–5 brought him into contact with Charles DIEHL, Gabriel Millet and Germaine Rouillard. He began teaching the history of the Byzantine state in the University of Breslau (now Wrocław) in 1928. In 1933 he moved to the chair of Byzantinology at Belgrade University, becoming active in the Serbian Academy after the hiatus of the war. In 1948 he founded the Byzantine Institute in Belgrade and in 1951 its *Zbornik Radova*, which he directed until his death. His contributions to Yugoslav Byzantine Studies include his edition of the *Fontes Byzantini historiam populorum Jugoslaviae spectantes* (1955–71) and were acknowledged when the Twelfth International Byzantine Congress met at Ohrid in 1961.

Ostrogorsky's influence is, however, wider than this might imply. Basically it lies in the dissemination of two works which became standard, particularly among western medieval historians. The first, on the Byzantine state, was published in Munich in 1940; translated into English in 1955, it underwent several revisions. This study of Byzantine political institutions remains a basic text which (although showing its age) has not been superseded. The second work, deriving from his doctorate, developed what may be termed the 'Ostrogorsky thesis', most fully expressed in his study of the Byzantine *pronoia* (roughly, 'fief') of 1951, which Henri Grégoire challengingly entitled '*Féodalité*' in his translation of 1954. It deals with the relationship of the Byzantine army, fisc, land and peasant, and argues that between the tenth and twelfth centuries great holders of land in *pronoia* interposed themselves between the state and its yeoman militia. It is a measure of the attraction of this thesis that while much has since been revised by Byzantinists (including Ostrogorsky himself), none has produced a convincing alternative synthesis, which must inevitably be more complex. On the state and Byzantine 'feudalism' one must still start with Ostrogorsky.

In his choice of topics and approach, Ostrogorsky was curiously unaffected by the prevailing ideologies of the countries in which he worked. Personally unassuming, a thoughtful host and greatly respected teacher, there were times when he had to walk warily. It was largely by coincidence that he shared contemporary Marxist interests. In fact Ostrogorsky regarded himself, and only just at second hand, as the successor of St Petersburg Byzantinists such as V. G. Vasilievsky and Theodore Uspensky, who were touched by the last, pre-revolutionary, generation of Russian social and economic historians. In English terms he was for Yugoslavia and Byzantine Studies something of a Paul VINOGRADOFF.

AAMB

Main publications

Geschichte des Byzantinischen Staates (Munich: 1940) trans. J. M. Hussey, *History of the Byzantine State* (Oxford: Blackwell, 1956; 1968); *Pronija* (Belgrade: 1951) French trans. Henri Grégoire, *Pour l'Histoire de la féodalité byzantine* (Brussels: Institut de Philologie et d'Histoire Orientales et Slaves, *Corpus Bruxellense Historiae Byzantinae Subsidia* I, 1954); revised edition, *Quelques problèmes de la paysannerie byzantine* (Brussels; Institut de Philologie et d'Histoire Orientales et Slaves, *Corpus Bruxellense Historiae Byzantinae Subsidia* II, 1956); about 180 other works reprinted, 6 vols, ed. Sabrana Dela (Belgrade: 1969).

Reading

Radojčić, Borislav: Georges Ostrogorsky (1902–1976).
Byzantina, 9 (1977) [an appreciation].
Zbornik Radova Vizantoloshkog Instituta 17 (1976) [an appreciation].

P

Palacký, František (b.1798, d.1876) The greatest of Czech historians and one of the most important of all historian-politicians, Palacký came from a humble background in eastern Moravia, and from the small Protestant minority which had long nourished a special grievance against the Austrian state. Educated at Protestant schools in nearby Hungary, he went to Bohemia only in 1823, but was soon established there as archivist to the patriotic noble family of Sternberg, historiographer to the Bohemian Estates, and editor (1827–38) of the journal of the newly founded National Museum, *Časopis Českého Muzea*. Palacký felt a strong romantic commitment to the Bohemian past as that of a peace-loving and democratic Slavonic people, the Czechs, progressively usurped by a German ruling class. In this spirit he conceived his life-work, a history of Bohemia which he completed only to 1526, and which appeared in parallel German and Czech editions with a subtle but significant difference in title. His conception of Hussitism, as a revolutionary national and progressive cause, grew particularly influential.

Meanwhile Palacký became involved with the contemporary political demands of the Czechs, as leader of the national movement which grew up from the 1840s. His famous rebuttal of the claims of the Frankfurt parliament, his proposals for the federal reconstruction of the Monarchy, and his bitter attacks on the compromise with Hungary in the 1860s were always underpinned by Palacky's historical learning ('We were before Austria: we shall be after her too!'). A member of the Austrian Academy of Sciences and of the upper house of the Austrian parliament from their establishment in 1847 and 1861 respectively, Palacký was a major and serious scholar, whose work remains fundamental to the study of medieval Bohemia, although he was sometimes credulous. His intellectual legacy to the Czechs, reformulated (as an ethical scheme) by T. G. Masaryk and (for the outside world) by DENIS, remained overwhelmingly important at least until the 1930s.   RJWE

Main publications

Würdigung der alten böhmischen Geschichtsschreiber (An assessment of the old Bohemian chroniclers) (Prague: 1830); *Geschichte von Böhmen* (History of Bohemia) 5 vols (Prague: 1836–67); *Dějiny národu českého v Čechách a v Moravě* (History of the Czech nation in Bohemia and Moravia) 5 vols (Prague: 1848–60); *Spisy drobné* (Occasional writings) 3 vols (Prague; 1898–1903); *Korrespondence a zápisky* (Correspondence and notes) ed. V. J. Nováček, 3 vols (Prague: 1898–1911); *Dílo* (Works) ed. J. Charvát, 4 vols (Prague: 1941–5).

Reading

Plaschka, R. G.: *Von Palacký bis Pekař* (From Palacký to Pekař) (Graz/Cologne: Wiener Archiv für Geschichte des Slawentums und Osteuropas, 1955).

Wurzbach, C. von: *Biographisches Lexikon des Kaiserthums Österreich* (Biographical lexicon of the Austrian empire) 21 (1870) 179–93.

Zacek, J. F.: *Palacký: the Historian as Scholar and Nationalist* (The Hague: Mouton, 1970).

palaeography and diplomatic The study of ancient handwriting, palaeography, and of the forms of documents, diplomatic, is essential to the use of manuscript sources, and has provided techniques upon which much historical scholarship now depends. Palaeography is required for the dating and authentication of original manuscripts, while diplomatic is essential for the assessment of records that survive only in copies. This is because a large part of diplomatic is concerned with the forms of words used for various transactions at different dates, the correct style of rulers and dignitaries, and the proper forms of dating clauses.

In both the study and its objects, Britain has had strong but intermittent connections with continental Europe. Writing was brought to England by missionaries from Rome in the late sixth century and was applied, exceptionally, not only to the Latin texts of the church but also to the Anglo-Saxon vernacular. A distinctive insular hand developed, which included elements of Celtic scripts. It was exported again to the Continent in the eighth century, by the missionary efforts of the English church, and then maintained some ground at home against the rise of the Carolingian minuscule, the reformed script which established clerical literacy in western Europe, and later inspired the typefaces Humanist italic and Times Roman.

The Norman Conquest brought a new infusion of continental European influences, and within a few generations extinguished the vernacular literary tradition. The church elaborated its liturgy, its administration, and a system of education which depended upon supplies not only of biblical and patristic texts, but also of secondary literature. Kings borrowed men and skills from the church, and secular administration devised its own styles of handwriting and forms which might differ from office to office, as did those of the Chancery and Exchequer in England. The decoration of liturgical manuscripts established the art of the illuminator and drew on a variety of native and exotic traditions.

Higher education in the middle ages is quite well documented, but we know little about the teaching of writing and its specialisms, although we can suppose apprenticeship and patronage to have been dominant. Until the invention of printing, and for some time afterwards, such accomplishments were practical, and hardly at all retrospective. Both secular and ecclesiastical institutions were de-veloped and defined with reference to the past through documentary evidence, but without a sense that all things, including handwriting, change with time. The increasingly angular forms of fifteenth-century English hands are strikingly different from the rounded shapes current in the thirteenth and early fourteenth centuries, but contemporaries showed little consciousness of the fact. There was practically no critical awareness of past ages, except for an occasional glance at the oddities of Anglo-Saxon, and such rare manifestations as the careful transcription of the eleventh-century script of Domesday Book in official exemplifications of its text.

That critical sense of the past emerged in the Renaissance and the Reformation of the church. The rebirth of classical Latin, together with the effects of printing in the vernaculars, brought the end of medieval Latin as a living language, and also changes in handwriting which were not all improvements. The English Chancery hand slowly fossilized in its late medieval forms, whilst ordinary business was recorded in a florid cursive. Changes in administrative practices, themselves related in part to the cheapness and abundance of paper, left medieval documents redundant and obscure. They were saved less by antiquarian sensibility, of which there was some, than by the demands of doctrinal controversy or by inertia. John Leland (c.1506–1552) surveyed the monastic libraries, on the eve of the Dissolution, in the hope of constructing a royal historical library. Matthew Parker (1504–1575) collected manuscripts to illustrate the viability and vitality of the English church. He and his secretary John Josselyn (1529–1603) were the first editors, perhaps strictly the first students, of Anglo-Saxon texts. They were followed closely by Sir Robert Bruce Cotton (1571–1631), a ruthless collector much involved in the politics of his own day, who raided public offices and private libraries to amass the Cottonian manuscripts.

During the seventeenth century historical technique advanced in two ways. Antiquaries like Sir William Dugdale (1605–1686) developed genealogical and topographical studies, which in time produced the classic county histories (see GENEALOGY). After the

315

Restoration a remarkable series of scholars established the critical study of sources. The greatest were probably Humphrey Wanley (1672–1726), the earl of Oxford's librarian, and Thomas MADOX (1666–1727), a clerk in the Augmentation Office, whose *History of the Exchequer* (1711) is the foundation of all subsequent work on medieval English administration, and whose *Formulare Anglicanum* (1702) offered historians of English law and institutions what Jean MABILLON's *De re diplomatica* (1702) gave European historiography at large. See MAURISTS, MURATORI, and NATIONAL RECORD SOCIETIES.

In all that work, despite the presence of Thomas Hearne (1678–1735) in Oxford, the universities played only an incidental part. Private endeavour, aristocratic patronage, and local patriotism were more powerful forces throughout the eighteenth century. The printing of Domesday Book for parliament in 1783 made its text available for study, and led on, through six Royal Commissions on the Public Records (1800–37), to the establishment of the Public Record Office in 1838, and the beginnings of a systematic survey of the riches of medieval administrative records. By that time Sir Frederick Madden (1801–73), who had worked on Anglo-Saxon manuscripts in his twenties, including the texts of Caedmon and the unique manuscript of *Beowulf*, was head of the department of manuscripts at the British Museum, where his successor, Sir Edward Bond (1815–1898) became principal librarian in 1878. Bond, with his successor Sir Edward Maunde Thompson, founded the Paleographical Society in 1873, to produce accurate facsimiles by photography. The Society, refounded in 1903 as the New Palaeographical Society, advanced the study of palaeography as a skill which any serious student of history might be expected to acquire.

The contribution of exceptionally gifted individuals remained central to the subject, in which what seems an instinctive sense ranks with minute observation and a patient application to detail. Maunde Thompson himself, like Bond and Madden, acquired much of his knowledge from work on the Class Catalogue of manuscripts in the British Museum, and his *Manual of Greek and Latin Palaeography* (1912)

is still the principal work in English. Montague Rhodes James (1862–1936) began his manuscript studies as a boy at Eton, and advanced them in the rich collections of Cambridge colleges. His range extended over all Europe, and he was as much a biblical scholar as a palaeographer and codicologist. His own handwriting was impenetrable, and some of his work is subject to correction in detail, but his general ability as an interpreter of manuscripts is unexcelled.

The principal exponents of palaeography since M. R. James's day have been the American scholar E. A. Lowe (1879–1969), the editor of the *Codices Latini Antiquiores*, who studied at Munich with Ludwig Traube's pupils, and Neil Ripley Ker (1908–1982) who succeeded Lowe as lecturer and reader at Oxford. Whilst palaeography remains a highly individual skill, diplomatic has advanced more broadly with the study of medieval institutions. Edmund Bishop (1846–1917) turned his palaeographical talents to liturgical studies. Hubert Hall (1857–1944) drew upon the public records for *Studies in English Official Historical Documents* (1908) and his *Formula Book of English Official Historical Documents* (1908–9). Neil Ker's friend and contemporary, Richard William Hunt (1908–1979), keeper of western manuscripts in the Bodleian Library, made distinguished contributions to both subjects.

Throughout this century the proliferation of record publishing societies and refined photographic techniques have made texts of all kinds available for comparative studies. With material more abundant than ever, much remains to be done on the work of individual scribes, on the teaching of handwriting and the diffusion of styles, on the use of formularies in the middle ages, and on the diplomatic of administrative records. The interaction of manuscript and print is also a relatively neglected subject. For those and other reasons diplomatic, itself in close association with palaeography, seems likely to hold its place in historical studies.   GHM

Reading

(Published by Clarendon Press, Oxford, unless otherwise stated.)

Bullough, R. A. and Storey, R. L. eds: *The Study of Medieval Records: Essays in Honour of Kathleen Major* (1971).
Cheney, C. R.: *Medieval Texts and Studies* (1973).
Denholm-Young, N.: *Handwriting in England and Wales* (Cardiff: University of Wales Press, 1954).
Douglas, D. C.: *English Scholars* (London: Cape, 1939).
Kitching, C. J.: Record publishing in England and Wales, 1957–1982, *Archives: Journal of the British Records Association* 17.73 (1985) 38–46.
Pfaff, R. W.: *Montague Rhodes James* (London: Scolar Press, 1980).
Thompson, E. Maunde: *Introduction to Greek and Latin Palaeography* (1912).

Palgrave, Francis (b.1788, d.1861) The first deputy keeper of the Public Records. Palgrave was born in London, the son of Meyer Cohen, a stockbroker. He became an Anglican, an act long remembered against him, on his marriage in 1823 to a daughter of Dawson Turner, the Norfolk antiquary, and changed his name to Palgrave. In 1826 he was called to the Bar and specialized in pedigree cases. He also became an experienced editor of medieval texts. Palgrave's knighthood in 1832 probably owed as much to his reformist sympathies as to his scholarship, but his historical acumen and forensic experience made him generally useful to the administration. He was made a member of the Municipal Corporations Commission, and in 1834 keeper of the records, predominantly those of the ancient Exchequer, stored in the Chapter House at Westminster. In 1836 he published *The Ancient Kalendars and Inventories of the Exchequer*. When the Public Record Office Act (1 & 2 Vict., *c*.94) emerged in 1838 from a prolonged debate Palgrave was appointed deputy keeper, answerable to the Master of the Rolls, Lord Langdale.

The new Office was established on the Rolls estate in Chancery Lane, and Palgrave's first task was to transfer records from some 50 repositories, including Westminster and the Tower, to the crowded accommodation in and around the Rolls chapel. At the same time he fought for funds for a new building, which was begun in 1851 to a design by Sir James Pennethorne. Palgrave retired from office in 1861 and died in the same year.

The significance of Palgrave's career lies not only in the establishment of the Public Record Office but in his wide view of an archivist's responsibilities. Although the management of the medieval records took up much of his energy, he was aware from the beginning of the importance of, and the archival problems inherent in, modern departmental papers. He was an intense, hypersensitive, and sometimes overbearing man, not the easiest of colleagues. His direction of the Office, complemented later by the work of Maxwell LYTE had a powerful effect on the development of historical scholarship.   GHM

Reading
Cantwell, J.: The 1838 Public Record Office Act and its aftermath: a new perspective. *Journal of the Society of Archivists* 7.5 (1984) 277–86.
Twenty-third Report of the Deputy Keeper of the Public Records London: HMSO, 1862.

Palmer, Robert Roswell (b.1909) Born in Chicago, Palmer graduated from the University of Chicago and taught for most of his academic career at Princeton, with intervals in the US army (1943–5), at Washington University, St Louis (1963–6), and at Yale (1969–77). He established himself as an authority on eighteenth-century France with *Catholics and Unbelievers in Eighteenth Century France* (1939) and *Twelve who Ruled* (1941), a biographical study of the 'great' Committee of Public Safety. In 1947 he published a translation of *Quatre-Vingt-Neuf* (*The Coming of the French Revolution*) by LEFEBVRE which introduced its author to the English-speaking world through his most concise and powerful work. Palmer is best known, however, for the argument that the western or 'Atlantic' world was swept by a single wave of democratic revolution in the late eighteenth century, in which aristocratic or oligarchical 'constituted bodies' were challenged by hitherto excluded groups. The thesis won support in France from Jacques GODECHOT, and was expounded at length by Palmer in his two-volume *Age of the Democratic Revolution* (I, *The Challenge*, 1959; II, *The Struggle*, 1963). It failed to persuade most other historians of the period however, who remained convinced that the French Revolution was a phenomenon of a

317

different order from the American, and that the upheavals in Geneva, Ireland, Holland, Belgium and Poland also invoked by Palmer as evidence for an Atlantic revolution were more striking for their differences than for their similarities. Nevertheless the idea stimulated much fruitful debate in the 1960s and 1970s. The two volumes of the 'Palmer thesis' were translated into German and Italian, and remain a remarkably wide-ranging survey of western political life in the late eighteenth century.   WD

Main publications

The world revolution of the West 1763–1801. *Political Science Quarterly* (1954); *The Age of the Democratic Revolution*, 2 vols (Princeton: Princeton University Press, 1959–63).

Reading

Amann, P.: *The Eighteenth Century Revolution: French or Western?* (London and New York: D. C. Heath, 1963).

Pares, Richard (b.1902, d.1958)   Eldest son of the Russian scholar Sir Bernard Pares, Richard Pares was educated at Winchester and at Balliol College, Oxford, taking a first in Literae Humaniores in 1924. His intention to follow Greats by reading modern history was cut short by election to a prize fellowship at All Souls. As a young man he was on easy terms with numerous brilliant Oxford contemporaries but was uncommitted to the excesses practised by some of them. For a time he contemplated a career in journalism but soon settled to an academic life. In the 1930s he held appointments at New College, Oxford and University College, London, and for the duration of the war he worked at the Board of Trade for which he was made CBE. From 1945 he was professor of history at Edinburgh until disabling illness forced him to resign in 1954. He returned to All Souls and spent the last four years of his life in Oxford.

Pares was an outstanding historian of the British empire of the eighteenth century, mastering the public records early in his career and later working extensively on merchants' papers. The copious notes he made served him well when visits to archives were no longer possible. Four substantial books

were the outcome, all highly skilled professional achievements. Their subject matter, however, was too specialized for a general readership and no more than marginal to the then preoccupations of most British historians. As a historian Pares was more admired than read.

Pares was aware of this. For his Ford Lectures at Oxford in 1952 he chose the more fashionable subject of George III. The book, published the following year, is still a compendium of common sense in a field intensively worked over by specialists. Pares was also a capable master of large themes as he showed in his review (reprinted in *The Historian's Business*) of Toynbee's *A Study of History*, the ten volumes of which he read in five weeks while on holiday in the Lake District. But for illness his talents and energy would have placed him in the front rank. He served his subject well as editor of the *English Historical Review* from 1939 to his death.   KGD

Main publications

War and Trade in the West Indies, 1739–1763 (Oxford: Clarendon Press, 1936); *Colonial Blockade and Neutral Rights, 1739–1763* (Clarendon Press, 1938); *A West-India Fortune* (London: Longmans, Green, 1950); *King George III and the Politicians* (Clarendon Press, 1953); *Yankees and Creoles* (Longmans, Green, 1956); *Merchants and Planters*, *Economic History Review*, Supplement 4, (Cambridge: Cambridge University Press, 1960); *The Historian's Business*, ed. R. A. and E. Humphreys (Clarendon Press, 1961).

Reading

Humphreys, R. A. and Shepperson, George: Richard Pares: a bibliography. *University of Edinburgh Gazette*, 21 (1958) 24–36.

Sutherland, Lucy S.: Introduction to *The Historian's Business* (see above).

Paris, Matthew   See ST ALBANS CHRONICLERS

Parkman, Francis (b.1823, d.1893)   A member of a prominent Boston family, Parkman graduated from Harvard in 1844 and from its Law School in 1846 though he never practised. Dogged by ill health he was often unable to produce more than six lines in a day but he drove himself to a very respectable output. After publishing *The Oregon Trail* in 1849 he turned his attention to the struggle between England and France in New World, producing eight major works. He also wrote a novel, *Vassall Morton* (1856) and a horticultural work on roses. The success of this brought him an unusual appointment to the chair of horticulture at Harvard in 1871.

Parkman was a transitional figure. He financed his own research and combined the romantic approach of Walter Scott with some of the methods of the new scientific German school. He could not have produced his work had not a previous generation, men like Jared Sparks, Lyman C. Draper, Edmund B. O'Callaghan, John G. Shea and Pierre Margry, discovered and established collections of records. Parkman's work showed little concern for economic forces and, despite personal interest in Indian tribes, little ethnological sense. Rather it reflected his patrician background and concerns that saw history as the creation of the talented and well-born. RAB

Main publications

The Oregon Trail (1849; Harmondsworth: Penguin, 1982); *Pioneers of France in the New World* (1865); *A Half-century of Conflict* (1892; New York: Collier Books, 1966).

Reading

Taylor, William R.: Francis Parkman. In *Pastmasters: Some Essays on American Historians*, ed. Marcus Cunliffe and Robin Winks (New York: Harper & Row, 1969) pp. 1–38.

Parrington, Vernon Louis (b.1871, d.1929) Parrington was a historian of literature whose reputation rests on one major work, *Main Currents in American Thought* (the first two volumes appeared in 1927 and won a Pulitzer prize; a third volume, uncompleted and less successful, was added posthumously in 1930).

Parrington was a westerner. He was born in Illinois of New England stock, but his father, a Union officer in the Civil War, took the family to Kansas while Vernon was a child. He began his studies at the College of Emporia, Kansas, and, with a Harvard degree, returned there to teach before moving on first to the University of Oklahoma and later to the University of Washington. Parrington then was a young man in Kansas at the height of the Populist movement there, but he seems to have been little affected. His interests at that time were literary and aesthetic, and the chief influences on him those of Ruskin and William Morris. Not until he moved to Washington in 1908 and met the Progressive political scientist, James Allen Smith, did Parrington begin to turn away from purely literary preoccupations and to organize his history of American thought. His work emphasized the distinctively American character of the writings he studied, but also the importance of environmental, economic, and even racial factors in determining it. The 'current' which he valued – his title might well have been in the singular, although his second volume, covering the years 1800 to 1860, gave full attention to sectional divisions – was the democratic, Jeffersonian ethos, and the struggle to advance it. Perhaps not only Morris but the unacknowledged Populists contributed to his brand of Progressivism.

Parrington was a dedicated and popular teacher, and reluctant to publish. By the time his work appeared, when he was well over 50, the Progressive movement had been nearly destroyed by a world war and a decade of prosperity. Parrington's Pulitzer prize owed much to a vigorous, attractive, and even romantic style; but his continuing success and influence owed still more to the onset of the great depression, which revived American radicalism even while strengthening American nationalism. That the advance of democracy was the main current in American thought, essentially American and giving American literature its peculiar quality, seemed plausible to many in the thirties. Parrington formed the views of a whole generation, the generation which was to create the new discipline of American Studies.

Parrington's work did not lack critics. 'A lively and aggressive patchwork of half-baked theories', wrote one. Of how many influential works could that be said! The most serious charge is that in emphasizing thought Parrington neglected style or artistry, and undervalued, therefore, not only conservatives who would not fit his scheme – though he gave them space as opponents – but also the apolitical. It was widely noticed that Poe, for example, was dismissed in a couple of pages.

PASTOR, LUDWIG VON

The partisan was often at odds with the scholar, and Parrington's work fell out of favour even as it had, in a sense, fallen into it. Even those who reject it, however, must reckon with it. The historian of American thought himself added a minor classic to the tradition he studied. AEC

Main publications

(All published by Harcourt Brace, New York.)
Main Currents in American Thought: an Interpretation of American Literature from the Beginnings to 1920. Vol. 1, *The Colonial Mind 1620–1800*, and vol. 2, *The Romantic Revolution in America 1800–1860* (1927), vol. 3, *The Beginnings of Critical Realism in America 1860–1920* [taken to 1900 only] (1930).

Reading

Eby, E. H.: Vernon Louis Parrington. In Parrington, *Main Currents*, vol. 3, pp. v–xvii.

Gabriel, Ralph H.: Vernon Louis Parrington. In *Pastmasters: some Essays on American Historians*, ed. Marcus Cunliffe and Robin W. Winks (New York: Harper & Row, 1969).

Harrison, Joseph B.: *Vernon Louis Parrington: American Scholar* (Seattle: University of Washington Chapbooks, no. 31, 1929).

Pastor, Ludwig von (b.1854, d.1928) Born at Aachen, Pastor was converted to Catholicism soon after the death of his Protestant father in 1864, and was brought up by his Catholic mother. At the gymnasium at Frankfurt he came under the influence of Johannes Janssen, whose *History of the German People*, a cultural history of Germany during the Reformation from a strongly Catholic viewpoint, Pastor later completed and edited. After studies at the universities of Louvain, Bonn, Berlin and Vienna, Pastor developed the ambition to write a *History of the Popes* to rival and counter that of the Protestant Leopold von RANKE. The completed work, which eventually ran to 40 volumes in the English edition, proved to be much more than a Catholic apologia. It did not hesitate to censure popes such as the Borgia Alexander VI and rested on a solid base of research, especially in the Vatican archives, to which he first gained access in 1879. Pastor's example and the impression he made upon the pope helped to bring about the famous opening of the archives to all scholars by Leo XIII in

1883. Unable to achieve recognition in Germany during the period of the Kulturkampf he became professor at the University of Innsbruck (1881–1901), was appointed director of the Austrian Historical Institute in Rome (1901) and Austrian ambassador to the Holy See (1920).

His monumental *History of the Popes*, from the Great Schism of 1378 to the death of Pius VI in the age of Napoleon, remains a prodigious achievement of historical stamina. It reflects the author's deep knowledge of archival materials, at Rome and further afield, which go well beyond the narrow confines of ecclesiastical history to cover the artistic and literary patronage of the popes and the topographical development of Rome, on which Pastor published several separate works. Its footnotes never cease to yield surprises, and its sustained scholarship outweighs some blindspots of interpretation, such as his dated view of Renaissance humanism. His remarkable industry and dedication are recorded in his published diaries (although to be treated with some care as a true contemporary record), which reveal him visiting libraries on his honeymoon and record his archival discoveries as well as his deep love of art galleries, museums and books. Many of his unpublished papers are in the Vatican library. AVA

Main publications

Geschichte der Päpste seit dem Ausgang des Mittelalters, 16 vols :1886–1933), English edn 40 vols (London: Routledge & Kegan Paul, 1891–1953).

Reading

Chadwick, O.: *Catholicism and History: the Opening of the Vatican Archives* (Cambridge: Cambridge University Press, 1978).

Pastor, L von: *Tagebücher, Briefe, Erinnerungen*, ed. W. Wühr (Heidelberg: F. H. Kerle Verlag, 1950) [incl. full list of his publications].

Pekař, Josef (b.1870, d.1937) The Czech historian Pekař first made his name with a penetrating critical and psychological study of Wallenstein (though this remained unknown to a wider public until the author's own German translation 40 years later) and buttressed it with critical contributions on the sources for Bohemian medieval history, and with innovatory work on the social and economic history of the seventeenth and eighteenth centuries. Pekař's evocation of life in the lordship of Kost, in the scenic Bohemian paradise where he had spent his youth, is a most telling piece of literature as well as of scholarship. Although Pekař admired PALACKÝ, he did much to revise the latter's views, and he took issue with the philosophy of history of T. G. (later president) Masaryk, seeking to rehabilitate Catholic traditions and the unfashionable baroque era. A moderate believer in Czech political claims before 1918, Pekař later moved more to the right (see SZEKFŰ in Hungary) and exercised a large influence upon Czechoslovak historical studies, editing the leading journal *Český Časopis Historický* for more than 30 years, and upon public life in general. An able polemicist and beautifully crisp writer, Pekař always maintained the highest standards of propriety, accuracy and relevance. He remains the foremost Czech historian since Palacký, and his execration since 1945 by Marxist scholars in his own country is unforgivable.   RJWE

Main publications

Dějiny Valdštejnského spiknutí, 1630–4 (History of Wallenstein's conspiracy) (1895), German trans., *Wallenstein, Tragödie einer Verschwörung*, 2 vols (Berlin: A. Metzner, 1936–7); *Kniha o Kosti* (The Book of Kost), 2 vols (Prague: 1909–11); *České katastry, 1654–1789* (Bohemian land registers) (Prague: 1915); *Bílá Hora: její příčiny a následky* (The [battle of the] White Mountain: its causes and consequences) (Prague: Vesmír, 1921); *Žižka a jeho doba* (Žižka and his times), 4 vols (Prague: Vesmír, 1927–33); *Smysl českých dějin* (The meaning of Czech history) (Prague: Historicky Klub, 1929).

Reading

Pachta, J.: *Pekař a pekařovština v českém dějepisectví* (Pekař and the Pekař School in Czech historiography) (Brno: Rovnost, 1950).
Plaschka, R. G.: *Von Palacký bis Pekař* (From Palacký to Pekař) (Graz/Cologne: Wiener Archiv für Geschichte des Slawentums und Osteuropas, 1955).
Vojtěch, T.: *Česká historiografie a pozitivismus* (Czech historiography and positivism) (Prague: Academia, 1984).

Pertz, Georg Heinrich (b.1795, d.1876)
The son of a Hanover court bookbinder, Pertz studied first theology and then history at Göttingen. His doctoral thesis of 1819 on the Carolingian mayors of the palace was widely praised and won him the attention of Karl, Freiherr von Stein, who was in the process of founding the Monumenta Germaniae Historica, a society for the editing of the medieval sources for the history of Germany. Pertz became the society's first general editor in 1823, a post he held until 1873. The society as Stein conceived it had a directorate of prominent people, with a general editor and a secretary to direct work in detail, and was financed by subscriptions and public grants. After Stein's death in 1831, and especially after 1844, the directorate practically ceased to exist. Pertz, together with the secretary Johann Friedrich Böhmer, ran the Monumenta as a personal fief in tandem with his other posts: from 1843 he was director of the Prussian State Library in Berlin. Towards the end of his life, the financing of the Monumenta having meanwhile become an entirely Prussian responsibility, Pertz grew increasingly autocratic; he regarded the Monumenta as a possession which he could hand on to his, unfortunately not very gifted, son. It was not until 1873 that he was finally persuaded to give up his grip on the institution and allow his former assistant, WAITZ, to assume the presidency.

Pertz was not a great historian; his claim to distinction rests entirely on his editorial work, which was mainly for the Monumenta, though he edited Leibniz's historical writings. He did publish a six-volume biography of Stein between 1849 and 1855, but this was unfavourably received by the critics as being merely 'collecting and editing' of materials without interpretation. Together with his assistants, who included Waitz and several other of the most distinguished German medievalists of the nineteenth century, he edited sixteen folio volumes of narrative sources and two folio volumes of Carolingian capitularies between 1826 and 1868. Pertz established principles for the edition of medieval texts which have remained valid until the present: the need to draw on the whole manuscript tradition and not, as had been generally customary up until then, simply take the nearest available manuscript; the importance of distinguishing between those parts of the text edited which were written by the author and those he compiled from earlier sources; and the need for an adequate commentary. These principles owed much to the contemporary revolution in classical philology led by Karl Lachmann, though the Monumenta were for a long time ahead of the classicists in their determination to search the libraries of Europe systematically for manuscripts. In effect Pertz, together with Waitz and others, invented the modern scholarly edition of medieval historical texts (together with the modern scholarly translation in the series Geschichtsschreiber der deutschen Vorzeit founded by Pertz), and through their editorial productivity gave German medievalists an advantage in the command of the available sources which they have in some ways retained to the present day.

TAR

Main publications

For Pertz's editions for the MGH, see the bibliography in *Monumenta Germaniae Historica: Gesamtverzeichnis* (Munich: Monumenta Germaniae Historica, 1986); *Das Leben des Ministers Freiherrn vom Stein*, 6 vols (Berlin: Reimer, 1849–55).

Reading

Autobiography and Letters of George Henry Pertz, ed. Leonora Pertz [his wife] (London: 1894).

Bresslau, H.: *Geschichte der Monumenta Germaniae Historica* (Hanover: Hahn, 1921).

Knowles, D.: The Monumenta Germaniae Historica. In *Great Historical Enterprises* (London: Nelson, 1963), pp. 64–97, esp. 68–84.

Oertl, A.: Georg Henrich Pertz. In *Derlinische Lebensbilder. Geisteswissenschaftler I*, ed. Michael Erbe (Berlin: Colloquium Verlag, in publication).

Petit-Dutaillis, Charles Edmund (b.1868, d.1947) Born at St Nazaire in 1868, Petit-Dutaillis studied at the Sorbonne, the École des Chartes and the École des Hautes Études. For a time he was professor at Lille and from 1908 to 1916 rector of the University of Grenoble.

In 1898 Petit-Dutaillis edited for publication *Le Soulèvement des travailleurs en Angleterre en 1381* by his undergraduate friend André Réville (d.1894), with a memoir of Réville and historical introduction by Petit-Dutaillis. An early interest in English history was evident in

his *Études sur la vie et le règne de Louis VIII* (1895). He contributed chapters on France, 1421–92, to the *Histoire de France* edited by Lavisse (1902), and on Louis IX to the *Cambridge Medieval History*, and covered the French theme for several centuries in *Les communes françaises: caractère et évolution des origines au 18ᵉ siècle* (1947); but his later work concentrated mainly on the comparative study of English and French institutions in the twelfth and thirteenth centuries. In 1913 he translated into French with notes, Stubbs's *Constitutional History of England*; these notes were translated and published in English as *Studies and Notes Supplementary to Stubbs' Constitutional History* (1914, 1929). Some of these were pioneering essays and are of uneven value; in general they have not worn well. His volume *La Monarchie féodale en France et en Angleterre* (1933) (originally *Académie des inscriptions*, 1930), was translated as *Feudal Monarchy in France and England* (1936) and found a wide public; it developed a view of French and English history in which likely trends were reversed by the opportunistic Philip Augustus and the near-lunatic John. He covered the same period in *L'Essor des états d'occident* (1937).

Petit-Dutaillis died in Paris in 1947. Though probably not the leading scholar among the French historians of institutions of his time, as Inspecteur Général de l'Instruction Publique, and Directeur de l'Office National des Universités he was an important official figure.

JFAM

Main publications

Studies and Notes Supplementary to Stubbs' Constitutional History (1914, 1929); *Feudal Monarchy in France and England* (1936); *L'Essor des états d'occident*, In *Histoire générale*. vol. 4.2 *Histoire du moyen âge* (Paris: PUF, 1937).

Phillips, Ulrich Bonnell (b.1877, d.1934) Born and brought up in Georgia, and a pioneer in the serious scholarly study of the old south, Phillips spent the last 23 years of his life at two northern universities, Michigan and Yale.

Phillips had a dominating influence on southern historiography in the first half of this century. His studies of slavery and southern society were based on detailed research in plantation records, but reveal profoundly conservative attitudes, particularly on matters of race. He believed that white supremacy was the central theme of southern history, but he was not simply a sentimentalist about the old south. He regarded slavery as benevolent but essentially inefficient, and as a brake on southern economic progress. His interpretation of slavery was largely overturned by Kenneth Stampp's *The Peculiar Institution*, published in 1956, but the Marxist historian, Eugene GENOVESE has paid tribute to Phillips's work.

PJP

Main publications

American Negro Slavery (New York: Appleton, 1918); *Life and Labor in the Old South* (Boston: Little, Brown, 1929).

philosophy of history It is usual to divide philosophy of history into two distinct branches, speculative and critical. Speculative philosophy of history is concerned with finding a pattern or meaning in history, frequently as the expression of some universal or cosmic design and having an ultimate goal. Critical or analytical philosophy of history is directed to defining the formal characteristics of history as a body of knowledge, principally through analysing the writings and procedures of historians.

Speculative philosophy of history was the traditional and, until about a century and a half ago, effectively the only kind of philosophy of history. Although speculation about the origins of the world and human society has been a continuous part of western thinking since the Greeks, as a specific view of human history it derives principally from Judaism and Christianity. The belief in the world as God's creation, which had its beginning in time and would run its ordained course, presented a unilinear view of history, in contrast to the predominantly cyclical views of the ancient world. The progress of time was marked by a series of central events in which Jewish expectations of the coming of a Messiah in the Old Testament received a Christian specification in the New Testament, in Christ's incar-

nation, crucifixion and resurrection, which would culminate in a last judgement of all mankind after the ending of the world. Paul and Augustine gave those themes lasting formulation. Nevertheless their importance was primarily eschatological, looking to what was to come in the next world, rather than in this one; and the kind of philosophy of history that it produced was prophetic rather than historical, exemplified in the doctrines of Joachim of Fiore (d.1202), author of the most elaborate as well as influential interpretation of history in the middle ages. What his and other Christian interpretations transmitted was the belief that history had a goal and that it proceeded by a series of stages with each phase or epoch having its own significance and its own divinely appointed agents.

Those features are also to be found in the main secularized versions which emerged in the eighteenth century. Although a case can be made for VICO as the first to give history a secular role in explaining the evolution of human societies, and the French philosophers of the Enlightenment such as CONDORCET who looked to history as the record of human progress, the true heirs to the Judaeo-Christian tradition were the German idealist philosophers, notably Kant, Herder, Schelling, Fichte and above all HEGEL. They discerned in history not simply a universal pattern of development, common to every human society, as Vico did — and from that standpoint was also cyclical — but the unfolding of a universal providential plan in which (except for Kant) the unit of change was a collective entity, a people or nation or state, and subsequently, with Marx and Engels, different economic and social classes. In each case these abstractions were the subject of universal history, holding for all mankind as the key to understanding humanity; and in Hegel's case the movement of history represented the progressive self-realization of the absolute spirit manifesting itself through successive world historical peoples. Marxism remains the one world-wide philosophy of history in that universal tradition, though its adherents claim, as Hegel did, that it is supported empirically. It also shares the widespread nineteenth-century confidence in history as scientific knowledge, doing for the understanding of mankind what the natural sciences were doing for the understanding of nature, an attitude expressed by social theorists, such as Comte and Spencer who, in the manner of Vico, saw science as the highest stage in the evolution through which all human societies passed. That cyclical element is also predominant in the systems of the two main representatives of speculative history in the twentieth century, SPENGLER and TOYNBEE, who took cultures and civilizations as their respective units. Unlike their nineteenth-century forerunners however they were more impressed by ultimate decline than apotheosis, although Toynbee in the later volumes of his *Study of History* came to regard civilizations as the bearers of the higher religions, whose emergence it was their function to serve.

Critical philosophy of history rose from the development of history as a systematic discipline, which also began in Germany, with NIEBUHR and above all RANKE. Like Hegel, Ranke saw the meaning of history as the realization of human freedom, and the means of portraying that freedom in the writing of universal history through the histories of different peoples and nations. The model was that of the natural sciences, exemplified by physics; the historian was the counterpart of the scientific inquirer whose task was to act as an impartial observer inductively discovering and correlating evidence, through critical study of the sources, which, as in the parallel study of natural phenomena, would eventually issue in complete knowledge of the past as it had actually happened. That view of both the purposes of history and the role of the historian became representative of much nineteenth-century academic thinking, as can be seen from the prospectuses of the new historical journals founded in the middle of the century, as well as in the circular sent by Lord Acton, as editor, to the contributors to the first *Cambridge Modern History of Europe*.

By the 1880s it brought a reaction, principally in Germany, from among neo-Kantians such as Windelband and Rickert, and most fully in an alternative philosophical approach to history from DILTHEY. They each in different ways maintained the distinctiveness of history as a separate kind of knowledge which placed it with cultural or human studies. According to Windelband and Rickert the latter were distinguished from the sciences of nature in being concerned with the particular; they were what Windelband called ideographic, as opposed to the universalizing, law-governed natural sciences, which were nomothetic. To Dilthey the difference lay not in their method but their subject, which for history and the human studies was mankind. Man's life and activities had to be grasped in a different way from natural events, as those of an intelligent being who acted according to conscious intentions and choices. History was therefore what Dilthey called 'mind-affected'. That view was developed by COLLINGWOOD between the two world wars. Opposing what he called the scissors-and-paste history of the positivists, who confined themselves to collating events recorded by their sources, Collingwood held that the proper study of history involved going beyond external occurrences to the thoughts which lay behind them. More uncompromisingly CROCE and later Oakeshott treated all history as the present knowledge of historians.

Recent critical philosophy of history, predominantly the preserve of professional analytical philosophers in the English-speaking world, has been more interested in its status as a branch of knowledge, in particular the character of its explanations and claims to objectivity. The first has largely concerned the attempts to assimilate explanations in history to those in the natural sciences, so far with little success. At present the weight of philosophical opinion, not to mention the practice of historians, is against the notion that historical knowledge is governed by universal, covering, historical laws. Among the arguments against the existence of such laws, apart from the difficulty of producing convincing examples, are that historical events are too complex and/or too different from one another to be subsumed under a single explanatory law; so that even assuming that such a law could be found and agreed upon for, say, the causes of the French Revolution, it could not simply be applied to the Russian Revolution. Much of the subject matter of history involves social and mental categories, such as tradition, authority or beliefs, which are not translatable into physical causal categories, while many of the topics of historical explanation are not concerned with identifying causes, still less with predicting or retrodicting their outcomes.

The problem of objectivity is connected especially with the problem of values, which are inherent in human actions. Here a distinction needs to be drawn between the values identified by the historian in studying past actions and his own values. In relation to the first he is no more compelled to pass judgement on them than he is on any other of the facts, whether the meaning of a particular ritual or the aims of two countries at war with one another. From that standpoint his approach to the meanings of actions or beliefs can be controlled by the same canons of conforming to the evidence and correct reasoning which govern the whole of history as a discipline. Nor are the evaluations involved in selection and interpretation of significance peculiar to history but common to all branches of knowledge. Even the evaluative language used to convey human activity can be converted into factual statements which correspond to what has occurred, such as describing a massacre or an act of magnanimity. The second aspect, of the historian's own value judgements upon the quality and character of his subjects, is, however, peculiar to history and the other humanities. It has to be recognized that historical events are open to an irreducible diversity of interpretations, as Shakespeare's plays are. The best that can be aspired to is informed interpretation made on the basis of proper qualified understanding; as such it is closer to a continuing discussion which, like much knowledge, is no less objective for being incomplete or indemonstrable.

GL

Reading

Atkinson, R. F.: *Knowledge and Explanation in History* (London: Macmillan, 1978).

Carr, E. H.: *What Is History?* (1961; 2nd rev. edn, London: Macmillan, 1986).

Collingwood, R.G.: *The Idea of History* (Oxford: Clarendon Press, 1946).

Leff, G.: *History and Social Theory* (London: Merlin, 1969).

Walsh, W. H.: *An Introduction to Philosophy of History* (3rd edn, London: Hutchinson, 1967).

Pirenne, Henri (b.1862, d.1935) Pirenne was the son of a woollen cloth manufacturer of Protestant descent and a pious Catholic mother; he was one of the first Belgians to be educated as a professional historian. In 1879 he entered the University of Liège, where Gottfried Kurth and Paul Fredericq were introducing the seminar on the model of Ranke, and worked with Giry, MONOD, FUSTEL DE COULANGES, Bresslau, WAITZ and others in Paris and Berlin before his appointment at Ghent in 1885. Pirenne was elected to the Commission Royal d'Histoire of the Belgian Academy in 1891. Through the Commission, of which he was secretary from 1907 until his death, he became the driving force of Belgian historical scholarship, overseeing the training of librarians and archivists and maintaining a constant flow of suggestions for research. The great generalizations for which he is best remembered owe their durability to their foundations in the critical scholarship which he led, and for which he set the standard in works such as his *Histoire de Dinant au moyen-age* (1889) and his edition of the chronicle of Galbert of Bruges (1891).

His interest in urban history brought Pirenne at once into confrontation with the problem of the continuity of ancient life. He quickly became convinced that urban life in Gaul petered out during the Merovingian period, and was rekindled by a great commercial revival in the eleventh century. His theses on the origins of the medieval city and on Muhammad and Charlemagne, as well as the framework of his greatest work, the *Histoire de Belgique*, which occupied him from 1894 until 1932, were all derived from one conclusion: that it was the ninth and not the fifth century which constituted a hiatus in European development — the period when Europe fell back into a natural 'economy of no outlets', its life and culture dominated by those who controlled the tillers of the soil. Hence, as he had concluded by 1895 but stated most fully in *Les anciennes démocraties des Pays-Bas* (1910) and most brilliantly in *Medieval Cities* (1922), though topography and communications might dictate that merchants — a new class broken free from the feudal structure — should settle on the sites of Roman cities, the social, legal and political institutions which they developed owed nothing to the Roman past.

Too simple, even too romantic though it was, Pirenne's merchant-settler theory was the first successful attempt to interpret urban history in social and economic terms, breaking free from the increasingly sterile controversy between those who described European institutions as the inheritance of the Roman past and those who argued that they descended from the military and legal customs of the Germanic settlers. He had founded a new way of writing general history, which was acclaimed with the publication of the first volume of the *Histoire de Belgique* in 1899. His lucid account of the creation and shaping of an entire community through the interplay of social, economic and cultural evolution — much of it never systematically explored before — presented (as the *échevin* of Brussels wrote, commending the book to all teachers)

the history of our country not as a conglomeration of duchies and counties with no connection between them except the identity of their feudal lord, but as that of a nation with its own identity, its distinctive personality, a common civilization making our territory a single region of intellectual culture. (Lyon: *Henri Pirenne*, pp. 135–6, *n. 75*.)

As one of the leaders behind his university's refusal to reopen under German auspices in 1916, Pirenne was interned at Holzminden. His encounter with refugees from all over central and eastern Europe — from some of whom he learnt Russian in return for lectures, which were published after his death as *The History of Europe* (1936) — stimulated his first formulation of the thesis now most firmly associated with his name. *Mahomet et Charlemagne*, completed only in draft when he died in October 1935, has been assailed and apparently destroyed many times, and remains not only one of the freshest and most persuasive accounts of the early middle ages for the novice but, in its essentials, one of the most inescapably influential. If few can quite agree that 'without Mahomet, Charlemagne would have been inconceivable' fewer still can conceive those centuries as though the civilization of antiquity vanished in the fifth century, or western Europe pursued its course thereafter unaffected by the vicissitudes of its richer and more advanced eastern neighbours.

Pirenne's prodigious achievement — he published more than 30 books and some 300 articles — owed much to robust health, a relaxed and sociable temperament which won the deep affection of scores of friends and pupils, and a family life of singular happiness, though clouded by the failure of three of his four sons to survive him. After the war his identification with resistance to the occupation made him a figure of great national popularity as well as a scholar of international influence. He played a prominent part in the International Committee of Historical Sciences (founded in 1898), a bold idea whose eventual outcome would have disappointed him. At Strasburg in 1919 he met Marc BLOCH and Lucien FEBVRE, who regarded him as the great pioneer of the more complete history which they sought. He felt unable to accept their repeated invitations to become the first director of *Annales* (see ANNALES SCHOOL) but did much to encourage its establishment. Bloch and Pirenne, two of the greatest historians of their generations, maintained a warm and regular correspondence until Pirenne's death.

RIM

Main publications

Histoire du meurtre de Charles le Bon, comte de Flandre (1127–1128) par Galbert de Bruges (Paris: 1891); *Histoire de Belgique*, 7 vols (Brussels: 1899–1932); *Les anciennes démocraties des Pays-Bas* (Paris: 1910) trans. as *Belgian Democracy* (Manchester: 1915) and *Early Democracies in the Low Countries* (New York: 1963); *Medieval Cities* (Princeton, NJ: Princeton University Press, 1925); Le mouvement économique et social au moyen-âge. In *Histoire Générale: Histoire du Moyen Age VIII*, ed. G. Glotz (Paris: 1933), part 2, trans. as *Economic and Social History of Medieval Europe* (London: 1936); *Mahomet et Charlemagne* (Brussels: 1937), trans. *Muhammad and Charlemagne* (London: 1939); *Les villes et les institutions urbaines*, 2 vols (Paris: 1939).

Reading

Lyon, Bryce: *Henri Pirenne: a Biographical and Intellectual Study* (Ghent: 1974).

Platina, Bartolomeo (b.1421, d.1481) Born Sacchi, Platina took his name from his place of birth, Piadena, near Cremona in north Italy. He wrote under the patronage of the Gonzaga family and an early work was a history of the dynasty. During the pontificate of Paul II Platina was in disfavour, but Sixtus IV appointed him librarian of the Vatican library. Platina wrote on many subjects, but his most important work was a *Lives of the Popes*, produced in 1474 and printed at Venice in 1479. The earlier sections leaned heavily upon a few standard sources, with little critical appraisal, but when dealing with the events of his own lifetime Platina commented more freely, repaying old debts with a particularly unflattering description of Paul II. Ludwig von PASTOR, who used Platina's work, wrote: 'instead of the confused and often fabulous chronicles of the Middle Ages, we find here for the first time, a clear and serviceable handbook of real history.' Platina's book was reprinted frequently, added to, and published in translation.

JAC

Main publication

Liber de vita Christi ac pontificum omnium (1474).

Reading

Hay, D.: *Annalists and Historians*. (London: Methuen, 1977).
Pastor, L. ed.: *History of the Popes* (London: Kegan Paul, 1891).

Plekhanov, Georgy Valentinovitch (b.1856, d.1918) Teacher of Lenin and originator of the expression 'dialectical materialism', Plekhanov is rightly considered the father of Russian Marxism. He possessed a cool, logical, systematic, and polemical mind which set great store by doctrinal orthodoxy. Born in Gudalovka, he left Russia in 1880 to avoid arrest for revolutionary activity. During the 1880s Plekhanov laid down the orthodox Marxist perspective for the development of the revolution in Russia in which he emphasized the hegemonic role of the proletariat and its intelligentsia. Plekhanov first reached a wide audience with *Development of the Monist View of History* (1894) which was the first systematic exposition of historical materialism in Russia. As against the eclecticism of Bernstein, he saw Marxism as a unified theoretical system. His monist view was based on a thoroughgoing materialism which looked favourably on Spinoza and Feuerbach, emphasized the debt of Marxism to French eighteenth-century materialism, and rejected any idea of mutually interacting 'factors'. These themes, which followed closely in the footsteps of Engels, were continued in his influential book *Fundamental Problems of Marxism* (1908). Plekhanov was distinctive in attributing a considerable role to purely geographical influences on historical development and in applying historical materialism to the study of aesthetics where he elaborated the view that the validity of art and literature depended on class values and thus that the ultimate criterion of judgement was the content and not the form. The most 'western' of Russian Marxists, Plekhanov remained outside Russia for the four decades preceding 1917.

DTM

Main publications

Development of the Monist View of History (1894); *The Role of the Individual in History* (1898); *Fundamental Problems of Marxism* (1908); *Selected Philosophical Works*, 5 vols (London: Lawrence & Wishart, 1961).

Reading

Baron, S.: *Plekhanov: the Father of Russian Marxism* (London: Routledge & Kegan Paul, 1963).
Haimson, L.: *The Russian Marxists and the Origins of Bolshevism* (Cambridge, Mass.: Harvard University Press, 1955).

Plucknett, Theodore Frank Thomas (b.1897, d.1965) Plucknett graduated from University College London, at the age of 18 and won the Alexander prize of the Royal Historical Society at the age of 20. The years from 1918 to 1921 were spent at Emmanuel College, Cambridge, from where he was nominated to a fellowship at the Harvard Law School. While professor of legal history at Harvard (1926−31), Plucknett composed his *Concise History of the Common Law* by dictation in a few weeks. This book, which went through five editions and was translated into Japanese among other languages, epitomizes Plucknett's qualities of wide-ranging knowledge combined with original research and a constant awareness that law touches real life. Probably at the instigation of Harold Laski, a chair of legal history was created for Plucknett in 1931 at the London School of Economics, where he remained until his retirement in 1963.

In London Plucknett devoted his scholarly energies primarily to the Selden Society, of which he was literary director from 1937 to 1963. He contributed, usually anonymously, to about 20 volumes. The books he published during his later years were all occasioned by invitations to lecture: the Ford lectures in 1947 at Oxford on the legislation of Edward I; the Maitland lectures in 1950 at Cambridge on early English legal literature; and the Wiles lectures in 1958 at Belfast on Edward I and the criminal law. His Creighton lecture in 1953 at London on the medieval bailiff contains Plucknett's *credo*: the historian should not be deterred by legal technicalities; after all, 'a technicality is nothing but a statement made with unusual brevity and exactness, and that is what a historian should prize most in his sources'. Plucknett was president of the Royal Historical Society from 1948 to 1952. Plucknett's work, like that of MAITLAND, endures as a model of how a historian should use legal records. MTC

Main publications

A Concise History of the Common Law (Rochester, New York: Lawyers' Cooperative Publishing Co., 1929); *Legislation of Edward I* (Oxford: Clarendon Press, 1949); *Early English Legal Literature* (Cambridge: Cambridge University Press, 1958); *Edward I and the Criminal Law* (Cambridge University Press, 1960); *Studies in English Legal History* (London: Hambledon Press, 1983).

Reading

Milsom, S. F. C.: Memoir: T. F. T. Plucknett. *Proceedings of the British Academy* 51 (1965) 505–19.

Plumb, John Harold (b.1911) Rising from a humble background and the small University College of Leicester, Plumb has reaped many of the highest honours open to a British historian. After research at Cambridge University and war service in the Foreign Office, he advanced to become professor of modern English history at Cambridge and master of Christ's College. A knighthood, fellowship of the British Academy, a DLitt., various honorary degrees and visiting professorships have all come his way. Although most famous as a prolific author, he has also been an effective administrator, a brilliant lecturer and a popular supervisor of research students.

Plumb is perhaps the most widely read of recent British historians. Though he is most famous for his work on English history between 1660 and 1760, his books cover an astonishingly wide geographical and chronological span and have been translated into many languages. Together with his editorship of several prestigious series, his pen has brought him a vast readership and a handsome income.

Plumb's fame and fortune rests, in part, upon his impressive mastery of a vast range of sources and his versatility, but it probably rests even more upon his creative imagination, his superb style and his optimistic belief in the progress of man and the value of history. He has a marvellous eye for both the grand sweep and the telling detail and his prose is almost unrivalled among historians for pace, vigour and flow. Always writing to be widely read, he has used his literary gifts to rescue history from arcane and specialized scholarship. His appeal to a wide audience owes much to his ability to make the past come alive and to his confidence in the material and even the moral progress of man. He has always tried to show that a more profound knowledge of the past would help to mould human attitudes and human action.

Plumb's determination to reach a very wide readership has almost certainly weakened his appeal to professional historians. Although he managed to combine a captivating style with the highest technical standards of professional scholarship, most notably in the first volume of his biography of Sir Robert Walpole and in *The Growth of Political Stability in England, 1675–1725*, his work has not generally matched the professional standards of Maitland, Elton or Namier. The second volume of his biography of Walpole sacrificed detailed content and deep analysis to style and popular appeal, and failed to explain Walpole's great achievements as a financier and political manager. Perhaps not surprisingly Plumb has not completed what once promised to be one of the great historical biographies. Moreover, although he has had innumerable admirers and a large number of research students, Plumb has never established a school of history. Nor has he adopted a methodology, in the manner of Namier, capable of influencing historians who have never met him. His historical gifts rest largely upon his own energy, imagination and creativity; they cannot easily be passed on to others.   HTD

Main publications

England in the Eighteenth Century (Harmondsworth: Penguin, 1950; New York: Penguin, 1951); *Sir Robert Walpole*, 2 vols (London: Cresset Press, 1956, 1960; repr. Allen Lane, 1972; Boston: Houghton Mifflin, 1956, 1961; repr. Clifton, NJ: A. M. Kelley, 1973). *The First Four Georges* (London: Batsford, 1956; Boston: Little, Brown, 1975); *Men and Places* (Cresset Press, 1963) pub. in USA as *Men and Centuries* (Westport, Conn.: Greenwood, 1979); *The Growth of Political Stability in England 1675–1725* (London: Macmillan, 1967) pub. in USA as *The Origins of Political Stability in England 1675–1725* (Atlanta Highlands, NJ: Humanities Press, 1977); *The Death of the Past* (London: Macmillan; Boston: Houghton Mifflin, 1969); with Huw Weldon, *Royal Heritage* (London: BBC, 1977) pub. in USA as *English Heritage* (Arlington Heights, Ill.: Forum Press, 1978).

Reading

McKendrick, N.: J. H. Plumb: a valedictory tribute. In *Historical Perspectives*, ed. McKendrick (London: Europa, 1974).

Plutarch (b.*c.*45, d.*c.*123) A moral essayist and biographer, Plutarch's lifelong home was in Greece in the small Boeotian town of Chaeronea, to which he was devoted. He travelled to Asia, Egypt, and Rome and Italy, and developed a wide circle of friends. These included Roman grandees, such as the consulars L. Mestrius Florus, to whom he apparently owed his Roman citizenship, and Q. Sosius Senecio, the dedicatee of the *Parallel Lives*; and also powerful figures from the Greek world, including two of the first to enter the Roman senate, C. Iulius Eurycles Herculanus of Sparta and King Philopappus of Commagene. Plutarch himself remained cool about such Roman careers: excessive ambition can destroy one's peace of mind, and young Greeks should be content to stay in Bithynia

or Galatia ('On quiet of mind', 470c–d). He won an international reputation, and received several imperial honours in his old age, but he was content to stay in Chaeronea, teaching a school of young disciples. For the last thirty years of his life he was also a priest at Delphi, serving the oracle at a time of revival under several emperors. In his essay 'Advice on public life' he counselled a young friend from Sardis not to seek municipal office, but to accept it if asked, and this was evidently his own practice: he tells of his friends' amusement at seeing him supervising minor building projects at Chaeronea, and he was doubtless also involved with the new buildings at Delphi. But such activity probably never exercised much of his energy or enthusiasm. His love was literature.

Plutarch's extant works (perhaps only half of his total production) include fifty biographies and some eighty miscellaneous works, which are normally grouped together under the loose Latin title *Moralia*: their range is extraordinary – declamation, political essays, popular and technical philosophy and religion, antiquarianism, literary criticism and 'table talk'. A disproportionately large number of these were apparently written after the death of the Emperor Domitian in 96; the *Parallel Lives*, his principal historical work, also belong to this productive late phase. He had earlier written his series of *Lives of the Caesars* from Augustus to Vitellius, of which only *Galba* and *Otho* survive, both rather weak. The *Parallel Lives* are much richer: 22 of those pairs survive, one of them the double pair *Agis, Cleomenes, and the Gracchi*, and we also have two Lives outside the series, *Aratus* and *Artaxerxes*. The technique of pairing a Greek with a Roman subject is important. 'Comparison' of political or literary figures was a standard rhetorical technique, but none of Plutarch's predecessors had developed it so elaborately, and often one Life's themes and emphases are influenced by those of its pair. Thus *Fabius* stresses Fabius Maximus' relations with the Roman *plebs* because a similar theme is important in its pair *Pericles*; *Aemilius* and its pair *Timoleon* both develop the theme of Fortune's mutability, and the capacity of a great man to bear it; *Philopoemen* and

329

Flamininus, the only pair to deal with two men of the same period, explore the consequences for Greece and for themselves of their ambition and contentiousness.

Plutarch clearly distinguished his biography from narrative history. His readers should not necessarily expect a full account of well-known historical events,

for it is not histories we are writing, but Lives. Nor is it always the most famous actions which reveal a man's good or bad qualities: a clearer insight into a man's character is often given by a small matter, a word or a jest, than by engagements where thousands die, or by the greatest of pitched battles, or by the sieges of cities.   (*Alexander* 1)

His interest is character. He will 'not collect the sort of historical information which is useless, but convey that which helps one to understand a man's nature and personality' (*Nicias* 1). The ultimate purpose is moral: he hopes that his audience (*Pericles* 1–2) – and indeed he himself (*Aemilius* 1) – will be inspired by examples of virtue; and a few instances of vice may also provide a helpful moral deterrent (*Demetrius* 1). *Demetrius and Antony*, and probably *Coriolanus and Alcibiades*, are pairs which fall into this last, negative category. Some Lives fit this general programme well: *Alcibiades* and *Cato minor*, for instance, are both extremely personal and moralistic Lives, giving strong impressions of their subject's personality but only a hazy sense of historical background. But at times Plutarch does display more interest in general historical points, for instance stressing the popular support which carried Pericles, the Gracchi and Julius Caesar to power, but left them vulnerable when it wavered. Still, such historical analyses are usually trite and perfunctory; his strength is rich and vivid narrative, for instance the night-time occupation of Thebes (*Pelopidas* 6–13), the Catiline conspiracy (*Cicero* 11–24), or the deaths of the younger Cato (*Cato minor* 66–70) or Antony and Cleopatra (*Antony* 76–86); and his insights into a great man's personality, and often his human vulnerability, can be moving and impressive.

Plutarch has always been widely read, and he has perhaps influenced popular perspec-

tives of Greek and Roman history more than any other ancient writer. His influence on the Renaissance was particularly great: in England, North's version (1579) of Amyot's French translation of the Lives (1559) was exploited by Shakespeare, particularly for *Julius Caesar, Coriolanus* and *Antony and Cleopatra*. Plutarch's sympathy for Liberators and Republicans – Dion, Timoleon, Brutus – later endeared him to intellectuals of the French Revolution. His prestige has waned in the last two hundred years, as advances in ancient historical technique have exposed the weaknesses of his narratives; but he is now re-emerging as an impressive intellectual and literary figure in his own right.   CBRP

Main writings

Lives, ed. and trans. B. Perrin (London: Loeb Classical Library, 1914).

Reading

Hamilton, J. R.: *Plutarch, Alexander; a Commentary* (Oxford: Oxford University Press, 1969) [especially Introduction].

Jones, C. P.: *Plutarch and Rome* (Oxford University Press, 1971).

Pelling, C. B. R.: *Plutarch's Life of Antony* (Cambridge: Cambridge University Press, 1988) [especially Introduction].

Russell, D. A.: *Plutarch* (London: Duckworth, 1973).

Wardman, A.: *Plutarch's Lives* (Berkeley and Los Angeles: University of California Press, 1976).

Pocock, John Greville Agard (b.1924)
The 'Machiavellian moment' comes to a people when they recognize the temporal finiteness of their civil order. From this departure point Pocock has reconstructed the history of early modern Englishmen by tracing the growth of their historical consciousness. His work, elaborated in *The Ancient Constitution and the Feudal Law* (1970) *Politics, Language and Time* (1971), and *The Machiavellian Moment* (1975), has led to the recovery of a classical republican tradition in Britain. It has also involved a reassessment of how systems of thought actually influence political behaviour. Both his substantive and his theoretical revisions have challenged the established Whig and Marxist explanations of England's pioneering role in the modernization of the

western world. In contrast to these schematized accounts of human destiny, Pocock has presented the history of a single political discourse as it shaped social perceptions and was in turn shaped by the events impinging upon its truths.

Where earlier interpretations of seventeenth- and eighteenth-century England had emphasized the progressive character of parliamentary government and commercial expansion, Pocock's interpretation is grounded in a radically different understanding of contemporary attitudes. He argues that the failure of the Puritans' Elect Nation alerted the English gentry to the terrors of history and plunged them into an intellectual engagement with strategies for securing stability. Inspired by Harrington, the figures in Pocock's histories are discovered in Renaissance writings on ancient prudence, a prescription for political health which called for a balanced constitution and a virtuous citizenry. For these men the fluidity of wealth introduced by Restoration prosperity threatened to undermine the independence of the citizen landholders, while fiscal innovations such as the Bank of England and the funding of the debt created dangerous forms of patronage. Within the classical republican model of politics these corrupting dependencies heralded the degeneration of the commonwealth itself. Because commerce was frequently seen as conveying change and corrupting virtue, its spread brought about a spiritual crisis for Englishmen using the language of civic humanism.

This notion of historical consciousness guiding a class of men in their world has served Pocock in two ways. It has justified his rejection of the proleptic view of English history as the story of the self-appointed torchbearers of liberty and progress. It has also formed the basis for his exploration of language. In this he has drawn from the sociology of knowledge. Languages figure in his work as socially-constructed systems of thought which organize people's response to events. Essentially conservative, languages distribute authority because they define what a person can say and therefore do. In pursuing these ideas Pocock has became part of a major in-

tellectual enterprise of the late twentieth century. In literature attention has shifted from texts and their authors to an examination of audiences and the communication of the texts. In science, the imaginative conceptions of nature have been dissociated from nature itself and in history the meaning attached to a people's experience has displaced the study of the import of the events in that experience. Focusing upon men and women as interpreters rather than doers, scholars influenced by these larger trends have incorporated semiotics, hermeneutics and linguistics into historical scholarship.

Born in London, Pocock grew up in New Zealand where he attended Canterbury University College. He subsequently studied in England with Herbert Butterfield at Cambridge. Drawn into a circle of scholars which included Peter Laslett, Quentin Skinner and John Dunn, Pocock became part of what he has termed a transformation in the understanding of political writings. Reading early modern texts as parts of a rhetoric shared by particular men, these scholars developed the tools to criticize Marxist emphasis upon the social determinants of thought, as well as the Whiggish evocation of transhistorical continuities. They examined political languages as sources of meaning, legitimation and authority for men seeking to understand themselves and their civil order in a specific time. Pocock's contribution to this effort includes studies of Harrington, Hobbes, Shaftesbury, Burke and Gibbon in addition to his work on the discourses centring on the common law, the ancient constitution and the Machiavellian tradition.

Returning to New Zealand in 1953 to teach at the University of Otago, Pocock subsequently developed the department of political science at the University of Canterbury. He has taught in the United States since 1965, spending ten years at Washington University, St Louis before moving to the Johns Hopkins University where he holds an appointment as professor of history.   JOA

Main publications

The Ancient Constitution and the Feudal Law (Cambridge: Cambridge University Press, 1970); *Politics,*

Language and Time (New York: Atheneum, 1971); *The Machiavellian Moment* (Princeton: Princeton University Press, 1975); editor. *The Political Works of James Harrington* (Cambridge University Press, 1977); *Virtue, Commerce and History* (Cambridge University Press, 1985).

Pokrovsky, Mikhail Nikolayevich (b.1868, d.1932) Son of a Muscovite civil servant, Pokrovsky was lucky enough to number among his university teachers both P. G. VINOGRADOFF and V. O. KLYUCHEVSKY. An early interest in economic history led towards Marxism; this in turn made it difficult for Pokrovsky to pursue an academic career. Nevertheless, he was able to carry on research and writing both in Russia and abroad. A four-volume *History of Russia since Ancient Times* was published between 1910 and 1914, and *Outlines of Russian Culture* in two volumes in 1915 and 1918. Pokrovsky was active as a speaker and journalist during the Russian Revolution, and produced a *Brief History of Russia* in 1920–3 to answer an urgent need for a work reflecting the outlook of the Soviet regime. During the 1920s he took on a number of administrative duties while continuing to edit collections of documents and to bring out essays, for example *The October Revolution* in 1929, and *Historical Science and the Class War* in two volumes in 1933. Soon after his death he was denounced by Stalin and his associates, but he has received rehabilitation and serious appraisal from 1956 onwards.

Pokrovsky's vast output moved through different phases, but his basic purpose might be summarized in his own words: 'Instead of puppets in crowns and in purple the author took the real tsar – Tsar Capital, autocratically ruling Russia from Ivan IV to Nicholas the Last.' He adopted the concept of 'merchant capital' as the primary motivater of social change, and argued that Russian absolutism was basically no different from European absolutism as a whole. Even Lenin found some of Pokrovsky's writing rather abstract, while for Stalin, the historian was guilty not only of Trotskyist ideological deviation but also of schematic interpretation of Russian history ill-suited to the patriotic doctrine of 'socialism in one country'. Now, he must be given the credit for putting the study of history

on firm new foundations in the 1920s, and for providing, perhaps unwittingly, an important link between historical scholarship of the nineteenth and twentieth centuries. PD

Main publications

Russkaia istoriia s drevneishikh vremen, 5 vols (Moscow: 1910–14), trans. *History of Russia from the Earliest Times to the Rise of Commercial Capitalism*, 2nd edn (Bloomington: Indiana University Press, 1966); *Russkaia istoriia v samom szhatom ocherke*, 3 vols (Moscow: 1920–3), trans. *Brief History of Russia*, 2 vols in 1 (Orono, Maine: University Prints, 1968); *Russia in World History: Selected Essays* (Ann Arbor: Michigan University Press, 1970).

Reading

Barber, J. D.: *Soviet Historians in Crisis, 1928–32* (London: Macmillan, 1981).
Enteen, G. M.: *The Soviet Scholar-Bureaucrat: M.N. Pokrovskii and the Society of Marxist Historians* (University Park: Pennsylvania State University Press, 1978).

Polish historiography The beginnings of modern Polish historiography can be traced to NARUSZEWICZ in the eighteenth century. His monarchical sympathies were challenged by the Romantic democrat LELEWEL who, in turn, was vigorously attacked by the 'pessimist' Cracow school led by BOBRZYŃSKI. The Lvov (Lwów) school led by K. Liske (1838–91) and T. Wojciechowski (1838–1919) shared Cracow's concern with the publication of sources but did not produce a synthesis of national history. Cracow's rivals were the Warsaw Positivists who sought 'optimistic' elements in Poland's development: A. Pawiński (1840–96) and A. Rembowski (1847–1906) wrote on the sixteenth century, and KORZON and W. Smoleński (1851–1926) on the eighteenth.

As modern Polish historical research expanded, the great schools of the nineteenth century fragmented in the first decades of the twentieth into narrower, more specialized yet pluralist groups of scholars. In Lvov, S. Askenazy (1866–1935) encouraged research in the diplomatic and political history of the eighteenth and nineteenth centuries. Economic and social history was given great impetus by F. Bujak (1875–1953) who wrote on prices, and above all by J. Rutkowski (1886–1949) in Poznań who studied the rural economy. The Marxist approach to economic history was initiated in Poland by N. Gąsiorowska-Grabowska (1881–1964); after 1953 she was to preside over the history institute of the Polish Academy of Sciences.

Constitutional and legal history was developed in Cracow by S. Kutrzeba (1876–1946), in Lvov by O. Balzer (1858–1933), and in Poznań by Z. Wojciechowski (1900–55). Kutrzeba also wrote on military history, and so did W. Tokarz (1873–1937) and M. Kukiel (1885–1973). Kukiel was one of a number of eminent historians who chose to remain in exile after 1945; another was O. Halecki (1890–1976) who produced a Catholic interpretation of Polish history. The interests of the liberal M. Handelsman (1882–1945), professor at Warsaw after 1919, centred on methodology, feudalism, and eighteenth- and nineteenth-century diplomatic history. He encouraged the medievalist 'Merovingian school' and a school of modern historians. A group of conservative historians working in Cracow, such as W. Konopczyński (1880–1952), an authority on the eighteenth century and first editor of the Polish biographical dictionary, is sometimes known as the 'new' Cracow school. The so-called Poznań school, which included K. Tymieniecki (1887–1968), concentrated on medieval history and Polish–German relations.

In 1948 officially sanctioned Marxism was imposed on the study and teaching of history, and since 1952 the Polish Academy of Sciences has coordinated much of historical research in Poland. Some Marxist scholars, such as KULA, have acquired an international reputation; nevertheless attempts at producing a definitive Marxist periodization of the whole of Polish history have repeatedly encountered political and ideological difficulties. S. Arnold's periodization, made during the Stalinist years, won little acclaim, and the Academy of Sciences made a fresh attempt after 1957, but its four-volume *History of Poland* stopped in 1918 and there are few signs of the work being completed. The pluralist traditions of Polish historiography have, not surprisingly, survived. WHZ

Reading

Backvis, C.: Polish tradition and the concept of history. *Polish Review* 6 (1961) 125–58.

Davies, N.: *God's playground: a History of Poland* (Oxford: Clarendon Press, 1981), I, pp. 3–22.

Grabski, A. F.: Interpreting history. *Polish Perspectives* 14 (1971) 18–28.

Maczak, A.: The style and method of history. *Polish Perspectives* 16 (1973) 12–17.

Rose, W.J.: Polish historical writing. *Journal of Modern History* 2 (1930) 569–85.

Pollard, Albert Frederick (b.1869, d.1948) Pollard was the principal force behind the setting up in 1921 of the Institute of Historical Research as a national and international centre for postgraduate studies at the University of London, a move of profound significance for historical studies especially in Britain and North America. For many years his photograph as first director gazed down from the wall of the Institute common room on generations of students who had never known him, an icon of intellectual rigour, confident purpose, adamantine professionalism and iron determination. Pollard is said to have had a lighter side and certainly he once broke a leg during high jinks following an Oxford dinner, but his sense of authority, leadership and hierarchy was strong, and during his 40-year reign over history at London, he was merciless in his domination of the system, his colleagues and his assistants, especially female ones (who included his wife).

Yet these austere qualities were desperately needed at London in 1903 when Pollard was appointed (at first part time) to the newly created chair of constitutional history at University College. There were two history graduates per year in the whole university and eight members of staff. By 1924 when Pollard retired as chairman of the Board of Studies in History (an institution he had virtually created) there were 250 undergraduates and 56 staff. Pollard in effect created the London History School. He was concerned also for the wider impact of the subject. This explains his many public lectures and the major role he played in setting up the Historical Association in 1906. A decade later, having finished three years as its president, he persuaded the Association to take over the periodical *History* and then, as editor, proceeded to raise it to the status of a major national journal.

Pollard owed his historical training to R. L. POOLE at Oxford (where he went from Felsted School in 1887) and to eight years as an assistant editor with the *Dictionary of National Biography*. He wrote widely on historical and public issues (often anonymously in *The Times* and its *Literary Supplement*), but his 500 biographies for the *Dictionary*, mainly on the Tudor period, established his specialism. He was also, as a characteristic product of Victorian nonconformity, convinced of the importance of the constitution and parliament (he was a candidate for parliament several times). The two interests came together in his later years in research into the members of the early Tudor parliaments, unfinished, but later bearing fruit under his pupil NEALE, S. T. Bindoff and the History of Parliament Trust.

Pollard's masterpiece is *Wolsey*. Beginning as the Ford lectures for 1927–8, it shows to perfection the author's greatest strength, his mastery of original sources, most of all the monumental *Letters and Papers, Foreign and Domestic, of the Reign of Henry VIII*, edited by J. S. Brewer and his team. It is true that Pollard did not often go behind printed texts and calendars to the original manuscripts, still less search for more, but the justification for this, apart from enormous administrative distractions (energetic and active though Pollard notoriously was), was that what Tudor studies in the early twentieth century required was precisely a scholar who would establish a general framework for the period on the basis of the major printed sources.

Pollard's interpretation became the accepted view of Tudor England. Indeed many of his books have only recently lost their status while *Wolsey* and numerous articles still retain a value. His intensive and perceptive use of *Letters and Papers* produced a quantum leap in historical sophistication which, coupled with the quality of his writing, stamped his authority on half a century of sixteenth-century scholarship. Add to this the creation of the History School at the University of London, undergraduate and postgraduate, the Histor-ical Association and *History*, and it is understandable why he refused to add a knighthood to his many academic honours. As with Christopher Wren, Pollard's true monument was there to be seen, all around.   EWI

Main publications

England under Protector Somerset (London: Kegan Paul, 1900); *Henry VIII* (Paris: Goupil, 1902; annotated edn, London: Longmans, Green, 1905); *Factors in Modern History* (London: Constable, 1907); *History of England from the Accession of Edward VI to the Death of Elizabeth* (Longmans, Green, 1910); *The Evolution of Parliament* (Longmans, Green, 1920; rev. 1926); *Wolsey* (Longmans, Green, 1929).

Reading

Galbraith, V. H.: *Proceedings of the British Academy* 35 (1949) 257–74.

Neale, J. E.: *English Historical Review* 64 (1949) 198–205.

The Times, 5 August 1949.

Williams, C. H.: *Bulletin of the Institute of Historical Research* 22 (1949) 1–10.

Polybius (b.*c*.200, d.*c*.118 BC) Born into a rich family in Megalopolis in southern Greece, Polybius received the education and training appropriate to a future statesman and military leader of the Achaean League. In 167, after serving as cavalry commander, he was exiled to Rome with 1,000 other Achaeans accused of insufficient devotion to the Roman cause during the recent Macedonian war. There he had the luck to become the friend and teacher of Scipio Aemilianus, who facilitated his later travels to Spain and north Africa, and – like Hannibal – across the Alps. In 146 he attended Scipio at the fall of Carthage and undertook a voyage of exploration in the Atlantic. Subsequently he mediated between Achaea and Rome after the disastrous Achaean war. He died aged 82 following a fall from his horse.

Polybius' main work was his *Histories*, 40 books in total, conceived at Rome but finished later. In this he showed how in under 53 years (i.e. 220–167 BC) the Romans had conquered virtually the whole inhabited world. The last ten books, covering 167–146 BC, he probably added when an old man, after the death of Scipio who figures prominently in them. In conscious reaction against the sensational and rhetorical forms of historiography then prevalent, Polybius intended his work to be sober and utilitarian. He calls it 'pragmatical', meaning however that it deals chiefly with political and military material. His purpose was to instruct statesmen and generals and to furnish the ordinary reader with moral training by recounting how historical characters had reacted to the vicissitudes of fortune.

Polybius writes clearly and claims that his work is truthful. This claim is mainly justified. But his self-righteous and frequently pedantic criticism of predecessors like Timaeus and Phylarchus and of contemporary historians like Zeno of Rhodes is not attractive. Petty prejudice obtrudes when he is discussing states hostile to Achaea, like the Aetolian League; and at Rome anyone connected with the Scipios comes out of it rather well. Polybius prides himself on writing 'universal history' covering the whole 'inhabited world'. This, he says, is unique, for it reflects events peculiar to his time, when Fortune's great achievement had been to unite the world under Rome. Though basically a rationalist, bent on eliminating 'chance' from a universe where events obey comprehensible laws of cause and effect, Polybius here introduces a concept of 'Fortune' not easily distinguishable from 'Providence'. This contradiction he nowhere wholly resolves.

Much of book 6 of *Histories* is taken up with a discussion of the Roman constitution, which Polybius considers largely responsible for Roman imperial success. In this a balanced mixture of kingship, aristocracy and democracy had evaded the tendency towards corruption inherent in the separate constitutional forms. This mixed constitution Polybius relates, not entirely satisfactorily, to a supposed cyclical evolution through a succession of alternating simple and corrupt forms, namely kingship, tyranny, aristocracy, oligarchy, democracy, mob-rule, monarchy and so once more back to kingship. Both models have their flaws but, directly or indirectly, have exercised great influence on later historians and political theorists down to MACHIAVELLI, VICO, MONTESQUIEU and TOYNBEE.

Five books survive intact. The rest consists of fragments taken mainly from collections of excerpts made in the ninth century and occasional citations in other writers.   FWW

Main writings

Histories, ed. text and trans. W. R. Paton (London: Loeb Classical Library/Heinemann, 1922–7); *Polybius: the Rise of the Roman Empire*, trans. I. Scott-Kilvert (Harmondsworth: Penguin, 1979) [a selection].

Reading

Momigliano, A. D.: Polybius' reappearance in western Europe. In *Entretiens Hardt 20: Polybe*, ed. E. Gabba (Geneva: Vandoeuvres, 1974) pp. 345–72.

——: *Polybius between the English and the Turks*, J. L. Myres Memorial Lecture (Oxford: Blackwell, 1974).

Walbank, F. W.: *Polybius* (Berkeley and London: University of California Press, 1972).

Poole, Reginald Lane (b.1857, d.1939) A member of a family of distinguished orientalists, Poole read history at Balliol College, Oxford, under STUBBS, and in 1882 took a doctorate at Leipzig. Returning to Oxford in 1886, he was from 1896 to 1927 university lecturer in diplomatic. In that position he was largely responsible for introducing the German scientific methods of history into England. Poole was assistant editor of the *English Historical Review* from its foundation in 1886, and sole editor from 1901 to 1920; more than anyone else, he was responsible for its form and style as a scientific journal. His own publications included works on Hebrew grammar, musical history and the Huguenots, but he is best known for his 'diplomatic' (especially on the Papal Chancery and the English Exchequer) and *Illustrations of the History of Medieval Thought* (1884).   RHCD

Main publications

Illustrations of the History of Medieval Thought (London: Williams & Norgate, 1884; 2nd edn London: S. P. C. K., 1920; repr. New York: Dover, 1960); *The Exchequer in the Twelfth Century* (Oxford: Clarendon Press, 1912); *Lectures on the History of the Papal Chancery* (Cambridge: Cambridge University Press, 1915); editor, John of Salisbury's *Historia Pontificalis* (Clarendon Press, 1927); *Studies in Chronology and History* (Clarendon Press, 1934; repr. 1969).

PORSHNEV, BORIS FEDOROVICH

Porshnev, Boris Fedorovich (b.1905, d.1972)
One of the Soviet Union's most eminent historians, Porshnev completed his graduate studies at the Institute of History of the Russian Association of Science Research Institutes in 1929. He subsequently taught in higher education institutions at Rostov-on-Don and at Moscow, becoming professor of history at the university. From 1957 to 1966 he chaired the section devoted to modern west European history at the Institute of History of the Soviet Academy of Sciences.

Porshnev's first major book, published in 1948, was a pioneering study of popular revolts in France before the Fronde. It did not appear in French until 1963. This delay notwithstanding, its impact was immense, triggering off a spate of investigations into French popular uprisings which has continued until the present day. Although Porshnev's approach was marked by the somewhat vulgarized concepts of class struggle prevalent during the Stalinist period, his achievement in giving historians of seventeenth-century France something other than great rulers to think about was considerable. Though few historians, Marxist or otherwise, have fully accepted his suggestion that the absolute state was a response to the pressure of an embryonic revolutionary class, his emphasis on the feudalization of the bourgeoisie still evokes much sympathy. In his later years Porshnev embarked on an ambitious trilogy endeavouring to bring together in a unified analysis the interaction of social, political and international relations at the time of the Thirty Years' War. The third part, *France, The English Revolution and European Politics* appeared in 1970, while the first volume devoted to Sweden's entry into the war and its significance for Muscovy was published posthumously in 1976. The volume which was to have dealt with East-West relations in the 1630s was never completed. DP

Main publications

Narodnye vosstaniia vo Frantsii pered Frondoi (the people's revolt in France before the Fronde) (Moscow: 1948) German trans., *Die Volksaufstande in Frankreich 1623–48* (Berlin: 1954) French trans., *Les soulèvements populaires en France de 1623 à 1648* (Paris: SEVPEN, 1963); *Feodalizm i narodny massye* (Feudalism and the popular masses) (Moscow: 1964); *Frantsiia, Angliiskaia revoliutsiia i evropeiskaia politika v seredine XVIIv* (France, the English revolution and European politics in the mid-seventeenth century) (Moscow: 1970).

Reading

Dukes, P.: Russia and mid-seventeenth-century Europe: some comments on the work of B. F. Porshnev. *European Studies Review* 4 (1974) 81–8.

Mousnier, R.: Recherches sur les soulèvements populaires en France avant la Fronde. *Revue d'histoire moderne et contemporaine* 5 (1958) 81–113.

Salmon, J. H.: Venal office and popular sedition in France. *Past and Present* 37 (1967) 21–43.

positivism The belief that the method of natural science provides the principal, or even the sole, model for the attainment of true knowledge. As applied to historical understanding it has a pedigree which can be traced back at least as far as Francis BACON and which must include a number of figures from the Enlightenment such as HUME, MONTESQUIEU, and CONDORCET.

The tension between scrupulous modesty and sublime assertiveness which was already apparent in the *philosophes'* efforts to construct a Newtonian 'science of society' remained a leading feature of the positivist enterprise as it developed during its nineteenth-century heyday. In the opening decades such stress characterized Henri de Saint-Simon's endeavours to discredit all so-called metaphysical approaches and to establish instead a 'positive philosophy' wherein gravitation would serve as the great model of systematic comprehension and of ultimate unity across every branch of knowledge. The strain also affected his associate Auguste COMTE, who coined the term 'positivism' and became the principal contributor to its subsequent popularity. The critical cautiousness discernible in Comte's *Cours de philosophie positive* (1830–42) had become, by the time of his *Système de politique positive* (1851–4), quite swamped by the revived mystical excesses associated with his aim to make science the basis for a new 'religion of humanity'. His record indicated that it was one thing to associate intellectual

336

progress with the strengthening of rigour and consistency in the sources and methods of understanding, but quite another and less defensible matter to identify the actual attainment of intellectual maturity with the supposed ability of natural science to yield some unitary, all-embracing pattern of eventual conclusions.

In historiography the more critical version of positivism was beneficial to the extent that it fortified the tendency (already emergent for largely independent reasons, as witnessed by NIEBUHR's reassessment of LIVY) to pay greater heed both to the collection and to the scrupulous handling of authentic primary evidence. It also underpinned the efforts of those, such as RANKE and MOMMSEN at Berlin, who strove to formalize the pedagogic and professional structures of a 'scientific history'. The Rankean quest to detail 'the facts' and so to recapture the past 'wie es eigentlich gewesen' (as it actually was) might be thought naive and bold enough. But that was not how matters seemed to the devotees of a still less critical positivism who agreed, explicitly or otherwise, with Comte's view of 'all phenomena being subject to invariable natural laws, whose precise discovery and reduction to the smallest number possible is the aim of all our effort'. For them, history would be fully scientific (and how indistinguishable from sociology?) only when it revealed these regularities, not just as operative in the past but also, by extrapolation, as predictively applicable. That is the spirit in which the nineteenth century's most ambitious exercises in positivistic historical synthesis were conducted, by commentators as diverse in their choice of general explanatory mechanisms as Gobineau, Spencer, BUCKLE, and TAINE. Most notable of all the manifestations − not least by virtue of its continuing influence on later historiography − was the economic interpretation of MARX and ENGELS, pivoting around modes of production and the concept of class struggle. Their effort eventually to make an ally of Darwinism is a particularly instructive example of the positivistic anxiety to render mutually compatible the most fashionable current ideas about natural evolution and their own notions of historical process.

Towards 1900 there developed 'a revolt against positivism' (see Hughes, 1958), especially in its more uncritical manifestations. Within this reaction, as applied to history, a leading part was played by such German neo-Kantians as Windelband, Rickert and DILTHEY. The last-named argued most powerfully of all against any hegemony of natural scientific models, by contending that Kant's differentiation between the phenomenal and noumenal spheres held the key to a proper distinction between two distinguishable but equally valuable roads to knowledge. History and the other 'human' sciences demanded that the investigator should probe beneath the surface of observable phenomena in order to tackle questions of thought, desire and emotion; to make linkages between 'lived experience' and the manner in which it is both expressed and comprehended; to exercise *Verstehen*, as a form of inner understanding or even sympathetic intuition. While WEBER strove to carve out a position in which some of these insights might still be kept compatible with a revamped positivism, the radical 'idealist' critique was further promoted during the early twentieth century by CROCE in Italy and COLLINGWOOD in Britain. The latter's treatment of BURY, as a scholar whose liberation from the philosophical errors of 'scientific history' in the Rankean sense was deemed to have been prematurely arrested, is a gem within the anti-positivistic literature.

Positivism, as a generator of systematic historical laws, has left two especially awesome twentieth-century monuments: SPENGLER's *Decline of the West* (1918−22) and TOYNBEE's *Study of History* (1934−61). In tracing the recurring cycles of cultures/civilizations, each comes ultimately to mimic the 'repeatability' of the laboratory experiment and produces an outcome owing more to mystical obfuscation than to science properly understood. Still more firmly shackled to the habits of uncritical positivism is the bulk of Soviet scholarship, which even today operates according to the spirit of Lenin's contention that the Marxist materialistic conception of the past can yield 'objective laws' capable of revealing the system of social relations prevailing at any point in history.

MDB

POSTAN, MICHAEL MOISSEY

Reading

Collingwood, R. G.: *The Idea of History*, Pt III, 9, and Pt IV, 1 (iv) (Oxford: Clarendon Press, 1946).

Haddock, B. A.: *An Introduction to Historical Thought*, chs 10–12 (London: Arnold, 1980).

Hughes, H. S.: *Consciousness and Society: The Re-orientation of European Social Thought, 1890–1930*, chs 1–2 (New York: Knopf, 1958).

Kolakowski, L.: *Positivist Philosophy: From Hume to the Vienna Circle* (New York: Doubleday, 1968).

Simon, W. M.: *European Positivism in the Nineteenth Century* (Ithaca, NY: Cornell University Press, 1963).

Postan, Michael Moissey (b.1899, d.1981)
Postan spent his first twenty years in Russia, and in consequence his later thinking was informed by broad international perspectives and personal knowledge of a peasant society. He never lost his interest in the social sciences, which he studied in Russian universities. In England in the 1920s and early thirties he worked as a student, researcher and lecturer in the University of London, often in close collaboration with Eileen POWER, whom he eventually married. His research into late medieval trade at this time bore fruit in a collection of essays edited by himself and Power, and in a chapter on the trade of northern Europe in the *Cambridge Economic History of Europe* (vol. II, 1952). In 1934 he moved to a post at Cambridge; he succeeded after four years to the chair of economic history, which he continued to occupy until 1965. His most original and influential contribution to medieval economic history was developed in a series of articles from 1937 to 1962. He explored the internal dynamics of medieval rural society, arguing that the period saw not a continuous progress towards cash rents, wage labour, and production for the market, but rather a cycle of expansion up to around 1300, and then a long-term decline. The two tendencies were linked, because the growth of population and the extension of cultivation of the thirteenth century built up critical pressures in the economy. Old cultivated lands produced less yield, mainly because of a lack of manure, and newly colonized lands ulti-mately failed. Food shortages and a major famine in 1315–17 caused a rising mortality, and ushered in a period of recession. Postan supported this thesis both with theoretical arguments, and with detailed empirical studies of livestock numbers and (with J. Z. Titow) of rates of peasant mortality. He explained the land market among peasants in terms of the 'natural' needs of families as children grew in number and then departed; he was here applying to medieval England the work of the Russian agricultural economist, A. V. Chayanov. He also argued against the idea that the aristocracy could counteract the effects of falling land values by exploiting the profits of war. He expounded his interpreta-tion of English economic development at length in the second edition of the *Cambridge Economic History* (vol.I 1966) and in his text-book.

Postan's influence has impinged on think-ing about pre-industrial societies throughout the western world. Never averse to contro-versy, he provoked criticism and lively argu-ment. The edifice of interpretation that he erected has received much underpinning from other writers, many associated with him at Cambridge. His opponents have scratched and dented the structure without yet under-mining it. Some of the most effective counter-arguments have challenged his assumption that a static technology prevented economic growth during the medieval crisis; others point to the lack of a strong social dimension in his analysis.

Postan's impact on the historical world ex-tended far beyond his major contribution to medieval studies. He never lost interest in the modern economy, writing in the 1930s about capital formation, and in the 1960s about post-war Europe. During the second world war he edited and wrote volumes for the official history on economic and technological matters. Postan brought vitality and enthu-siasm to teaching and conference debates. As editor of the *Economic History Review* and the *Cambridge Economic History* and also through his personal influence, he made English his-torians more aware both of international de-velopments and of the importance of theory.

CCD

Main publications

(Published by Cambridge University Press, Cambridge unless otherwise stated.)
Medieval agrarian society in its prime: England. In *Cambridge Economic History of Europe*, vol. I, 2nd edn (1966) pp. 548−632; *Medieval Trade and Finance* (1973); *Essays on Medieval Agriculture and General Problems of the Medieval Economy* (1973); *The Medieval Economy and Society* (London: Weidenfeld & Nicolson, 1972).

Reading

Postan, M. M.: *Fact and Relevance: Essays on Historical Method* (Cambridge: Cambridge University Press, 1971).
Miller, E.: Memoir. *Proceedings of the British Academy* 69 (1984) 543−57.

Potter, David Morris (b.1910, d.1971) An American southerner by birth, Potter spent most of his academic life in the north, and brought to his studies of the Civil War era a blend of critical detachment and deep-rooted understanding of his native region. Having obtained his undergraduate degree from Emory University, he took his MA and PhD at Yale, where he taught from 1942 to 1961. For the last ten years of his life he was Coe professor of American history at Stanford. He was Harmsworth professor at Oxford in 1947−8, and gave the Commonwealth Fund lectures at University College London, in 1963. At the time of his death he was president of both the American Historical Association and the Organization of American Historians.

A man of calm authority, unflagging energy and unassuming manner, Potter bore with fortitude various tragedies in his private life. Perhaps less well known to the wider public than some of his contemporaries he had an immense influence over his fellow historians. His work was ambitious and wide ranging; he was essentially an interpretative and analytical, rather than a narrative, historian − a man of ideas enriched by a prodigious range of reading.

Potter wrote in a crisp, lucid and economical style but found great difficulty in completing book-length projects. Many of his books were either collections of essays and articles or based on lecture series; no fewer than five of his books appeared posthumously and were completed and prepared for publication only through the dedicated editorial work of former colleagues, notably Don E. Fehrenbacher. Some of his most important and influential work is to be found in two volumes of collected essays: *The South and the Sectional Conflict* (1968) and *History and American Society* edited by Fehrenbacher (1973). Both contain the masterly essay, a quintessential Potter product, on 'The historian's use of nationalism and vice versa'. Probably the most widely read and discussed of all his books, *People of Plenty: Economic Abundance and the American Character* (1954), explored two of Potter's favourite themes: American national character, and the relationship between history and the social and behavioural sciences. The key to the distinctive features of the American national experience was to be found, he suggested, in economic abundance, which was 'by technology out of environment'. The book retains its fascination even in an age when abundance is neither so peculiarly American nor so secure as it seemed in the 1950s.

Potter's more specialized work centred on the era of the American Civil War. His first book, *Lincoln and his Party in the Secession Crisis*, was an intricate study of the months between Lincoln's election and the outbreak of the war. For the last decade and a half of his life, Potter wrestled with the task of writing the volume for the New American Nation Series on the coming of the Civil War. The book, still unfinished at his death, finally appeared in 1976, thanks to Fehrenbacher's unselfish editing and his completion of the final chapters. *The Impending Crisis 1848−1861* won, posthumously for Potter, a Pulitzer prize. It offered a subtle and discriminating analysis of the issues at stake, and never lost sight of the alternatives open to the protagonists, nor of the many roads not taken.

Without rigid ideological commitments, and distrustful of catch-all explanations, Potter combined clarity of argument and style with a deep sense of the essential complexity of the past. He epitomized much that was best in American historiography between the second world war and Vietnam.   PJP

Main publications

Lincoln and his Party in the Secession Crisis (New Haven, Conn.: Yale University Press, 1942); *People of Plenty: Economic Abundance and the American Character* (Chicago: University of Chicago Press, 1954); *The South and the Sectional Conflict* (Baton Rouge: Louisiana State University Press, 1968); *The South and the Concurrent Majority*, ed. Don E. Fehrenbacher and Carl N. Degler (Louisiana State University Press, 1972); *Division and the Stresses of Reunion, 1845–1876* (Glenview, Ill.: Scott Foresman, 1973); *History and American Society*, ed. Don E. Fehrenbacher (New York: Oxford University Press, 1973); *Freedom and its Limitations in American Life*, ed. Don E. Fehrenbacher (Stanford, Calif.: Stanford University Press, 1976); *The Impending Crisis, 1848–1861*, completed and ed. Don E. Fehrenbacher (New York: Harper & Row, 1976).

Reading

Brogan, D. W.: David M. Potter. In *Pastmasters: Some Essays on American Historians*, ed. Marcus Cunliffe and Robin W. Winks (New York: Harper & Row, 1969), pp. 316–44.

Degler, Carl N.: David M. Potter. *American Historical Review* 76 (1971) 1273–5.

Power, Eileen (b.1889, d.1940)   From Girton College Cambridge Eileen Power went to London University in 1921, and held in turn the posts of lecturer, reader and professor of economic history at the London School of Economics. She wrote prolifically on a variety of medieval subjects, from nunneries to Essex clothiers, and also worked on the modern period, notably as co-editor with R. H. Tawney of *Tudor Economic Documents*. Her special expertise lay in the English wool trade, on which she delivered the Ford Lectures in 1939, and she contributed a long essay to the book on fifteenth-century trade based on the seminar chaired by herself and her husband, M. M. POSTAN. Those who knew her felt the charisma of her personality. She combined, said one contemporary, the grace of a butterfly with the industry of a bee. All assessments of her as a person and a scholar are tinged with a sense of tragedy because of her early death, before she was able to complete her full-length book on the wool trade. She has left work that is characterized by simple and lucid writing, without many statistics or heavy apparatus, yet learned and precise. She was an able popularizer, writing books for a lay readership and for schoolchildren. A posthumously published fragment shows that she was preparing an important work on the history of women.   CCD

Main publications

Medieval People (London: Methuen, 1924); ed. with M. M. Postan, *Studies in English Trade in the Fifteenth Century* (London: Routledge & Kegan Paul, 1933); *The Wool Trade in English Medieval History* (Oxford: Oxford University Press, 1941).

Reading

Tawney, R. H.: Obituary. *Economic History Review* 10 (1939–40) 92–4.

Powicke, Frederick Maurice (b.1879, d.1963)   Powicke was educated at Stockport Grammar School, Owens College, Manchester, and Balliol College, Oxford. In 1903 he returned to Manchester as a research fellow under T. F. TOUT, who appointed him an assistant lecturer in 1906. In 1908 he was elected a prize fellow of Merton College, Oxford. The next year he became professor of history at Belfast and remained there until he once more returned to Manchester, this time as professor, in 1919. From 1928 to 1947 he was regius professor at Oxford. He was knighted in 1946.

Powicke's first book concerned *The Loss of Normandy* in 1204. His masterpiece, *Stephen Langton*, similarly concerns the strife of John's reign. Instead of treating his subject merely as the struggle of king and archbishop, Powicke describes Langton's career from a variety of angles, most notably as a teacher at Paris, presenting a rounded person. His talent for biography is also demonstrated in journal articles and in his work on Ailred of Rievaulx. However, in his most ambitious book, *King Henry III and the Lord Edward*, his biographical touch is less sure: the king and his son are swamped by a mass of discursive information. The discursiveness is deliberate, as Powicke was aiming to recreate the disconnected reality of human experience. This is 'history as perhaps Proust might have written it', Sir Richard SOUTHERN commented. But Powicke lacked the requisite information, as he had failed to examine the manuscript rolls of the Chancery, Exchequer, and courts of law in the Public

Record Office. This was uncharacteristic of him, as he had made a meticulous study of *The Medieval Books of Merton College* and, in his capacity as president of the Royal Historical Society from 1933 to 1937, had promoted cooperative research which produced annual bibliographies, the *Handbook of British Chronology*, and a new edition of Wilkins's *Concilia*. Powicke's last book, *The Thirteenth Century*, intended as a textbook for undergraduates, is a political narrative along much the same lines as *King Henry III and the Lord Edward*. Powicke's best political analysis for the general reader had been done 20 years earlier, in *Medieval England 1066–1485*, when his energies were at their height.   MTC

Main publications

The Loss of Normandy (Manchester: Manchester University Press, 1913); *Stephen Langton* (Oxford: Clarendon Press, 1928); *Medieval England 1066–1485* (Oxford: Oxford University Press, 1931); *The Medieval Books of Merton College* (Clarendon Press, 1931); *King Henry III and the Lord Edward* (Clarendon Press, 1947); *The Life of Ailred of Rievaulx by Walter Daniel* (London: Thomas Nelson, 1950); *The Thirteenth Century* (Clarendon Press, 1953).

Reading

Hunt, R. W., Pantin, W. A. and Southern, R. W.: *Studies in Medieval History Presented to F. M. Powicke* (Oxford: Clarendon Press, 1948).
Southern, R. W.: Memoir: F. M. Powicke. *Proceedings of the British Academy* 50 (1964) 275–304.

Prado, Caio Jr (b.1907)   Holder of a law degree from São Paulo, Caio Prado was prominent in politics, held elected office in São Paulo and, after the communist revolt of 1935, was gaoled and left Brazil, returning in 1939. In 1947 he was elected state deputy for the Brazilian Communist Party (PCB). In 1969 a governmental decree forced him to retire from his chair of political economy at the University of São Paulo and deprived him of his political rights. His scholarship is characterized by a Marxist interpretation.

His *Formação do Brasil* (which, together with FREYRE's *Casa-Grande e Senzala* and BUARQUE DE HOLANDA's *Raizes*, was a landmark in Brazilian historiography) is an overview of Brazilian history before independence, and an inquiry into factors contributing to the situation at the beginning of the nineteenth century. This is a critical examination of the historical evolution of an economic structure characterized by speculative exploitation of natural resources, latifundia, monoculture, an export economy and slave labour, and related social factors. Prado's interpretation of the cattle industry as a unifying factor is original. Political independence (1822) notwithstanding, for Prado the Second Empire (1840–89) represented the transition from colony to modern Brazil. His synthesis of economic history has spurred controversy by interpretations and mode of analysis. Prado's work is characterized by originality of research, of documentation, and of interpretation and is informed by his view of the past as being part of the present in Brazil.   AJRR-W

Main publications

Evolução Politica do Brasil (São Paulo: Editora Brasiliense, 1934); *Formação do Brasil Contemporaneo* (São Paulo: Livraria Martins, 1942) trans. Suzette Macedo *The Colonial Background of Modern Brazil* (Berkeley and Los Angeles: University of California Press, 1967); *História Economica do Brasil* (São Paulo: Editora Brasiliense, 1945).

Prawer, Joshua (b.1917)   Born in Breslau, Prawer settled in what is now the state of Israel in 1936 and taught in the Hebrew University of Jerusalem where he became professor of medieval European history in 1958. In the course of a distinguished career he has been chairman of the Humanities Section of the Israel Academy of Sciences and Humanities and editor-in-chief of the *Encyclopaedia Hebraica*.

Prawer has been enormously influential in the study of the medieval history of the Holy Land, in particular in the period of the Crusades. A pupil of Richard KOEBNER, he established his international reputation through a series of studies on the crusaders' colonization activities and the social, economic and agrarian structures in the Latin East in the twelfth and and thirteenth centuries. These studies began to appear in the early 1950s and were later refashioned in book form as *Crusader Institutions* (1980). He has also made notable contributions to the history of the Jewish communities in the Holy Land in the same period. PWE

Main publications

Histoire du royaume latin de Jérusalem, 2 vols, (Paris, CNRS, 1969–71); *The Latin Kingdom of Jerusalem: European Colonialism in the Middle Ages* (London; Weidenfeld & Nicolson, 1972); *Crusader Institutions* (Oxford: Clarendon Press, 1980).

Reading

Kedar, B.Z, Mayer, H.E. and Smail R.C.: Joshua Prawer : an appreciation, In *Outremer: Studies in the History of the Crusading Kingdom of Jerusalem presented to Joshua Prawer*, ed. Kedar et al. (Jerusalem: Izhak Ben-Zvi Institute, 1982).

Prescott, William H. (b.1796, d.1859)   An unlucky accident in the dining hall of Harvard University left young William Prescott nearly blind. Unable to practise law, he devoted himself with good humour and rigorous discipline to becoming a man of letters. Narrative history was the form of literature that attracted him; his subject was the story of the rise of Spain, beginning with *The Reign of Ferdinand and Isabella*. More notable for dramatic incidents and characters than for depth of historical analysis, this first book opened doors for Prescott in Europe. The distinguished scholars Pascual de Gayangos and Martín Fernández de Navarrete became his friends; public and private archives allowed their documents to be copied for his collection.

Prescott's subsequent work on the reigns of Charles V and Philip II show his mastery of these materials as well as his imagination and magniloquent style, but it was in Spain's overseas empire that he discovered the epic themes exactly fitted to his talents. *The Conquest of Mexico* and *The Conquest of Peru* endure as great adventure stories. ATB

Main publications

History of the Reign of Ferdinand and Isabella, the Catholic, 3 vols (London: John Foster Kirk, 1841); *History of the Conquest of Mexico, with a Preliminary View of the Ancient Mexican Civilization, and the Life of the Conqueror, Hernando Cortés*, 3 vols (New York: Harper & Bros, 1843); *History of the Conquest of Peru, with a Preliminary View of the Civilization of the Incas*, 2 vols (New York: Harper & Bros, 1847); *History of the Reign of Philip the Second, King of Spain*, 3 vols (Boston: Phillips, Sampson, 1855–8).

Reading

Humphreys, R. A.: William Hickling Prescott: the man and the historian. *Hispanic American Historical Review* 39 (1959) 1–19.

Procopius of Caesarea (*fl.* sixth century AD)   The chief historian of the reign of Justinian (AD 527–65), Procopius tells us that he had been the secretary/aide of the general Belisarius whom he accompanied on many of his campaigns on the eastern frontier, in North Africa and Italy from AD 527 to at least 540. An eye-witness of the plague which struck Constantinople in 542, he probably remained in the capital thereafter.

Procopius composed three works, at first sight very different, or even mutually contradictory. His history of the wars, *De bellis*, comprised eight books of which I–VII, finished in 550/51, carry the narrative of Justinian's wars of reconquest from 527 to that date, and are divided geographically; two are concerned with the wars against Persia, two with the campaigns against the Vandals, and three with the war against the Goths in Italy. *Wars*, Book VIII, added in 554/55, carried the story on all fronts up to that year. Procopius also wrote a panegyric in six books, *De aedificiis* (*Buildings*), which catalogue and praise Justinian's activity as builder, especially of churches and fortifications; all parts of the empire are included except Italy. The work is variously dated to 554/55 or 560. In addition, he was the author of the so-called *Secret History* (*Anecdota*), which is a violent attack on Justinian, his wife Theodora (d. 548) and several chief ministers including Belisarius. On internal grounds this work can be assigned to 550/51 and is therefore contemporary with the completion of *Wars* V–VII. Thus Procopius seems within the space of a few years to have both praised and criticized Justinian's regime.

When the *Secret History* was found in a manuscript in the Vatican library in the early seventeenth century, its discoverers denied that it could be by Procopius. More recently however, and especially since the work of its Teubner editor, J. Haury, at the end of the nineteenth century, scholars have found an explanation of the differences in a reconstruction of Procopius' biography: some personal disaster ('schizophrenia' according to several) accounted for the *Secret History*, an imperial commission cynically executed for the *Buildings*. Yet we have next to no information about Procopius outside the works themselves; moreover, discontent with Justinian's policy is also observable in the later parts of *Wars* I–VII, and again in VIII. The *Secret History*, then, represents the underside of the arguments expressed in the more circumspect *Wars*; the *Buildings*, the imperial ideal to which, despite recent disappointments, Procopius still clung.

All three works are written in the classicizing Greek of the educated elite in the early Byzantine period. The *Wars*, the most impressive surviving work of its kind, provides, despite its literary apparatus of speeches and digressions, a vivid and often eye-witness narrative of Justinian's wars, and as such has formed the backbone of all modern histories of the period, while the *Buildings* gives a record of sixth-century monuments all the more valuable as interest in the urban history of the period increases. All Procopius' works express the conservative attitudes of the landowning provincial elites in the face of an autocratic and interventionist ruler. In the same way, while admiring Justinian's return to imperial ideals, and often admitting the conventional Christian views of his time, Procopius also criticizes the emperor for his preoccupation with doctrinal issues and persecution of heretics. All three works have suffered in the past from an over-literal interpretation, yet they still yield a high percentage of reliable and often unique historical information.   AMC

Main writings

Wars I–VIII; *Buildings*; *Secret History*, ed. J. Haury, rev. G. Wirth (Leipzig: Teubner, 1962–4).

Reading

Cameron, Averil: *Procopius and the Sixth Century* (London: Duckworth, 1985).

profession of history Professions and professionals are the subject of a large and growing literature that has spawned many competing definitions of the concept. Perhaps the neatest and least controversial frame of reference is provided by John HIGHAM. A profession, he says, is 'a body of individuals with a particular skill who by co-operative action establish and maintain their own standards of achievement instead of obeying some external authority'. If we accept this definition three distinct phases in the process of professionalization become evident. First, the emergence of the particular skill; second, the recognition of it as the province of a specialist; and third, the promotion by the specialists themselves of a self-conscious and dynamic professional ethic. The drive to professionalization finds its locus in formal association which, by excluding the unsuitable and unqualified from recognition, serves further to define and delineate the exclusive nature of the specialism.

Using this model it is clear that the professionalization of historical scholarship in Europe and the United States is a nineteenth-century phenomenon. Generalizations, however, should be treated with caution. The process of professionalization is easier to describe than to explain, and stages, rates and styles of change varied markedly between individual nations.

The preliminary stage was the adoption by scholars at the turn of the eighteenth century of a critical historical attitude. The new breed of critical historians differed from their Enlightenment counterparts in two fundamental ways. First, in their attitude to the past. Political, social and economic revolutions were transforming Europe. The gulf between the past and the present engendered a new 'historical habit of mind' which aimed, in Ranke's words, to see the past from the inside, 'as it really was'. Emphasis was placed on change and development in human character and institutions. Actions were to be understood in their own context rather than judged against fixed laws of reasonable conduct. The second crucial difference was in their treatment of sources. Historians had used documentary evidence since the seventeenth century, but the new breed applied to it the sophisticated techniques of analysis developed by lawyers, philologists, and biblical scholars.

These developments served gradually to

343

separate historians from philosophers and 'men of letters', while a growing concentration on national history and the evolution of institutions of government increased the gulf between historians and the parochial, fact-gathering antiquarians on the one side, and archaeologists concentrating on excavations and artefacts relating to pre-literate societies, on the other.

The emergent specialism quickly became institutionalized. This took two forms. First, the surviving fragments of the national past were centralized in record offices and archives, where, often under state supervision, the work of calendaring and editing records attained the status of an industry. Second, history became an academic descipline. As part of the educational reconstruction of the Napoleonic era it took root in Germany – at the university of Berlin in 1810 – and then in France, at the Sorbonne in 1812. In more stable socio-political environments it was much slower to develop, not being taught formally in England until 1848, or in the United States until the 1870s.

These institutions began gradually to supervise the training of new scholars and as they expanded, and historical techniques became more specialized, they became the locus for a growing community of historians. The mid-nineteenth century scholar was keen to distance himself from the 'man of letters'. He did so in two fundamental ways. First, he stressed his 'scientific objectivity', both in the scrupulous application of rigorous techniques to verifiable evidence, and in the insistent desire to establish 'the truth' as independent of political or religious affiliation. Second, he rejected the claims of a popular audience and disclaimed all desire to entertain. The new historical scholar wrote for the edification of fellow specialists. Herein lay the essence of the drive to professionalization. The community of scholars was bound by common agreement on method, scope, purpose and standards of scholarship. This series of 'invisible colleges', loyalty to which transcended the relationship that particular individuals maintained with the institution they served, was cemented by formal association: societies, journals and from 1898 international congresses.

By 1900 historians in Europe and the United States had developed, defined and delineated their own particular skill. They had begun to establish for themselves a career structure in institutions of education and in government service for which they regulated admission and training requirements. A historical profession was clearly in evidence. It did not encompass everyone who wrote history, or who claimed to be or was recognized as a historian, but as standards of scholarship rose in the twentieth century and as specialization increased and sources multiplied it came increasingly to do so.   PRHS

Reading

Goldstein, D. The organisational development of the British historical profession 1884–1921. *Bulletin of the Institute of Historical Research* 55 (1982) 180–93.

Heyck, T. W.: *The Transformation of Intellectual Life in Victorian England* (London: Croom Helm, 1982).

Higham, J., Kreiger, L. and Gilbert, F.: *History* (Englewood Cliffs, NJ: Prentice Hall, 1965).

Levine, P.: *The Amateur and the Professional: Antiquarians, Historians, and Archaeologists in Victorian England 1838–1886* (Cambridge: Cambridge University Press, 1986).

Millerson, G.: Education in the professions. In *Education and the Professions*, ed. T. G. Cook for the History of Education Society (London: Methuen, 1973) pp. 1–18.

Reader, W. J.: *Professional Men: the Rise of the Professional Classes in Nineteenth-Century England* (London: Weidenfeld & Nicolson, 1966).

Slee, Peter R. H.: *Learning and a Liberal Education: the Study of Modern History in the Universities of Oxford, Cambridge and Manchester 1800–1914* (Manchester: Manchester University Press, 1986).

prosopography A word popularized since the 1930s for the collective study of individual lives and careers, together with family relationships and patronage connections. The technique was pioneered in America by Charles BEARD, for classical studies by F. Münzer, and for English history by L. B. NAMIER. British prosopographers were heavily dependent upon compilations such as the *Dictionary of National Biography*, published from 1882 onwards, *Alumni Oxonienses* (from 1891), the *Complete Peerage* (from 1910) and *Alumni Cantabrigienses* (from 1922). The technique continues to be used, particularly by classical historians such as Ronald SYME and A. H. M. JONES. Though of value for the investigation of elites and certain institutions and groups, such as parliaments or political parties, it was pushed too hard as an alternative to narrative. The areas to which it can usefully be applied are limited and it can easily lead to purely mechanistic explanations. See GENEALOGY and STRUCTURAL ANALYSIS.   JAC

Reading

Stone, L.: *The Past and the Present* (Boston: Routledge & Kegan Paul, 1981) ch. 2.

Prothero, George Walter (b.1848, d.1922) Though neither an outstanding nor a productive historian, Prothero's contribution to the professionalization of the discipline in Britain was considerable.

The first was strong commitment to what C. H. Firth called 'the historical teaching of history': the view that the distinct, objective methodological techniques developed by historians had a unique educational value and should therefore be taught as an intrinsic component of every university history course. Appointed tutor at King's College, Cambridge, in 1876 and university lecturer eight years later, it was Prothero who in 1884 argued most convincingly for the addition to the historical tripos of a special subject based on the study of documentary sources. His chief and most enduring work of scholarship was a compilation of statutes and documents intended for students and teachers of Tudor and Stuart history which went into four highly influential editions.

Prothero was appointed to the newly created chair of history at Edinburgh in 1894, but resigned it five years later in favour of the editorship of the *Quarterly Review*. No longer a teacher of history, Prothero now took on a new role in promoting the idea of community and cooperation in British scholarship. He was elected president of the Royal Historical Society in 1901 and fellow of the British Academy in 1903. He worked as co-editor of the Cambridge Modern History from 1901 to 1912, and as historical adviser to the Foreign Office between 1917 and 1919, where he

edited the official series of peace handbooks. He was made KBE in 1920.   PRHS

Main publications

Select Studies and other Documents Illustrative of the Reigns of Elizabeth and James I (Oxford: Clarendon Press, 1894).

Reading

Crawley, C. W.: Sir George Prothero and his Circle. *Transactions of the Royal Historical Society* 5.20. (1970) 101–28.

Prynne, William (b.1600, d.1669) A Puritan lawyer and pamphleteer, Prynne wrote more than 200 pamphlets in a lifetime marked by energy, courage, disputatiousness and repetitiveness. Most of what he wrote is not readable today, and much of it was not readable then according to some of his critics, including Milton. Yet F. W. MAITLAND called Prynne a 'heroic' figure: he was not referring to the mutilation of Prynne's ears – twice – at the hands of Archbishop Laud; rather, he was thinking of the contribution which Prynne made to historical scholarship in preserving manuscripts as Keeper of Records in the Tower of London after the Restoration. This task, records Prynne, was 'so filthy and unpleasant that Mr. Riley and others would not soil their hands, or clothes, nor endanger their healths to assist me in it.' Anthony à WOOD recorded how generously Prynne in 1667, 'in his black and taffaty-cloak', received the young research student from his old university, introduced him to historical documents, and 'seemed to be glad that such a young man as he was should have inclinations towards venerable antiquity'.

J. G. A. POCOCK has shown how the seventeenth-century respect for the 'ancient constitution' was undermined (unintentionally) by antiquarian research. This process is beautifully illustrated by Prynne's career. He began his writing career as the uncritical champion of Coke and was the official apologist for the sovereignty of parliament in the civil war; he ended it ridiculing Coke's belief that the *Modus Tenendi Parliamenti* was written in the time of Edward the Confessor, and stating his preference for Sir Henry SPELMAN as a

345

scholar to Coke, who simply did not have the leisure to master original sources.

Prynne used Sir Robert Filmer's researches in 1648 to argue for the supremacy of the House of Lords over the Commons. Similarly, after the Restoration he used his own researches among the manuscripts to buttress the case of Lords against Commons in the impeachments of Lord Mordaunt and CLARENDON and in the dispute between Skinner and the East India Company. But Prynne was no court lackey at the end of his life either: on Clarendon's impeachment he said flatly, 'the King cannot do it; it is against his Coronation Oath and Magna Charta.'

Though contemporaries were puzzled by a career shot through with contradictions, historians can now recognize more easily how a basically conservative Erastian adapted a simplified earlier view of the 'ancient constitution' to the more complex model thrown up by his researches in original manuscripts.   WML

Main publications

Histrio-Mastix (London: 1633); *The Soveraigne Power of Parliaments* (London: 1643); *A Plea for the Lords* (London: 1648); *An Exact Chronologicall History*, 4 vols (London: 1666–70).

Reading

Lamont, W. M.: *Marginal Prynne* (London: Routledge & Kegan Paul, 1963).

Pocock, J. G. A.: *The Ancient Constitution and the Feudal Law* (Cambridge: Cambridge University Press, 1957).

Pufendorf, Samuel (b.1632, d.1694)   After a meteoric career which brought him the first chair of natural law in Germany, at Heidelberg in 1661, a disagreement with his employer sent Pufendorf into Swedish exile until 1688, when he was appointed court-historian to Frederick William the Great, Elector of Brandenburg. The greatest natural lawyer of his day, Pufendorf used his historical skills to penetrating effect in his exposé of the state of the Holy Roman Empire, probably the most influential political work published in Germany in the seventeeth century.   TCWB

Main publications

De statu imperii germanici ('Utopiae', 1667); *Commentariorum de rebus Suecicis libri XXVI ab expeditione Gustavi Adolphi in Germaniam ad abdicationem usque Christinae* (Utrecht: 1686).

R

Radzinowicz, Leon (b.1906) Radzinowicz was born in Poland and had a cosmopolitan legal education in Warsaw, Paris, Geneva and Rome, followed by a distinguished university career in Geneva and Warsaw before he came to England in 1937. He became director of the department of criminal science in the law faculty at Cambridge in 1949. Radzinowicz's academic distinction and his powerful, confident personality were, in 1959, instrumental in securing for Cambridge the establishment of Britain's first Institute of Criminology and for himself appointment as its director and Wolfson professor of criminology. Knighted in 1970, he retired from his Cambridge posts in 1973, but has continued to publish.

Radzinowicz's academic career has been that of a lawyer and a criminologist rather than a historian. Indeed, as Britain's first professor of criminology and in his capacity as first director of the Cambridge Institute he has been the single most influential figure in the development of British criminology since the second world war. As befits the work of a man with such a cosmopolitan academic background, Radzinowicz's criminology has always had a strong comparative element, which has embraced both cross-national and historical comparisons. Despite the fact that the bulk of Radzinowicz's published work has not been directly historical, his reputation as a scholar in the English-speaking world has been founded on a work of history − his monumental *History of the English Criminal Law and its Administration from 1750*, published in five volumes between 1948 and 1986.

These five volumes set out to locate the reform of the criminal law, of policing and of punishment during the eighteenth and nineteenth centuries in its social context. Although the project has, in its massive scope and its concern to document and explain administrative reform, some similarities with the administrative histories of the Webbs, the originality of its conception was remarkable. In 1949 most existing accounts of crime and the criminal law by historians were either anecdotal or narrowly administrative. Those offered by legal historians were almost entirely based on case law. Radzinowicz's work, by contrast, was grounded in a comprehensive exploration of eighteenth- and nineteenth-century books, pamphlets and official printed sources. The fruits of this enormous research were woven by Radzinowicz into an explanation of the pace and character of reform which emphasized the tension between, on the one hand, pressures for change arising out of new ideas about the administration of the criminal law and new problems of crime and disorder, and, on the other, the inertia which characterized a law enforcement system deeply rooted in a political and social order profoundly resistant to change.

From the appearance of the first volume in 1948, Radzinowicz's *History* was acknowledged as a work of outstanding scholarship. Yet it took a long time for its findings to be assimilated by historians. In part, this was a consequence of the lack of interest among historians in the 1950s and early 1960s in its subject matter. Only since the late 1960s, with the explosion of interest in the social and legal history of crime and the criminal law, has Radzinowicz's work received the attention it deserves. With attention has inevitably come criticism. Radzinowicz has been taken to task for his reliance on official sources, his failure to take the work of the courts seriously, his Whiggish enthusiasm for the prejudices of eighteenth- and nineteenth-century reformers. It is a striking testimony to his scholarship, however, that the questions he addresses and the information he provides continue to serve as a framework within which many of his critics work.

JAS

Main publications

A History of English Criminal Law and its Administration from 1750, 5 vols, (London: Stevens, 1948–86) vol. 1: *The Movement for Reform* (1948), vol. 2: *The Clash between Private Initiative and Public Interest in the Enforcement of the Law* (1956), vol. 3: *Crosscurrents in the Movement for the Reform of the Police* (1956), vol. 4: *Grappling for Control* (1968), vol. 5, with R. Hood: *The Emergence of Penal Policy* (1986); *Sir James Fitzjames Stephen 1829–1894 and his Contribution to the Development of Criminal Law* (London: Bernard Quaritch, 1957); *Ideology and Crime* (London: Heinemann, 1966).

Reading

Hay, Douglas: Property, authority and the criminal law. In *Albion's Fatal Tree*, ed. D. Hay, *et al.* (London: Allen Lane, 1975).

Innes, Joanna and Styles, John: The crime wave: recent writing on crime and criminal justice in eighteenth-century England. *Journal of British Studies* 25 (1986) 380–435.

[Thompson, Edward]: Law as part of a culture. *Times Literary Supplement* 3504 (1969) 425–7.

Ralegh, Walter (b.1554, d.1618) 'Only my father would keep such a bird in a cage', was the comment of Henry, Prince of Wales when James I sent Ralegh to the Tower. But at least the bird sang, and after 11 years Ralegh published his *History of the World*, one of the glories of the English language. Its success was immediate, perhaps because James tried ineffectually to suppress it as 'too saucy in censuring princes'. Hampden, Lilburne, Milton, Cromwell and Locke all read and admired it.

The scale of the work, as originally conceived, was enormous, and the tone majestic. In three sections, Ralegh was to deal with the rise and fall of pre-Christian civilizations, the Christian era, and the history of Britain. But with the death of Prince Henry in 1612, under whose encouragement the work had been written, the heart went out of Ralegh's enterprise, and his published volumes reached no further than the second century BC, ending with the celebrated apostrophe to death. The intention was didactic and exemplary. It was the duty of the historian, wrote Ralegh, to demonstrate God's will in the world and to show how evil deeds were punished. There was no sense of progress. For Ralegh, 'the long day of mankind' was 'drawing fast towards an evening and the world's tragedy and time near at an end'.

In his preface, Ralegh apologized for not bringing his history closer to the seventeenth century, but added, with nice irony: 'whosoever in writing a modern history, shall follow truth too near the heels, it may haply strike out his teeth'. But he frequently diverted from ancient times to refer to recent or contemporary events and this undoubtedly helped to give the work appeal. Many of the monarchs of Britain were reviewed and found wanting, and Henry VIII was held up as a supreme example of a merciless prince:

For how many servants did he advance in haste, (but for what virtue no man could suspect), and with the change of his fancy ruined again, no man knowing for what offence? To how many others, of more desert, gave he abundant flowers from whence to gather honey, and in the end of harvest burnt them in the hive?

As one might expect, both from Ralegh's opinions and from his predicament, some of the most memorable passages illustrate the transitoriness of human success and the vicissitudes to which all people are subject in this 'ridiculous world': 'there is no man so assured of his honour, of his riches, health or life, but that he may be deprived of either, or all, the very next hour or day to come.' The same was true of empires and of civilizations: 'and yet hath Babylon, Persia, Egypt, Syria, Macedon, Carthage, Rome and the rest no fruit, no flower, grass nor leaf springing up on the face of the earth of those seeds. No! Their very roots and ruins do hardly remain.'

Such an attitude was poetic and moralistic rather than historical and Ralegh's *History* declined sharply in popularity in the following

348

century, which was less receptive to his heavy, doom-laden grandeur. Johnson paid tribute to the 'elegance' of Ralegh's style but did not think that the book itself was more than a 'historical dissertation'. Though Ralegh took pains with his sources and made efforts to compare them, a more sceptical age found it hard to take seriously his effort to demonstrate the exact dimensions of Noah's Ark. His work led nowhere, observed a modern commentator, and it remains true that its political influence, in helping to provide justification for resistance to Stuart monarchs, was more important than its historiographical.   JAC

Main publications

The Discoverie of the Large ... Empyre of Guiana (London: Robert Robinson, 1596); *The History of the World* (London: W. Burre, 1614).

Reading

Firth, C. H.: Sir Walter Raleigh's 'History of the World'. *Proceedings of the British Academy* 8 (October 1918) 427–46.

Trevor-Roper, H.: The last Elizabethan: Sir Walter Raleigh. In *Historical Essays* (London: Macmillan, 1957), pp. 103–7.

Ramsay, James Henry (b.1832, d.1925) The tenth baronet of an ancient Scottish family with strong academic interests, Ramsay devoted over forty years of his working life to producing *The Scholar's History of England*, an eight-volume narrative history of England up to 1500 from original sources. Factual and annalistic, it had much the same value for English students as the *Jahrbücher des deutschen Reichs* in Germany. His most enduring achievement was his pioneer work on the revenues of the kings of England, based on account rolls in the Public Record Office.

          MMC

Main publications

(All published by Oxford University Press, Oxford.) *The Scholar's History of England*, 8 vols, (1892–1913) vols 1–2: *The Foundations of England* (1898), vol. 3: *The Angevin Empire, 1154–1216* (1903), (vol. 4: *The Dawn of the Constitution, 1216–1307*, (1908), vols 5–7: *The Genesis of Lancaster, 1307–1399* (1913), vol. 8; *Lancaster and York, 1399–1488* (1892); *The Revenues of the Kings of England, 1066–1399* (1925).

Ranke, Leopold von (b.1795, d.1886) A writer of narrative history on a grand scale and famous for his claim to write it as it actually was ('wie es eigentlich gewesen'), Ranke was born in Wiehe, Thuringia, a lawyer's son – though his forebears were Lutheran pastors. He was educated at a famous school, the Schulpforta, and at Leipzig university.

Upon publication of his first work, *The Roman and German Peoples*, in 1824 Ranke gained fame, and an appointment as professor of history at Berlin university, where he remained until 1871. The preface to the book contained the notorious and misunderstood claim cited above. Ranke did not mean that he would achieve a God-like impartiality, but that he would write history as he found it rather than to prove any dogma. Ranke inaugurated the writing of history from a wide range of manuscript documents; he used private letters, diplomatic dispatches, and diaries in Latin, French, German, Italian, Spanish and English. To these he applied the critical standards developed by the historians of Greece and Rome, Niebuhr and Mommsen. He made tours of archives in Germany, Austria and Italy during the years 1827 to 1831 and 1834 to 1837, and later visited those in Paris, London and Oxford. The idea which led him to plan six histories was that during the barbarian invasions six peoples – the Italian, French, Spanish (called Roman); and German, English and Scandinavian (called German) – formed a Latin, Christian European community. This was consolidated by the crusades, and then by rivalry in overseas discovery. The six peoples did not unite but during the Italian Wars of 1494 to 1515 (the subject of Ranke's first book) and the subsequent conflict between the Catholic Spanish monarchy and the French monarchy with Protestant and Ottoman allies, they formed the modern European state system.

Ranke's second work was on the Ottomans and Spain but his archival tour deflected him and he published *German History, 1555–1618* third. The history of the popes followed, then *German History in the Age of the Reformation* and, after an interval, the French history and the English history. In the interval he began the nine, eventually extended to twelve, books of Prussian history which overweighted the German part of his originally symmetrical plan. Ranke's marriage in 1840 to Clara Graves, an Englishwoman he met in Paris, and the birth of his children anchored him in his immediate surroundings. He was close to Frederick William IV, was ennobled and became the friend of Max of Bavaria. Ranke also covered much contemporary history in his university courses and in his contributions to the *Historisch-politische Zeitschrift* of which he was editor.

Supremely conscious of the unceasing flow of events Ranke wrote about long periods, often casting back to the middle ages or earlier. He wrote of the men and women who, he believed, caused events and the persons of his drama were relatively few. He showed imagination in the reconstruction of motives, sensitivity in the depiction of character, dramatic sense in choosing when to introduce a particular person into the story. His narrative art is well worth study. But he was also handling the material of philosophy and more than one writer has inquired into the relationship between Ranke and HEGEL.

Ranke saw in history 'freedom' and 'necessity' which contended against each other and penetrated each other. Thus in acting the powerful individual was both free and constrained. First, the choice of action was based upon an appropriate, if not the only, means of achieving a goal: Frederick William I of Prussia had to build an army because he could only survive by maintaining a balance of military strength among his neighbours. Second, the action was directed by human psychology and the character of things: Charles V kept on fighting after achieving his aims 'because it is not in the nature of man to be content with limited gain'. Henry IV of France and Elizabeth of England (favourites with Ranke) so well understood the character of things that they seemed to fuse themselves with the situations in which they worked. In contrast Louis XIV so sought to impose his will on people and things that he flew in the face of necessity. Third, the career of every individual of historical importance was in part predetermined by the driving power in events themselves. This does not mean that Ranke believed in historical inevitability. It means that he accepted Kant's distinction between the particular and the general which allowed, for example, particular French people to be Protestants but the general character of France to be Catholic. It means also that he accepted Herder's notion of the moral energy in communities and nations which inclined them to grow further in a direction once taken. Applied to the French monarchy this notion explained why the feudal, aristocratic and national forces which might have successfully resisted its centralizing habit failed to do so. Finally it meant that Ranke believed that God had brought certain people into the world at a particular time as chosen instruments and that he recognized God's purpose in the world's order. But Ranke's religious sense was too subtle for him to claim to know what God's purpose was or even to discern it in an accumulation of events trending in one direction. Mortals must live with the mystery of world history.   AR

Main publications

Leopold von Rankes Sämmtliche Werke (Collected works), 54 vols (Leipzig: Duncker & Humblot, 1867−90);. vols 33−4, *Geschichten der romanischen und germanischen Völke* (Histories of the Roman and German peoples) (1824); vols 37−9, *Die romanischen Päpste* (The Roman Popes) (1834), vols 1−6, *Deutsche Geschichte im Zeitalter der Reformation* (German history in the age of the reformation) (1839−47).

Reading

Fuchs, W. P.: *Leopold von Ranke Das Briefwerk* (Letters) [also a biography; Fuchs is the authority on Ranke] (Hamburg: Hoffman & Campe, 1949).
Gay, P.; *Style in History* (London: Jonathan Cape, 1975) pp. 59−94.
Von Laue, T. H.: *Leopold von Ranke: the Formative Years* (Princeton: Princeton Univeristy Press, 1950).

Rapin-Thoyras, Paul de (b.1661, d.1725) A French Huguenot, of a family of lawyers. After the revocation of the Edict of Nantes, Rapin-Thoyras accompanied William of Orange to England and then to Ireland. He spent the rest of his life at The Hague or in Germany. In 1717 he published a *Dissertation sur l'origine du gouvernement de l'Angleterre* and from 1723 to 1725 brought out a series of volumes of *Histoire de l'Angleterre*. The attitude was Whiggish. Rapin took some pains with his research and printed some historical documents, though he was not familiar with English state papers. Translated into English by Nicholas Tindal (1725–31), the book had a great success and remained the standard history until superseded by Hume and Goldsmith. JAC

Main publications

Dissertation sur l'origine du gouvernement de l'Angleterre (The Hague: 1717); *Histoire de l'Angleterre* (The Hague: 1723–5).

Rashdall, Hastings (b.1858, d.1924) Rashdall became a historian by accident. He wanted to teach philosophy at Oxford, but a disappointing second in final schools crushed his hopes of a college fellowship. There was only one alternative. He had won the Stanhope Prize in 1879; perhaps another success in open competition would override his poor examination results. His ploy worked. In 1883 he won the Chancellor's prize and the offer, subject to revision, of publication. Revision took twelve years. It became an obsession. Rashdall would not, could not go to press before 'every published document relating to any medieval university' and every relevant work of contemporary scholarship had been consulted. A once slim essay became three weighty volumes published in 1895 as *The Universities of Europe in the Middle Ages*.

It was an astonishing achievement. Acclaim was instant and remains undiminished. The short sections on intellectual life were weak, unconvincing, and soon rendered obsolete. But the core of the work – a comparative study of the institutional structures and constitutional features of European universities based on detailed studies of printed documentary sources – has never been surpassed.

Publication coincided with Rashdall's appointment to a tutorship in philosophy at New College, Oxford. The combination of events had a cathartic effect on him. He never wrote history again. By developing instead the notions of 'personal idealism' and 'ideal utilitarianism' he became one of the leading English religious thinkers of the early twentieth century. PRHS

Main publications

The Universities of Europe in the Middle Ages, 3 vols (Oxford: Clarendon Press, 1895).

Reading

Matheson, P. E.: *Life of Hastings Rashdall* (London: Oxford University Press, 1928).

Rashid al-Din (b.1247, d.1318) Born in Hamadan in western Persia, Rashid al-Din Fadl Allah was trained as a physician. His family was Jewish, but he was converted to Islam at the age of 30. From 1298 until his execution in 1318 he was the leading statesman of the Mongol kingdom in Persia and Iraq, the Ilkhanate, which had been set up in the 1250s by Hulegu, grandson of Genghis Khan. Rashid al-Din occupied, jointly with a succession of colleagues, the post of *wazir*, head of the Persian bureaucracy which served the ruling Mongol military aristocracy.

The Ilkhan Ghazan (reigned 1295–1304) asked Rashid al-Din to write a history of the Mongols and their conquests. Subsequently Ghazan's brother and successor Oljeitu (reigned 1304–16) suggested that the history should be expanded to include all the peoples with whom the Mongols had come into contact. The result was the *Jami' al-tawarikh* (Collection of histories), a lengthy work which ranks as the most important single source in any language for the history of the Mongol world empire, as well as being, for its date and place of origin, uniquely wide ranging. Rashid al-Din also left works of Islamic theology and a volume of letters (which may be spurious).

The first part of the *Jami' al-tawarikh* contains the more important material. For its account of the career of Genghis Khan it drew on Mongolian sources which are now lost; and for the history of Mongol Persia it was based on the author's own wide experience of government. In particular it preserved the texts of many of Ghazan's edicts which were designed to repair the ravages of seven decades of Mongol misgovernment. Being the work of a prominent bureaucrat it is exceedingly well informed, if hardly objective. The second part is interesting historiographically. It includes accounts of China, India, the Turks, the Jews, the Franks, etc., and thus has some claim to be

351

regarded as a world history. In this respect it had neither predecessors nor immediate successors in the Muslim Persian historiographical tradition. (See ISLAMIC HISTORIOGRAPHY.)

DOM

Main writings

Jami' al-tawarikh [only part available in English] trans. J. A. Boyle, *The Successors of Genghis Khan* (New York and London: Columbia University Press, 1971); other sections trans. into French, German, and especially Russian. For a flavour of the 'world history' see *Histoire des Francs*, ed. and trans. K. Jahn (Leiden: E. J. Brill, 1951).

Reading

Boyle, J. A.: Introduction to *The Successors of Genghis Khan*. [See above.]
Morgan, D. D.: *The Mongols* (Oxford: Basil Blackwell, 1986).

Raynal, Guillaume Thomas François (b.1713, d.1796) Born in Languedoc, Raynal was educated by the Jesuits, joined them, and taught in Jesuit colleges until the age of 34. He then became a freelance writer in Paris, and was editor of the *Mercure de France* between 1750 and 1754. He knew all the major figures of the Parisian Enlightenment, and between the late 1740s and 1762 published various descriptive and historical works. His name was established, however, in 1772 with the publication of *Histoire philosophique des deux Indes*, the founding work of anti-colonialism. It denounced European expansion as a tragedy and disaster for the rest of the world. Raynal never left Europe, but wide reading had convinced him that wherever they went the Europeans had brought cruelty, greed and exploitation. These convictions were expressed in lurid, provocative language which did much to boost the book's sales; but it was a compendium, unique in its time, on the history of Europe's overseas expansion. Raynal's was not the only hand involved; Diderot, d'Holbach and other *philosophes* are known to have supplied much material, and the text was constantly revised and amended in the light of contemporary events. One of the greatest best-sellers of its day, it went through three editions and 30 impressions in Raynal's lifetime, and was translated into Spanish and English. It was originally published anonymously, with even a false publication date (1770) and was banned as subversive throughout the French and Spanish dominions. When Raynal admitted authorship in 1780 he was compelled to leave the country and on his return was not allowed to live in Paris. When he reappeared there in 1791 it was to denounce the excesses of a Revolution of which many considered him a precursor. He died in poverty in Marseilles.

WD

Main publications

Histoire philosophique et politique des établissements et du commerce des Européens dans les deux Indes, 6 vols (Amsterdam: 1770).

Reading

Wolpe, H.: *Raynal et sa machine de guerre. L' 'Histoire des deux Indes' et ses perfectionnements* (Stanford, Calif.: Stanford University Press, 1957).

Redlich, Josef (b.1869, d.1936) An Austrian historian, intellectual, and politician of Moravian Jewish extraction, Redlich was a lawyer by training and fascinated by constitutions and structures of government. He engaged in an exhaustive study of English administration and the procedures of the House of Commons, which gained him a speciaiist reputation in Britain. He then made a political career in Austria, serving as minister of finance in the last months of the Monarchy and again in 1931. His fascinating diaries, posthumously published, are a prime source for the public life of Austria-Hungary before and during the war. After 1918 Redlich had the enforced leisure to produce two major works of pure history: a biography of Emperor Francis Joseph which still rules the field and, above all, a majestic analysis of the constitutional question in the Habsburg lands between 1848 and 1867. Given Redlich's catholic interests, including a chair at Harvard from 1926, even this monumental investigation remained a torso (he planned it to continue to 1918); yet its unerring grasp of political realities and its finely-nuanced analysis of the problems of empire qualify it as one of the few undoubted masterpieces of Austrian historiography.

RJWE

Main publications

Englische Lokalverwaltung (1901) trans. as *Local Government in England*, ed. F. W. Hirst, 2 vols (London: Macmillan, 1903); *Das österreichische Staats- und Reichsproblem*, 2 vols (Leipzig: P. Reinhold, 1920–6); *Kaiser Franz Josef von Österreich: Eine Biographie*, (1928) trans. as *Emperor Francis Joseph of Austria* (London: Macmillan, 1929).

Reading

Fellner, F.: Introduction to Redlich's *Schicksalsjahre Österreichs, 1908–19*, 2 vols (Graz/Cologne: Veröffentlichungen der Kommission für neuere Geschichte Österreichs, 1953–4).

Ritter, Gerhard (b.1888, d.1967) Born in Bad Sooden, Ritter's education took him from Magdeburg to three universities: Heidelberg, Hamburg and Freiburg. Ritter was appointed to Freiburg in 1925, where he remained, apart from a period of detention in 1944–5, and achieved emeritus status in 1956.

The range of Ritter's scholarship made him one of the most formidable historians of his generation. The topics which engaged his attention fell firmly into a traditional concern with great men and the political and ethical dilemmas confronting them. He wrote a substantial history of the University of Heidelberg and Martin Luther early engaged his attention. He began a long connection with the *Archiv für Reformationsgeschichte* (Archive for Reformation history). All his life he remained fascinated by Luther, though he confessed in the English version of his biographical study that he had earlier been too swayed by nationalist sentiment in his interpretation.

In 1913 Ritter published a study of Prussian conservatism and Bismarck's German policy. After the war, he again turned to the problem of Prussia's relationship to Germany. His biography of Stein appeared in 1931 and soon established itself as a major interpretation. That was followed, in 1936, by a historical profile of Frederick the Great. These were not easy years for historians to concern themselves with such issues. Ritter thought of himself as a realist in his recognition of the inescapable facts of military power; he was not an Anglo-Saxon pacifist. Nevertheless, might was not right. The second world war therefore inevitably caused him much anguish. His study of Carl Goerdeler and the German resistance movement (1955) was no detached essay. It drew upon his own experiences at a time of national turmoil. In his post-war writings he struggled to come to terms with the German catastrophe in such works as *Die Dämonie der Macht* (Demonic of power) (1947) and *Europa und die deutsche Frage* (Europe and the German question) (1948). His final major study of the relationship between military and civil power, *Staatskunst und Kriegshandwerk*. was a fitting climax to a lifetime's concern in one way or another with this issue. Its range remains impressive, reflecting Ritter's long personal and historical agonizing over Germany's past. But it was also the climax of a particular historiographical tradition, and in his old age Ritter found himself engaged in controversy with FISCHER concerning Germany's role in 1914. The encounter was a clash of generations and political assumptions. Only after a quarter of a century is it possible to appreciate the virtues of both approaches.   KGR

Main publications

Die preussischen Konservativen und Bismarcks deutsche Politik, 1858 bis 1876 (The Prussian conservatives and Bismarck's German Policy, 1858 to 1876) (Heidelberg: 1913); *Stein: eine politische Biographie* (Stein: a political biography) (Stuttgart: Deutsche Verlags-Anstalt, 1931); *Friedrich der Grosse: ein historisches Profil* (1936) English trans. *Frederick the Great: a Historical Profile* (London: Eyre & Spottiswoode, 1968); *Staatskunst und Kriegshandwerk* (1954–68) English trans. *The Sword and the Sceptre* (London: Allen Lane, 1969–73); *Carl Goerdeler und die deutsche Widerstandsbewegung* (1955) English trans. *Carl Goerdeler and the German Resistance Movement* (London: Allen & Unwin, 1958); *Luther: His Life and Work* (London: Collins, 1963).

Reading

Iggers, G. G.: *New Directions in European historiography* (Middletown, Conn.: Wesleyan University Press, 1975).

Roberts, Michael (b.1908) A Lancastrian by birth, Roberts graduated from Worcester College, Oxford in 1931. After a year at Princeton he spent two years as lecturer in Oxford and Liverpool before being appointed, still aged only 31, to the chair of modern history at Rhodes University, Grahamstown. After two years in the army, in 1944 he became British Council representative in Stockholm. His two years in the Swedish capital gave him what proved to be a lifelong interest in Swedish history, particularly in the seventeenth century. The first-fruit of this was the finest of all his rich scholarship, a two-volume study of Sweden during the reign of Gustav II Adolf. The first volume was completed in South Africa. The second followed in 1958, four years after Roberts had returned to the United Kingdom to succeed G. O. Sayles in the chair of history at the Queen's University Belfast. It contains a survey, unlikely to be surpassed in any language, of Swedish society at the time of the king's accession. Roberts's work has won deep respect in the Swedish academic world and he has been awarded membership of the Swedish Academies of Science and of Letters, History and Antiquities.

At Belfast Roberts did much to encourage the teaching of Irish history and was largely instrumental in the establishment of the Wiles Lectures, to which he himself contributed after his retirement with 'The Swedish Imperial Experience'. He managed to find time in the midst of his teaching and administrative commitments to continue to add to our knowledge of sixteenth- and seventeenth-century Sweden in the form of books and articles (most of which were reprinted in *Essays in Swedish History*). In these he discussed the motivation for Swedish territorial expansion, questioning the economic interpretation favoured by a number of Swedish scholars in favour of one which stressed strategic considerations. He retired in 1973 to live in South Africa, but continues to publish, now principally on eighteenth-century topics.   SPO

Main publications

Gustavus Adolphus, a History of Sweden 1611–1632 (London: Longmans, Green, 1953, 1958); *Essays in Swedish History* (London: Weidenfeld & Nicholson, 1967); *The Early Vasas* (Cambridge: Cambridge University Press, 1968); *British Diplomacy and Swedish Politics 1758–1773* (London: Macmillan, 1980); *The Age of Liberty: Sweden 1719–1772* (Cambridge University Press, 1986).

Reading

Bossy, John and Jupp. Peter eds.: Essays Presented to Michael Roberts (Belfast: Blackstaff Press, 1976) pp. vii–ix.

Robertson, William (b.1721, d.1793) A minister's son, educated at Dalkeith Grammar School and Edinburgh University, Robertson took up his first living in 1743 at Gladsmuir, East Lothian, and in 1756 moved to the first of his Edinburgh ministries. He became a powerful political figure, leading the Moderate group within the Church of Scotland from 1751. The patronage of Lord Bute helped him to become principal of Edinburgh University from 1762 and Historiographer Royal for Scotland, a lucrative but less demanding position. His energy and forcefulness helped to secure Moderate strength in the General Assembly and to make Edinburgh University such a flourishing institution by the end of the century.

Robertson was regarded by his contemporaries as an immensely succesful historical writer. Hume regarded his rapid achievements with some envy. Some 1250 copies of the first edition of his first major work, the *History of Scotland* (1759) sold out in a month. Though it purported to be a history of Scotland up to the sixteenth century, very little space was given to any period before then. His interest in early modern Europe grew, and he devoted both his two following works, the *History of the Reign of the Emperor Charles V* (1769), and the *History of America* (1777) to it. Robertson was distinguished among his contemporaries for his scrupulousness and his eagerness to search for primary sources in British and European libraries, and even through questionnaires sent to Spaniards and to missionaries to the American Indians. He was also an admirable narrator and his skills are seen at their best in his account of the discovery of America.

Robertson's historical outlook was shaped in some respects by factors he shared with HUME and SMITH: an interest in the growth of the broad pattern of European civilization and a strong emphasis on the material circumstances shaping that civilization. Unlike them, he introduced some sense of a divine, providential framework to historical study, seen in an early sermon, *The Situation of the World at the Time of Christ's Appearance* (1755). His emphasis on the sixteenth century, and his dismissal of much of the European medieval past as mere barbarism and superstition sprang from his view of the later period as one in which reason came to play a more effective part in political affairs, and the European state system began to achieve something like a balance of power, moving recognizably towards the commercial and civilized world of his own day.

Robertson shared with Smith an approach to historical writing which stressed material and environmental factors. In his *History of America* he tried to offer a comparative study of the levels of existence of different indigenous American peoples. While demonstrating the important point that the origin of the American tribes was likely to be found in the crossing from Asia, he saw as a more fundamental study for the historian, the record of progress through the different stages of society. Whether describing the poverty of North American tribes or the relative wealth of the Aztec or Inca cities, he did not lose sight of that progression, or its ultimate goal in the levels achieved by western European civilization.   JR

Main publications

History of Scotland, 2 vols (London: 1759); *History of the Reign of the Emperor Charles V, with a View of the Progress of Society in Europe* ... 3 vols (London: 1769); *History of America*, 2 vols (London: 1777); *Historical Disquisition concerning the Knowledge which the Ancients had of India* (London: 1791).

Reading

Humphreys, R. A.: William Robertson and his 'History of America'. In *Tradition and Revolt in Latin America and other essays* (London: Weidenfeld & Nicolson, 1969).
Meek, R. L.: *Social Science and the Ignoble Savage* (Cambridge: Cambridge University Press, 1976).
Stewart, D.: *Account of the Life and Writings of William Robertson D. D.* In *The Works of William Robertson*, 12 vols (London: 1817).

Rodrigues, José Honorio (b.1913, d.1987) Born and educated (in law) in Rio de Janeiro, Rodrigues's visits to the United States and England taught him the tools of the trade of a professional historian. He promoted the introduction into Brazilian universities of courses in methodology, research, and historiography. Rodrigues directed the Division of Rare Books and Publications of the national library and was director of the National Archives (1958–64). He enjoyed an international re-

putation for historiographical studies, edited collections of documents, and critical editions. An interpretive historian, his work is characterized by meticulous archival research, and his studies into the nature of historical inquiry led him to urge the preservation of archives and documents. His work on the colonial period is complemented by the historical perspective which he brings to contemporary social and economic problems of Brazil.

AJRR-W

Main publications

Civilização Holandesa no Brasil (Rio de Janeiro: Companhia Editora Nacional, 1940); *A Teoria da História do Brasil* (São Paulo: Instituto Progresso Editorial, 1949); *Historiografia e Bibliografia do Dominio Holandes no Brasil* (Rio de Janeiro: Instituto Nacional do Livro, 1949); *A Pesquisa Histórica no Brasil* (Rio de Janeiro: Instituto Nacional do Livro, 1952); *Historiografia del Brasil: Siglo XVI* (Mexico City: Editorial Libros de Mexico, 1957); *Brasil e Africa* (Rio de Janeiro: Editora Civilização Brasileira, 1961); *Historiografia del Brasil: Siglo XVII* (Mexico City: Editorial Libros de Mexico, 1963); *Brazil and Africa* trans. R. A. Mazzara and S. Hileman (Berkeley and Los Angeles: University of California Press, 1965; *Independencia, Revolução e Contrarevoluçãs*, 5 vols (Rio de Janeiro, 1975–6); *O Parlamento e a Consolidação do Império* (Brasília, 1982).

Roger of Howden (d.1201/2) Roger of Howden obtained his name from his connections with the township of Howden in the East Riding of Yorkshire where he succeeded his father as parson in or before 1174. The chronicler must have been often absent from his parish, for probably shortly before 1174 he became a clerk at the court of Henry II. To judge from the diarial quality of his writings, the appointment led to a life centred on the royal court until shortly after the death of Henry II when he lost his position under Richard. In his last twelve years Roger of Howden participated in the Third Crusade before returning to his Yorkshire parish where he found service with Hugh du Puiset, Bishop of Durham, who had an episcopal residence at Howden.

Roger of Howden's *Gesta Regis Henrici Secundi* has often been erroneously ascribed to Benedict of Peterborough. It consists of annals covering the period between 1170 and 1192 and was written and revised throughout that period with the help of information and documents gathered at the royal court. The *Chronica*, which covers the period 732 to 1201, was commenced in 1192 or 1193. It has annals to 1169, composed from a variety of written sources among which the *Historia post Bedam* was most used which served as a preface to a revised edition of the *Gesta* which provides the basis of the *Chronica's* coverage of the period to 1192. Subsequently Roger added details of contemporary events as they became available in the years up to his death. The edition of the *Chronica* now represented by British Library Royal MS 14.C.2 and Bodleian Library Laud MS 582, which are in part written in the author's own hand, was produced in the last two or three years of his life.

It has often been asserted that the writings of Roger of Howden, unlike those of some of his contemporaries, lack a personal touch because they rarely display anything more than the slightest prejudice. He has been called a trimmer, but careful analysis of his work is beginning to show that there is little sign of trimming in the discussion of issues which involved those from whom he received employment.   DJC

Main writings

Gesta Regis Henrici Secundi Benedicti Abbatis (Rolls Series XLIV); *Chronica Rogeri de Houedene* (Rolls Series LI).

Reading

Corner, D. J.: The *Gesta Regis Henrici Secundi* and *Chronica* of Roger, Parson of Howden. *Bulletin of the Institute of Historical Research* 56 (1983) 126–44.

Roger of Wendover See ST ALBANS CHRONICLERS.

Rogers, James Edwin Thorold (b.1823, d.1890) Rogers began academic life with a classics degree at Oxford (1846). While a tutor in classics his radicalism, inspired by Bright, Cobden and Mill, led him to agitate for university reform; he also turned to teach economic sciences (at King's College, London), and held the chair of political economy at Oxford in 1862–7, renewal being prevented by conservative opposition. He belonged to the group of academics who agitated for political reform in the 1860s, at which time Rogers advocated manhood suffrage and other progressive causes. After a period as a Liberal MP (1880–6), he was re-elected to the Oxford chair for the last two years of his life. He wrote on philosophy, politics and religion, but is best known as an economic historian. For him politics and history were closely linked: the purpose of history was 'to examine the causes of modern evils . . . before remedying them'. In opposition to the classical economists he believed that industrialization had impoverished the working man, and that social change could be achieved by political action. In *Six Centuries of Work and Wages* he showed in vigorous and direct prose that the condition of wage-earners had deteriorated after the fifteenth century. The arguments that he advanced were influential (the book went through eleven editions by 1912), but are now largely superseded. However, the basis of his work, the *History of Agriculture and Prices*, is still used and stands as a monument to his industry and scholarship.   CCD

Main publications

A History of Agriculture and Prices in England, 7 vols (Oxford: Clarendon Press, 1866–1902); *Six Centuries of Work and Wages* (London: Swan & Sonnenschein, 1884).

Reading

Harvie, C.: *Lights of Liberalism* (London: Allen Lane, 1976).

Rostovtzeff, Michael Ivanovitch (b.1870, d.1952) (His name appears in a wide variety of spellings; this is the form which he regularly used in the last part of his life.) One of the leading historians of the ancient world, Rostovtzeff's upbringing and experiences had a profound effect on his interests and attitudes. He was the son of the director of a gymnasium near Kiev in the south-western part of the Tsarist empire. This region was noted for its dependence on agriculture and for its ethnic diversity. Cultural interaction and the social structure of ancient agriculture were central concerns in Rostovtzeff's later reseach. Having attended the universities of Kiev and then St Petersburg, from where he graduated in 1892, he taught for a time and then spent three years travelling in central Europe and the Mediterranean countries, where his visit to Pompeii stimulated a long-lasting pre-occupation.

On his return to Russia Rostovtzeff began teaching Latin at the University of St Petersburg, where he was made a professor in 1903 after completing important works on state contracts in the Roman empire (his master's thesis) and on Roman lead tesserae (his doctorate). In the years running up to the Russian Revolution he turned his attention to southern Russia, the region from which he originated. Tackling this area with its complex cultural history and phenomenal richness of material remains led him to emphasize that archaeology provided an independent source as important as written texts for the historian. His publications were always to be profusely illustrated with material evidence not as a mere adornment but as important in its own right. Even when absorbed in the problems of the past, current political developments were never far from his mind. His work on the Roman colonate system of land tenure included a comparison between one of the most important Roman decrees and P. A. Stolypin's edict of November 1906 which enabled Russian peasants to depart from their communal organizations and turn themselves into yeoman farmers. In his study of the northern Black Sea littoral he claimed that the area generated a long-lived culture 'which no German or Mongolian invaders were able to destroy'. Published in 1921, these words clearly alluded to the German occupation of the Ukraine in 1918 and to Rostovtzeff's feeling for the vicissitudes of his country.

A committed anti-Bolshevik, Rostovtzeff emigrated from Russia and found sanctuary for a short time at Queen's College, Oxford, where he combined scholarly research on papyri with the writing of vituperative anti-Soviet pamphlets. Then came an invitation to the chair of ancient history at Wisconsin, followed in 1925 by a move to Yale as he accepted the Sterling professorship of ancient

history. New Haven was to be his home for the rest of his life.

In 1928 Yale took over from the French the funding of the excavation of the remarkable site of Dura-Europos on the Euphrates, which successively had been a Hellenistic fortress, Parthian caravan city and Roman frontier stronghold. The diversity of its cultural influences was an obvious attraction for Rostovtzeff, as was the remarkable state of preservation of its ruins which Rostovtzeff compared with Pompeii. For ten years he supervised the work of the expedition, and nurtured the talents of a group of colleagues and pupils who emerged as the golden generation of American ancient historians and became one of Rostovtzeff's most potent legacies to scholarship.

Rostovtzeff was a tireless writer. His bibliography, spanning 58 years of research, runs to nearly 500 items. He never set subjects aside and was constantly revising his work in the light of new discoveries. Two of his most significant works appeared at about the same time in the mid-1920s. If his *History of the Ancient World* now seems very dated, his massive *Social and Economic History of the Roman Empire* has been described as 'the source, the inspiration and the despair of scholars'. For Rostovtzeff the difference in the social and economic structure of the ancient world from the modern era was quantitative, not qualitative. He was quite happy to describe ancient society in language more appropriate to the modern world. Further he was moved by what a friendly critic called 'a Platonist belief that civilization can only be created and maintained by a small upper class which remains continuously endangered by barbarian mass movements' (F. M. Heichelheim, review of *The Social and Economic History of the Hellenistic World*, *JHS* vol. 63, 1943, p. 129). His bitterness about what had happened in Russia was carried over into his bleak, unforgiving, and deeply distorted picture of the late Roman empire in which the civilized ambitions of an urban aristocracy are blotted out by the barbarianism of the lower classes. By 1941 cooler and shrewder judgement inspired his *Social and Economic History of the Hellenistic World*, one of the landmarks of historical writing in the twentieth century. If Rostovtzeff did not create the Hellenistic period, then his work certainly defined the fundamental characteristics of Greek society in the centuries after Alexander the Great.

In many ways Rostovtzeff belongs to the traditions of nineteenth-century scholarship. His lack of interest in sociological theory, the straightforwardness of his methodological approach, and a tendency to high-minded moralizing have not endeared his work to the more knowing of recent classical scholars.

DBS/JJP

Main publications

Geschichte der Staatspacht in der römischen Kaiserzeit bis Diokletian (Ergänzungsband IX: *Philologus*, 1902), pp. 331ff.; *Studien zur Geschichte des römischen Kolonates* (Beiheft I: *Archiv für Papyrusforschung*, 1910); *Iranians and Greeks in South Russia* (Oxford: Clarendon Press, 1922); *A Large Estate in Egypt in the Third Century B.C.* (Madison: University of Wisconsin Studies in the Social Sciences and History, No. 6, 1922); *The Social and Economic History of the Roman Empire* (Clarendon Press, 1926; 2nd edn rev. P. M. Fraser, 1957); *A History of the Ancient World*, vols 1 and 2, trans. J. D. Duff (Clarendon Press, 1926–7); *Skythien und der Bosporus*, vol. 1, trans. E. Pridik (Berlin: Hans Schoets, 1931); *The excavations of Dura-Europos conducted by Yale University and the French Academy of Inscriptions and Letters, Preliminary Reports*, ed. M. Rostovtzeff (New Haven, Conn.: Yale University Press, 1929–52); *The Social and Economic History of the Hellenistic World*, 3 vols (Clarendon Press, 1941).

Reading

Gilliam, J. F.: Addenda to the bibliography of M. I. Rostovtzeff. *Historia* 36 (1987) 1–8.

Vernadsky, G.: *Russian Historiography: a History* (Cambridge, Mass.: Nordland Publishing, 1978), pp. 449–54.

Welles, C. B.: M. I. Rostovtzeff. *Gnomon* 25 (1953) 142–4.

——: Bibliography – M. Rostovtzeff. *Historia* 5 (1956) 358–81.

Rostow, Walt Whitman (b.1916) Born in New York and educated at Yale and Oxford, Rostow's first academic post was as an instructor in economics at Columbia University (1940–1). After army service he served with the State Department. He was elected to the Harmsworth professorship of American history at Oxford in 1946 and to the Pitt professorship of American history at Cambridge in 1949. In 1951 he became professor of economic history at the Massachusetts Institute of Technology and a member of MIT's Center for International Studies. In 1961 he once again entered government service as a presidential assistant. From 1966 until 1969 he was Special Assistant to President Johnson and was much involved with South-East Asian affairs. In 1969 he went to the University of Texas where he became professor of political economy.

This mixture of academic and political life shows up strongly in Rostow's writing. His list of publications is prodigious, including no fewer than 16 books and nearly 40 articles on historical themes. In addition, he has published a large number of articles and addresses on political and public issues. He has done much to popularize the subject and to suggest that it has direct relevance to major political and economic issues. His writing is shot through with highly speculative ideas expressed by means of 'semantic inventions', as they have been described: for example, the terms 'preconditions', 'take-off', 'self-sustaining growth' and 'leading sector'.

The wide appeal of Rostow's work also owes much to his acute sense of timing. In particular, he provided an apparent historical pedigree for the new and handsome creature of the post-1945 world: economic growth. In 1953 he published *The Process of Economic Growth* and the themes he outlined there were brought to their highest level in 1960 in *The Stages of Economic Growth: a Non-Communist Manifesto*. Rostovian semantics were given full rein to produce a fusion of economic history and mild polemic. The stages were derived from a categorization, or taxonomy, of historical evidence (mainly based on British experience) and then presented as a universal process which ultimately led to major choices for political leaders in advanced economies. It was a view of the world based on the nation state. But it was fundamentally ahistorical because it was a closed analysis. Each country was considered in isolation and international factors which cut across national boundaries were given no place. Similarly, it paid no attention to the manner in which a given phase of economic development affected subsequent ones, and this major omission was particularly relevant to the question of the emergence of third world economies. Careful investigation of Rostow's claims as to the nature of the process were soon found to be incongruent with historical evidence. As a manifesto for growth it was soon remaindered.

The devastating professional criticism of his work should not be allowed to detract from what are perhaps Rostow's more long-lasting achievements. His ability to provoke widespread academic debate should be counted among these. More fundamentally his early work promoted the application of theory, quantification and dynamic models to the narrative of historical change. *The British Economy of the Nineteenth Century* (1948) and *The Growth and Fluctuation of the British Economy, 1790–1850* (1953) are splendid demonstrations of the newly discovered power of economic logic in historical explanation.

In the 1970s, Rostow reverted to the grand theme of global economic development. While the focus of these studies was on the dynamics of scientific and technical change in relation to the political economy of national development, and the same speculative approach was evident as in his earlier work, they lacked freshness and novelty. Furthermore, he pronounced a bright future for third world economies which few have found convincing.

For all the verve and vitality with which Rostow's ideas have been expressed they have not led to a school of historical analysis. His concepts are seriously under-specified and cannot be brought together effectively into either a theory or a typology of economic development over time. In this respect his work has been greatly overshadowed by that of Gerschenkron. Yet the seductive language Rostow invented has been a means of illuminating the truth that economic development is part of a complex process of *historical change* and not the consequence of the short-term application of economic prescriptions. In an age when a professional economist has become both soothsayer and prophet this is no mean achievement.   BWEA

Main publications

Essays in the British Economy of the Nineteenth Century (Oxford: Clarendon Press, 1948, repr. Westport, Conn.: Greenwood, 1981); *The Process of Economic Growth* (New York: W. W. Norton, Oxford: Clarendon Press, 1953; 2nd edn 1960); with Arthur D. Gayer, Anna Jacobson Schwarz, with the assistance of Izaiah Frank, *The Growth and Fluctuation of the British Economy, 1790–1850*, 2 vols (Oxford: Clarendon Press, 1953, 2nd edn, Brighton: Harvester, 1975); editor, *The Economic Take-off into Sustained Growth* (London: Macmillan, New York: St Martin's, 1963); *How It All Began: Origins of Modern Economy* (New York: McGraw-Hill, 1975); *The World Economy: History and Prospect* (Austin: University of Texas Press, London: Macmillan, 1978); *Why the Poor Get Richer and the Rich Slow Down: Essays in the Marshallian Long Period* (Austin: University of Texas Press; London: Macmillan, 1980).

Reading

Supple, Barry: Revisiting Rostow. *Economic History Review* 37 (1984) 107–14.

Roth, Cecil (b.1899, d.1970) One of the pioneers of Anglo-Jewish history, and probably the foremost of those who lived and worked in England. At the same time however Roth made outstanding contributions to the history of Italian Jewry and to that of the Marranos. His move from the City of London School to Oxford was interrupted by infantry service during the first world war, but in the autumn of 1919 he went to Merton College, Oxford, and gained a doctorate, *The Last Florentine Republic (1527–30)*, which was published in 1925 and translated into Italian in 1929. As an undergraduate he had developed an interest in Anglo-Jewish history and this was to change the direction of his career. There were then few opportunities for the academic study of modern Jewish history, and he was in effect an autodidact. There were virtually no academic appointments in 'modern' Jewish history, certainly none in Oxford until his own as reader in 'Post-Biblical Jewish Studies' in 1939; the necessity he faced to make a career as a freelance writer and researcher dictated the range of his publications in these years. Another factor was the need to be a publicist for Jewry in the face of growing Nazi anti-Semitism.

The bulk of Roth's work, and certainly that by which he will be remembered, lies in the field of Anglo-Jewish history, especially in the period before 1858. He was interested in individuals, families and small groups, rather than in 'the masses' or the applications of 'social sciences' to historical research, so that to many his approach seemed curiously old-fashioned and out-moded. He was firmly rooted in Jewish traditions, arguing vehemently for the validity of 'Jewish' history. But in addition to pursuing his own research he was always anxious to encourage others, so that even those who followed other lines of research could find encouragement from him, and the continuance during the second world war of the Jewish Historical Society of England was the result of his devotion to his subject. AN

Main publications

Magna Bibliotheca Anglo-Judaica (1937), *History of the Jews in England* (1941, 3rd edn, 1964).

Reading

Rabinowicz, O. K.: A bibliography of the writings of Cecil Roth. In *Remember the Days: Essays on Anglo-Jewish History presented to Cecil Roth*, ed. J. M. Shaftesley (1966).
Roth, Irene: *Cecil Roth, Historian Without Tears* (1982) [a memoir].

Round, John Horace (b.1854, d.1928) Round brought the standards of modern historical scholarship into the drawing-rooms of the professional and landowning classes of late Victorian and Edwardian England. This was the world into which he had been born, from which he inherited private means, interests both genealogical and literary, and a weak constitution. It was a world he never left, but which accident and ability enabled him for a time to transcend. At Oxford in the 1870s he sat at the feet of William Stubbs. Letters to his father criticized the sermons in Balliol College chapel, and commented on his contemporaries, among whom were T. F. Tout ('an unfortunate scholar'), R. Lane Poole and C. H. Firth.

Thereafter comment and criticism mounted up: 16 books and pamphlets and 812 articles and notes are listed in *Family Origins*, and that list is incomplete. Of the books *Geoffrey de Mandeville* comes closest to being more than a collection of articles: on the dating of a few charters was hung the picture of a baron who exemplified 'the feudal and anarchic spirit of the age' of King Stephen. The beginnings of *Feudal England* were firmly placed at the Norman Conquest, and the 1166 quotas were used for a classic study of the introduction of knight service into England. The volume contains also part of the fallout from one of Round's famous controversies, that with E. A. FREEMAN, whom Round found too careless with his texts and far too fond of the Anglo-Saxons. At the time of his greatest influence, however, the 1880s and 1890s, Round was more of a cooperative scholar than is sometimes allowed: he was involved from the beginning with the Pipe Roll Society (founded 1883), the *English Historical Review* (founded 1886), and the *Victoria County History* (*VCH*) project (launched 1899). He wrote introductions to the Domesday texts of 12 counties for the *VCH*, and set standards for the whole enterprise. His views on Domesday Book were highly influential. They stressed its fiscal importance and the artificiality of the assessments for taxation, and may have deflected F. W. MAITLAND from more promising lines of inquiry. From 1903 to his death he lived at 15 Brunswick Terrace, Brighton, the house in which he had been born. 'We are all anarchists in a way', Round wrote to the once unfortunate Tout in 1914, congratulating him on 'giving historical and antiquarian workers a lead'; but the price of order has been professionalism, a subject increasingly divorced from the local and family roots which to him were so important. EK

Main publications

Geoffrey de Mandeville (London: Longmans, Green, 1892); *Feudal England* (London: Swan Sonnenschein, 1895); editor, *Calendar of Documents preserved in France. Vol. I, 918–1206* (London: HMSO, 1899); *The Commune of London and Other Studies* (Westminster: Constable, 1899); *Studies in Peerage and Family History* (Constable, 1901); editor, *Rotuli de Dominabus* (Pipe Roll Society 35, 1913).

Reading

King, E. J.: John Horace Round and the 'Calendar of Documents preserved in France', *Anglo-Norman Studies* 4 (1981) 93–103, 202–4.

Page, W.: Memoir of Dr J. Horace Round. In *Family Origins and Other Studies*, ed. Page (London: Constable, 1930).

Powell, W. R.: J. H. Round, the county historian. *Essex Archaeology and History* 3.12 (1980) 25–38.

Rudé, George (b.1910) After graduating from Trinity College, Cambridge, Rudé spent the first thirty years of his adult life as a schoolmaster. In 1950, he received a doctorate from the University of London for a dissertation on 'The Parisian wage-earning population and the insurrectionary movements of 1789–91', which explored a number of themes that were later to be developed in his published work on the history of the crowd. Despite the originality of his research, no British university appointment was forthcoming for Rudé, who was a supporter of the Communist party. In 1960 he left Britain for a university post in Australia and by 1964 had been appointed to a chair at an Australian university. Subsequently he taught at universities there and in Canada.

Rudé was one of the pioneers of the 'new' social history. In three books published between 1959 and 1964 – *The Crowd in the French Revolution*, *Wilkes and Liberty* and *The Crowd in History* – he transformed the history of what he chose to call the crowd (in preference to more pejorative terms such as riot or mob). Rudé went back into legal records, tax lists, petitions and poll books in order to restore to the faces in the crowd something of their social identity – in particular their occupations and their places of residence – and to reconstruct the rationalities which informed crowd behaviour.

Rudé suggested that the European 'pre-industrial' crowd in the period 1730–1840 was composed neither of criminals nor even just of the labouring poor but of a cross-section of the working population. The crowd actions in which these people participated he revealed as disciplined and often ritualized acts of protest, associated with economic grievances, sophisticated political beliefs and opposition, in defence of customary rights, to capitalist innovation.

It is above all Rudé's approach to identifying the faces in the crowd that has been widely admired and copied. Criticisms of his method have focused less on its intrinsic shortcomings than on its limitations. Rudé's attempt to distinguish rioters from criminals failed to take account of the fact that those prosecuted for criminal offences appear to have come, like the participants in his crowds, from a cross-section of the working population. His emphasis on the identity and actions of the members of the crowd resulted in a disappointingly superficial analysis of their ideas and beliefs. His promotion of the term crowd has not enjoyed universal acceptance.

Rudé produced a number of successful general works on eighteenth-century European and British history. His recent studies of crime and protest during the first half of the nineteenth century (*Captain Swing*, which he co-authored with Eric Hobsbawm, excepted) have been criticized as superficial, both empirically and conceptually.   JAS

Main publications

(Published by Clarendon Press, Oxford, unless otherwise stated.)
The Crowd in the French Revolution (1959); *Wilkes and Liberty* (1962); *The Crowd in History: a study of popular disturbances in France and England, 1730–1848* (Chichester: Wiley, 1964); *Revolutionary Europe, 1783–1815* (London: Fontana, 1964); with E. J. Hobsbawm, *Captain Swing* (1969); *Paris and London* (London: Collins, 1970); *Protest and Punishment* (1978); *Criminal and Victim* (1985).

Reading

Krantz, Frederick, ed.: *History from Below: Studies in Popular Protest and Popular Ideology in Honour of George Rudé* (Montreal: Concordia University Press, 1985).

Linebaugh, Peter: Eighteenth-century crime, popular movements and social control. *Bulletin of the Society for the Study of Labour History* 25 (1972) 11–15.

Runciman, Steven (b.1903) After Eton, Runciman read history at Trinity College, Cambridge, where he was fellow from 1927 and lecturer from 1932 to 1938. Apart from his professorship in Byzantine history and art at Istanbul University (1942–5), this was

Runciman's only period of formal teaching; and, apart from a walk round the Backs at Cambridge with J. B. BURY, he had no formal mentor in Byzantine history. Runciman's fellowship thesis of 1927 on Romanos Lekapenos is arguably his most important work. His most impressive and best-loved achievement is a history of the Crusades in three volumes, perhaps the last on that scale to be attempted by a single hand. It is a majestic narrative with Runciman's own manifesto in the preface: 'History-writing today has passed into an Alexandrian age, where criticism has overpowered creation ... I believe that the supreme duty of the historian is to write history, that is to say, to attempt to record in one sweeping sequence the greater events and movements that have swayed the destinies of man.'

Runciman was in the diplomatic service in Sofia, Cairo and Jerusalem from 1940 to 1942 and re-established the British Council in Athens in 1945−47. His unabating writings over sixty years have a range, style and accessibility which is matched by a courteous readiness seriously to address audiences of all sorts from Los Angeles to Lockerbie. Here this shy, yet gregarious, polyglot has welcomed countless visitors to his library and automata, drawings by Edward Lear and good genealogical gossip. The doyen of British Byzantine studies, Runciman was made a Companion of Honour in 1984.   AAMB

Main publications

(Published by Cambridge University Press, Cambridge, unless otherwise stated.)
The Emperor Romanus Lecapenus and his Reign (1929, 1963); *A History of the First Bulgarian Empire* (London: G. Bell, 1930); *A History of the Crusades*, 3 vols (1951−4); *The Eastern Schism* (Oxford: Clarendon Press, 1955); *The White Rajahs* (1960).

Reading

Byzantine and Modern Greek Studies 4 (1978) [a festschrift].
Connell, J.: *The House by Herod's Gate* (London: Sampson Low, Marston, 1944).
Cullen, Rachel: Interview on Runciman's eightieth birthday, *The Times*, (7 July 1983).
Plante, David: 'Profile'. *New Yorker* (November 1986) 53−80.
Vidal, G.: *Reflections upon a sinking ship* (London: Heinemann, 1969).

Russian historiography   Although there is a considerable amount of archaeological evidence for the earliest years, the written record is comparatively sparse. *The Russian Primary Chronicle* dealing with the period from legendary origins to about 1100 was composed probably in Kiev in the early twelfth century. In variant forms, it is used as an introduction to other accounts produced in such principalities as Vladimir and Suzdal. Like their counterparts in other lands, the Russian chronicles were overlaid with new material according to locality and date, usually to reinforce the claims or to emphasize the goodness and justice of the princes in whose domains they were composed. Arabic, Bulgarian and especially Byzantine sources were adapted to these major purposes, as were folklore, myths and rumours. The commercial centre of Novgorod has left us birchbark records of commercial transactions as well as developing its own chronicle tradition. In the early fifteenth century, as Moscow was establishing its ascendancy over the other principalities, the *Troitsky* or *Trinity Chronicle* was composed as a justification. By the sixteenth century, this and other such compilations became a powerful weapon in the struggle for national unification under the dominance of Moscow. Unfortunately many of these medieval documents were destroyed in the great Moscow fire of 1812.

In the seventeenth century the new *Stroganov*, *Yesipov* and *Remezov Chronicles* did much to incorporate Siberia, although the chronicle in general was declining in importance. In 1674 Innokenty Giesel, an Archimandrite of Prussian origin at the Monastery of the Kiev Crypt, produced *The Synopsis*, a simple historical account from Kievan to Muscovite times drawn from a considerable range of domestic and foreign sources, with the purpose of maintaining the autonomy of the Ukraine within a framework of harmonious relations between Kiev and Moscow. This work went through thirty editions between 1674 and 1881, and Giesel exerted a considerable influence on his successors. So did Aleksey Ilich Mankiyev, the author of *The Basis of the Russian Empire: Information that might satisfy the Curious*, which was still in progress at the author's death in 1723 and not published until 1770.

In 1720 Peter the Great decreed that 'all letters, historical manuscripts and books be examined, copied and sent to the Senate from all monasteries, dioceses and cathedrals formerly granted charters'. Through example of his remarkable life as well as by such an edict, Peter gave an impetus to the study of the Russian past. One of his many admiring collaborators, V. N. Tatishchev, may be considered the first modern historian, using a wide range of materials including diplomatic correspondence, collections of laws and local records as well as the chronicles to write a more discriminating narrative than his predecessors: *Russian History from the Earliest Times* up to 1557 in five parts. Work developed throughout the eighteenth century on foundations laid not only by Tatishchev and his Russian contemporaries but also by a remarkable series of immigrant German scholars. There was dissension between Russian and German historians over the part played by earlier Scandinavian immigrants in the formation of the Kievan state, but there was also more discovery of sources and more writing by, for example Prince M. M. Shcherbatov and G. F. Müller.

The earlier part of the nineteenth century was marked by the publication of large numbers of documents, notably more than 50 volumes of the *Complete Collection of Laws of the Russian Empire* from 1830 onwards, and by a greater measure of historiographical refinement, not least as demonstrated by N. M. KARAMZIN. However, the controversy between Westerners and Slavophiles led to the adoption of extreme positions as well as acting as a scholarly stimulus. Professional history made its appearance in 1851 with the first volume of the *History of Russia from the Earliest Times* by S. M. Solovyev, professor of Russian history at the University of Moscow from 1844. The 29 volumes up to 1774 contained a vast amount of raw material somewhat imperfectly processed: the subject was presented as an organic whole, but in a 'scissors and paste' manner. Solovyev's achievement was surpassed in an all-round fashion by his former pupil V. O. KLYUCHEVSKY. The late tsarist period witnessed impressive developments in several directions: the state school did good work in the field of institution and law;

economic, social and cultural aspects of the subject were opened up by individuals such as P. N. MILYUKOV in his *Studies of Russian Culture* (1896–1903); and regional and federalist interpretations were advanced to counter the dominant Great Russian centralist version. Marxism made its appearance before the October Revolution, after which it soon established a monopoly. During the 1920s no historian was more significant than M. N. POKROVSKY, but his reputation fell steeply with the ascendancy of Stalin in the 1930s. Some worthwhile achievements were somehow completed during the difficult circumstances persisting through to the death of Stalin, but only since then has Soviet historiography managed to demonstrate a full variety and quality within its circumscribed limits. Among those Soviet historians who have achieved an international reputation have been M. N. Pokrovsky, E. A. Kosminsky and B. F. PORSHNEV.   PD

Reading

Mazour, A. G.: *The Writing of History in the Soviet Union* (Stanford, Calif.: Hoover Institution, 1971).
——: *Modern Russian Historiography*, rev. edn (London and Westport, Conn.: Greenwood, 1975).
Wieczynski, J. L. ed.: *Modern Encyclopedia of Russian and Soviet History* (Gulf Breeze, Florida: Academic International, 1976–).

Rymer, Thomas (b.1641, d.1713) The first Historiographer Royal fully to deserve the title, Rymer had been a mediocre drama critic before his appointment by William III in 1692. Commissioned to edit a collection of the treaties and alliances of English monarchs, he produced fifteen large volumes of public records, not all of them diplomatic, covering the period from 1101 to 1543; and a further five were completed by his assistant, Robert Sanderson. Though sometimes uncritical, this first great collection of English historical documents is a fundamental source for medieval history.   PAS

Main publications

Foedera, 20 vols (London: 1704–35).

Reading

Douglas, D.: *English Scholars 1660–1730* (London: Eyre & Spottiswoode, 1939).

363

S

St Albans chroniclers The origins of the medieval tradition of chronicle writing at St Albans remain in doubt. Contrary to the views of POWICKE and GALBRAITH, an examination of the sources used either side of the annal for 1188 in Roger of Wendover's *Flores historiarum* suggests that there was a St Albans compilation of earlier material which was perhaps produced by Abbot John de Cella in the early years of the thirteenth century. In spite of such complications, the view that Wendover created the first known piece of original historical writing at St Albans is nevertheless acceptable inasmuch as the treatment in the *Flores* of the period from the early years of Henry III's reign to the work's conclusion in the annal for 1234 is based on no surviving literary authority.

Roger of Wendover was a St Albans monk who became prior of the cell of Belvoir, from which position he was dismissed in 1219 or soon afterwards. He began to write his *Flores* at a date somewhere between 1204 and 1231, perhaps in the period shortly after his deposition from office. The work is a general history concentrating on English affairs, based on a variety of well-known sources for the period from the Creation to 1202, and on a lost source also used by the *Annales Sancti Edmundi* which probably provided material involving events as late as 1214. When it becomes an original work, the tone of the *Flores* is perhaps best judged by the fact that Matthew Paris thought it in need of literary embellishment, documentary additions and an extra portion of rhetoric in order to sharpen up its already hostile view of church and state authorities.

Paris's revision of Wendover's *Flores* occurs in his *Chronica majora*. This chronicle was begun in about 1240. It covers the period from the Creation to 1259 and is an independent work from its annal for 1236 onwards. The *Chronica* was Paris's greatest historiographical enterprise, but he also wrote and illustrated shorter national chronicles, a book of documents, works of local history and a substantial amount of hagiography in both Latin and Anglo-Norman, in prose and in verse. Paris took the habit at St Albans in 1217 and, despite several excursions in England and one visit to Norway, spent most of his life in that monastery which, through its geographical situation, the popularity of its guest-house and the distribution of its cells, proved to be an excellent centre for the accumulation of information. Paris, in fact, collected so much material that he had to index and summarize it for the benefit of his readers. Nothing, however, holds his vast *Chronica* together more effectively than the homiletic fervour of his approach, most evident in his criticisms of the king, the pope and such groups as aliens and mendicants. After 1250, Paris sought to modify some of his more excessive outbursts because they might be 'offensive to friends'. He has, nevertheless, left an invaluable insight into what sorts of thirteenth-century development were particularly offensive to a committed Benedictine.

In the hundred or so years after Paris's death in 1259, St Albans produced only two anonymous continuations of his *Chronica*, a single continuation of his *Gesta abbatum monasterii Sancti Albani*, and a few historical treatises which were originally independent of the Wendover/Paris tradition. Thomas Walsingham, who was precentor at St Albans by 1380 and remained in that office until 1394 when he become prior of the cell at Wymondham, produced in this period of his career a short history of the world from the Creation to 1392 and texts of more local interest. Around the same time he wrote his *Chronica majora* as a continuation of Paris's *Chronica*. Up to its annal for 1377 this text is no more than a compilation based on a number of sources including a continuation of Higden's *Polychronicon* (which may have been Walsingham's earliest work). But eventually the text becomes a large-scale contemporary history. At Wymondham, Walsingham produced a shorter chronicle, covering the years between 1327 and 1392, which was an abbreviation of his *Chronica majora* and probably developed from an earlier abbreviation made before 1393. Despite a growing interest in the Latin classics, after his return to St Albans in 1396–7, Walsingham continued to work on his *Chronica majora* up to 1420 and on his shorter chronicle up to 1419 or, perhaps, 1422. Between 1419 and 1422, he also wrote his *Ypodigma Neustriae* (The making of Neustria). Many attempted comparisons of Paris and Walsingham have been invalidated by a failure to appreciate the different political and intellectual concerns of thirteenth- and fifteenth-century England. It is, however, evident that Walsingham was impressed by the techniques which Paris had adopted in order to structure his material, and that Paris would have been excited by the vivid prose in which Walsingham was able to condemn the degeneracy of some of Richard II's knights and to celebrate the victories of Henry V in France.

Walsingham was the last representative of the medieval tradition of chronicle writing established at St Albans. John Whethamstede, who was abbot of St Albans from 1420 to 1440 and from 1452 to 1465, was, in many senses, Walsingham's equal as a historian and as a stylist but he chose to produce registers rather than chronicles. Under Whethamstede desultory annals were written in the monastery up to 1440, but such efforts were not of the quality of the works of Wendover, Paris and Walsingham, which had, in the name of St Albans, created a single national history stretching from the Creation to the fifteenth century.   DJC

Main writings

Wendover, Roger of: *Flores historiarum* (Rolls Series LXXXIV).
Paris, Matthew: *Chronica majora* (Rolls Series LVII).
Walsingham, Thomas of: *The St Albans chronicle*, ed. V. H. Galbraith (Oxford: Clarendon Press, 1937).

Reading

Gransden, Antonia: *Historical Writing in England*, vols 1–2 (London: Routledge & Kegan Paul, 1974 and 1982).
Vaughan, Richard: *Matthew Paris* (Cambridge: Cambridge University Press, 1958).

Sainte-Beuve, Charles Augustin (b.1804, d.1869)   Poet, novelist, critic and literary historian, Sainte-Beuve was the posthumous son of a tax collector. While still a medical student in Paris he became involved in journalism, writing literary reviews for the liberal newspaper *Le Globe* from 1825. He became a friend of Victor Hugo and was a prominent member of his circle, the *Cénacle*. Sainte-Beuve's flirtation with Romanticism ended with his falling in love with Hugo's wife, Adèle; his novel, *Volupté* (1834), drew upon his feelings for her and provided an interesting psychological study. During these years he entered with enthusiasm into the current cultural and intellectual trends, but each time moved on, finally returning to the critical frame of mind for which he became most famous in his essays.

In 1837 Sainte-Beuve began his five-volume masterpiece, the *Histoire de Port Royal* (1840–59), the first substantially researched portrait of the Jansenist movement in the seventeenth century. His fame would have been assured had he left only this work, but he had already published several volumes of literary portraits and from 1845 he went on to write a weekly article, in the Bonapartist newspaper *Le Constitutionnel*. These *Causeries du lundi* (Monday chats) ran to 15 volumes, followed by a further 13 volumes of *Nouveaux lundis*. Some are pure historical studies, but most are critical reviews of literary and historical publications which concentrate upon the psychology of the writer and the delineation of character. Although he was an unhappy, embittered man, much caricatured in the nineteenth century, his urge for truth and honesty stands out today.　　　　　PRC

Main publications

Histoire de Port Royal, 7 vols, 4th edn (Paris: Hachette, 1878); *Les grands écrivains français: études des 'Lundis' et des 'Portraits'*, 23 vols, ed. M. Allem (Paris: Garnier, 1926–30); *Causeries du lundi*, 8 vols, trans. E. J. Trenchman (London: Routledge, 1909).

Reading

Nicholson, H. *Sainte-Beuve.* (London: Constable, 1957).

Sallust (b.86 BC, d.35 BC)　Gaius Sallustius Crispus came from Amiternum, a central Italian town about 50 miles from Rome. He was, it may be presumed, a member of the local landowning gentry. In increasing numbers in the first century BC such men looked beyond the confines of their home town to a public career in Rome itself. How, and under whose patronage, Sallust made the transition is irrecoverable. Nothing is known of his early career until he appears as a troublesome tribune in a turbulent year, 52 BC.

The political backlash against his activities came in 50 BC when the censors removed his name from the roll of the Senate. Although the primary motive for their action was probably political vindictiveness, it may have been cloaked in terms of moral censure. Certainly there was a tradition which attacked Sallust's personal behaviour, including an allegation of adultery in high places. Such charges were standard fare in Roman political life.

At that time there was one place to go which held the prospect of reviving one's fortune. Julius Caesar in Gaul found himself increasingly at odds with those in power in Rome and was ready to welcome anyone to his camp. Sallust was just one of a large number who found their way there. In the civil war which followed, Sallust commanded a legion and later, in 47 BC, was one of those sent to try to quell the rash of mutinies in Caesar's army — without success but, unlike two other envoys, he escaped with his life. In 46 BC Sallust was

praetor and accompanied Julius Caesar on his campaign in North Africa, where he distinguished himself in collecting supplies for the army. A final surprise came when Caesar appointed him as the first governor of the newly annexed territory of Africa Nova (part of Algeria). Sallust seized this opportunity in a manner all too typical of his age. He pillaged his province, or so it was alleged, to such an extent that on his return to Rome he faced a prosecution from which he was saved only by Caesar's intervention. At this point Sallust gave up politics or, perhaps, politics gave him up. In the introductions to his two monographs Sallust loftily represented himself as turning aside with disdain from the corruption of the chase for political honours. This somewhat disingenuous apology soon attracted critics who pointed out that the severe tone of moralizing in his writings was undermined by the nature of his own career.

In the last century of the Republic a public career could be frustrating, even hazardous. Some very distinguished men chose to opt out and to retire to their estates. However, the robust values of the Roman aristocracy had little time for such quietism. Sallust went out of his way to emphasize that he had not been tempted by such pursuits; instead he turned to the writing of history, an activity which he felt was worthy of a gentleman. Indeed, up to his own time the composition of history had been virtually the exclusive preserve of the senatorial upper class. Yet by the first century BC nothing had been produced in Rome which could rival the achievements of the Greeks. In Cicero's opinion what Roman historical writing needed was style. That was just what Sallust gave it, although not as Cicero would have wished. Sallust developed a highly self-conscious and artificial way of presenting history, characterized by a predilection for archaic and poetic words, startling sentence structure in which phrases are cut off abruptly and words appear in an unexpected order, and a tautness of expression which was such that no single word could be extracted without destroying the sense of the whole. All these had been features of the writings of THUCYDIDES and Sallust was trumpeted as his Roman rival.

Sallust possessed a deep historical pessimism. For him the Roman Republic was in a state of inevitable decline and his two monographs were designed to illustrate moments in that decline. The first, *The War with Catiline*, recounted the famous events of Catiline's alleged conspiracy which was exposed by Cicero in 63 BC. Catiline, presented as a man of talent with a warped mind, was seen as a product of the corruption of the age. *The War with Jugurtha* told of the trouble which Rome experienced in the late second century with Numidia. Apart from the obvious attractions of a military narrative, one reason for Sallust's choice of subject must have been the allegations of bribery and corruption which had been brought against the various, incompetent members of the nobility in charge of the war. For Sallust this represented a falling-away from the high standards of an earlier and more successful age. He also began, but never completed, a *Histories* which now survives only in fragments and covered the years 78−67 BC. In Sallust goodness gets but brief mention, while the psychology of corruption is extensively analysed. Even in those rare cases where he concentrates on characters he approved of, most notably in the famous comparison between Caesar and Cato in the *Catiline*, his assessments are rich in ambiguity.

Sallust had a profound effect on his successors, most of all on TACITUS who inherited and refined his approach and shared his cynicism. Sallust's pessimism about human nature meant that he was always popular with Christian writers and in the Renaissance he was second only to Livy in many people's estimation.   JJP

Main writings

The War with Catiline, The War with Jugurtha, Histories and works dubiously ascribed to Sallust − *Letters to Caesar When an Old Man, Invective against Cicero*, all in *Sallust*, text, trans. and ed. by J. C. Rolfe (Cambridge, Mass.: Loeb Classical Library, Harvard University Press, 1921); the full fragments of the *Histories* in *C. Sallustii Crispi Historiarum Reliquiae*, ed. B. Maurenbrecher (Leipzig: Teubner, 1891−3).

Reading

Earl, D. C. *The Political Thought of Sallust* (Amsterdam: Hakkert, 1966).
La Penna, A.: *Sallustio e la 'rivoluzione' romana* (Milan: Feltrinelli, 1968).

Syme, R.: *Sallust* (Berkeley: University of California Press, 1964).

Sarpi, Paolo [Pietro] (b.1552, d.1623)   The son of a merchant, Paolo Sarpi, also known as 'Pietro', became a Servite and a scholar of prodigious range with many contacts among European intellectuals. His religious stance has been variously interpreted as that of a Catholic reformer, a Protestant sympathizer, even an atheist. Appointed in 1606 official adviser to a Venetian senate locked in jurisdictional conflict with the papacy, he wrote his account of the Interdict of 1606−7 in the affair's immediate aftermath. While that account remained unpublished in his lifetime, Sarpi's greatest historical work, his history of the Council of Trent, appeared, in England under a pseudonym, three years after its completion in 1616. Sarpi aimed to expose the moral and institutional decay of the church and to show how the reform movement had failed at the Council of Trent. This failure sprang from the Roman curia's political purposes which in turn were a function less of its representatives' self-interested motivation than of the constraints which institutional structures imposed upon them. Though coloured by Sarpi's hostility towards papal universalism, his contempt for the narrowness of scholastic theology and his commitment to the autonomy of the secular state, the *History* stands as a monument to detailed narration based upon extensive documentation as the key to historical understanding of events and their significance.   HALJ

Main publications

Historia del Concilio Tridentino (1619) (London: 1676); *Historia particolare delle cose passate tra il Sommo Pontefice Paolo V e la Serenissima Repubblica di Venetia* (1624) (London: J. Bill, 1626).

Reading

Bouwsma, W. J.: *Venice and the Defense of Republican Liberty* (Berkeley: University of California Press, 1968).
Wootton, D.: *Paolo Sarpi: between Renaissance and Enlightenment* (Cambridge: Cambridge University Press, 1983).

Savigny, Friedrich Carl von (b.1779, d.1861)   From a Protestant family that had left France in 1630, Savigny was professor of Roman law in the universities of Marburg (1800–04), Lanďshut (1808–10) and Berlin (1810–42). He was Prussian minister for the revision of legislation from 1842 to 1848. In 1803 he married Kunigunde Brentano, sister of the poet Clemens Brentano.

Although first and foremost a lawyer, Savigny was also a leading historian and the founder of the Historical School of Law. His essential idea was that law is based neither on the abstract dictates of universal and immutable reason nor on legislation, particularly not in its codified form, but is the result of the organic evolution of the national spirit. Law is but one of the manifestations of a particular people's culture, the *Volksgeist*, and no attempt should be made to fix it at any given moment: hence Savigny's rejection of legal codification as 'unorganic'. His ideas were forcefully expressed in 1814 in his *Vom Beruf unsrer Zeit für Gesetzgebung und Rechtswissenschaft* (On the vocation of our age for legislation and jurisprudence) in which he attacked the plea for codification published the same year by A. F. Thibaut under the title *Über die Nothwendigkeit eines allgemeinen bürgerlichen Gesetzbuchs für Deutschland* (On the necessity of a general civil code for Germany). Savigny's approach should be seen in the light of the general enthusiasm of the nineteenth century for the application of the historical method in the most diverse disciplines. It also stemmed from his traditionalism, his attachment to monarchy and feudalism, his rejection of the French Revolution and his aversion to arbitrary legislation as a source of law.

His own direct contribution to legal history was an encyclopaedic history of Roman law in the middle ages, the first modern work on the subject. In it Savigny tried to bridge the gap between the law of antiquity and the modern Roman-based *jus commune*, which was influential throughout Europe and 'received' as national law in Germany. Savigny was more interested in the law as a product of learning (hence his concentration on authors, works, manuscripts, editions, teaching methods and universities) than as a reflection of political developments and social currents. Although the view of law as a purely cultural phenomenon would now be considered rather narrow, there is no doubt that Savigny was a father-figure for modern legal history.   RCvC

Main publications

Das Recht des Besitzes (1803) French trans. C. Faivre d'Audelange (Paris: 1845); *Geschichte des römischen Rechts im Mittelalter*, 6 vols (Berlin: 1815–31, 2nd edn, 7 vols, 1834–51), English trans., vol 1, E. Cathcart (Edinburgh: A. Black, 1829), French trans., incomplete, 4 vols, C. Guenoux (Paris: 1839), Italian trans., 3 vols, complete and enlarged, E. Bollati (Turin: Ghiringhello, 1854–7); *System des heutigen römischen Rechts*, 8 vols (Berlin: 1840–9), French trans. C. Guenoux (Paris: 1840–51), Italian trans. V. Scialoja (Rome: 1886–98).

Reading

Coing, H., ed.: *Vorträge zum 200. Geburtstag von F. C. von Savigny* (Ius Commune, 8) (Frankfurt: Vittorio Klostermann, 1979).

Ebel, F.: *Savigny Officialis. Vortrag gehalten vor der Juristischen Gesellschaft zu Berlin am 22. Oktober 1986* (Schriftenreihe der Juristischen Gesellschaft zu Berlin, 104) (Berlin: Walter de Gruyter, 1987).

Gaudemet, J.: Histoire et système dans la méthode de Savigny. *Hommage à René Dekkers* (Brussels: Bruylant, 1982) pp. 117–134.

Gmür, R.: *Savigny und die Entwicklung der Rechtswissenschaft* (Münster: Aschendorff, 1962).

Hattenhauer, H.: *Thibaut und Savigny. Ihre programmatischen Schriften* (Munich: Franz Vahlen, 1973).

Marini, G.: *Savigny e il metodo della scienza giuridica*, (Bologna: Riccardo Patron, 1965).

Schröder, H.: *Friedrich Karl von Savigny. Geschichte und Rechtsdenken beim übergang vom Feudalismus zum Kapitalismus in Deutschland* (Frankfurt: Peter Lang, 1984).

Stoll, A.: *F. K. v. Savigny. Ein Bild seines Lebens mit einer Sammlung seiner Briefe*, 3 vols (Cologne: C. Heymann, 1927–39).

Thieme, H.: Savigny und das deutsche Recht. *Zeitschrift der Savigny-Stiftung für Rechtsgeschichte*, G. A. 80 (1963) 43–92.

Saxo 'Grammaticus' (*fl. c.*1200)   Denmark's most important medieval writer, the only one with a European reputation; yet very little is known about him. Commissioned by archbishop Absalon (d.1201) he wrote a history of Denmark from the foundation of the state by a mythical king 'Dan' to *c.*1185. This large work, first called *Gesta Danorum* (*GD*) *c.*1300, is divided into 16 books, the first nine dealing with pagan, the last seven with Christian times. Saxo drew on a wide variety of sources, for example, Paul the Deacon, BEDE, ADAM OF BREMEN and the *Roskilde Chronicle*, taking great liberties with them all. He also drew on oral traditions, mentioning both Icelanders and Absalon as informants. Undoubtedly his account of contemporary history was deeply influenced by traditions cherished by his patron's own family, the powerful Hvides of Zealand.

Like GEOFFREY OF MONMOUTH's *Historia*, *GD* is a 'national history', reflecting the twelfth-century renaissance and the revival of interest in classical writers, who influenced not only Saxo's vocabulary, syntax and concepts but also his poetry. Saxo has been considered a propagandist for royal political ideas, but it can be shown that, thanks to a highly sophisticated technique of writing on two levels (implicitly questioning what he explicitly states), Saxo was able to oppose what he was commissioned to support. No complete manuscript of *GD* has been preserved; it was first printed in 1514, but it was used earlier, for example by Albert Krantz, through whom Shakespeare may have learnt about prince Hamlet. BSS

Main writings

Saxonis Gesta Danorum, ed. J. Olrik and H. Ræder (Hauniae: Levin & Munksgaard, 1931), English trans. P. Fisher, *Saxo Grammaticus: History of the Danes* (Cambridge: Brewer/Rowland & Littlefield, 1979, and E. Christensen, *Saxo Grammaticus, Danorum Regum Heroumque Historia*, vols I–III (Oxford: British Archaeological Reports 84, 1980–1).

Reading

Friis-Jensen, K. ed.: *Saxo Grammaticus: a Medieval Author Between Norse and Latin Culture* (Copenhagen: Museum Tusculanum Press, 1981).
Sawyer, B.: Valdemar, Absalon and Saxo: Historiography and Politics in Medieval Denmark. *Revue Belge de Philologie et d'Histoire* 43 (1985) 685–705.

Scandinavian historiography The remarkable series of vernacular works produced in Iceland in the twelfth and thirteenth centuries are considered to be the starting point of Scandinavian historiography. These works concern either the history of the island from its settlement at the end of the ninth century, or the history of Norway whence most of the settlers came. To the first category belong Ari

Thorgilsson's *Islendingabók* and *Landnámabók*, the authorship of which is uncertain. The latter provided a source for the *Sagas of the Icelanders*, largely anonymous accounts of the fortunes of the leading families of the island in the tenth and eleventh centuries but containing much fictional material. Of the second category, the most remarkable is the *Heimskringla* by SNORRE STURLUSON. In Denmark the earliest historical writing of any importance dates from the late twelfth century, when Sven Aggesen produced a brief history of the country in Latin and SAXO 'GRAMMATICUS' composed the much more ambitious *Gesta Danorum*. Swedes began to record their past appreciably later; monastic annals did not appear until the thirteenth century. These formed the bases for the rhymed chronicles: *Erikskrönikan*, which covers the thirteenth century, and *Karlskrönikan*, the early fifteenth. The national consciousness of the period of the Kalmar Union with Denmark and Norway is reflected in the Latin *Chronica Gothorum* by Ericus Olai, the first Swedish historian known by name. The title suggests the emerging myth of the Swedish origins of the Goths, who were supposed to have laid the foundations of European civilization after the Roman Empire. 'Gothicism' was born.

In the sixteenth century, the leading figure of the Swedish reformation, Olaus Petri, in his *Svenska krönika* provided his country with its first vernacular history in prose (to 1520), which treated 'Gothicism' with a healthy scepticism. The theory was, on the other hand, elaborated on with some conviction in the exiled Johannes Magnus's *Historia de omnibus gothorum sueonumque regibus*, published in Rome in 1554. His brother Olaus followed this with his own even more ambitious *Historia de gentibus septentrionalibus*, still a valuable source of information about life in Scandinavia in the sixteenth century. To match such figures as these, Denmark had only Arild Huitfeldt, who around 1600 composed a number of king's chronicles which were landmarks in their use of the rich source material available to the author as the kingdom's chancellor.

The collection and publication of historical manuscripts gathered pace in both Denmark and Sweden in the seventeenth century; the Icelander Arni Magnusson began to assemble in Copenhagen his great collection of medieval manuscripts. But at the same time the 'Gothic' tradition reached its culmination in Olaus Rudbeck's *Atlantica* (1679), in which he identified Sweden with the mythical Atlantis. Such ideas were effectively scotched in the eighteenth century by Olof von Dalin, whose *Svea rikes historia* (1747, 1750 and 1760−1) represents a significant advance in historical method. A similar task was performed in Denmark by Ludvig Holberg, whose *Danmarks riges historie* (1732−5) effectively questioned much that he found in the earlier books of Saxo. As a medieval historian, however, Holberg was far surpassed by the Swede Sven Lagerbring, whose four-volume *Svea rikes historia* (1769−83, 1907) reached the year 1463.

In the nineteenth century, Norwegian and Finnish historiography was strongly influenced by the national and political struggles of the age. In Norway, Ernst Sars was the leading liberal nationalist historian, while the younger Halvdan Koht and Edvard Bull represented more radical trends at the end of the century. Sakari Yrjö-Koskinen interpreted Finland's past in a nationalist spirit. Danish liberal nationalist writing was symbolized by Carl Ferdinand Allen, whose most important work was, however, a study of all three Scandinavian kingdoms at the beginning of the sixteenth century and was remarkable for its sympathetic treatment of the 'tyrant' Christian II. In the early part of the century Swedish historical writing was dominated by Erik Gustaf Geijer, whose history of Sweden until the middle of the seventeenth century appeared in the 1830s. His conservative pro-monarchical views were strongly criticized by his contemporary Anders Fryxell, who in his highly popular work, *Berättelser ur svenska historien*, found more to praise in the noble-dominated Age of Liberty of the eighteenth century than in the Age of Greatness in the seventeenth.

The twentieth century has been marked in all the Scandinavian countries by a growing interest in social and economic history. This has been particularly marked in Sweden,

where HECKSCHER has been followed by a large number of younger historians, many strongly influenced by Marxist ideas. Medieval history also, however, benefited from the work of the 'Lund School' associated with Lauritz and Curt Weibull, who stressed a Scandinavian outlook and a close attention to source criticism. Both Norway and Finland have led the way in research into local history, while the importance of agriculture in Danish economy has been reflected in an extensive study of rural history there.   SPO

Reading

Hatton, Ragnhild: Some notes on Swedish historiography. *History* n.s. 37 (1952) 97−113.

Westergaard, Waldemar: Danish history and Danish historians. *Journal of Modern History* 24 (1952) 167−179.

Scheel, Heinrich (b.1915) From a proletarian background in Berlin, Scheel joined the Communist Youth League in 1932, became involved in the *Rote Kapelle* resistance movement, was arrested in 1942 and spent the rest of the war in concentration camps. He has since emerged as one of the most prolific and influential historians in the German Democratic Republic. His most original work, informed by a rigorously Marxist-Leninist approach, has been on the 'German Jacobins' of the 1790s.   TCWB

Main publications

Süddeutsche Jakobiner (Berlin: Akademie, 1962); *Die Mainzer Republik*, 2 vols (Berlin: Akademie, 1975, 1981).

Schlegel, Friedrich von (b.1772, d.1829) Born at Hanover into a family of bureaucrats and clergymen, Schlegel's chequered career exemplified the difficulties experienced by professional writers in Germany in earning a living by their pen. Despite their importance for the romantic movement, none of the periodicals Schlegel edited survived for more than a few issues. After a peripatetic existence, which included spells at Leipzig, Dresden, Jena, Berlin and Cologne, he finally settled in Vienna in 1808, where he converted to Roman Catholicism and entered Habsburg service.

Most active and best known as a literary critic and theorist, Schlegel expounded his views on history in two influential courses of lectures given in Vienna and subsequently published: *Über die neuere Geschichte* (1810) and *Philosophie der Geschichte* (1828). Characteristically romantic was his emphasis on the history of thought, religion and political institutions at the expense of war, diplomacy and high politics. An admirer of the French Revolution in the 1790s, by the time of the 1810 lectures he was singing the praises of both the Holy Roman and Habsburg Empires for their reconciliation of unity with diversity and, more specifically, their achievement of true liberty and the proper relationship between church and state. Even after its demise was confirmed in 1815, the Holy Roman Empire remained his ideal and informed his view of the past.

TCWB

Main publications

A Course of Lectures on Modern History, trans. Lyndsey Purcell and R. H. Whitelock (London: Bohn, 1849); *The Philosophy of History*, trans. A. J. W. Morrison (London: Bohn, 1847) [incl. a memoir].

Reading

Eichner, H.: *Friedrich Schlegel* (New York: Twayne, 1970).
Peter, K.: *Friedrich Schlegel* (Stuttgart: Metzler, 1978).

Schlesinger, Arthur Meier, Jr (b.1917)
Son of the eminent American historian Arthur M. Schlesinger, Schlesinger Jr published his first book, *Orestes Brownson: a Pilgrim's Progress* (1939) at the age of 22. It was the subject of his honours thesis at Harvard University where he graduated in 1938. At the age of 28 he won a Pulitzer prize for history with *The Age of Jackson* (1945). Since then he has been a highly visible political activist and a prolific writer of books and essays on politics in twentieth-century America. More than any other contemporary academic historian, Schlesinger has earned wide recognition both as a writer and as adviser to prominent national politicians.

Much of Schlesinger's energy has assisted liberal causes. A founder of the Americans for Democratic Action in 1947, he also advised Democratic presidential candidate Adlai Stevenson in 1952 and 1956. His writings focused on the reform activity of progressive American presidents from Jackson to the present. *The Age of Roosevelt*, published in three volumes between 1957 and 1960, presented a highly favourable account of FDR and the New Deal. Schlesinger then left Harvard, where he had taught since 1946, to serve as a special adviser to President Kennedy. He later published two large, widely acclaimed books on the Kennedys: *A Thousand Days: John F. Kennedy in the White House* (1965), which won a second Pulitzer (for biography); and *Robert F. Kennedy and His Times* (1978).

Schlesinger left the White House after the assassination of President Kennedy, and has since been less directly engaged in politics. From 1967 he served as Albert Schweitzer professor of the humanities at the City University of New York. In 1973 he published *The Imperial Presidency*, a sweeping and often critical account of the growth of presidential power in American history. A fluent stylist, Schlesinger has also written numerous essays and reviews, of film as well as of books. As in the past, many of these have stoutly defended a mainstream liberal agenda, a 'vital center' as he had called it in the 1940s, calling for progressive social reforms as well as for prudent internationalism in the area of foreign affairs.

JTP

Main publications

(Published by Houghton Mifflin, Boston, Mass., unless otherwise stated.)
Orestes Brownson: a Pilgrim's Progress (Boston: Little, Brown, 1939); *The Age of Jackson* (Little, Brown, 1945); *The Vital Center: the Politics of Freedom* (1949); with Richard H. Rovere, *The General and the President and the Future of American Foreign Policy* (New York: 1951); *The Age of Roosevelt*, vol. 1: *The Crisis of the Old Order, 1919–1933* (1957), vol. 2: *The Coming of the New Deal* (1958), vol. 3: *The Politics of Upheaval* (1960); *The Politics of Hope* (Little, Brown, 1962); *A Thousand Days: John F. Kennedy in the White House* (1965); *The Bitter Heritage: Vietnam and American Democracy, 1941–1966* (1966); *The Crisis of Confidence: Ideas, Power, and Violence in America* (1969); *The Imperial Presidency* (1973); *Robert F. Kennedy and His Times* (1978); *The Cycles of American History* (1986).

SCHOLEM, GERSHOM GERHARD

Scholem, Gershom Gerhard (b.1897, d.1982) Scholem occupied a commanding position among historians of the Jewish religion. He grew up in Berlin in an assimilated German–Jewish family, but, as he relates in his autobiography, he was drawn early to the academic study of Hebrew texts. His doctoral dissertation, *Das Buch Bahir*, was published in 1923, immediately establishing him as a master of the mystical thought of the thirteenth-century kabbalists. The most striking feature of this and subsequent studies was the demonstration of continuities in the Jewish mystical tradition reaching back to the days of the Temple. His work on the divergent strands of Jewish mysticism culminated in a series of lectures given in New York in 1938, and later published as the highly readable *Major Trends in Jewish Mysticism* (1941). Identifying a powerful undercurrent of mysticism in the tradition and practice of Judaism, Scholem brought to light the work of several significant mystical writers such as the Spaniard Abraham ben Samuel Abulafia, and placed the key work, known as the *Zohar*, in its wider context. Kabbalah and mystical pietism were no longer presented as somewhat disreputable species of underground religion, but as an integral and formative element in the development of Judaism. What concerned Scholem was the existence of a secret, or rather, secretive, tradition that represented more truly the meaning of Jewish intellectual history than did the rationalism and 'science' of the nineteenth-century German–Jewish scholars; indeed the word 'kabbalah' actually means 'tradition'.

Scholem expressed his own commitment to Judaism by a strong belief in the Zionist movement. He settled in Jerusalem in 1923 and from 1933 he was professor of mysticism. He was awarded the prestigious Israel Prize in 1958. He continued to expound Jewish mysticism to wide audiences, and turned his attention to the career of the self-proclaimed Messiah Shabbetai Zvi, to whom he devoted one of his most important books. But he did not lose touch with the cultural world of his youth, maintaining with the German–Jewish littérateur, Walter Benjamin, an eager correspondence in which he acerbically criticized the materialistic, Marxist creed of his friend.

For Scholem it was precisely the irrational that underlaid the history of the Jews, though existing in a state of tension with the orderly rationalism of the Wissenschaft des Judentum and similar movements: 'half-articulated mutterings about mystical secrets, symbols and images, all rooted in the world of esoterica and in the abstruse speculations of the kabbalists, became transformed, in my eyes, into invaluable keys to an understanding of important historical processes.'   DSHA

Main publications

Major Trends in Jewish Mysticism (New York: Schocken, 1941); *Jewish Gnosticism* (New York: The Jewish Theological Seminary of America, 1960); *The Messianic Idea in Judaism and other essays* (London: Allen & Unwin, 1971); *Sabbetai Sevi, the mystical Messiah, 1626–1676* (London: Littman Library, 1973); *Kabbalah* (New York: New York Times Library of Jewish Knowledge, 1974); *From Berlin to Jerusalem: Memories of my Youth* (Schocken, 1980) [autobiographical]; *Walter Benjamin: the Story of a Friendship* (Philadelphia: Jewish Publication Society of America, 1981; London: Faber, 1982) [autobiographical].

Reading

Biale, D.: *Gershom Scholem: Kabbalah and Counter-history* (Cambridge, Mass.: Harvard University Press, 1979).

Dan, J.: *Gershom Scholem and the Mystical Dimension of Jewish History* (New York: New York University Press, 1987).

Schweid, E.: *Judaism and Mysticism according to Gershom Scholem* (Atlanta, Ga.: Scholars' Press, 1985).

Studies in Mysticism and Religion Presented to G. G. Scholem on his 80th Birthday (Jerusalem: 1977) [incl. bibliography].

science, history of With the stupendous transformation of science in early modern times, the question of science's history became an important problem for historical inquiry; and leading scientists of the time, such as Francis Bacon and Johannes Kepler, set about producing a 'usable past'. Repudiating the traditional idolatry of Greek science, some occult authors proposed instead an even earlier 'ancient wisdom' (*prisca sapientia*) in natural philosophy, perhaps deriving from Moses, which it was hoped could be recovered. But increasingly during the seventeenth century, the interpretation of the history of science became enmeshed in the Ancients vs. Moderns dispute (could and did contemporaries surpass Antiquity in knowledge?). New scientific discoveries formed a key weapon in the Moderns' armoury, and so, not surprisingly, science's history was increasingly written as a progressive success story. Newton had superseded Ptolemy, Harvey had disproved Galen, Bacon had demonstrated the importance of observation and experiment, and, between them, Galileo and Descartes had championed mathematics and the mechanical philosophy. New discoveries would dispel old dogmas. The direction of science was thus the march of progress.

This vision was largely taken over by the Enlightenment and subsequently by Positivism. For both movements, science became the paradigm case of human endeavour regarded not as degeneration or merely cyclical change, but rather as unlimited improvement. For many nineteenth-century social movements, not least Marxism, particularly as developed by Engels and Lenin, the progress of science seemed the key factor distinguishing the forward march of western society from the allegedly stagnant civilizations of the east. In that sense, the success of science underwrote the very idea of 'scientific history' and 'scientific socialism'.

Many compendious histories of science in general and of particular branches of it were written during the last century, mainly by practising scientists. Full of detail, they are generally short of interpretation, proceeding on the 'Whiggish' assumption that science is unproblematically cumulative. Over the last fifty years, however, academic study of science's history has made great strides, with close attention being paid for the first time to, for example, scientists' manuscript evidence rather than just to their published findings. Major controversies have arisen in the discipline. These have particularly focused upon whether science has been socially determined or has been relatively autonomous.

From the 1930s, an influential group of Marxist scientists, in particular Joseph NEEDHAM and J. D. Bernal, argued that the triumphs of western science were to be explained as a function of the overthrow of feudal society by the bourgeoisie, and as responses to the technological needs of an emergent capitalist economy. In turn the Industrial Revolution called into being the new sciences of chemistry and electricity. Such a reading was criticized as reductionist and economistic by a new generation of academic historians of science who rose to prominence after the second world war, inspired by the emigré Russian philosopher, Alexandre Koyre. They argued that the Marxist interpretation grossly neglected the theoretical (as distinct from the practical) dimensions of modern science. Transformations in thought were more important than the accumulation of useful facts. They contended that the great discoveries of what they newly called the 'Scientific Revolution' (roughly, the period from Copernicus to Newton) were the achievements of truth-loving individual geniuses contemplating the wonders of nature largely in isolation. Major statements of this approach include A. Rupert Hall's *The Scientific Revolution, 1500–1800* and C. C. Gillispie's *The Edge of Objectivity*.

Over the last twenty years, this so-called 'internalist' interpretation of science's history has in turn been challenged by 'externalists' who find this 'privileging' of science's autonomy unconvincing. One line of 'externalist' history has argued that non-scientific traditions of ideas have played a major part in the shaping of scientific theories. Thus, following Frances Yates's explorations of Hermeticism, it has been argued that magic, neo-Platonism, astrology, alchemy, and the like, were not repudiated by the scientific revolution, but rather made it possible (for example, by stressing number and cosmic harmony). Similarly, political economy and Malthusian population theory are claimed to have influenced Darwin's theory of evolution by natural selection. Today's scholarship — for example, on Newton's heretical theological views — is revealing how involved scientists have been in the total thought-worlds of their time.

Another current has attempted a new, nonreductionist, social history of science. Neo-Marxists such as R. M. Young have stressed that 'science *is* social relations'; non-Marxist sociologists of knowledge such as Barry

Barnes have claimed we should grasp science through the material interests which propel it. Rejecting theories of inspired flashes of genius, such scholars have explored the complex social fabrics within which the processes of scientific inquiry take place, giving due emphasis to the culture of laboratory life, scientific institutions, funding and communication, and the wider 'social system' of science. Science's claims to be objective and neutral are here taken not at face value, but rather as successful strategies for social integration, and the ideological role played by science in establishing public criteria of rationality and normalcy, for example in forming gender and racial stereotypes, is given much attention.

The question, in turn, of the impact of science upon society remains similarly contested. For instance, there is little dissent from the view that science played some part in the technological changes of the Industrial Revolution, possibly by instilling a more quantitative approach or a greater disposition to experiment. But it remains dubious whether technological breakthroughs such as the steam engine actually drew upon new scientific theories. Similarly, science's impact upon general culture and consciousness is not easy to evaluate. The notion, for example, that the Victorian crisis of faith was largely a response to Darwinism is probably mistaken. Nineteenth-century science may have bolstered religion as much as it undermined it, and the old idea of a centuries-long struggle between science and theology is certainly misplaced. In assessing the interplay of science and society it must be remembered that for many centuries science remained the pursuit of a tiny élite of scholars and gentlemen amateurs. Only during the last hundred years have the needs of state and the pressures of professionalization drawn the scientist fully within society.   RP

Reading

Corsi, P. and Weindling, P. eds: *Information Sources in the History of Science and Medicine* (London: Butterworth, 1983).

Durbin, P. T. ed.: *A Guide to the Culture of Science, Technology and Medicine* (London, Collier Macmillan, 1980).

Gillispie, C. C.: *The Edge of Objectivity* (Princeton, NJ: Princeton University Press, 1960).

Hall, A. R.: *The Revolution in Science, 1500–1750*, rev. edn of *The Scientific Revolution, 1500–1800*, (1954) (London: Longman, 1983).

Isis 1924– [American journal, valuable source on new developments. Incl. annual annotated bibliography of histories of science, technology and medicine.]

Scott, Walter (b.1771, d.1832) A product of the Edinburgh society which led David Hume to describe eighteenth-century Scotland as 'the historical nation', Scott added to formal training in law – which sharpened his sense of fair play and respect for documentary evidence – an extraordinarily comprehensive and varied interest in the past, especially the past of his own land. Adam Ferguson, the father of historical sociology, happened to be a family friend. To the framework of sociological inquiry which characterized Ferguson's *Essay on The History of Civil Society* (1767), Scott added a passionate interest in acquiring through print, word of mouth, or other means all out-of-the-way information, whether concerning ballads, battles, social customs, or old buildings. In his writings on history he displayed exceptionally wide-ranging general curiosity, a bias towards antiquarianism, and at least the essential outlines of the intellectual inheritance which marked the philosophical historians of the Scottish Enlightenment. He was knighted in 1820.

Scott's formal contributions to history include an influential essay on 'Chivalry' (1818), an edition of *The Provincial Antiquities of Scotland* (1819–26), the widely popular *Tales of a Grandfather* (1827–30) and a *History of Scotland* (1829–30). There were, too, editions of historical source materials, among them *The State Papers of Sir Ralph Sadler* (1809), and the *Secret History of James I* (1811). His *Life of Napoleon Buonaparte* (1827), written for money but also out of conviction, incorporated new material, including recollections supplied by the Duke of Wellington; it ranged widely over the political and military history of Scott's own time. Inevitably, this large-scale biography proved highly controversial; Scott wrote in his journal in September 1827 of a

French general, Baron Gourgaud, who had objected to the way in which his comments on Napoleon's conditions while on St Helena had been quoted: 'I wonder he did not try to come over and try his manhood other wise. I would not have shund him nor any frenchman who ever kissd Bonaparte's breech.'

Scott's most vital contributions to historical writing were made in his prose fiction; to a considerable extent in the accompanying notes which he supplied as a matter of course for his long poems and for such 'literary' publications as *The Minstrelsy of the Scottish Border* (1802–3); and in the copious introductions and notes which he added late in his life to the Magnum edition of his novels. A modern Scottish historian cites his account of the Porteous Riots in Edinburgh in the opening chapters of *The Heart of Midlothian* as still our most informative historical account of that event. It combines clarity, narrative energy, and a grasp of the social forces at work in the place and period in question. If elsewhere there are inevitable inaccuracies in Scott's vivid portrayals of historical characters and incidents, it remains true that his fiction has taught readers more history than have most history books. In particular, *Waverley* (1814) and *Redgauntlet* (1824) trace the inception and the consequences of the 1745 Rebellion and its aftermath with massive imaginative authority. Scott did not set out consciously to write history 'from underneath'; but it is lastingly to his credit that his vision of life often places humble people, beggars, soldiers, servants, and the like on centre stage, while statesmen and monarchs are never allowed to claim more attention that their varying individual significance makes reasonable.

What Scott contributed, above all, was a deeply human vision of the past. It was his ability to bring innumerable characters to life, against a backcloth of history, which caught the imagination of writers throughout Europe, America, and Russia, making possible the development of the historical novel. Carlyle summed up his achievement as follows:

these Historical Novels have taught all men this truth, which looks like a truism, and yet was as good as unknown to writers of history and others, till so

taught: that the bygone ages of the world were actually filled by living men, not by protocols, state-papers, controversies and abstractions of men. Not abstractions were they, not diagrams and theorems; but men, in buff or other coats and breeches, with colour in their cheeks, with passions in their stomach, and the idioms, features and vitalities of very men. It is a little world; inclusive of great meaning! (Cited in Hayden, *Scott: the Critical Heritage* p. 367)

DAL

Main publications

(Published by Cadell, Edinburgh, unless otherwise stated.)
Waverley Novels, 48 vols (1830–34); *Poetical works*, 12 vols, ed. J. G. Lockhart (1833–4); *Miscellaneous Prose Works*, 28 vols, ed. J. G. Lockhart (1834–6); *Minstrelsy of the Scottish Border* (1802), 4 vols, ed. T. F. Henderson (Edinburgh: Blackwood, 1902); *Journal*, ed. W. E. K. Anderson (Oxford: Clarendon Press, 1972).

Reading

Crawford, Thomas: *Walter Scott* (Edinburgh: Scottish Academic Press, 1982).
Hayden, John O.: *Scott: the Critical Heritage* (Routledge & Kegan Paul, 1970).
Johnson, Edgar: *Sir Walter Scott: The Great Unknown*, 2 vols (London: Hamish Hamilton, 1970).

Scottish historiography 'O do not read history, for that I know must be false', said Sir Robert Walpole, and false indeed were many of the tall tales, myths and legends which until Walpole's time made up Scotland's vision of its glorious past. As late as 1686, Sir George Mackenzie of Rosehaugh (1636–1691), leading Scottish lawyer, antiquarian and founder in 1682 of the Advocates Library, had published his *Antiquity of the Royal Line of Scotland Further Cleared and Defended*, which came close to accusing two English bishops of treason when they dared to question the myth which made the Scottish – and therefore the British – royal house the oldest in Europe.

Yet it was in this era that the study of Scottish history was revolutionized, from a most unlikely quarter. Fr Thomas Innes (1662–1744), son of impoverished Aberdeen Catholics, went with his brother Louis to the Scots College in Paris. They were remarkable men. Louis became principal of the college. Thomas, from 1698, worked in the Catholic mission in the Highlands. But with the foolhardy courage of the utterly dedicated scholar, he also went to Edinburgh and London, where 'Mr Fleming' risked discovery for the sake of working in the Advocates and Cottonian Library. (It is a nice comment on something which is now a familiar Scottish historiographical obsession that the Cottonian librarian, Dr Smith, gave Innes all he wanted, except for material on Mary Queen of Scots which he reserved for his own work.) In 1729 came the results of these labours: *A Critical Essay on the Ancient Inhabitants of the Northern Parts of Britain or Scotland*. With impeccable courtesy and a level of critical record scholarship which was wholly new, this acquaintance of Jean MABILLON and reader of Pierre BAYLE demolished the myths. And it is pleasant to record that the Presbyterian city of Glasgow honoured the achievements of the Catholic priest, this 'monkish, bookish man', by making him a burgess in 1739.

Thereafter, two themes came to dominate Scottish historiography: a passion for publishing texts, and an uncertainty, born of union with England, about what to make of them. In the first half of the eighteenth century there were four printing houses in Edinburgh, the most notable being that of Thomas Ruddiman, grammarian and antiquary; by 1779 there were 27, including that of William Smellie, first editor of the *Encyclopaedia Britannica* (1768). Enlightenment Scotland witnessed the editions of James Anderson's *Diplomata et Numismata Scotiae* (1739); Walter Goodall's edition of the *Scotichronicon* of John of Fordun, with its continuation by Walter Bower (1759), a major late-medieval source which is only now being revised and re-edited; and of course a welter of material about the Reformation, about that great hero John Knox, and — with magnificent indifference to inconsistency — that equally great heroine Mary Queen of Scots.

The habit of pouring scholarly time and energy into the editing of texts continued into the nineteenth century, immensely helped by the founding of publishing clubs. The idea came from the Roxburghe Club, founded in London in 1812, but the movement was more generally inspired by the influence and enthusiasm of Sir Walter SCOTT, admitted to the Roxburghe in 1823 and founder of the Bannatyne Club in Edinburgh in the same year. In 1833 Glasgow responded with the Maitland Club. In 1839 Aberdeen got its outlet for the publication of north-eastern material with the Spalding, and the romance though not, alas, the energy of the Highlander found brief expression in the single volume produced by the Iona Club, *Collectanea de Rebus Albanicis* (1847). In addition, there was a major drive to put government and legal records into print; hence the massive twelve volumes of the *Acts of the Parliaments of Scotland* (1814–75), the *Register of the Privy Council* (1877 onward), the *Registrum Magni Sigilli* (1882–1914) and *Secreti Sigilli* (1908 onward). Meanwhile, the creator of the chair of Scottish history in Edinburgh, Sir William Fraser, was producing single-handedly a series of splendid red-bound volumes containing muniments and papers of many of the great Scottish families, and the original clubs were giving way to new publishing ventures such as the Scottish Text Society (founded 1882), the Scottish History Society (founded 1886), and the Stair Society, established in 1934 for the publication of legal records and texts. Historians of Scotland were, proportionately, deeply fortunate in the sheer quantity of material in print.

But what were they doing with it? One answer was to debate endlessly the morals of Mary Queen of Scots; from the battle waged in the 1750s between Goodall and William Robertson to the modern biography by Antonia Fraser (1969) and beyond, that violent bedroom drama has exercised a baleful and voluminous fascination. Equally romantic, once they were no longer feared, were the Highlands; the Iona Club may have failed, but there has long been a ready market for clan histories. And Scottish pride was sustained by accounts of the triumph of the Calvinist over the Catholic church. Yet there remained a problem, a crisis of identity for historians of Scotland. Scott himself appealed to nationalist feelings all over Europe, but not in Scotland; for this was still the age of the north Briton. Union with England produced a dual reaction to the past, already detectable in the seventeenth century, and pride in Scotland's achievements became mingled with apology for the violence and poverty of the kingdom and its institutions – as compared, inevitably, with England. Despite the production of the tools of the trade, detailed research was remarkably lacking; instead, the fashion was for the overview, and many histories of Scotland were produced, from that of Patrick Fraser Tytler, originally published in eight volumes and completed in 1843, to those of P. Hume Brown (3 volumes, 1911), W. C. Dickinson and G. Pryde (2 volumes, 1961), Rosalind Mitchison (1970) and others, while between 1965 and 1975 the parallel to the monumental *Oxford History of England* appeared in the four-volume Edinburgh *History of Scotland*, and in the 1980s the volumes of the *New History of England* were accompanied by the much shorter *New History of Scotland*. In these, one can detect the need felt by Scottish historians to compare, for better or worse, their society with others; they do not match the self-confidence of English historians that their subject is of obvious importance in its own right. Nevertheless, as an academic subject – for all the efforts of Jean Plaidy and others to keep the 'thud and blunder' or romantic approach going – there has been a revolution in Scottish historical publishing since the second world war, and today, thanks largely to the existence of a single publishing house in Edinburgh, John Donald, a steady stream of monographs is putting the study of Scotland on a footing recognizable to historians of other societies. With the work of scholars such as G. W. S. Barrow, G. Donaldson, T. C. Smout and many others, Scottish history is flourishing.

JW

Reading

Ash, M.: *The Strange Death of Scottish History* (Edinburgh: Ramsay Head, 1980).
Rae, T. I.: Historical scepticism in Scotland before David Hume. In *Studies in the Eighteenth Century*, vol. 2, ed. R. F. Brissenden (Canberra: Australian National University Press, 1973).
Scots Antiquaries and Historians (Abertay Society) 16 (1972).

Seebohm, Frederic (b.1833, d.1912) Born in Bradford, the son of an immigrant German Quaker wool merchant, Seebohm received his education at Bootham School, York, and after reading law at the Middle Temple, settled in Hitchin as a partner in a banking firm. He remained there for the rest of his life. His deep religious convictions were reflected in his first important published work, a study of the three 'Oxford reformers', Erasmus, More and Colet. His most important contribution to scholarship did not, however, appear for a further sixteen years, in 1883. Convinced of the error of Thorold ROGERS's theory of a medieval golden age, he began to investigate the origins of the medieval rural community, in particular of the manor. The result of painstaking research, based on the principle of working back 'from the known to the unknown', was *The English Village Community*. In this he rejected the ideas of the 'Germanists' like STUBBS and FREEMAN, who saw the roots of the community as found in the thirteenth century in a primitive free Germanic organization which had been only gradually 'manorialized'. In tune with the continental 'Romanists', like FUSTEL DE COULANGES, whose findings he introduced into British historiography, he saw the origin of the manor and of villeinage in the Roman villa and the slavery of the ancient world; the open field system was, he claimed, developed to protect villagers during the disturbed period following the fall of the Roman Empire in the west. While VINOGRADOFF sided with the Germanists on origins, both he and Seebohm were to be criticized for generalizing too freely from the examples of Midland ecclesiastical estates, on which most of their research was done, to build up a picture of a 'typical' manor which was supposed to exist also in other parts of England, and for exaggerating the extent to which the English peasant had been enserfed after the Conquest. Seebohm was certainly inclined to treat customs and institutions from different periods as contemporary and to make unduly bold inferences from inadequate evidence. But his vivid portrayal of English medieval rural society, much modified as it subsequently was, did much to stimulate interest in the manor and to encourage the work of historians such as MAITLAND, STENTON and Joliffe. His later work on Welsh tribal organization and Anglo-Saxon law, in which

377

he stressed the importance of patriarchal authority, were not up to the standard of his work on the manor. Seebohm never held an academic appointment but was awarded honorary degrees by the universities of Cambridge, Edinburgh and Oxford. Head of a family of five daughters and a son, he played an active role in his Hertfordshire community as, among other things, a JP and school governor.

SPO

Main publications

(All published by Longmans, Green, London.)
The Oxford Reformers (1867); *The English Village Community* (1883); *The Tribal System in Wales* (1895); *Tribal Custom in Anglo-Saxon Law* (1902).

Reading

Vinogradoff, P.: Obituary — Frederic Seebohm (1833–1912). In *Collected Papers of Paul Vinogradoff*, vol. I (Oxford: Oxford University Press, 1928), pp. 272–6.

Seeley, John Robert (b.1834, d.1895) Seeley was an influential figure in the development of the historical profession in nineteenth-century England, exemplifying the shift from the gentleman scholar of eclectic interests to the full-time academic. Born in London, he read classics at Christ's College, Cambridge, and was appointed professor of Latin at University College London in 1863. In 1869 he succeeded Kingsley to the chair of modern history at Cambridge. Of an Evangelical background, Seeley was much influenced by POSITIVISM, which led him to argue that a science of history could be established as a school for statesmen. His inaugural lecture at Cambridge, in which he advanced this thesis, is said to have produced a classic example of academic acidity, the master of Trinity departing with the words, 'how little did one think we should so soon have been regretting poor Kingsley'. Seeley had a great popular success with a life of Christ, *Ecce Homo*, in 1866, and his *Expansion of England* in 1883 caught and swelled the imperial tide. He was knighted in 1894 on Rosebery's recommendation, and on his death his friends established the History Faculty Library at Cambridge in his honour.

JAC

Main publications

Ecce Homo (Cambridge: 1866); *The Life and Times of Stein* (Cambridge: 1878); *The Expansion of England* (London: Macmillan, 1883); *A Short History of Napoleon* (London: Seeley, 1886); *The Growth of British Policy* (Cambridge University Press, 1895).

Reading

Gooch, G. P.: *History and historians in the nineteenth century* (London: Longmans, 1913).

Kitson Clark, G.: A hundred years of the teaching of history at Cambridge, 1873–1973. *Historical Journal* 16 (1973) 535–53.

Peardon, T. P.: Sir John Seeley, pragmatic historian in a nationalist age. In *Nationalism and Internationalism*, ed. E. M. Earle (New York: Columbia University Press, 1950).

Rein, A.: *John Robert Seeley: eine Studie über den Historiker* (Langensalza: 1912).

Shannon, R.: John Robert Seeley and the idea of a national church. In *Ideas and Institutions of Victorian Britain*, ed. R. Robson (London: Bell, 1967).

Wormell, D.: *Sir John Seeley and the Uses of History* (Cambridge: Cambridge University Press, 1980).

Selden, John (b.1584, d.1654) Educated at Oxford and the Inner Temple, jurist, antiquarian, MP and orientalist, Selden was probably the most erudite scholar of his day. Although his productions were voluminous, and won contemporary acclaim, he is best known to later generations for his posthumously published *Table Talk*, and to historians for the practical uses to which he put his formidable scholarship. In this latter capacity his association with Sir Edward Coke, and the contribution which he made to the defence of constitutional liberties against crown encroachments in the early part of the seventeenth century, have been widely recognized.

Historians now would question the importance of both these points. Whereas Coke emphasized common law as the law of reason, Selden's analysis is a more hard-headed explanation of its historical determinants. His demonstration, in a series of books published between 1607 and 1617, of the *differences* between feudal practices in England and those of his own day, may be his most lasting contribution to historiography. He was on parliament's side during the civil war, not out of Cokeian reverence for an 'ancient constitution', but because Commissions of Array in

1641 were to him as historically unwarranted as billeting of soldiers in 1628. Of his most celebrated work he claimed in the preface that it was not moved by animus against the clergy: it was 'a mere narrative of the History of Tythes'. This was disingenuous. When the full minutes of the Westminster Assembly of Divines are published (and the only printed version we have so far is highly selective), Selden's role in using his historical erudition in the service of Erastianism may be seen to be of equal importance to his more celebrated contributions in the Commons in exposing the unhistorical basis of prerogative claims.　WML

Main publications

Titles of Honour (London: 1614); *History of Tythes* (London: 1618); *Mare Clausum* (London: 1635); *Fleta* (London: 1647).

Reading

Christianson, Paul: John Selden, the five Knights' case, and discretionary imprisonment in early Stuart England. *Criminal Justice History* 6 (1985) 65–87.

Pocock, J. G. A.: *The Ancient Constitution and the Feudal Law* (Cambridge: Cambridge University Press, 1957).

Pollock, F. ed.: *Table Talk* (London: 1927).

Tuck, Richard: The ancient law of freedom: John Selden and the civil war. In *Reactions to the English Civil War 1642–1649*, ed. J. Morrill (London: Macmillan, 1982) pp. 137–63.

Seton-Watson, Robert William (b.1879, d.1951)　A Scotsman educated at Winchester and Oxford, Seton-Watson travelled extensively as a young man in France, Germany and Italy, but from 1905 he concentrated his attention on the nationalities of Austria-Hungary. Blessed with private means, he devoted himself wholeheartedly to learning the languages of the two countries, writing about their difficulties, becoming acquainted with their leaders, and attempting to persuade the British Foreign Office of the ways in which their problems could be resolved. His periodical *The New Europe* (1916–20) exercised an influence quite disproportionate to its maximum circulation of 5,000 copies. When the frontiers of Europe were redrawn after the first world war Seton-Watson became the first occupant of the Masaryk chair of central

European history at London University's School of Slavonic Studies (1922) and subsequently professor of Czechoslovak studies at Oxford (1945–9). He was elected fellow of the British Academy and president of the Royal Historical Society, but never turned into a study-bound academic. The title of his 1922 inaugural lecture, 'The historian as a political force in central Europe', implied a link between the armchair and the public forum which he sought always to maintain. However naive, his belief that 'nationalism, if properly conceived, is not a "cul-de-sac" of hate and insularity, but . . . the only sure road . . . to the international standpoint' enabled him to make significant contributions to the foundation of Yugoslavia and Czechoslovakia and the emasculation of Hungary.　DBS

Main publications

Racial Problems in Hungary (London: Constable, 1908); *The South Slav Question and the Habsburg Monarchy* (London: Constable, 1911); *A History of the Roumanians* (London: Cambridge University Press, 1934); *A History of the Czechs and Slovaks* (London: Hutchinson, 1943).

Reading

Seton-Watson, H. and C.: *The Making of a New Europe: R. W. Seton-Watson and the Last Years of Austria-Hungary* (London: Methuen, 1981).

Simiand, François (b.1873, d.1935)　Born in Gières, France, Simiand trained as a philosopher. His formative intellectual influences were the librarian of the École Normale, Lucien Herr, who encouraged him to become an active socialist, and Lévy-Bruhl and Durkheim under whose influence he turned towards sociology, becoming one of the group which founded *L'Année sociologique* (1896). His career was spent both in the civil service and in institutions rather marginal to the university mainstream, such as the École Pratique des Hautes Études, Conservatoire National des Arts et Métiers and, at the very end of his life, the Collège de France.

Simiand's own research was concerned mainly with the evolution of wages and prices and the development of quantitative techniques. In particular he employed statistics on money supply and analysis of its influence upon prices and incomes in order to define long-term phases of growth (phase A) and of regression (phase B), as well as shorter term inter-cyclical movements. These he believed would provide the key to an understanding of social and political behaviour, although he accepted that the complex responses of groups such as employers or workers interacted with the basic economic mechanisms to reduce their regularity. The onset of the world economic depression in the 1930s and the desire to identify the causes of such crises intensified his commitment and sense of purpose.

Although criticized in recent years because of its excessive emphasis on monetary factors, its neglect of technological change, and because its obsession with statistical information led to the serious undervaluing of less quantifiable information, Simiand's approach has had a considerable influence upon the work of French historians particularly through the mediation of LABROUSSE. In historiographical terms, his contribution from the 1890s to the critique of conventional historical scholarship was perhaps even more fundamental. In an article published in 1903 he condemned the *histoire historisante*, the essential empiricism of leading academic historians such as Seignobos, and their overwhelming concern with political history and great individuals to the neglect of social phenomena. He insisted upon the need to adopt an analytical approach, based upon sociological method and wherever possible employing statistics. This critique was of considerable significance in the intellectual development of the school exemplified by Marc BLOCH and Lucien FEBVRE who in 1929 established the *Annales d'histoire économique et sociale*. Simiand's original article was republished in *Annales ESC* in 1960 to help young historians to 'appreciate the importance of the dialogues between history and the social sciences'.   RDP

Main publications

Méthode historique et science sociale, étude critique à propos des ouvrages récents de M. Lacombe et de M. Seignobos. *Revue de synthèse historique* 6 (1903) repr. in *Annales ESC* 15 (1960) 83–119; *Statistique et expérience: remarques de méthode* (Paris: Rivière, 1922); *Le Salaire, l'évolution sociale et la monnaie; essai de théorie expérimentale du salaire*, 3

vols (Paris: Alcan, 1932); *Les Fluctuations économiques à longue période et la crise mondiale* (Paris: Alcan, 1932); *Recherches anciennes et nouvelles sur le mouvement général des prix du XVIe au XIXe siècles* (Paris: EPHE, 1933).

Reading

Bouvier, J: Feu François Simiand? *Annales ESC* 28 (1973) 1173–92.

Lévy-Leboyer, M.: L' Héritage de F. Simiand: prix, profit, et termes de l'échange au XIXe siècle, *Revue historique* 1 (1970) 77–120.

Sismondi, Jean Charles Léonard Simonde de (b.1773, d.1842) Son of a Swiss pastor, Charles Simonde was apprenticed in a Lyons business house until the December 1792 revolutionary coup in Geneva which drove his family to England. He returned home in 1794 and was incarcerated for a short time, subsequently emigrating to farm in Tuscany. Briefly imprisoned three times in the political upheavals there, Simonde returned in 1800 to Geneva by then annexed to France). He adopted the original family name, Sismondi, and began to write. Companion to Mme de Staël, favourable to neither Bonaparte nor the Bourbons, under Constant's influence he supported the emperor on his return from Elba in 1815. After Waterloo, however, Sismondi returned to Switzerland where, after marrying in England in 1819, he lived for most of the rest of his life.

A prolific writer, Sismondi's passion was the advancement of human happiness. His 16-volume *Histoire des Républiques italiennes du moyen âge* (1807–17) recounted the triumph of despotism and the consequent eclipse of Italy. A three-volume novel, studies of Tuscan agriculture, political economy, southern European literature and the fall of the Roman empire stand beside his *Histoire des Français* (1821–44), 29 volumes of which, from Roman Gaul to Louis XV, occupied him to his death. Didactic, Protestant, scorning military glory and all absolute power, he measured national prosperity and greatness by the liberty of a people's institutions. Historians, he wrote, must consider less the reputation of the dead than the salvation of the living. Judgemental, iconoclastic, without great literary art, he was innocent of historicism and lacked an essential historical imagination. His alibi was the outsider's detachment, hard work in the printed sources, understanding of the place of economic change, and devotion to 'the progress of morality and happiness in human society'.

Though the public was cool, scholars welcomed the earliest volumes (J. S. Mill dared call them 'sprightly, and frequently eloquent'). Honours came during the July monarchy. But, overtaken by younger historians, Sismondi apparently grew bored with his immense enterprise, and critics said that this showed. His place is none the less with the great nineteenth-century pioneers of documented history.   JCC

Main publications

Histoire des Républiques italiennes du moyen âge, 16 vols (1809–18) (English trans. London: Routledge, 1906); *Histoire des Français* (continued from the accession of Louis XVI up to the assembly of the Estates General in 1789 by A. Renée), 31 vols (1821–44).

Reading

Gooch, G. P.: *History and Historians in the Nineteenth Century* (London: Longmans, Green, 1952), pp. 159–62.

Salis, J. R. de, *Sismondi, 1773–1842; la vie et l'oeuvre d'un cosmopolite philosophe* (Paris: Librairie Ancienne Henri Champion, 1932).

Slavonic historiography The Slavonic peoples have been held together historically by considerable similarities in their languages and significant cultural overlaps, though their political and social evolution has diverged widely. Over many centuries of chroniclers, from the twelfth-century Nestorian Chronicle of Kiev onwards, some consciousness of common origins was regularly evinced, and the linguistic bond advanced as evidence of the extent and homogeneity of the Slavonic world. Such notions received dramatic stimulus in the years around 1800, especially through the writings of Herder, the great ethnographer of Baltic-German stock who publicized the uncorrupted, democratic and peaceable traditions of the Slavs and prophesied future glory for them. A wave of Romantic sentiment encouraged research into Slavonic history, much of it highly imaginative, and sometimes not averse to forging suitable evidence (for example, the notorious 'manuscripts' of ostensibly thirteenth-century provenance perpetrated by Václav Hanka in Bohemia). Literary and linguistic history made giant strides, particularly in the work of Josef Dobrovský (1753–1829), Jernej Kopitar (1780–1844) and Pavel Josef Šafárik (1795–1861).

Yet the movement soon fell into contradiction, since the sources revealed at least as much diversity as cohesion, while particular nationalisms asserted their primacy, a process accelerated by the growth and institutionalization of a historical profession in the different countries inhabited by Slavs. Russian scholarship, though heavily influenced from abroad, paid little attention to the Slav cause as a whole (see KARAMZIN), except to assert hegemony for the tsarist state or the Orthodox community. The Poles were largely alienated from the Russians: indeed, their first outstanding modern historian, LELEWEL, led the insurrection of 1830–1. Even PALACKÝ among the Czechs, whose vision of the past owed most to Herder, concentrated on the history of his own nation. South Slavs developed their own regional version of the ideal, describing it first as Illyrian and then as Yugoslav, which was propagated by historians such as Kukuljević-Sakcinski and Rački. The sense of solidarity lived on as a political myth, dubbed 'pan-Slavism' especially by its enemies. Yet its traces survived in historiography and have been periodically revived by those who, as scholarly persuasion or ideological weapon, sought to assert the essential unity and distinctivenes of Slavonic or Eastern Europe.   RJWE

Reading

Dvornik, F.: *The Slavs in European History and Civilization* (New Brunswick, NJ: Rutgers University Press, 1962).

Kohn, H.: *Pan-Slavism: Its History and Ideology* (Notre Dame, Ind.: Indiana University Press, 1953).

Macůrek, J.: *Dějepisectví evropského východu* (Prague: Historický Klub, 1946).

Slicher van Bath, Bernhard Hendrik (b.1920) Spending most of his academic life at the Agricultural University of Wageningen,

Slicher van Bath is one of the foremost Dutch agrarian historians of the post-war period. He developed his ideas about the evolution of the rural economy during the course of undertaking local studies devoted to limited districts within the Netherlands, but which covered a time span stretching from the high middle ages to the nineteenth century. Of these the most important was *A Society in Tension* about the province of Overijssel. He then turned to a wider canvas and in 1960 published his *Agrarian History of Western Europe (500–1850)*, an interpretative work which set out to explain the alternating episodes of expansion and contraction in the agrarian history of the medieval and post-medieval west, and which had a profound influence on a whole generation of agricultural and economic historians. The most important feature of Slicher van Bath's approach was the use of local data on things such as crop yields, and his identification of the strategies adopted by farmers in the face of long-term price changes. Subsequently he turned his attention to the history of Latin America.   CC

Main publications

Een Samenleving onder Spanning: Geschiedenis von het Platteland in Overijssel (Assen, Holland: Van Gorcum, 1957); *De Agrarische Geschiedenis van West-Europa (500–1850)* (1960; Eng. trans., London: Arnold, 1963).

Smith, Adam (b.1723, d.1790)   Smith's life and work as a political economist are well known, yet his work was only one part of what he planned to be a systematic account of the general principles of law and government, informed by historical evidence and understanding.

The historical themes developed in Smith's lectures as professor of moral philosophy at the University of Glasgow from 1752 to 1764 survive only in the form of student notes but these ideas, perhaps traceable to earlier lectures given in Edinburgh in 1748, were fundamental to the concerns of the *Wealth of Nations* (1776). In particular, Smith has been seen as the inspirer in Scotland of the 'four stages theory'.

Though the framework of these lectures was inherited from the natural law of PUFEN-

DORF, Smith transformed the content into the history of jurisprudence and government according to a universal framework and applicable to all societies. All would pass through four stages, each defined by the mode of subsistence: the hunting stage, the age of shepherds, the age of agriculture, the commercial stage. All aspects of a society – its law, culture, government and family – could be related to its mode of subsistence. Such history rested on conventional record, on comparisons with contemporary peoples – particularly, for the early stages, such groups as the American Indians – and to some degree on 'conjecture'. Such a scheme with, at its apex, eighteenth-century commercial civilization was an attractive one to contemporaries and subsequent writers such as ROBERTSON, and it posed some critical questions about the nature of the transition from one stage to another which Smith was to address in the *Wealth of Nations*.   JR

Main publications

Lectures on Jurisprudence, ed. R. L. Meek, D. D. Raphael and P. G. Stein (Oxford: Oxford University Press, 1978); *The Wealth of Nations*, ed. R. H. Campbell and A. S. Skinner, 2 vols (Oxford University Press, 1976).

Reading

Haakonssen, K.: *The Science of a legislator: the natural jurisprudence of David Hume and Adam Smith* (Cambridge: Cambridge University Press, 1981).
Meek, R. L.: *Social Science and the Ignoble Savage* (Cambridge University Press, 1976).

Smith, Henry Nash (b.1906, d.1987)   Born in Texas, Smith graduated from Southern Methodist University, and received his MA and PhD from Harvard. He soon became recognized as one of the major figures in the new American studies movement which wanted to fuse the strengths of literary and historical approaches to the study of culture. His interdisciplinary interests led him to look at the meaning of the west for American culture, not in terms of facts but as symbol and myth. The result led to *Virgin Land* (1950), an extraordinarily successful and long-lasting investigation which won both the Bancroft and John H. Dunning prizes. Its great impact helped make the study of myth respectable and helped change the direction of cultural studies from its concentration on 'high' culture. Though the work can be seen as a criticism of Frederick Jackson TURNER's 'Frontier thesis' it did re-emphasize the important hold which the west has had on the American imagination. From 1953 until retirement Smith was professor of English at Berkeley, his major interest having become Mark Twain. This was recognized in his appointment as literary editor of the Mark Twain papers.   RAB

Main publications

Virgin Land (Cambridge, Mass.: Harvard University Press, 1950); *Mark Twain: the Development of a Writer* (Cambridge, Mass.: Belknap Press, 1962); editor *Popular Culture and Industrialism* (New York: New York University Press, 1967); *Democracy and the Novel* (New York: Oxford University Press, 1978).

Reading

Ethridge, James M. ed. Henry Nash Smith. In *Contemporary Authors*, vol. 4 (Detroit: Gale Research Company, 1963).

Snorre Sturluson (b.1179, d.1241) A member of the powerful Sturlunga family in Iceland. Brought up by the chieftain Jón Loptsson, a grandson of Sämund the Wise, Snorre acquired an intimate knowledge of Icelandic and Norwegian poetry and traditions. He inherited the large farm at Borg, once owned by his maternal ancestor, the poet Egil Skallagrimsson. In his early twenties Snorre was one of Iceland's most powerful chieftains and later he also became lawspeaker (leader of the *Althing*). In Iceland he displayed a ruthless ambition for money and glory. When, in 1218, he went to Norway, he was well received by King Håkon Håkonsson, whose man he became. He promised to work for the subordination of Iceland to the Norwegian king, but after returning home in 1220 he failed to do so. During his next visit to Norway (1237–39) he quarrelled with the king, who prohibited his return to Iceland. When Snorre disobeyed, he was held a rebel whose life was forefeit. His Icelandic enemies were not slow to take advantage of this; in 1241 he was killed by men commissioned by his brother-in-law,

Gizurr Thorvaldsson. Snorre's most important work is *Heimskringla*, the history of Norwegian kings from a mythical beginning to 1177. It is not clear whether he wrote or merely supervised the production of this collection of kings' sagas, which incorporates old material. It is generally agreed that the creator of *Heimskringla* is identical with the author of the later *Edda*, a 'course-book' for poets, presenting the pagan mythology, poetic devices and metres. In this work the author justified an interest in pagan poetry by proving that pagan beliefs prefigured Christian truth.   BSS

Main writings

Heimskringla 3 vols, ed. Bjarni Aðalbjarnarson (Reykjavik: Islenzk Fornrit 26–28, 1941–51) English trans. L. M. Hollander, *Heimskringla: History of the Kings of Norway* (Austin: University of Texas Press, 1977); *Edda Snorra Sturlusonar*, ed. Finnur Jónsson (Copenhagen: 1931) English trans. A. Faulkes, *Snorri Sturlusen Edda* (London: Dent, 1987).

Reading

Sveinsson, Einar Ól.: *The Age of the Sturlungs* (Ithaca, NY: Cornell University Press, 1953).

Turville-Petre G.: *Origins of Icelandic Literature* (Oxford: Clarendon Press, 1967).

Soboul, Albert Marius (b.1914, d.1982) A prolific and combative historian of the French Revolution, Soboul earned a reputation for his extensive knowledge of the Parisian working class and the peasantry. His professional interests sprang largely from his own humble origins. The son of a carpenter from the Ardèche Department who settled in Algeria in 1910, Soboul spent his early years on a farm where the stony soil made it difficult to make a living. His father was killed early in the first world war and his mother died in 1922, leaving the young orphan in the care of his maiden aunt Marie Soboul. The headmistress of a women's teachers college in Nîmes and a scientist, she impressed her strong republican feelings on her nephew.

In the local lycée Soboul demonstrated genuine academic promise and with the aid of scholarships he pursued his education at Montpellier and then Paris. His studies at the Sorbonne enabled him to pass his *agrégation* in history and geography in 1938. His first published work, a study of Saint-Just, demonstrated that he had acquired a taste for revolutionary history. Marked by the agitation that the Popular Front aroused, he involved himself in Communist youth activities and joined the party itself by 1939.

After military service during the second world war, he began his teaching career at the Lycée of Montpellier. In 1942 resistance activity led to his dismissal by the Vichy regime. But he found employment at the Musée des arts et traditions populaires in Paris, where, under the direction of Georges Henri Rivière, he spent the duration of the war studying peasant life. With the Liberation, Soboul resumed his classroom instruction, first at Montpellier, then in the capital.

Undertaking research for his doctoral dissertation, Soboul came under the influence of Georges LEFEBVRE, well known for his work on the peasantry. In 1958 he successfully defended his massive thesis dealing with the Parisian *sans-culottes* of the Year II. It stressed that these urban shopkeepers and artisans were not a coherent class but did desire popular democracy and social equality. Soboul taught at the University of Clermont-Ferrand before being named in 1967 to the chair of the history of the French Revolution at the Sorbonne. President of the Société des études robespierristes and editor of *Annales historiques de la Révolution française*, Soboul emerged as the leading French authority on the Revolution. He achieved international recognition as his works were translated into various foreign languages and he made frequent trips abroad to lecture.

Soboul's writings stressed the importance of social conflict, especially the demands made by the lower classes. He considered the eighteenth century as a period when the mercantile and professional bourgeoisie sought political power at the expense of the aristocracy. Inspired by the critiques of Enlightenment *philosophes*, this ambitious class moved to secure domination when the old regime monarchy lost control over the nation's finances by 1789. Soboul insisted that the bourgeoisie reformed French institutions in their own image. They depended, however, on the active support offered by the *sans-culotte*

and peasant majority. As the bourgeoisie gradually divided and France struggled against the Allied coalition, internal political, social and economic stresses led to increased popular demands for democracy and economic justice. This new revolutionary wave threatened the ruling elite who responded partly through timely concessions, partly by effective suppression of militant leadership during the Terror. The contradictions inherent in such a policy, Soboul maintained, weakened the popular base of the government of the Year II and led to its overthrow in 1794. Middle-class politicians who then controlled France eventually allowed themselves to fall under the sway of the victorious general Bonaparte. Soboul deemed Babeuf's Conspiracy of the Equals an effort to install popular government, one that despite its failure would guide future generations towards revolutionary action.

Throughout his later career Soboul engaged in numerous polemics with critics who found his historical schema too ideologically rigid. Yet he repeatedly denied that he was a Marxist historian; rather, he considered himself part of the 'classical' and 'scientific' school of historiography represented by TOCQUEVILLE, JAURÈS and Lefebvre. Certainly, Soboul opened new vistas on 'history from below'.   JF

Main publications

La Révolution française (1789–1799) (Paris: Éditions Sociales, 1948); *Les Sans-culottes parisiens en l'an II: mouvement populaire et gouvernement révolutionnaire, 2 juin 1793–9 thermidor an II* (Paris: Clavreuil, 1958); *Les Soldats de l'an II* (Paris: Club français du livre, 1959); *Le Procès de Louis XVI* (Paris: Julliard, 1966); *Paysans, sans-culottes et Jacobins* (Clavreuil, 1966); *La Première république, 1792–1804* (Paris: Calmann-Lévy, 1968); *La Civilisation et la Révolution française*, 3 vols (Paris: Arthaud, 1970–82); *Problèmes paysans de la Révolution, 1789–1848* (Paris: Maspero, 1976); *Comprendre la Révolution* (Maspero, 1981); *La Révolution française* (Éditions sociales, 1982).

Reading

Cobb, R.: Albert-Marius Soboul: a tribute. In *People and Places* (Oxford: Oxford University Press, 1985) pp. 46–92.
Hommage à Albert Soboul. *Annales historiques de la Révolution française* 54 (1982) 513–670.

Huard, R. and Naudin, M. J.: Entretiens avec Albert Soboul. *Cahiers d'histoire de l'Institut de recherches marxistes* 21 (1985) 119–44.

social history From its inception social history has been presented as an alternative, at times self-consciously oppositional, form of historical inquiry. The radicalism may have been genuinely political, as it was with the Fabians and liberals who developed the subject in Britain and the Marxists who proved so central to its development in western Europe during the 1950s and 1960s, but it has generally been presented by its practitioners as offering the alternative to some supposed mainstream of historical writing. One might trace the beginnings of social history in Britain to the Scottish Enlightenment and Adam Ferguson's *An Essay on the History of Civil Society* (1767), but sustained growth came only in response to the institutional and intellectual professionalization of history in the later nineteenth century. Fabian and liberal-radical intellectuals took a prominent part in creating the subject in Britain between those years and the second world war; the writings of Sidney and Beatrice WEBB, R. H. TAWNEY, J. L. and Barbara HAMMOND and H. N. Brailsford shaped its continuing identity as tied to that other fledgeling discipline of economic history while being primarily concerned with the condition and movements of the lower classes. The title of G. D. H. COLE and Raymond Postgate's influential *The Common People* (1938) tells us much about the populist concerns that have rarely been absent from social history in Britain.

This closeness to ECONOMIC HISTORY, through the founding of the *Economic History Review* (1927) and of many university departments of economic and social history, had by the 1960s become a problem for social historians, and the subject then entered a new and professedly oppositional phase. Economic history's increasing concern with theory, economic growth and statistical analysis made it a less congenial partner for a social history that was at the same time attacking as narrow and elitist the constitutional and traditional political history which prevailed in university degree courses. The rapid growth of higher education in these years provided the basis for an unprecedented expansion of social history.

It was not only in Britain that social history presented itself, whether politically or intellectually, as an alternative. When Lucien FEBVRE and Marc BLOCH founded *Annales d'histoire économique et sociale* in Strasburg (1929) they sought to shift historical inquiry away from the event and the formal public record towards those long processes in human history and the forces that lie behind them which they felt historians had hitherto largely ignored. In Germany, social history found it far more difficult to make space in an academic world dominated by political history, but the critical social history that developed there from the 1960s presented itself as an argumentative alternative to orthodoxy. However, far from seeking an alternative approach rooted in the long economic and demographic processes beloved of the ANNALES SCHOOL, the historians around Jurgen Kocka, Hans-Ulrich Wehler and the journal *Geschichte und Gesellschaft* (founded 1975) have tried to answer through social history those questions relating to Germany's distinctive political development that have long been central to German historiography. The French and German experiences – and that in Britain with *Past and Present* (1952) – indicate the critical role of journals rather than institutions in the growth of social history.

The generally oppositional stance and the rapid expansion since the 1960s together divert the eye from real tensions within social history, a subject easier to define negatively than positively. Two tendencies stand out, however: the first analysing aspects of human life previously neglected; the second seeking to write the history of society. The first of these tendencies came to dominate, and social history began to proliferate subjects and specialisms. The result of this centrifugal impulse was that, by the 1970s, it became difficult to discern a core to the discipline. Social history had become essentially the study of social aspects of the past, as implied by G. M. TREVELYAN's often misunderstood description of social history as 'the history of the people with the politics left out'. Some of these proliferating sub-disciplines provided a temporary stopping place for those seeking a more ambitious social history. This was particularly true of LABOUR HISTORY and URBAN HISTORY during the 1960s and 1970s. Others thrived as specialist sub-groups of a larger social history that could serve as little more than an umbrella. In this way the 1970s and 1980s saw the specialist growth of family history, the history of leisure, women's history, DEMOGRAPHIC HISTORY and many more, including ORAL HISTORY which created a subject around a source.

Social history has indeed struggled since its beginnings with the potential vastness of its subject matter. A second tendency therefore developed, expressing the imperialist ambitions of some social historians to make their subject the history of all society. The total history pursued by Febvre and BRAUDEL was but an early and very specific expression of this tendency. In its development in recent decades this social history has attempted to organize those concerns for social structure, classes, social movements and protest, structures of wealth and inequality, power and authority, ideology and culture which have provided the centre of a subject with such centrifugal impulses.

This presentation of social history as the history of society, able to incorporate all other histories, has been strongest where the social sciences have influenced its growth. This is true of the USA, where the work of Charles Tilly and of the large-scale Philadelphia social history project exemplify in their different ways the impact of sociology on social history. The German social historians around *Geschichte und Gesellschaft* added the subtitle 'A Journal for Historical Social Science', and have projected a broader social history firmly rooted in the analysis of power, subordination and political development. Indeed, social history has been particularly receptive to the influence of other disciplines. If this has at times proved to be a search for conceptual maps in a terrain where the social historian could get lost in a morass of empirical observations, the relationship has often been a great deal more creative. Demography spawned a significant sub-area within social history, and, if sociology's relationship with history in Britain failed to fulfil early expectations, recent contacts with cultural and social anthropology have proved more fertile, above all in the study of *mentalités* and popular culture.

Social anthropology has helped specialists on the early modern period resolve some of the problems that have faced all social historians – that their focus on the historically inarticulate, and on the less formal aspects of the lives of the articulate, creates immense problems of source identification and analysis. The need to wrestle with fragmentary and awkward data must in part explain the methodological and conceptual innovativeness of the best social history. It also explains the arrival of the local or regional study as the bedrock of the discipline.

Social history in Britain has been broadly identified with the study of the lower classes, and E. P. THOMPSON's manifesto in the preface to his *The Making of the English Working Class* is but the most eloquent expression of this view. Only in the 1980s has there appeared a substantial broadening of the social focus. The periods of chronological concentration have however been more varied. In its early decades, social history was particularly concerned with medieval and early modern societies (Eileen POWER, R. H. Tawney). The expansive mood of the 1960s and 1970s, the belief in growth and sociology, encouraged a concentration on the nineteenth century (the present century remains neglected except by oral historians). From the perspective of the late 1980s, the early modern period appears as perhaps the most imaginative area of social historical analysis, reflecting in its concerns a wider shift in social history towards questions of ideology and culture. GC

Reading

Crossick, Geoffrey: L'histoire sociale de la Grande-Bretagne moderne: un aperçu critique des recherches récentes. *Le mouvement social* 100 (1977) 101–20.

Hobsbawm, E. J.: From social history to the history of society. *Daedalus* 100 (1971) 20–45.

Thane, Pat and Sutcliffe, Anthony: Introduction. In *Essays in Social History*, vol. 2, ed. Thane and Sutcliffe (Oxford: Oxford University Press, 1986), pp. vii–xxxiv.

sociology and history Like social anthropology, sociology deserved more attention from the historical profession than it generally received up to a few years ago. Despite well-known denunciations by Richard COBB and Edward THOMPSON (whose target was really one particular style of sociology), social historians in particular may find – and some of them have found – that sociological concepts, models and methods are of use in their work. Historians of the recent past, for example, are following the lead of sociologists in gathering information by interview, while the comparative method and the random sample are of wider relevance. Even the recent trend towards 'microhistory', which is a reaction against broad sociological generalizations, involves procedures not unlike the case studies and community studies of the sociologists (as some microhistorians, such as LE ROY LADURIE, are well aware).

If some historians still claim to describe social reality 'as it actually is', others, such as Lawrence STONE, admit (as do the sociologists) to using models of 'ideal types', in the sense of intellectual constructs which simplify in order to allow analysis. In regard to concepts, 'social role', 'social deviance', 'social control', 'social stratification' and 'social function' are becoming more and more part of the vocabulary of social historians. These terms are not neutral and they should not be employed uncritically, but to follow the debates on 'control' and 'function' within sociology is itself a valuable corrective to the hyper-empiricism which a historical education still encourages (at least in Britain).

However, the area in which we are most likely to see closer co-operation in the future is that of social change. Like historians, sociologists are concerned with change; unlike historians, they approach the subject in a theoretically self-conscious way. Their traditional approach to change, from Auguste COMTE to Talcott Parsons, was in terms of social 'evolution', in other words change which is gradual rather than sudden or violent and develops internally rather than being imposed from outside. This approach, which when applied to the Industrial Revolution by Parsons's pupil Neil Smelser drew down on him the wrath of Edward Thompson, is now generally discredited. The main alternative,

the Marxist approach, emphasizing conflict rather than consensus and revolution rather than evolution, is of course well known to historians. There are, however, other sociological theories with which historians ought to be familiar.

In the first place, there are the ideas of Max WEBER, who deserves to be remembered for much more than the provocative little book on the Protestant Ethic. His thoughts on the 'disenchantment' (or secularization) and the 'bureaucratization' of the world (for better or worse, or both) still deserve to be taken seriously by social historians. In the second place, rather more recently, a group of sociologists (notably Pierre Bourdieu) have emphasized the importance of what they call the 'reproduction' of the society or culture in the family, in schools, at work and elsewhere. In other words, they are suggesting that 'tradition', as it used to be called, ought to be seen as problematic, that it requires explanation no less than change does. More generally, sociologists in Britain and elsewhere are becoming increasingly interested in the relation between action or agency and structure, and in particular in what is sometimes called the problem of 'structuration', the process of the 'constitution' of structures by recurrent practices. Recent publications suggest that sociologists are beginning to take history more seriously than at any time since the 1920s. UPB

Reading

Abrams, P.: *Historical Sociology* (Shepton Mallett: Open Books, 1982).
Burke, P.: *Sociology and History* (London: Allen and Unwin, 1980).
Giddens, A.: *The Constitution of Society* (Cambridge: Polity Press, 1984).

Sorel, Albert (b.1842, d.1906) Son of a manufacturer of Honfleur (Calvados), Sorel was a career civil servant with no historical training. After six eventful years in the ministry of foreign affairs (years that included the Franco-Prussian War) he was appointed in 1872 professor of diplomatic history at the École des sciences politiques, and served from 1876 to 1902 as secretary-general to the president of the Senate. Between 1875 and his death he wrote extensively on both diplomatic history and eighteenth-century literature. A perceptive short essay (1877) on the eastern question in the eighteenth century was followed between 1885 and 1904 by his eight-volume masterpiece *L'Europe et la révolution française*, in which he argued that so far from transforming international relations the French Revolution merely deepened and prolonged the power relationships based on geography and national traditions that already existed. Although the later volumes deteriorated in quality the first, on the political traditions of the old regime, has never been surpassed as a portrait of eighteenth-century international relations and did much to establish a picture of them that has endured into the historiography of our own day.   WD

Main publications

La Question d'Órient au XVIIIᵉ siècle (1877); *Europe and the French Revolution. The Political traditions of the Old Regime* (1885) English trans. (London: Fontana, 1969).

Southern, Richard William (b.1912) From the Royal Grammar School, Newcastle, Richard Southern went to Balliol College, Oxford, where he was taught by V. H. GALBRAITH. After graduating in 1932 he studied in Oxford and Paris (under F. M. POWICKE and Ferdinand LOT). His early work on St Anselm was interrupted by the war, which called him to service with the Durham Light Infantry, and later with the RAC. Retiring as a major he returned to his fellowship at Balliol (1937–1961). From 1961–9 he was Chichele professor of modern history in the University of Oxford (and a fellow of All Souls), and from 1969–81 he was president of St John's College Oxford. He was elected a fellow of the British Academy in 1960, and was knighted in 1974.

Southern has consistently centred attention on (in his own words) 'the study of the thoughts and vision, moods and emotions and devotions of articulate people'. His first book, *The Making of the Middle Ages* (1953), earned immediate acclaim, for its breadth of outlook, for a luminous capacity to encapsulate a major point in a striking illustration, and for its

shrewd and highly individual perception of the relation between great movements of thought and their social and economic context. It has been translated into 27 languages. The same qualities marked the mature work in which his lifelong interest in St Anselm bore fruit (1963). His other subsequent writings include *Western Views of Islam*, *Western Society and the Church*, his brilliant (and sometimes controversial) papers on the twelfth-century schools and on medieval Platonism, and his articles on the writing of history in the middle ages (these last being the addresses that he delivered as president of the Royal Historical Society, 1968–72). His latest book, a seminal reappraisal of Robert Grosseteste, was published in 1986.

Oxford has known Richard Southern as a magnetic teacher, who has had a profound influence in moving English medieval historical studies away from their traditional institutional bias. A slender, handsome man, of wit and great charm, he remains in his seventies a working historian of high originality and stature.   MHK

Main publications

The Making of the Middle Ages (London: Hutchinson, 1953); *Western Views of Islam in the Middle Ages* (Cambridge, Mass.: Harvard University Press, 1962); *The Life of St Anselm by Eadmer* (London: Nelson Medieval Texts, 1962); *St Anselm and his Biographer: a study of monastic life and thought* (Cambridge: Cambridge University Press, 1963); *Western Society and the Church in the Middle Ages* (Harmondsworth: Penguin, 1970); *Medieval Humanism and the Other Studies* (Oxford: Blackwell, 1970); *Robert Grosseteste* (Oxford: Oxford University Press, 1986).

Spelman, Henry (b.c.1564?, d.1641) Spelman graduated from Trinity College, Cambridge, in 1583 and studied at Lincoln's Inn before returning to his Norfolk estates. His first work of scholarship, *Aspilogia*, a systematic study of heraldry, was probably written before 1595. Like much of Spelman's work, it was composed in Latin and only published after his death. At this time he was also transcribing medieval charters. Through the Society of Antiquaries in London, to which he was elected in 1593, he got to know CAMDEN, Cotton and other scholars. His first paper for them was on the medieval coinage in 1594.

After serving as a member of parliament and high sheriff of Norfolk, Spelman moved to London in 1612 to pursue a life of scholarship.

The great product of this period is Spelman's *Archaeologus*, a dictionary of medieval legal terminology. The first volume, from A to L, was published in 1626. Its composition in Latin made it comprehensible to continental European scholars, with whom Spelman conducted an extensive correspondence. Its best known definition is that of *feodum*, which Spelman expanded into a pamphlet in 1641. Taking his cue from international scholarship, he argued that feudal tenures had not always existed in English common law; they were introduced by William the Conqueror. (The question as to whether the Normans introduced feudalism into England is still a matter of debate today.) In the conflict between Charles I and parliament, Spelman's scholarship tended to ally him with the royalists, as he showed that English institutions, including parliament, had specific historical origins rather than being embedded in an immemorial Anglo-Saxon past. To promote the scholarly study of Anglo-Saxon, Spelman endowed a readership at Cambridge in 1635.

The high point of Spelman's scholarship was his volume of documents, arranged chronologically up to 1066, on the legislation of the English church. This is the *Concilia*, which Dugdale completed in 1664, Wilkins enlarged in the eighteenth century, and Powicke initiated a revision of in the twentieth. Discovering, dating, collating, and criticizing the documents was Spelman's pioneering achievement, even though many emendations have been made subsequently. 'What great monuments of antiquarian knowledge he has left to the world', wrote Aubrey. Through his work on feudal and ecclesiastical records in Latin and Anglo-Saxon, Spelman is the father of medieval documentary scholarship in England. He is also the first user of the term 'the middle ages' to describe the period between the church fathers and the Reformation.   MTC

Main publications

Concilia (London: R. Bodger, 1639); *Aspilogia*. In *Nicolai Upton de Studio Militari* (London: J. Martin & J. Allestrye, 1654); *Archaeologus or Glossarium Archailogicum* (London: A. Warren, 1664); Treatise of Feuds and Tenures by Knight-service in England. In *Reliquiae Spelmanniae*, ed. E. Gibson (London: A. & J. Churchill, 1698).

Reading

Cronne, H. A.: The study and use of charters. In *English Historical Scholarship in the 16th and 17th centuries*, ed. L. Fox (London: Oxford University Press, 1956).
Pocock, J. G. A.: *The Ancient Constitution and the Feudal Law*, Reissue (Cambridge: Cambridge University Press, 1987).

Spengler, Oswald (b.1880, d.1936) Spengler's renown came suddenly, in the year 1918, when the ex-schoolmaster published the first half of his *Decline of the West* and earned adulation from his German compatriots. Amid defeat they gained consolation particularly from the fact that this global history (completed in 1922) highlighted the hollowness of Allied victory. Readers admired the ambitiousness and dogmatism of Spengler's attempt to pattern not only the past but also the West's doom-laden future. Spengler sought legitimation by stressing his debts to Goethe, as mentor in romantic method, and (more justly) to Nietzsche, as hammer of progressivist complacency. *The Decline of the West* focuses on eight main 'cultures': the Egyptian, Indian, Babylonian, Chinese, Mexican, Greco-Roman and Magian (Islamic), together with the ominously-named Faustian variety dominant during the West's last millennium. Each has been largely self-contained, internally unified by a distinctive spiritual orientation. Yet the 'comparative morphology' of their history shows that all have been fated to follow identical rhythms and laws of development. The master-images are those of flowering and the seasons. Winter always comes at last, bringing tyrannies, endemic warfare, the devouring 'world-city' and the triumph of materialism. Thus Culture gives way to mere Civilization, 'the thing-become succeeding to the thing-becoming, death following life'. The predictions about an imminent brutal Caesarism seemed fulfilled in Hitler's rise, and Spengler certainly used his new-found fame to help undermine the Weimar Republic. But Nazism was too optimistically redemptive to earn his unqualified approval. Today *The Decline of the West* (still in print, and allegedly once recommended by Henry Kissinger as President Nixon's bedtime reading) retains in certain passages a bracing suggestiveness. But most of the work now stands revealed as fantasy – a warning to those who, when challenged by metahistorical questions, believe almost any answer to be better than none. MDB

Main publications

Der Untergang des Abendlandes, 2 vols (1918, 1922) trans. as *The Decline of the West*, 2 vols (London: Allen & Unwin, 1926, 1928; many reprints): *Der Mensch und die Technik* (1931) trans. as *Man and Technics* (London: Allen & Unwin, 1932); *Jahre der Entscheidung* (1933) trans. as *The Hour of Decision*, (London: Allen & Unwin, 1934).

Reading

Hughes, H. S. *Oswald Spengler: a Critical Estimate* (New York and London: Scribner, 1952).

Srbik, Heinrich von (b.1878, d.1951) Srbik was a leading Austrian historian of the inter-war years, and a prominent teacher in the high Germanic tradition. His early work on Austrian government since the seventeenth century culminated in the massive biography of Metternich, perhaps too sympathetic to its subject, but balanced and perceptive, for which he is now best remembered. Like many conservative intellectuals of his generation, Srbik could not reconcile himself to the rump Austrian Republic, though he served it as minister of education in 1929–30. He backed the *Anschluss* with Hitler's Germany (for which he was rewarded with the presidency of the Austrian Academy of Sciences) and his later writings examine the whole course of modern Austro-German relations in great detail. Despite their tendentiousness, they contain much of lasting worth. RJWE

Main publications

Der staatliche Exporthandel Österreichs von Leopold I bis Maria Theresia (Austria's state export trade from Leopold I to Maria Theresa) (Vienna/Leipzig: 1907); *Wallensteins Ende* (Wallenstein's End) (Vienna: L. W. Seidel, 1920); *Metternich, der Staatsmann und der Mensch* (Metternich: the statesman and the man), 3 vols (Munich: F. Bruckman, 1925–54); *Deutsche Einheit* (German unity), 4 vols (F. Bruckman, 1935–42).

Stenton, Frank Merry (b.1880, d.1967) Stenton's early education was mostly at home. In 1897 he went to study music at the Extension College, Reading (later Reading university), and in 1899 to read modern history at Keble College, Oxford. In 1908, after some years as a schoolmaster, he returned to Reading as research fellow and remained, from 1912 as professor, from 1946 till his retirement in 1950 as vice-chancellor. His eight honorary degrees indicate the wide respect in which he was held. (For comparison: F. M. Powicke had ten, V. H. Galbraith five, C. H. Firth five, A. J. Toynbee five, L. B. Namier four.) The keystone of his achievement was *Anglo-Saxon England* (1943), volume II in the Oxford History of England. It is unusual for such a book to occupy such a position; that this one did reflects the way in which the study of Anglo-Saxon history developed.

The turn of the century had seen the transformation of knowledge of Anglo-Saxon England. In 1892 VINOGRADOFF's *Villainage in England* appeared and Plummer's edition of the *Chronicle*; in 1895 Napier and Stephenson's *Crawford Charters*; in 1896 Plummer's *Bede*; in 1895 ROUND's *Feudal England*; in 1897 Skeat's *Place Names of Cambridgeshire*; in 1901 the first volumes of LIEBERMANN's *Gesetze* and of Baldwin Brown's *Arts in Early England*; in 1906 Stevenson's *Asser*. Until 1943 there was no authoritative guide to Anglo-Saxon England in the light of the new learning. The current manuals (for example by Ramsay, T. Hodgkin and Oman) were obsolescent narratives. R. H. Hodgkin ended his *History of the Anglo-Saxons* (1935) with King Alfred and did not have Stenton's learning. *Anglo-Saxon England* provided what was lacking: a guide to, and a foundation for, Anglo-Saxon studies.

Stenton was peculiarly qualified to write such a work. As an undergraduate he came under the influence of Vinogradoff. He attended Napier's lectures on Old English, a very unusual thing for a historian to do. For some of R. L. POOLE's lectures on diplomatic he formed the entire audience. By the time he was thirty-three, he had published *William the Conqueror* (1908), a trenchant, well-judged introduction to its subject; *Types of Manorial*

Structure in Northern Danelaw (1910), with original conclusions argued from complicated sources with clarity and control; *Place-Names of Berkshire* (1911); and *The Early History of the Abbey of Abingdon* (1913), for many years the only such study based on the close analysis of early charters.

The main lines of his interests were by this time established. Place-names always attracted him. He was co-author of fourteen English Place Name Society volumes between 1925 and 1950. Equally strong was his interest in Danelaw institutions. A collection of documents on the Danelaw (1920) and a treatise on its peasantry (1926) were followed by his Raleigh Lecture of 1927 in which he argued, too forcefully, that the free peasants of the Danelaw were the descendants of Danish warrior-settlers. He continued to work on charters from the seventh century to the twelfth. There resulted an epoch-making paper on 'The supremacy of the Mercian kings' and his Ford lectures of 1929 which drew largely on charters to illuminate 'The first century of English feudalism'.

The success of *Anglo-Saxon England*, which had been on the stocks since before 1929, was well-deserved. The learning behind the book gave it magisterial weight, and a pregnant quality such that often a single sentence gives a clue to a whole train of thought. Its principal defect is insularity. Stenton showed little interest in considering English history in the light of continental developments and parallels.

Stenton played a creative and nergetic part in the establishment and/or organization of institutions important in relation to the study of history in England: the English Place Name Society, the Pipe Roll Society, the Lincolnshire and Northamptonshire Record Societies, the History of Parliament. He built up a good history school at Reading.

His personal history and circumstances do much to explain his work. That he lived to be eighty-seven, the son of a father born in 1825, gave a particular resonance to his observation about the early annals of the *Chronicle*: 'It is easy to underestimate the length of time covered by two good memories.' His Danelaw interests had deep roots. He came from a

family long established in Southwell and he owned a strip of open field in Nottinghamshire until 1965. He was married to the distinguished historian D. M. Stenton (once his pupil) and had no children. His domestic life was organized to protect his work; his wife cut his hair, and for many years he would not admit a telephone to the house. Stenton's life and work had a particular kind of unity and he was the last scholar to link the days of John Horace Round to our own. He was knighted in 1948.   JC

Main publications

(All published by Oxford University Press, Oxford.) *The First Century of English Feudalism* (1932, 2nd edn 1961); *Anglo-Saxon England* (1943, 2nd edn 1950, 3rd edn 1971); *Latin Charters of the Anglo-Saxon Period* (1955); *The Free Peasantry of the Northern Danelaw* (1969) [originally pub. in the *Bulletin* of the Royal Society of Lund, 1925–6]; *Preparatory to Anglo-Saxon England; being the Collected Papers of Frank Merry Stenton*, ed. D. M. Stenton (1970) [incl. bibliography].

Reading

Slade, C. F.: Doris Mary Stenton. *Liber Memorialis* (Pipe Roll Society 79, n.s. 41).
Stenton, D. M.: Memoir: Frank Merry Stenton. *Proceedings of the British Academy* 54 (1968) 315–24.

Stephen, Leslie (b.1832, d.1904)   Father of Virginia Woolf and younger brother of James Fitzjames Stephen, the jurist, Leslie Stephen was educated at Eton which he disliked, and Trinity Hall, Cambridge, where he took holy orders. Assailed by religious doubt, he gave up his fellowship in 1864 to pursue a literary career in London as editor, critic and reviewer. His main contribution to historical scholarship was as founding editor of the *Dictionary of National Biography*, from 1882 to 1891. He wrote 387 articles himself, many of them on major literary and historical figures. But his *History of English Thought in the Eighteenth Century* (1876) and its successor *The English Utilitarians* (1900) are still of value. Stephen was knighted in Edward VII's coronation honours list of 1902.   JAC

Main publications

History of English Thought in the Eighteenth Century, 2 vols (London: Smith Elder, 1876); *Life of Samuel Johnson* (London: Macmillan, 1878); *Life of Sir*

STEPHENSON, CARL

James Fitzjames Stephen (Smith Elder, 1895); *The English Utilitarians*, 3 vols (London: Duckworth, 1900); *Studies of a biographer*, 4 vols (Duckworth, 1898–1902).

Reading

Annan, N.: *Leslie Stephen: the godless Victorian* (New York: Random Honse, 1984).

Grosskurth, P.: *Leslie Stephen*. Vol. 207, *Writers and their work* (1968).

Himmelfarb, C.: *Victorian minds* (New York: Knopf, 1968).

Maitland, F. W.: *Life and letters of Leslie Stephen* (London: Duckworth, 1906).

Stephenson, Carl (b.1886, d.1954) The career of Stephenson shows the characteristic strengths of American medieval scholarship in the first half of the twentieth century. His first teacher at Harvard was Charles Gross, who encouraged him to work on English towns; after Gross's death in 1909 C. H. HASKINS encouraged him to look to the European continent for a comparative perspective. A scholarship which allowed him to study with Henri PIRENNE at Ghent in 1924 was a further and crucial influence on his intellectual development.

Stephenson is best known for his book *Borough and Town*, in which, following Pirenne's views on the key importance of long-distance commerce, he was led to discount the degree of urbanization in pre-Conquest England. The book was influential, not least because it stimulated James TAIT to a rebuttal, *The Medieval English Borough*. On the evidence then available, Tait carried the day, but Stephenson's time may come again, as recent excavations in London and elsewhere show the second half of the eleventh century as a period of major economic growth. He also contributed notable articles (printed in *Medieval Institutions*) on the origins of feudalism. The medievalists of his day were missionaries in America, their texts essential for evangelization. Stephenson's texts were the texts for his generation. A wandering scholar in the first half of his career, he settled at Cornell in 1930, retiring a few months before his death.   EK

Main publications

Borough and Town: a Study of Urban Origins in England (Cambridge, Mass.: Harvard University Press, 1933); with G. F. Marcham, *Sources of English Constitutional History* (New York: Harper, 1937); *Medieval Feudalism* (Ithaca, NY: Cornell University Press, 1942); *Medieval Institutions. Collected Essays* (Cornell University Press, 1954; repr. pbk, 1967) [incl. memoir by B. D. Lyon].

Stone, Lawrence (b.1919) Educated at Charterhouse, Stone studied at the Sorbonne in 1938 and then returned to England where he graduated from Christ Church, Oxford in 1946. He was Bryce research student 1946–7, before holding a lectureship at University and Corpus Christi Colleges between 1947 and 1950. In the latter year he became fellow of Wadham College, a position he held until he moved to the Dodge chair of history at Princeton University in 1963.

Stone is a prolific and controversial writer, with interests ranging from sculpture (*Sculpture in Britain* was his first book) through the history of literacy and education to the work for which he is best known, on the English aristocracy. Always ready to consider new methods and to reject them if and when they were found wanting, Stone's shifting preoccupations have included Marxism (although he was never a Marxist), sociology and anthropology. His earliest historical work was associated with the 'gentry controversy'. Much influenced by TAWNEY and the crisis of feudalism, in 1948 he published an article on the Elizabethan aristocracy which supported Tawney's thesis by exposing the extravagance and financial irresponsibility of many sixteenth-century English noblemen. This was savagely attacked by Hugh TREVOR-ROPER. Stone accepted some of the criticism and continued his research on the sixteenth-century aristocracy, although his first major history book was on an Elizabethan banker. But he was already moving away from the economic history of Tawney's generation to ideas coming from the ANNALES SCHOOL. As his interest in the 'new history' developed, in 1958 he joined the board of the journal *Past and Present*, but in 1963, tired of fourteen to sixteen hours of tutorials a week at Wadham and frustrated by his inability to reform the Oxford history syllabus, Stone left for Princeton. Two years later his major work on the aristocracy appeared, *The Crisis of the Aristocracy, 1558–1641*. It was the most substantial product of the gentry crisis, but it also reflected Stone's own recognition that the debate had revealed the shoddy base on which much historical methodology was built in the later 1940s. The book was, however, widely criticized in regard both to its methods and to its statistics.

Once settled in the United States Stone broadened the horizons of his scholarship. Influenced by sociology, and affected by contemporary events in the third world, he wrote *The Causes of the English Revolution, 1529–1642* (1972). He also became interested in demography and social anthropology, as well as being introduced to CLIOMETRICS. From cliometricians he learned statistical techniques which he used first in 1972 but which came to fruition only in *An Open Elite? England, 1540–1880*, published in 1984 but conceived in 1965, long before Stone had concluded that cliometrics was becoming completely unintelligible to the average historian. Unconvinced of the value of number crunching, Stone moved during the 1970s towards anthropology. From this interest came *The Family: Sex and Marriage In England, 1500–1800* (1977), a book which reflected his concern with the context of individual behaviour and an enthusiasm for the history of the family. By the late 1970s Stone was disillusioned with much of the 'new history', including quantification, the *annalistes* and sociology, and he accepted that narrative history had recaptured much of the ground it had previously lost.

In 1943 Stone married Jeanne C. Fawtier, with whom *An Open Elite?* was written. He became a naturalized American in 1970, but is still a regular visitor to England. He is a fellow of the American Academy of Arts and Sciences and since 1968 has been director of the Shelby Cullom Davis Center for Historical Studies at Princeton.   JVB

Main publications

The Crisis of the Aristocracy, 1558–1641 (Oxford: Clarendon Press, 1965); *Social Change and Revolution in England, 1540–1640* (London: Longmans, Green, 1965); *The Causes of the English Revolution, 1529–1642* (London: Routledge & Kegan Paul, 1972); *Family and Fortune: Studies in Aristocratic Finance in the Sixteenth and Seventeenth Centuries* (Clarendon Press, 1973); *The University in Society* (Princeton, NJ: Princeton University Press, 1974); *The Family: Sex and Marriage in England, 1500–1800* (London: Weidenfeld & Nicolson, 1977); *The Past and the Present* (Boston: Routledge & Kegan Paul, 1981); with Jeanne C. Fawtier Stone, *An Open Elite? England, 1540–1880* (Clarendon Press, 1984).

Reading

Kenyon, J.: *The History Men* (London: Weidenfeld & Nicolson, 1983).
Times Higher Education Supplement, 23 October 1983.

Stow, John (b.1525, d.1605)   Stow (or Stowe) was the first important English historian of the city. The son of a London tallow-chandler, he spent all his life in the metropolis, becoming a freeman of the Merchant Taylors Company in 1547. From the 1560s he was increasingly engaged in antiquarian pursuits, editing the works of Geoffrey Chaucer and various chronicles. His *Summarie of Englyshe Chronicles* appeared in 1565, *The Chronicles of England from Brute unto the Present Year of Christ* in 1580 and *The Annales of England* in 1592. Stow's antiquarian reputation led to his inclusion in the circle of scholars associated with Archbishop Parker in the early part of Elizabeth's reign, and he subsequently became a member of the Society of Antiquaries. Another member was William Lambarde whose pioneering *Perambulation of Kent* published in 1576 was the model for Stow's most important work, *The Survey of London* (1598). Stow's approach was strongly topographical, taking each ward and parish of the city in turn and recounting its history, relying on a mixture of archival sources, civic tradition and observation. In addition there were sections on the social, political and religious life of the city. A man of conservative sympathies (including suspected Catholicism) Stow provides a nostalgic record of a city landscape which was rapidly being transformed by metropolitan expansion in the sixteenth century. At the same time, his work was also suffused with pride as a Londoner in the capital's burgeoning economic and political greatness. The format of the *Survey* was copied by successive London antiquaries up to the mid-eighteenth century; it also influenced a number of provincial town histories after the Restoration. By continental standards of historiography Stow's work was somewhat old-fashioned and unimaginative, but in England the *Survey* stood head and shoulders above most other town histories until George III's reign.   PAC

Main publications

The Annales of England (London: 1592, several edns to 1631); *A Survey of London* (1598, several further edns) ed. C. L. Kingsford (Oxford: Clarendon Press, 1908).

Reading

Kingsford, C. L.: Introduction. In *A Survey of London* [see above].
Ashton, R.: Stow's London. *London and Middlesex Archaeological Society*, 29 (1978) 137–43.

structural analysis   The name given to the technique associated with L. B. NAMIER's book *The structure of politics at the accession of George III*, published in 1929. Namier's intention was to examine the mechanics of the governmental system, the men who ran it, and their relationships and he attempted to quantify as much as possible in order to avoid vague, impressionistic or anecdotal history. He saw structural analysis as an adjunct to narrative exposition, as he explained subsequently in *Avenues of History*:

> As History deals with concrete events, fixed in time and space, narrative is its basic medium – but guided by an analytic selection of what to narrate. ... What matters in history is the great outline and the significant detail; what must be avoided is the deadly morass of irrelevant narrative.

D. A. Winstanley, reviewing Namier, wrote that no previous historian had ever made 'so thorough and gallant an attempt to discover the *actual workings* of the political system of the eighteenth century'.

It can scarcely be claimed that Namier lived up to his own high ideal. Like most historians, he delighted in detail, and his work was shot through with glimpses, often highly entertaining, of parliamentary beggars, bastards, members who went mad, and the like. Nor can his account of the complex relationship between Bute and Newcastle escape the charge of detail for its own sake. Nevertheless, the technique attracted great interest, and in the 1950s extravagant claims were made for it as a method that would revolutionize the writing of history, allowing an objective, almost cartesian, purity of analysis. It also attracted fierce opposition, notably from Herbert BUTTERFIELD, who devoted a whole volume to denouncing it as a technique that could produce desiccated, splintered and mechanistic history.

In retrospect, and particularly in its use of the techniques of PROSOPOGRAPHY, structural analysis can be seen to have been less novel than some claimed. Burke had included a famous analysis of the composition of the National Assembly of France in his *Reflections on the French Revolution*, and a number of works in the Victorian period had started to identify and analyse the members of the landed élite who governed England. In the Edwardian period the Porritts published important pioneering work in Namier's own parliamentary history, and W. T. Laprade had made use of the parliamentary papers of John Robinson to examine the role of patronage in Hanoverian political life. J. E. NEALE in his work on Tudor history, and H. H. Scullard in his analyses of Roman elites, had employed similar methods. During the 1950s Brunton and Pennington showed that the method could be employed to scrutinize the members of the Long Parliament and Frank Eyck, in 1968, applied it to the Frankfurt Parliament of 1848–9. Since the controversies of the 1950s, the technique has been accepted as a valuable part of general historical method, but one with severe limitations and considerable dangers. In particular, the concentration on government and authority gives it an in-built tendency to deny the importance of ideology and of opinion generally, a limitation which Laprade had noted when he wrote that a serious weakness of Namier's book had been its failure to 'make adequate use of newspapers, periodicals and pamphlets'.   JAC

Reading

Blaas, P. B. M.: *Continuity and anachronism: parliamentary and constitutional development in Whig his-*

toriography and in the anti-Whig reaction between 1890 and 1930 (The Hague: Martinus Nijhoff, 1978).

Butterfield, H.: *George III and the historians* (London: Collins, 1957).

Cannon, J. A.: Lewis Namier. In *The Historian at work*, ed. J. A. Cannon (London: George Allen & Unwin, 1980).

Plumb, J. H.: The Atomic historian. *New Statesman* 78 (1 August 1969) 141−3.

Price, J. M.: Party, purpose and pattern: Sir Lewis Namier and his critics. *Journal of British Studies* 1 (November 1961) 71−93.

Stubbs, William (b.1829, d.1901) Stubbs was the first important English historian to teach and publish as a member of a university. He came of a Yorkshire yeoman family which he himself later traced back to the fourteenth century, and received early training in reading charters and deeds from his father, a Knaresborough solicitor. He was educated at Ripon Grammar School and (from 1844 and through the influence of C. T. Longley) Christ Church, Oxford, where he was favoured by Dean Gaisford and allowed full use of Christ Church library. In 1848 he attained a first in classics and a third in mathematics. Immediately after graduating he was ordained, and elected to a fellowship of Trinity College, Oxford, which he held for two years.

All his life Stubbs was an assiduous worker; his vast knowledge of the sources of medieval English history, acquired while he was the diligent incumbent of the college living of Navestock, Essex, led to his nomination as regius professor of modern history at Oxford (and fellow of Oriel College) in 1866. During his professorship the number of undergraduates studying modern history increased greatly: among those who were much influenced by Stubbs were T. F. TOUT, J. H. ROUND, R. L. POOLE and C. H. FIRTH; the Stubbs Society, still in existence, is the descendant of the seminars which Stubbs held. Stubbs introduced himself to his first audience as 'a worker at history', and performed his professorial duties conscientiously. Every year of his professorship except two was marked by some important publication. He continued his researches and writings until they were made impossible by his nomination as bishop of Chester (1883−8) and then of Oxford (1888 to death). He was a conscientious pastoral and preaching bishop, active on the Anglican commission on ecclesiastical courts; he enjoyed his return to Oxford but lamented the requirement to reside in his palace outside the city.

Stubbs's first publication (1858) was the *Registrum Sacrum Anglicanum* (2nd edn, 1897), a work showing the 'course of episcopal succession' in England. Sequels were his *Councils and Ecclesiastical Documents of the Anglo-Saxon church* (1878) and over 500 articles in the *Dictionary of Christian Biography* (4 vols, 1877−87). But a much more famous and seminal work was his *Select Charters and Other Documents Illustrative of English History* (1860) which ran to eight editions in his lifetime. He meant this to be 'primarily a treasury of reference', designed to illuminate the 'polity' of England. The selection was most skilfully done, and Stubbs's handbook of texts remains invaluable and immensely influential. His single lectures and courses of lectures, collected by others but not well edited, included: *Seventeen Lectures on the Study of Medieval and Modern History and Kindred Subjects* (1886; 3rd edn, with additions, 1900); *Lectures on Early European History* (1904); *Lectures on Early English History* (1906); *Germany in the Early Middle Ages 476−1250* (1908). Stubbs edited 19 volumes of the Rolls series, 15 while he was professor; his valuable introductions were later collected as *Historical Introductions to the Rolls Series*. His greatest work was his *Constitutional History of Medieval England in its Origin and Development*, first published in three volumes (1873−8). This was the first treatment of the subject apart from a sketch by Hallam. The Anglo-Saxon and Norman sections have been much criticized, and his view of the development of the English medieval parliament is incomplete, but for the reign of Henry II and his sons Stubbs's knowledge of the sources enabled him to produce a well-informed account of lasting value, though his stern disapproval of King John on moral grounds has been outmoded by the work of J. C. Holt. Stubbs desired, but never held, the Oxford regius chair of ecclesiastical history in his original college, but he wrote five useful historical appendices to the Report of the Commission on Ecclesiastical Courts and other valuable

STUKELEY, WILLIAM

sketches in his episcopal Ordination Addresses and Visitation Charges. All his life he enjoyed close and fruitful friendships with German and English scholars (F. LIEBERMANN, R. Pauli, G. WAITZ, E. A. FREEMAN, J. R. GREEN) but not with French. (Indeed he despised the French and their 'detestable emperor'.)

Stubbs was a lifelong Tory (as a boy he waved a Tory flag in the face of the Whig Lord Chancellor Brougham), a firm High Churchman, and a man of strong family affections. He loathed dinner parties and smoking, but was a humorous person with a gift for comic verse. His work as an editor raised English editorial scholarship to the level of that of continental Europe; he left an enduring mark on the new Oxford School of Modern History, and four volumes (the *Select Charters* and the *Constitutional History*) which have determined the development of much institutional and political history written since his time.   JFAM

Main publications

Select Charters and Other Documents of English History (1860, 9th edn 1911); Historical Introductions to the Rolls Series (1902); *Constitutional History of Medieval England in its Origin and Development*, 3 vols (1873–8, 1891–8).

Reading

Hutton, W. H.: *Letters of William Stubbs, Bishop of Oxford, 1825–1901* (London: Constable, 1904).

Richardson, H. G. and Sayles, G. O.: *The Governance of Medieval England* (Edinburgh: Edinburgh University Press, 1963).

Stukeley, William (b.1687, d.1765) Born in Lincolnshire and educated at Cambridge, Stukeley became the leading antiquarian of early Hanoverian England. By profession a doctor, he took holy orders and held a living at Stamford from 1730 to 1740, and subsequently in London. Of a fanciful turn of mind and obsessed by the Druids, Stukeley was not immune to embarrassing errors and was completely taken in by the forger Charles Julius Bertram. His early work on Stonehenge and Avebury was careful and scholarly and remains of value.   JAC

Main publications

Itinerarium Curiosum (London: 1724); *Stonehenge, a Temple Restored to the British Druids* (London: 1740);

Abury, a Temple of the British Druids (London: 1743); *An Account of Richard of Cirencester* (London: 1757).

Reading

Piggott, S.: *William Stukeley: an Eighteenth-Century Antiquary* (Oxford: Clarendon Press, 1950).

Suetonius (b.*c.*70, d. after 122) Gaius Suetonius Tranquillus, like his Greek contemporary PLUTARCH, was one of the founders of historical biography in antiquity. He would probably not have welcomed characterization as a historian, but his *De vita Caesarum* started a tradition of lives of emperors which came to substitute for history.

Suetonius was the son of an officer of equestrian rank, Suetonius Laetus. The discovery of a career inscription at Hippo Regius on the north African coast makes plausible an African origin; the area was sufficiently Romanized to produce a string of significant literary figures by the second century AD. Suetonius was educated partly at Rome, in Domitian's reign, probably under such men as the rhetorician Quintilian and the grammarian Valerius Probus. He secured the benefits of the support of the influential Younger Pliny. Towards the end of Trajan's reign, and at the beginning of Hadrian's, he held a string of prestigious posts in the imperial secretariat (precise dating and sequence remain obscure). As secretary *a bibliothecis* he had charge of the extensive imperial libraries of the capital, and may have overseen the establishment by Trajan of the new libraries of his monumental forum complex; his post *a studiis* was similarly one requiring a man of learning; finally under Hadrian he became secretary *ab epistulis* (technically in charge of correspondence), one of the most influential posts in the secretariat. His name is closely linked with that of another friend of Pliny, Septicius Clarus, as praetorian prefect the most powerful military and judicial subordinate in the imperial entourage. Suetonius is known to have dedicated his imperial lives to Septicius while still in office. He and Septicius fell from favour together and were relieved of office, probably in 122 during Hadrian's tour of Britain (128 now seems a less likely date). The grounds of dismissal, as reported by the Life of Hadrian, were 'excessive familiarity with the empress Sabina'; internal palace intrigue, of which they were surely victims, regularly took the form of accusations of sexual links with the imperial family. How long Suetonius survived the termination of his office is unknown.

His literary chronology has too few fixed points, but there is a long list of works to accommodate, of scholarly, philological and antiquarian nature in addition to his biographies. On internal grounds it is probable that the imperial lives were written last, after and in many respects in the style of his successful lives of literary figures (*De viris illustribus* (About illustrious men') is a conjectural title), of which those of the grammarians, rhetors and a few poets survive. These were themselves surely sequels to the series of lesser philological and antiquarian essays. A letter of Pliny dated *c*.105 shows Suetonius had nothing published at that date but his appointment to imperial posts, perhaps within a decade, argues a substantial body of publication by then. His literary biographies might have been completed before his appointment as *ab epistulis* in *c*.117. The first book at least of the imperial lives appeared before his fall from office, though it is arguable whether other books were published at the same time or subsequently.

The importance of Suetonius' imperial lives, starting (interestingly) with Julius Caesar not Augustus, and ending with Domitian (i.e. before the reigning dynasty), apart from their value as a source of information and anecdotes (more or less reliable) lies in its contrast with traditional Roman historiography. It makes a show of scholarly method, foreign to the historiographical tradition, though understandable against the author's own literary background, with citation of documentary evidence and unfamiliar sources, avoidance of chronological disposition, and a show of scholarly objectivity. In fact it is a colourful and distinctly slanted picture of the early Caesars, reflecting the dominant ideology of the early Antonine period. Suetonius' weaknesses were more extensively imitated than his strengths by later surviving writers of imperial biography.   AW-H

Main writings

De vita Caesarum, ed. M. Ihm (Stuttgart: Teubner, 1908); trans. J. C. Rolfe, *The Lives of the Caesars*

(London: Loeb Classical Library, 1913); trans. Robert Graves, *The Twelve Caesars* (Harmondsworth: Penguin, 1957); *De Grammaticis et Rhetoribis*, ed. G. Brugnoli (Leipzig: Teubner, 1960); trans. J. C. Rolfe (London: Loeb Classical Library, 1913); [commentaries on individual Caesars] *Divus Augustus*, ed. J. M. Carter (Bristol: Classical Press, 1982); *Nero*, ed. B. H. Warmington (Bristol: Classical Press, 1977) and ed. K. P. Bradley (Brussels: Collection Latomus, 1978).

Reading

Baldwin, B.: *Suetonius* (Amsterdam: Hakkert, 1983).

Gascou, J.: *Suétone historien* (Rome: École Française de Rome, 1984).

Wallace-Hadrill, A.: *Suetonius: the Scholar and his Caesars* (London: Duckworth, 1983).

Sutherland, Lucy Stuart (b.1903, d.1980) Born in Australia, educated in South Africa, Sutherland moved to Oxford as an undergraduate in 1925, where she spent the rest of her life except for the years between 1941 and 1945 during which she was a temporary civil servant. After her Oxford degree she chose the eighteenth century as her field of research, and all her work thereafter sprang from this root. In the first years of her research Lewis NAMIER published his *Structure of Politics*, a work which had a marked effect upon her thinking and approach, even though she was never in any formal sense a 'Namierite'. By the outbreak of the war she had already laid down the patterns of her writing, drawing attention to the links between the political and economic life of the century, and already looking in detail at the activities of the East India Company.

She had been appointed to an assistant tutorship (later to be a tutorship and fellowship) at Somerville College; immediately after the war she withdrew from a possible contest for election as principal of Somerville only to be eagerly sought by Lady Margaret Hall. As Head of House she took a leading part in university life and as a prominent university figure she was called on frequently for service either on national university committees or Royal Commissions. None of this diminished her flow of publications. Her *East India Company in Eighteenth-Century Politics* was paralleled by her various articles and lectures on 'The City of London in eighteenth-century politics', and her reputation was crowned by her fellowship of the British Academy in 1954 and her D. Litt. in 1955. Her range of scholarship is evidenced by her editorial work on the Burke Correspondence, her contributions to the *History of Parliament*, and her outstanding work on the eighteenth-century history of the University of Oxford. Her collected essays, *Politics and Finance in the Eighteenth Century*, equally illustrate the depth and cohesion of all her work. The regard in which she was held by fellow historians was marked by the presentation to her of a *Festschrift*, and her contribution to national life was marked by her appointment as DBE. AN

Main publications

Her individual essays are reprinted in *Politics and Finance in the Eighteenth Century*, ed. Aubrey Newman.

Reading

Whiteman, Anne, Bromley, J. S. and Dickson, P. G. M.: *Statesmen, Scholars and Merchants: Essays in Eighteenth-Century History presented to Dame Lucy Sutherland* (Oxford: 1973) [incl. bibliography].

Whiteman, Anne: Memoir. *Proceedings of the British Academy* 69 (1983) 611–30.

Sybel, Heinrich von (b.1817, d.1895) One of the trinity of great German scholars (along with DROYSEN and TREITSCHKE) who together make up the 'Prussian school', Sybel's career appeared conventional and even predictable. A pupil of RANKE, he taught at several German universities, moving to Bonn in 1861 and becoming director of the Prussian State Archives in 1875. He was also the founder and first editor of what is still the leading German-language historical journal, the *Historische Zeitschrift*, which began publication in 1859. But what set Sybel apart from the conventions established by his mentor Ranke was his rejection of the latter's doctrine of moral neutrality in historical writing. Sybel believed that history had a distinct political role, declaring on one occasion that he was 'four-sevenths politician and three-sevenths professor'. Through his lectures, pamphlets and books he aimed to influence contemporary events. Like many German historians in the middle decades of the nineteenth century Sybel played an active part in the political struggles of his time, becoming in later life a firm supporter of Bismarck and, at times, an apologist for his policies.

Sybel's political preoccupations were apparent in his writings. He was initially a medieval historian, publishing on the First Crusade and on the origins of German kingship during the Dark Ages. But his concern with contemporary political struggles drew him towards more modern history. In the 1850s he wrote a multi-volume history of the French Revolution, particularly in its international and diplomatic aspects. After the completion of German unification he produced a large-scale work on the founding of the German empire, the final volume of which appeared in the year before his death. This was essentially an official history of German unification from the viewpoint of Prussia and of Bismarck.

Sybel's historical works were coloured by strong and deeply held prejudices: he was hostile towards the Catholic church, towards France and the French, and towards Austria, and he seldom rose above a narrow Prussian viewpoint. This reduced the value of his historical writings, though they were based on massive archival research. Sybel's most enduring contribution to scholarship was probably the series of major documentary publications that he sponsored and encouraged as director of the Prussian State Archives. HMS

Main publications

Geschichte der Revolutionszeit von 1789 bis 1800, 5 vols (1853–58; 2nd edn, 4 vols, Frankfurt-am-Main, 1872–79) English trans. 3 vols (London and Leipzig: 1867–9); *Die Begründung des Deutschen Reiches durch Wilhelm I*, 7 vols (Munich and Leipzig: 1890–94) English trans. 3 vols (New York: 1890–1, repr. London: Greenwood, 1968).

Reading

Flaig, H.: The historian as pedagogue of the nation. *History* 59 (1974) 18–32.

Gooch, G. P.: *History and Historians in the nineteenth century*, chs 7–8 (London: Longmans, Green, 1913).

Iggers, G. G.: *The German conception of history* (Middletown, Conn.: Wesleyan University Press, 1968) chs 4–5.

Syme, Ronald (b.1903) Born in New Zealand, Syme read classics at Wellington University and became lecturer at Auckland; in 1925 he came to Oxford — to which he has been attached ever since — to read *literae humaniores*. Fellow of Trinity College (1929–49) and Camden professor of ancient history (1949–70), he then became a fellow of Wolfson College. In the 1920s and 1930s he travelled widely in Europe, especially in the Danube–Balkan region. He was already deeply imbued with German scholarship in the fields of epigraphy, prosopography and military history: this was reflected in his first writings which included articles on legions and provinces, and chapters on the frontiers in volumes X and XI of the *Cambridge Ancient History*. The influence of Münzer's work on the republican nobility is apparent in Syme's articles on senators of the late republic, which prepared the way for *The Roman Revolution*, published in the summer of 1939. Appreciation was immediate, sharpened by the outbreak of war; but this delayed its long-term impact and interrupted Syme's career. He was attached to British Embassies, in Belgrade and Ankara, before becoming professor of classical philology at Istanbul from 1942 to 1945.

The echoes of recent events were eloquent, if nowhere explicit, in *The Roman Revolution*. 'Pessimistic and truculent' in tone, written in a powerful, pointed and epigrammatic style, it demolished the standard view of Augustus as a beneficent saviour; instead he emerged as a cynical politician, consciously destroying the republic he pretended to restore. Syme did not focus on Augustus alone or on other 'great men' such as Caesar and Cicero; with meticulous scholarship he dissected the oligarchy which formed Augustus' 'party'. If the first book is his most formally perfect, the massive (856 pages) *Tacitus*, which consolidated his position as the foremost living historian of Rome, has perhaps been more influential, inspiring a whole series of studies of ancient authors in their context. He himself has contributed similar works on Sallust and Ovid. A regular participant for over twenty years in the annual Bonn *Historia-Augusta-Colloquia*, Syme has produced four studies of this mysterious and much misused source: what might in other

hands be arid and laboured is transformed by his elegant scholarship, flavoured with a subtle wit. In the meantime his astonishing production continues unabated: more than forty articles were composed between 1981 and 1985, together with a substantial monograph, in which he returned to an earlier theme, *The Augustan Aristocracy*.

A fellow of the British Academy from 1944, knighted in 1959, a member of the Order of Merit since 1976, Syme has received honorary degrees and other distinctions in four continents. He was secretary-general of the International Council for Philosophy and Humanistic Studies from 1952 to 1971 and its president from 1971 to 1975.   ARB

Main publications

(Published by the Clarendon Press, Oxford unless otherwise stated.)
The Roman Revolution (1939); *Tacitus*, 2 vols (1958); *Colonial élites — Rome, Spain and the Americas* (1958); *Sallust* (Berkeley and Los Angeles: University of California Press, 1964); *Ammianus and the Historia Augusta* (1968); *Ten Studies in Tacitus* (1970); *Emperors and Biography* (1971); *The Historia Augusta: a Call for Clarity* (Bonn: Habelt, 1971); *Danubian Papers* (Bucharest: Bibliothèque d'études du sud-est européen, 1971); *History in Ovid* (1978); *Roman papers* I–IV (1979–1988); *Some Arval Brethren* (1980); *Historia Augusta Papers* (1983); *The Augustan Aristocracy* (1986).

Reading

Alföldy, G.: Review-discussion of *Roman Papers* I–II, *American Journal of Ancient History* 4 (1979) 167–85.
——: *Sir Ronald Syme, 'Die römische Revolution' und die deutsche Althistorie* (Heidelberg: Winter, 1983).
Bowersock, G. W.: The emperor of Roman history. *New York Review of Books* 6 May (1980) 8–13.
Millar, F.: Style abides. *Journal of Roman Studies* 71 (1981) 144–52.

Szekfű, Gyula (b.1883, d.1955) The greatest Hungarian historian of the twentieth century, Szekfű entered the professional arena by dropping a bombshell: his first substantial work, published in 1913, sought to divest Ferenc Rákóczi, the greatest hero in the national pantheon, of much of his nimbus. Yet Szekfű was a good patriot, in his own conservative fashion, and his critique seven years later of the liberal and capitalist excesses over

SZEKFŰ, GYULA

'three generations', which he held responsible for the collapse of the old Hungarian state, made him into a leading public figure between the wars. This extraordinarily persuasive work led to another, yet more influential: the post-medieval sections in a comprehensive history of Hungary which Szekfű compiled with Bálint Hóman. Unlike Hóman, however, who served as minister in increasingly quasi-fascist governments and was later executed as a war criminal, Szekfű disliked Nazi Germany and moved to a reconciliation with the political opposition. After 1945 he served for a time as Hungarian ambassador in Moscow. Though an unrepentant advocate of the rights of the Magyars as the 'political nation' in historic Hungary, Szekfű's extensive writings show a consistent originality, finesse, and power of (often iconoclastic) argument.   RJWE

Main publications

A száműzött Rákóczi (Rákóczi in exile) (Budapest: Magyar Tudományos Akadémia, 1913); *Három nemzedék. Egy hanyatló kor története* (Three generations. History of a decline) (Budapest: Királyi Magyar Egyetemi Nyomda, 1920); *Iratok a magyar államnyelv kérdésének történetéhez, 1790–1848* (Documents on the history of the question of Hungarian as state language, 1790–1848) (Budapest: Magyar Történelmi Társulat, 1926); with B. Hóman, *Magyar történet* (History of Hungary) 8 vols (Budapest: Királyi Magyar Egyetemi Nyomda, 1928–34); *Bethlen Gábor* (Budapest: Magyar Szemle Társaság, 1929); *État et nation* (Paris and Budapest: Presses Universitaires de France, 1945).

Reading

Dénes, I. Z.: *A 'realitás' illúziója: a historikus Szekfű Gyula pályafordulója* (The illusion of 'reality': the historian Gyula Szekfű's volte-face) (Budapest: Akadémiai Kiadó, 1976).

Glatz, F.: *Történetíró és politika* (The historian and politics) (Budapest: Akadémiai Kiadó, 1980).

Németh, L.: *Szekfű Gyula* (Budapest: Bólyai Akadémia, 1940).

T

Tabari, Muhammad ibn Jarir (b.839, d.923) Tabari was the compiler of, among several other works, a vast universal history in Arabic which is our most important and detailed source for the first 300 years of Islam.

The name by which he is generally known, Tabari, is derived from the Persian province of Tabaristan (Mazandaran), south of the Caspian; in its capital, Amol, he was born and brought up. Tabari's father, inspired by a dream foretelling his son's greatness, financed him to begin his travels in search of knowledge. This was part of the traditional education of a Muslim scholar, and Tabari travelled to Iraq, Syria and Egypt seeking oral and written material about history, law, exegesis of the Koran, and the traditions of the Prophet Muhammad. Settling eventually in Baghdad, he devoted himself to writing and teaching. His industry was formidable and can have left little time for much else, for he is reported to have written 40 folios a day for 40 years. Nevertheless his life was not without controversy. His attempt to found a school of law aroused the hostility of many of the people of Baghdad, and he acquired a reputation among some for political and religious heterodoxy. It is even said that he had to be buried secretly at night because of the enmity of the Baghdadis. Nevertheless, his scholarly reputation triumphed, and by the thirteenth century his fame had led some of the people of Cairo to claim that he was buried there rather than in Baghdad.

The great value of Tabari's history is that it preserves a large selection of earlier sources which would otherwise be lost to us. The extracts from these earlier sources are placed side by side, complete with their contradictions and inconsistencies, with little explicit editorial intervention on Tabari's part. This does not mean, as has sometimes been thought, that Tabari gives us these sources in pristine condition. By his time they had already been subject to a long process of oral and written transmission and it is probably impossible for us to reconstruct them in their original form. In effect his work presents a wide cross-section of the historical consensus of Islam as it had evolved during its first three centuries.

The edition of Tabari's history published at Leiden between 1879 and 1901 runs to nearly 13 volumes but, even so, may be a considerable abbreviation of the original text. His other most important work, devoted to the exegesis of the text of the Koran, consists of 30 volumes in the printed Cairo edition of 1903–10. One of his pupils spent seven years copying the text and then lent it to a friend who spent two years perusing it from beginning to end. It was returned with the comment: 'On the surface of the earth there is no one more knowledgeable than Tabari!'.   GRHt

Main publications

The History of al-Tabari, English trans., 38 volumes planned (Albany: State University of New York Press, 1985 onward).

Reading

Al-Tabari. In *Encyclopaedia of Islam*, 1st edn (Leiden: 1913–42).

Sezgin, F.: *Geschichte des arabischen Schrifttums*, i, (Leiden: 1967) 323–8.

Tacitus, Cornelius (b.AD 56/7)   Born probably in northern Italy or modern Provence, Tacitus married the daughter of Agricola

401

(governor of Britain) in 77, entered the senate as quaestor in 81 or 82, and eventually became consul in 97 and proconsul of Asia in 112/13 or 113/14. His date of death is unknown.

In AD 98 Tacitus published his first works, *Agricola* and *Germania*. The former, a biography of his father-in-law, obeys the conventions of Graeco-Roman biography and largely heroizes its subject. The latter, an ethnographical and geographical monograph on the German people, likewise obeys the conventions of its genre and provides little factual information but rather the tralaticious material which Greeks and Romans thought appropriate to all foreigners. Tacitus' third work, the *Dialogue*, is a monograph which was perhaps written at the turn of the century but of which the dramatic date is 74/5: in it Tacitus treats the decline of oratory in dialogue form in the Ciceronian manner.

Each of these three short works touches on topics which seem relevant to Tacitus' own age. In the first he raises the key question of how to live one's life under an oppressive autocracy such as that of the emperor Domitian, and suggests that the answer lies in moderation and virtual quietism. In the second, by treating the Germans as 'noble savages', Tacitus implies criticism of contemporary materialism at Rome. And in the third the decline of eloquence is explained in terms of the decline of personal and political freedom which the imperial system of government entailed.

Tacitus' reputation as the greatest Roman historian, however, rests chiefly on the *Annals* and *Histories*, which together produced a total of 30 volumes and, when complete, began with the death of the emperor Augustus in AD 14 and ended 82 years later with the death of Domitian in AD 96. The scale of treatment, which is ample, and the annalistic format, which is rigorously sustained throughout, together serve to remind readers that Tacitus was writing history in the grand manner, which had been sanctioned by tradition and was represented above all by LIVY.

The *Histories*, on which Tacitus was engaged in 106/7, is the earlier of the two works. Though originally it comprised 12 or 14 volumes (the exact number is unknown) and covered the years 69–96, only the first four volumes (together with a quarter of the fifth) have survived. The extant narrative thus covers no more than the civil war which raged through most of 69, and the very beginning of Vespasian's principate in 70 – although in a retrospective section of his preface Tacitus surveys events from Nero's death in June 68. Elsewhere in the preface Tacitus, like THUCYDIDES, rouses his readers' expectations by listing the topics with which he will deal and by stressing their potential for exciting and dramatic treatment. He thus announces his work as a characteristic example of CLASSICAL HISTORIOGRAPHY of the type which Cicero had recommended. In the narrative itself he is as good as his word, and book 3 in particular – where he describes the second battle of Cremona, Vespasian's march on Rome, the firing of the Capitol, the fighting in the city, and the murder of the rival emperor Vitellius – is commonly hailed as a masterpiece.

The writing of the *Annals* is assigned to various periods between the years 109 and 120. Though originally it comprised 16 or 18 volumes (the exact number is again uncertain) and covered the period 14–68, only books 1–4, a fragment only of book 5, book 6, books 11–15, and a portion of book 16 have survived. We thus lack his account of some of Tiberius' reign, all of Caligula's, much of Claudius', and the death of Nero; what remains, however, is compulsive reading, and quite enough to establish Tacitus as a writer of historical narrative of the first rank. The *Annals* is rightly seen as the culmination of his literary career.

Tacitus delighted in demonstrating that the political life of the early empire was a sham and that appearances consistently differed from the reality. Conversely, and paradoxically, he also delighted in misleading his own readers: as has been remarked, 'there are many occasions when we have to read him very closely indeed to perceive that he has in fact denied what one thought he had said.' He was also a master of the unexpected. In the *Histories* he had promised that his next work would be an encomiastic history of contemporary society, but the *Annals* is a vituperative account of a still earlier period. Similarly, most first-century AD historians had modelled their styles on the smoothness of Cicero and Livy, but Tacitus chose to imitate the iconoclastic style of SALLUST. Such inversion of the normal also characterized his treatment of events. Instead of appearing as the protectors of their citizens, Tiberius and Nero are portrayed as the chief instigators of civil war against them: Nero, for example, fires the city of Rome and 'plunders' the provinces of his own empire to rebuild the city as his personal capital, while the citizens for their part vie with one another in vice, criminality and servile flattery.

There can be no doubt that this inverted and one-sided approach to early imperial history was intended to be understood on more than one level: as an attack on the imperial system in general and on its operation in his own day in particular. Yet why should Tacitus attack a system from which, as he says himself, his own political career had benefited so conspicuously? Perhaps he was bitter at having risen from relative obscurity to distinguished offices of state which had long since been stripped of much of their real power by successive emperors. Yet his remarks about the republic are hardly less critical than those about the empire, and he attacks the opponents of emperors with as much cynicism as he attacks the emperors themselves. It is hard to resist the conclusion that Tacitus was a dissenter by nature rather than by conviction, never happy unless, like one of the characters in his own *Dialogue*, he was assuming the role of a critic.   AJW

Main writings

Historiae, text, ed. H. Heubner (Stuttgart: Teubner, 1978); *P. Cornelius Tacitus: Die Historien*, commentary by H. Heubner, vols 1–5 (Heidelberg: Winter, 1963–82); *A Historical Commentary on Tacitus' 'Histories'*, G. E. F. Chilver, vols 1 [Books 1–2] and 2 [Books 4–5] (Oxford: Clarendon Press, 1979–85); *Tacitus: the 'Histories' Book III*, commentary by K. Wellesley (Sydney: Sydney University Press, 1972); *Annales*, text, ed. H. Heubner (Stuttgart: Teubner, 1983); *Cornelius Tacitus: Annalen*, commentary by E. Koestermann, vols 1–4 (Winter, 1963–8); *The Annals of Tacitus*, text, with commentary by F. R. D. Goodyear, vols 1–2 [Books 1–2] (Cambridge: Cambridge University Press, 1972–81); *The Annals of Tacitus*, text, with commentary by H. Furneaux, vols 1–2 (Oxford: Clarendon Press, 1896–1907).

Reading

Martin, Ronald: *Tacitus* (London: Batsford, 1981).
Syme, Ronald: *Tacitus* (Oxford: Clarendon Press, 1958).
Walker, B.: *The 'Annals' of Tacitus: a Study in the Writing of History* (Manchester: Manchester University Press, 1952).

Taine, Hippolyte (b.1828, d.1893)   Taine's life was marked by early misfortunes: the death of his father when he was 13, an unhappy experience at school in Paris; his failure to pass the *agrégation* when a student at the École normale supérieure and the rejection of his doctoral thesis. For a time he was a teacher in provincial schools, until in 1852 he settled in Paris and earned his living as a private tutor and professional writer. Since he no longer had any expectation of an academic post he felt free to study widely, especially in physiology, anatomy and psychology, and to write voluminously on a great variety of subjects. In 1853 he published a study of the fables of La Fontaine; in 1855 a guidebook to the Pyrenees which came to be considered a classic; in 1856 a study of Livy. He published a vast number of essays which were collected and were very successful: *Les Philosophes français du XIXᵉ siècle* (1857); *Essais de critique et d'histoire* (1858) which contained studies of Balzac and Michelet; and *Histoire de la littérature anglaise* (1863).

In 1863 Taine accepted the post of admissions examiner at the military College of Saint Cyr and in 1865 he became professor of aesthetics and the history of art at the École des beaux arts. These posts gave him the opportunity to travel and write about the provinces and about Italy, as well as to publish his lectures (*La Philosphie de l'art*, 1885). His philosophy was expressed in *De l'Intelligence* (1870), and in 1871, shortly before giving a course of lectures at Oxford, he started on his major historical work, *Les Origines de la France contemporaine*, which was published in six volumes between 1874 and 1893, the year of his death.

Taine had earlier put forward his conviction, which was to become famous, that the three vital forces that shape and determine the nature of a people are *la race*, *le milieu* and *le moment.* He had used Balzac as his model for considering that the psychology, institutions, beliefs, thought and organization of any historical generation must be symmetrically related. History demands, he wrote, the understanding that mankind is not a collection of objects lying next to one another, but a machine of functionally interrelated parts. It was because he believed that history was a totality, that he sought to demonstrate that France's experience from the sixteenth century to his own time could be demonstrated as a connected whole.

Taine exercised considerable influence over several generations, and is thought to have been one of the major influences on writers of the naturalist school, such as Émile Zola. The positivist philosopher in Paul Bourget's novel *Le Disciple* (1889) is thought to have been modelled on Taine. But his historical work has been sharply criticized, especially his treatment of the Revolution, where he was accused of seeing only the Terror.

AULARD, who exposed Taine's poor scholarship, once said that no student at the Sorbonne who quoted Taine would receive a degree. Few took the risk. But, despite this and more general objections that he viewed the course of history as determined by a series of mechanistic and inflexible laws, Taine's work remained an inspiration to twentieth-century right-wing historians such as GAXOTTE. Moreover, his magnificent style and his belief that a historical moment such as the French Revolution could only be understood by the analysis of social forces maintain his reputation as one of the great classic historians.   DJ

Main publications

Les origines de la France contemporaine, 6 vols (1874–93) [Selected chapters] trans. as *The Origins of Contemporary France*, ed. and intro. Edward T. Gargan (Chicago, Ill.: University of Chicago Press, 1974); *L'Ancien régime* (Paris: 1875); *La Révolution*, vol. 1: *L'Anarchie* (Paris: 1878), vol. 2: *La Conquête jacobine* (Paris: 1881), vol. 3: *Le Gouvernement révolutionnaire* (Paris: 1884); *Le Régime moderne*, vol. 1 (Paris: 1891), vol. 2 (Paris: 1893).

Reading

Cardonell, Charles-Olivier: *Histoire et historiens: une mutation idéologique des historiens français 1865–1885* (Toulouse: 1976).

Chevrillon, André: *Taine: formation de sa pensée* (Paris: 1932).
Kahn, Sholom J.: *Science and Aesthetic Judgement: a Study in Taine's Critical Method* (New York: 1953).

Tait, James (b.1863, d.1944)   Tait was a shy, unassuming, singular man who devoted his quiet life entirely to scholarship. He was a medievalist who maintained that a thorough understanding of the mechanics of medieval society could best be secured by detailed local and regional studies. Tait was born and educated in Manchester, and after three undergraduate years at Balliol College, Oxford, in 1887 he returned to Manchester to take up an assistant lectureship at Owens College. Raised to lecturer in 1896 and elected to a chair in 1902, Tait remained in Manchester and accordingly was directed to work on the records closest to hand and in the region he knew best. Between his two big books, *Medieval Manchester and the Beginnings of Lancashire* (1904) and *The Medieval English Borough* (1936), he contributed to the eight volumes of *The Victoria County History of Lancashire* (1906–14), edited *The Domesday Survey of Cheshire* (1916), and served as president of the Chetham Society (1915–28). He was elected fellow of the British Academy in 1921.

Tait never married and rarely socialized. His spare time was spent reviewing for the *English Historical Review*, and it is here that the weight of his learning was most influential. His published work is a polished mirror of his becalmed personality: cautious, balanced, precise. Tait found teaching tiresome. While conscientious in his duties, he was uninspiring and the sleeping partner in Tout's development of the Manchester History School.   PRHS

Main publications

The Medieval English Borough (Manchester: Manchester University Press, 1936); [review] Domesday Book and beyond, by F. W. Maitland. *English Historical Review* 12 (1897) 768–77.

Reading

Galbraith, V. H.: James Tait. *English Historical Review* 60 (1945) 129–135.

Talmon, Jacob Leib (b.1916, d.1980) Born in Poland, Talmon obtained a doctorate from the London School of Economics in 1943. After devoting some of his time to politics and diplomacy he eventually became professor of modern history at the Hebrew University of Jerusalem. He is mainly remembered for his investigation into the causes of modern totalitarianism, which he traced back to the influence of Rousseau. The first of the three volumes that he devoted to this subject, *The Origins of Totalitarian Democracy* (1952), was not well received by historians of the French Revolution. It developed an unfashionable line of argument that had first been advanced by TAINE and Cochin and was later to be taken up by FURET. In his *Romanticism and Revolt* (1967), Talmon expressed the view that the statistical and sociological approach to history had been taken far enough and he preferred the study of 'patterns of mind and behaviour' and 'human drama'. Taste in history has caught up with him and he seems likely to get more justice from posterity than he did from his contemporaries.

NH

Main publications

(All published by Secker & Warburg, London.)
The Origins of Totalitarian Democracy (1952); *Political Messianism: the Romantic Phase* (1960); *Romanticism and Revolt* (1967); *The Myth of the Nation and the Voice of Revolution: the Origins of Ideological Polarization in the Twentieth Century* (1981).

Tawney, Richard Henry (b.1880, d.1962) Born in Calcutta, Tawney was educated at Rugby School and at Balliol College, Oxford. Between 1906 and 1908 he taught political economy at Glasgow University, and he also pioneered adult education classes at Rochdale and Longton. In 1908 he accepted the post of lecturer for the Workers' Educational Association (WEA) tutorial classes under Oxford University which he held until 1914. Tawney had joined the executive committee of the WEA in 1905, and remained a member for 42 years, serving as vice-president from 1920, and as president from 1928 to 1943. In 1914 he became director of the Ratan Tata Foundation at the London School of Economics (LSE). After war service he was elected in 1918 to a Balliol fellowship but a year later moved back to the LSE where he became reader in 1923 and professor in 1931.

Tawney's major writings encompassed a wide range of historical concerns although he did not have much time for the Industrial Revolution or the nineteenth century, and he was primarily interested in restraints on economic drive rather than on commercial and industrial enterprise. His concerns were predominantly with shifting attitudes and relationships, but over time there was a significant change in his historical thinking.

The first phase of Tawney's writing, until the mid-1920s, was concerned with the resistance of groups and individuals to the imposition of capitalist modes of thought and behaviour. He wrote in the preface to *The Agrarian Problem in the Sixteenth Century* (1912) that the interest of economic history was in the light it shed on the presuppositions about social expediency which influenced statesmen and humble individuals and classes alike. He saw the act of moral judgement as central to the historian's task and this was one of the major themes of the long introduction to his 1925 edition of Thomas Wilson's *Discourse upon Usury* of 1569, and of his most important historical work *Religion and the Rise of Capitalism* (1926). The latter book examined relations between economic practice and moral principle during the sixteenth and seventeenth centuries and reflected *The Agrarian Problem* in its concern with the resistance of men to the erosion of traditional standards of social behaviour. It ranks with *The Acquisitive Society* (1921) and *Equality* (1931) as the most important of Tawney's books.

A second phase in Tawney's historical work dates from the 1930s when his focus moved away from the ethical problems of past economic activity towards the study of the economic roots of political dominance and revolution. It was a shift of thought entirely in keeping with the world economic crisis and the advance of Italian fascism. This concern with the relationship between political and economic power resulted in articles on the rise of the gentry (1941), which sparked off the long-running gentry controversy of the 1950s and 1960s, and Tawney's British Academy

Raleigh Lecture 'Harrington's Interpretation of his Age'. In these writings and in his unpublished Ford Lectures at Oxford in 1935, Tawney concluded that as the centre of social gravity shifted before the English civil war, so political power moved with it. Indeed political change in seventeenth-century England was to be seen in terms of determinism. This emphasis on the structural limits of political action carried through into his last book, which was a study of Lionel Cranfield as merchant and minister in the early seventeenth century. A central argument of this book concerned the constraints on the actions of men arising from the machinery of social and economic power. The weight of his writings on the period 1540–1640 led to this period being known by the 1950s as 'Tawney's century'.

The range of Tawney's interests was enormous. Throughout his life he wrote extensively on education, and he served on numerous commissions and committees including the Coal Industry Commission which reported in 1919, and the University Grants Committee (1943–8). After helping to found the Economic History Society in 1926 he co-edited its *Review* from 1927 to 1934. Between 1918 and 1928 he stood unsuccessfully as an Independent Labour candidate at three general elections, and became a major political influence. The Labour party manifesto of 1928 was largely his work. Among his books were *Minimum Rates in the Chain-making Industry* (1914); *Land and Labour in China* (1932), a brilliant survey of China's agrarian problems following an eight-month visit to the country, in which Tawney drew on his knowledge of pre-industrial agriculture to highlight the parallels between Chinese and western development; and, during a year in America in 1942, a short history placing developments in the American labour movement firmly within the context of the growth of American industrial society. Tawney's achievements were widely appreciated, although his reputation as a historian has suffered since his death, largely on the grounds that he allowed his political opinions to influence his conclusions. He was a fellow (1918–21) and honorary fellow (1938 onwards) of Balliol College, a member of the American Philosophical Society, and a fellow of the British Academy. Although he did not proceed to his Oxford MA Tawney received honorary doctorates from universities across the world. Despite his comfortable origins in India his lifelong dislike of privilege led him to refuse high honours including the peerages offered to him by MacDonald and Attlee. JVB

Main publications

The Agrarian Problem in the Sixteenth Century (London: Longmans, Green, 1912); *Religion and the Rise of Capitalism* (London: Murray, 1926); *Land and Labour in China* (London: Allen & Unwin, 1932); The rise of the gentry. *Economic History Review* II (1941) 1–38; Harrington's interpretation of his age. *Proceedings of the British Academy* 27 (1941) 119–223; *Business and Politics under James I: Lionel Cranfield as Merchant and Minister* (Oxford: Oxford University Press, 1958).

Reading

Terrill, R.: *R. H. Tawney and his Times* (London: Deutsch, 1973).
Williams, J. R., Titmuss, R. M. and Fisher, F. J.: *R. H. Tawney, a Portrait by Several Hands* (London: WEA, 1960).
Winter, J. M.: Tawney the historian. In *History and Society: Essays by R. H. Tawney*, ed. Winter (London: Routledge & Kegan Paul, 1978) pp. 1–40.

Taylor, Alan John Percivale (b.1906) A. J. P. Taylor is one of the few major historians whose work has gained the respect of academics and has appealed also to a wide general public. He was born on 25 March 1906 at Birkdale near Southport, then part of Lancashire. His family was well-to-do and involved in the cotton trade; his father sold out his interests in 1920, economically at just the right time. Alan Taylor was educated at Bootham, York, the Quaker public school, and at Oriel College, Oxford. He became a lecturer at Manchester University in 1930, then moved to Magdalen College, Oxford where he was a fellow from 1938 to 1976 (and thereafter an honorary fellow).

Taylor's nonconformist background was to be much in evidence throughout his career. From it he drew the moral, 'I am no better than anyone else, but no one is better than me.' His father had transferred his loyalties from the Radicals to the Labour party after the first world war. Taylor was to be an individualistic socialist throughout his career, even being briefly a member of the Communist party as an undergraduate. He has been very much part of the English radical tradition which has run, as he has commented, 'from Wilkes to Michael Foot'. During the time that he was a leading figure in CND, he took great pleasure in noting that some of his speeches were being given in halls where John Bright had denounced the Corn Laws a century earlier. When invited to give the Ford Lectures at Oxford in 1956, he chose to speak of his radical heroes, and from these lectures came his favourite of his books, *The Trouble Makers* (1957).

From 1934 to 1961 Taylor's main works were on diplomatic and Central European history. Diplomatic history was much in vogue, given the very widespread interest in the origins of the first world war when Taylor began research in Vienna in 1928. Indeed his mentor, A.F. Pribram, had moved from studying Cromwell to the origins of the Great War. Taylor, who had intended his research to be linked to British parliamentary radicals of the 1830s and 1840s, worked instead on the problem of northern Italy in European diplomacy in 1848; research which, when supplemented by work in archives in London and Paris, led to his first book in 1934. Further books on Austria-Hungary, Germany and diplomatic history culminated in his major survey of diplomatic history, *The Struggle for Mastery in Europe 1848–1918* (1954).

Taylor's best known and most controversial book was *The Origins of the Second World War* (1961), his last major book on European diplomatic history. It caused immense controversy in both Europe and America. It challenged entrenched orthodoxies about the 1930s at a time when cold war certainties were beginning to crumble in the west. In fact it was a traditional, narrowly defined, diplomatic history, focusing on the concerns of London, Paris and Berlin, and reliant on such published sources as were available. Many of his interpretations which shocked in 1961 had been expressed by Taylor in earlier writings. Especial outrage was caused by his denial that *Mein Kampf* was a valuable guide to Hitler's actions and by his portrayal of Hitler's and Stalin's foreign policy as traditional not diabolical. The brilliance of Taylor's style, his seemingly endless questioning of hitherto established views and his broad analysis of the background to war in Europe in 1939 have ensured that the book continues to be read and argued about.

As a result of the storm over this book Taylor's Oxford University lectureship was not renewed in 1963, in spite of his record of publications and his skill as a lecturer. But he was not new to controversy. During the latter part of the second world war and immediately after it, when he had been a regular broadcaster on BBC radio, his views on Anglo-Soviet relations and Yugoslavia had become increasingly unpalatable to the Establishment. During the 1950s and 1960s he had been an early 'media personality', appearing with Michael Foot, Robert Boothby and W.J. Brown in very popular current affairs discussion programmes on television and writing columns in the *Sunday Pictorial*, the *Daily Herald* and the *Sunday Express*. He was passed over for chairs of history at Oxford and the London School of Economics, and chose not to take a professorship elsewhere.

After *The Struggle for Mastery in Europe* Taylor increasingly concentrated on British history. In 1959 and 1961 he gave important lectures on 'Politics in the First World War' and on Lloyd George, at the British Academy and at Cambridge University. These were followed by his second major survey volume, *English History 1914–1945* (1965). This was characteristic Taylor, full of paradoxes and aphorisms, sparkling in style, revealing his radical and irreverent *persona*, yet relying, perhaps, too much on his intuition.

Taylor's friendship with Lord Beaverbrook led him to accept the honorary directorship of the Beaverbrook Library, off Fleet Street (1967–75). This brought Taylor into contact with scholars from all countries working on modern British history, while he wrote *Beaverbrook* (1972) and *The Second World War* (1975).

Taylor was a dedicated lecturer for the Historical Association. He was elected to the British Academy in 1956 but resigned, amid much publicity, in 1980 during the controversy over Anthony Blunt's membership. CJW

TAYLOR, GEORGE V.

Main publications

The Italian Problem in European Diplomacy 1847–1849 (Manchester: Manchester University Press, 1934); *Germany's First Bid for Colonies 1884–1885* (London: Macmillan, 1938): *The Habsburg Monarchy 1815–1918* (Macmillan, 1941; 2nd edn 1948; New York: Harper, 1965); *The Course of German History* (London: Hamish Hamilton, 1945; New York: Coward McCann, 1946); *The Struggle for Mastery in Europe 1848–1918* (Oxford: Oxford University Press, 1954); *Bismarck: The Man and the Statesman* (Hamilton, 1955; New York: Knopf, 1955); *The Trouble Makers* (Hamilton, 1957); *The Origins of the Second World War* (Hamilton, 1961; new edn 1963; New York: Atheneum, 1962 with 'Preface for the American Reader'); *English History 1914–1945*, Oxford History of England (Oxford University Press, 1965); *Beaverbrook* (Hamilton, 1972; New York: Simon & Schuster, 1972); *A Personal History* (Hamilton, 1983). See also Wrigley, C.: *A. J. P. Taylor: A Complete Bibliography* (Brighton: Harvester, 1980).

Reading

Journal of Modern History 49 (1977) [issue devoted to Taylor].

Louis, W. R., ed.: *The Origins of the Second World War: A. J. P. Taylor and his Critics* (New York: Wiley, 1972).

Martel, G., ed.: *The Origins of the Second World War Reconsidered* (London: Allen & Unwin, 1986).

Sked, A. and Cook, C. eds: *Crisis and Controversy: Essays in Honour of A.J.P. Taylor* (London: Macmillan, 1976).

Taylor, George V. (b.1919) Educated in his native New Jersey, after majoring in history at Rutgers University, Taylor originally trained for business before war service in the Pacific. Subsequent postgraduate work at the University of Wisconsin led to a dissertation on French businessmen and the Revolution. Between 1952 and 1985 he taught at the University of North Carolina, Chapel Hill. His reputation rests on a handful of articles which in the 1960s, together with the contemporaneous writings of COBBAN, transformed historians' perceptions of the origins of the French Revolution. Cobban's role was largely negative, pointing out the flaws in existing orthodoxies; Taylor's conclusions are unlikely to be substantially modified. Early work on the structure of eighteenth-century French business led to a definitive analysis (1964) of the types of capitalism existing before 1789, which demonstrated the relatively limited role of classic commercial and industrial capitalism. In 1967 he argued that the structure of wealth in France as a whole was overwhelmingly noncapitalist, even among the bourgeoisie, concluding that the traditional picture of a capitalist bourgeoisie overthrowing a feudal nobility in 1789 could no longer be sustained. This much-anthologized and deeply influential article suggested that the causes of the Revolution were not primarily social at all. With this conviction, Taylor went on to analyse what the French wanted in 1789 on the evidence of the *cahiers* (grievance lists) drawn up then. He found little that would explain the subsequent radicalism of the National Assembly, and concluded that the political process itself was the main radicalizing force. His research on the *cahiers* continues.

WD

Main publications

Types of capitalism in eighteenth-century France. *English Historical Review* 79 (1964) 478–497; Noncapitalist wealth and the origins of the French Revolution. *American Historical Review* 72 (1967) 469–496; Revolutionary and nonrevolutionary content in the cahiers of 1789: an interim report. *French Historical Studies* 7 (1972) 479–502.

Tellenbach, Gerd (b.1903) After taking a doctorate in Freiburg in 1926, Tellenbach worked from 1928 to 1932 on the *Repertorium Germanicum* in Rome and was habilitated at Heidelberg in 1933. After a period in which he made his living as a replacement for other professors on sabbatical he was appointed to a chair at Giessen in 1938, whence he moved to Münster in 1942 and Freiburg in 1944. The long delay in securing a permanent appointment was probably due to his attitude to the Nazi regime; though not himself a member of any resistance circle his stance was one of critical distance.

In 1936 and 1940 appeared the texts which set the direction of Tellenbach's scholarly work: a study of the Gregorian idea of *libertas* and two pathbreaking studies on the origins of the kingdom of Germany, which coined the term 'the imperial aristocracy' for the leading families of the Carolingian empire, whose possessions and interests extended across the borders of the various Carolingian subkingdoms. After a long period from 1945 to 1955 in which his main preoccupation was the re-establishing of the University of Freiburg, these two themes re-emerged in a flood of studies by himself and his pupils (the so-called Freiburg school) on the German aristocracy of the early and high middle ages and on monastic reform movements. The connection between the two lay in the Freiburg school's exploitation of sources which had long been known but had seemed to have little to offer the historian: *libri memoriales*, the confraternity books of monasteries, which consist largely of long lists of names. Tellenbach and his pupils were able to show the value of these sources both for the genealogy of the high nobility and for the study of the shifts of interest and emphasis within the numerous monastic reform movements of the tenth and eleventh centuries. Especially after it became possible to apply new techniques of data processing to the often formidable bulk of the material, the approach pioneered by Tellenbach and his pupils led to a substantial reappraisal of the early history of Germany, one which is still in progress, as is the edition and indexing of the *libri memoriales* themselves.   TAR

Main publications

Libertas: Kirche und Weltordnung im Zeitalter des Investiturstreites (Stuttgart: Kohlhammer, 1936) trans. as *Church, State and Christian Society in the Period of the Investiture Contest* (Oxford: Blackwell, 1939); *Königtum und Stämme in der Werdezeit des Deutschen Reiches* (Weimar: Böhlau, 1939); *Die Entstehung des Deutschen Reiches* (München: Callweg, 1940); *Studien und Vorarbeiten zur Geschichte des grossfränkischen und frühdeutschen Adels* (Freiburg: Albert, 1957); editor, *Liber memorialis von Remiremont* (Zürich: Weidmann, 1970).

Reading

Adel und Kirche. Gerd Tellenbach zum 65. Geburtstag dargebracht von Freunden und Schülern (Freiburg: Herder, 1965) [incl. bibliography] pp. 581–7.
Tellenbach, G.: *Aus erinnerter Zeitgeschichte* (Freiburg: Verlag der Wagnerschen Universitätsbuchhandlung, 1981) [autobiography].

Thietmar of Merseburg (b.975, d.1018) Major historian of Ottonian Germany. Thietmar's *Chronicon*, written from 1012 onwards, at first sought to record only the fortunes of the see of Merseburg. Yet it soon burst this modest frame and became a history of the *Reich*, its kings, its ruling circles (especially the Saxon aristocracy) and, last, but not least, a memoir of Thietmar himself. He belonged to this wealthy nobility, being the son of an East-Saxon Count, Siegfried, whose seat and family sanctuary lay at Walbeck on the Aller. Destined for the church as a boy, Thietmar enjoyed an excellent education at the Magdeburg Cathedral school, and by the year 1000 was a beneficed member of the cathedral community. It was Archbishop Tagino of Magdeburg who in 1008/9 recommended him to Henry II for the vacant see of Merseburg.

Thietmar was a small, unsightly man but with an indefatigable memory and understanding for the situation about him, for his kin, their neighbours and rivals, and for the Saxon-Slav south-eastern frontiers. He was a compulsive writer driven towards history and memoirs by a restless pastoral conscience. He felt deeply about the eternal welfare of those he commemorated in his pages. Full of self-reproach he hoped that his readers and successors would intercede for him. His *Chronicon* breaks off in 1018 but he was still dictating it to a scribe as he lay ill and dying. The manuscript at Dresden with many entries in his own hand survives in a facsimile edition, the original having suffered grievously in 1945.

Thietmar's diction is complex, his style idiosyncratic – not to say crotchety – despite his classical learning, but this makes him all the more intimate and communicative long before historians sought such close relations with their readers. He divided his work into eight books and wrote programmatic verse prologues for some of them. The first he devoted to Henry I, the next to Otto the Great to whose times he looked back as a golden age. Books III and IV dealt with Otto's son and grandson and Thietmar excelled in decribing the succession crises of 983–985 and 1002. From book V onwards he wrote ever more closely to events and he became well acquainted with Henry II, who often stayed at Merseburg. For the earlier tenth century Thietmar had used WIDUKIND OF CORVEY as a source; for the later, up to 998, he drew on the Quedlinburg Annals. His own experiences, journeys, participation in the campaigns against Boleslas Chrobry of Poland, the promotions and deaths of archbishops of Magdeburg, the misdeeds of his cousin Werner, the Saxon nobles' outrages against their bishops, the feuds of the Lower Rhine region and some news from further afield, like King Swein's plunder of England, dominate the later books. More than any other writer of the Ottonian ambit the bishop of Merseburg conveys a sense of place and occasion, the milieu of the ruling families and the parameters of their outlook and feelings. Throughout his mood is sombre, sometimes ironical, always profoundly religious. His work lived on and joined the mainstream of twelfth-century Saxon historiography.   KJL

Main writings

Thietmari Merseburgensis Episcopi Chronicon, ed. R. Holtzmann, 2nd edn (Berlin: *Monumenta Germaniae Historica* n.s. *SRG* 1955) same text with German trans. by W. Trillmich, *Thietmar von Merseburg Chronik, Ausgewählte Quellen zur deutschen Geschichte des Mittelalters*, IX (Darmstadt: Wissenschaftliche Buchgesellschaft, 1970).

Reading

Holtzmann, R.: Introduction to *Thietmari Merseburgensis Episcopi Chronicon*.
Lippelt, H.: *Thietmar von Merseburg Reichsbischof und Chronist, Mitteldeutsche Forschungen*, 72 (Cologne and Vienna: Böhlau, 1973).
Trillmich, W.: Introduction to *Thietmar von Merseburg Chronik*.

Thirsk, Joan (b.1922) After completing her doctorate at London, Thirsk moved in 1951 to the University of Leicester as senior research fellow in agrarian history in the department of English local history. Here she developed an influential approach to agrarian history which stresses farming practice and regional differences in rural economies and which is exemplified in her contributions to *The Agrarian History of England and Wales*. She has also published widely on the economic history of early modern England. In 1965 she succeeded W. G. HOSKINS as reader in economic history at Oxford.   MO

Main publications

English Peasant Farming: the Agrarian History of Lincolnshire from Tudor to Recent Times (London: Rout-

ledge & Kegan Paul, 1957); *The Agrarian History of England and Wales*, vol. IV (1967) and vol. V (1984–5) (Cambridge: Cambridge University Press); *Economic Policy and Projects* (Oxford: Oxford University Press, 1978); *The Rural Economy of England: Collected Essays* (London: Hambledon Press, 1984).

Thomas of Walsingham   (See ST ALBANS CHRONICLES.

Thomas, Keith Vivian (b.1933) Although he has spent the whole of his career in what might appear to be the conservative confines of the Oxford History School, Keith Thomas is arguably the most innovative of English social historians. The son of a South Wales farmer, educated at Barry Grammar School and Balliol, he was for many years fellow and tutor at St John's College, becoming successively reader and professor of modern history in the university. Since 1986 he has been president of Corpus Christi College. He has an unusually wide range. He has written important articles on political thought and radical sects in seventeenth-century England, but his greatest achievement has been to map out new areas for research in social and intellectual history.

In 'History and Anthropology' (1963) he argued that historians should extend their sympathies and the appeal of their subject by responding to new insights from social anthropology; and in *Religion and the Decline of Magic* (1971) he showed in detail what such an approach could yield. Hailed on its appearance as a masterpiece of historical reconstruction, this book altered the standard picture of early modern English men and women by demonstrating that the witch, the cunning man and the astrologer were as influential in popular culture as the priest, and how beliefs in ghosts and fairies, prophecies and omens were an integral and comprehensible part of people's mental equipment in a preindustrial world. His later work has been less overtly influenced by anthropology, but he has continued to illuminate past habits of mind and patterns of social behaviour, writing on such subjects as age, literacy, animals and jokes. Based on a remarkable command of sources and presented with a clarity which makes original perceptions appear self-evident, his work goes a long way towards satisfying his own requirement for historical study, that it should 'enhance our self-consciousness'.   PAS

Main publications

History and Anthropology. *Past and Present* 24 (1963) 3–24; *Religion and the Decline of Magic* (London: Weidenfeld & Nicolson, 1971); *Age and Authority in Early Modern England* (London: British Academy, 1976); *Man and the Natural World: Changing Attitudes in England 1500–1800* (London: Allen Lane, 1983).

Reading

Geertz, H. and Thomas, K.: An Anthropology of Religion and Magic. *Journal of Interdisciplinary History* 6 (1975) 71–109.

Thompson, Edward Palmer (b.1924) Although he spent many years in the extramural department at Leeds University and a few years at the Centre for the Study of Social History at Warwick University, E. P. Thompson is mainly celebrated as a political activist working for the Communist party's Historians' Group 1946–56, then for the New Left and, most recently, for the peace movement. His historical works are only a small part of his output, but they have aroused both intense admiration and vigorous criticism.

Thompson has done a prodigious amount of historical research and his works are lengthy, detailed and written with elegance and panache. Concerned to write history from the bottom up, he has been determined to rescue the labouring poor 'from the enormous condescension of posterity'. While he has not detailed the economic consequences of the growth of agrarian and industrial capitalism, he has devoted considerable attention to their impact on the social, moral and cultural experiences of the poor. His perceptive imagination has led to a number of profound and original insights into the lives of ordinary people. He has written much that is stimulating and challenging about class consciousness, class struggle and class formation; about the law as an ideological weapon in the hands of the ruling class; and about the motives of the poor who took direct action to protect their concept of justice and rights. Thompson can

also be credited with making his ideological stance and methodological approach quite explicit. He often discusses at length the character of historical inquiry and the role of human agency in history, and he is always prepared to admit that historical knowledge is provisional, incomplete and approximate.

On the other hand Thompson's critics have detected serious flaws in his historical works. He is not always rigorous in his scrutiny of evidence and he relies too much on inferences, conjectures and hearsay. His assumptions are sometimes tendentious and some of his arguments undoubtedly go beyond what his evidence will bear. More fundamental are the criticisms which condemn his view of class as being too subjective, which question his claim that the working class was made by the 1830s, and which accuse him of both reading the present into the past and using historical examples to inspire contemporary struggles. In endeavouring to do justice to the experiences and activities of the labouring poor Thompson has often been unjust to their political, social and economic superiors.   HTD

Main publications

William Morris: Romantic to Revolutionary (London: Lawrence & Wishart, 1955; New York: Pantheon, 1977); *The Making of the English Working Class* (London: Gollancz, 1963; New York: Pantheon, 1964); The Moral Economy of the English Crowd in the Eighteenth Century. *Past and Present*, 50 (1971) 76–136; *Whigs and Hunters* (London: Allen Lane, 1975; New York: Pantheon, 1976); *The Poverty of Theory and other essays* (London: Merlin, 1978; New York: Monthly Review, 1979).

Reading

Anderson, Perry: *Arguments with English Marxism* (London: Verso; New York: Schocken, 1980).

Donnelly, F. K.: Ideology and early English working-class history: Edward Thompson and his critics. *Social History* 2 (1976) 219–38.

Kaye, Harvey J.: *The British Marxist Historians* (Cambridge: Polity; New York: Blackwell, 1984).

Thompson, James Matthew (b.1878, d.1956) Educated at Winchester and Christ Church College, Oxford, Thompson was ordained as a clergyman and it was in this capacity that he became a fellow of Magdalen College in 1904. He left the Church of England when he could no longer accept the literal truth of the New Testament, became a professional historian when he was already forty, and was retained by his college. Between the wars he was the only British authority on the French Revolution. His lack of personal dogmatism and his interest in people, both revolutionaries and undergraduates, made him a sympathetic and exciting tutor rather than the founder of any particular school. He wrote what is still the best biography of Robespierre, even if the tortuous psychology of his subject was sometimes too much for Thompson's humane and reasonable mind to probe. In 1943 he published *The French Revolution*, in which his enormous erudition and eye for significant detail enabled him to recreate a world without trying to make it conform to any pattern of his own devising.   NH

Main publications

(All published by Blackwell, Oxford.)
Robespierre (1935); *The French Revolution* (1943; repr. 1985); *Louis Napoleon and the Second Empire* (1954).

Reading

Goodwin, A.: Memoir. *Proceedings of the British Academy* 43 (1957) 271–291.

Thucydides (b.*c*.460, d.*c*.400 BC) Little is known about Thucydides, son of Olorus, besides what he considered his readers should be told; from *The Peloponnesian War* (I 1.1, V 26.1 and 5) we learn:

Thucydides the Athenian wrote the history of the war fought between Athens and Sparta, beginning the account at the very outbreak of the war [431 BC], in the belief that it was going to be a great war and more worth writing about than any of those which had taken place in the past... The history of this period also [after 421 BC] has been written by the same Thucydides, an Athenian, keeping to the order of events as they happened by summers and winters, down to the time when the Spartans and their allies put an end to the empire of Athens and occupied the Long Walls and Piraeus [404 BC]. By then the war had lasted altogether twenty-seven years... I lived through the whole of it, being of an age to understand what was happening, and I put my mind to the subject so as to get an accurate view of it. It happened, too, that I was banished from my country for twenty years after my command at Amphipolis [424 BC]; I saw what was being done on both sides, particularly on the Peloponnesian side, because of my exile, and this leisure gave me rather exceptional facilities for looking into things.

At II 48.3 Thucydides adds that he caught, but recovered from, the plague whose symptoms he there describes. In a sense, the information is enough: he wrote about what he lived through, what he saw at first hand, what he 'looked into' and 'put his mind to' in order to understand it accurately.

Thucydides' method was 'not to write down the first story that came my way', but to seek out eye-witness accounts and check them carefully against each other (I 22.2). Unlike HERODOTUS, he never names his authorities, gives alternative versions or admits uncertainty. He has done the work, formed his opinion of what happened, and the reader must take his word for it. Modern historians, trying to combine Thucydides' account with what can be inferred from the documentary evidence of inscriptions and from contemporary and later authors, are apt to find his reticence frustrating. What is that dense and detailed narrative based on? More important, what did he leave out, and why? Thucydides does not say.

What we are told is the purpose of Thucydides' enterprise. This war was the greatest his world had ever seen; he employed all his powers to understand what was happening and why it was happening; to pass on that understanding would be something gained for ever (I 22.4, '*ktema es aei*'). All the dispassionate detail of the narrative is the means to a greater end, that of understanding human behaviour under extreme political stress. Why do men choose one course rather than another? How far is rational foresight possible? Is altruism compatible with self-interest? The constant pressure of such questions no doubt accounts for Thucydides' notorious concession about speeches: where he or his informants could not remember the exact words used, he put into the speaker's mouth 'what, in my opinion, was called for by each situation' (I 22.1). The detailed record of what happened is not enough; Thucydides evidently needed the freedom to invent appropriate material for his readers to have the chance of understanding the complexities of motivation.

The structure of the history also reflects its purpose. Although it is unfinished – the narrative stops in book VIII, late in 411 BC – it is a reasonable guess that he was aiming at a total of ten books, and that the transition from book V to book VI was a calculated turning point. If so, then one part of Thucydides' aim was to explain what our age might term the psychopathology of Athenian imperialism. In the Funeral Speech at the beginning of the war, Pericles is made to boast of the ideals of democratic Athens: 'we obey the laws themselves, especially those which are for the protection of the oppressed, and those unwritten laws [of justice and altruism] which it is an acknowledged shame to break' (II 37.3). But war is a teacher of violence, as Thucydides explains in his paradigmatic account of the civil strife in Corcyra; under its stress, 'men take it upon themselves to begin the process of repealing those general laws of humanity which are there to give a hope of salvation to all who are in distress' (III 84.3). Even, and especially, the Athenians. At the end of book V, at the turning point of his narrative, Thucydides inserts an extraordinary dramatic dialogue between the representatives of Athens and those of Melos, an island the Athenians intend to enslave. The desperate Melians put their trust in justice, hope, and the gods. The Athenians are contemptuous: 'the strong do what they have the power to do and the weak accept what they have to accept' (V 89); hope is a mere delusion, and 'our opinion of the gods and our knowledge of men lead us to conclude that it is a general and necessary law of nature to rule wherever one can' (V 105.2). Halfway through the story, Athens is at a peak of power and arrogance.

Book VI begins with the Athenians sending a vast armada to conquer Sicily in 415. Excessive hope eventually proves delusive. The great force is destroyed, and the surviving remnants are reduced to the same state of desperation as the Melians. Thucydides gives their doomed leader a final speech:

Throughout my life I have worshipped the gods as I ought, and my conduct towards men has been just and without reproach. Because of this I still have a strong hope for the future... If any of the gods was angry with us at our setting out, by this time we have

been sufficiently punished. Other men before us have attacked their neighbours, and after doing what men will do have suffered no more than what men can bear. So it is now reasonable to hope that the gods will be kinder to us, since by now we deserve their pity rather than their jealousy... (VII 77.2–4).

In that cruel irony lies the justification of Thucydides' way with speeches. The work of the greatest historian of antiquity was also a work of dramatic art, tragic and inexorable.

TPW

Main writings

The Peloponnesian War, trans. Rex Warner (Harmondsworth: Penguin, 1954, rev. edn, intro. M. I. Finley, 1972 [from which the quotations are taken]).

Reading

Connor, W. R.: *Thucydides* (Princeton, NJ: Princeton University Press, 1984).
Cornford, F.M.: *Thucydides Mythistoricus* (London: Arnold, 1907).
Gomme, A. W., Andrewes, A. and Dover, K. J.: *A Historical Commentary on Thucydides* (Oxford: Oxford University Press, 1945–81).
Romilly J. de: *Histoire et raison chez Thucydide* (Paris: Les Belles Lettres, 1956).
Stahl, H.-P.: *Thucydides: die Stellung des Menschen im geschichtlichen Prozess* (Munich: Beck, 1966).

Tocqueville, Alexis de (b.1805, d.1859) The scion of an aristocratic Norman family, Tocqueville grew up in a world in which the consequences of the French Revolution were omnipresent: his maternal grandfather was one of the defence lawyers in the trial of Louis XVI before the Convention; his father narrowly escaped the guillotine, being saved when the Thermidor reaction brought the Terror to an end. The significance and results of the *Grande Révolution* always held a central place in his thought. Educated at the *lycée* in Metz, where his father served as prefect under the restored Bourbon monarchy, he trained in the law and became a magistrate at Versailles. Unlike his father, who refused to take the oath of allegiance to Louis-Philippe, he continued to serve under the House of Orleans.

In 1831 Tocqueville was given leave to visit the United States to study the American penal system. Among the results of that visit was the publication, in 1835 and 1840, of the two

413

volumes of *Democracy in America*. These constitute a work of social analysis rather than history: their importance is, in part, that they gave Tocqueville a reputation in England as well as in France; but still more that he developed a method of work which he was able to apply later to historical writing. In visits to England he gained the friendship of such men as Nassau Senior, John Stuart Mill and George Cornewall Lewis; he married an Englishwoman, Mary Mottley.

Resigning from the magistracy Tocqueville entered politics, serving as a deputy in the Chamber from 1839 and as a member of the Constituent Assembly of the Second Republic in 1848. For a few months in 1849 he was minister for foreign affairs, but his active political life ended with the coup d'état of 1851 which he wholeheartedly condemned. Like Burke, the author whom he most frequently quoted, he therefore had practical experience of political life and was perpetually interested in the relationship between political theory and political practice.

Souvenirs, which was written in 1850–1, record Tocqueville's experiences during the Second Republic, and remain entertaining and enlightening. They reveal a skill in penportraiture which seldom appears in his other works: he depicts his contemporaries vividly and with some acerbity, though without real malice.

After retiring from politics Tocqueville planned to write a history of the revolutionary and Napoleonic era. Initially he seems to have intended a work centring on the personality and achievements of Napoleon, with an introductory chapter or two on the old régime. But the introduction became a volume, *L'Ancien Régime et la Révolution*, published in 1856, the only part of his *magnum opus* to be completed. After his death, fragmentary drafts for later volumes were found among his papers; but it is on this one book that Tocqueville's reputation as a historian rests.

Unlike earlier writers on the revolution of 1789 – Lamartine, MICHELET and Thiers, for example – Tocqueville hoped to produce not a narrative of events but an analysis of French society. He claimed to have written 'without prejudice, but not without passion';

no doubt his feelings were deeply engaged and this gives the book the power to grip the reader, a power which it still holds after 130 years. The material of *Democracy in America* was derived from personal contacts and interviews; *L'Ancien Régime* is based on documentary evidence; but both books show the same flair for drawing convincing general conclusions from a vast accumulation of detailed material. Tocqueville did not start from literary sources but from administrative archives, because he regarded administration as the essential framework of society; he drew on material from both central and local repositories. Finding in Paris few records of the *généralité* of the Ile-de-France of earlier date than 1787, he spent much time in the archives at Tours where he was helped by the interest and co-operation of the curator Grandmaison. He investigated the *terriers* of many private estates and, according to Lefebvre, was the first historian to use the deeds of sale of national property after 1790 as a means of discovering the truth about land ownership before the revolution. He also used the *cahiers de doléance*, or grievance lists, brought by the deputies to the Estates-General of 1789. Only after absorbing these materials did he turn to the work of eighteenth-century writers and commntators. There are no footnotes; such notes as appear at the end of the book are really short explanatory essays on contentious points. But Tocqueville offered to supply detailed references to anyone who required them and no doubt he could have done so: seventeen large bundles of material relating to *L'Ancien Régime* were found among his papers after his death.

Though his focus was always on France, Tocqueville argued that the problems of eighteenth-century France were shared by much of Europe. He used both England and Germany for purposes of comparison and towards the end of his life he was studying the German language and planning extended work in the German archives. This plan remained unfulfilled: Tocqueville died at his home in Normandy in 1859.

Tocqueville's work has stood the test of time though, not surprisingly, modern historians have been able to point out errors and omissions. He assumed that administrative practice was everywhere the same as in those *généralités* which he had closely studied. He failed to appreciate that the eighteenth-century *intendant* was not necessarily or even normally 'a man of humble birth' and that the nobility was closing its ranks and regaining a measure of political importance. Lefebvre accuses him of giving too much space to the nobility and too little to the third estate; within the third estate he concentrates on the peasantry and pays little attention to the bourgeoisie and the artisans. An aristocrat himself, for all his devotion to liberty he had an aristocratic preoccupation with land and with those who lived on and by the land. He is less aware than twentieth-century historians of the Atlantic, as distinct from the European, connections of the French Revolution. It has been suggested that his critique of the old régime is essentially a veiled critique of the equally centralized Second Empire under which he was writing. But his work remains essential reading for serious students and provides a framework of reference for those making detailed studies of different localities in France. His outstanding merits lie in his sense of the continuity of history and his appreciation that causation can seldom, if ever, be attributed to a single factor. And his lapidary style, though a severe test for translators, reminds us that reading history can be a pleasure.   JMT

Main publications

The complete works of Tocqueville, ed. J. P. Mayer, have been published under the auspices of the *Commission Nationale pour l'édition des oeuvres d'Alexis de Tocqueville* (1951 onwards) vol.2 incl. *L'Ancien Régime et la Révolution*, English trans. by Stuart Gilbert, intro. Hugh Brogan, *The Ancien Régime and the Revolution* (London: Fontana, 1966).

Reading

Herr, R.: *Tocqueville and the old Régime* (Princeton, NJ: Princeton University Press, 1962).

Lively, J.: *Social and Political Thought of Alexis de Tocqueville* (Oxford: Clarendon Press, 1962).

Mayer, J.P: *Prophet of the Mass Age* (London: Dent, 1939).

Redier, Antoine: *Comme disait Monsieur de Tocqueville* (Paris: Perrin, 1925).

Tout, Thomas Frederick (b.1855, d.1929) Tout was born in Norwood, London, educated at Southwark Grammar School and Balliol College, Oxford, and was elected to the chair of history and English literature at St David's College, Lampeter, in 1881. He took up his appointment at a time when, following the report of the Royal Commission on Academical Organization, the duties of a professor were becoming more clearly defined. They were threefold: teaching, administration and scholarship. Tout was quick to master all three and in so doing transformed the tiny history department at Lampeter. Success bred success. In 1890 he was elected to the chair of history at Owens College, Manchester, where he found still greater scope for the exercise of his remarkable abilities. On his retirement in 1926 he was the most widely respected professional academic historian in Britain.

Fierce in debate and redoubtable in committee Tout was a natural administrator. He was actively involved in the campaign for an independent University of Manchester. He was instrumental in founding the University Press, and was an influential supporter of women's education in Manchester. But Tout's greatest achievement was the creation in Manchester of a history school of European renown. Under his inspirational leadership the training it gave in the methods of historical research was unequalled in Britain.

Tout served a lengthy scholastic apprenticeship. For almost 30 years he contented himself by reviewing for the *English Historical Review*, contributing articles to the *Dictionary of National Biography* and by displaying his impressive grasp of the outlines of English medieval history in a series of popular school textbooks. But in 1908 after reading Eugène Deprez's *Études de la diplomatique anglaise* he discovered a new sense of direction and began to cut and shape his own research tools and with them to fashion a new interpretation of medieval constitutional history. A more sophisticated and functionalist refinement of the French 'histoire événementielle', Tout's studies of medieval administration exercised the most profound influence on British historiography since Stubbs. Attention was shifted forcibly from monarch and constitution to household, chancery and wardrobe; away from traditional notions of power and authority invested in king and parliament to the day-to-day maintenance of the administrative machinery of government. Tout wrote three major books on this theme: *The Place of the Reign of Edward II in English History* (1914); *France and England: their Relations in the Middle Ages and Now* (1922), in which he stressed the underlying similarity of French and English institutions, and most important, the massive six-volume *Chapters in the Administrative History of Medieval England* (1920–1933). None of the work is pretty, for Tout was neither a finished scholar nor an elegant stylist. But it is solid, accurate and durable, and the *Chapters* remains among the outstanding achievements of English historical scholarship.

Towards the end of his life Tout was pre-eminent among English medieval historians. He was elected fellow of the British Academy in 1911 and president of the Royal Historical Society in 1926.   PRHS

Main publications

The Place of the Reign of Edward II in English History (Manchester: Manchester University Press, 1914); *Chapters in the History of Medieval England, The Wardrobe, the Chamber, and the Great Seals*, 6 vols (Manchester University Press, 1920–33); *The Collected Papers of Thomas Frederick Tout, with a Memoir and Bibliography*, 3 vols (Manchester University Press, 1932).

Reading

Blaas, P. B. M.: *Continuity and Anachronism: Parliamentary and Constitutional Development in Whig Historiography and the Anti-Whig Reaction between 1890 and 1930* (The Hague: Martinus Nijhoff, 1978).

Powicke, F. M.: Memoir. In *The Collected Papers of T. F. Tout* vol. I [see above] pp. 1–24.

Toynbee, Arnold Joseph (b.1889, d.1975) Farming in the Lincolnshire fens was the Toynbee family background, though Arnold's grandfather was a well-known surgeon and his short-lived uncle (of the same name) was a legend in Oxford and in Whitechapel where 'Toynbee Hall' was his monument. The younger Toynbee showed little sign of following the same path; nor did he hint at his future obsession with religion as a guarantor of civi-

lization. At Winchester and Balliol College, Oxford, where he was a contemporary and friend of the brilliant young Pole, Lewis Bernstein NAMIER, Toynbee showed interest in the ancient world for its own sake rather than as the model for a universal pattern of social development. A period as fellow and tutor of Balliol between 1912 and 1915 was brought to an end by the demands of war, and from 1915 until 1919 Toynbee immersed himself in war work of various kinds. In 1919 the task became peace work: he joined the Middle Eastern section of the British delegation to the peace conference at Versailles. This concern with foreign policy set the tone of Toynbee's preoccupations for the rest of his professional life; after briefly holding the Koraes chair in Greek at London University, in 1925 he became director of studies at the Royal Institute of International Affairs, more familiarly known as Chatham House, and held that post for a full thirty years. From this vantage point, rather than from a university chair, Toynbee developed the historical thinking that found expression in his masterwork, *A Study of History*, which appeared in twelve volumes between 1934 and 1961.

In this immensely long career the two world wars played a decisive role: during the first Toynbee discovered civilization; during the second, religion.

Toynbee's realization that civilization was threatened after 1914 raised in his mind the problem of its origins and development. Why did some civilizations thrive and others, seemingly no less advantaged, fail? 'This question was simmering in my mind when, in the summer of 1920, Professor Namier ... placed in my hands Oswald Spengler's *Untergang des Abendlandes*.' Toynbee quickly outgrew his initial fascination with SPENGLER's *Decline of the West* though the names of the two men continue to be linked as both saw the past as a pattern of repeated developments. For Spengler's mechanical and fatalistic model Toynbee substituted one turning on his discovery of 'challenge and response': a theory that explained the origins of a successful civilization by considering the stimulating effects of the problems its society confronted or, in the case of a retarded culture, escaped.

A second axiom, the law of 'withdrawal and return', showed how the élites, whom Toynbee took to be crucial to the process of maintaining and expanding a civilization, imposed their doctrines and then themselves suffered social conditioning before returning all the stronger for their experience to lead their societies into the next phase of development. But, according to Toynbee, eventually the mindless proletariat breaks out from the control of its guiding minority in a catastrophic schism and the civilization dies away.

A Study of History charts the rise and fall of the twenty or so 'cycles' of this process that Toynbee identified in his reading of ancient and modern historical experience. But it does not do so consistently. Volumes I–III (1934) depict the cycles as history *pur et simple*; but after the second world war the cycles are informed by God's purposes. They revolve no longer like catherine wheels but rather like those on a locomotive: 'after all, if a vehicle is to move forward on a course which its driver has set, it must be borne along on wheels that turn monotonously round and round'. The engine for this rolling programme of social advance appears in the *Study of History* as the 'universal church' to which civilizations give rise in the desperation of their fall. Almost all of Toynbee's writing in the later years of his life celebrated and amplified this concept.

Together with his work on the annual *Survey of International Affairs*, Toynbee's writing made a major historiographical statement. No less evidently, his sculptured and contoured vision of the past gave rise to rigorous criticism, most persistently from the distinguished Dutch historian Pieter GEYL. The accusation that Toynbee had squashed historical evidence into categories it would not fit proved difficult to rebut convincingly, and by the time of his death in 1975 none of Toynbee's central contentions was still credible among professional historians.   MB

Main publications

A Study of History, 12 vols (London: Royal Institute of International Affairs, 1934–61); *Survey of International Affairs* (Royal Institute of International Affairs, annually, 1925–46); *Civilization on Trial* (New York: Oxford University Press, 1948); *Greek Historical Thought from Homer to the Age of Heraclius*

(London and Toronto: Dent, 1950); *Some Problems of Greek History* (London and New York: Oxford University Press, 1969); *Acquaintances* (Oxford University Press, 1969); *Experiences* (Oxford University Press, 1969).

Reading

Bebbington, D. W.: *Patterns in History* (Leicester: Leicester University Press, 1979).

Cowling, Maurice: *Religion and Public Doctrine in Modern England*, vol. I (Cambridge: Cambridge University Press, 1980) ch. 2.

Geyl, Pieter: *Debates with Historians* (Glasgow: Collins, 1962).

——: *Encounters in History* (London: Collins, 1963).

Montagu, M. F. A.: *Toynbee and History: critical essays and reviews* (Boston, Mass.: Porter Sargent, 1956).

Treitschke, Heinrich von (b.1834, d.1896) Treitschke, the prophet of German unification, was born in Saxony, the son of a general in the Saxon army. He studied and taught at several German universities before succeeding Ranke as professor of history at the university of Berlin in 1874. The *History of Germany in the Nineteenth Century* traced the German liberal national movement up to 1848 discussing literature, learning and painting as well as politics, and identified Germany with Prussia. Treitschke's contributions to the *Preussische Jahrbücher* of which he was editor from 1866 to 1889 covered much contemporary history. Beginning as a political liberal, claiming extensive rights for the individual against the state, between 1864 and 1874 he came to deny the individual any ultimate rights at all. He believed that only a large state had a complete social life and perfect cultural coherence; that the spirit of the nation, the *Volksgeist*, determined its political structure; that both size and spirit were the inevitable outcome of a historical process. His doctoral dissertation published as *Science of Society* (1859) was on political thought and his university lectures on this subject, publicly attended, made propaganda for the Bismarckian *Reich*. Treitschke, despite his deafness, was a member of the Reichstag from 1871 to 1884.   AR

Main publications

Deutsche Geschichte im neunzehnten Jahrhundert, 5 vols (1879–94); *Historische und politische Aufsätze*, 4

vols (1863–97) [collected essays including 'Die Republik der vereinigten Niederlande', 'Bundesstaat und Rechtsstaat' and 'Unser Reich'].

Reading

Bussmann, W.: *Treitschke, sein Welt- und Geschichtsbild* (Göttingen: Musterschmidt Wissenschaftlicher Verlag, 1952).
Dorpalen, A.: *Heinrich von Treitschke* (New Haven, Conn.: Yale University Press, 1976).

Trevelyan, George Macaulay (b.1876, d.1962) By his own admission, Trevelyan was a traditional historian rather than an innovator. He was close to being a predestined history man. His great-uncle was Macaulay and the *History of England* was written in Wallington Hall, Trevelyan's Northumberland home. His father, Sir George Otto Trevelyan, published a biography of Macaulay and a celebrated early life of Charles James Fox. The traditions of the family were Whig, with a radical tinge.

After Harrow, Trevelyan went to Trinity, Cambridge, the college of his father and great-uncle, which he loved and of which he subsequently became master. He arrived in time to be told by SEELEY, then a dying man, that history was a science and that Macaulay and Carlyle were charlatans. In 1903, BURY, in his inaugural lecture at Cambridge, repeated Seeley's dictum. Trevelyan reacted strongly against these views, and insisted that history, though containing scientific elements, must be presented in decent literary form. For Trevelyan, the attraction of history was largely poetic and its function mainly educative: by poetic he did not mean imaginative, but human, compassionate and emotional. The most sustained exposition of his views was a long essay, 'Clio, a muse', published in 1913, but based on an earlier article, in which he demanded good narrative: 'the idea that histories which are delightful to read must be the work of superficial temperaments, and that a crabbed style betokens a deep thinker or conscientious worker, is the reverse of the truth. What is easy to read has been difficult to write.'

In 1896 Trevelyan gained a first and a dissertation on Lollardy led to his election to a Trinity fellowship. The dissertation was the basis of his first book, *England in the Age of Wycliffe* (1899). Trevelyan saw the period as a critical one in the evolution of religious and political liberty – concerns which demonstrated his Whig pedigree. But his next move was less predictable. In 1903 he left Cambridge for London, partly because he found the historical climate uncongenial; in addition, the release from routine academic duties allowed him to concentrate full-time on writing. His next volume, *England under the Stuarts* (1904) enabled him to revisit Macaulay territory and he began it with a social survey not unlike the famous third chapter. An enormously successful textbook, it ran to more than 20 editions and was still being reprinted in 1977.

Trevelyan first visited Italy in 1895 and, at the time of his wedding in 1904, Bernard Pares gave him Garibaldi's memoirs as a present. It was the trigger needed to set him to work on a remarkable trilogy on Garibaldi and Italy, published between 1907 and 1911. Trevelyan worked at a furious pace and, in best Macaulay tradition, prepared for his task by tramping the Italian peninsula. The volumes established him as one of the best known of British historians.

After the first world war, which he spent with an ambulance unit in Italy, Trevelyan resumed his remarkable output. *Lord Grey of the Reform Bill* (1920) was too indulgent towards that fretful politician to be wholly successful and *Manin and the Venetian Revolution* (1923) did not quite match the Garibaldi volumes. But *British History in the Nineteenth Century* (1922) and a *History of England* (1926) sold splendidly. In 1927, by a pleasant irony, Trevelyan succeeded Bury in the Regius chair of modern history and made a triumphant return to Cambridge. But though the advocates of 'scientific history' were no longer as formidable, there were new historical dangers. In 1929 and 1930, NAMIER published two great volumes, which not only dented the main theme of Trevelyan's Romanes Lectures of 1926 – the continuity of party history – but advocated STRUCTURAL ANALYSIS as an alternative to sterile narrative. In 1931, Herbert BUTTERFIELD brought out *The Whig Interpretation of History*, with its strictures on historians who took sides in history, and though

Butterfield prudently did not identify those historians, it was difficult to find a historian more Whig than Trevelyan. Trevelyan's star began to wane among professional historians who, as Kitson Clark later wrote, felt that he did not address himself to the right questions. Trevelyan himself recognized that he had drifted: 'I am a mere survival' he told his brother in 1939. But against this were enormous compensations. Honours showered upon him. He was awarded the Order of Merit in 1930, became master of Trinity in 1940, and chancellor of the University of Durham in 1950. In 1935 he was invited to write George V's jubilee orations to both houses of parliament and put into the monarch's mouth an impeccably Whig view of British history. With the general public, his popularity remained high. His *England in the Age of Queen Anne*, another trilogy, came out in the early 1930s — 'my best work, except perhaps the Garibaldis', Trevelyan wrote.

Trevelyan's last major book, *English Social History*, published at the end of the second world war, demonstrated the gulf that had opened between his standing in his profession and among the public. His definition of social history as 'history with the politics left out' seemed casual and inadequate, and the review in *History* complained of an 'absence of any satisfactory intellectual construction . . . a lack of analysis'. Others found Trevelyan's outlook too comfortable and nostalgic. But once again Trevelyan caught the popular tide and his success with the general reader was phenomenal, 400,000 copies being sold in five years. Plumb's summary of him as 'a poet at large in history' was kindly, but, at the very least, it can be said that few people can ever have succeeded more completely in the task of bringing history to the people.   JAC

Main publications

(All published by Longmans, London.) *England in the age of Wycliffe* (1899); *Garibaldi's Defence of the Roman Republic* (1907); *Garibaldi and the Thousand* (1909); *Garibaldi and the Making of Italy* (1911); *Clio, a Muse, and other Essays* (1913); *Lord Grey of the Reform Bill* (1920); *Manin and the Venetian Revolution of 1848* (1923); *England under Queen Anne: I, Blenheim* (1930); *England under Queen Anne: II, Ramillies* (1932); *England under Queen Anne: III, The Peace and the Protestant Succession* (1934); *Grey of Fallodon* (1937); *English Social History: a Survey of Six Centuries* (1944).

Reading

Trevelyan, G. M.: *An autobiography and other essays* (London: Longmans, Green, 1949).

Moorman, M.: *G. M. Trevelyan, a memoir* (London: Hamilton, 1980).

Plumb, J. H.: *G. M. Trevelyan*. Vol. 14, *Writers and Their Work* (1951).

Kenyon, J.P.: *The History Men* (London: Weidenfeld & Nicolson, 1983).

Clark, G. Kitson: G. M. Trevelyan as an historian, *Durham University Journal* 55 (1962–3) 1–4.

Trevor-Roper, Hugh Redwald (b.1914) Trained in classics, Trevor-Roper switched to history before spending the second world war in the Intelligence Corps. After more than 30 years teaching at Oxford where he was regius professor of history from 1957 to 1980, he moved to Cambridge to become master of Peterhouse. A conservative in politics, his declared recreations are 'field sports'. He was created Baron Dacre of Glanton in 1979.

Trevor-Roper began his historical career with a biography of Archbishop Laud, but he first made his name with a piece of research done in uniform: the investigation into the circumstances of Hitler's death. Brilliantly written, *The Last Days of Hitler* became a bestseller. Trevor-Roper then returned to the seventeenth century, and became involved, along with — or rather in opposition to — R. H. TAWNEY and Lawrence STONE, in the notorious 'gentry controversy', in which he espoused the view that it was not so much the rise of the gentry as the decline of part of it which best explains the outbreak and the course of the English civil war. Suspicious of professionals and specialists, he prefers to spread himself over what he calls 'some scattered parts of a great subject'. He has tended to concentrate on three areas: early modern Europe, twentieth-century Germany, and the history of historical writing. In all three he has put forward ideas which are original and fertile.

Trevor-Roper appears to enjoy controversy, whether the subject is Hitler's war aims (which he once debated with A. J. P. TAYLOR) or the anatomy of the Elizabethan aristocracy.

419

Indeed, he is often most sparkling, if not most perceptive, when writing about individuals or groups he dislikes – Laud, Hitler, the clergy, the Scots. It is a pity that he has written relatively little on a movement with which he is actually in sympathy, the Enlightenment. It is also to be regretted that he has dissipated his intellectual energies on a variety of themes (the most eccentric, perhaps, being the biography of Backhouse, the 'hermit of Peking') rather than giving us the major study of seventeenth-century European politics and culture of which he is capable.   UPB

Main publications

Archbishop Laud (London: Macmillan, 1940); *The Last Days of Hitler* (Macmillan, 1947); *The Gentry, 1540–1640 Economic History Review* Supplement (Cambridge: Cambridge University Press, 1953); *Religion, the Reformation and Social Change* (Macmillan, 1967); *The European Witch-Craze* (Harmondsworth: Penguin, 1970); *Princes and Artists* (London: Thames & Hudson, 1976); *Renaissance Essays* (London: Secker & Warburg, 1985).

Trotsky, Leon [Lev Davidovich Bronstein] (b.1879, d.1940) Lev Davidovich Bronstein was the son of Ukrainian Jewish farming parents. Like many other Russian revolutionaries, he adopted a pseudonym, Leon Trotsky, by which he became known. Trotsky's secondary education was interrupted by his arrest in 1898 for revolutionary activities and subsequent exile to Siberia. He escaped, and eventually joined Lenin and other Social Democrats in London. For a time chief spokesman for the Mensheviks, he later adopted an independent position between the latter and the Bolsheviks. Returning to Russia in 1905, he became one of the leaders of the first soviet, in St Petersburg. After revolutionary defeat, he was again exiled to Siberia. He escaped to western Europe, editing *Pravda* in Vienna for several years. Trotsky was in the USA when the February Revolution broke out in 1917; he arrived back in Petrograd (St Petersburg) in May and joined the Bolsheviks in the summer. He proved an eloquent and influential party member, becoming chairman of the Petrograd Soviet.

In the Soviet government Trotsky was initially commissar for foreign affairs, concluding the peace negotiations of Brest-Litovsk, then commissar for war — a post he held until 1925. He also founded the Red Army and, with Lenin, was co-founder of the Third International. After Lenin's death and the ensuing power struggle with Stalin, Trotsky was expelled from the party; in 1929 he was deported to Turkey from where he wrote his *History*. He spent his final years of exile in France, Norway and finally Mexico, where he was working on a biography of Stalin when he died at the hands of a Stalinist agent.

Trotsky's historical interests were wide-ranging, a reflection of his commitment as a revolutionary and intellectual to understanding the forces behind political, social and economic change. His chief historical writings may be divided into three broad categories: those concerned with Russia before and during 1917, post-revolutionary Russia and the emergence of Stalinism, and the more recent political and social history of Spain, Germany and China. For Trotsky, the revolutions of 1905 and 1917 grew out of the effects of war on Russia while the notion of 'permanent revolution', perhaps his most important contribution to revolutionary theory, though understating the complexity of history, developed directly from the experiences of 1905. His *History* described and explained the success of Bolshevism in 1917; other works assess its problems. In *The New Course*, Trotsky provided his own analysis of, and solution to, the bureaucratization that he believed had developed during the civil war, while *The Revolution Betrayed* analysed developments in the USSR after Lenin's death, and the causes of Stalinism in particular.

A lucid and colourful writer, Trotsky was serious in his endeavours though not always historically accurate. This can partly be blamed on the shortcomings of study facilities in exile, but it was also due to his tendency to focus on abstractions of historical events rather than on what actually happened. Nothing illustrates this better than his use of analogy in the French Revolution. His observations and perceptions, moreover, are those of a key participant in the revolutionary events analysed within a Marxist perspective, the only possible approach, Trotsky maintained, for comprehending the totality of the Soviet experience.   JCh

Main publications

1905 (1909) English trans. (London: Allen Lane, 1972); *The New Course* (1923) English trans. (Ann Arbor: University of Michigan Press, 1965); *The Permanent Revolution* (1929) English trans. (New York: Pathfinder, 1969); *The Spanish Revolution 1931–39*, Pathfinder, 1972); *The History of the Russian Revolution* (1931) English trans. (London: Gollancz, 1965); *The Revolution Betrayed* (1936) English trans. (Pathfinder, 1972); *Stalin – An Appraisal of the Man and His Influence* (unfinished 1940) English trans. (New York, London: Harper, 1941).

Reading

Beilharz, P.: Trotsky as Historian. *History Workshop Journal* 20 (1986) 36–55.

Deutscher, Isaac: *The Prophet Armed* (1954), *The Prophet Unarmed* (1959), *The Prophet Outcast* (1963); 3 vols (Oxford: Oxford University Press).

Knei-Paz, Baruch: *The Social and Political Thought of Leon Trotsky* (Oxford: Clarendon Press, 1978).

Lubitz, W. ed.: *Trotsky Bibliography* (Munich, New York, London and Paris: K.G. Saur, 1982).

Wolfe, B.D.: Leon Trotsky as Historian. *Slavic Review*. 203 (1961) 495–502.

Turner, Frederick Jackson (b.1861, d.1932) Born in Portage, Wisconsin, the son of a newspaper publisher and minor politician, Turner studied first at the University of Wisconsin and received his doctorate from The Johns Hopkins University (1891). He was a member of the University of Wisconsin faculty from 1885 to 1910, taught at Harvard from 1910 to 1924, and served as senior research associate at the Huntington Library from 1927 until his death. An especially gifted orator, who taught both rhetoric and history for several years, Turner was a remarkably talented teacher whose undergraduate and graduate students responded warmly to his enthusiastic advocacy of history. Turner won friends by the warmth of his personality and captivated his colleagues and students with his extensive knowledge and the novelty of his ideas.

Turner's interests were remarkably broad. He not only initiated research and made important contributions to many fields in American history but also pioneered new methodologies, in particular the use of maps and statistics, and challenged historians of his era to study closely the research done in cognate disciplines and apply it when possible in their own work. His subjects, methods and sources were often so different from those of traditional scholars that some of them questioned whether he should be identified as a historian; but Turner felt that historians should use whatever knowledge and tools were available to them, and he often pleaded with historians to utilize the data and skills of geographers, statisticians, economists, and sociologists. He encouraged his students and colleagues to escape from parochial studies of New England and the Seaboard South and directed their attention to the study of immigration and assimilation, diplomacy, economic history, political behaviour, social and cultural history, and the frontier experience.

Turner's scholarly contribution stemmed from his personal experiences. The fact that he grew up in a recently settled part of the United States made a lasting impression on him. And he was trained by two excellent scholars, William F. Allen at Wisconsin and Herbert Baxter ADAMS at Johns Hopkins, both of whom endorsed the scientific methods of historical investigation then taught in German universities. Adams, a leading figure in American scholarship, propounded the so-called 'germ theory', which stressed continuities and argued that all American institutions derived from the Germanic tribal experience. Turner's dissertation, 'The character and influence of the Indian trade in Wisconsin' (1891) only partly accepted Adams's ideas.

Early in his career Turner developed lasting friendships with Woodrow Wilson, Charles Homer Haskins, Max Farrand, J. Franklin Jameson, and several others, who shared his interest in the professionalization of history as a discipline. They were the beginnings of a network that came to dominate the field, controlling appointments to major institutions, sitting on editorial boards, and working closely together on professional issues. Turner was the most influential of the group not only because he trained the largest number of students but also because his scholarly influence became pervasive.

TURNER, FREDERICK JACKSON

Turner's essay, 'The significance of the frontier in American history' (1893), which rejected the 'germ theory', was a landmark work in American historical scholarship. Within a decade of its publication Turner's thesis that the process of settling the American frontier had made a lasting if not permanent impact on the American character and American society became the cardinal organizing principle of American historical studies. It has remained a subject of controversy. Turner believed that the American historical experience was unique and that it offered a laboratory to study the evolution of a society. Although profoundly influenced by natural science, he accepted multiple causation and was not a determinist. Moreover, he felt that each generation of scholars must reinterpret the past in a contemporary context.

The purpose of history in Turner's view was to reveal how a variety of interacting forces formed a society, an aim which led him to look at American history in a different way. The result was an evocative but less successful idea explained in an essay, 'The significance of the section in American history' (1925), which integrated political and cultural attitudes with geographical units and economic interest groups. The American body politic, he theorized, had found through its unique structure a means of resolving acute problems that in Europe had resulted in wars. This sectionalism thesis never became a serious organized principle in American historical scholarship, but in a modified form it influenced the way that some economists, geographers and political scientists have looked at the past.

Although his work was sharply criticized almost from the start, Turner, his disciples and students dominated teaching and research in American universities until the Great Depression. His ideas enjoyed a renaissance after the second world war, but in modified form. His methodological concerns, especially his search for a means of correlating numerical data, identify him as a forerunner of the new social and political history.

Turner was president of the American Historical Association in 1910 and won a Pulitzer prize for a collection of his essays entitled, *The Significance of Sections in American History*. MR

Main publications

(Published by H. Holt, New York, unless otherwise stated.)
The Rise of the New West (New York: Harper, 1906); *The Frontier in American History* (1920); *The Significance of Sections in American History* (1932); *The United States, 1830–1850: the Nation and its Sections* (1935).

Reading

Billington, R. A.: *The American Frontier Thesis: Attack and Defense* (Washington, DC: American Historical Association, 1971).

——: *Frederick Jackson Turner: Historian, Scholar, Teacher* (New York: Oxford University Press, 1973).

Edward, Everett E.: *The Early Writings of Frederick Jackson Turner* (Madison, Wisconsin: University of Wisconsin Press, 1938).

Hofstadter, Richard: *The Progressive Historians* (New York: Knopf, 1968).

Mattson, Vernon E. and Marion, William E.: *Frederick Jackson Turner: a Reference Guide* (Boston: G. K. Hall, 1985).

Noble, David: *Historians Against History* (Minneapolis: University of Minnesota Press, 1965).

U

Ullmann, Walter (b.1910, d.1983)   Austrian by birth and education, Ullmann was one of the distinguished group of European scholars who moved to Britain during the pre-war years. Most of his career was spent at Cambridge, where he was an outstanding teacher, and his abundant published work covers a wide range of interests. It was centred on canon law, which had previously been little used by British historians even in the study of medieval political theory and government. After the Maitland Memorial Lectures of 1947–8 (published as *Medieval Papalism*) and *The Growth of Papal Government* (1955), it has become impossible to ignore the significance of canon law as a source for ideas and administration. Ullmann's approach was both thorough and learned; it also rested on rigid assumptions about the consistency of papal theory over long periods and about its hierocratic character. His schemata have not been generally accepted by other scholars, and the current work on medieval canon law in North America, while it has learned from Ullmann's methods, displays a quite different theoretical character. Another area in which Ullmann made a major contribution was the study of the early roots of the Renaissance in European thought. He was an influential and benevolent figure in British historical circles generally, professor of medieval history at Cambridge from 1965 to 1978, and a fellow of the British Academy. CM

Main publications

Medieval Papalism: the Political Theories of the Medieval Canonists (London: Methuen, 1949); *The Growth of Papal Government in the Middle Ages* (Methuen, 1955); *Principles of Government and Politics in the Middle Ages* (Methuen, 1961); *The Individual and Society in the Middle Ages* (Baltimore and London: Methuen, 1966).

Reading

Kempf, F.: Die päpstliche Gewalt in der mittelalterlichen Welt, *Miscellanea Historiae Pontificiae* 21 (1959) 117–69.

Barion, H. and Kempf, F.: *Zeitschrift der Savigny-Stiftung für Rechtsgeschichte* 46 (1960) 112–34 and 47 (1961) [development of discussion by Kempf, see above].

Oakley, F.: Celestial hierarchies revisited. *Past and Present* 60 (1973) 3–48.

Tierney, B. and Linehan, P. eds: *Authority and Power: studies on mediaeval law and government presented to Walter Ullmann on his seventieth birthday* (Cambridge: Cambridge University Press, 1980) [incl. bibliography].

Unwin, George (b.1870, d.1925)   The first economic historian of note with a working-class background, Unwin held the first chair of economic history in Britain. He was the eldest of six children of a Stockport railway clerk, left school at 13, and went to work in the offices of a local hat-making firm. He was extremely intelligent and read voraciously. When he was 20, on the advice of an uncle who was a Cardiff schoolmaster, he sat for, and won, a scholarship to the University College there. He studied literature, philosophy and religion for three years before proceeding, on another scholarship, to Lincoln College, Oxford where he read classics for another four. He attained a first but failed to secure a teaching post even as an extramural lecturer. He did, however, win yet another scholarship which enabled him to study economics in

Berlin for six months in 1898. There he became interested in economic history and determined to do some research on the history of hatting when he came home. Sidney and Beatrice Webb provided financial help, first from the funds of the recently established London School of Economics and then by securing for him the post of secretary to Leonard Courtenay, a leading politician, married to one of Beatrice Webb's many sisters. Unwin found himself with spare time to work in the archives of London livery companies and the City Corporation. In September 1900 'A seventeenth century trade union' appeared in the *Economic Journal* and two important books followed: *Industrial Organisation in the Sixteenth and Seventeenth Centuries* (1904) and *The Gilds and Companies of London* (1908). He also contributed a valuable chapter on industries to the *Victoria County History of Suffolk*, vol. II (1907) and on social history to vol. I which appeared four years later in 1911.

In 1908 he was appointed to a lectureship in economic history at Edinburgh University but, never strong physically, he could withstand neither the heavy teaching load nor the Scottish winter. The University of Manchester came to the rescue and created a chair of economic history for him in 1910, establishing, for a considerable time, Manchester's leadership in this field. In a part of the country familiar to him Unwin (in Tawney's words) showed 'to an unusual degree the power of kindling enthusiasm for his subject in those who worked with him'. His remaining two books, *Finance and Trade under Edward III* (1918) and *Samuel Oldknow and the Arkwrights* (1924), were both the fruits of this friendly collaboration between a professor with an unrivalled knowledge of sources and method and keen students who welcomed the opportunity of working with such a master. Of special interest is the last work, the product of a wealth of business records, traced to a disused cotton mill with the help of an enterprising boy scout who had been found distributing eighteenth-century weavers' pay tickets which he had found there. The resulting book, a very early, if not the first, substantial British business history, led historians to begin to revise their ideas about the pace of change during the Industrial Revolution.

Overwork, caused by heavy administrative duties, together with the unhappiness of a pacifist in time of war and intense dislike of state activity growing at the expense of individual and group effort, all eventually undermined Unwin's weak constitution. He died when only in his mid-50s, much admired for his selflessness and his scholarship. It was a great tribute to this 'saint' (Ashton's word for him) that Tawney, whose views on the role of the state differed completely from Unwin's, wrote a memoir which Ashton later described as 'one of the outstanding academic biographies of our time'. TCB

Main publications

Industrial Organisation in the Sixteenth and Seventeenth Centuries (Oxford: Clarendon Press, 1904; repr. London: Cass, 1957); *The Gilds and Companies of London* (London: Methuen, 1908; repr. London: Cass, 1963); *Finance and Trade under Edward III* (Manchester: Manchester University Press, 1918); *Samuel Oldknow and the Arkwrights: the Industrial Revolution at Stockport and Marple* (Manchester: Manchester University Press, 1924).

Reading

Ashton, T. S.: Introductory memoir. In *Industrial Organisation* [Cass reprint, as above].

Tawney, R. H.: Introductory memoir. In *Studies in Economic History: the Collected Papers of George Unwin*, ed. Tawney (London: Macmillan/Royal Economic Society, 1927; repr. London: Cass, 1958) [incl. full bibliography].

urban history The rise of urban history as a recognized academic field has been a development from the 1950s in North America, from the 1960s in Britain and to a lesser extent in western Europe. Growing interest in the field has generated a flood of publications and the appearance of specialist publications such as the American *Journal of Urban History* (1974–) and the British *Urban History Yearbook* (1973–). Institutionalization has also come with the establishment of the British Urban History Group in 1962, the Canadian and Australian Urban History Groups, le Groupe International d'Histoire Urbaine, and urban history centres at Munster, Bordeaux, Winnipeg and Leicester.

To some extent the growth of urban history reflects the general fragmentation of historical studies into a host of specialisms. But the modern subject has an important pre-history. In England there has been a strong tradition of urban antiquarianism since the time of John STOW. From the late eighteenth century until the late Victorian period a spate of books appeared on individual British towns, often written to applaud local achievements. The same tradition contributed to the printing of town records and the establishment of civic record societies. The nineteenth century also saw the emergence, in both Britain and the United States, of another current of urban literature, concerned more with the social and moral problems of major cities. This prepared the way for the Chicago School of urban sociologists, formed in the 1920s and including R. E. Park and E. W. Burgess. Their 'ecological theory of the city' with its emphasis on the social fragmentation and residential segregation caused by large-scale urbanization had widespread influence on geographers and historians. Other writers in the early twentieth century also contributed to the growing debate on the significance of the city in western history: the German sociologist Max WEBER elucidated the communal institutions of the classical and medieval city, the Belgian historian Henri PIRENNE stressed the link between medieval urban growth and the development of long-distance trade, and the American architectural historian Lewis Mumford described the decay of civilization in terms of the rise of the industrial city.

These diverse interests in the city developed into a rigorous scholarly field after the war through the work of a number of key historians. In the United States Eric Lampard, Oscar Handlin and Stephan Thernstrom wrote persuasively on the social and demographic processes of urbanization, principally on the experience of the larger American cities. In Britain Asa BRIGGS and H. J. DYOS were the founding fathers of the study of the modern city. Briggs's splendidly written and widely read *Victorian Cities* (1963) showed the effect of American writing in its concern with the disruptive social and political effects of large-scale urban growth in metropolitan centres

such as Birmingham and Manchester. Dyos's work on London revealed similar preoccupations and had a major impact through his involvement in the British Urban History Group. The ideas of Briggs and Dyos set the parameters for much of the subsequent generation of work by British urban historians. The prime concern has been with the largest urban centres and with the demographic, social and spatial processes of urbanization. Less emphasis has been given (until recently) to political and cultural developments or to urban experience outside the metropolitan centres. A different methodological approach has been evident among British scholars working on early modern and medieval towns. The crucial figure here was the local historian W. G. HOSKINS whose research on Exeter, Leicester and other provincial towns reflected the old tradition of English urban antiquarianism.

Hoskins's concern with the whole network of English towns and their social, economic and political structure had a growing impact on younger historians in the 1960s and led to a major revival of interest in the pre-modern town. Of particular importance in the new generation of work was the 1967 study by Alan Everitt, a colleague of Hoskins, of English market towns in the period 1500–1640.

In western Europe outside Britain urban history has developed more patchily. In France work has concentrated on the leading provincial cities such as Bordeaux, Lyons and Toulouse, reflecting strong regional traditions of historiography. In Germany historians have focused principally on medieval and Reformation cities. In the Low Countries the golden age of urbanization from the late middle ages to the seventeenth century has received most attention. Recent trends suggest however that there is a growing realization in many European countries of the value of a more sustained, wide-ranging and comparative approach to the analysis of urban development and its impact on society.

The advance of urban history has not gone unchallenged, particularly in Britain. A number of historians have questioned whether the study of the city, particularly in the modern period, is a legitimate academic subject. There is concern at the distinctive role and impact of the urban community at a time during the nineteenth century when the urban dimension appears to pervade much of national society. The methodological identity of urban history has also been debated. Though growing numbers of historians, geographers and others have studied the historical development of the city, they have been less willing to learn from each other or to devise a common analytical approach. But despite some growing pains the subject remains vigorously alive, with increasing work on earlier periods, the involvement of a widening circle of disciplines (most notably archaeology) and the growth of international comparative studies in Europe and elsewhere giving a new depth and perspective to research in the field.   PAC

Reading

Briggs, A.: *Victorian Cities* (London: Odhams, 1963).

Clark, P. ed.: *The Early Modern Town* (London: Longman, 1976) ch. 1.

Everitt, A.: 'The Market Town' and 'The Open Market'. In *The Agrarian History of England and Wales*, vol. IV: *1500–1640* (Cambridge: Cambridge University Press, 1967).

Fraser, D. and Sutcliffe, A. eds: *The Pursuit of Urban History* (London: Edward Arnold, 1983).

Martindale, D. and Neuwirth, G. eds: Introduction to M. Weber, *The City* (London: Collier-Macmillan, 1966).

Park, R. E., Burgess, E. W. and McKenzie, R. D.: *The City*; new edn M. Janowitz (Chicago: University of Chicago Press, 1967).

V

Valla, Lorenzo (b.c.1407, d.1457) Born in Rome, where he also died, Valla's reputation as a stylist and as an analyst of style was exemplified in his *Elegantiarum Latinae Linguae* (1471). His other works were examples of polemical philosophy and perhaps revealed his scepticism (it is hard to be sure with works constructed as dialogues). As a historian he is known for his mediocre *Historiarum Ferdinandi regis Aragoniae* (1521), a product of his years in Naples (1435–1448) and his devastating proof of the falsity of the 'Donation of Constantine' (1440). This last was in large measure the product of Aragonese hostility to the papacy, which had relied for centuries on the rights acquired from the so-called Donation. In fact Valla's demonstration was mainly philological, pointing out how the language of the document was anachronistic. His clever and querulous nature was aimed at the pope himself, and as a result his history was not published for a century. DH

Main writings

De falso credito et ementita Constantini donatione (1570) trans. and ed. C. B. Coleman *The Treatise of Lorenzo Valla on the Donation of Constantine* (New Haven, Conn.: Yale University Press, 1922).

Reading

Cochrane, Eric: *Historians and Historiography in the Italian Renaissance* (Chicago, Ill.: University of Chicago Press, 1981).

Varnhagen, Francisco Adolfo de (b.1816, d.1878) Son of a German engineer and his Portuguese wife, Varnhagen was born in Sorocaba (Brazil) and educated at the Royal Military College in Lisbon. He took Brazilian citizenship (1841) and served in the corps of engineers and as secretary to Brazilian legations in Lisbon and Madrid. Resigning his military commission he became ambassador to several South American countries and in 1868 was named Minister Plenipotentiary in Vienna. He was created Baron and Viscount of Porto Seguro (1874).

Varnhagen was a polygraph with studies of Portuguese medieval poetry, Brazilian literature, poetry, ethnology, philology and diplomacy, and wrote a historical novel and historical drama. Known as the 'father of modern Brazilian historical scholarship', his approach was characterized by indefatigable archival research in Europe and Brazil, rigorous methodology, critical scholarship, attention to detail, and the search for historical truth. He was influenced by French and German historical traditions, most notably by Jean Mabillon and Leopold von RANKE. His comprehensive *História Geral* reveals personal support of monarchy, patriotism and nationalism, and emphasizes European contributions to Brazil. Varnhagen's heroic approach does not prevent this being a valuable compendium on the economics, administration, and society of the colony. Obsession with facts and detail precluded a high level of conceptualization and prevented Varnhagen from producing a truly interpretive work of synthesis. He engaged in major polemics, most notably with Abreu e Lima over plagiarism, over the letters of Vespucci, his unsympathetic treatment of the Indian, and an allegedly anti-Jesuit stance. AJRR-W

Main publications

História Geral do Brasil, 2 vols (Madrid: Imprensa da Va de Dominguez, 1854); *História das Lutas com os*

VASARI, GIORGIO

Holandeses no Brasil (History of the struggles with the Dutch in Brazil) (Vienna: C. Finsterbeck, 1871); *História da Independencia do Brasil* (Rio de Janeiro: Imprensa Nacional, 1917).

Reading

Schwartz, Stuart B.: Francisco Adolfo de Varnhagen: diplomat, patriot, historian. *Hispanic American Historical Review* 47.2 (May 1967) 185–202.

Vasari, Giorgio (b.1511, d.1574) Born in Arezzo, Vasari practised as an artist chiefly in Florence and Rome. He was an able architect (responsible for the Uffizi, Florence) and a rather lesser painter of large and speedily executed frescoes. His greatest achievement is as one of the first and most influential historians of art.

In 1550 he published *Le vite de' più eccellenti pittori, scultori, et arcitettori* (*Lives of the Artists*). This was followed by a much revised and enlarged second edition in 1568. In the *Vite* Vasari sought to describe, in three stages, the revival of the visual arts from the time of Cimabue and Giotto in the late thirteenth century, through the progress achieved by Brunelleschi, Donatello, Masaccio and others, to its culmination in Leonardo da Vinci, Raphael and above all Michelangelo.

The *Vite* was based on a tireless accumulation of information collected during Vasari's extensive travels in Italy, his wide artistic contacts and his pioneering use of documentary sources. Though concerned with the causes of the rise and decline of artistic styles, his approach was essentially biographical. His book is enlivened by anecdotal material that has subsequently been criticized for its inaccuracies. Nevertheless Vasari remains our fundamental source for Renaissance art and the basic outline and critical assessments that he presents have remained remarkably lasting.

JGB

Main publications

Le opere di Giorgio Vasari, 9 vols, ed. G. Milanesi (Florence; 1878–85) trans. A. B. Hinds, *The Lives of the Painters, Sculptors and Architects* (London: Dent, 1963).

Reading

Boase, T. S. R.: *Giorgio Vasari: the Man and the Book* (Cambridge, Mass.: Princeton University Press, 1979).

Velleius Paterculus (*b.c.*19 BC, d. after AD 30) Descended from Campanian stock, Velleius began his military career in Thrace and Macedonia and continued it under the generalship of the future emperor Tiberius in Germany in AD 4–6, in Illyricum in 6–9 and then in Germany again until 12. He was designated quaestor in AD 6 and recommended (along with his brother) by Augustus in 14 for the praetorship.

Velleius wrote a two-volume universal history which he dedicated to M. Vinicius, consul in AD 30 (the presumed date of publication). Book 1 was planned to cover early Greek legend and history to Rome's destruction of Carthage in 146 BC but only two fragments (amounting to 18 chapters) survive. Book 2 (amounting to 131 chapters) has survived intact and continues the narrative down to AD 29. 'I know hardly any historical work', said Macaulay, 'of which the scale is so small, and the subject so extensive.' Valleius' compression is indeed uncharacteristic of CLASSICAL HISTORIOGRAPHY in general; but his work, like that of Cornelius NEPOS earlier (the now lost *Chronica*) and that of FLORUS later, belongs to the sub-genre of the historical summary. It is for this reason that he constantly draws attention to his brevity throughout his work.

Yet Velleius' treatment of events naturally becomes more expansive as he nears his own times. Well over half of book 2 is devoted to the emperors Augustus (chs 59–93) and Tiberius (94–131); and his account of the latter is so encomiastic, especially in comparison with those of TACITUS and others, that it has had the effect of discrediting Velleius' work as a whole. Yet his account has intrinsic value by presenting the 'establishment' view of events for which Tacitus, from the safe perspective of the second century AD, supplied an 'opposition' view.

In fact Velleius is the only Latin historian of Roman affairs to have survived from the period between LIVY and Tacitus. He was an active participant in many of the events he describes, and he regularly provides information on topics about which we would otherwise be ignorant. So far from deserving discredit, his is perhaps the most underrated narrative in Roman historiography.

AJW

Main writings

Histoire romaine, text, French trans. and notes by J. Hellegouarc'h, (Paris: Les Belles Lettres, 1982); *The Caesarian and Augustan Narrative*, ed. A. J. Woodman (Cambridge: Cambridge University Press, 1983) [incl. commentary]; *The Tiberian Narrative*, ed. A. J. Woodman (Cambridge University Press, 1977) [incl. commentary].

Reading

Sumner, G. V.: The truth about Velleius Paterculus: prolegomena. *Harvard Studies in Classical Philology* 74 (1970) 257–97.

Woodman, A. J.: Questions of date, genre, and style in Velleius. *Classical Quarterly* 25 (1975) 272–306.

Venturi, Franco (b.1914) Born in Rome, Venturi is the most notable living historian of Italian origin. He went with his father, an art historian, into exile in 1931, and became a student at the Sorbonne, where he wrote a thesis (published in 1940) on D. F. Vasco, a lesser figure of the Italian Enlightenment, and did pioneering work on Diderot (*La Jeunesse de Diderot*, 1939) and the French *Encyclopédie* (*Le origini dell'Enciclopedia*, 1946). During the second world war he was interned by the Fascists, then fought and wrote for the resistance in Italy. As cultural attaché at the Italian embassy in Moscow after the war he had the opportunity to do research on the thought and action of opponents of the Tsarist regime in nineteenth-century Russia. The chief fruit of this work was *Il populismo russo* (1952), translated into English as *Roots of Revolution* (1960), a study of the Russian populists between 1848 and 1881.

Since returning to Italy Venturi has held chairs at Cagliari, Genoa and Turin, and his work has concentrated on the Enlightenment. He has edited and written substantial introductions to volumes 3 (1958), 5 (1962) and 7 (1965) of the series *Illuministi italiani*, in which writings of eighteenth-century Italian reformers are reprinted. He published in 1965 a major edition of the most famous work of the Italian Enlightenment, Cesare Beccaria's *Dei delitti e delle pene* (Crimes and punishments). Since 1959 he has edited the *Rivista storica italiana*, the principal Italian historical journal, and has himself written numerous weighty articles for it. Some of these, with other essays of his, have appeared in English, edited by S. J. Woolf, as *Italy and the Enlightenment* (1972). Venturi gave the Trevelyan lectures at Cambridge in 1969, published in English in 1971 as *Utopia and Reform in the Enlightenment*. He has also written on some great modern historians, especially Jean Jaurès.

Venturi's grandest enterprise is a vast and still incomplete study called *Settecento riformatore* (The reforming eighteenth century). The first volume (1969) deals with Italian reformist thought between the 1730s and the 1760s; the second (1976) with the confrontation between church and state in Catholic Europe between 1758 and 1774; the third (1979) with the first crisis of the *ancien régime* between 1768 and 1776; and the fourth (two parts, both 1984) with its 'fall', down to 1789. The fifth, of which the first part appeared in 1987, returns to the Italian Enlightenment in the period after 1764.

Venturi's work on both nineteenth-century Russia and eighteenth-century Europe has concentrated on reformers, radicals, secularists and revolutionaries, consciously neglecting the conservatives and the clericals; and he has paid particular attention to the republics that survived into the eighteenth century. But, though sympathizing with the Left, he has explicitly rejected Marxist interpretations. Specifically in relation to Russia, he sees the ill-organized and utopian populists as making a constructive contribution to the revolutionary movement. Generally, he believes that in history 'in the last analysis the decisive element is the action and reaction of individuals' (*Settecento riformatore*, vol. 2, p. xii), and he considers the conscious thought of individuals to be of immense historical significance and to develop to a great extent independently of social and material factors. He emphasizes the importance of publications designed to achieve practical results, as against writings notable for their literary and philosophical distinction. His critics accuse him of over-using and over-valuing Italian and progressive writings, and of concentrating too much on the history of thought at the expense of political, diplomatic and economic history. But his ability to study and deploy sources in almost every European language makes his coverage uniquely wide, and his special brand of intellectual history involves an exceptionally broad frame of reference. His work on Russia has won the admiration of western and communist scholars alike; and he has transformed the study of the Enlightenment, both by showing the importance of Italian thinkers and reformers and by making fresh appraisals of rulers and writers, greater and lesser, not only from every European country but also from the rebellious American colonies.   DEDB

Main publications

La Jeunesse de Diderot (Paris: Skira, 1939); *Le origini dell'Enciclopedia* (Rome: Edizioni U 1946); *Il populismo russo* (Turin: Einaudi, 1952); *Roots of Revolution* (London: Weidenfeld & Nicolson, 1960); *Italy and the Enlightenment*, ed. S. J. Woolf (London: Longman, 1972); *Utopia and Reform in the Enlightenment* (Cambridge: Cambridge University Press, 1971); *Settecento riformatore* (vol. 1, 1969, vol. 2, 1976, vol. 3, 1979, vol. 4, 1984, vol. 5, part 1, 1987) (Einaudi, ongoing.)

Vergil, Polydore (b.*c*.1470, d.1555) Vergil arrived in England in 1502 as the deputy to Adriano Castellesi, bishop of Hereford, collector of papal taxes and future cardinal. He had little in the way of taxes to remit but made himself useful in various ways as an intermediary between Englishmen and the papal curia; he was patronized by the new dynasty of the Tudors, managed to keep out of serious political trouble and after other promotions was finally made archdeacon of Wells. When he arrived in 1502 he was already the author of two works destined to be popular: the *Adagia* (1498), eclipsed by Erasmus's collection of proverbs; and the *De inventoribus rerum* (1499), an antiquarian survey of 'first begetters' which was widely read and translated into most European languages. Besides the *De inventoribus rerum* Vergil's most celebrated and influential book was the *Anglica Historia*. The manuscript of this was written in 1512–13 and is now in the Vatican Library. The book was first published as a handsome folio at Basle in 1534. After a chapter describing England and sections dealing with early government, the history then advanced, a book to a reign, to the death of Henry VII (1509), a pattern followed by narrative historians almost

to our own day. Revised in detail this was reprinted in 1546; in 1555 after further revision the author added a further book covering events up to 1538. Other reprints followed until 1603. Intended to appeal to the *literati* of Europe, the *Anglica Historia* remained for long the standard book for continental scholars. No English translation was published until portions of a mid-sixteenth-century version were printed in two volumes of the Camden Series in 1844 and 1846; in 1960 the same series published an edition and translation of the Vatican MS from 1485 to 1513, followed by a text and translation of the 1955 edition covering the period 1513–1537. Vergil's history was contemporary with Thomas More's *Richard III*, and, like it, defended the new Tudor dynasty against its critics. They were both absorbed into Hall's *Chronicle* and so came to influence the historical dramatists, notably Shakespeare. Vergil followed his main texts faithfully, depending on standard accounts such as Matthew Paris and the St Albans chroniclers, the London town chronicles and, where they were relevant, ancient authorities such as Caesar. He also produced an edition of the sixth-century work of Gildas, *De calamitate, excidio et conquestu Britanniae*, to reinforce his sceptical attitude to the Arthurian legend. This came out, probably at Antwerp, in 1525.   DH

Reading

Clough, C. H.: *English Historical Review* 82 (1967) 772–83.
Copenhaver, Brian P.: The historiography of discovery in the Renaissance. *Journal of the Warburg and Courtauld Institutes* 41 (1978), 112–214.
Gabrieli, V.: L'Anglica Historia di Polydoro Vergilio. *La Cultura* 24 (1986), 64–97.
Hay, Denys: *Polydore Vergil: Renaissance Historian and Man of Letters* (Oxford: Oxford University Press, 1952).

Vernadsky, George (b.1887, d.1973) The son of a distinguished Russian scientist, grandson of an influential political economist, Vernadsky was born to the academic purple. Gold medallist at his Moscow gymnasium, he spent some time in Berlin and at the University of Freiburg before entering Moscow University in the autumn of 1906 (where his mentors included KLYUCHEVSKY). As a post-graduate he worked on Russia's colonization of Siberia and Russian freemasonry in the reign of Catherine the Great, and defended his dissertation three days before the Bolshevik takeover in St Petersburg. He then taught modern Russian history at the universities of Perm and Taurida, but soon left Russia for Constantinople, Athens, Prague (1922–7) and, finally, the United States, where he taught at Yale. Like E. H. CARR he became controversial only in middle and old age. His major work, a series of volumes on Russian history from the earliest times to the end of the seventeenth century, lay in a field remote from his early specialisms and appeared between 1943 and 1969. It embodied the doctrine of 'Eurasianism', a creed formulated by a small group of Russian émigrés in the 1920s who held that Russia belonged neither to Europe nor to Asia but constituted a unique entity, 'Eurasia'. The political implications of Eurasianism were reactionary. In order to establish the uniqueness of the proposed geographical unit, advocates of the doctrine had to assign a low priority to the western elements in Russian culture and emphasize the oriental, with the result that they appeared more right-wing even than the Slavophils of the nineteenth century. In his first Eurasianist effusion, written in 1922, Vernadsky presented the entire history of attempts at reuniting the western and eastern churches as as tale of justly resisted Catholic subterfuge. In his major volumes, he assigned far greater importance to Khazars and Mongols than they had received in the work of earlier scholars. He did not carry his *magnum opus* beyond the accession of Peter the Great, but its thrust was hostile to Russia's eighteenth- and nineteenth-century westernization. Vernadsky was too good a scholar to be blinded by his assumptions, and expressed himself more guardedly in the last decades of his life, but he remained true to Eurasianism for 50 years. His autobiographical fragments cover only the years before his departure from Russia and offer no explanation of his subsequent historiographical orientation. It is tempting to say that, in Prague in the 1920s, he came to reject the highly western, intellectual, and even cosmopolitan

environment in which he had been reared, and therefore he turned from the modern Russian history which he had been studying to the medieval period which served his purposes better. Yet at the very time of his most ardent Eurasianism he continued to publish work on the chances of western-style constitutional development in eighteenth- and ninteenth-century Russia. Not a man to wear his heart on his sleeve, he failed to provide enough information for the ambiguities in his outlook to be resolved; but he would certainly have understood the legitimacy of asking questions about historians' motives, for he was the author of a massive (unfinished) survey of Russian historiography.   DBS

Main publications

(Published by Yale University Press, New Haven, Conn., unless otherwise stated.)
Russkoe masonstvo v tsarstvovanie Ekateriny II (Russian Freemasonry in the reign of Catherine II) (Petrograd: 1917); *Gosudarstvennaia ustavnaia gramota rossiiskoi imperii 1820 goda: istoriko-iuridicheskii ocherk* (The Russian empire's state constitutional charter of 1820: an historico-juridical essay) (Prague: 1925); (French trans., *La Charte Constitutionelle de l'Empire Russe de l'an 1820*, Paris: 1933); *Ancient Russia* (1943); *Kievan Russia* (1948); *The Mongols and Russia* (1953); *Russia at the Dawn of the Modern Age* (1959); *The Tsardom of Moscow 1547–1682* (1969); *Russian Historiography: A History* (Belmont, Mass.: Nordland, 1978).

Reading

Halperin, C. J.: George Vernadsky, Eurasianism, the Mongols, and Russia. *Slavic Review* 41 (1982) 477–93.

Riasanovsky, N. V.: The Emergence of Eurasianism. *California Slavic Studies* 4, (1967) 39–72.

Vicens Vives, Jaume (b.1910, d.1960)   From his native Girona, Vicens went to Barcelona University, where he graduated in history in 1930, obtained his doctorate in 1936, and lectured; but after the civil war he was 'exiled' to Andalusia, to teach history in Baeza grammar school. He returned to hold the chair of modern history at Zaragoza University (1947), and then, at Barcelona, those of modern history (1948–60) and economic history (1954–60). Intelligent, handsome, charming, hospitable, he attracted many disciples, young and old, historians and non-historians.

VICO, GIAMBATTISTA

Vicens's work is best understood in terms of the censorship under which most of it was produced, and of the historiographical tradition from which it was descended and against which it was a reaction. Wealthy, nationalistic and with the biggest medieval archives in continental Europe, Catalonia had the strongest historiographical tradition of any region in Spain. This tradition, one of Romantic nationalism, idealized the 'independent', 'democratic' Catalonia of the middle ages, and reviled Ferdinand the Catholic for subjecting it to the despotism of Castile. In his doctoral thesis, on Ferdinand and Barcelona, Vicens showed, with ample documentation, that Ferdinand's reforms had been made in good faith and had in fact benefited the city and all Catalonia; he broke the stranglehold of Romantic nationalism on Catalan historical studies, and made it possible to examine other problems more openly and objectively. He himself followed up his thesis by similar justifications of Ferdinand's policies towards the peasantry, parliament and overseas interests, and by a masterly biography of Ferdinand's father, John II, another bogy of the Romantic nationalist tradition.

That tradition had been discredited, not only methodologically but also politically, by its collapse in the civil war; and Franco's censorship prevented its voice from being heard. There was thus room for a revisionist history which would be well-documented, open to new ideas and ready to remove, especially, the anti-Spanish errors from Catalan historiography, without being either anti-Catalan or pro-Franco.

Vicens was the ideal leader for this new school. A keen traveller, he learned enthusiastically but eclectically from Marxists, demographers, the Annales school and others; and he began to expand into economic history and into Spain's neglected nineteenth century. He wrote on industrialists in politics, assembled a new group of researchers, founded a periodical, *Estudios de Historia Moderna*, to publish their findings and created the first research centre devoted to Spain's modern history. He set up his own publishing house, Teide, which issued numerous good text-books, mainly written by himself and his disciples, and used the profits to publish important works of research; and, perhaps his greatest achievement, he founded the *Indice Histórico Español*, a unique periodical which lists, in theory, every work newly published on Spanish history, together with a brief critical review. Lastly, he wrote brief distillations of his basic ideas about Catalan and Spanish history which show clearly his perspicuity, eclectic methods, powers of synthesis and broad perspective. Had he not died prematurely of cancer, he would undoubtedly have dominated both Spanish historiography and Catalan culture in the sixties and seventies; even now most Catalan historians are his academic descendants, and no historian of Spain anywhere escapes his influence.   DWL

Main publications

Ferran II i la ciutat de Barcelona (1479–1516) 3 vols (Barcelona: University of Barcelona, 1936–37); *Historia de los remensas en el siglo XV* (Barcelona: Consejo Superior de Investigaciones Científicas, 1945); *Aproximación a la historia de España* (University of Barcelona, 1952) English trans. (Berkeley: University of California Press, 1970); *Juan II de Aragón 1398–1479* (Barcelona: Teide, 1953); *Noticia de Cataluña* (Barcelona: Ancora, 1954); *Els Trastàmares (Segle XV)* (Teide, 1955); with M. Llorens, *Industrials i polítics del segle XIX* (Teide, 1959); *Historia económica de España* (Teide, 1959) English trans. (Princeton, N.J: Princeton University Press, 1969).

Reading

Batllori, M.: La doble lección de Jaime Vicens y Vives, 1910–1960. *Razón y Fe* 752 (1960) 261–272.

Galera Cuffi, P.: Bibliografía de Jaime Vicens Vives (1910–1960). *Indice histórico español* 6 (1960) 1–16.

Pinell, J. M. et al.: Homenatge a Jaume Vicens i Vives. *Serra d'Or* II, 11 (1960) 1–23.

Vico, Giambattista (b.1668, d.1744) Vico worked for most of his adult life as a lowly professor of rhetoric at the University of Naples. He had little sympathy for the intellectual fashions of his day, preferring the severe styles of scholarship associated with Roman law and classical literature to methods of study based upon the latest innovations in mathematics and the natural sciences. But though his intellectual predilections seemed quaintly outmoded to his contemporaries, he succeeded in establishing a philosophical foundation for methods and procedures appropriate to the historical and cultural sciences. His *Principi di una scienza nuova* (*New Science*) (first published in 1725) has come to be seen as a landmark in the history of ideas, offering a new conception of the significance of the past.

Vico's views were formed after painstaking criticism of prevalent theories of knowledge. In his early treatises, *De nostri temporis studiorum ratione* (1709) and *De antiquissima Italorum sapientia* (1710), he took Descartes and his school to task for proposing a general approach to different fields of study which could not accommodate the sheer contingency of human affairs. At this stage of his career he had yet to elaborate a clear conception of historical knowledge; but he had recognized the absurdity of disregarding the practical and qualitative judgements which give human life its distinctive character.

It was through studies of law (issued between 1720 and 1722) that Vico came to grasp the importance of setting judgements about the past in a proper frame of reference. Conceptions of law, in his view, had been distorted because of the failure of historians and philosophers to recognize that law itself was but an aspect of a wider culture, intelligible in terms of assumptions which would change in the course of historical development. Without an adequate understanding of the way cultures changed, the original meaning or significance of legal ideas and practices would be shrouded in mystery.

The problem of reconstructing past modes of thought and practice was the centre-piece of Vico's *New Science*. He combined two conceptions which in most discussions of philosophy of history are kept separate: a substantive conception of the past and an analysis of the sources of historical error. In his account of historical judgement, he generalized the insight of his legal studies: misconceptions were attributable to the casual imposition of present assumptions on the relics of distant ways of life. What was required, if anachronistic judgements were to be avoided, was an account of the way cultures assumed a specific guise in relation to different sets of circumstances. Vico argued that certain modes of social life (which he termed 'poetic') were a necessary precondition for the emergence of the attitudes of mind characteristic of developed civilizations. To judge the practices of primitive cultures in terms of the ethos of later (more refined) cultures would be the grossest anachronism. It would not only foreclose the possibility of an historical understanding of remote societies but would also prevent a developed society from penetrating its own past. And since men were the products of their societies, they would be denied the possibility of understanding themselves.

In Vico's account, then, history was cast as the central discipline in the humanities. Philosophical questions about the nature of man had become secondary to the determination of how and why practices had emerged. And though few scholars would find Vico's detailed account of the transformation of cultures persuasive, his approach to the past had conferred fresh significance upon the various kinds of evidence. His conception of the unity of a culture enabled him to treat any artefact from a given period as evidence for the recovery of a particular cast of mind. Narrow etymological exercises, for example, could assume wider importance as epitomes of cultural history; and well documented episodes in a particular society's history could be used as points of reference for the interpretation of artefacts from other societies at a similar stage of development.

Vico's achievement was not restricted to the theory of history. Within the *New Science* he sought to illustrate the implications of his theories by means of substantive exercises in historical reconstruction. His accounts of Homer and Roman law attracted the attention of scholars in his own day who were but little interested in his more general speculations. And prior to the *New Science* he had completed two historical works of note. The first, *Principum neapolitanorum coniurationis anni MDCCI historia* (1702), was a celebration of the suppression of a revolt of nobles at Naples in 1701; the second, *De rebus gestis Antonii Caraphaei* (1716), was a life of a particularly ruthless soldier employed by the Austrians to suppress disorders in Hungary. Both were commissioned works and reflect earlier conventions of historical scholarship (following classical models, using set speeches to emphasize particular issues, aiming rather to celebrate a point of view than to present a balanced account).

But it is as a philosopher of history (see PHILOSOPHY OF HISTORY) that Vico is chiefly remembered. Whatever the shortcomings of his detailed scholarship, he had shown that people's understandings of themselves were directly related to their views of the past. Possession of a historical sense was a distinctive human attribute. Hence recovery of the past served a wider (philosophical) purpose.

BAH

Main publications

(All published by Felice Mosca, Naples, unless otherwise stated.)
De nostri temporis studiorum ratione (1709) trans, *On The Study Methods of our Time* (Indiana: Bobbs-Merrill, 1965); *De antiquissima Italorum sapientia* (On the ancient wisdom of the Italians) (1710); *Il diritto universale* (Universal law) (1720–22); *Principi di una scienza nuova* (1725, important rev. edns 1730 and 1744) trans. *The New Science*, 3rd edn (Ithaca, NY: Cornell University Press, 1984).

Reading

Berlin I.: *Vico and Herder: Two Studies in the History of Ideas* (London: Hogarth, 1976.)
Burke, P.: *Vico* (Oxford: Oxford University Press, 1985).
Nicolini, F.: *Vico storico* (Naples: Morano, 1967).
Pompa, L.: *Vico: A Study of the 'New Science'* (London: Cambridge University Press, 1975).

Villani, Giovanni (b.*c.*1276, d.1348) The best-known Italian medieval chronicler and founder of the Florentine historiographical tradition which culminated in Machiavelli and Guicciardini, Villani brought to the writing of history the experience of an active life in business and politics. A partner and associate of the Peruzzi and Buonaccorsi companies of international bankers, Giovanni travelled extensively to Flanders, Rome and Naples; he settled in Florence from about 1308 where his experience was further enriched by the holding of a succession of public offices. Although he claimed to have experienced a Gibbon-like inspiration during a visit to the Roman Jubilee of 1300, it was not until 1322 that Villani began to keep a continuous record of events which he maintained until he was a victim of the Black Death of 1348. The earlier chapters show signs of having been revised between 1333 and 1341.

The first six books of Villani's chronicle, which have sometimes been taken as an attempt at a universal chronicle, are in fact a skilful weaving together of sacred and secular traditions to establish the historic credentials of Guelph Florence, daughter of imperial Rome, upholder of the church and papacy and faithful ally of the royal house of France. The next two and a half books follow the fortunes of the city as it reached the climax of its medieval prosperity. Because of this and the overlap of themes and incidents with those referred to by Dante, which cannot be due to chance but which have not been satisfactorily explained, this section of the chronicle has been intensively exploited by later scholars, yet, being based on a mixture of inadequate chronicles, personal memory and hearsay, it is the most insecure part of the work. By contrast the last part, from 1322 onwards, where the narrative is detailed and contemporary, has attracted relatively little attention, apart from the celebrated chapters (XI.91–4) in which Villani gives a statistical account of the city and its government.

Villani accepted the typical medieval view that history demonstrated the judgements of God but he was too honest an observer not to see that virtue and vice did not always seem to receive their due deserts. In the latter part of his chronicle he can be seen wrestling with this problem and becoming increasingly critical of the government of his native city with a pessimism which was doubtless accentuated by his own financial ruin following the sudden collapse of the Buonaccorsi bank in 1342. Since it was written in an attractive vernacular and enlivened with incidents of immediate human interest, Villani's chronicle was widely read in Florence and has been essential reading for every historian of the city since his time. His greatest achievement was to direct the attention of his successors towards the search for human as well as supernatural causes for historic events and to show by his example how a chronicle could be used to convey serious and sustained criticism of contemporary politics and society. His brother Matteo's continuation down to 1363 is an important work in its own right.   JKH

Main writings

Cronaca [also *Cronica*, or *Istorie Fiorentine*] several edns incl.: L. A. Muratori: *Rerum Italicarum Scriptores* (1729) vol. 13; G. Antonelli, 8 vols in 4 (Florence: 1823); F. G. Dragomanni, 4 vols (Florence: 1844–5); A. Racheli, 2 vols (Trieste: 1857); selections in *Villani's Chronicle: Being Selections from the First Nine Books of the Chroniche Fiorentine*, 2nd rev. edn, trans. Rose E. Selfe, ed. Philip H. Wicksteed (London: Constable, 1906).

Reading

Green, L.: *Chronicle into History* (Cambridge: Cambridge University Press, 1972) pp. 1–43, 155–169.

Vinogradoff, Paul Gavrilovitch (b.1854, d.1925) After graduating from Moscow in 1875, Vinogradoff went to study in Berlin with MOMMSEN. His first book was on the origins of feudal relations in Lombard Italy. Searching for the foundations of feudal society, he came to London in 1883 to study in England's rich medieval archives. His collection of essays entitled *Villainage in England* shows his wide knowledge of manuscripts in London, Oxford and Cambridge. He is believed to have introduced MAITLAND to the Public Record Office: certainly Maitland dedicated his first book to him in 1884. Maitland learned about more than archives from Vinogradoff; the Russian could tell him also of BRUNNER'S work in Berlin and the international dimensions of legal history. Vinogradoff was above all an internationalist, speaking many languages, tirelessly travelling in Europe and also to America and India. In 1901 he left Moscow, in protest at police pressure in the university, and became professor of jurisprudence at Oxford in 1903. He was knighted in 1917 for his services to Anglo-Russian relations in the war.

During his 20 years and more at Oxford, Vinogradoff promoted research through his professorial seminar run on the Prussian model. His books on *The Growth of the Manor* and *English Society in the 11th Century* were products of the seminar, as were his editions of the survey of Denbigh and the year books of Edward II. As well as aiding their professor's research, the seminar members were encouraged to publish their first monographs in his series of 'Oxford Studies in Social and Legal History' or to edit texts for his British Academy 'Records of Social and Economic History'. In their distinguished names Vinogradoff can be seen to have trained a new generation of medievalists: Cam, Douglas, Jacob, Lennard, Levett, Putnam, Salter and Stenton, among others.   MTC

Main publications

Villainage in England (Oxford: Clarendon Press, 1892); *The Growth of the Manor* (London: Swan Sonnenschein, 1905); *English Society in the 11th Century* (Clarendon Press, 1908); *Roman Law in Medieval Europe* (London: Harper, 1909); editor with F. Morgan, *Survey of the Honour of Denbigh, 1334* (London: Oxford University Press, 1914); editor with L. Ehrlich, *Year Book for Michaelmas 6 Edward II* (London: Selden Society, 34, 1917 and 38, 1921).

Reading

Fisher, H. A. L.: *The Collected Papers of Paul Vinogradoff* (Oxford: Clarendon Press, 1928).

Powicke, F. M.: Sir Paul Vinogradoff. *English Historical Review* 26 (1926) 236–243.

Voltaire, François-Marie Arouet (b.1694, d.1778) Voltaire was the most striking eighteenth-century example of the man who raised himself by his own talent from comparatively humble origins to become the most famous man of letters in Europe, the correspondent of an empress and the guest of a king. A stormy youth saw him twice sent to the Bastille and then exiled to England where he lived from 1726 to 1729. On his return to France he spent several years in the provinces with Mme du Châtelet and then enjoyed a period of semi-favour at the French court, where he was protected by Mme de Pompadour and made historiographer royal. At the invitation of Frederick II he lived at the Prussian court at Potsdam from 1750 to 1753 and then established himself in Switzerland before making his final home at Ferney, just across the French border.

Voltaire displayed to perfection the universality of the *philosophe*. He first established his reputation as a tragedian and epic poet. He introduced the work of Newton to France, wrote many allegorical fables, of which the most famous is *Candide*, contributed to most of the intellectual controversies of his time and towards the end of his life conducted a crusade against religious persecution. In constant contact with like-minded writers, he can almost be regarded as the managing director of the Enlightenment. He also wrote history: biographies of Charles XII of Sweden and Peter the Great and two volumes on the ages of Louis XIV and XV. His most ambitious historical work was his *Essai sur les moeurs*, begun about 1734 but not published until 1751. This was a history of the world from the origins of civilization until the beginning of the period covered by his *Louis XIV*.

Voltaire belonged to the eighteenth-century school of 'philosophical' historians. He was contemptuous of mere erudition and saw no point in historical writing that was not designed to extract from the past lessons for the present. These could be as conventional as the example of good and bad rulers. He himself said that the moral of his *Charles XII* was the futility of wars of conquest: if even his exceptional military genius had done Charles no good, Voltaire hoped that the example would discourage subsequent rulers. This did not prevent Voltaire from devoting the greater part of his *Siècle de Louis XIV* to the military history of the period. Another favourite target was the Christian – or more particularly the Catholic – church as a source of intolerance, persecution and disorder. In the *Essai sur les moeurs* he described Christianity as one of the main causes of the downfall of a Roman empire that 'contained more monks than soldiers'. His general outlook in this work was materialist, in the sense that he ascribed the progress of civilization to the interaction between man and his environment and he saw religion itself, and the different forms of religious practice, as environmentally conditioned. At times this brought him close to MONTESQUIEU but, despite his contempt for historians who merely purveyed information, when he himself turned to biography most of what he wrote was a fairly conventional synthesis of memoirs and the reminiscences of eye-witnesses. To this he appended chapters on administrative, cultural and religious history, without trying to relate these to his political narrative. The fact that he regarded the age of Louis XIV as one of the four great periods of European history (the previous three being the ages of Alexander, Augustus and the Renaissance) suggested that his historical sympathies lay with enlightened autocracy. Despite his admiration for England, Voltaire was no Whig.

No one is likely to read Voltaire's history today for its factual content. His historical works – especially the *Essai sur les moeurs* – are nevertheless fascinating illustrations of the attempt by a mind of exceptional power, supported by an encyclopaedic knowledge of the information available to an eighteenth-century intellectual, to explain man's past in terms of the preconceptions of the period. Voltaire's objective was to entertain and to instruct. If his reasonable guesses have often been invalidated by the research of specialists into more fields than any individual can now hope to encompass in his lifetime, history may have gained in accuracy but it has lost something in breadth and its ability to hold the attention of the intelligent non-historian. NH

Main publications

Charles XII (1731); *Lettres philosophiques* (1734) English trans. *Letters on England* (Harmondsworth: Penguin, 1980); *Essai sur les moeurs et l'esprit des nations* (1751); *Le Siècle de Louis XIV* (1756).

Reading

Brumfitt, J.M.: *Voltaire historian* (London: Oxford University Press, 1958).
Gay, P.: *Voltaire's politics* (Princeton, NJ: Princeton University Press, 1959).

Vovelle, Michel (b.1933) The son of teachers, Vovelle was educated first in Chartres and then Paris, where he attended the lycée Louis-le-Grand and then the École Normale in Saint-Cloud. After graduating in 1958 he taught there until 1965 when he moved to a lectureship at the University of Aix-en-Provence, where he became a professor in 1976. He is now a professor at the Sorbonne and, in succession to Albert Soboul, director of the Institut d'histoire de la révolution française.

Vovelle's first major work, a *thèse d'état*, was an influential study of attitudes towards death in eighteenth-century Provence as traced through the quantitative sources of wills and testaments. A further work on the perception of death through the imagery of altar-pieces widened the scope of this approach to religious sociology. These works describe a change in the procedures relating to death during the eighteenth century, and therefore a change in the conception of death. In spite of such lengthy studies on the subject, he has not given a firm explanation of this change in attitude. He has subsequently enlarged his field of inquiry to encompass other attitudes held by the mass of the population. In parallel with M. Agulhon, Vovelle has worked on popular religion, festivals and sociability — currently an influential concept — and has concentrated not upon the economic infrastructure of society but upon the mainly unconscious ideological superstructure of the common people. Like many contemporary Marxists he has found the concepts of *mentalité* and ideology a stimulating field of research in spite of the rather imprecise definitions given to these terms. During the 1960s and 1970s most of his research was concentrated upon Provence, apart from a book on his native Chartres; the move to Paris has encouraged a wider perspective in his writings, exhibited in his book on death in western Europe from 1300 to the present day (not translated) and an interesting work of synthesis entitled *La Mentalité révolutionnaire* (The revolutionary mentality) (1985).

PRC

Main publications

La Chute de la monarchie, 1787–1792, (Paris: Seuil, 1972) English trans. *The Fall of the French Monarchy, 1787–1792* (Cambridge: Cambridge University Press, 1984); *Piété baroque et déchristianisation en Provence au XVIIIe siècle: les attitudes devant la mort d'après les clauses des testaments* (Paris: Plon, 1973); *Idéologies et mentalités* (Paris: Maspero, 1982); *La mentalité révolutionnaire* (Paris: Éditions Sociales, 1985).

W

Waitz, Georg (b.1813, d.1886) From a merchant family in Schleswig-Holstein, Waitz studied law and history first at his local university in Kiel and then from 1833 in Berlin. Guided by RANKE, his interests soon turned to medieval history. He made a brilliant debut in 1835 with a prize-winning essay on the reign of Henry I, subsequently elaborated in the *Jahrbücher* (1885), and from 1836 worked at the Monumenta Germaniae Historica under PERTZ until 1842 when he became professor at Kiel.

In the following five years appeared the first two volumes of the *Deutsche Verfassungsgeschichte*. Volumes 3–4, on the Frankish kingdom, appeared in 1860–1; volumes 5–8, on the kingdom of Germany to the end of the twelfth century, between 1874 and 1878; and a substantially revised edition of volumes 1–4 was published in 1880–1. In its final form this was a magisterial survey of the political, constitutional and legal history of the Germanic peoples from antiquity to the high middle ages. It served as a model for STUBBS's equally influential *Constitutional History of England*, and like Stubbs's work, can still be read with great profit. It is remarkable for both its firm grasp and clear insights – which have often only been obscured by subsequent scholarship – and for its comprehensive coverage of the sources. It is seldom that the modern historian, confronted with a puzzling passage in a charter or chronicle, will not find a helpful discussion in Waitz, together with references to all the other relevant sources. Though it shares with almost all constitutional history of the nineteenth and early twentieth century a tendency to systematize, in Waitz's own time the criticism of the work was rather that it presented the Germanic polity as having been more fluid and formless than it could possibly have been in reality.

Early in his adult life Waitz formed connections with the Göttingen circle which included Dahlmann and the Grimms, and like them he was a liberal constitutionalist. As such he took part as a delegate from Schleswig-Holstein in the deliberations of the Frankfurt parliament in 1848–9, where he was a prominent member of the Casino party. In 1847 he had accepted a professorship at Göttingen. He remained there for nearly 30 years, and after the Danish annexation of Schleswig-Holstein gradually severed his connections with his homeland. In 1854, however, he published the first two volumes of a projected three-volume history of Schleswig-Holstein, which was followed in 1864 by a short one-volume history intended as a contribution to the debate on the future of the duchy.

Waitz's Göttingen period was one of immense productivity. As late as 1896, ten years after his death, it was estimated that some 30 of his pupils held chairs at German universities, and if numbers alone are to be the criterion, he was probably a more influential teacher even than his own teacher RANKE. His influence spread far beyond the circle of his immediate pupils, however. He was a founding member of the Historische Kommission, a regular contributor to and reviewer in Sybel's *Historische Zeitschrift*, and in 1869 he produced a revised edition of Dahlmann's bibliography of German history, familiar to generations of scholars as 'Dahlmann-Waitz'.

On the death of Georg Heinrich Pertz in

1875 Waitz moved to Berlin as the chief director of the Monumenta Germaniae Historica, to which he brought a new vigour, reviving its journal, *Neues Archiv*, and introducing a series of new and separate editions of the most important narrative sources (*Scriptores Rerum Germanicarum*), much superior to the editions in the folio *Scriptores*.

Unlike his teacher Ranke, Waitz was not a narrative historian; his strength lay in the analysis of details and the ability to relate them to their surroundings. In this he was characteristic of the new type of professional historian that emerged in Germany in the nineteenth century: prolific both in discovering new sources and in interpreting them; an able organizer and teacher; and politically active. He stood above most of his contemporaries, however, in both the range and the quality of his writings.   TAR

Main publications

Deutsche Verfassungsgeschichte, 8 vols (Kiel and Berlin: 1844–78); *Jahrbücher des deutschen Reiches unter König Heinrich I* (Leipzig: Duncker & Humblot, 1863); F. C. Dahlmann, *Quellenkunde der deutschen Geschichte*, 3rd edn. by G. Waitz (Göttingen: Dieterich, 1869); *Gesammelte Abhandlungen* 1 (Göttingen: Dieterich, 1896).

Reading

Bresslau, H.: *Geschichte der Monumenta Germaniae Historica*, (Hanover: Hahn, 1921).

Wallerstein, Immanuel Maurice (b.1930) Receiving his doctorate at Columbia University, Wallerstein has taught at Columbia (1958–71), McGill University (1971–76), and the State University of New York at Binghamton, where in 1976 he was appointed professor of sociology and director of the new Fernand Braudel Center for the study of economies, historical systems and civilizations.

Defining the nation (in *The Road to Independence*) as 'the only complete social system' in the modern world, Wallerstein has inquired into the role of voluntary associations in fostering individuality and new forms of social integration (see SOCIOLOGY AND HISTORY) in Black Africa. But under the impact of the university upheavals of the 1960s, he turned to a new macro-unit of analysis, world-economy (from Fernand BRAUDEL's *économie-monde*,

derived in turn from German *Weltwirtschaft*). Borrowing also from Latin American dependency theory, founded in part on German conceptions of territoriality, he identified three kinds of world-systems: world-empires, world-economies, and mini-systems of food gatherers and hunters.

World-empires, Wallerstein affirms, operate as political units on principles of redistribution. World-economies function as an abstract market but in the framework of rival political states. Rejecting the ideas of mixed economy and orthodox dependency theory (dual economy), Wallerstein believes that every world-system has but one mode of production. Since the sixteenth century and even more since the mid-eighteenth century, moreover, there has been only one world-economy, namely, capitalism. Capitalism functions however as a tripartite territorial system: a core or politically and economically dominant state; a group of peripheral states that divert local resources to world-economic needs; and a group of semi-peripheral states that thwart polarization by associating for some purposes with the core and for others with the periphery.   TS

Main publications

The Road to Independence: Ghana and the Ivory Coast (Paris, The Hague: Mouton, 1964); *The Modern World-System*, vols. 1 & 2 (New York: Academic Press, 1974–80); *The Capitalist World-Economy: Essays* (Cambridge: Cambridge University Press; Paris: Éditions de la Maison des sciences de l'homme, 1979); Braudel, le '*Annales*' e la storiografia contemporanea. *Studi storici* 21 (January–March 1980) 5–17.

Walpole, Horace (b. 1717, d. 1797) Walpole's *Memoirs* of the reigns of George II and George III represent contemporary history written by an active participant. They are not impartial, but they do not claim impartiality. He wrote in his *Memoirs of the Reign of George II* (1985 edn, II 2), 'I am no historian, I write casual memoirs; I draw characters; I preserve anecdotes, which my superiors the historians of Britain may enchase into their weighty annals or pass over at their pleasure.'

Horace was the fourth son of Robert Walpole, who was to become the first Earl of Orford.

WALTER OF GUISBOROUGH

He did not enter public life until the last years of his father's Premiership. After his father's death Horace became devoted to his father's memory, defending it against all criticism, and looking at many of his contemporaries in the light of their supposed attitudes to his father. He played a minor part in the political manoeuvrings of the 1740s and 1750s, secretly engaging in opposition journalism without ever allowing himself any public commitment. His nearest approaches to direct involvement were attempts to influence events through more significant politicians. When these failed he would become disillusioned, often enough underlining his new opinions with unflattering sketches of former associates. Always a prominent member of 'Society' and of the literary world, he increasingly concentrated on his antiquities, his private printing press, and the pursuit of the 'Gothick' into architecture and literature.

Walpole's analysis of the contemporary scene is demonstrated in part through the voluminous correspondence in which he engaged, choosing carefully the recipients of his letters on a wide variety of subjects, and in part through the *Memoirs* which increasingly represented his particular interpretation of contemporary events. The belief that the wicked minister (Bute) had allied with the designing Princess Dowager in order to distort the British constitution runs through his *Memoirs* even though it does not appear in his letters. The publication of his *Memoirs* in the early nineteenth century led to his views becoming almost uncritically accepted by many of the historians who followed him and thus becoming part of the tradition of British historiography.

The sinecures bestowed on Horace by his father allowed him a financial independence and the illusion of impartiality. But he was always dependent on his political contacts, and when these failed him the result was that his narrative lacked credibility. None the less without his *Memoirs* it would be very difficult, if not almost impossible, to write the history of the second half of the eighteenth century.   AN

Main publications

Correspondence of Horace Walpole, reconstructed and repr. by W. S. Lewis (New Haven, Conn.: Yale University Press); the only recommended edition of his *Memoirs of the Reign of George II* is ed. John Brooke [who had intended to re-edit the other volumes].

Reading

Brooke, John: Introduction. In *Memoirs of the Reign of George II* by H. Walpole.

—: Biography. In *The History of Parliament, 1754–1790* by H. Walpole.

Sedgwick, Romney: Biography. In *The History of Parliament, 1715–1754* by H. Walpole.

Smith, W. H. ed.: *Horace Walpole: Writer, Politician, and Connoisseur* (New Haven, Conn.: Yale University Press, 1967).

Walter of Guisborough (*fl.* 1300) An Augustinian monk, Walter wrote his chronicle between 1301 and 1312. For the period from the 1280s he is a valuable original source for Edward I's wars, especially in Scotland. Guisborough priory is in north Yorkshire and Walter writes as a partisan of the English, giving lively accounts, with dramatized dialogue, of battles such as that at Stirling Bridge in 1297. Before Rothwell's edition of 1957, Walter was known as 'Walter of Hemingburgh', or 'Hemingford', or 'Gisburn'.   MTC

Main writings

The Chronicle of Walter of Guisborough, ed. H. Rothwell (London: Camden Society, 3rd ser. 89, 1957).

Reading

Gransden, A.: *Historical Writing in England*, vol. 1 (London: Routledge, 1974).

war, historiography of Historical writing on war has been marked more by its quantity than its quality. Military history today enjoys a popular market which few, if any, other areas of historical inquiry can match, and in the past generals have been as ready as politicians to write their memoirs. The best of both genres deserves the respect of the academic: writers in military history such as Correlli Barnett, Georges Blond, Max Hastings, Walter Millis, and John Terraine have succeeded in being both stimulating and provocative, and have done much to bridge the divide between the researcher and the 'intelligent general reader'. But most books on the subject are repetitive, self-justificatory and frequently militaristic, setting out to glorify war rather than to illuminate it.

The dominant motive in the more serious writing on the history of war has been didactic. Soldiers have tried to establish clearly defined principles of war, which are constant through time and whose validity can be proved by illustrations from history. Needless to say much of this writing is selective and self-serving. But without the didactic use of military history there would have been little of quality published in the field before 1945. The growth and development of military history is therefore closely linked to the growth and development of professional armies: the former provided the latter with instruction and with a sense of continuity and self-regard.

In the eighteenth century, classical authors — XENOPHON, CAESAR, and Vegetius — formed the backbone of professional reading. The first modern campaigns to attract serious attention were those of Frederick the Great: participants who left accounts included Archenholtz, Lloyd, Tempelhoff, and Warnery; while others, such as Guibert, used Frederick's campaigns as the vehicles for their own ideas. But it was Napoleon who marked the real arrival of military history for didactic purposes, and whose achievements attracted the greatest efforts of synthesis and analysis before 1914. Pre-eminent among his interpreters was A. H. Jomini, whose writings on the conduct of war became required reading in the burgeoning military academies of Europe. Jomini, a self-important and ambitious Swiss who served on Ney's staff, eventually settled in Russia, and died in 1869. His desire to rationalize Napoleon's achievements and to instruct his readers — though resulting in misrepresentation — should not be allowed to swamp the scale of his contribution to military history: his accounts of the wars of Frederick and of Napoleon are still required reading. Most military writing in Europe in the nineteenth century was caught in Jomini's thrall; and notable among his imitators was William NAPIER whose six volumes on the Peninsular War (1828–40), despite their polemicism, are the foundation-stone of British military history. Very different, more demanding and less popular in his approach to

the understanding of Napoleon was Carl von Clausewitz (1780–1831). Clausewitz's best-known work, *On War* (1832), is a theoretical study, but Clausewitz — like his mentor Scharnhorst — was also a military historian. For military history was, in Clausewitz's view, the key to the development of the soldier's judgement. It had to be accurate history, not a version which discarded facts that failed to fit the pattern suggested by prescriptive theory. History that was honest and put events in their proper contexts would enable the student to see how things actually happened: theory should be the means of subsequently criticizing and clarifying those events.

During the second half of the nineteenth century the institutional developments in armies, the establishment of staff colleges and the emergence of general staffs, continued to be the main impetus to the writing of military history. Historical branches of the general staff, pioneered in Germany, attracted able men, and their industry produced works of great detail and scholarship. As serving officers they could not avoid some national and service biases, but in France, for example, the work of Jean Colin came closer to the essence of Napoleonic warfare than anything published hitherto. In the United States A. T. MAHAN, a serving naval officer and the son of an instructor at West Point, applied a Jominian approach to British naval supremacy in the eighteenth and early nineteenth centuries. His doctrinal commitments to the ideas of sea power, capital ships and fleet action, affected his historical judgement, but he became president of the American Historical Association and his writings influenced policy makers before 1914 and are still read by historians today. The two world wars of the twentieth century marked the arrival of 'official history': again, whatever the institutional biases in their writing, the scale of these undertakings and their grounding in primary sources will ensure their continued importance. Furthermore, official history has increasingly become the domain of academic historians, and not of serving officers: that of West Germany for the second world war has been in the hands of the *Militärgeschichtliche Forschungsamt*, a research institute staffed by professional historians. It has, therefore, less of the didactic tone which marked the general staff histories of the nineteenth century. But the spirit of Jomini lives on: J. F. C. Fuller and Basil Liddell Hart are two military theorists of this century who have unashamedly used military history to advance their own arguments.

The more purely academic study of military history has suffered from a Whig or liberal approach which has seen war as an aberration in human affairs. Distinguished political historians such as Leopold von RANKE, Archibald ALISON and Otto HINTZE discussed war, but as an adjunct to political history. However, their approach did at least enable Clausewitz, with his emphasis on war as a political instrument, to act as a bridge between academic history and the more self-contained and teleological professional study of campaigns. The most outstanding exponent of Clausewitz's approach was Hans Delbrück, whose *Geschichte der Kriegskunst im Rahmen der politischen Geschichte* (4 vols, 1900–20), fully lives up to its title, and is still a major work in the field. Delbrück wrote primarily for historians, and only incidentally for soldiers, but − although an academic − he never received the recognition his scholarship deserved, for not until the nuclear age did it become relatively respectable to study modern military history within the confines of a university. After 1945 war was self-evidently too important to be omitted from any study of the modern world, and the outstanding military historians since then, Gordon Craig, Werner Hahlweg, Michael Howard, Peter Paret and Gerhard Ritter, have been Clausewitzian in their wish to see armies and war in a political context. Obviously, too, military history has benefited from the postwar expansion in higher education, and from the concomitant proliferation of subjects. Much recent research, like that of André Corvisier, has been concerned not with the conduct of war but with armies as institutions, their social composition and their role in society: here the findings of sociologists (especially Morris Janowitz) and of political scientists (for example Samuel P. Huntington) have informed the questions set by a new generation of researchers. Characteristic of this eclectic approach is the provocative opening chapter of John Keegan's *The Face of Battle* (1976), which sets an agenda for an entirely

new range of writing, looking at the individual soldier and his response to the ordeals of combat.   HFAS

Reading

Bucholz, Arden: *Hans Delbrück and the German Military Establishment: War Images in Conflict* (Iowa: University of Iowa Press, 1985).

Howard, Michael: Military history as a university study. *History* 41 (1956) 184–91.

Howard, Michael: The use and abuse of military history. In *The Causes of Wars* (London: Temple Smith, 1961; repr. 1983).

Jessup, John E. and Coakley, Robert W.: *A Guide to the Study and Use of Military History* (Washington: Center of Military History, United States Army, 1979).

Paret, Peter: The history of war. *Daedalus* 100 (1971) 376–96.

——: *Clausewitz and the State* (Oxford: Clarendon Press, 1976).

——: *Makers of Modern Strategy from Machiavelli to the Nuclear Age* (Oxford: Clarendon Press, 1986).

Skaggs, David Curtis: Michael Howard and the dimensions of military history. *Military Affairs* 49 (1985) 179–83.

Wattenbach, Wilhelm (b.1819, d.1897)   Like his slightly older contemporary WAITZ, with whom he was closely associated, Wattenbach was born in Schleswig-Holstein and studied from 1837 in Bonn, Göttingen and Berlin. Wattenbach succeeded Waitz as editor of the Monumenta Germaniae Historica, and in the following years produced a number of major editions, including one of the chronicle of Monte Cassino and a full edition of the complexly interrelated Austrian annals. Though Wattenbach had habilitated himself in 1851 it was not until 1862 that he was appointed to a chair, at Heidelberg.

From 1855 to 1862 he was archivist at Breslau, and here, besides contributing to the edition of Silesian charters then getting under way, he produced in 1858 his survey of the sources for German medieval history, which went through six revisions in his lifetime and, greatly revised and expanded by subsequent generations of scholars, is still the standard work of reference on the subject. During this period he continued to edit for the Monumenta, and indeed a substantial proportion of the first 20 folio volumes of the *Scriptores*, the narrative sources for the history of medieval Germany, were edited by him. His other major work, a study of script and scribes in the middle ages, appeared in 1871. From 1872 he was professor for the auxiliary historical sciences (meaning in his case largely palaeography) in Berlin, and from 1875 he was a member of the Zentraldirektion of the Monumenta Germaniae Historica, and edited the society's journal. On Waitz's death in 1886 he might reasonably have expected to succeed him as president, but he evidently had enemies who were able to use the Prussian government's desire for firmer control over the Monumenta to block his appointment. In consequence he largely severed his ties with the institution, after having worked in and for it for 40 years. The disappointment seems to have affected him deeply, as his once prolific output (largely in the form of short studies and editions of hitherto unknown sources) declined substantially in the last decade of his life. His last major contribution to scholarship was to produce in collaboration with Loewenfeld, Ewald and Kaltenbrunner a revised and greatly expanded edition of Jaffe's papal regesta, which appeared in 1885–8.   TAR

Main publications

Das Schriftwesen im Mittelalter (Leipzig: Hirzel, 1871); *Deutschlands Geschichtsquellen im Mittelalter*, 2 vols, 6th edn, (Berlin: Hertz, 1893–4).

Reading

Bresslau, H.: *Geschichte der Monumenta Germaniae Historica* (Hanover: Hahn, 1921).

Dümmler, E.: Wilhelm Wattenbach. *Neues Archiv der Gesellschaft für ältere deutsche Geschichtskunde* 23 (1898) 569–75.

Webb, Sidney (b.1859, d.1947) and **Beatrice** (b.1858, d.1943) The Webbs married in 1892 and for their honeymoon went to Glasgow and Dublin to research into the records of early trade unions. So began the famous partnership. All their lives they engaged in Fabian socialist education and propaganda, sometimes in practical affairs as with Sidney's long association with the educational activity of the London County Council, through the work and publications of the Fabian Society, or with their own voluminous output of historical and political writing.

The Webbs were pioneers in a wide range of British social and administrative history. Their *History of Trade Unionism* (1894) which was followed by the two volumes of *Industrial Democracy* (1897) represented a remarkable body of original research whose interpretation has continued to influence successive generations; and their monumental history of local government from 1688, in nine volumes, was a scholarly achievement of high order.

In their early years the Webbs were consciously anti-Marxist, although they themselves worked within a framework of clearly defined assumptions. The 'inevitability of gradualness' – the core of the Fabian philosophy – was based on the understanding that the continued extension of political democracy could not be halted; and that such extension would bring about the social and economic changes for which the Fabian society constantly provided the blueprints. All their contemporary political arguments were encapsulated within a historical perspective, the most illuminating example being their massive documentation for the Poor Law Commission of 1905–9.

The many historical works the Webbs produced have dated, but a substantial number remain as classics indispensable to the research worker. Only the large-scale study of Soviet communism, written in the last decade of their lives, must be judged separately from the main corpus of their writing. Beatrice Webb produced two volumes of autobiography and a diary, now published in full, which will remain essential reading for the student of her period. Their collaboration was a remarkable exercise in personal and intellectual harmony.   JS

Main publications

(All published by Longmans, Green, London, unless otherwise stated.)
Webb, S. and B.: *English Local Government from the Revolution to the Municipal Corporations Act*, 9 vols (1906–29); Webb, B.: *My Apprenticeship* (1926); *Our Partnership*, ed. B. Drake and M. I. Cole (1948); *The Diary of Beatrice Webb*, 4 vols, ed. N and J. Mackenzie, (London: Virago, 1982–5).

Reading

Bellamy, J. M. and Saville, J. eds: *Dictionary of Labour Biography*, vol. 2 (London: Macmillan, 1974) [incl. bibliography, pp. 389–96].

McBriar, A. M.: *Fabian Socialism and English Politics 1884–1918* (Cambridge: Cambridge University Press, 1962).

WEBB, WALTER PRESCOTT

Tawney, R. H.: *Memoir: Beatrice Webb.* Proceedings of the British Academy, 29 (1945) 285–311.

Webb, Walter Prescott (b.1888, d.1963) Webb was born in east Texas but brought up in west Texas. As one consequence his life and work reflected southern and western influences. He believed that history could be an instrument for social change, that it showed that west and south had both been victims of northern interests, and that he should use the writing of history to help redress the balance. He attempted this most notably in *Divided We Stand* (1937), written in haste and anger as a protest against the Supreme Court's decisions on the National Industrial Recovery Act (NIRA) and Agricultural Adjustment Act (AAA). Though both his wife and daughter belonged to the United Daughters of the Confederacy, Webb tried to persuade the south to forget racial politics and concentrate on economic growth. Towards the end of his life he became worried about the effects of rising population and increasing exploitation on the west.

Webb is mainly remembered as a historian of the west, in particular for his successful broadening of the 'Frontier Thesis' of Frederick Jackson TURNER, especially in *The Great Frontier* (1952), where he extended it to explain the effects of European expansion globally. He also showed concern at what would happen to democracy and capitalism with what he took to be the closing of the global frontier. RAB

Main publications

The Great Plains (Boston: Ginn and Company, 1931); *The Texas Rangers* (Boston, Mass.: Houghton Mifflin, 1935); *Divided We Stand* (New York: Farrar & Rinehart, 1937); *The Great Frontier* (Houghton Mifflin, 1952).

Reading

Frantz, Joe B. et al.: *The Walter Prescott Webb Memorial Lectures: Essays on Walter Prescott Webb* (Austin: University of Texas Press, 1976).

Weber, Max (b. 1864, d. 1920) Probably the most influential social scientist of the century, advocate of a distinctive method of social and historical analysis, Weber's expertise encompassed law, economics, politics, history, sociology, and philosophy. Educated at the universities of Heidelberg and Berlin, he was awarded a chair at Heidelberg in 1896 and spent most of his academic life there. His political ambitions – he was a nationalist, but opposed to the Kaiser and the Junker class – surfaced at the end of the first world war, but remained unfulfilled.

Weber's earlier work, culminating in *The Protestant Ethic and the Spirit of Capitalism*, published in two articles in 1904–5, examined particular aspects of specific historical processes and periods; with the magisterial *Agrarian Sociology of Ancient Civilisations* of 1909, a greater interest in an elaboration of comparative sociological concepts is evident. In 1909 he began the work with which he was to be occupied, on and off, for much of the rest of his life: *Economy and Society*, a compendious manifesto for, and example of, the historically-based sociology that had become his core concern. However, at all stages Weber's work reveals his central preoccupations: the development of a method appropriate to the study of the uniqueness of historical processes, through the elaboration of concepts that are necessarily comparative and theoretical; and a presentation of these historical processes as involving competing groups struggling for supremacy in ways that simultaneously involve political domination, economic interests, and religious values.

These themes came together in his studies of the distinctiveness of Western capitalism and the world order to which it has given rise, and his claims here reveal an interesting tension between Weber's explicit approach to history and his drive for theoretical systematization: his rejection of the very possibility of any teleological philosophy of history seems radical and complete, yet the development of modernity itself is presented as a remorseless, dynamic process whereby the rational mastery of the world becomes an 'iron cage' of subjection to that very process.

Weber took a distinct stance in the methodological and historiographical controversies that split the German academic establishment of the time. He argued that history is nothing if it is not scientific, but the influence of the neo-Kantians and their stress on the distinctive problems of cultural analysis is very strong in his work: Rickert's advocacy of the use of models in historical analysis, models that are elaborated in the light of the historian's values, is reflected in Weber's development of the concept of the ideal type; and the emphasis in DILTHEY on the need for *verstehen* ('understanding') influenced Weber's claim that the viewpoint of the typical actor in his distinctive cultural context is the starting point for historical interpretation, even though the aim may be to embody this understanding in a study of the causation of complex historical processes.

In the *Protestant Ethic*, then, we find the claim that the religious dilemmas of obscure puritan divines, and the way these were translated into everyday action, turn out to have been centrally implicated in the causation of Western capitalism and its transformation of the world; and this is not because this outcome bears any relation to their original intentions, or because of the general importance of 'ideas' in history, but because the social practices in which these religious values were embedded proved, in that political and economic context, to be essential stimulants of the motivational patterns that contributed to the 'work ethic' in the period of early capital accumulation.

'Ideal types' are intended to be coherent 'accentuations' of aspects of reality that enable the historian to define his topic of investigation, in the light of his own values and interests, thereby being able to clarify and systematize the goals of his investigation. They can never grasp the 'essence of history', for there is none; there is no History, only histories, but these are not lacking in order and coherence, so long as we realize that these relate inescapably to the interests that lead us to lend significance to some phenomena and ignore others.

The success of Weber's attempt to develop a coherent strategy for historical analysis that is irreducible to either positivist or idealist presuppositions, while clearly influenced by them, remains a matter for debate. But perhaps, in the end, it is Weber's stress on the inseparability of history and sociology that may prove most fruitful: for Weber, sociology is essentially a higher-level, theoretically informed history, and history can only exist through the self-conscious use of comparative concepts that are inherently sociological. So Weber's lasting legacy − and challenge − to history and sociology may well be the denial that they can exist separately at all. JJ

Main publications

Die protestantische Ethik und der Geist des Kapitalismus, *Archiv für Sozialwissenschaft und Sozialpolitik* (1904−5), trans. *The Protestant Ethic and the Spirit of Capitalism* (New York: Charles Scribner, 1958); Agrarverhältnisse im Altertum. *Handwörterbuch der Staatswissenschaften*, 1 (1909) 52−188, trans. *The Agrarian Sociology of Ancient Civilisations* (London: New Left Books, 1976); *Wirtschaftsgeschichte* (München: Duncker & Humblot, 1923), trans. *General Economic History* (London and New York: Allen & Unwin, 1927); *Gesammelte Aufsätze zur Wissenschaftslehre* (Tübingen: J. C. B. Mohr, 1951), trans. [incomplete] *The Methodology of the Social Sciences* (Glencoe, Ill.: The Free Press, 1949); *Wirtschaft und Gesellschaft* (Tübingen: J. C. B. Mohr, 1956), trans. *Economy and Society* (Berkeley, Calif.: University of California Press, 1978).

Reading

Bendix, R.: *Max Weber* (Garden City, New York: Doubleday, 1962).
Freund, J.: *The Sociology of Max Weber* (Harmondsworth, Middlesex: Allen Lane, 1968).
Marshall, G.: *In Search of the Spirit of Capitalism* (London: Hutchinson, 1982).
Parkin, F.: *Max Weber* (Chichester and London: Ellis Horwood and Tavistock, 1982).

Wedgwood, (Cicely) Veronica (b.1910) After reading modern history at Oxford, Wedgwood pursued a productive career without holding a university appointment, though she was awarded many honorary degrees and was an honorary lecturer at University College London. Her first book, a rather idealized life of Strafford (1935; 'revaluated' 1961), initiated an abiding interest in biography and in the early Stuarts. Her studies of the early Stuarts culminated in her (unfinished) trilogy, *The Great Rebellion*, surveying the events as they unfolded without the benefit or disadvantage of the after-comment on their consequences. Her second book, *The Thirty Years War* (1938), which she interpreted as 'a meaningless conflict', revealed concern for early modern Europe. It was followed by biographies of William the Silent (1944) and Richelieu (1949). Elegant and undogmatic, history as a 'velvet study', as pleasing as edifying, her work has appealed to professional historians and lay readers alike. Her most recent work, *The Spoils of Time* (1984), a world history to 1550, is uncharacteristic. IAR

Main publications

The Thirty Years War (London: Jonathan Cape, 1938); *The Great Rebellion*, vol. I: *The King's Peace 1637–1641*, vol 2: *The King's War 1641–1647* (London: Collins, 1955, 1958); *The Trial of Charles I* (London: Collins, 1964).

Reading

Ollard, R. and Tudor-Craig, P. eds: *For Veronica Wedgwood These: Studies in Seventeenth Century History* (London: Collins, 1986) [a festschrift].
Richardson, R. C.: *The Debate on the English Revolution* (London: Methuen, 1977), pp. 127–9.

Wells, Herbert George (b.1866, d.1946) His father's china shop in Bromley supplied the first of Wells's many false starts (as draper's apprentice, chemist, schoolteacher) before he found his métier as a popularizer of science. His brief studies under T. H. Huxley left him with an exaggerated belief in his capacity to identify great historical processes, which found some expression in his scientific extravaganzas such as *The Time Machine* (1895) and *Anticipations* (1901). But he was not a historian before 1918 and not much of one thereafter. His total historical output amounted to *The Outline of History* (1920) and *The Short History of the World* (1922) into which it grew (see WORLD HISTORY). Yet between them these sold millions of copies, and many among the generation of A. J. P. Taylor looked back on them, as he did, with affection. Wells had a conception of the past precisely because he had an image of the future. It was the point of his history to reveal the future that the Great War had implied, 'the great peace to which all history seems to be pointing'. But in fact Wells failed to create a genuine *Weltgeschichte*: his treatment of extra-European history remained cursory, and encyclopaedias constituted his central source. The merit of his books lay simply in their verve and clarity. 'I have a brain good for outlines,' he wrote in his autobiography; that talent best commends his history. MB

Main publications

The Outline of History (1919–20); *The Short History of the World* (1922; Harmondsworth: Penguin, 1970).

Reading

Cowling, Maurice: *Religion and Public Doctrine in Modern England*, vol. 2 (Cambridge, Cambridge University Press, 1985).
Wells, H. G.: *Experiment in Autobiography*, 2 vols (1934; new edn, London Faber & Faber, 1984).
West, Anthony: *H. G. Wells* (London: Hutchinson, 1984).

Welsh historiography Welsh history may be said to have begun in the sixth–seventh centuries AD, after the battles of Deorham (577) and Chester (613), when the inhabitants of Wales were cut off from those who, elsewhere in Britain, spoke their tongue or something very similar. For many centuries their own awareness of their history was intertwined with origin myths and legendary traditions allegedly going back to a pre-Roman period. These notions found their classical formulation in GEOFFREY OF MONMOUTH'S *Historia Regum Britanniae* (c. 1136). Geoffrey claimed to have translated an ancient British chronicle and may have made use of sources such as Gildas's sixth-century *De Excidio Britanniae* and the ninth-century compilation, *Historia Brittonum*, attributed to NENNIUS. Much of his material, however, came from his own fertile imagination. He ascribed to the British a long and illustrious history from the legendary Brutus, grandson of Aeneas, down to Arthur and ending with Cadwaladr in 664. His work was widely accepted as genuine in the middle ages and was nowhere more enthusiastically received than in Wales, where many manuscript copies survive of the Welsh translation. Severely criticized by Polydore Vergil in the sixteenth century, Geoffrey's account was hotly defended by scholars in England and Wales, of whom the ablest were Sir John Price (1502?–1555) and John Lewis of Llynwene (d.1616). It continued to command some credence in Wales until the nineteenth century.

Genuine sources of earlier Welsh history are the work of Bede and other English historians who mention the country. The primary native source was *Brut y Tywysogyon* (Chronicle of the Princes). Three main recensions of it exist: the Red Book of Hergest and associated versions; the Peniarth MS 20 version; and the composite source, *Brenhinedd y Saeson* (Kings of the English) made up of the Brut and an English chronicle. They were independent translations of Latin originals, of which *Annales Cambriae* may represent skeleton outlines, and *Cronica de Wallia* the nearest Latin source. Begun at St David's in the eighth century, the *Brut* moved to Llanbadarn *c.* 1099, and from 1175 to 1332 was a Strata Florida chronicle. A few important ecclesiastical texts, like *Liber Landavensis* and the Red Book of St Asaph, have also survived. Native Welsh laws, first promulgated in writing, perhaps, in the reign of Hywel the Good (*c.*910–*c.*950), survive in about seventy manuscripts of which half were transcribed in the medieval period. Welsh poets, associated first with the princes and, after 1282, with the aristocracy, had a recognized duty to preserve the history of Wales. The large corpus of their poetry, stretching from the sixth century to the seventeenth, though difficult to interpret satisfactorily, is a potentially valuable source of historical information and consciousness.

The Tudor and early-Stuart era saw the emergence of new antiquarian interest in Wales. The translation by Humphrey Llwyd (1527–68) of *Brut y Tywysogyon* was augmented by David Powel (1552?–98), whose *Historie of Cambria* (1584) took the subsequent history of Wales briefly down to the Tudor period. Re-issued in 1697 by William Wynne with notes from the seventeenth-century antiquary Robert Vaughan (d.1697), it remained for centuries the main 'authority' on which Welsh medieval history was founded. Welsh ecclesiastical history was drastically revised in 1567 by Richard Davies and William Salesbury, who contended that the Reformation represented a return to the pristine purity of the early British church. Antiquarians and topographers comparable with those found in England were George Owen (*c.*1552–1613), whose *Description of Pembrokeshire* is much the best Welsh example of its kind, Rice Merrick in Glamorgan (d.1586–7), and John Wynn (1553–1627), whose *History of the Gwydir*

Family remains useful for fifteenth-century history. The work of all three remained in manuscript for centuries.

The revival of English antiquarian scholarship in the 1680s was extended into Wales by Edward Lhuyd (1660–1709), a brilliant and rigorous scholar who awakened new interest in language, local history and the early association of the Welsh with other Celtic peoples. His successors failed to measure up to his standards. Henry Rowlands (1655–1723) in his *Mona Antiqua Restaurata* (1723) became entangled in Druidic myths; and the *Drych y Prif Oesoedd* (Mirror of the Chief Ages) (1740) of Theophilus Evans (1693–1767), though immensely popular, was more notable for its prose style than for its historical content. The patriotic London–Welsh societies, though enthusiastic for Welsh history, achieved little in practice. Iolo Morganwg (1747–1826), exceptionally gifted and learned, was fatally bedevilled by his passion for Druidic and other legends. More promising was Thomas Pennant (1726–98), whose *Tours in Wales* (1778–81) produced a revived antiquarian interest. It led to a crop of county histories, of which much the best was Theophilus Jones's *Breconshire* (1805–09). The earliest and one of the most accomplished denominational histories, *Hanes y Bedyddwyr* (History of the Baptists), by Joshua Thomas (1718–97) appeared about this time (1778).

Increased literacy and more interest in Welsh writing led to the publication of two notable histories in Welsh. One was by Thomas Price (Carnhuanawc, 1787–1848) on the history of the Welsh until 1282 (1836–42) and the other by an exceptionally gifted self-taught historian, R. J. Pryse (Gweirydd ap Rhys, 1807–89) on the history of the Britons and the Welsh (1873–6). The growing influence of organized historical study began to be felt in Wales. John Williams ('Ab Ithel', 1811–62) produced a sub-standard Rolls Series edition of *Annales Cambriae* and the *Brut*; he was also one the joint founders in 1846 of the Cambrian Archaeological Association, whose journal, *Archaeologia Cambrensis*, remains a potent force in historical studies. The revived Cymmrodorion Society began publishing its *Transactions* (1877 – '), *Y*

Cymmrodor (1877–1949), its record series (1893–1936) and its one-volume *Dictionary of National Biography* (1953, 1959). Late in the nineteenth century the first-fruits of a new generation of university-trained historians appeared. John Rhys (1840–1918) and D. Brynmor-Jones (1852–1921) published *The Welsh People* (1900), based very largely on material compiled by the Welsh Land Commission. O. M. Edwards, a wonderfully gifted popularizer of Welsh history, published his influential *Wales* (1901) and *A Short History of Wales* (1906). The culmination was reached in 1911 with the appearance of J. E. Lloyd's (1861–1947) magisterial two-volume *History of Wales* down to 1283. The most accomplished piece of writing ever to appear on the history of Wales, its standards have never been equalled let alone surpassed.

During the twentieth century Welsh history has continued to gain a great deal from the institutionalization of historical study. The foundation of the National Library and the National Museum in 1907 did much to make essential sources better housed and catalogued and easier of access. It also encouraged the development of historical study. In 1911 the Royal Commission on Ancient Monuments (Wales) was founded and has published a series of inventories on Welsh counties. The first Welsh county history society, the Powisland Club of Montgomeryshire, has published its transactions since 1868. During this century its example has been followed by most of the other historic counties and since the 1930s a county record office has been opened in most of them. Some counties embarked on county histories: Carmarthenshire published two volumes (1935, 1939), Glamorgan five (1936–84), and Merioneth one (1967).

Notable exceptions such as Goronwy Edwards and Kenneth Morgan notwithstanding, the biggest contribution to Welsh historiography has come from the University of Wales. Each of its four older university colleges has paid particular attention to the discipline. Secure foundations were laid at Aberystwyth by E. A. Lewis, David Williams and T. Jones Pierce, at Bangor by Lloyd, A. H. Dodd, R. T. Jenkins and Glyn Roberts, at Cardiff by William Rees and at Swansea by Ernest Hughes. All the colleges continue to maintain a vigorous programme of research and publication. The University's Press Board has been the most important publisher of Welsh historical studies. Its Board of Celtic Studies has regularly commissioned major volumes and publishes two journals, the *Bulletin* of the Board of Celtic Studies (1921–) and the *Welsh History Review*.   GW

Reading

A Bibliography of the History of Wales (Cardiff: University of Wales Press, 1962; new edn in prep.).

Jack, R. I.: *Medieval Wales* (London: Hodder & Stoughton, 1972).

Kendrick, T. D.: *British Antiquity* (London: Methuen, 1950).

Morgan, P. T. J.: *The Eighteenth Century Renaissance* (Llandybie: Christopher Davies, 1981).

Williams, G.: Local and National History. *Welsh History Review* 5 (1970) 45–66.

Whig interpretation of history   This term was popularized by Herbert BUTTERFIELD in 1931 in his book of the same title, but a distinction must be made between the meaning attached to the term by Butterfield and the looser sense in which it came to be used by others.

Butterfield criticized as Whig historians those who wrote with one eye on the present, who were preoccupied with the study of origins and who were obsessed with the evolution of political, civil or religious liberty. The development of representative institutions or religious freedom had too often been traced in simple evolutionary terms, with the people of the past too neatly divided into the advocates and enemies of progress. What had passed for moral judgements in history had often been political rather than ethical in inspiration. Instead of fastening on superficial similarities between the past and the present the historian ought to concentrate on defining unlikenesses and making these intelligible. Instead of using the past to justify the present the historian should study the past for its own sake, analysing the interplay of forces which had transformed the past into the present. Compassion ought to be extended to the defeated, such as Tories or Catholics, and not restricted to the victors such as Liberals or Protestants. Butterfield claimed that historians had often put the wrong questions: instead of asking To whom do we owe our religious liberty? the historian should ask How did religious liberty arise? Later in 1944 Butterfield published *The Englishman and his History* which suggested that the unique relationship between Whig history and English politics had made a positive contribution to the national consciousness, but this did not prevent the earlier work from maintaining its dominance. As a result the Whig interpretation was condemned, often in ways that were too sweeping and that distorted what Butterfield had actually said.

Butterfield's argument had always been controversial. Critics had pointed out that if there had been Whig, Liberal or Protestant distortions of history there were also Tory, Marxist or Catholic ones. There was confusion about the identity of the Whig historians. Most people had assumed that Butterfield had had in mind the main figures in English historical writing: MACAULAY, FREEMAN, GREEN, STUBBS, TREVELYAN. In fact his chief target had been ACTON, and a careful reading of Butterfield's text showed that he had not claimed that only Liberals wrote Whig history. Whig history was so deeply embedded in the English tradition that men who were Tories in their own time, such as HALLAM or STUBBS, had written history with a Whig flavour. Although he had failed to name them Butterfield had insisted that the worst examples of crude Whig history were to be found in the work of textbook writers and popularizers. In any case by 1931 there was already a reaction against traditional liberal history. On a scholarly level MAITLAND and NAMIER had exposed many familiar assumptions, and the general reaction against all things Victorian had meant that even popularizers were standing Victorian history on its head. Whig history came to be synonymous with Victorian history; the Whig interpretation became a pejorative term, used lightly to decry historians who excelled in narrative or who believed in representative government or individual freedom.

In many ways the Whig interpretation was an unsatisfactory term. Not all English historians had been Whig – HUME, GIBBON and CARLYLE could hardly be described as Whigs – and not even historians who were Whig had been as consistently Whig in what they had written as many people assumed. Even Macaulay had been less Whig in his attitude to eighteenth-century politics than might have been expected, as Butterfield himself pointed out.

Although the warnings contained in Butterfield's essay were widely regarded and may now appear platitudinous the designation Whig obscured the fact that he had been preoccupied with denouncing faults in the writing of history rather than dissociating himself from a particular political tradition. Butterfield did not intend to revive a Tory tradition in historical writing and he was equally opposed to attempts by left-wingers to exploit history to justify current ideologies or to discern the movements of the future.

In some respects the suggestion that history should have a utilitarian purpose lay at the heart of the controversy. Some historians, such as CARR, sought to reassert the usefulness of history and its relevance to contemporary concerns, arguing that the relationship between the past and the present, between fact and interpretation, was more complex than Butterfield had suggested. But Butterfield himself had affirmed that each generation had to rewrite history. He had not denied the relationship between past and present; indeed, he had emphasized the role of the historian in making the past explicable to the present. His chief anxiety had been to liberate the study of the past from being subordinated to contemporary values, but he also recognized that new questions would be asked, new evidence would come to light, new dimensions would be added to historical understanding. History did not offer absolute or final conclusions. The only cure for bad history was more and better history.

The notion of a Whig interpretation has now become so riddled with qualifications that it has outlived its value. But the controversy helped to free history from shallow attempts to make the study of the past a mere resource for buttressing fashionable contemporary assumptions. Even when these assumptions are far from being Whig the dangers remain. Only when the study of the past is secure from partisan exploitation does it have a value in heightening each generation's awareness of the richness and variety of human experience and in making people conscious of the challenge implied by every attempt to enter into minds different from one's own.   JWD

Reading

Butterfield, H.: *The Whig Interpretation of History* (London: Bell, 1931).

——: *The Englishman and his History* (Cambridge: Cambridge University Press, 1944).

——: *History and Human Relations* (London: Collins, 1951).

Carr, E. H.: *What is History?* (1961; 2nd rev. edn, London: Macmillan, 1986).

Whitelock, Dorothy (b.1901, d.1982) Dorothy Whitelock was educated at Leeds High School, Leeds University and Newnham College, Cambridge, She took the English tripos and came under the influence of H. M. Chadwick. Six years of research were completed in 1930 by the publication of her invaluable *Anglo-Saxon Wills*. In that year she went to St Hilda's College, Oxford, teaching Old and Middle English there until 1957 when she was elected to the Elrington and Bosworth chair at Cambridge. She wrote widely. Particularly important were her studies of Archbishop Wulfstan. Her *English Historical Documents c.500–1042* contained translations of many of the sources, with extensive bibliographies and comments and has been valuable to all students of Anglo-Saxon history. Her short book on Anglo-Saxon society (1952), though unanalytical, was packed with matter. In historical judgements Dorothy Whitelock followed Sir Frank STENTON closely, and the injustice of her review (*American Historical Review*, 1961) of E. John's seminal book on land tenure is attributable to concern to defend Stenton. Her learning was unusually wide and exact; she played a key part in the maintenance of Anglo-Saxon studies.   JC

Main publications

English Historical Documents c.500–1042 (London: Eyre & Spottiswoode, 1955, 2nd edn, 1979); *From Bede to Alfred* (London: Variorum, 1980) [Collected papers]; *History and Law and Literature in Tenth and*

Eleventh Century England (Variorum, 1981) [Collected papers]; *Councils and Synods with other documents relating to the English church*, pt 1:*871–1066*, ed. D. Whitelock, M. Brett and C. N. L. Brooke (Oxford: Oxford University Press, 1981).

Reading

Loyn, H.R.: Dorothy Whitelock 1901–82. *Proceedings of the British Academy* 70 (1986) 543–53.

Widukind of Corvey (*fl.* tenth century) Masterly historian of tenth-century Ottonian Saxony. Most of what is known about Widukind's life and work is the little he chose to tell his readers: a monk of Corvey who entered the monastery when perhaps 15 years old, *c.*940; he came from a noble family, quite likely the *stirps Widukindi*, the descendants of Charlemagne's foremost Saxon enemy. Matilda, the wife of Henry I, was deemed to belong to this kin. The three books of his *Res Gestae Saxonicae* have the character of an epic and convey vividly the strains of tragic conflict within Saxon aristocratic society and its ruling family during the decades of their most rapid expansion and booty-laden triumphs. In the opening words of the *Res Gestae Saxonicae* Widukind informed his readers that he would now turn to the deeds of his princes, of his own kind and people, having first written about the triumphs of the warriors of the highest Emperor, God. The choice of words and images strikes the note of all that follows: the wars of Henry I and the great crises of Otto I's reign.

Three versions of his work have been traced through the manuscripts. The second of these he dedicated to Otto I's twelve-year-old daughter Matilda, Abbess of Quedlinburg, in 968, without however setting aside his stem saga of the Saxon people's origins and land seizures from an earlier draft in which the Ottonians did not yet hold so special a place. The last and final version ends with the death of Otto I, his followers' lament, and their oaths to his son Otto II next day, 8 May 973. It is now thought that the first version had been concluded only a short while before the dedication rather than in 958. Widukind's prose is steeped in SALLUST, and in his descriptions of the Liudolfings he owed something to EINHARD's *Life of Charlemagne*, but his *Res*

Gestae do not quite breathe Einhard's secularity. At great crises and in desperate situations it was God who saved Otto I from his enemies and gave him victory against the odds, but Widukind also dwelt on the king's iron nerve and unshakable resolve. At the Battle of the Lech (955) Otto is made to say to his men that they had divine protection, more *virtus* and far better weapons than their Magyar enemies. *Dilatatio inperii* was Widukind's theme but he also knew its risks. In this suspense between the known and the unknown, the natural and the supernatural shaping the historical process, lies Widukind's enduring literary strength. His work lived on and was received by later Saxon and East-Frankish historians such as THIETMAR, Frutolf and the Lotharingian Sigebert of Gembloux.   KJL

Main writings

Widukindi Monachi Corbeiensis Rerum Gestarum Saxonicarum Libri Tres, ed. P. Hirsch and H. E. Lohmann, 5th edn, (Hanover: *Monumenta Germaniae Historica*, SRG, 1935).

Reading

Beumann, H.: *Widukind von Korvei* (Weimar: Böhlau, 1950).
——: Historiographische Konzeption und politische Ziele Widukinds von Corvey. In *Wissenschaft vom Mittelalter*, Beumann (Cologne and Vienna: Böhlau, 1972).
Hirsch, P.: Introduction. In ed. edn (1935) [see above].

William of Malmesbury (*fl.*1095–1143) William, England's most important historian following Bede, was an almost careerless man, and his personality is opaque to us. No one wrote about him, and he was reticent about exposing himself in his voluminous works. Born of mixed (Anglo-Norman) parentage somewhere in Wiltshire, he entered the ancient abbey of Malmesbury as a child, and there ended his days. He held the office of precentor by *c.* 1137 and was a candidate for the abbacy in the following year. But it seems clear that most of his interest was focused on scholarly reading and writing.

William was one of the best-read Europeans of his day, with a special love for the Latin classics. Although much of his scholarship was directed towards historical research, he also compiled a *florilegium*, a set of miracles of the Virgin, and a biblical commentary. He has always been best known as a general historian of England, consciously attempting to bring BEDE's *Ecclesiastical History* up to date. This he did in two separate works, the *Gesta Regum Anglorum* (Deeds of the English kings), dealing with political history, and the *Gesta Pontificum Anglorum* (Deeds of the English prelates), dealing with ecclesiastical history. The first was completed in 1125, twice revised by 1135, and continued in the *Historia Novella*, which ends in 1142, the last date William is known to have been alive. The *Gesta Pontificum* was also completed in 1125 and revised over the succeeding decade. Both works achieved rapid popularity, especially the *Gesta Regum*, known on the European continent before 1200, and adapted and plundered over succeeding centuries by other general or national chroniclers.

The traditions and written resources of English Benedictine houses supplied most of the material and inspiration for William's historical work. It is not surprising, therefore, that he was 'commissioned' to write local history and hagiography, by his own abbey, by Glastonbury and Worcester. His *Antiquities of Glastonbury*, once infamous because of the spurious additions made to William's account by local monks, has now been purged and William's reputation restored as a critical evaluator and reliable reporter of his sources. The last book of the *Gesta Pontificum* is devoted to his own abbey, and includes a life of its founder and patron Aldhelm.

This astonishing output presupposes a good education and lengthy preparations. William describes his early studies, but does not say where they were undertaken. His preparation consisted in augmenting his abbey's library, and in travelling up and down England investigating the libraries, archives and oral traditions of other religious houses. Sometimes William obtained manuscripts or had complete works copied; but he also made compendia and collections to be used as reference tools for his more original works. His version of the papal chronicle, the *Liber Pontificalis*, was made after 1119, and we have a collection of sources for Roman history written, partly in his own hand, in 1129.

451

WILLIAM OF POITIERS

Comments by William in his major writings reveal his conception of the historian's task: to select sources intelligently, to employ them truthfully and imaginatively, and to render them in elegant Latin. He was unusual in sometimes using non-literary material such as monuments, inscriptions and oral testimony. Although the impingement of the Norman Conquest on English ecclesiastical traditions supplied the context for much of his historical writing, William's vision was a European one. Thus his *Gesta Regum* includes accounts of the Investiture Dispute, the First Crusade, and the appearance of new monastic orders on the continent of Europe.   RMT

Main writings

Gesta Regum Anglorum, 2 vols, ed. W. Stubbs (London: Rolls Series, 1887–9); *Gesta Pontificum Anglorum*, ed. N. E. S. A. Hamilton (London: Rolls Series, 1870); *Antiquities of Glastonbury*, ed. and trans. J. Scott (Woodbridge: Boydell & Brewer, 1981); *Vita Dunstani*. In *Memorials of St. Dunstan*, ed. W. Stubbs (London: Rolls Series, 1874); *Vita Wulfstani*, ed. R. Darlington. In *Camden Third Series* 11 (1928); *Historia Novella*, ed. and trans. K. Potter (London: Nelson, 1955).

Reading

Gransden, A.: *Historical Writing in England c.550 to c.1307* (London: Routledge, 1974) ch. 9.

Southern, R. W.: Aspects of the European Tradition of Historical Writing IV: the Sense of the Past. *Transactions of the Royal Historical Society* 5.23, (1973) 243–63.

Thomson, R. M.: *William of Malmesbury* (Woodbridge: Boydell & Brewer, 1987).

William of Poitiers (*fl.*1050–77)   Author of a laudatory *Life* of William the Conqueror, *c.*1077. The first part is closely connected with the *Gesta Normannorum Ducum* of William of Jumièges, but there has been much dispute as to which writer borrowed from the other. The second part, concerning the Conquest of England, is of the first importance since William of Poitiers was, or had been, one of the Conqueror's chaplains and was writing in his lifetime.   RHCD

Main writings

Guillaume de Poitiers: Histoire de Guillaume le Conquérant, ed. and trans. by Raymonde Foreville (Paris: Les Belles Lettres, 1952) [recommended edn], partial trans. in *English Historical Documents*. Vol. 2,

1042–1189, ed. David C. Douglas (London: Eyre & Spottiswoode, 1953) pp. 217–31.

Reading

Davis, R. H. C.: William of Poitiers and his *History of William the Conqueror*. In *The Writing of History in the Middle Ages: Essays Presented to Richard William Southern*, ed. R. H. C. Davis and J. M. Wallace-Hadrill (Oxford: Oxford University Press, 1981) pp. 71–100.

William of Tyre (b.*c.*1130, d.1184)   Born in Jerusalem the child of first or second generation settlers after the First Crusade, William spent almost twenty years studying in the Schools of Paris, Orleans and Bologna before returning to the Holy Land in 1165. He thereupon embarked upon a successful career as royal servant and ecclesiastic, serving King Amalric of Jerusalem as an ambassador to the Byzantine empire and tutor to his son, the future Baldwin IV. In 1174 he was appointed chancellor of the Kingdom of Jerusalem and the following year he became archbishop of Tyre.

William was the author of a history of the Islamic world and of an account of the Third Lateran Council of 1179, neither of which are extant, and of a history of the First Crusade and the subsequent history of the Latin East to 1184, which has survived. From the late 1120s this work is almost our only informed account of the European settlements in the east, and it is especially valuable for the reigns of William's contemporaries, Amalric (1163–74) and Baldwin IV (1174–85). This period was marked by an increasing threat from the Muslims under Saladin, and in his history William tried to inspire people to greater efforts by reminding them of their past and to provide the west with an *apologia* for the Kingdom of Jerusalem which might be read in conjunction with appeals for aid. Like most attempts to educate people through history it was a failure, and in 1187, shortly after his death, Jerusalem fell to Saladin.

William wrote in Latin, and his history is generally regarded an outstanding example of medieval historiography. If the number of surviving manuscripts and their distribution can be taken as a guide, however, it had a limited readership. A thirteenth-century translation

452

into French with continuations to bring it up to date was evidently far more successful. PWE

Main writings

Willelmi Tyrensis Archiepiscopi Chronicon [Latin text] ed. R. B. C. Huygens (*Corpus Christianorum: Continuatio Mediaevalis* 63–63a) (Turnhout: Brepols, 1986); English trans. with notes, E. A. Babcock and A. C. Krey, *A History of Deeds Done Beyond the Sea* (New York: Columbia University Press, 1941).

Reading

Davis, R. H. C.: William of Tyre. In *Relations between East and West in the Middle Ages*, ed. D. Baker (Edinburgh: Edinburgh University Press, 1973) pp. 64–76.

Edbury, P. W. and Rowe, J. G.: *William of Tyre: Historian of The Latin East* (Cambridge: Cambridge University Press, 1988).

Hiestand, R.: Zum Leben und zu Laufbahn. Wilhelm von Tyrus *Deutsches Archiv* 34 (1978) 345–80.

Huygens, R. B. C.: Guillaume de Tyr étudiant, un chapitre (XIX, 12) de son 'Histoire' retrouvé. *Latomus* 21 (1962) 811–29.

Williams, Eric Eustace (b.1911, d.1981) Born into the family of a Trinidadian minor civil servant, Williams died 70 years later as the first prime minister of Trinidad and Tobago. Before leading his nation into independence he was successively a scholar at St Catherine's, Oxford, a professor at Howard University in Washington, DC, a civil servant with the Anglo-American Caribbean Commission and the founder of Trinidad's dominant political party (PNM).

Williams was particularly proud of playing a many-faceted role in the dramatic dissolution of the European empires. He identified closely with the generation of colonials educated in Britain on the eve of the second world war, seeing himself as much an educator and popular historian as political mobilizer. His declaration of independence speech for his nation in 1962 was by way of a history of the people of Trinidad and Tobago.

Williams's major scholarly study was also his personal declaration of independence from British imperial historiography. When *Capitalism and Slavery* was first published (1944), the dominant approach to British slavery and its abolition rested on a fundamental disjunction between the economic forces which sustained the system and the

humanitarian idealism which destroyed it. For Williams this interpretation minimized the role of slavery in British economic history and allowed imperial historians to justify their empire in the afterglow of a nineteenth-century crusade.

Capitalism and Slavery shifted the Afro-Caribbean economy to the centre stage of world history. The older materialist/idealist dichotomy was discarded. Slavery provided the capital and the trade network for the British industrial revolution. Its fall was driven by hard-headed capitalists, regrouping against an institution in continuous decline following the American Revolution.

Williams's biting style, rapid-fire factuality and assault on the prevailing tradition quickly assured his study a high place among colonial and radical students in Britain and the Caribbean. By the mid-1970s his influence was widespread in the mainstream of Anglo-American scholarship on slavery, its abolition, and third world dependency.

As *Capitalism and Slavery* became more recognized as a historiographical landmark, specialists subjected its theses to rigorous analysis and systematic statistical testing. As a result many of his sharply delineated arguments on causes, effects and ideological shifts eluded empirical verification. Nevertheless, the work has remained more than just a pioneer classic of third world historical rhetoric. Its enduring message, that British economic growth could not be abstracted from overseas exploration and that abolition of slavery could not be addressed independently of general economic development, retains its power to enliven scholarly debate. SD

Main publications

Capitalism and Slavery (Chapel Hill: University of North Carolina Press, 1944; London, 1964); *British Historians of the West Indies* (Port of Spain: PNM Publishing, 1964; New York, 1972); *From Columbus to Castro: the History of the Caribbean 1492–1969* (New York: Harper & Row, 1970).

Reading

Beckles, H.: Capitalism and slavery: the debate over Eric Williams. *Social and Economic Studies* 33 (1984) 171–85.

Drescher, S. Eric Williams: British capitalism and British slavery. *History and Theory* 26 (1987) 180–96.

Morner, M.: The study of black slavery, slave revolts and abolition: recent studies. *Tydschift voor geschiedenis* 98 (1985) 353—65.

Solow, B. L. and Engerman, S. L.: *British Capitalism and Caribbean Slavery: The Legacy of Eric Williams* (Cambridge: Cambridge University Press, 1988).

Willis, Browne (b.1682, d.1760)   A distinguished local historian and antiquarian, Willis was a gentleman of property in Buckinghamshire. Educated at Westminster and Christ Church, Oxford, he represented Buckingham in parliament from 1705 to 1708. In 1717 he helped to refound the Society of Antiquaries. His two most important works were an architectural and historical survey of the cathedrals of England, published in 1727 and 1730, and a parliamentary history of the counties, cities and boroughs. Many of his notes and memoranda passed to the Bodleian Library at his death. Willis's extensive travels in connection with his writings were said to have damaged his ample estate and left him, at the end of his life, looking like a beggar.   JAC

Main publications

A Survey of the Cathedrals of York, etc. (1727, 1730); *Notitia Parliamentaria* (1715, 1716, 1750); *History of the Mitred Parliamentary Abbies*, (1718–9); *History and Antiquities of Buckingham* (1755).

Reading

Nichols, J. *Illustrations of the Literary History of the Eighteenth Century* (1817–31).

Wilson, Charles Henry (b.1914)   Professor of modern history at Cambridge from 1965 to 1979, Wilson specialized in economic and social history. Two major themes dominate his work: English and Dutch rivalry during the seventeenth and eighteenth centuries, and business history in more recent times.

His first major work was *Anglo-Dutch Commerce and Finance in the Eighteenth Century* (1941). Subsequently he published *Profit and Power: a Study of England and the Dutch Wars* (1957) and a masterly concise exposition of seventeenth- and eighteenth-century economic theories in *Mercantilism* (1958). The fruits of his researches and syntheses of the work of others appeared in his own chapters and work

as editor of volume 4, with E. E. Rich (1967) and volume 5 (1977), of *The Cambridge Economic History of Europe*.

In developing business history his *History of Unilever* gave insights concerning many aspects of economic activity, in manufacturing, marketing and investment, with international ramifications. The first two volumes (1954) dealt with the origins of the British and Dutch companies forming Unilever and the third volume (1968) examined the expansion of the company internationally from 1945 to 1965. With W. J. Reader he wrote *Men and Machines: a History of D. Napier and Sons, Engineers, Ltd.* (1958) and he examined retailing in *First with the News: W. H. Smith* (1985).

Among his other publications were *The Dutch Republic and the Civilisation of the Seventeenth Century* (1968) and *Queen Elizabeth and the Revolt of the Netherlands* (1970). For the general reader he provided illumination in *England's Apprenticeship, 1603—1763*.   IJEK

Main publications

Anglo-Dutch Commerce and Finance in the Eighteenth Century (Cambridge: Cambridge University Press, 1941); *Profit and Power: a Study of England and the Dutch Wars* (London: Longmans, 1957); *Mercantilism* (1958); editor, *The Cambridge Economic History of Europe* (1967), vol. 4 (With E. E. Rich), vol. 5 (1977); *History of Unilever*, 3 vols (London: Weidenfeld & Nicolson, 1954—68); with W. J. Reader, *Men and Machines: a History of D. Napier and Sons, Engineers, Ltd.* (London: Cassell, 1958); *First with the News: W. H. Smith* (London: Jonathan Cape, 1985).

Winckelmann, Johann Joachim (b.1717, d.1768)   German art historian and archaeologist, Winckelmann was the son of a poor Prussian cobbler. He developed an early passion for classical antiquity, though it was not until 1755 that he visited and settled in Rome and he was never to reach Greece itself. In Rome he became librarian to the notable collector Cardinal Albani and prefect of papal antiquities. By the time of his murder at Trieste he was recognized as Europe's leading authority on Greek and Roman sculpture.

Before he reached Rome he published his *Gedanken über die Nachahmung der griechischen Werke in der Malerei* (1755) (*Reflections on the painting and sculpture of the Greeks*) in which he argued for the primacy of the ideals of Greek art in the classical tradition. His most important historical work was his *Geschichte der Kunst des Altertums* (1764) (*History of ancient art*). In this he broke with the biographical emphasis of previous histories of art to focus on the works themselves. He provided a systematic account of the stylistic development of antique art, set within the whole context of classical civilization. Both his methodology and the specific stylistic and chronological categories that he defined have had a lasting influence on art history. It was, however, his lyrical descriptions of individual works such as the Laocoön and Apollo Belvedere that captured the popular imagination. His writings and his friendship with the painter Mengs greatly influenced the development of neo-classicism, and his publication of the finds at Pompeii and Herculaneum prepared the way for modern archaeology.   JGB

Main publications

Gedanken über die Nachahmung der griechischen Werke in der Malerei (1755) English trans. (London: 1765); *Geschichte der Kunst des Altertums* (1764) English trans. (Boston: 1880).

Reading

Irwin, David: *Winckelmann: Writings on Art* (London: Phaidon, 1972).

Wölfflin, Heinrich (b.1864, d.1945)   Born in Switzerland of a wealthy Basle family, Wölfflin was a pupil and friend of Jacob BURCKHARDT and succeeded him in the chair of art history at Basle in 1893. In 1901 he was appointed to the prestigious chair at Berlin. Later he moved to Munich and Zurich.

His most important books were concerned with defining styles of art. His first book *Renaissance und Barock* (*Renaissance and Baroque*), published when he was 24, defined Baroque architecture as a distinct style with its own formal values. In 1899 he published his hugely influential analysis of High Renaissance painting and sculpture, *Die klassische Kunst* (*Classic Art*). The principles of formal analysis received their fullest exposition in 1915 in his *Kunstgeschichtliche Grundbegriffe* (*Principles of Art History*). The evolution of style was seen as a process of development between two poles

defined by five pairs of opposite concepts (linear versus painterly; plane versus recession etc.). To illustrate this in lectures he developed the use of twin slide projection – now standard practice for art history teaching.

The limitations of Wölfflin's formal analysis, that it ignores both content and context, are clear enough. His essentially static view of the High Renaissance, as the attainment of a conceptualized ideal that owes much to a nineteenth-century understanding of Greek art, has also been much criticized. However his theoretical views were based on a remarkably precise and sensitive examination of individual works. This has given his books a lasting value and they remain standard textbooks.   JGB

Main publications

Renaissance und Barock (1888) English trans. (London: Collins, 1964); *Die klassische Kunst* (1899) English trans. (London: Phaidon, 1952); *Kunstgeschichtliche Grundbegriffe* (1915) English trans. (London: G. Bell, 1932).

Wood, Anthony (b.1632, d.1695)   Antiquary, historian and chronicler of Oxford, Wood lived as a recluse opposite his old college, Merton, collecting books, hoarding manuscripts, making enemies, and writing classics of antiquarian scholarship. Based on extensive original research, his histories of the university and colleges and his lives of Oxford worthies remain valuable works of reference, and his autobiography and diaries give a vivid and sometimes caustic picture of his own times.   PAS

Main publications

Athenae Oxonienses (London: 1691, 1692); *The History and Antiquities of the University of Oxford* (Oxford: 1792, 1796); *The Life and Times of Anthony Wood*, ed. A. Clark (Oxford: Oxford Historical Society, 1891–5) [autobiography and diaries].

Woodward, Comer Vann (b.1908)   Born and brought up in Arkansas, Woodward spent much of his earlier career at southern universities, and his friendships included leading figures in the southern literary renaissance. He taught for 14 years at The Johns Hopkins

WORLD HISTORY

University, Baltimore (1947–61) before moving to Yale. He combines a deliberate, reflective, courteous manner with a readiness to challenge received historical wisdom.

Woodward has been a leading figure among southern liberals and the most influential southern historian of his time. In his earlier work, on Tom Watson, and especially on the *Origins of the New South*, he rewrote much of the history of the south after the Civil War by liberating it from dogmatic insistence on the solidarity of the south and the continuity of its history. His later work on the history of race relations, notably *The Strange Career of Jim Crow*, spoke directly to the concerns of his own time. Collections of his essays, which are models of wit, style and insight, focus on race and on the southern identity. His editorial work on the Civil War diary of Mary Chesnut won him a Pulitzer prize.

His view of history is essentially pessimistic, and shows a fascination with irony and paradox. His lifelong devotion to the craft of history, and his strong belief in the public duty of the historian, have been reflected in his service to the American historical profession. He has the rare distinction of having served as president of the American Historical Association, the Organization of American Historians and the Southern Historical Association.   PJP

Main publications

Tom Watson, Agrarian Rebel (New York: Macmillan, 1938); *Reunion and Reaction* (Boston: Little, Brown, 1951); *Origins of the New South, 1877–1913* (Baton Rouge: Louisiana State University Press, 1951); *The Strange Career of Jim Crow* (New York: Oxford University Press, 1955, 3rd edn 1974); *The Burden of Southern History* (Louisiana State University Press, 1960); *American Counterpoint* (Boston: Little, Brown, 1971); editor, *The Comparative Approach to American History* (New York: Basic Books, 1968); editor, *Mary Chesnut's Civil War* (New Haven, Conn.: Yale University Press, 1981).

Reading

O'Brien, M.: C. Vann Woodward and the burden of southern liberalism. *American Historical Review* 78 (1973) 589–604.

Roper, John H.: *C. Vann Woodward, Southerner* (Athens, Ga.: University of Georgia Press, 1988).

Woodward, C. Vann: *Thinking Back: the Perils of Writing History* (Baton Rouge: Louisiana State University Press, 1986).

world history   The idea of world history as history considered within the framework of the entire world (not simply the known world) as opposed to, say, a national or cultural framework, is very recent. It is quite distinct both from the PHILOSOPHY OF HISTORY and from general history. Since OROSIUS, many thinkers have tried to encapsulate the entire historical process within a speculative and necessarily teleological system; the last of these to enjoy widespread influence was perhaps HEGEL. Equally, many historians have used techniques of systematic and comparative historical analysis in an attempt to identify general or universal principles governing the operation of human societies. Such a purpose has been ascribed to POLYBIUS and to IBN KHALDUN, but in the context of modern historiography it is usually seen as a characteristic product of the Enlightenment.

VOLTAIRE's *Essai sur les moeurs* (1757) is regarded as the first universal history, less for its account of the development of civilizations beyond Europe than for the breadth of its concern with human progress in general, breaking away from mere political narrative. Its successors in this respect might be said to include both the MARXIST INTERPRETATION OF HISTORY and the *histoire globale* of the ANNALES SCHOOL, whose primary concern is to seize all aspects of social or historical processes and relate them to each other, rather than to describe them comprehensively in a world context. Nevertheless, all of these have contributed to the growth of interest in non-European societies which is necessary for the study of world history.

If the goal of world history was agreed to be, as J. G. Schlözer of Göttingen put it in 1785, 'to show how the earth and humanity as a whole had come to the state in which they now stood' (see Butterfield, *Man on his Past*, p. 49), the result up to the first world war was invariably, and perhaps inevitably, to lead Europeans to identify their own history as its dynamic. For RANKE, as for the Göttingen school, the European state system had mobilized the energies which dominated the world in the centuries after 1500; for Marx the unfolding contradictions of European productive forces created and unleashed capitalist imperialism.

The dilemma as to whether or not Asia can be fitted into the succession of modes of production, which Marx and his followers have not succeeded in resolving, is a particular case of a general presumption now seen as characteristic of nineteenth- and twentieth-century orientalism: that Asian society is essentially unchanging; that it has, in effect, no history, except in the most trivial sense. However, the positivist goal of complete scholarly knowledge required the history of the whole world to be established as firmly and scientifically as possible. The great general histories of the late nineteenth and early twentieth centuries, led by the collection of Gustave Glotz and the collaterals and descendants of the Cambridge Modern History whose publication is still in progress, are sometimes denied the title of world history on the ground that they are composed of series of national or regional histories. Yet whatever their philosophical or historiographical inadequacies, they have constituted an indispensable foundation for world history.

The view that European development has been the principal source of historical change is neither wholly invalid nor by any means moribund, but it could not survive unchallenged through the present century. *Outline of History* (1920), by H. G. WELLS, was offered to those who 'had been taught history in nationalist blinkers, ignoring every country but their own' (p. 2), on the ground that nothing less than world history would serve a world that had become one. Among professional historians, naturally enough, the first to write on that basis were those concerned with the diplomatic and military history of the two previous centuries. An influential definition argued in 1963 that since before that time 'even the total effect of these great movements [barbarian invasions, etc.] was not to create a permanent and constant interaction between developments in each continent ... true world history is of necessity recent history' (David Thomson, *World History*). Such puritanism, however, even if persuasive in itself, is undermined by the ability of a W. H. McNEILL to construct a world history precisely on the basis of continuing and formative interactions between peoples and civilizations since

the earliest times. This reflects some of the most fruitful preoccupations of modern historiography, such as the interest of PIRENNE and the Annales school in the repercussions of long-distance trade and the impact on history of archaeology, and reinforces the increasing dissatisfaction of contemporary social science with a conception of societies as sharply delimited and self-contained entities.

This is one of the issues currently in contention about the writing of world history; others include whether and how a vantage point can be identified from which it can be written − a view from the moon as it were, rather than from London or Peking; whether it is possible or desirable to establish a periodization which, unlike Europe's 'ancient, medieval and modern', can be satisfactorily applied to the world as a whole, and so on. World history is still in its infancy, and must endure the same doubts and difficulties as other historiographies have done in their time. But a striking and rapid development of the last few years is that debate is no longer about whether, but about how world history is to be done, that the amount of historical discussion conducted in world perspective grows annually in quantity and quality, and that the results are beginning to be reflected in the teaching of history in schools and universities in most parts of the world. RIM

Reading

Barraclough, G.: *Main Trends in History* (New York: Holmes & Meier, 1979).

Butterfield, H.: *Man on His Past* (Cambridge: Cambridge University Press, 1955).

Thomson, D.: *World History 1914−61* (Oxford: Oxford University Press, 1963).

Wolf, E. R.: *Europe and the People Without History* (Berkeley and London: University of California Press, 1982).

Wrigley, Edward Anthony (b.1931) Professor of population studies at the London School of Economics since 1979, E. A. Wrigley is England's leading demographic historian. He has spent most of his career in Cambridge, where he was fellow of Peterhouse and (until 1974) university lecturer in geography. His first publications were on the Industrial Revolution and he has retained a lively interest in the causes and consequences of industrialization and urbanization, on which he continues to write penetrating and influential articles. But his outstanding contribution has been to historical demography. In 1964, with Peter LASLETT, he founded the Cambridge Group for the History of Population and Social Structure, of which he is associate director. He was responsible for initiating and supervising its demographic work, applying the techniques pioneered by French demographers to English parish registers (see DEMOGRAPHIC HISTORY). He undertook the first exercise in family reconstitution for an English parish (making the Devonshire village of Colyton famous in the process); and he directed the collection and analysis of data from more than 400 parishes, which led to his *magnum opus*, *The Population History of England 1541–1871*, written with R. S. Schofield. Methodologically inventive and exhaustively documented, this remarkable book has transformed historical understanding of English population, and also thrown searching light on the long-term processes of social and economic change in the past.

PAS

Main publications

Industrial Growth and Population Change (Cambridge: Cambridge University Press, 1961); *Population and History* (London: Weidenfeld & Nicolson, 1969); with R. S. Schofield, *The Population History of England 1541–1871* (London: Edward Arnold; Cambridge, Mass.: Harvard University Press, 1981); *People, Cities and Wealth* (Oxford: Blackwell, 1987).

X

Xenophon (d. after 355 BC) Like other wealthy young men out of sympathy with radical democracy, Xenophon was an associate of Socrates and stayed in Athens during the oligarchic interlude of 404–3. In 402–1 he left to join the younger Cyrus' unsuccessful rebellion against Artaxerxes II. On returning to western Anatolia in 399 he joined the Spartan camp, gained the friendship of king Agesilaus and, when Athens declared war on Sparta in 395, actually fought against fellow Athenians at Coronea (394). Exiled in consequence (if not earlier) he never returned to Athens, even though the sentence was perhaps revoked as early as 370 and his sons, having been educated at Sparta, served in the Athenian cavalry in 362. He settled first near Olympia (on an estate granted by Sparta) but during the upheavals after Leuctra (371) moved to Corinth where he remained until his death.

Once retired from active military service Xenophon turned to literature and produced some 15 works (all extant). He was not so much a historian as a moralizing and didactic writer some 40 per cent of whose output recorded contemporary political and military activities and could therefore be called historical. Not that politics and warfare were absent elsewhere. The *Constitution of the Spartans* describes Spartan institutions (attributed, unhistorically, to a single ancient Lawgiver); *Resources* offers Athens advice on raising revenues; *Hieron* makes a Syracusan tyrant denounce tyranny in conversation with the poet Simonides. Political theorizing appears occasionally in *Memorabilia*, and in *Oeconomicus* Persian royal interest in agriculture and Cyrus' horticultural predilections illustrate a discourse

on estate-management. *Hipparchicus* outlines techniques of cavalry warfare and leadership. The last is a characteristic Xenophontic theme and dominates his longest work, *Cyropaedia*. Purportedly a biography of the Elder Cyrus, founder of the Persian empire, it is valueless as a historical record, being riddled with flagrant inaccuracies, and should be regarded as the first extant historical novel (Ctesias' work on oriental history is an inadequately preserved predecessor) and as having historical worth only in so far as the story's institutional assumptions may sometimes reflect actual conditions. But Xenophon's willingness to use pseudo-historiography in order to illustrate techniques of leadership, and perhaps to suggest that acquisition of an empire can corrode even the virtues of a Cyrus, is worth bearing in mind when approaching his properly historical works, and the choice of a Persian subject is typical of a writer whose compositions are always apt to display intimate connections with their author's personal history and predilections. This is obviously also true of *Agesilaus*, a work which can only charitably be called historical, since it is an encomium of Xenophon's friend consisting of a brief chronological account (frequently almost *verbatim* identical with the appropriate passages of *Hellenica*) and a more lengthy, and tedious, laudation of the king's character, virtue by virtue. Even more 'personal' is *Anabasis*, which recounts the adventures of Cyrus' mercenaries. During the period until a month after the decisive defeat at Cunaxa, Xenophon keeps himself entirely out of sight. But thereafter the account is dominated by his role in the army's safe return to the Aegean via north

459

XENOPHON

Mesopotamia, Armenia and the north Anatolian coast and in their subsequent sojourn in Thrace. Other, and different, accounts existed (one is summarized in DIODORUS). Xenophon's is surely not innocent of apologia and self-advertisement, and his recollection may sometimes be faulty (the account of Cunaxa is puzzling, for example). Some have also detected an implicit argument that the empire would be vulnerable to concerted Greek attack, but the preoccupation with arts of leadership and military stratagem is more obvious — despite which *Anabasis* is not only the source of much information about Persian Anatolia and Mesopotamia, but also an extremely good read, much the most obviously attractive of Xenophon's writings and deservedly popular in antiquity.

The same cannot be said of *Hellenica*, which completed THUCYDIDES and then in the separately composed bulk of the work continued the story of Greek city rivalries down to 362 BC and which was never accorded any special authority in antiquity. This is understandable: it is of uneven literary quality (the prevailing clumsy blandness being relieved only by occasional flashes of colour) and, whatever the merits of Xenophon and his rivals where their versions disagreed (the modern tendency consistently to condemn Xenophon in such cases is to be viewed with suspicion), his account as a whole was simply too prone to startling omissions: a historian who fails to name the Theban architect of Sparta's defeat at Leuctra or to refer either to the Second Athenian Confederacy or to Athens's Aegean policies of the 360s could not be the standard one for his period. Naturally, Xenophon knew about these and many other ignored or underplayed topics, but his purposes (or prejudices) did not require (or permit) their rehearsal. What those purposes were is a nice question. The outline of an answer is suggested by the lack of admiration for any of the major city-states (Sparta, for whom Xenophon is too often casually assumed to be an unthinking propagandist, Athens and Thebes); the recurrent theme that aspirations of empire and power provoke divine displeasure (Xenophon was ever a religious man) and are the source of no joy to those who entertain them; and the probability that Xenophon was addressing an Athenian audience (in need of admonition about imperial delusions) and writing hastily and without extensive special research. *Hellenica* was, in fact, a curious compromise between political pamphlet for the 350s and true history. Eclipsed in popularity by *Anabasis*, *Cyropaedia* and the Socratic writings, it was incapable of providing a particular model or stimulus to later historians: characteristically, ARRIAN, who projected himself as a second Xenophon, wrote nothing which could be regarded as an imitation *Hellenica*, although the rest of the Xenophontic corpus is well-reflected in his output.　　CJT

Main writings

Anabasis trans. R. Warner as *The Persian Expedition*, and *Hellenica*, trans. R. Warner as *History of my Times* (Harmondsworth: Penguin Classics, 1972 and 1979).
[The standard modern editions of Xenophon's works are those of the Oxford, Teubner and Budé series. Trans. of all appear in the Loeb Classical Library.]

Reading

Anderson, J. K.: *Xenophon* (London: Duckworth, 1974).
Cawkwell, G. L.: Introductions. In *The Persian Expedition* and *History of my Times* [see above].
Higgins, W. E.: *Xenophon the Athenian* (Albany, NY: State University of New York Press, 1979).

Y

Yates, Frances Amelia (b.1899, d.1981) Educated at the University of London, where she read French, Yates was associated with the Warburg Institute for nearly 40 years, and acknowledged a considerable intellectual debt to its members, notably Fritz Saxl, Gertrud Bing, Perkin Walker and Ernst Gombrich. Her work was mainly concerned with art, literature and ideas in Renaissance England, France, Germany and Italy, but she was well aware of the importance of classical and medieval traditions. Her training as a literary historian directed her interests from Shakespeare to Giordano Bruno and so to astrology, magic, cabala and other forms of the occult. She also wrote on art and politics, more especially on Renaissance courts and their festivals. Yates worked by herself, immersing herself in her texts until she could 'see', rather than work out, what they meant. Her strong imagination was held in check — until her last years — by a sturdy, empiricist common sense. Relatively unknown until her sixties, though something of a cult figure in her old age, her influence on the study of history was exercised through the Warburg Institute and her graduate students.   UPB

Main publications

(Published by Routledge & Kegan Paul, London, unless otherwise stated.)
The French Academies of the Sixteenth Century (London: Warburg Institute, 1947); *The Valois Tapestries* (Warburg Institute, 1959); *Giordano Bruno and the Hermetic Tradition* (1964); *The Art of Memory* (1966); *The Rosicrucian Enlightenment* (1972); *Astraea* (1975).

Reading

Burke, P.: The last of the Magi: Frances Yates and the occult philosophy. *Bulletin of the Society for Renaissance Studies* 2. 1 (1982) 29–33.

Z

Zavala, Silvio (b.1909)   With a doctorate in law from Madrid, Zavala finds it natural to reconstruct the Spanish American empire upon primarily legal foundations. Showing uncommon versatility, he addresses the entire colonial period and writes on Peru, Argentina, Guatemala and Mexico. Zavala's body of publications reveals his enduring interests in the philosophy of conquest, the unity and diversity of hemispheric history and, most especially, the varying forms of Indian servitude. Prominent in public service as well as scholarship, Zavala was Mexican ambassador to France (1966–75).   ATB

Main publications

La encomienda indiana (Madrid: Centro de Estudios Históricos, 1935); *Las instituciones jurídicas en la conquista de América* (Madrid: Centro de Estudios Históricos, 1935); *La Utopía de Tomás Moro en la Nueva España y otros estudios* (1937) (London: Hispanic & Luso-Brazilian Councils, 1955); *Ensayos sobre la colonización española en América* (Philadelphia: University of Pennsylvania Press, 1943); *La filosofía política en la conquista de América* (1947) (Mexico: Fondo de Cultura Económica, 1953); *El mundo americano en la época colonial*, 2 vols (Mexico: PAIGH, 1967); *Los intereses particulares en la conquista de América* (Mexico: UNAM, 1964); *Los esclavos indios en Nueva España* (Mexico: Colegio Nacional, 1968); Los esclavos indios en Guatemala. *Historia Mexicana* 19 (1969–70; 459–65) *Orígenes de la colonización en el Rio de la Plata* (Mexico: Colegio de México, 1978); *El servicio personal de los indios en el Perú*, 3 vols (Mexico: Colegio de México, 1978–80); *El servicio personal de los indios en la Nueva España*, 2 vols (Colegio de México, 1984–5).

Reading

Bakewell, Peter: An Interview with Silvio Zavala. *Hispanic American Historical Review* 62 (1982) 553–68.

Zeldin, Theodore (b.1933)   Educated in London and in Oxford, Zeldin has been at St Antony's College, Oxford, since 1963. He first appeared as a specialist on the Second Empire. His study of Napoleon III's system of government discussed many of the questions which Namier had raised on eighteenth-century politics (for example, why men went into parliament). In particular his work illuminated the person of Emile Ollivier and examined certain controversial elements in his career, such as why he deserted the Republicans in order to lead Napoleon's Liberal Empire and why he changed his mind and advocated making war on Prussia. The year 1973 saw the appearance of the first volume of a considerable work, *France 1848–1945*, in the Oxford History of Europe. This book, and its successor which appeared four years later, caused a considerable stir. Zeldin did not present a simple chronological account of events, but aimed at disentangling the different elements and aspects of French life. His emphasis was, as he put it, on understanding values, human relationships and the forces that influenced thinking. The subtitles of the two volumes indicate much of the nature of this original work. Volume I is *Ambition, Love, Politics*; volume II, *Intellect, Taste, Anxiety*. After this major contribution to the study of French history Zeldin wrote a more sociological and immediate work, *The French*, which enjoyed great success in France.   DJ

Main publications

The Political System of Napoleon III (London: Macmillan, 1958); editor, *Emile Ollivier and the Liberal*

Empire of Napoleon III (Oxford: Oxford University Press, 1963); editor, *Conflicts in French Society* (Oxford: 1970); *France 1848–1945* (Oxford History of Modern Europe) (Oxford University Press, vol. I, 1973, vol. II, 1977); *The French* (London: Collins, 1983).

Zosimus (*fl.*500 AD)   A former court functionary at Constantinople, Zosimus was the author of a *New History* of the Roman empire. He began with the regime of Augustus (of which he was highly critical) and briefly surveyed the Roman emperors as far as the mid-third century. From that point a fuller narrative extends to 410 (although the account of the years 282–305 is missing). The surviving history breaks off before the catastrophe of Alaric's sack of Rome, and the evidence suggests that it was never completed. As a Greek writing about Rome, Zosimus claimed to model himself on POLYBIUS, and to chart the decline of Roman greatness as Polybius had described its growth. Although a historian much inferior to his model, Zosimus is out-ranked only by AMMIANUS MARCELLINUS as a source for late antiquity.

Zosimus derived his history entirely from earlier works, and his inadequacies as a historian are evident in his failure to eliminate the confusion and contradictions which arose from this amalgam. He was a convinced pagan in what was now a Christian Roman empire, and this religious standpoint gives his history its particular interest. It is the only surviving account of late antiquity to place the desertion of the old gods at the root of Rome's decline and to produce a hostile portrayal of those emperors who were the architects of the Christian empire, Constantine and Theodosius.

EDH

Main writings

Histoire Nouvelle, ed. and trans. F. Paschoud (Paris: Les Belles Lettres, 1971 onward); *New History*, trans. with commentary by R. T. Ridley (Sydney: Australian Association for Byzantine Studies, *Byzantina Australiensia* 2, 1982).

Reading

Paschoud, F.: Zosimos. *Realencyclopädie* II. 19 (1972) 795–841.

Index

The Editors and Publishers are grateful to Mary Norris who compiled the index.
Page references to major entries on a subject are in bold type.

INDEX

INDEX